Die erst Epistel Sanct Johannis.

Das erst Capitel.

DAs do vom anfang war.
das wyr gehoret haben.
das wyr gesehen haben mit vnsern au
gen/das wyr beschawet haben/vnnd
vnser hende betastet haben / von dem
wort des lebens/vnd das leben ist er-
schynen / vnd wyr haben gesehen vnd
zeugen vnnd verkundigen euch das le-
ben dz ewig ist / wilchs war bey dem
vater vñ ist vns erschynen / Was wyr
gesehen vnd gehort habẽ/das verkun-
digen wyr euch / auff das auch yhr
mit vns gemeynschafft habet/vnd vn
ser gemeynschafft sey mitt dem vatter
vnd mit seynem son Jhesu Christo / vnnd solchs schreyben wyr euch
auff das yhr euch frewet vnd ewer freud vollig sey.

Vnd das ist die verkundigung/die wyr von yhm gehort haben vnd
euch verkundigen/das Gott eyn liecht ist/ vnnd ynn yhm ist keyn fin-
sternis/So wyr sagen/das wyr gemeynschafft mit yhm haben/vnd
wandelln ym finsternis / so liegen wyr vnd thun nicht die warheyt/
Szo wyr aber ym liecht wandelln/wie er ym liecht ist/so haben wyr
gemeynschafft vnternander / vnd das blutt Jhesu Christi macht vns
reyn von aller sunde.

Szo wyr sagen/wyr haben keyne sund/so verfuren wyr vns selbs/
vnd die warheyt ist nicht vns/so wyr aber vnsere sunde bekennen/szo
ist er trew vnd gerecht/das er vns die sunde erlesset / vnd reyniget vns
võ aller vngerechtikeyt/So wyr sagen/ wyr habẽ nicht gesundiget/
so machen wyr yhn zum lugener/ vnd seyn wort ist nit ynn vns.

Das ander Capitel.

MEyn kindlin/solchs schreybe ich euch/auff das yhr nit sun-
diget/vnd ob yemand sundiget/so haben wyr eynen fursspre
Roma.3. chen bey Gott/Jhesum Christ/ der gerecht ist / vñ der selb
ist die versunung fur vnser sunde / nit alleyn aber fur die vn-
sere/sundern auch fur der gantzen wellt/Vnd an dem erkennen wyr/
das wyr yhn erkand haben/so wyr seyne gepott hallten/Wer da sa-
get/ich habe yhn erkand / vnnd helt seyne gepot nicht/der ist eyn lug
ner/vñ ynn solchem ist keyn warheyt/ Wer aber seyne wort hellt/ ynn
solchem ist warlich die liebe Gottis volkomẽ/Daran erkennen wyr/
das wyr ynn yhm sind /Wer da saget/das er ynn yhm bleybet /der
soll auch wandelln/ gleych wie er gewandellt hatt.

hermeneia

Hermeneia
—A Critical
and Historical
Commentary
on the Bible

The Johannine Letters

A Commentary on 1, 2, and 3 John

by Georg Strecker

Translation by Linda M. Maloney
Edited by Harold Attridge

Fortress Press

Minneapolis

The Johannine Letters

A Commentary on 1, 2, and 3 John

Cover and interior design: Kenneth Hiebert
Production management by Publishers' WorkGroup
Typesetting by Polebridge Press

Library of Congress Cataloging-in-Publication Data

Strecker, Georg, 1929–
[Johannesbriefe. English]
The Johannine letters : a commentary on 1, 2, and 3 John / by Georg Strecker ; translation by Linda M. Maloney ; edited by Harold Attridge.
p. cm. — (Hermeneia—a critical and historical commentary on the Bible)
Includes bibliographical references and indexes.
ISBN 0-8006-6047-1 (alk. paper)
1. Bible. N.T. Epistles of John–Commentaries. I. Attridge, Harold W. II. Bible. N.T. Epistles of John. English. New Revised Standard. III. Title. IV. Series.
BS2805.3.S75513 1996
227'.94077–dc20 95-36570
CIP

The paper used in this publication meets the minimum requirements of American National Standard for Information Sciences—Permanence of Paper for Printed Library Materials, ANSI Z329.48–1984.

Manufactured in the U.S.A. AF 1–9683

99 98 97 96 95 1 2 3 4 5 6 7 8 9 10

BELOVED, LET US LOVE ONE ANOTHER, BECAUSE LOVE IS FROM GOD; EVERYONE WHO LOVES IS BORN OF GOD AND KNOWS GOD.
—1 JOHN 4:7

The Author

Georg Strecker (1929–1994) was Professor of New Testament at the University of Göttingen 1968–1994. He earned a doctorate at the University of Marburg under Rudolf Bultmann. He was the author of a number of books, including *Das Judenchristentum in die Pseudoklementinen* (1958), *Der Weg der Gerechtigkeit: Untersuchung zur Theologie des Matthäus* (1962), *Die Bergpredigt. Ein exegetischer Kommentar* (1984) translated into English as *The Sermon on the Mount* (Abingdon 1989), *Konkordanz zu den Pseudoklementinen* (1986/89), and *Literaturgeschichte des Neuen Testaments* (1992).

Contents

The Third Epistle of John

The name *Hermeneia*, Greek ἑρμηνεία, has been chosen as the title of the commentary series to which this volume belongs. The word *Hermeneia* has a rich background in the history of biblical interpretation as a term used in the ancient Greek-speaking world for the detailed, systematic exposition of a scriptural work. It is hoped that the series, like its name, will carry forward this old and venerable tradition. A second, entirely practical reason for selecting the name lies in the desire to avoid a long descriptive title and its inevitable acronym, or worse, an unpronounceable abbreviation.

The series is designed to be a critical and historical commentary to the Bible without arbitrary limits in size or scope. It will utilize the full range of philological and historical tools, including textual criticism (often slighted in modern commentaries), the methods of the history of tradition (including genre and prosodic analysis), and the history of religion.

Hermeneia is designed for the serious student of the Bible. It will make full use of ancient Semitic and classical languages; at the same time, English translations of all comparative materials—Greek, Latin, Canaanite, or Akkadian—will be supplied alongside the citation of the source in its original language. Insofar as possible, the aim is to provide the student or scholar with full critical discussion of each problem of interpretation and with the primary data upon which the discussion is based.

Hermeneia is designed to be international and interconfessional in the selection of authors; its editorial boards were formed with this end in view. Occasionally the series will offer translations of distinguished commentaries which originally appeared in languages other than English. Published volumes of the series will be revised continually, and eventually, new commentaries will replace older works in order to preserve the currency of the series. Commentaries are also being assigned for important literary works in the categories of apocryphal and pseudepigraphical works relating to the Old and New Testaments, including some of Essene or Gnostic authorship.

The editors of *Hermeneia* impose no systematic-theological perspective upon the series (directly, or indirectly by selection of authors). It is expected that authors will struggle to lay bare the ancient meaning of a biblical work or pericope. In this way the text's human relevance should become transparent, as is always the case in competent historical discourse. However, the series eschews for itself homiletical translation of the Bible.

The editors are heavily indebted to Fortress Press for its energy and courage in taking up an expensive, long-term project, the rewards of which will accrue chiefly to the field of biblical scholarship.

The editor responsible for this volume is Harold W. Attridge of the University of Notre Dame.

Frank Moore Cross	*Helmut Koester*
For the Old Testament	For the New Testament
Editorial Board	Editorial Board

This new edition of the commentary on the Johannine Letters cannot be released without an acknowledgment of respect and gratitude to Rudolf Bultmann, my teacher at Marburg in 1949–1950. To him I owe the theological standards I apply to the exegesis of the New Testament. That will be clear from the following interpretation, which makes reference more often than is usually the case to the previous edition, the mature work of Rudolf Bultmann completed in 1967. My interpretation is made in a spirit both of critical acceptance and critical distance, and attempts to unfold the Johannine writings not so much by means of detailed literary-critical dissection as from a redaction-critical point of view, in order to remain aware of the vitality of the oral tradition as it is revealed in the Johannine "school," not least through the discussions that took place there. In my essays "Die Anfänge der johanneischen Schule" (1986) and "Chiliasm and Docetism in the Johannine School" (1990), I presented a preliminary sketch of these matters. Above all, I seek critical readers who are open-minded enough to question traditional positions.

It is true of this commentary on the Johannine Letters, as it has been of all the volumes produced in the "Kritisch-exegetischer Kommentar über das Neue Testament" since its founding, that its proper goal is not scholarly discussion, but the unity of theory and praxis in service of the church's preaching. In this connection, the description of the first letter of John by the reformer Martin Luther may not only receive acknowledgment, but may also find an expansive interpretation: that this "honest, apostolic epistle paints Christ for us in a beautiful and loving way; for it is a glorious treasure-house of many spiritual and heavenly truths."

It is my pleasant duty at this point also to thank those whose advice aided me in the preparation of the German edition: Pastor Klaus Fricke, retired, in Göttingen-Nikolausberg; and my former assistant, Friedrich Wilhelm Horn, Th.D., now Professor of New Testament at the University of Duisburg. My special thanks to Professor Linda Maloney, who took on the arduous task of preparing the English translation and exercised great care in bringing it to completion. She was kind enough also to incorporate necessary additions to the German edition, including the correction of typographical errors and inadvertent omissions, so that this American edition has been brought in line with the latest state of research to the fullest extent possible.

Göttingen
15 January 1993

Georg Strecker

Reference Codes

1. Sources and Abbreviations

Abbreviations for ancient sources follow, with minor modifications, the *Theological Dictionary of the New Testament,* ed. Gerhard Kittel and Gerhard Friedrich, trans. Geoffrey W. Bromiley, vol. 1 (Grand Rapids: Eerdmans, 1964) xvi–xl. Abbreviations in text-critical notes follow the Nestle-Aland, 26th edition (Eberhard Nestle, Erwin Nestle, Kurt Aland, et al., *Novum Testamentum Graece* [Stuttgart: Deutsche Bibelstiftung, 1979]; abbreviated Nestle-Aland^{26}). The following abbreviations have also been used:

AB	Anchor Bible
'Abot R. Nat.	*'Abot de Rabbi Nathan*
Act. Thom.	*Acts of Thomas*
Aeschylus	
Ag.	*Agammemnon*
AGJU	Arbeiten zur Geschichte des antiken Judentums und des Urchristentums
AGLB	Aus der Geschichte der lateinischen Bibel
AGWG.PH	Abhandlungen der Gesellschaft der Wissenschaften zu Göttingen. Philologisch-historische Klasse
AKG	Arbeiten zur Kirchengeschichte
AnBib	Analecta biblica
ANF	Ante-Nicene Fathers
ANRW	*Aufstieg und Niedergang der römischen Welt*
ANTT	Arbeiten zur neutestamentlichen Textforschung
Ap. Const.	*Apostolic Constitutions*
Ap. John	*Apocryphon of John* (NHC 2, 1)
Apoc. Abr.	*Apocalypse of Abraham*
Apoc. Mos.	*Apocalypse of Moses*
Apoc. Pet.	*Apocalypse of Peter*
Apoc. Zeph.	*Apocalypse of Zephaniah*
2 Apoc. Jas.	*Second Apocalypse of James* (NHC 5, 4)
Aristotle	
Nic. Eth.	*Nicomachean Ethics*
Rhet.	*Rhetorica*
Asc. Isa.	*Ascension of Isaiah*
As. Mos.	*Assumption of Moses*
ASNU	Acta seminarii neotestamentici upsaliensis
AsSeign	*Assemblées du Seigneur*
AThANT	Abhandlungen zur Theologie des Alten und Neuen Testaments
AUSS	*Andrews University Seminary Studies*
b.	Babylonian Talmud
BAGD	W. Bauer, W. F. Arndt, F. W. Gingrich, and F. W. Danker, *A Greek-English Lexicon of the New Testament*
2 Bar.	Syriac *Apocalypse of Baruch*
BAW	Bibliothek der Alten Welt
BBB	Bonner biblische Beiträge
BBET	Beiträge zur biblischen Exegese und Theologie
BDF	F. Blass, A. Debrunner, and Robert W. Funk, *A Grammar of the New Testament and Other Early Christian Literature* (Chicago: University of Chicago Press, 1961)
BDR	F. Blass, A. Debrunner, and F. Rehkamp, *Grammatik des neutestamentlichen Griechisch*
Ber.	*Berakot* (tractate of Mishna and Talmud)
BEThL	Bibliotheca ephemeridum theologicarum Lovaniensium
BEvTh	Beiträge zur evangelischen Theologie
BFCTh	Beiträge zur Förderung christlicher Theologie
BGU	*Ägyptische Urkunden aus den Kgl. Museen zu Berlin*
BHTh	Beiträge zur historischen Theologie
Bib	*Biblica*
BJRL	*Bulletin of the John Rylands University Library of Manchester*
BJS	Brown Judaic Studies
BKV	Bibliothek der Kirchenväter
BSac	*Bibliotheca sacra*
BT	*The Bible Translator*
BTB	*Biblical Theology Bulletin*
BU	Biblische Untersuchungen
BZ	*Biblische Zeitschrift*
BZNW	Beihefte zur *ZNW*
CBQ	*Catholic Biblical Quarterly*
CBSC	Cambridge Bible for Schools and Colleges
CChr	Corpus Christianorum
CD	The Cairo (Geniza Text of the) Damascus (Document)
Chrysostom	
Hom. in Joh.	*Homilies on John*
CIG	*Corpus inscriptionum graecarum*
1 Clem.	*The First Epistle of Clement*
2 Clem.	*The Second Epistle of Clement*
Clement of Alexandria	
Div.	*Quis Dives Salvetur*
Exc. Theod.	*Excerpta ex Theodoto*
Hyp.	*Hypotyposeis*

Paed.	*Paedagogus*
Strom.	*Stromata*
CNEB	Cambridge Bible Commentary on the New English Bible
CNT	Commentaire du Nouveau Testament
ConNT	Coniectanea Neotestamentica
Corp. Herm.	*Corpus Hermeticum*
CR	Corpus reformatorum
CSCO	Corpus scriptorum christianorum orientalium
CSEL	Corpus scriptorum ecclesiasticorum latinorum
CuBi	*Cultura bíblica*
DBM	Δελτίο Βιβλικῶν Μελετῶν
DBSup	*Dictionnaire de la Bible, Supplément*
Did.	*Didache*
Dio Chrysostom	
Or.	*Orationes*
Diogenes Laertius	
Vit. phil.	*Vitae philosophorum*
Diogn.	*Epistle to Diognetus*
DRev	*Downside Review*
DT	*Divus Thomas*
EB	Echter Bibel
EdF	Erträge der Forschung
EDNT	Horst Balz and Gerhard Schneider, eds., *Exegetical Dictionary of the New Testament*
EeV	*Ésprit et Vie*
EKKNT	Evangelisch-katholischer Kommentar zum Neuen Testament
EKL	*Evangelisches Kirchenlexikon*
1 Enoch	*Ethiopic Enoch*
Ep.	*Epistola(e)*
Ep. Arist.	*Epistle of Aristeas*
Epictetus	
Diss.	*Dissertationes*
Epiphanius	
Pan.	*Panarion*
EstBib	*Estudios bíblicos*
EtB	Études bibliques
EThL	*Ephemerides theologicae lovanienses*
Euripides	
Cycl.	*Cyclops*
Iph. T.	*Iphigeneia at Tauris*
Phoen.	*Phoenician Women*
Eusebius	
Dem. Ev.	*Demonstratio evangelica*
Hist. eccl.	*Historia ecclesiastica*
Praep. Ev.	*Praeparatio evangelica*
EvQ	*Evangelical Quarterly*
EvTh	*Evangelische Theologie*
EWNT	Horst Balz and Gerhard Schneider, eds., *Exegetisches Wörterbuch zum Neuen Testament*
Exp.	*The Expositor*
ExpT	*Expository Times*
frg.	fragment
FRLANT	Forschungen zur Religion und Literatur des Alten und Neuen Testaments
FThSt	Freiburger theologische Studien
FTS	Frankfurter theologische Studien
FZPhTh	*Freiburger Zeitschrift für Philosophie und Theologie*
GCS	Griechische christliche Schriftsteller der ersten drei Jahrhunderte
GKT	Grundkurs Theologie
GNT	Grundrisse zum Neuen Testament
Gos. Phil.	*Gospel of Philip* (NHC 2, 3)
Gos. Thom.	*Gospel of Thomas* (NHC 2, 2)
GThA	Göttinger Theologische Arbeiten
GuL	*Geist und Leben*
Herm.	*Shepherd of Hermas*
Man.	*Mandates*
Sim.	*Similitudes*
Vis.	*Visions*
HeTr	Helps for Translators
Hippolytus	
Ref.	*Refutation of All Heresies*
HKAW	Handbuch der klassischen Altertumswissenschaft
HKNT	Handkommentar zum Neuen Testament
HNT	Handbuch zum Neuen Testament
HNTC	Harper's New Testament Commentaries
Homer	
Il.	*Iliad*
Od.	*Odyssey*
HSNT	Die Heilige Schrift des Neuen Testaments
HThKNT	Herders theologischer Kommentar zum Neuen Testament
HUT	Hermeneutische Untersuchungen zur Theologie
Hyp. Arch.	*Hypoatasis of the Archons* (NHC 2, 4)
IB	*Interpreter's Bible*
ICC	International Critical Commentary
Ignatius	
Eph.	*Letter to the Ephesians*
Magn.	*Letter to the Magnesians*
Phld.	*Letter to the Philadelphians*
Pol.	*Letter to Polycarp*
Rom.	*Letter to the Romans*
Smyrn.	*Letter to the Smyrnaeans*
Trall.	*Letter to the Trallians*

ILS	Hermann Dessau, ed., *Inscriptiones latinae selectae*
Int	*Interpretation*
Irenaeus	
Adv. haer.	*Adversus haereses (Against the Heresies)*
ITQ	*Irish Theological Quarterly*
JAC	Jahrbuch für Antike und Christentum
JBC	Raymond E. Brown, et al., eds., *The Jerome Biblical Commentary*
JBL	*Journal of Biblical Literature*
JEA	*Journal of Egyptian Archeology*
Jos. Asen.	*Joseph and Aseneth*
Josephus	
Ant.	*Antiquities of the Jews*
Ap.	*Against Apion*
Bell.	*Bellum Judaicum (The Jewish War)*
JPTh	*Jahrbücher für protestantische Theologie*
JSHRZ	Jüdische Schriften aus hellenistisch-römischer Zeit
JSNTSup	Journal for the Study of the New Testament Supplement Series
JTS	*Journal of Theological Studies*
Justin	
1 Apol.	*First Apology*
Dial.	*Dialogue with Trypho*
KD	*Kerygma und Dogma*
KEK	Kritisch-exegetischer Kommentar über das Neue Testament
KJV	*King James Version*
KIT	Kleine Texte
KTA	Kröners Taschenausgabe
LSJ	Liddell-Scott-Jones, *Greek-English Lexicon* (Oxford: Clarendon, 1968)
Lucian	
Hermot.	*Hermotimus*
LXX	Septuagint
m.	Mishna
Mart. Pol.	*Martyrdom of Polycarp*
Midr. Ps.	*Midrash on the Psalms*
MNTC	Moffatt New Testament Commentary
MT	Masoretic Text
MThS	Münchener theologische Studien
MThS.H	Münchener theologische Studien. Historische Abteilung
MThZ	*Münchener theologische Zeitschrift*
NCB	*New Century Bible*
NEB	*New English Bible*
NedThT	*Nederlands theologisch tijdschrift*
Neot	*Neotestamentica*
Nestle-Aland^{26}	Eberhard Nestle, Kurt Aland, et al., *Novum Testamentum Graece* (26th ed.; Stuttgart: Deutsche Bibelstiftung, 1979)
NGWG	Nachrichten der Gesellschaft der Wissenschaften in Göttingen
NHC	Nag Hammadi Codex
NHLE	James M. Robinson, ed., *The Nag Hammadi Library in English* (3d ed.; San Francisco: Harper, 1988)
NICNT	New International Commentary on the New Testament
NKZ	*Neue kirchliche Zeitschrift*
NovT	*Novum Testamentum*
NovTSup	*Novum Testamentum*, Supplements
NRSV	*New Revised Standard Version*
NRTh	*La nouvelle revue théologique*
NTAbh	Neutestamentliche Abhandlungen
NTApoc^{1}	Edgar Hennecke and Wilhelm Schneemelcher, eds., *New Testament Apocrypha* (2 vols.; trans. A. J. B. Higgins, et al.; ed. R. McL. Wilson; London: Lutterworth; Philadelphia: Westminster, 1963–64)
NTApoc^{2}	Wilhelm Schneemelcher, ed., *New Testament Apocrypha* (2 vols.; rev. ed.; trans. Ernest Best, et al.; ed. R. McL. Wilson; Louisville: Westminster/John Knox, 1991)
NTD	Das Neue Testament Deutsch
OBO	Orbis biblicus et orientalis
Odes Sol.	*Odes of Solomon*
Orig. World	*On the Origin of the World* (NHC 2, 5)
Origen	
C. Cels.	*Contra Celsum*
Comm. in Joh.	*Commentary on the Gospel According to John*
Comm. in Matt.	*Commentary on the Gospel According to Matthew*
Comm. in Rom.	*Commentary on the Epistle to the Romans*
Orat.	*De oratione*
Princ.	*De principiis*
ÖTK	Ökumenischer Taschenbuchkommentar zum Neuen Testament
OTP	James H. Charlesworth, ed., *The Old Testament Pseudepigrapha* (2 vols.; Garden City: Doubleday, 1983–85)
P.	Papyrus
P. Eger.	Egerton Papyrus
P. Flor.	Florentini Papyrus
P. Lond.	London Papyrus

P. Oxy.	Oxyrhynchus Papyrus
P. Ryl.	Rylands Papyrus
Pass. Andr.	*Passio Andreae*
PETSE	Papers of the Estonian Theological Society in Exile
PG	Migne, *Patrologia graeca*
PGM	K. Preisendanz, ed., *Papyri graecae magicae*
Ph	*Philologus*
Philo	
Abr.	*De Abrahamo*
Agric.	*De agricultura*
Cher.	*De cherubim*
Conf. ling.	*De confusione linguarum*
Decal.	*De decalogo*
Det. pot. ins.	*Quod deterius potiori insidiari solet*
Deus imm.	*Quod Deus sit immutabilis*
Ebr.	*De ebrietate*
Flacc.	*In Flaccum*
Fug.	*De fuga et inventione*
Gig.	*De gigantibus*
Jos.	*De Josepho*
Leg. all.	*Legum allegoriae*
Leg. Gaj.	*Legatio ad Gajum*
Migr. Abr.	*De migratione Abrahami*
Mut. nom.	*De mutatione nominum*
Op. mun.	*De opificio mundi*
Poster. C.	*De posteritate Caini*
Praem. poen.	*De praemiis et poenis*
Q. Exod.	*Quaestiones in Exodum*
Q. Gen.	*Quaestiones in Genesim*
Rer. div. her.	*Quis rerum divinarum heres sit*
Sacr. AC	*De sacrificiis Abelis et Caini*
Sobr.	*De sobrietate*
Som.	*De somniis*
Spec. leg.	*De specialibus legibus*
Virt.	*De virtutibus*
Vit. Mos.	*De vita Mosis*
Pindar	
Nem.	*Nemean Odes*
Pyth.	*Pythian Odes*
PL	Migne, *Patrologia latina*
Plato	
Leg.	*Leges (Laws)*
Prot.	*Protagoras*
Rep.	*Republic*
Theaet.	*Theaetetus*
Tim.	*Timaeus*
Plotinus	
Enn.	*Enneads*
Plutarch	
Ei Delph.	*De Ei apud Delphos*
Is. et Os.	*De Iside et Osiride*
Quaest. Rom.	*Quaestiones Romanae*
Stoic. rep.	*De Stoicorum repugnantiis*
Polycarp	
Phil.	*Letter to the Philippians*
Porphry	
Abst.	*De abstinentia*
Ps-Clem. Ep.	*Pseudoclementine Homilies, Introductory Epistle*
Ps.-Clem. Hom.	*Pseudoclementine Homilies*
Ps.-Clem. Rec.	*Pseudoclementine Recognitions*
Ps.-Plato	
Def.	*Definitions*
Ps. Sol.	*Psalms of Solomon*
Ps.-Tertullian	
Adv. haer.	*Adversus omnes haereses*
Q	Qumran
1QH	*Thanksgiving Hymns* from Qumran Cave 1
1QM	*Milḥāmāh (War Scroll)* from Qumran Cave 1
1QpHab	*Pesher on Habakkuk* from Qumran Cave 1
1QS	*Manual of Discipline* from Qumran Cave 1
1QSa	Appendix A to 1QS
2QFlor	*Florilegium* from Qumran Cave 2
4QTestim	*Testimonia* from Qumran Cave 4
QD	Quaestiones disputatae
RAC	*Reallexikon für Antike und Christentum*
RB	*Revue biblique*
RechBib	Recherches bibliques
RechSR	*Recherches de science religieuse*
RefR	*Reformation Review*
RevExp	*Review and Expositor*
RGG	*Religion in Geschichte und Gegenwart* (2d ed.; Tübingen: Mohr [Siebeck], 1927–32; 3d ed., 1957–62)
RHPhR	*Revue d'histoire et de philosophie religieuses*
RivB	*Rivista biblica*
RNT	Regensburger Neues Testament
RQ	*Römische Quartalschrift für christliche Altertumskunde und Kirchengeschichte*
RSV	*Revised Standard Version*
RThom	*Revue thomiste*
RVV	Religionsgeschichtliche Versuche und Vorarbeiten
SANT	Studien zum Alten und Neuen Testament
SBEc	*Studia biblica et ecclesiastica*
SBFLA	*Studii biblici franciscani liber annuus*
SBJ	*La sainte bible de Jérusalem*
SBLDS	SBL Dissertation Series
SB (PC)	*La sainte bible.* Published under the general direction of Louis Pirot and continued by A. Clamer

SBS	Stuttgarter Bibelstudien
SBT	Studies in Biblical Theology
SC	Sources chrétiennes
SCHNT	Studia ad corpus hellenisticum Novi Testamenti
Seneca	
Ben.	*De beneficiis*
Ep.	*Epistulae morales*
Prov.	*De providentia*
Sextus Empiricus	
Adv. log.	*Adversus logicos*
Adv. math.	*Adversus mathematicos*
Sib. Or.	*Sibylline Oracles*
Sipra Lev.	*Sipra on Leviticus*
Sipra Num.	*Sipra on Numbers*
Sipre Deut.	*Sipre on Deuteronomy*
SJT	*Scottish Journal of Theology*
SNT	Schriften des Neuen Testaments
SNTSMS	Society for New Testament Studies Monograph Series
Sophocles	
Phil.	*Philoctetes*
SPAW.PH	Sitzungsberichte der preussischen Akademie der Wissenschaften. Philosophisch-historische Klasse
StB	Studia Biblica
StEv	*Studia evangelica*
Stobaeus	
Ecl.	*Ecloge*
StPat	*Studia Patavina*
StPatr	*Studia Patristica*
Str-B	H. Strack and P. Billerbeck, *Kommentar zum Neuen Testament*
SUNT	Studien zur Umwelt des Neuen Testaments
SVF	Johannes von Arnim, *Stoicorum veterum fragmenta*
SWJT	*Southwestern Journal of Theology*
T. 12 Pat.	*Testaments of the Twelve Patriarchs*
T. Benj.	*Testament of Benjamin*
T. Dan	*Testament of Dan*
T. Iss.	*Testament of Issachar*
T. Jud.	*Testament of Judah*
T. Naph.	*Testament of Naphtali*
T. Reub.	*Testament of Reuben*
T. Sim.	*Testament of Simeon*
T. Zeb.	*Testament of Zebulon*
TBC	Torch Bible Commentaries
TBLNT	Lothar Coenen, et al., eds., *Theologisches Begriffslexikon zum Neuen Testament* (ET: *New International Dictionary of New Testament Theology*, ed. Colin Brown [3 vols., Grand Rapids: Zondervan, 1975–78])
TDNT	G. Kittel and G. Friedrich, eds., *Theological Dictionary of the New Testament*

TDOT	G. J. Botterweck and H. Ringgren, eds., *Theological Dictionary of the Old Testament*
Tertullian	
Ad mart.	*Ad martyros*
Adv. Marc.	*Adversus Marcionem*
Adv. Prax.	*Adversus Praxean*
Bapt.	*De baptismo*
Idol.	*De idololatria*
Pud.	*De pudicitia*
Scorp.	*Scorpiace*
Tg.	*Targum*
ThBü	Theologische Bücherei
THBW	Theologisch-homiletisches Bibelwerk
Theoph	Theophaneia
ThGl	*Theologie und Glaube*
ThHKNT	Theologischer Handkommentar zum Neuen Testament
ThJb	*Theologische Jahrbücher* (Tübingen)
ThLZ	*Theologische Literaturzeitung*
ThQ	*Theologische Quartalschrift*
ThR	*Theologische Rundschau*
ThSt	*Theologische Studien* (Munich)
ThStK	*Theologische Studien und Kritiken*
ThWAT	G. J. Botterweck and H. Ringgren, eds., *Theologisches Wörterbuch zum Alten Testament*
ThWNT	G. Kittel and G. Friedrich, eds., *Theologisches Wörterbuch zum Neuen Testament*
TNTC	Tyndale New Testament Commentaries
TRE	*Theologische Realenzyklopädie*
TS	*Theological Studies*
TThZ	*Trierer theologische Zeitschrift*
TU	Texte und Untersuchungen zur Geschichte der altchristlichen Literatur
TZ	*Theologische Zeitschrift*
UCB	Urchristliche Botschaft
UNT	Untersuchungen zum Neuen Testament
VC	*Vigiliae christianae*
VD	*Verbum Domini*
VF	*Verkündigung und Forschung*
VL	Vetus Latina
v.l.	*varia lectio* (variant reading)
VS	Verbum salutis
VT	*Vetus Testamentum*
WA	M. Luther, Kritische Gesamtausgabe (= "Weimar" edition)
WBC	Word Biblical Commentary
WMANT	Wissenschaftliche Monographien zum Alten und Neuen Testament
WTJ	*Westminster Theological Journal*

WUNT	Wissenschaftliche Untersuchungen zum Neuen Testament
Xenophon	
Hell.	*Hellenica*
Mem.	*Memorabilia Socratis*
Resp. Lac.	*Respublica Lacadaemoniorum*
y.	Talmud Yerushalmi, Jerusalem Talmud
ZBK	Zürcher Bibelkommentar
ZKG	*Zeitschrift für Kirchengeschichte*
ZKTh	*Zeitschrift für katholische Theologie*
ZNW	*Zeitschrift für die neutestamentliche Wissenschaft und die Kunde der älteren Kirche*
ZP	Zauberpapyri
ZThK	*Zeitschrift für Theologie und Kirche*
ZWTh	*Zeitschrift für wissenschaftliche Theologie*

2. Short Titles of Commentaries, Studies, and Articles Often Cited

Works mentioned more than twice are regularly cited by short title. In all cases full bibliographical information accompanies the first citation.

Aland and Aland, *Text*
Kurt and Barbara Aland, *The Text of the New Testament: An Introduction to the Critical Editions and to the Theory and Practice of Modern Textual Criticism* (trans. Erroll F. Rhodes; Grand Rapids: Eerdmans, 1987; 2d ed., 1989); ET of *Der Text des Neuen Testaments: Einführung in die wissenschaftlichen Ausgaben sowie in Theorie und Praxis der modernen Textkritik* (Stuttgart: Deutsche Bibelgesellschaft, 1982).

Balz, "Johanneische Theologie"
Horst R. Balz, "Johanneische Theologie und Ethik im Licht der 'letzten Stunde,'" in Wolfgang Schrage, ed., *Studien zum Text und zur Ethik des Neuen Testaments: Festschrift für H. Greeven* (BZNW 47; Berlin: de Gruyter, 1986) 35–56.

Balz, "Johannesbriefe"
Horst R. Balz, "Die Johannesbriefe," in Horst Balz and Wolfgang Schrage, *Die "Katholischen" Briefe: Die Briefe des Jakobus, Petrus, Johannes und Judas* (NTD 10; 2d ed.; Göttingen: Vandenhoeck & Ruprecht, 1980) 156–222.

Bauer, *Orthodoxy and Heresy*
Walter Bauer, *Orthodoxy and Heresy in Earliest Christianity* (trans. by a team from the Philadelphia Seminar on Christian Origins; ed. Robert A. Kraft and Gerhard Krodel; Philadelphia: Fortress, 1971); ET of *Rechtgläubigkeit und Ketzerei im ältesten Christentum* (ed. Georg Strecker; BHTh 10; 2d ed.; Tübingen: Mohr [Siebeck], 1964).

Bauernfeind, "Fürbitte"
Otto Bauernfeind, "Die Fürbitte angesichts der 'Sünde zum Tode,'" in *Von der Antike zum Christentum: Festgabe für Victor Schultze* (Stettin: Fischer & Schmidt, 1931) 43–54.

Behm, "*παράκλητος*"
Johannes Behm, "*παράκλητος*," *TDNT* 5 (1967) 800–814.

Betz, *Paraklet*
Otto Betz, *Der Paraklet: Fürsprecher im häretischen Spätjudentum, im Johannes-Evangelium und in neu gefundenen gnostischen Schriften* (Leiden: Brill, 1963).

Black, "Johannine Epistles"
C. Clifton Black II, "The Johannine Epistles and the Question of Early Catholicism," *NovT* 28 (1986) 131–58.

Böcher, "Antichrist"
Otto Böcher, "Antichrist II," *TRE* 3 (1978) 21–24.

Bonnard, "La première épître"
Pierre Bonnard, "La première épître de Jean est-elle johannique?" in Marinus de Jonge, ed., *L'Évangile de Jean* (BEThL 44; Gembloux: Duculot, 1977) 301–5.

Bonnard, *Les épîtres johanniques*
Les épîtres johanniques (CNT 2/13c; Geneva: Labor et Fides, 1983).

Botterweck, "ידע"
G. J. Botterweck, "ידע," *TDOT* 5.461–81.

Bousset, *Antichrist*
Wilhelm Bousset, *The Antichrist Legend: A Chapter in Christian and Jewish Folklore* (trans. with prologue on the Babylonian dragon myth by A. H. Keene; Satanism series; London: Hutchinson, 1896); ET of *Der Antichrist in der Überlieferung des Judentums, des Neuen Testaments und der Alten Kirche* (Göttingen: Vandenhoeck & Ruprecht, 1895).

Bousset, *Kyrios Christos*
Wilhelm Bousset, *Kyrios Christos: A History of the Belief in Christ from the Beginnings of Christianity to Irenaeus* [trans. John E. Steely; Nashville: Abingdon, 1970); ET of *Kyrios Christos: Geschichte des Christusglaubens von den Anfängen des Christentums bis Irenaeus* (FRLANT 21; 6th ed.; Göttingen: Vandenhoeck & Ruprecht, 1967).

Bousset, *Offenbarung Johannis*
Wilhelm Bousset, *Die Offenbarung Johannis* (KEK 16; 1906; 6th ed.; Göttingen: Vandenhoeck & Ruprecht, 1966).

Bousset and Gressmann, *Die Religion des Judentums*
Wilhelm Bousset and Hugo Gressmann, *Die Religion des Judentums im späthellenistischen Zeitalter* (HNT 21; 4th ed.; Tübingen: Mohr, 1966).

Braun, *Gesammelte Studien*
Herbert Braun, *Gesammelte Studien zum Neuen Testament und seiner Umwelt* (3d ed.; Tübingen: Mohr [Siebeck], 1971).

Braun, "Literar-Analyse"
Herbert Braun, "Literar-Analyse und theologische Schichtung im ersten Johannesbrief," *ZThK* 48 (1951) 262–92, reprinted in idem, *Gesammelte Studien zum Neuen Testament und seiner Umwelt* (3d ed.; Tübingen: Mohr [Siebeck], 1971, 210–42).

Brooke, *Epistles*
Alan England Brooke, *A Critical and Exegetical Commentary on the Johannine Epistles* (ICC 43; Edinburgh: Clark; New York: Scribner's, 1912; reprinted Edinburgh: Clark, 1957).

Brown, *Epistles*
Raymond E. Brown, *The Epistles of John* (AB 30; Garden City: Doubleday, 1982).

Brown, *John*
Raymond E. Brown, *The Gospel According to John* (2 vols.; AB 29, 29a; Garden City: Doubleday, 1966–70).

Brox, "Doketismus,"
Norbert Brox, "Doketismus: Eine Problemanzeige," *ZKG* 95 (1984) 301–14.

Brox, *Zeuge*
Norbert Brox, *Zeuge und Märtyrer: Untersuchungen zur frühchristlichen Zeugnis-Terminologie* (SANT 5; Munich: Kösel, 1961).
Büchsel, *Johannesbriefe*
Friedrich Büchsel, *Die Johannesbriefe* (ThHKNT 17; Leipzig: Deichert, 1933).
Büchsel, "μονογενής"
Friedrich Büchsel, "μονογενής," *TDNT* 4 (1967) 737–39.
Bultmann, "Analyse"
Rudolf Bultmann, "Analyse des ersten Johannesbriefes," in Rudolf Bultmann and Hermann Freiherr von Soden, eds., *Festgabe für A. Jülicher zum 70. Geburtstag* (Tübingen: Mohr, 1927) 138–58, reprinted in Erich Dinkler, ed., *Exegetica: Aufsätze zur Erforschung des Neuen Testaments* (Tübingen: Mohr [Siebeck], 1967) 105–23.
Bultmann, *Epistles*
Rudolf Bultmann, *The Johannine Epistles* (trans. R. Philip O'Hara with Lane C. McGaughy and Robert W. Funk; ed. Robert W. Funk; Hermeneia; Philadelphia: Fortress, 1973); ET of *Die drei Johannesbriefe* (KEK 14; 2d ed.; Göttingen: Vandenhoeck & Ruprecht, 1969).
Bultmann, *Exegetica*
Erich Dinkler, ed., *Exegetica: Aufsätze zur Erforschung des Neuen Testaments* (Tübingen: Mohr [Siebeck], 1967).
Bultmann, "γινώσκειν"
Rudolf Bultmann, "γινώσκειν, κτλ.," *TDNT* 1 (1964) 689–719.
Bultmann, *John*
Rudolf Bultmann, *The Gospel of John: A Commentary* (trans. G. R. Beasley-Murray, et al.; Philadelphia: Westminster; London: Blackwell, 1971); ET of *Das Evangelium des Johannes* (KEK; Göttingen: Vandenhoeck & Ruprecht, 1964), with *Ergänzungsheft* (1966).
Bultmann, "Redaktion"
Rudolf Bultmann, "Die kirchliche Redaktion des ersten Johannesbriefes," in Werner Schmauch, ed., *In Memoriam E. Lohmeyer* (Stuttgart: Evangelisches Verlagswerk, 1951) 189–201; reprinted in Erich Dinkler, ed., *Exegetica: Aufsätze zur Erforschung des Neuen Testaments* (Tübingen: Mohr [Siebeck], 1967) 381–93.
Bultmann, "ζάω"
Rudolf Bultmann, Gerhard von Rad, and Georg Bertram, "ζάω, κτλ.," *TDNT* 2 (1964) 832–75.
Bultmann and Lührmann, "φανερόω"
Rudolf Bultmann and Dieter Lührmann, "φανερόω," *TDNT* 9 (1974) 3–6.
Cernuda, "Engañan"
Antonio Vicent Cernuda, "Engañan la oscuridad y el mondo; la luz era y manifiesta lo verdadero," *EstBib* 27 (1968) 153–75, 215–32.
Chaine, *Les épîtres catholiques*
Joseph Chaine, *Les épîtres catholiques* (EtB; 2d ed.; Paris: Gabalda, 1939).
Chapman, "Historical Setting"
John Chapman, "The Historical Setting of the Second and Third Epistles of St. John," *JTS* 5 (1904) 357–68, 517–34.
Conzelmann, "Anfang"
Hans Conzelmann, "'Was von Anfang war,'" in Walther Eltester, ed., *Neutestamentliche Studien für Rudolf Bultmann* (BZNW 21; Berlin: Töpelmann, 1957) 194–201, reprinted in Conzelmann, *Theologie als Schriftauslegung: Aufsätze zum Neuen Testament* (BEvTh 65; Munich: Kaiser, 1974) 207–14.
Conzelmann, *1 Corinthians*
Hans Conzelmann, *1 Corinthians: A Commentary on the First Epistle to the Corinthians* (trans. James W. Leitch; Hermeneia; Philadelphia: Fortress, 1975).
Conzelmann, "φῶς"
Hans Conzelmann, "φῶς," *TDNT* 9 (1974) 310–58.
Culpepper, *Johannine School*
R. Alan Culpepper, *The Johannine School* (SBLDS 26; Missoula: Scholars Press, 1975).
Deissmann, *Light from the Ancient East*
Gustav Adolf Deissmann, *Light from the Ancient East* (trans. Lionel R. M. Strachan; New York: George H. Doran, 1927; reprinted Grand Rapids: Baker, 1978); ET of *Licht vom Osten: Das Neue Testament und die neuentdeckten Texte der hellenistisch–römischen Welt* (4th ed.; Tübingen: Mohr, 1923).
Delling, "τελειόω"
Gerhard Delling, "τελειόω," *TDNT* 8 (1972) 81–82.
Dobschütz, "Studien"
Ernst von Dobschütz, "Johanneische Studien I," *ZNW* 8 (1907) 1–8.
Dodd, *Epistles*
Charles Harold Dodd, *The Johannine Epistles* (2d ed.; London: Hodder & Stoughton, 1947).
Ehrhardt, *Framework*
Arnold Ehrhardt, *The Framework of the New Testament Stories* (Manchester: Manchester University Press; Cambridge: Harvard University Press, 1964).
Ernst, *Gegenspieler*
Josef Ernst, *Die eschatologischen Gegenspieler in den Schriften des Neuen Testaments* (BU 3; Regensburg: Pustet, 1967).
Flusser, "The Hubris of the Antichrist"
David Flusser, "The Hubris of the Antichrist in a Fragment from Qumran," *Immanuel* 10 (1980) 31–37.
Foerster, *Gnosis*
Werner Foerster, *Gnosis: A Selection of Gnostic Texts* (2 vols.; ed. R. McL. Wilson; Oxford: Clarendon, 1972–74).
Francis, "Form and Function"
Fred O. Francis, "The Form and Function of the

Opening and Closing Paragraphs of James and I John," *ZNW* 61 (1970) 110–26.

Funk, "Form and Structure"
Robert W. Funk, "The Form and Structure of I and II John," *JBL* 86 (1967) 424–30.

Haenchen, "Neuere Literatur"
Ernst Haenchen, "Neuere Literatur zu den Johannesbriefen," in idem, *Gesammelte Aufsätze*, vol. 2: *Die Bibel und Wir* (Tübingen: Mohr [Siebeck], 1968) 235–311 (= *ThR* 26 [1960] 1–43, 267–91).

Häring, "Gedankengang"
Theodor Häring, "Gedankengang und Grundgedanke des ersten Johannesbriefs," in Adolf von Harnack, et al., eds., *Theologische Abhandlungen: Carl von Weizsäcker zu seinem siebzigsten Geburtstage 11. Dezember 1892 gewidmet* (Freiburg: Mohr [Siebeck], 1892) 171–200.

von Harnack, *History of Dogma*
Adolf von Harnack, *History of Dogma*, vol. 1 (trans. Neil Buchanan, from 3d ed.; New York: Russell & Russell, 1958; reprinted New York: Dover, 1961); ET of *Lehrbuch der Dogmengeschichte*, vol. 1 (5th ed.; Tübingen: Mohr, 1931).

von Harnack, *Johannesbrief*
Adolf von Harnack, *Über den dritten Johannesbrief* (TU 15/3b; Leipzig: Hinrichs, 1897).

von Harnack, *Marcion*
Adolf von Harnack, *Marcion: The Gospel of the Alien God* (trans. John E. Steely and Lyle Bierma; Durham: Labyrinth Press, 1990); ET of *Marcion: Das Evangelium vom fremden Gott* (TU 45; 2d ed.; Leipzig: Hinrichs, 1924; reprinted Darmstadt: Wissenschaftliche Buchgesellschaft, 1960).

von Harnack, "Zur Textkritik"
Adolf von Harnack, "Zur Textkritik und Christologie der Schriften des Johannes: Zugleich ein Beitrag zur Würdigung der ältesten lateinischen Überlieferung nach der Vulgata," SPAW.PH 5/2 (Berlin: Reimer, 1915) 534–73, reprinted in *Studien zur Geschichte des NT und der Alten Kirche*, vol. 1: *Zur neutestamentlichen Textkritik* (AKG 19; Berlin: de Gruyter, 1931) 105–52.

Heise, *Bleiben*
Jürgen Heise, *Bleiben: Menein in den johanneischen Schriften* (HUT 8; Tübingen: Mohr, 1967).

Herkenrath, "Sünde zum Tode"
Josef Herkenrath, "Sünde zum Tode," in Theodor Steinbüchel and Theodor Müncker, eds., *Aus Theologie und Philosophie: Festschrift für Fritz Tillmann* (Dusseldorf: Patmos, 1950) 119–38.

Hilgenfeld, *Ketzergeschichte*
Adolf Hilgenfeld, *Die Ketzergeschichte des Urchristentums* (Leipzig: Fues [Reisland], 1884; reprinted Hildesheim: Olms, 1963).

Hirsch, *Studien*
Emanuel Hirsch, *Studien zum vierten Evangelium* (BHTh 11; Tübingen: Mohr, 1936).

Houlden, *Commentary*
James Leslie Houlden, *A Commentary on the Johannine Epistles* (HNTC; Black's New Testament Commentaries; London: Black; New York: Harper & Row, 1973; 2d ed.; London: Black, 1994).

Huther, *Handbuch*
Johann Eduard Huther, *Kritisch-exegetisches Handbuch über die drei Briefe des Apostels Johannes* (KEK 14; 4th ed.; Göttingen: Vandenhoeck & Ruprecht, 1880).

Jonas, *Gnosis*
Hans Jonas, *Gnosis und spätantiker Geist* (2 vols.; 2d ed.; Göttingen: Vandenhoeck & Ruprecht, 1954).

Jülicher and Fascher, *Einleitung*
Adolf Jülicher and Erich Fascher, *Einleitung in das Neue Testament* (7th ed.; Tübingen: Mohr, 1931).

Käsemann, "Ketzer und Zeuge"
Ernst Käsemann, "Ketzer und Zeuge," *ZThK* 48 (1951) 292–311, reprinted in idem, *Exegetische Versuche und Besinnungen* (2 vols.; 6th ed.; Göttingen: Vandenhoeck & Ruprecht, 1970) 1.168–87.

Käsemann, "Paul and Early Catholicism"
Ernst Käsemann, "Paul and Early Catholicism" (trans. Wilfred F. Bunge), in *New Testament Questions of Today* (trans. W. J. Montague and Wilfred F. Bunge; Philadelphia: Fortress, 1969) 236–51.

Kilpatrick, "Two Johannine Idioms"
George D. Kilpatrick, "Two Johannine Idioms in the Johannine Epistles," *JTS* n.s. 12 (1961) 272–73.

Klein, "Das wahre Licht"
Günther Klein, "'Das wahre Licht scheint schon.' Beobachtungen zur Zeit- und Geschichtserfahrung einer urchristlichen Schule," *ZThK* 68 (1971) 261–326.

Klos, *Sakramente*
Herbert Klos, *Die Sakramente im Johannesevangelium* (SBS 46; Stuttgart: Katholisches Bibelwerk, 1970).

Kühner-Gerth, *Grammatik*
Raphael Kühner and Bernhard Gerth, *Ausführliche Grammatik der griechischen Sprache* (2 vols.; 4th ed.; Leverkusen: Gottschalk, 1955).

Kümmel, *Introduction*
Werner Georg Kümmel, *Introduction to the New Testament* (trans. Howard Clark Kee; 3d ed.; Nashville: Abingdon, 1975); ET of *Einleitung in das Neue Testament* (1964; 21st ed.; Heidelberg: Quelle & Meyer, 1983).

Leipoldt, *Geschichte*
Johannes Leipoldt, *Geschichte des neutestamentlichen Kanons*, vol. 1: *Die Entstehung;* vol. 2: *Mittelalter und Neuzeit* (Leipzig: Hinrichs, 1907–1908).

Lidzbarski, *Ginza*
Mark Lidzbarski, *Ginza: Der Schatz, oder Das Grosse Buch der Mandäer* (Göttingen: Vandenhoeck & Ruprecht; Leipzig: Hinrichs, 1925).

Lieu, *Epistles*
Judith M. Lieu, *The Second and Third Epistles of John: History and Background* (Studies of the New Testament and Its World; ed. John Riches; Edinburgh: Clark, 1986).

Lohmeyer, "Aufbau"
Ernst Lohmeyer, "Über Aufbau und Gliederung des ersten Johannesbriefes," *ZNW* 27 (1928) 225–63.

Lohse, *Märtyrer*
Eduard Lohse, *Märtyrer und Gottesknecht: Untersuchungen zur urchristlichen Verkündigung vom Sühnetod Jesu Christi* (FRLANT 64; 2d ed.; Göttingen: Vandenhoeck & Ruprecht, 1963).

Luz, "Erwägungen"
Ulrich Luz, "Erwägungen zur Entstehung des 'Frühkatholizismus,'" *ZNW* 65 (1974) 88–111.

Malatesta, *Interiority and Covenant*
Edward Malatesta, *Interiority and Covenant: An Exegetical Study of* εἶναι ἐν *and* μένειν ἐν *in the First Letter of Saint John* (AnBib 69; Rome: Biblical Institute Press, 1978).

Marshall, *Epistles*
I. Howard Marshall, *The Epistles of John* (NICNT; Grand Rapids: Eerdmans, 1978).

Mealand, "Language of Mystical Union"
David L. Mealand, "The Language of Mystical Union in the Johannine Writings," *DRev* 95 (1977) 19–34.

Metzger, *Text*
Bruce Metzger, *The Text of the New Testament: Its Transmission, Corruption, and Restoration* (3d ed.; New York: Oxford University Press, 1992).

Moulton, *Grammar*
James Hope Moulton, et al., *A Grammar of New Testament Greek* (3 vols.; 3d ed.; Edinburgh: Clark, 1908–63).

Nagl, "Gliederung"
Erasmus Nagl, "Die Gliederung des ersten Johannesbriefes," *BZ* 16 (1924) 77–92.

Nauck, *Tradition*
Wolfgang Nauck, *Die Tradition und der Charakter des ersten Johannesbriefes* (WUNT 3; Tübingen: Mohr, 1957).

Norden, *Agnostos Theos*
Eduard Norden, *Agnostos Theos: Untersuchungen zur Formgeschichte religiöser Rede* (Leipzig/Berlin: Teubner, 1913; reprinted Darmstadt: Wissenschaftliche Buchgesellschaft, 1974).

Nötscher, *Zur theologischen Terminologie*
Friedrich Nötscher, *Zur theologischen Terminologie der Qumran-Texte* (BBB 10; Bonn: Hanstein, 1956).

Osten-Sacken, *Gott und Belial*
Peter von den Osten-Sacken, *Gott und Belial* (SUNT 6; Göttingen: Vandenhoeck & Ruprecht, 1969).

Percy, *Untersuchungen*
Ernst Percy, *Untersuchungen über den Ursprung der johanneischen Theologie* (Lund: Gleerup, 1939).

Peterson "'Ἀγάπη,"
Eric Peterson, "'Ἀγάπη" *BZ* 20 (1932) 378–82.

Porsch, *Pneuma und Wort*
Felix Porsch, *Pneuma und Wort* (FTS 16; Frankfurt: Knecht, 1974).

Poschmann, *Paenitentia*
Bernhard Poschmann, *Paenitentia secunda: Die kirchliche Busse im ältesten Christentum bis Cyprian und Origenes* (Theoph 1; Bonn: Hanstein, 1940; reprinted 1964).

de la Potterie, "Anointing of the Christian by Faith"
Ignace de la Potterie, "Anointing of the Christian by Faith," in Stanislaus Lyonnet, *The Christian Lives by the Spirit* (trans. John Morriss; Staten Island: Alba House, 1971) 79–143; ET of "L'onction du chrétien par la foi," *Bib* 40 (1959) 12–59.

de la Potterie, *La vérité*
Ignace de la Potterie, *La vérité dans Saint Jean* (2 vols.; AnBib 73–74; Rome: Biblical Institute Press, 1977).

de la Potterie, "Sin Is Iniquity"
Ignace de la Potterie, "Sin Is Iniquity," in Stanislaus Lyonnet, *The Christian Lives by the Spirit* (trans. John Morriss; Staten Island: Alba House, 1971) 37–55; ET of "Le péché, c'est l'iniquité (I Joh III,4)," *NRTh* 78 (1956) 785–97.

Prucker, Γνῶσις Θεοῦ
Eugen Prucker, Γνῶσις Θεοῦ (Classiciacum 4; Würzburg: Rita-Verlag und Druckerei, 1937).

Radermacher, *Neutestamentliche Grammatik*
Ludwig Radermacher, *Neutestamentliche Grammatik: Das Griechisch des Neuen Testaments im Zusammenhang mit der Volkssprache* (HNT 1; 2d ed.; Tübingen: Mohr [Siebeck], 1925).

Reitzenstein, *Hellenistic Mystery-Religions*
Richard Reitzenstein, *Hellenistic Mystery-Religions: Their Basic Ideas and Significance* (trans. John E. Steely; Pittsburgh: Pickwick, 1978).

Richards, *Classification*
William L. Richards, *The Classification of the Greek Manuscripts of the Johannine Epistles* (SBLDS 35; Missoula: Scholars Press, 1977).

Rudolph, *Gnosis*
Kurt Rudolph, *Gnosis: The Nature and History of Gnosticism* (trans. P. W. Coxon and K. H. Kuhn; ed. R. McL. Wilson; 3d ed.; San Francisco: Harper & Row, 1990); ET of *Die Gnosis: Wesen und Geschichte einer spätantiken Religion* (2d ed.; Göttingen: Vandenhoeck & Ruprecht, 1980).

Schlier, "Bruderliebe"
Heinrich Schlier, "Die Bruderliebe nach dem Evangelium und den Briefen des Johannes," in Albert Descamps and André de Halleux, eds., *Mélanges bibliques en hommage au R. P. Beda Rigaux* (Gembloux: Duculot, 1970) 235–45.

Schlier, "Vom Antichrist"
Heinrich Schlier, "Vom Antichrist: Zum 13. Kapitel der Offenbarung Johannis," in Ernst Wolf,

ed., *Theologische Aufsätze: Festschrift für Karl Barth* (Munich: Kaiser, 1936) 110–23, reprinted in idem, *Die Zeit der Kirche: Exegetische Aufsätze und Vorträge*, vol. 1 (2d ed.; Freiburg: Herder, 1958) 16–29.

Schlier, "παρρησία"
Heinrich Schlier, "παρρησία, παρρασιάζομαι," *TDNT* 5 (1967) 871–86.

Schmithals, "γινώσκω"
Walter Schmithals, "γινώσκω," *EDNT* 1 (1990) 248–51.

Schmitz, *Frühkatholizismus*
Hermann-Josef Schmitz, *Frühkatholizismus bei Adolf von Harnack, Rudolph Sohm und Ernst Käsemann* (Düsseldorf: Patmos, 1977).

Schnackenburg, *Epistles*
Rudolf Schnackenburg, *The Johannine Epistles: Introduction and Commentary* (trans. Reginald and Ilse Fuller; New York: Crossroad, 1992).

Schnackenburg, *Johannesbriefe*
Rudolf Schnackenburg, *Die Johannesbriefe* (HThKNT 13/3; 7th ed.; Freiburg: Herder, 1984).

Schnackenburg, *John*
Rudolf Schnackenburg, *The Gospel According to St. John* (trans. Kevin Smyth, et al.; 3 vols.; New York: Crossroad, 1980–82); ET of *Das Johannesevangelium* (3 vols.; HThKNT 4/1–3; Freiburg: Herder, 1965–84).

Schneider, "Briefe"
Johannes Schneider, *Die Briefe des Jakobus, Petrus, Judas und Johannes: Die Katholischen Briefe* (NTD 10; 9th ed.; Göttingen: Vandenhoeck & Ruprecht, 1961).

Schnelle, *Antidocetic Christology*
Udo Schnelle, *Antidocetic Christology in the Gospel of John* (trans. Linda M. Maloney; Minneapolis: Fortress, 1992); ET of *Antidoketische Christologie im Johannesevangelium* (FRLANT 144; Göttingen: Vandenhoeck & Ruprecht, 1987).

Schottroff, *Glaubende*
Luise Schottroff, *Der Glaubende und die feindliche Welt* (WMANT 37; Neukirchen-Vluyn: Neukirchener Verlag, 1970).

Schrenk, "ἐντολή"
Gottlob Schrenk, "ἐντολή," *TDNT* 2 (1964) 554–55.

Schunack, *Briefe*
Gerd Schunack, *Die Briefe des Johannes* (ZBK NT 17; Zurich: Theologischer Verlag, 1982).

Schürmann, "Auf der Suche"
Heinz Schürmann, "Auf der Suche nach dem 'Evangelisch-Katholischen,'" in Paul-Gerhard Müller and Werner Stenger, eds., *Kontinuität und Einheit: Festschrift for Franz Mussner* (Freiburg/Berlin/Vienna: Herder, 1981) 340–75.

Schwartz, *Über den Tod*
Eduard Schwartz, *Über den Tod der Söhne Zebedai: Ein Beitrag zur Geschichte des Johannesevangeliums* (AGWG.PH 7/5; Berlin: Weidmann, 1904; reprinted Göttingen: Kraus, 1970).

Schwertschlager, "Der erste Johannesbrief"
R. Schwertschlager, "Der erste Johannesbrief in seinem Grundgedanken und Aufbau" (diss., Gregoriana; Coburg, 1935).

Segond, "1re Epître"
Albert Segond, "1re Epître de Jean, chap. 5,18–20," *RHPhR* 45 (1965) 349–51.

Smalley, *1, 2, 3 John*
Stephen S. Smalley, *1, 2, 3 John* (WBC 51; Waco: Word, 1984).

Sparks, *Apocryphal OT*
Hedley Frederick Davis Sparks, ed., *The Apocryphal Old Testament* (Oxford: Clarendon, 1985).

Staerk, *Soter*
Willy Staerk, *Soter: Die biblische Erlösererwartung als religionsgeschichtliches Problem, vol. 1: Der biblische Christus* (BFCTh 2/31; Gütersloh: Bertelsmann, 1933).

Stauffer, "ἀγαπάω"
Ethelbert Stauffer, "ἀγαπάω, κτλ.," *TDNT* 1 (1964) 21–55.

Stott, *Epistles*
John R. W. Stott, *The Epistles of John* (TNTC 19; Grand Rapids: Eerdmans, 1964).

Strecker, "Anfänge"
Georg Strecker, "Die Anfänge der johanneischen Schule," *NTS* 32 (1986) 31–47.

Strecker, *Sermon*
Georg Strecker, *The Sermon on the Mount: An Exegetical Commentary* (trans. O. C. Dean, Jr.; Nashville: Abingdon, 1988); ET of *Die Bergpredigt: Ein exegetischer Kommentar* (2d ed.; Göttingen: Vandenhoeck & Ruprecht, 1985).

Strecker, *Weg*
Georg Strecker, *Der Weg der Gerechtigkeit* (FRLANT 82; 3d ed.; Göttingen: Vandenhoeck & Ruprecht, 1971).

Thompson, "Psalm 119"
P. J. Thompson, "Psalm 119: A Possible Clue to the Structure of the First Epistle of John," *StEv* II (TU 87; Berlin: Akademie, 1964) 487–92.

Trilling, *Der zweite Brief*
Wolfgang Trilling, *Der zweite Brief an die Thessalonicher* (EKK 14; Zurich: Benziger; Neukirchen-Vluyn: Neukirchener Verlag, 1980).

Tröger, *Gnosis und NT*
Karl-Wolfgang Tröger, ed., *Gnosis und Neues Testament* (Gütersloh: Mohn, 1973).

Vellanickal, *Divine Sonship*
Matthew Vellanickal, *The Divine Sonship of Christians in the Johannine Writings* (AnBib 72; Rome: Biblical Institute Press, 1977).

Venetz, "Zeuge des Erhöhten"
Hermann-Josef Venetz, "Zeuge des Erhöhten: Ein exegetischer Beitrag zu Joh 19,31–37," *FZPhTh* 23 (1976) 81–111.

Vielhauer, *Geschichte*
Philipp Vielhauer, *Geschichte der urchristlichen Literatur* (Berlin/New York: de Gruyter, 1975).

Weigandt, "Doketismus"
P. Weigandt, "Der Doketismus im Urchristentum und in der theologischen Entwicklung des 2. Jahrhunderts" (diss., Heidelberg, 1961).

Weiss, *Briefe*
Bernhard Weiss, *Die drei Briefe des Apostel Johannes* (KEK 14; 6th ed.; Göttingen: Vandenhoeck & Ruprecht, 1899).

Wendt, "Der 'Anfang'"
Hans Hinrich Wendt, "Der 'Anfang' am Beginne des I Johannesbriefes," *ZNW* 21 (1922) 38–42.

Wengst, *Brief*
Klaus Wengst, *Der erste, zweite und dritte Brief des Johannes* (ÖTK 16; Gütersloh: Mohn, 1978).

Wengst, *Häresie und Orthodoxie*
Klaus Wengst, *Häresie und Orthodoxie im Spiegel des ersten Johannesbriefes* (Gütersloh: Mohn, 1976).

Westcott, *Epistles*
Brooke Foss Westcott, *The Epistles of St. John* (2d ed.; London: Macmillan, 1886; new ed. with introduction by Frederick F. Bruce; Abingdon: Marcham Manor; Grand Rapids: Eerdmans, 1966).

Wikenhauser and Schmid, *Einleitung*
Alfred Wikenhauser and Josef Schmid, *Einleitung in das Neue Testament* (6th ed.; Freiburg: Herder, 1973).

Windisch and Preisker, *Die Katholischen Briefe*
Hans Windisch and Herbert Preisker, *Die Katholischen Briefe* (HNT 15; 3d ed.; Tübingen: Mohr, 1951).

Wischmeyer, "Vorkommen und Bedeutung"
Otto Wischmeyer, "Vorkommen und Bedeutung von Agape in der ausserchristlichen Antike," *ZNW* 69 (1978) 212–38.

Zahn, *Geschichte*
Theodor Zahn, *Geschichte des neutestamentlichen Kanons* (2 vols.; Erlangen: Deichert, 1888–92).

Zahn, *Grundriss*
Theodor Zahn, *Grundriss der Geschichte des neutestamentlichen Kanons: Eine Ergänzung zu der Einleitung in das Neue Testament* (2d ed.; Leipzig: Deichert, 1904).

Zerwick, *Biblical Greek*
Maximilian Zerwick, *Biblical Greek Illustrated by Examples* (4th ed.; trans. Joseph Smith; Rome: Biblical Institute Press, 1963).

Editor's Note

The English translation of the Johannine Epistles is based on the German translation of Professor Strecker and reflects his exegetical decisions. Other biblical texts are usually from the *New Revised Standard Version.* Quotations from Latin and Greek authors, except where noted, follow the texts and translations of the Loeb Classical Library or other standard editions. Translations of the Dead Sea Scrolls are normally from Geza Vermes, *The Dead Sea Scrolls in English* (3d ed.; London: Penguin, 1987).

The endpapers display the opening page of 1 John from Marin Luther's "September Bible" of 1522. They are provided courtesy of The John Work Garrett Library of The Johns Hopkins University, Baltimore, Maryland.

1. Patristic Witnesses

The light of historical tradition falls relatively early on at least part of the Johannine writings. The letter of Polycarp of Smyrna (died 156) to the Philippians (7.1) already has an indirect citation: "For 'whosoever does not confess that Jesus Christ has come in the flesh is antichrist'; and whosoever does not confess the testimony of the cross 'is of the devil' (ἐκ τοῦ διαβόλου); and whosoever perverts the sayings of the Lord to suit [that one's] own lusts (πρὸς τὰς ἰδίας ἐπιθυμίας) and says there [is] neither resurrection nor judgment—such a one is the firstborn of Satan (πρωτότοκός ἐστι τοῦ σατανᾶ)." At this point Polycarp is no doubt referring to 1 John 4:2–3, according to which "every spirit that confesses that Jesus Christ has come in the flesh is from God," and laying the responsibility for rejection of this confession on the spirit of the "antichrist." In addition, the words ἐπιθυμία and διάβολος seem to be borrowed from 1 John.[1]

While other possible connections to contemporary or earlier literature, such as *1 Clement*,[2] the *Didache*,[3] Ignatius of Antioch,[4] or the *Shepherd of Hermas*,[5] are uncertain, one can establish with great probability, on the basis of Justin, that 1 John was being used in the churches at the latest by the middle of the second century.[6] This is shown also by the witness of Papias, who in his "accounts of the Lord's sayings"—as Eusebius (*Hist. eccl.* 3.39.17) reports—referred to 1 John and 1 Peter,[7] and apparently did not rely merely on the oral tradition of the presbyter from Asia Minor but may also have used 3 John.[8] Other, somewhat later witnesses are the *Epistle to Diognetus*[9] and the letter from the communities at Lyons and Vienne, written about 177.[10]

The Muratorian Canon, which may go back to the end of the second century, is of special importance. It contains a listing and description of NT and apocryphal NT writings, and quotes directly both from the Gospel of John and from 1 John (1:1, 4).[11] The following explanation, "for so he confesses (himself) not merely as an eye- and ear-witness, but also a writer of all the marvels of the Lord in order,"[12] makes clear that in the

1 Polycarp *Phil.* 7.1. Translation adapted from Cyril C. Richardson, ed., *Early Christian Fathers* (New York: Macmillan, 1970) 134. Cf. 1 John 2:16–17 and 3:8, 10. That Polycarp at this point is not citing the related text of 2 John 7 is evident from the infinitive ἐληλυθέναι instead of the participle ἐρχόμενον (against Theodor Zahn, *Geschichte des neutestamentlichen Kanons* 1/2 [Erlangen: Deichert, 1889] 905 n. 1).

2 *1 Clem.* 49.1 (1 John 5:1–3); *1 Clem.* 49.5; 50.1 (1 John 2:5; 4:18).

3 *Did.* 10.5 (1 John 4:12, 18; cf. John 17:23); *Did.* 11.7 (1 John 4:1). Cf. *Did.* 16.4 (2 John 7).

4 Ignatius *Eph.* 14.2 (1 John 3:6; 5:18).

5 *Herm. Vis.* 1.1.8 (1 John 2:15–16); *Herm. Man.* 12.3.5 (1 John 5:3); *Herm. Sim.* 9.18.1 (1 John 4:17–18); *Herm. Sim.* 9.24.4 (1 John 4:13). Cf. Bernhard Weiss, *Die drei Briefe des Apostel Johannes* (KEK 14; 6th ed.; Göttingen: Vandenhoeck & Ruprecht, 1899) p. 1 n.; Hans Windisch and Herbert Preisker, *Die Katholischen Briefe* (HNT 15; 3d ed.; Tübingen: Mohr, 1951) 125–26, 130–31.

6 Justin *Dial.* 123.9 (1 John 3:1–2); not only the expression τέκνα θεοῦ, but also the sentence construction points to the passage in 1 John here indicated; beyond this, the combination with the obligation "to keep Christ's commandments" echoes 1 John 2:3 (as well as 3:22, 24).

7 Cf. 1 John 2:3 (ἐὰν τὰς ἐντολὰς αὐτοῦ τηρῶμεν); 5:2 (ὅταν τὸν θεὸν ἀγαπῶμεν καὶ τὰς ἐντολὰς αὐτοῦ ποιῶμεν) with Eusebius *Hist. eccl.* 3.39.3 (οὐδὲ τοῖς τὰς ἀλλοτρίας ἐντολὰς μνημονεύουσιν).

8 Cf. Eusebius *Hist. eccl.* 3.39.3 (ἀπ᾽ αὐτῆς . . . τῆς ἀληθείας); 3 John 12 (ὑπὸ αὐτῆς τῆς ἀληθείας).

9 *Diogn.* 10.2–3 (1 John 4:9, 19; 1:4); *Diogn.* 11.4 (1 John 1:1; 2:7, 13–14).

10 Eusebius *Hist. eccl.* 5.1.10 (1 John 3:16).

11 "Quid ergo mirum, si Johannes tam constanter singula etiam in epistulis suis proferat, dicens in semetipsum: 'quae vidimus oculis nostris et auribus audivimus et manus nostrae palpaverunt, haec scripsimus vobis'" (lines 26–31); text in Theodor Zahn, *Grundriss der Geschichte des neutestamentlichen Kanons: Eine Ergänzung zu der Einleitung in das Neue Testament* (2d ed.; Leipzig: Deichert, 1904) 78; Hans Lietzmann, *Das Muratorische Fragment und die Monarchianischen Prologue zu den Evangelien* (KIT 1; 2d ed.; Berlin: de Gruyter, 1933) 5–7. Translation: "What wonder then if John, being thus always true to himself, adduces particular points in his epistles also, where he says of himself: 'What we have seen with our eyes and have heard with our ears and our hands have handled, that we have written to you' " (*NTApoc*² 1.35).

12 Lines 32–34: "Sic enim non solum visorem se et

Muratorian Canon the author of 1 John is identified with the evangelist and described as an eyewitness. After describing, in the next forty lines, the Acts of the Apostles, the Pauline Letters, and the writings falsely ascribed to Paul, as well as the Letter of Jude, the unknown author writes: "superscriptae Johannis duae in catholica habentur" ("two [letters] with the title [or: two of the above mentioned] John are accepted in the catholic [church]" lines 68–69). In current research the dominant opinion is that these lines are connected with the earlier statement about 1 John, thus representing a reference to 1 and 2 John.[13] For this position one may also refer to the testimony of Irenaeus, and perhaps to Clement of Alexandria as well, both of whom seem to know only these two Johannine Letters.[14] Still, the physical separation of this statement from lines 32–34, as well as the word *superscriptae,* apparently with denigrating intent,[15] expresses a certain reservation that leads one to suspect that the author of the Muratorian fragment held somewhat the same opinion as Origen and Eusebius, and did not wish to acknowledge 2 and 3 John, the two letters of the presbyter, as genuine Johannine writings.[16] The canon of the Roman synod of 382 and the church father Jerome make a similar distinction: Jerome calls the presbyter "another John" (*De viris illustribus* 9; a different opinion is found in his *Epistula* 53.9 [CSEL 54]). While Irenaeus also identifies the author of 1 John with the evangelist,[17] the attribution of 2 and 3 John to the apostle and evangelist John is first attested with some degree of clarity by Origen (Eusebius *Hist. eccl.* 6.25.10), Dionysius of Alexandria (Eusebius *Hist. eccl.* 7.25.11), and Eusebius (*Dem. Ev.* 3.5.88; see the different statement in his *Hist. eccl.* 3.25.3).

2. The History of the Text

The three Johannine Letters are included among the Catholic Letters in the major biblical manuscripts ℵ A B C, and belong to that group of NT writings that is, on the whole, well attested. In earlier scholarship the classification of the textual tradition as belonging to the groups $\mathfrak{H}$ (Egyptian or Alexandrian text), and $\mathfrak{K}$ (Byzantine or Imperial text), as well as the Caesarean, Western, or Palestinian text (H. von Soden), had great authority. As regards the text of the Johannine Letters in particular, however, this division cannot be applied without some serious reservations. They are almost

auditorem, sed et scriptorem omnium mirabilium domini per ordinem profiteretur." Cf. also Georg Strecker, "Canon Muratori," *RGG*³ 4 (1986) 1191 (with bibliography).

13 This is the opinion, for example, of Weiss, *Briefe,* 163; Johannes Leipoldt, *Geschichte des neutestamentlichen Kanons* (2 vols.; Leipzig: Hinrichs, 1907–1908) 1.234; Rudolf Schnackenburg, *The Johannine Epistles: Introduction and Commentary* (trans. Reginald and Ilse Fuller; New York: Crossroad, 1992) 46–47, 274; Horst R. Balz, "Johannesbriefe," in Wolfgang Schrage and Horst R. Balz, *Die "Katholischen" Briefe: Die Briefe des Jakobus, Petrus, Johannes und Judas* (NTD 10; 2d ed.; Göttingen: Vandenhoeck & Ruprecht, 1980) 156; Alan E. Brooke, *A Critical and Exegetical Commentary on the Johannine Epistles* (ICC 43; Edinburgh: Clark; New York: Scribner's, 1912; reprinted Edinburgh: Clark, 1957) lvii; Klaus Wengst, *Der erste, zweite und dritte Brief des Johannes* (ÖTK 16; Gütersloh: Mohn, 1978) 228; Judith Lieu, *The Second and Third Epistles of John: History and Background* (Studies of the New Testament and Its World; ed. J. Riches; Edinburgh: Clark, 1986) 23; a different opinion was already voiced by Johann Eduard Huther, *Kritisch-exegetisches Handbuch über die drei Briefe des Apostels Johannes* (KEK 14; 4th ed.; Göttingen: Vandenhoeck & Ruprecht, 1880) 20. Walter Thiele has pointed out the different textual traditions of the Johannine writings. It seems, therefore, that the Latin tradition is not uniform; in particular, there is a difference in the Latin version of 3 John compared with the first two Johannine Letters. From this fact he concludes that the translation and tradition of the Latin texts were independent of one another (*Wortschatzuntersuchungen zu den lateinischen Texten der Johannesbriefe* [AGLB 2; Freiburg: Herder, 1958]). There is certainly a problem in applying this circumstance to the interpretation of the lines of the Muratorian Canon cited above, since the latter may well have been written in Greek. This is particularly true with regard to the original relationship of the three Johannine Letters. Cf. also n. 18 below.

14 On this, see nn. 38 and 42 below.

15 Cf. *NTApoc*² 1.36 ("with the title").

16 Cf. Zahn, *Geschichte,* 1.219–20; idem, *Grundriss* 20 (on the basis of Eusebius *Hist. eccl.* 6.25.10, according to which Origen, in his commentary on the Gospel of John, indicates his doubts about the Johannine authorship of 2 and 3 John).

17 Irenaeus *Adv. haer.* 3.16.5 (1 John 2:18–22); cf. *Adv. haer.* 3.16.8 (2 John 7–8).

entirely absent from the most important representative of the so-called Western text, Codex D (05 = Bezae Cantabrigiensis). Because of a gap of 67 sheets, only 3 John 11–15 and the signature to 3 John are transmitted by this primary Western witness. The Old Latin manuscripts that are cited as witnesses of the Western text type vary in their content as regards the Catholic Letters (1 John and 1 Peter being the best attested), and there are gaps, even though in individual instances they offer some readings deserving attention, since they rest on Greek textual models.[18] The Old Syriac witnesses, which often contain a Western text, must be eliminated, since they do not contain the Catholic Letters. Only in the Peshitta do we find 1 John, and all three letters are contained in the Philoxenian version.[19] The assignment of manuscripts to the so-called Caesarean text is problematic. Muriel M. Carder has attempted to ascribe minuscule 1243 to the Caesarean type,[20] but serious doubts have been raised against this.[21] Moreover, the supposition of a Caesarean text type witnessed by W, 28, 565, 700, and the manuscript families f^1 and f^{13} is highly questionable, and not only for the Johannine letters.[22]

18 The most important Old Latin manuscripts for the Johannine Letters are the minuscules h (no. 55 in the Vetus Latina edition of Beuron, a 5th-century palimpsest from Fleury, containing 1 John 1:8—3:20), r (64, the Freising fragment, 7th century, containing 1 John 3:8—end), d (5, from the 5th century, containing 3 John 11–15), l (67, from the 7th century, containing 1 John 1:5—2:10, 14–16; 2:24—3:12; 3:22—4:18; 4:20—end; 2 John 1–6, 8–end; 3 John 1–10), w (32, from the 6th century, containing 1 John 1:6–7; 2:6–11, 15–17; 3:6–9, 13–21; 4:9–21), z (65, from the 8th century, containing 1 John 1:1—3:15). Older forms of the Old Latin text can be found in Cyprian, Pseudo-Cyprian, Augustine (1 John), Pseudo-Augustine's *Speculum* (m); cf. Hermann Josef Frede, *Kirchenschriftsteller: Verzeichnis und Sigel* (VL 1/1; 3d ed.; Freiburg: Herder, 1981). Walter Thiele (*Epistulae Catholicae* [VL 26/1; Freiburg: Herder, 1956–69] 97*–99*, and earlier, idem, "Untersuchungen zu den altlateinischen Texten der drei Johannesbriefe" [diss., Tübingen, 1956], with the summary in *ThLZ* 82 [1957] 71–72) distinguishes a number of textual groups: group K, witnessed primarily by Cyprian and Pseudo-Cyprian, is said to be closest to the Western text; group T (including minuscules 67, 32, 55, 64, 65) designates the "European type," in which the African and Western texts recede; V = Vulgata is understood as an accommodation to the Greek *Vorlage*, i.e., as a revision of the Old Latin, and not as a new translation. Adolf von Harnack still wanted to regard the Vulgate as an important instance of textual criticism, since for him Jerome was a thorough reviser of the Vulgate, including its NT part. Cf. Adolf von Harnack, "Zur Textkritik und Christologie der Schriften des Johannes: Zugleich ein Beitrag zur Würdigung der ältesten lateinischen Überlieferung nach der Vulgata," *SPAW.PH* 5/2 (Berlin: Reimer, 1915) 534–73, reprinted in *Studien zur Geschichte des NT und der Alten Kirche* vol. 1: *Zur neutestamentlichen Textkritik* (AKG 19; Berlin: de Gruyter, 1931, 105–52, esp. 146); however, on Jerome's editorial work in the NT part of the Vulgate, cf. Kurt and Barbara Aland, *The Text of the New Testament: An Introduction to the Critical Editions and to the Theory and Practice of Modern Textual Criticism* (trans. Erroll F. Rhodes; 1987; 2d. ed.; Grand Rapids: Eerdmans; Leiden: Brill, 1989) 191–92. On the Latin tradition, see also Brooke, *Epistles*, 197–223 (including reproduction of sources).

19 Edition: John Gwynn, *Remnants of the Later Syriac Versions of the Bible*, vol. 1: *New Testament: The Four Minor Catholic Epistles in the Original Philoxenian Version* (London: Williams & Norgate, 1909); cf. also Andreas Juckel, *Das Neue Testament in syrischer Überlieferung*, vol. 1: *Die grossen Katholischen Briefe* (ed. Barbara Aland; ANTT 7; Berlin/New York: de Gruyter, 1986).

20 Muriel M. Carder, "A Caesarean Text in the Catholic Epistles?" *NTS* 16 (1969/70) 252–70: "The circumstance adds weight to the impression received that MS 1243 is a witness to the Caesarean text here" (p. 269). See also her dissertation, "An Enquiry into the Textual Transmission of the Catholic Epistles" (Victoria University, 1968).

21 Cf. Kurt Aland, "Bemerkungen zu den gegenwärtigen Möglichkeiten textkritischer Arbeit aus Anlass einer Untersuchung zum Cäsarea-Text der Katholischen Briefe," *NTS* 17 (1970/71) 1–9 (the principal objection is the lack of a collation with Origen and Eusebius, as well as the fact that no *Sitz im Leben* has been established for the postulated text group).

22 Cf. Werner Georg Kümmel, *Introduction to the New Testament* (trans. Howard W. Kee; rev. ed.; Nashville: Abingdon, 1975) 552, according to whom the Caesarean text cannot be shown to exist outside the textual tradition of Mark; cf. also Kurt and Barbara Aland, who call it "purely hypothetical" (*Text*, 66); Bruce Metzger, *The Text of the New Testament: Its Transmission, Corruption, and Restoration* (3d ed.; New York: Oxford University Press, 1992) 215 ("the least

Beginning with the 26th edition of the Nestle text, Kurt Aland has introduced the symbol 𝔐 to represent the "majority text," which "for practical purposes" corresponds to the symbol 𝔎, and thus (being based on the great majority of the minuscule manuscripts) reproduces the Byzantine Koine. It is true that the "constant witnesses" are also subsumed under this symbol, to the extent that they correspond to 𝔐. These include, in part, important manuscripts such as ℵ ABCPKL Ψ, as well as 𝔓^{9} (partially) and 𝔓^{74}. These, together with a number of minuscules, are listed separately when they deviate from 𝔐.[23] It was a necessary consequence of this reorganization of the manuscript witnesses that in Nestle-Aland^{26} not only the group symbol 𝔎 but also the symbol ℌ would be dropped. For the latter "not infrequently . . . represented a conjecture,"[24] so that the users of the *Novum Testamentum Graece* are again referred to the evaluation pro and con, as developed on the basis of the individual manuscripts listed. When Kurt Aland expresses himself more positively at a later point, and says that he regards the Alexandrian text, as well as D and 𝔎, as "incontestably verified," in contrast to the Caesarean and Jerusalem text,[25] he apparently refers to an accepted form of the text that has not been evaluated for the text construction itself, since the Egyptian text type exists only in a few manuscripts that, in addition, are influenced by the Byzantine tradition.[26] Accordingly, the exegesis of the Johannine Letters may not ignore the insecurity of the acceptance of manuscript text groups, and the following discussion must deal with the question of the original reading not primarily by applying general criteria but differently from one case to another. In this process, it is not the external manuscript witnesses but the internal criteria that must be the decisive factors in determining the quality of one reading or another.[27]

3. The Place of the Johannine Letters in the History of the Canon

As far as their status within the history of the canon is concerned, the Catholic Letters come after the Gospels and the Pauline corpus, since they found their fixed place in the NT canon only at a relatively late date, and, unlike the Synoptic Gospels and the Pauline Letters, were transmitted as a not very homogeneous group. Nevertheless, the great majuscule manuscripts placed them after the Acts of the Apostles as a unified group of writings,[28] and they are known to have had a secure place in the NT canon since the beginning of the fourth century. One should mention first the index of Codex Claromontanus, if it is dated to the end of the third or beginning of the fourth century.[29] Here the three Johannine Letters are listed in the context of the Catholic Letters, after the Pauline Letters, the two

homogeneous").

23 See Klaus Junack and Winifred Grunewald, *Das Neue Testament auf Papyrus*, vol. 1: *Die katholischen Briefe* (with a foreword by Kurt Aland; ANTT 6; Berlin/New York: de Gruyter, 1986) 9–10 (𝔓^{9}), 25–26 (𝔓74); and Nestle-Aland^{26}, 9*.

24 Nestle-Aland^{26}, 8*.

25 Aland and Aland, *Text*, 67.

26 Nestle-Aland^{26}, 8*; Aland and Aland, *Text*, 64–65. The so-called Egyptian text is also represented by the two Coptic translations, sa and bo. Cf. also Schnackenburg, *Epistles*, 43–44.

27 The most thorough investigation of the textual tradition of the Johannine Letters has been recently presented by William L. Richards (*The Classification of the Greek Manuscripts of the Johannine Epistles* [SBLDS 35; Missoula: Scholars Press, 1977]), although it is now somewhat out of date since it was based on the 25th edition of Nestle-Aland. Nevertheless, this work remains impressive because of its copious statistical comparisons. Its conclusion is that there are three principal text groups: A (Alexandrian type), B (Byzantine type), and M ("mixed text"). In addition, a number of subordinate groups are assigned to each principal group. By comparison to Hans von Soden's classification, it again appears that the positing of a "Palestinian text" is questionable. The question of the original text is set aside, so that this work has little import for the determination of the origins of the text.

28 Thus in Codex Vaticanus (the order is: Acts of the Apostles, Catholic Letters, Pauline Letters), and in Codex Sinaiticus (Pauline Letters, Acts of the Apostles, Catholic Letters); the Roman canon of 382 also mentions, after the Acts of the Apostles, seven "epistulae canonicae": two letters of the apostle Peter, a letter of the apostle James, a letter of the apostle John, "two letters of the other John, the presbyter," and a letter of the apostle Jude Zelotes; cf. Zahn, *Grundriss*, 83.

29 Thus Zahn, *Geschichte*, 2.172; differing, Adolf Jülicher and Erich Fascher, *Einleitung in das Neue Testament* (7th ed.; Tübingen: Mohr, 1931) 596–97 ("probably around 500"); Aland and Aland, *Text*, 110

letters of Peter and the Letter of James, but before the letters of Jude and Barnabas.[30] Next there is the canon of Cyril of Jerusalem, who, in his catecheses delivered in the Church of the Resurrection in Jerusalem around the year 348, also discusses the "divine Scriptures" and places "seven Catholic Letters" (James, 1 and 2 Peter, 1–3 John, and Jude) between the Acts of the Apostles and the Letters of Paul.[31] While here the connection between the Acts of the Apostles and the Catholic Letters as "*apostolos*" is evident, we also have an appendix to the fifty-ninth canon of the synod of Laodicea, held around 360,[32] that lists the seven Catholic Letters after the Acts of the Apostles and before the Letters of Paul.[33] The same order is found in an important official church document, Athanasius's Easter letter of 367.[34] With this, the construction of the NT canon was concluded in many areas, even though the Syrian church, for example, did not include the Catholic Letters until the Philoxenian version.

By contrast, one can reconstruct the prehistory of canonical acceptance, especially its beginnings, only in a general way. Discussion of canonicity began much earlier. Eusebius accepted Origen's division of the NT writings into three parts, distinguishing among ὁμολογούμενα ("accepted"), ἀμφιβαλλόμενα ("disputed"), and ψευδῆ ("spurious") writings.[35] He counts 1 John, as well as 1 Peter, among the "accepted" writings, but locates 2 and 3 John among the "disputed" parts of the canon.[36] In doing so, he apparently relies on Origen's own position; Origen also (although the details of this are in need of interpretation) distinguished 2 and 3 John from the acknowledged Johannine writings.[37] Origen represents the state of the canon at the beginning of the third century, which should be distinguished from an actual reference to the Johannine Letters. When NT and OT writings are cited with approval, this does not necessarily mean that the citation presupposes the canonical validity of those writings, especially since an NT canon of more or less fixed extent developed only in the course of time. Thus the quotations from the Johannine Letters that are found in the writings of Clement of Alexandria are also to be evaluated only tentatively in terms of canonical criticism. While Clement adduced 1 and 2 John, together with the four Gospels and fourteen Pauline Letters, as authorities,[38] in his work called *Hypotyposeis* ("Sketches" or "Outlines"), only a few fragments of which have survived, he is supposed to have interpreted the Catholic

(6th century).

30 Text in Zahn, *Geschichte*, 2.159.

31 Cf. Zahn, *Geschichte* 2.172–80, 179.

32 For the dating of the synod, cf. Zahn, *Geschichte*, 2.193–202; the list of the Scriptures in the fifty-ninth canon of the synod at Laodicea in Asia Minor was probably a secondary addition: see Zahn, *Geschichte*, 2.197–201; Leipoldt, *Geschichte*, 1.94.

33 Text in Zahn, *Geschichte*, 2.202.

34 Text in Zahn, *Geschichte*, 2.211.

35 Cf. Origen *Comm. in Joh.* 5.3; *Comm. in Matt.* 14.21; 17.35; *Orat.* 14.4, etc.; cf. also *Princ.*, Praef. 8 (on the "doctrina Petri," which Origen does not count among the church's Scriptures). On this subject, see Hans von Campenhausen, *The Formation of the Christian Bible* (trans. J. A. Baker; Philadelphia: Fortress, 1972) 320–21.

36 Eusebius *Hist. eccl.* 3.25.

37 Cf. Eusebius *Hist. eccl.* 6.25.9–10: here Eusebius describes Origen's canon of Scripture, in which he counted among the Johannine writings the Fourth Gospel and the Apocalypse of John, declaring thereafter: "In addition, he [John] left an epistle of a very few lines, and possibly two more, though their authenticity is denied by some. Anyway, they do not total a hundred lines between them." If the second and third letter mentioned here are to be identified, as it seems, with 2 and 3 John, the statement about the epistle "of a very few lines" must refer to 1 John, which is regarded as genuine. This conclusion is not improbable, for Origen can also say of Paul's letters to the churches, some of which are longer, that they contained "only a few lines" (Eusebius *Hist. eccl.* 6.25.7).

38 Cf. *Strom.* 3.4.32.2 (1 John 1:6–7); 3.5.44.5 (1 John 2:4); 3.6.45.2 (1 John 2:18–19); 3.5.42.6 (1 John 3:3); 4.16.100.4 (1 John 3:18–19); 5.1.13.1 (1 John 4:16); 4.16.100.5 (1 John 4:18; 5:3); 2.15.66.4 (1 John 5:16–17); *Paed.* 3.12.98.2–3 (1 John 2:2–6); 3.11.82.1 (1 John 4:7; 5:3); *Div.* 37.6 (1 John 3:15); *Hyp.* (GCS) 17.215.3 (2 John 1); 215.5 (2 John 5–6); 215.7 (2 John 7); 215.6 (2 John 9); 215.10 (2 John 10); 215.12 (2 John 11).

Letters,[39] so that one might easily conclude that he acknowledged all three Johannine Letters.[40] This example shows that the patristic witness as such remains controverted and in no way offers a clear determination on the canonical acceptance of an NT writing. For Tertullian one may conclude that, of the traditional apostolic writings, he accepted thirteen letters of Paul, 1 John, 1 Peter, and James.[41] It is established that Irenaeus used 1 and 2 John.[42] The unevenness in the witnesses[43] is evident also in the Muratorian Canon, which—as stated above—not only knows the Gospel of John but also cites 1 John and probably mentions the other two Johannine Letters as accepted in the Catholic church, without itself wishing to defend their canonical authority.[44]

One may thus presuppose that the three Johannine Letters were already in use in the churches in the second century, even if their inclusion in the NT canon took place under differing circumstances. Undoubtedly, 1 John was most widely accepted. Its relatively early attestation by Polycarp and Papias makes it clear that this longest of the Johannine Letters, because of the power of its theological statement, had no difficulty in finding a hearing in the ancient church. Of the other two Johannine Letters, 2 John, which is occasionally cited alongside 1 John,[45] was evidently better known. This may be explained by its direct opposition to false teachers, which was useful in the church's concrete confrontations with gnostic groups. By contrast, 3 John, apparently a private letter of the presbyter aimed at a special situation, the controversy with Diotrephes, was more difficult to adapt to the theological and ecclesial tasks of the great church as it came into being.[46] It thus shared the fate of the Letter to Philemon, the most personal of Paul's letters, which is not attested in the literature of the great church before Tertullian.

The Johannine Letters are a clear example of the disparity of factors that led to the construction of the NT canon. Undoubtedly the principle of apostolicity, that is, authorship by an apostle, played a role in the canonization of the Johannine Letters as well; the identification of the author with an apostle is relatively early, even though it is not universally attested.[47] General use and acceptance, that is, the principle of catholicity,[48] may also have been influential, although the Johannine writings were at first restricted to the region of Asia Minor, and ecumen-

39 Eusebius *Hist. eccl.* 6.14.1: "In the *Outlines*, to put it briefly, [Clement] has summarized all canonical Scripture, even including the Disputed (ἀμφιβαλλόμενα) Books, namely the Epistle of Jude and the other Catholic Epistles, the Epistle of Barnabas, and the 'Revelation of Peter.'"

40 3 John, however, is not included in the Latin translation of Clement of Alexandria's interpretation (*Adumbrationes*), nor is it mentioned by Cassiodorus, who commissioned a translation in the sixth century, in his "Institutiones divinarum litterarum" (8.4). This finding could support the thesis that Clement knew only 1 and 2 John. Cf. William Sanday, *The Cheltenham List of the Canonical Books of the Old and New Testament and of the Writings of Cyprian* (SBEc 3; Oxford: Clarendon, 1891) 248–49; Leipoldt, *Geschichte,* 1.232–33; Lieu, *Epistles,* 19–20.

41 Tertullian *Scorp.* 12–13; *Pud.* 2.14; *De Anima* 15–17; *Idol.* 2 (on 1 John); cf. also Leipoldt, *Geschichte,* 1.235.

42 Cf. Irenaeus *Adv. haer.* 3.16.5 (identification of the author of 1 John with "Joannes domini discipulus," the evangelist); at this point he cites 1 John 2:18–22; also 3.16.8 (1 John 4:1–3; 5:1); quotations from 2 John at 1.16.3 (2 John 11); 3.16.8 (2 John 7–8).

43 Add to this that Hippolytus, who does not mention the Johannine Letters in his better-known writings, cites 1 John in his homily (preserved in Georgian) on the story of David and Goliath, at 3.2 (1 John 4:14); 7.1 (1 John 4:14, "salvator mundi"); 7.11 (1 John 5:19). Cf. *Traités Hippolyte sur David et Goliath* (trans. Gerard Garitte; CSCO 264; Louvain: Secrétariat de Corpus SCO, 1965) 2.6.9; *Biblia patristica: Le troisième siècle (Origène excepté)* (Paris: Éditions du centre national de la recherche, 1977) 447–48.

44 See above, Introduction, part 1. Zahn (*Geschichte* 1.209–11) observes correctly that the citation of an individual letter as "the letter of John" does not exclude a knowledge of the other Johannine Letters.

45 Cf. the citations in Clement of Alexandria and Irenaeus (nn. 38 and 42 above).

46 Leipoldt points out that the institution of "itinerant apostles," upheld by the presbyter, practically died out near the end of the second century, when the NT canon was gradually being established (*Geschichte,* 1.236).

47 As shown above, the author of 1 John is more frequently identified with the apostle and evangelist than is the author of 2 and 3 John, since the designation "the presbyter" suggested a distinction between this person and the apostle John (see above, Introduction, part 1). On the question of the principle of apostolicity in the construction of the canon, cf. Franz Overbeck, *Zur Geschichte des Kanons* (Chemnitz: Schmeitzner; New York: Steiger, 1880;

ical acceptance would not have been achieved without the equation of the author with John the evangelist. The fortunes of 3 John within the history of the canon, in comparison with the other Johannine Letters, give an indication that the "form" of an NT writing also weighted the scales in the decision about canonization, since a letter written in the form of a private communication could not simply be ranked alongside the other, "official" letters. If one further considers the differing degrees of acceptance in the different regions, one may acknowledge that the factor of "accident" cannot be completely excluded.[49] Despite this variability in canon-critical influences, and despite their differing degrees of applicability to the individual Johannine writings, there can be no doubt that all these documents, as well as the Gospel of John, enjoyed great esteem in the region of their origin,[50] even though their acknowledgment as canonical was accomplished only through a process lasting several centuries.[51]

4. The Johannine School

The Johannine Letters and the Gospel of John are so closely related, both in their language and in the scope of their ideas, that earlier scholarship has been able to speak of a "Johannine circle."[52] This is a useful concept for explaining the lines of connection among the Johannine writings as well as their literary independence of one another. But one can speak with more accuracy of a "school of John," since the differences and agreements among the Johannine writings point to school traditions and presume teacher-pupil relationships that are also determinative for the definition of the concept of a "school." In antiquity, school traditions played an essential role in the process of creation and handing on literary and preliterary sayings and speeches. Examples are the schools of the Pythagoreans, the Stoics, the Essenes, of Philo, of Rabbi Hillel, and—in the Christian era—the Antiochene and Alexandrian schools.[53] Such schools are always traced to a "founder," who represents

reprinted Darmstadt: Wissenschaftliche Buchgesellschaft, 1965) 31.

48 On this, see Adolf von Harnack, *Das Neue Testament um das Jahr 200* (Freiburg: Mohr [Siebeck], 1889) 55–58.

49 Cf. the judgment on the Muratorian canon: "according to it, want of principle was the Church's principle in the preparation of the new canon" (Jülicher and Fascher, *Einleitung,* 495; quoted in *NTApoc*[1] 1.36).

50 The text-critical evidence suggests that the three Johannine writings were originally handed on together: in 81 manuscripts only 16 textual witnesses vary the text type "in one or two of the epistles" (Richards, *Classification* 195–98; table 46).

51 It is significant that it is not the Fourth Gospel but 1 John that (through Polycarp) has the earliest historical attestation. Manuscript or patristic evidence for the Gospel of John is lacking for the first half of the second century, since $\mathfrak{P}^{52}$ and P. Eger. 2 are not absolutely reliable witnesses (against Alfred Wikenhauser and Josef Schmid, *Einleitung in das Neue Testament* [6th ed.; Freiburg: Herder, 1973] 343–44; on this, see n. 78 below). Only with Tatian, Theophilus of Antioch, and Irenaeus, i.e., in the second half of the second century, do undisputed citations from the Fourth Gospel occur. This is confirmed by the *Epistula Apostolorum,* although definite bases for the dating of this writing are lacking. (See the translation by C. Detlef G. Muller in *NTApoc*[2] 1.249–84.) This is a document from the antignostic struggle of the great church, then coming into being. It presumes the existence of four canonical Gospels, including the Gospel of John.

52 Thus Oscar Cullmann (*The Johannine Circle* [trans. John Bowden; Philadelphia: Westminster, 1976] 87) sought to draw a line extending from the "Johannine community" by way of the "special Hellenist group in the early community in Jerusalem," and the Johannine circle of disciples (beloved disciples) to the historical Jesus, the disciples of the Baptizer, and members of a "heterodox marginal Judaism." In his opinion, the Johannine circle was characterized by common community structures, missionary interests, polemic against false teachers, and the effort to demonstrate the legitimacy of their own group . He does not attribute the Johannine Apocalypse, the only NT writing that explicitly mentions an author named "John" (Rev 1:1), to the Johannine circle. Even if the Johannine Apocalypse may not, in the strict sense, be attributed to the Johannine school, its unique apocalyptic character points to a common basis that it shares with the Johannine theology of the Fourth Gospel and the Johannine Letters.

53 Cf. Wilhelm Bousset, *Jüdisch-Christlicher Schulbetrieb in Alexandria und Rom* (FRLANT 6; Göttingen: Vandenhoeck & Ruprecht, 1915; reprinted Hildesheim: Olms, 1975). In studying the writings of Philo, Bousset came to the conclusion that Philo was reworking the tradition of the Jewish exegetical schools in Alexandria. Something similar may be said of Clement of Alexandria. Here "the teaching activity of the catechetical school of Alexandria is clearly evident" (p. 267). Similar traditions are also

the decisive authority for the traditional teaching and confirms its independence from comparable communities.[54]

Even apart from the Johannine writings, one may raise the question whether other schools and their traditions are to be detected in the NT writings. Even in the relationship between John the Baptizer and his pupils, and especially in that between Jesus and his disciples, there may have been basic elements of a "school," although the urgency of Jesus' demand for conversion would have excluded any intention to found a lasting school tradition.[55] The evangelist Matthew uses traditional literary units shaped by Christian scribes and designated as school traditions.[56] There are good

visible in Irenaeus and Justin (pp. 152–54, 263–71). R. Alan Culpepper defines the concept of "school" through nine characteristics: (1) emphasis on φιλία and κοινωνία; (2) gathering around a founder, who is honored as an example of wisdom or goodness; (3) obedience to the teachings of the founder; (4) members of the school are pupils of the founder; (5) teaching and learning are community activities; (6) common meals are often celebrated as a memorial of the founder; (7) rules and practices determine the life of the members; (8) distance from human society; (9) development of organizational forms that ensure the continuation of the school (*The Johannine School* [SBLDS 26; Missoula: Scholars Press, 1975] 258–59).

54 Here one should distinguish, with Culpepper (*Johannine School,* 249) between "active" and "passive" founders. Not only teachers who actively influenced the building up of a community of pupils (e.g., Epicurus or Jesus) enjoy high regard but also other authority figures "who were later adopted by schools as their hero or 'founder'" (e.g., Hillel or Zeno).

55 The thesis of Martin Hengel is certainly not very helpful: "At all events, . . . the pressing proximity of God's rule itself did not leave any time for the development of a teacher-pupil relationship and for scholarly studies in the rabbinic fashion" (*The Charismatic Leader and His Followers* [trans. James Greig; Edinburgh: Clark; New York: Crossroad, 1981], 80). That Jesus could not apply himself to "scholarly studies in the rabbinic fashion" is already evident from the fact that a rabbinic tradition of study, in the proper sense of the word, is discernible only near the end of the first century CE, while its literary evidence first appears much later, and for that reason can be used only with great caution in NT exegesis. On this, cf. Birger Gerhardsson, *Memory and Manuscript: Oral Tradition and Written Transmission in Rabbinic Judaism and Early Christianity* (ASNU 22; Uppsala: Uppsala Universitet, 1961) 85–92. Despite attempts to trace rabbinic traditions back to the pre-NT era, Rainer Riesner has also acknowledged the pluralistic ("protorabbinic") character of scribal learning in the time of Jesus (*Jesus als Lehrer: Eine Untersuchung zum Ursprung der Evangelienüberlieferung* [WUNT 2/7; Tübingen: Mohr, 1981] 173–76). Nonetheless, one should not deny that the proclamation of the approaching reign of God was associated with the incorporation of Jewish wisdom traditions in Jesus' teaching. Joachim Jeremias correctly points to certain features that marked Jesus' preaching, and that also entered into early Christian tradition, even though the details remain subject to debate (*Abba: Studien zur neutestamentlichen Theologie und Zeitgeschichte* [Göttingen: Vandenhoeck & Ruprecht, 1966] 15–19, 145–52, and elsewhere; for an English translation of these essays, see Joachim Jeremias, *The Prayers of Jesus* [Studies in Biblical Theology 2/6; trans. John Bowden; London: SCM; Naperville: Allenson, 1967] 11–57, 108–15).

56 Thus Krister Stendahl (*The School of St. Matthew and Its Use of the Old Testament* [ASNU 20; Uppsala: Uppsala Universitet, 1954]) infers a school as *Sitz im Leben* of the theological work of the evangelist Matthew, especially in light of Matthew's inclination to systematize the tradition, fondness for casuistry, and reflections on the position of community leaders. Here one must note the distinction between tradition and redaction. If the first evangelist is to be called a Christian scribe (cf. Matt 13:52), still he had doubtless read the OT in Greek, and it has not yet been proved that he was knowledgeable in Hebrew or Aramaic, or that he was responsible for the style of the allusive quotations where it deviates from that of the LXX, even though numerous interpretations have been built on the basis of this hypothesis (e.g., Robert H. Gundry, *The Use of the Old Testament in St. Matthew's Gospel with Special Reference to the Messianic Hope* [NovTSup 18; Leiden: Brill, 1967]). On this subject, cf. Georg Strecker, *Der Weg der Gerechtigkeit: Untersuchung zur Theologie des Matthäus* (FRLANT 82; 3d ed.; Göttingen: Vandenhoeck & Ruprecht, 1971) 15–35, 49–85.

reasons for speaking also of a "school of Paul." No doubt Paul stood in a teacher-pupil relationship with his coworkers, who are sometimes named as cosenders of his letters. This is evident not only from the Pauline reception of Jewish wisdom traditions,[57] but also from distinct units in the Pauline Letters that should not be interpreted from a purely literary standpoint, but strongly suggest that they are the outgrowth of school discussions.[58]

The suggestion that a "school" forms the background for the Johannine writings should also be kept in mind in explaining gaps and abrupt transitions in the Johannine Letters. These could indicate nonliterary, oral units of tradition that were formed and handed on within the Johannine school; thus they would not necessarily point to the existence of source documents. Accordingly, on the one hand the agreements in language and content throughout the Johannine writings are to be traced to a common school tradition. On the other hand the differences and the unique characteristics of the individual Johannine writings, as well as tensions within the text of a single work, may represent keys that will aid us in understanding the conflicts and developmental tendencies within the school, which of course affected the authors of the Johannine writings as well.

One starting point for approaching the question about the origins and history of the Johannine school could be the self-designation of the sender of 2 and 3 John, ὁ πρεσβύτερος (2 John 1; 3 John 1). This name could be understood as a reference to age ("the elder") or as an official title ("the presbyter").[59] In any case, it indicates that the community addressed in 2 John and also Gaius, the recipient of 3 John, were well acquainted with the person named here, and that they acknowledged the superior authority of the person so designated. It is possible that because of this person 2 and 3 John, the two shortest letters in the NT, found entry into the canon. On this basis, one may easily suppose that these two letters are original documents of the founder of the Johannine school.

Papias of Hierapolis, a resident of Asia Minor, testifies to a presbyter tradition in that peninsula that is helpful in solving the problem of the origins of the Johannine school:

> I shall not hesitate to furnish you, along with the interpretations, with all that in days gone by I carefully learnt from the presbyters (*παρὰ τῶν πρεσβυτέρων*) and have carefully recalled, for I can guarantee its truth. Unlike most people, I felt at home not with those who had a great deal to say, but with those who taught the truth; not with those who appeal to commandments from other sources but with those who appeal to the commandments given by the Lord to faith and coming to us from truth itself. And whenever anyone came who had been a follower of the presbyters (*τοῖς πρεσβυτέροις*), I inquired into the words of the presbyters (*τοὺς τῶν πρεσβυτέρων λόγους*), what Andrew or Peter had said, or Philip or Thomas or James or John or Matthew, or any other disciple of the Lord (*τις ἕτερος τῶν τοῦ κυρίου μαθητῶν*), and what Aristion and the presbyter (*ὁ πρεσ-*

57 Thus Hans Conzelmann, according to whom the Pauline school was located at Ephesus: "Paulus und die Weisheit," *NTS* 12 (1965/66) 231–44 (cf. 233); cf. also his "Die Schule des Paulus," in Carl Andresen and Gunter Klein, eds., *Theologia Crucis—Signum Crucis: Festschrift für E. Dinkler* (Tübingen: Mohr, 1979) 85–96, and Peter Müller, *Anfänge der Paulusschule* (AThANT 74; Zurich: Theologischer Verlag, 1988).

58 Cf. H. Ludwig, "Der Verfasser des Kolosserbriefes—ein Schüler des Paulus?" (diss., Göttingen, 1974), excursuses 1 and 2: In the first excursus, the author treats "from pre- and extra-Christian to the first Christian schools" (pp. 201–10); here it is evident that Jewish rabbinic schools and Hellenistic philosophical schools are only approximately comparable, and that they are very different in their educational ideals and the material of their teaching; Christian schools are associated with the names of Justin, Clement of Alexandria, and Origen. In the catechetical school at Alexandria introductory and advanced instruction were separated, something that undoubtedly had its roots in earliest Christianity; on this, cf. Heb 5:12–14; 6:1–2; 1 Cor 3:2. In the second excursus, Ludwig describes the "indications of a Pauline school in the authentic letters of Paul and in Acts" (pp. 211–28); here Ludwig correctly points out that there are esoteric units within the letters of Paul that can be traced to school discussions (examples: Rom 5:12–21; 1 Cor 10:1–10; 2 Cor 3:7–18).

59 See the detailed exposition below, on 2 John 1.

βύτερος) John, disciples of the Lord, were still saying (*οἱ τοῦ κυρίου μαθηταὶ λέγουσιν*).[60]

The close relationship between this tradition and the Johannine linguistic world is obvious. The absolute concept of *ἀλήθεια* ("the truth" here authorizes the "commandments" just as does "the Lord") recalls the usage in 2 and 3 John and indicates the possibility of a connection between Papias and this representative of the Johannine school.[61] In the presbyter traditions used by Papias, one should distinguish on the one hand between the *πρεσβύτεροι*, who are among Jesus' twelve disciples and could not have been personally known to Papias, simply because of the lapse of time, and Aristion and the presbyter John on the other hand. It is true that these last two are, like the others, called "disciples of the Lord," and also, like them, fall within the category of *πρεσβύτεροι*,[62] but—unlike the apostles—these two live in Papias's own time, as seems probable from the present tense, *λέγουσιν*.[63] Eusebius also understood it this way, since he explains that Papias reported having listened personally to Aristion and John the presbyter.[64] From all this, one may readily conclude that the presbyter John who is mentioned by Papias is identical with the "presbyter" who wrote 2 and 3 John.[65] The equation of the John in Asia Minor (who is still clearly distinguished by Eusebius from John the son of Zebedee)[66] with the founder of the Johannine school makes it understandable why the circle that produced the Johannine writings—wherever they were located—was associated only with the name of "John."[67]

60 Eusebius *Hist. eccl.* 3.39.3–4 (ET: Eusebius, *The History of the Church from Christ to Constantine.* Trans. and with an introduction by G. A. Williamson [Harmondsworth: Penguin, 1965]).

61 2 John 1; 3 John 1, 8; esp. 3 John 12 (*ὑπὸ αὐτῆς τῆς ἀληθείας*); a connection with John 14:6, as occasionally supposed, is less likely (see Gerhard Maier, *Die Johannesoffenbarung und die Kirche* [WUNT 25; Tübingen: Mohr [Siebeck], 1981] 51–52, with further literature).

62 Eusebius *Hist. eccl.* 3.39.3, line 10 (ET by Williamson); what is noteworthy is that it is not Aristion but the presbyter John to whom the title is attached.

63 Eusebius *Hist. eccl.* 3.39.4, line 20 (ET by Williamson).

64 *Hist. eccl.* 3.39.7, line 12 (*αὐτήκοον ἑαυτόν φησι γενέσθαι*). When Eusebius here states that Papias "learned the words of the apostles from their former followers, but says that he listened to Aristion and the presbyter John with his own ears," this does not mean that Aristion and the presbyter are to be counted among those of the apostolic generation, but merely that Papias accords their authoritative teaching a special place, which was all the more important because he had immediate access to them. At another point (3.39.14) Eusebius says that Papias "gives us accounts of the Lord's sayings obtained from Aristion or learned direct from the presbyter John." This statement does not contradict the status of Papias as a direct hearer, as previously described, since the "traditions of the presbyter" could, obviously, have been transmitted orally. Gerhard Maier ignores the problem in this passage when he allows only the following alternatives: "One can either understand the fragment in such a way that Papias asked the pupils of the presbyters about the presbyters' traditions of Andrew, etc. . . . or else that Papias understood the presbyters to mean the previous, apostolic generation, so that the pupils of the presbyters had direct traditions from Andrew, etc." (*Die Johannesoffenbarung und die Kirche* [WUNT 25; Tübingen: Mohr [Siebeck], 1981] 54). In reality, what is at issue is the tradition of John the presbyter and/or of Aristion, whom Papias acknowledges as independent representatives of the presbyterial tradition, without identifying them with the apostolic teaching or relating them to that teaching alone. Only by forcing the material is it possible to dispute the distinction between two Johns in the words of Papias (and in Eusebius *Hist. eccl.* 3.39.5). That Papias refers to Aristion and John the presbyter as *τοῦ κυρίου μαθηταί* (3.39.4, line 20) cannot be eliminated on the basis of the omission of these words in the Syrian tradition, it is true, but this is a general designation that cannot be restricted to the generation of Jesus himself (cf. Wilhelm Bousset, *Die Offenbarung Johannes* [KEK 16; 6th ed.; Göttingen: Vandenhoeck & Ruprecht, 1906, reprinted 1966] 39–40). *Μαθητής* is also used in this general sense in Eusebius *Hist. eccl.* 3.36.9 (= Ignatius *Rom.* 5.3); cf. also Eusebius *Hist. eccl.* 3.36.1: Polycarp as companion of the apostles (*τῶν ἀποστόλων ὁμιλητής*).

65 For the consequences of this conclusion for the temporal location of the Johannine writings and their location in the region of Asia Minor, see below.

66 Eusebius *Hist. eccl.* 3.39.6: "He thus confirms the truth of the story that two men in Asia had the same name, and that there were two tombs in Ephesus, each of which is still called John's"; cf. *Hist. eccl.* 7.25.19: "I think there was another John among the Christians of Asia [who wrote Revelation], as there are said to have been two tombs at Ephesus, each

What one can learn about the "presbyter" from 2 and 3 John indicates that he understood himself as the leading representative of a church community (cf. 2 John 13), so that there is no contradiction between "community" and "school." Moreover, 2 John shows that the presbyter was not only acknowledged in his immediate surroundings but was able to make his authority effective in other communities as well, and was active in spreading Christian teaching and making the love commandment a reality among Christians. His missionary activity is expressed particularly in 3 John, addressed to the Christian Gaius, who is counted among the followers of the presbyter (3 John 4: τὰ ἐμὰ τέκνα). Here it is also clear that the presbyter sends out "brothers and sisters" who are active in spreading the "truth" in other communities and who found support among the presbyter's followers, but rejection from his opponents (3 John 5–8).

Diotrephes is specifically mentioned as one of the opponents. He was an outstanding, ambitious person in the community addressed by the presbyter, and had attempted to destroy the presbyter's influence by applying disciplinary measures within the church: he refused to receive the envoys sent by the presbyter (3 John 9–10). This conflict was not yet ended at the time 2 and 3 John were written, for the presbyter announces his own imminent arrival (3 John 14). This visit would not be only to Gaius, but would also affect the church community to which Diotrephes belongs and with which Gaius was also closely associated. By contrast, the Demetrius who is also mentioned in the letter to Gaius was apparently a messenger from the presbyter; favorable testimony about him is specifically mentioned (3 John 12).

If, on the basis of 2 and 3 John, the outlines of an image of the thought and activity of the presbyter begin to emerge, still other questions must be raised at this point. With regard to the relationship between the presbyter and the Beloved Disciple in the Fourth Gospel, one may ask whether the Gospel speaks of one and the same figure throughout, or whether one must distinguish between the Beloved Disciple in the body of the Gospel and in the appended chapter, where this figure is clearly identified with the evangelist (John 21:24). One should also ask whether, or to what extent, the fourth evangelist associated a historical or theological reality with this figure. It is possible that what is at stake here is the authority of the Johannine school, which, at the level of the evangelist, secures the truth of the Gospel.[68] This would mean that, in the course of the transmission of traditions within the Johannine school, the presbyter, as author of 2 and 3 John, became a figure within the Gospel tradition, and that genuine Johannine theology

reputed to be John's."

67 It was only from the time of Origen that the same writing group (Gospel of John, Johannine Letters, as well as the Johannine Apocalypse) was called Johannine, and the author identified with the son of Zebedee; cf. Eusebius *Hist. eccl.* 6.25.9–10, and n. 37 above.

68 It is not very likely that the founder of the Johannine school is historically identical with the Beloved Disciple, as Culpepper (*Johannine School*, 288) wishes to deduce from the expression ἀπ' ἀρχῆς (1 John 2:7, 24; 3:11; 2 John 5–6). There is an extensive redaction-critical analysis of these texts in Thorwald Lorenzen, *Der Lieblingsjünger im Johannesevangelium* (SBS 55; Stuttgart: Katholisches Bibelwerk, 1971). Here an equation of the Beloved Disciple with the founder of the Johannine school is excluded, as is the symbolic interpretation (as found in Bultmann, Dibelius, Lietzmann, Käsemann, Kragerud, and others). Instead, this author regards the Beloved Disciple as "a concrete, individual, historical person," of whom one should suppose "that this was an important and familiar person in the Johannine community" (p. 82). For this discussion, see also Hartwig Thyen, "Entwicklungen innerhalb der johanneischen Theologie und Kirche im Spiegel von Joh 21 und der Lieblingsjüngertexte des Evangeliums," in Marinus de Jonge, ed., *L'Évangile de Jean: Sources, rédaction, théologie* (BEThL 44, Gembloux: Duculot, 1977) 259–99, according to whom all the Beloved Disciple texts can be traced to the author of John 21. He also defends the idea that "in the 'Beloved Disciple' of the Gospel . . . a literary monument has been erected to the author of the two shorter Johannine Letters" (p. 290).

was interpreted through the genre of "gospel." This is all the more likely since the truth proclaimed by the presbyter drew its support from the "teaching of Christ" (2 John 9).

The answers to these and other questions are intimately related to the definition of the relationship of the Johannine writings to one another. This, too, can only be sketched at this point. The present commentary proceeds from the thesis that one and the same author stands behind 2 and 3 John. This appears not merely from the identity of the titles given to the sender in each case (2 John 1; 3 John 1: ὁ πρεσβύτερος), but also from the situation presupposed by both letters (2 John 12; 3 John 13: the author indicates that he will come), as well as from the formal and linguistic correspondences (e.g., the closing formulae in 2 John 12 and 3 John 13). If both are genuine, and not falsified documents,[69] then 2 John probably preceded 3 John, since the sending and reception of 2 John seems to be reflected in 3 John.[70] The definition of the relationship of these two letters to 1 John will be detailed in the exegesis below. But I may note here that the differences in form and content make an identical authorship unlikely in this case. The author of 1 John does not call himself ὁ πρεσβύτερος. His writing also diverges from the two shorter Johannine Letters from a form-critical perspective. Unique features are discernible in the realms of theology and church discipline, so that what one finds here is an independent author in the Johannine school tradition, even though the fundamental structures of the Johannine Letters unite them not only with one another but also with the Gospel of John. This is to say that the thesis of a Johannine school tradition is opposed to a linear literary analysis of the text. The assumption of written sources on which an author, and then, in turn an (ecclesiastical) redactor is dependent—an assumption that excludes all other tradition-critical explanations—should be viewed with skepticism. Such a thesis is in danger of underestimating the liveliness of the discussions that are presumed by the Johannine writings and that shape their content. No sufficient evidence can be presented to show that the author of the Johannine Letters used the Fourth Gospel, as I will demonstrate below.[71] But also the various forms of a theory based on the analysis of sources, even though in the recent past these have distanced themselves more and more from Rudolf Bultmann's three-stage theory, still posit the presence of a *sēmeia* source.[72] One must therefore question whether they allow sufficient scope for the conflicts that occurred in advance of the Fourth Gospel.[73]

As far as the place of composition of the Johannine writings is concerned, what has already been said gives some indication: If there is a close connection with the presbyter traditions of Papias, the peninsula of Asia Minor becomes a probable place of origin. The patristic witnesses also favor this location. The citation by Polycarp of Smyrna, the oldest testimony, places 1 John in Asia Minor.[74] This corresponds to the patristic testimony about the Fourth Gospel (rather late, it is true), as found in Irenaeus and Clement of Alexandria, and makes it possible to consider Ephesus as the seat of the Johannine school,[75] without thereby restricting it to

69 Rudolf Bultmann differs: "The letter form should probably be taken as a fiction" (*The Johannine Epistles* [trans. R. Philip O'Hara with Lane C. McGaughy and Robert W. Funk, ed.; Hermeneia; Philadelphia: Fortress, 1973] 1). Cf. on 2 John below.

70 See below on 3 John 9 (ἔγραψα as a reference to 2 John).

71 Cf. esp. on 1 John 1:1–4; 5:13.

72 Thus Robert T. Fortna tried to reconstruct a christological source document underlying the Gospel of John, which would have traced Jesus' way from the first miraculous signs to his death and resurrection (*The Gospel of Signs* [SNTSMS 11; London: Cambridge University Press, 1970]). Against this, Udo Schnelle (*Antidocetic Christology in the Fourth Gospel* [Minneapolis: Fortress, 1992]) has critically examined the arguments advanced for the presence of a "semeia source" and persuasively demonstrated the unity of "miracles and *doxa*" in the theology of the fourth evangelist, which also includes Jesus' "semeia." (See pp. 144–50 of that work.)

73 On this, see Georg Strecker, "Die Anfänge der johanneischen Schule," *NTS* 32 (1986) 31–47.

74 Polycarp *Phil.* 7.1 (1 John 4:2–3; 2 John 7); see the Introduction, part 1 above.

75 Irenaeus *Adv. haer.* 2.22.5: "as the Gospel and all the elders testify; those who were conversant in Asia with John, the disciple of the Lord, [affirming] that John conveyed to them that information. And he remained among them up to the times of Trajan" (ANF 1:392); *Adv. haer.* 3.1.1: "Afterwards, John, the disciple of the Lord, who also had leaned upon His breast, did himself publish a Gospel during his residence at Ephesus in Asia" (ANF 1:414). Clement

one of the churches of Asia Minor. Instead, one may well suppose that the Johannine school exercised its influence on a majority of the communities and cities in Asia Minor. This seems probable from the correspondence and missionary activity of the presbyter that are documented in 2 and 3 John.

Regarding the time of composition, one should also keep in mind the citation in Polycarp. It indicates that 1 John existed in the first half of the second century. If one adds to this the testimony about John the presbyter, according to which he was personally known to Papias, one may consider the probable time of writing of the two shorter Johannine Letters to have been around 100 or later.[76] For the writing of the Gospel of John, the witness of P^{52}, especially if it is dated to the year 125,[77] or that of Papyrus Egerton appears to have great weight. Still, an opinion shared rather broadly among researchers is that these two papyri should be dated to the middle of the second century. Moreover, in recent years some new points have come to light that need to be evaluated in terms of a later dating.[78] In addition, great weight must

---

of Alexandria (*Hyp.* 6.8, in Eusebius *Hist. eccl.* 6.14.7): "Last of all, aware that the physical facts had been recorded in the gospels, encouraged by his pupils and irresistibly moved by the Spirit, John wrote a spiritual gospel" (ET by Williamson).

76 The *terminus ante quem* is set by Papias, who, according to broad consensus, wrote his "interpretations" around 130 (between 120 and 160), and who had had contact with John the presbyter (cf. Eusebius *Hist. eccl.* 3.39.4).

77 Cf. Aland and Aland, *Text,* 85–87, 99.

78 P. Eger. 2 (P. Lond. Christ. 1) delivers four fragments of Gospel pericopes, the first being of the Johannine type (John 5:39, 45–46; 9:29), while Synoptic overtones dominate the others. Although the papyrus is generally dated around the "middle of the second century" (Philip Vielhauer, *Geschichte der urchristlichen Literatur: Einleitung in das Neue Testament, die Apokryphen und die Apostolischen Väter* [2d rev. repr.; Berlin/New York: de Gruyter, 1978] 636; thus also the first editors: Harold I. Bell and Theodore C. Skeat, *Fragments of an Unknown Gospel and Other Early Christian Papyri* [2d ed.; London: Trustees of the British Museum, 1935] 1; and Charles H. Dodd, "A New Gospel," in idem, *New Testament Studies* [1953; 2d ed.; Manchester: Manchester University Press, 1954] 12), Helmut Koester has suggested a date "into the beginning of the II CE," presuming that the papyrus reflects a stage of pre-Johannine and pre-Synoptic tradition (*Introduction to the New Testament: History and Literature of Early Christianity* [2 vols.; Philadelphia: Fortress; New York/Berlin: de Gruyter, 1982] 2:182). In contrast, Franz Neirynck ("Papyrus Egerton 2 and the Healing of the Leper," *EThL* 61 [1985] 153–60) has attempted to establish the use of the Synoptic gospels as probable. Since the first fragment seems to presume the Gospel of John, there are contacts with all four Gospels, whose material has been "reproduced from memory" (thus Joachim Jeremias and Wilhelm Schneemelcher, "Papyrus Egerton 2," in *NTApoc*[2] 1:96). Since in any case it is a question of free quotations, a great degree of uncertainty remains in the identification of the underlying texts. According to recent research, the origin of the papyrus could be dated around the year 200 or in the third century (cf. M. Groenewald, "Unbekanntes Evangelium oder Evangelienharmonie," *Abhandlungen der Rheinisch-Westfälischen Akademie der Wissenschaften, Sonderreihe Papyrologica Coloniensia* 8 [Kölner Papyri VI; Opladen: Westdeutscher Verlag, 1987] 136–37). In no event should the importance of P. Eger. 2 for an early dating of the Gospel of John be overestimated.

The "family similarity" to P. Eger. 2 was an important argument for the editor, C. H. Roberts, in dating 𝔓[52] (P. Ryl. Greek 457), which is supposed to have been written in the first half of the second century (*An Unpublished Fragment of the Fourth Gospel in the John Rylands Library* [Manchester: University of Manchester Press, 1935] 11). With the altered evaluation of P. Eger. 2, the early dating of 𝔓[52], which contains John 18:31–34, 37–38, becomes problematic, all the more so as the reasons given are certainly not adequate to establish the results desired. Thus the paleographic analysis leads to differing conclusions, since the absence of the *iota adscript* points rather to a later time, and the writing out of the *nomina sacra* can only be inferred, as no *nomen sacrum* appears in the text as it stands. It is indicative that the editor adduced only older papyri for the handwriting comparison, without verifying whether other manuscripts, dated near the end of the second or in the third century, might reveal similarities. There is urgent need for a new analysis of 𝔓[52] that would objectively set out the pros and cons of a possible dating; it might reveal that the favored dating "around A.D. 125," unusually precise for such a papyrus (Aland and Aland, *Text,* 69), should be relegated to the realm of the creation of pious legends, especially since the reference to "general consensus" (Kurt Aland, "Der Text des Johannes-

be accorded to internal criteria. From them one can infer that, at the beginning of the Johannine tradition, the presbyter wrote 2 and 3 John, and that the Johannine school tradition thereafter branched out into the writing of 1 John and the Gospel of John, independently of the earlier letters. The origins of the last two writings are to be placed in the first half of the second century.

5. Outline of 1 John

The many attempts to establish a thematically oriented train of thought in 1 John have been recorded in a variety of proposed outlines of the letter.[79] In the schemata that are by far the most widely preferred, 1 John is divided into two[80] or three[81] units, excluding the prologue and conclusion. Beyond this, there has been no

evangeliums im 2. Jahrhundert," in Wolfgang Schrage, ed., *Studien zum Text und zur Ethik des Neuen Testaments: Festschrift zum 80. Geburtstag von Heinrich Greeven* [BZNW 47; Berlin/New York: de Gruyter, 1986] 1) cannot stand without critical examination. Cf. also the tendencies in modern papyrological research that—without scholarly justification—have attracted wide respect: e.g., Anton Fackelmann, "Präsentation christlicher Urtexte aus dem ersten Jahrhundert geschrieben auf Papyrus. Vermutlich Notizschriften des Evangelisten Markus?" *Anagennesis* 4 (1986) 25–36; Carsten P. Thiede, *The Earliest Gospel Manuscript? The Qumran Papyrus 7Q5 and Its Significance for New Testament Studies* [Exeter: Paternoster, 1992]), together with the convincing criticism of this work by H. U. Rosenbaum, "Cave 7 Q! Gegen die erneute Inanspruchnahme des Qumran-Fragments 7 Q 5 als Bruchstück der ältesten Evangelien-Handschrift," *BZ* n.s. 31 (1987) 189–205.

79 Literature: Herbert Braun, "Literar-Analyse und theologische Schichtung im ersten Johannesbrief," *ZThK* 48 (1951) 262–92, reprinted in idem, *Gesammelte Studien zum Neuen Testament und seiner Umwelt* (3d ed., Tübingen: Mohr [Siebeck], 1971, 210–42); Friedrich Büchsel, "Zu den Johannesbriefen," *ZNW* 28 (1929) 235–41; Rudolf Bultmann, "Analyse des ersten Johannesbriefes," in Rudolf Bultmann and Hermann Freiherr von Soden, eds., *Festgabe für A. Jülicher zum 70. Geburtstag* (Tübingen: Mohr, 1927) 138–58, reprinted in Erich Dinkler, ed., *Exegetica: Aufsätze zur Erforschung des Neuen Testaments* (Tübingen: Mohr [Siebeck], 1967) 105–23; Bultmann, "Die kirchliche Redaktion des ersten Johannesbriefes," in Werner Schmauch, ed., *In Memoriam E. Lohmeyer* (Stuttgart: Evangelisches Verlagswerk, 1951) 189–201, reprinted in Bultmann, *Exegetica*, 381–93; Ernst von Dobschütz, "Johanneische Studien I," *ZNW* 8 (1907) 1–8; Fred O. Francis, "The Form and Function of the Opening and Closing Paragraphs of James and I John," *ZNW* 61 (1970) 110–26; Giorgio Giurisato, "Struttura della prima lettera di Giovanni," *RivB* 21/4 (1973) 361–81; Theodor Häring, "Gedankengang und Grundgedanke des ersten Johannesbriefs," in Adolf von Harnack, et al., eds., *Theologische Abhandlungen: Carl von Weizsäcker zu seinem siebzigsten Geburtstage 11. Dezember 1892 gewidmet* (Freiburg: Mohr [Siebeck], 1892) 171–200; P. R. Jones, "A Structural Analysis of I John," *RevExp* 67 (1970) 433–44; Ernst Lohmeyer, "Über Aufbau und Gliederung des ersten Johannesbriefes," *ZNW* 27 (1928) 225–63; Domenico Muñoz León, "El origen de las fórmulas ritmias antitéticas en la Primera Carta de San Juan," *Miscelánea José Zunzunegui* (Vitoria: Editorial Eset, 1975) 221–44; Erasmus Nagl, "Die Gliederung des ersten Johannesbriefes," *BZ* 16 (1924) 77–92; Wolfgang Nauck, *Die Tradition und der Charakter des ersten Johannesbriefes* (WUNT 3; Tübingen: Mohr, 1957); C. Clare Oke, "The Plan of the First Epistle of John," *ExpT* 51 (1939–40) 347–50; Otto A. Piper, "I John and the Didache of the Primitive Church," *JBL* 66 (1947) 437–45; R. Schwertschlager, "Der erste Johannesbrief in seinem Grundgedanken und Aufbau" (diss., Gregoriana; Coburg, 1935); Albin Skrinjar, "De divisione epistolae primae Joannis," *VD* 47 (1969) 31–40; idem, "De unitate epistolae 1 J," *VD* 47 (1969) 83–95; P. J. Thompson, "Psalm 119: A Possible Clue to the Structure of the First Epistle of John," *StEv* II (TU 87; Berlin: Akademie-Verlag, 1964) 487–92; Kozue Tomoi, "The Plan of the First Epistle of John," *ExpT* 52 (1940–41) 117–19; Arthur Westcott, "The Divisions of the First Epistle of St. John. Correspondence between Drs. Westcott and Hort," *Exp.* 7, series 3 (1907) 481–93.

80 Thus Raymond E. Brown, *The Epistles of John* (AB 30; Garden City: Doubleday, 1982) 123–29 (sections: prologue; 1:5—2:28; 2:29—5:12; epilogue); similarly Tomoi (sections: 1:5—2:28; 2:29—5:13). Francis divides between 1:5—2:29 and 3:1—5:12; thus also André Feuillet, who also wishes to demonstrate such extensive parallels between the Gospel of John and 1 John that they reflect a common conception of the "structure of the Christian life," understood as community with "trinitarian life," with the emphases in both writings falling on faith and love ("Étude structurale de la première épître de saint Jean") in Heinrich Baltensweider and B. Reicke, eds., *Neues Testament und Geschichte: Historiches Geschehen und Deutung im Neuen Testament: Oscar Cullmann zum 70. Geburtstag* [Zurich: Theologischer Verlag; Tübingen: Mohr (Siebeck), 1972] 307–27).

shortage of original attempts at division. An effort has been made to show that this writing was produced according to the model of other literary forms, or in dependence on known texts. Thus J. C. O'Neill attempted to distinguish twelve subunits that could have originated in a Jewish-sectarian collection of admonitory speeches.[82] Psalm 119 has also been proposed as a formative text behind 1 John.[83] Better known is the thesis of Ernst Lohmeyer, according to which the external form not only of 1 John but also of the Johannine Apocalypse and the Gospel of John is determined by the number seven.[84] Raymond E. Brown thinks he can demonstrate that the Gospel of John furnished the principle of division.[85] An attempt has also been made to divide 1 John according to a fixed progression of thought. Erasmus Nagl saw a "fixed outline" in the rhythmic succession of three theses: (1) God is light (1:5—2:28); (2) God is just (2:29—4:6); (3) God is love (4:7—5:19).[86] But for the most part 1 John is seen as a relatively loose series of various trains of thought hung together on the basis of association. Many exegetes therefore regard their suggested outlines more as aids to the reader's understanding than as genuine attempts to discover a clear-cut form within the letter.[87]

Nonetheless, Theodor Häring has discovered a principle behind the succession of the individual units in 1 John: "after repeated readings, one cannot doubt that the two basic ideas, the signs by which one may recognize this community, resulting from the nature of their community with God ('faith in Christ,' and 'love of the brothers and sisters') are presented in a constant alternation; more precisely, in such a way that they first appear repeatedly one after the other, and then in their internal bondedness with one another."[88] Even if one does not follow Häring's suggested divisions in detail, one can discover in 1 John an alternating shift between parenetic and dogmatic sections. While Häring, in line with the liberal tradition, has especially regarded "the inseparable unity of faith and love," the emphasis on the "ethical character of our religion,"[89] as the letter's unifying idea, in this book I must give greater stress to the polemical thrust of 1 John; this is true for the outline as well. Moreover, the exegesis will show that the conflict with the opposing teachers is restricted mainly to the dogmatic sections, for 1 John, as a unified whole, is not

81 Thus very frequently, e.g., by Charles H. Dodd, *The Johannine Epistles* (2d ed.; London: Hodder & Stoughton, 1947) xxii (1:5—2:28; 2:29—4:12; 4:13—5:13); Huther, *Handbuch*, 12 (1:5—2:28; 2:29—3:22; 3:23—5:17); Schwertschlager, "Der erste Johannesbrief" (1:5—2:27; 2:28—4:6; 4:7—5:17); Wengst, *Brief*, 28–29 (1:5—2:17; 2:18—3:24; 4:1—5:12); Edward Malatesta divides the letter into the three sections, 1:5—2:28; 2:29—4:6; 4:7—5:13, each headed "Exposition of Criteria of New Covenant Communion with God," which, however, is not persuasive, since there is no covenant terminology in 1 John (*Interiority and Covenant: An Exegetical Study of εἶναι ἐν and μένειν ἐν in the First Letter of Saint John* [AnBib 69; Rome: Biblical Institute Press, 1978]). Other advocates of a three-part schema include Häring and Nagl (see below). There is a comprehensive list of the various attempts at division in Brown, *Epistles*, 764.

82 J. C. O'Neill, *The Puzzle of 1 John: A New Examination of Origins* (London: SPCK, 1966).

83 Thompson, "Psalm 119."

84 Lohmeyer, "Aufbau." For a critique, see Braun, "Literar-Analyse," esp. 270.

85 Brown, *Epistles*, 123–29.

86 Nagl, "Gliederung" (cf. esp. 77). For an overview of these and other attempts see Schwertschlager, "Der erste Johannesbrief," 9–16.

87 Thus even Augustine (*Prologus in Epistulam Ioannis* [SC 75; Paris: Cerf, 1961] 104) thought that "John" spoke constantly and comprehensively of love. Vielhauer is more precise: "The document does not follow any strict train of thought, but joins together a loose series of admonitory, instructive, and polemical remarks, often mingling them with one another. There is also no shortage of repetitions" (*Geschichte*, 461). Cf. also Kümmel, who sees his proposed outline as "nothing more than an attempt" (*Introduction*, 436).

88 Häring, "Gedankengang," 9 (cf. also p. 6), with the following subunits: "Undeniably, 1:1–4 speaks of the revelation of eternal life, that is, of faith in Jesus Christ; 1:5—2:17 concerns walking in light, not sinning, doing what is just, and love of the brothers and sisters; 2:18–27 again speaks of faith in Christ; 2:28—3:24 takes up the subject of love once more; the former appears again in 4:1–6. Then 4:7–21 is about the love that is inseparable from faith; 5:1–12 concerns the faith that is inseparable from love. In the final section, 5:13–21, this fundamental idea of two-sided unity is repeated in urgent phrases."

89 Häring, "Gedankengang," 10.

to be understood on the basis of the existing polemical situation but from the author's affection for the Christian community. Consequently, I propose the following divisions:

	1:1–4 *Prelude*	What we have seen, we declare to you.
I.	*1:5—2:17* *Parenesis*	Communion with God must be realized in freedom from sin and in mutual love
II.	*2:18–27* *Dogmatic exposition*	False teaching
III.	*2:28—3:24* *Parenesis*	Whoever keeps God's commandments has a well-founded hope
IV.	*4:1–6* *Dogmatic exposition*	On discernment of spirits (truth and error)
V.	*4:7—5:4a* *Parenesis*	The love of God revealed in the Son obliges us to love our brothers and sisters
VI.	*5:4b–12* *Dogmatic exposition*	Faith founded on the testimony of water, blood, and Spirit
VII.	*5:13–21* *Final parenetic remarks*	The power of prayer

1 John

In both form and content, 1 John must be categorized differently from 2 and 3 John. Whereas 2 John is a letter to a *κυρία*, presumably a single congregation, and 3 John is addressed by the presbyter to an individual (Gaius), 1 John lacks the essential external marks of a letter. It has neither a prescript with the necessary information about the sender and addressee nor a proemium; the epistolary conclusion is also lacking. Nonetheless, the unknown author addresses the readers as "children" (*τεκνία, παιδία*), or even as "beloved ones" (*ἀγαπητοί*),[1] and the frequent use of "write" (*γράφειν*) seems appropriate to the situation of a letter.[2] This is no abstract meditation; rather, the author is giving concrete advice, as indicated by the attention paid to the different classes of persons within the community (2:12–14). The address is to readers who "believe in the name of the Son of God" (5:13). These readers apparently belong to multiple congregations that make up the community as a whole, rather than to a particular local congregation. From this point of view it seems that one should regard the writing as a combination of letter and sermon, and designate it a *homily in the form of a letter,* a homiletic writing addressed to the whole church,[3] but without thereby eradicating the immediate horizon of the Johannine community. As such, 1 John is neither an occasional letter nor a theological treatise. Instead, as a homily, it contains theoretical (dogmatic) and practical (parenetic) sections. This is clear from the outline: following an introduction (1:1–4), parenetic and dogmatic teachings alternate. Of course, an absolute stringency should not be expected here (for example, the "dogmatic" section beginning at 4:1 opens with an imperative challenge to test the spirits). Specific basic concepts contribute to the unity encompassing the various sections: these include, among others, "fellowship of God" (*κοινωνία θεοῦ*), "love of God" (*ἀγάπη θεοῦ* and *ἀγαπᾶν τὸν θεόν*), as well as "sin" (*ἁμαρτία*) and "hating the brother or sister" (*μισεῖν τὸν ἀδελφόν*). These expressions echo typical Johannine terminology, and this raises the question of the place of this document within the tradition history of the Johannine writings.

As regards its *relationship to 2 and 3 John,* one should first point to the literary independence of these two older letters from the other Johannine writings. They contain a good many hapax legomena as well as expressions that recall the language of other NT writings.[4] Beyond this, it

1 See below on 1 John 2:1 (n. 2); 2:12, 14; and 3 John 1.

2 See below on 1 John 2:12 (n. 5).

3 Among the NT writings, Hebrews is most nearly in homiletic form, especially if one acknowledges that the epistolary conclusion, because of its Pauline elements, must be regarded as secondary. The address *ἀδελφοὶ ἅγιοι* adds to the homiletic character (3:1). It is less appropriate to call 1 John a "religious treatise" (Windisch and Preisker, *Die Katholischen Briefe,* 136; Martin Dibelius, *Geschichte der urchristlichen Literatur* [ThBü 58; 1926; 2d ed.; ed. Ferdinand Hahn; Munich: Kaiser, 1975] 2.61–63; Vielhauer, *Geschichte,* 462; Joseph Chaine [*Les épîtres catholiques* (EtB; 2d ed.; Paris: Gabalda, 1939) 120] calls it a mixture of theological treatise and letter; Friedrich Büchsel [*Die Johannesbriefe* (ThHKNT 17; Leipzig: Deichert, 1933) 1] has a similar opinion), since this designation does not really take into account 1 John's direct address to its audience. But such expressions as "manifesto" (Jülicher and Fascher, *Einleitung,* 226; Rudolf Bultmann, "Johannesbriefe," *RGG*³ 3 [1959] 836–39) or "appeal in the form of a sermon" (Balz, "Johannesbriefe," 161) do not really give adequate scope to the theoretical character of the writing. The designation "homily" is also found in the work of Lohmeyer, "Aufbau," 256–57; Dodd, *Epistles,* xxi, lx.

4 Among the hapax legomena in 2 and 3 John (differing from 1 John and the Fourth Gospel) are: *φιλοπρωτεύειν, φλυαρεῖν, μέλαν, χάρτης, κάλαμος*, and not least the reference to the sender as *ὁ πρεσβύτερος*; all expressions that do not occur in the other Johannine writings but are present in non-Johannine documents, e.g.: *ἐχάρην λίαν* (2 John 4; 3 John 3; cf. Phil 4:10); *βλέπειν ἑαυτούς* (2 John 8; cf. Mark 13:9); *μισθὸν πλήρη ἀπολαμβάνειν* (2 John 8; cf. Matt 5:12; 10:41–42 par.); *συνεργοὶ γίνεσθαι* (3 John 8; cf. 1 Cor 3:9; 2 Cor 1:24); *ἀγαθοποιεῖν* (3 John 11; cf. Luke 6:9, 33, 35; 1 Pet 2:15; 3:6, 17). On this, see Eduard Schwartz, *Über den Tod der Söhne Zebedai: ein Beitrag zur Geschichte des Johannesevangeliums* (AGWG.PH 7/5; Berlin: Weidmann, 1904; reprinted, Göttingen: Kraus, 1970) 47–48, 52–53; Jülicher and Fascher, *Einleitung,* 236–37; Emanuel Hirsch, *Studien zum vierten Evangelium* (BHTh 11; Tübingen: Mohr [Siebeck], 1936) 177–78; Schnackenburg, *Epistles,* 270; Lieu, *Epistles,* 217–22.

can be shown that the Johannine imaginative and literary world, with its dualism and dialectical forms of speech, is present here only in its rudimentary beginnings.

The situation is quite different in the case of 1 John. It is clear already from the handing on of the "old" and "new" *agapē* commandments that this document represents a fuller, more reflective, and later stage of tradition than the other two minor Johannine writings.[5] This is evident from the polished style, recalling the Fourth Gospel, which has led to the thesis that 1 John is using a source document characterized by antithetic parallelisms.[6] Besides this stylistic factor, weighty material reasons favor the independence of 1 John from the two subsequent letters: the absence of the reference to the author as "the elder" (*ὁ πρεσβύτερος*); the plural use of the word "antichrist" (*ἀντίχριστος*);[7] the Christ's having "come in the flesh";[8] the general, temporally undifferentiated statement that "no one can see God";[9] and the word "children" (*τεκνία*).[10] Finally, just as 3 John presupposes 2 John (cf. 3 John 9), the author of 1 John, in using the aorist "I wrote" (*ἔγραψα*) in 1 John 2:14, is probably not pointing to this present writing,[11] but instead intends to suggest the idea of a previous letter, which could refer to 2 (and 3) John. In any case, the author of 1 John presupposes a ramified discussion within the Johannine school traceable to the beginnings of that school in the still more distant past, beginnings that appear to be attested in 2 and 3 John.[12]

With regard to the *relationship between 1 John and the Fourth Gospel*, the suggestion that 1 John is to be

---

5 See below. Many proposals that are advanced in favor of the dependency of 2 and 3 John on 1 John presuppose the conclusion and are unpersuasive: for example, the opinion that 2 John 5 refers to 1 John 2:7–8 (the old and new commandment) or to John 13:34 (the new commandment) and shows "a clear line of development from the Gospel of John through 1 John to 2 John." It is obvious that the designation of the opponents as antichrists (2 John 7; 1 John 2:18; 4:3) not only historicizes eschatology in general but also reveals a shift from 2 John to 1 John (where it is plural!)—see n. 7 below and the remarks on 2 John 7. The thesis that the saying about the completion of joy (2 John 12) is only a stereotypical reference to 1 John 1:4 cannot be established; neither can the assumption that 1 John 3:6 ("seeing God"), as a claim by the opponents, has priority over the corresponding passage in 3 John 11. As regards the differing attitudes toward opponents in 1 and 2 John, it is difficult to conclude from that situation to the dependency of 2 John on 1 John. The conclusion should rather be that different authors are arguing at different times and in different situations against opponents who are, in each case, independent of one another. (This is said in response to Wengst, *Brief*, 230–31.)

6 Thus Dobschütz, "Studien," and Bultmann, *Epistles;* modified by Braun, "Literar-Analyse"; on this, see the critical review by Eduard Lohse in *The Formation of the New Testament* (trans. M. Eugene Boring; Nashville: Abingdon, 1981) 183–92. Brown (*Epistles*, 124–25) still presumes that 1 John presupposes the Gospel of John and, following the thesis of James L. Houlden (*A Commentary on the Johannine Epistles* [HNTC; Black's New Testament Commentaries; London: Black; New York: Harper & Row, 1973; 2d ed.; London: Black, 1994] 31) and André Feuillet ("The Structure of First John: Comparison with the 4th Gospel," *BTB* 3 [1973] 194–216), believes he can demonstrate the presence of the outline of the Fourth Gospel within 1 John. This approach, however, leads to an overvaluation of the caesura in 1 John 3:10/11.

7 1 John 2:18; against 2 John 7 (singular); the singular is also found in 1 John 2:22; 4:3. Apparently the author of 1 John, in emphasizing the "many antichrists," presumes the language of 2 John 7, but modifies it with a view to this author's own situation, different from that of 2 John.

8 1 John 4:2; cf. John 1:14; against 2 John 7.

9 1 John 4:12a; John 1:18; different 3 John 11: "whoever does evil has not seen God." On this, see n. 27 below on 1:1.

10 1 John 2:1, 12, 28; 3:7, 18; 4:4; 5:21; John 13:33. Cf. the Papias fragments, in which we find the title *παῖδες* for community members: *τοὺς κατὰ θεὸν ἀκακίαν ἀσκοῦντας "παῖδας" ἐκάλουν ὡς καὶ Παπίας δηλοῖ βιβλίῳ πρώτῳ τῶν κυριακῶν ἐξηγήσεων καὶ Κλήμης ὁ Ἀλεξανδρεὺς ἐν τῷ Παιδαγωγῷ* (Maximus the Confessor, *Scholia in Dionysium Areopagitam, de ecclesiastica hierarchia* 2: "those who, in harmony with God, practice no evil, they called 'children,' as does Papias also in the first book of the expositions of the Lord [i.e., the words of the Lord] and Clement of Alexandria in the *Paidagogos*"). Cf. Erwin Preuschen, *Antilegomena* (Giessen: Ricker, 1901) 57–58. 2 John 1, 4, 13; 3 John 4 are similar; but cf. also *τέκνα (τοῦ) θεοῦ*: 1 John 3:1–2, 10; 5:2; John 1:12; 11:52.

11 Cf. v. 14a with v. 3; v. 14b with v. 13a; v. 14c with v. 13b. Cf. Brooke, *Epistles*, 41–43; more extensively Schnackenburg, *Epistles*, 118 (according to whom this is an "epistolary aorist").

understood as a "Johannine pastoral letter"[13] has exercised great influence in the discussion of this problem. Nevertheless, after what has been said one should ask whether in this connection the temporal priority of the Fourth Gospel is not presumed too automatically, and whether the independent character of 1 John with respect to the Gospel is not generally underestimated.

On the one hand, one must acknowledge that the Gospel and 1 John share common elements. These are both linguistic[14] and material in character, since the key Johannine concepts of "truth" (ἀλήθεια) and "love" (ἀγάπη), among others, appear in both books.[15] If these common elements are based on the tradition of the Johannine school that is fundamental to both these writings, there may be the further factor that the situation of the Johannine circle in which that tradition arose is different from that of 2 and 3 John, and that both the Gospel and 1 John are to be assigned to an advanced stage in the history of the tradition.[16]

On the other hand, one may justly point out that the two documents are strikingly different in both form and content. The "form" of the Fourth Gospel is that of a *vita Jesu,* less tightly constructed than the Synoptics but obviously planned with great care, as is evident from its beginning and ending.[17] The result is a different placement of theological accents and a difference in theological concepts, for the author of 1 John betrays no knowledge of any traditions about the life of Jesus. Whereas 1 John is ecclesiologically oriented, the orientation of the Gospel is christological.

Of further material importance is that specific theological ideas are present in only one of these two documents of the Johannine circle. Thus, while John 1:29 alludes to the atoning character of the death of

---

12 See above, part 4 of the Introduction ("The Johannine School"); Strecker, "Anfänge," esp. 40–42.

13 Hans Conzelmann, "'Was von Anfang war,'" in Walther Eltester, ed., *Neutestamentliche Studien für Rudolf Bultmann* (BZNW 21; Berlin: Töpelmann, 1957) 194–201, reprinted in idem, *Theologie als Schriftauslegung: Aufsätze zum Neuen Testament* (BEvTh 65; Munich: Kaiser, 1974) 207–14, esp. 214; cf. earlier Otto Baumgarten, *Die Johannesbriefe* (SNT 4; 3d ed.; Göttingen: Vandenhoeck & Ruprecht, 1918) 185 ("pastoral circular letter").

14 The linguistic style of the Fourth Gospel in relation to that of 1 John has been investigated frequently and in depth. Cf. Heinrich Julius Holtzmann, "Das Problem des ersten johanneischen Briefes in seinem Verhältnis zum Evangelium II," *JPTh* 8 (1882) 128ff.; Brooke, *Epistles,* i–xxvii; Chaine, *Les épîtres catholiques,* 104–18. According to Hirsch, the Gospel of John is the authoritative Gospel for 1 John (*Studien,* 171). Haenchen's conclusion is similar ("Neuere Literatur zu den Johannesbriefen," in idem, *Gesammelte Aufsätze,* vol. 2: *Die Bibel und Wir* [Tübingen: Mohr (Siebeck), 1968] 235–311 [= *ThR* 26 (1960) 1–43, 267–91] 249–50). In contrast, Dodd (*Epistles,* xlvii–lvii) emphasizes the differences and concludes from them that a different audience is in view. Others emphasize the common linguistic elements in the two documents; see, e.g., Wilbert F. Howard, "An Examination of the Linguistic Evidence Adduced against the Unity of Authorship of the First Epistle of John and the Fourth Gospel," *JTS* 48 (1947) 12–25; W. G. Wilson, "The Common Authorship of the Johannine Gospel and Epistles," *JTS* 49 (1948) 147–56; Alwyn P. Salom, "Some Aspects of the Grammatical Style of 1 John," *JBL* 74 (1955) 96–102; George D. Kilpatrick, "Two Johannine Idioms in the Johannine Epistles," 272–73; so also Wikenhauser and Schmid, *Einleitung,* 621–23; cf. Schnackenburg, *Epistles,* 34 and elsewhere (see n. 22 below).

15 Cf. also Windisch and Preisker, *Die Katholischen Briefe,* 109–10. They mention as common elements the close association of Father and Son, the sending of the Son into the world, his becoming flesh, water, and blood (1 John 5:6–8; John 19:34–35), dualism of God and world, God and the devil, love and hate, light and darkness, death and life, as well as the formulas of immanence.

16 Here I can only make brief reference to the problem of "early catholicism" in the Fourth Gospel. No doubt there are pastoral elements that are customarily attributed to early catholicism not only in 1 John but in the Gospel as well. Thus Brown (*Epistles,* xiii–xxi) also understands the Johannine Paraclete sayings as a response to the early Christian problem of the delay of the parousia and the loss of the eyewitnesses.

17 Hans Windisch already supported the thesis that John knew the Synoptics (*Johannes und die Synoptiker: Wollte der vierte Evangelist die älteren Evangelien ergänzen oder ersetzen?* [UNT 12; Leipzig: Hinrichs, 1926]).

Jesus, only 1 John (1:7, 9; 2:2; 4:10) expressly states it; the case is similar with the concept of "hope" (ἐλπίς; 1 John 3:3) and with the word παρουσία (1 John 2:28). And while future eschatological elements are not absent from the Fourth Gospel, they retreat significantly in favor of a present eschatology. There is also a differing use of the concepts of the Paraclete (παράκλητος; in John it refers to the "Spirit," in 1 John 2:1 to Jesus Christ), "light" (φῶς; John 8:12 and frequently elsewhere for Christ; 1 John 1:5 for God). The Fourth Gospel does not directly mention any "false teachers," but includes them within the idea of the world or the unbelief of the Jews.[18] By contrast, 1 John describes them polemically and at length as "antichrists" (1 John 2:18) and "false prophets" (1 John 4:1).[19] The ecclesiologically important terms χρῖσμα, σπέρμα, κοινωνία, and παρρησία are found only in 1 John, whereas the absolute christological concept of λόγος appears only in John 1:1, 14.[20] Similarly, 1 John also lacks the terminology of "glory" (δόξα), as well as the statements about Christ's ascent and descent (ἀνα- and καταβαίνειν) and the terms σώζειν, σωτηρία, κρίσις, ὑψοῦν, and πνεῦμα ἅγιον. These examples show that the conceptual material is marked by differing christological or ecclesiological tendencies. But the differences go beyond mere variety of expression or expressive intention.[21] Moreover, the common features of the two documents are not so extensive that one must posit a single author for both.[22] The terminological differences and agreements are explained, rather, when one presupposes that both documents originated as mutually independent writings of the Johannine school.

Concerning the question of literary unity, one cannot deny that 1 John reveals a whole series of apparent leaps that could invite literary-critical division. Rudolf Bultmann went far in that direction: he wished to use his linguistic observations to isolate a source document used as a model by the author of 1 John. This document would have contained twenty-six antithetical couplets[23] and would have been closely related, in both form and content, to the "revelatory discourse source" Bultmann postulated for the Fourth Gospel.[24] The linguistic observations on which Bultmann based his literary-critical conclusions remain of structural-analytical value even when one agrees with Ernst Haenchen that Bultmann's reconstruction is based on parallelisms that are too mechanically paired in their construction[25] and

18 On Jewish unbelief, see John 5:10, 15–16, 18; 7:1, 13; 8:48, 52, 57; 9:18, 22; 10:24, 31, 33; 11:8; 18:12, 14, 31, 36, 38; 19:7, 12, 14, 31, 38; 20:19, as well as Rev 2:9; 3:9. The suggestion that the stereotypical opposition to the "world" or the "Jews" may point to an older period and that the opposition to false teaching within the Christian community in 1 John belongs to a later period is not persuasive (Bultmann, *Epistles*, 1).

19 Compare the sharp conflict between the presbyter and the πλάνοι ("deceivers") in 2 John 7.

20 Compare this with the genitive expression λόγος τῆς ζωῆς (1 John 1:1), or λόγος τοῦ θεοῦ as "word of God" (1 John 2:14; cf. 1:10; 2:5, 7; also John 10:35). The general use of λόγος/λόγοι (1 John 3:18; 3 John 10; John 4:37; and frequently elsewhere) is less closely related.

21 Against Wikenhauser and Schmid, *Einleitung*, 622, according to whom the unique features of 1 John in contrast to the Fourth Gospel find "their unforced explanation in its opposition to the gnostic heresy."

22 Dodd is correct in arguing against a common authorship for John and 1 John. When, in opposing him, W. F. Howard and W. G. Wilson emphasize that the linguistic differences do not require one to conclude that different authors are at work (see n. 14 above), the problem of the Johannine school is left out of the discussion. The idea of a Johannine school tradition was also advanced by Dodd, even though in a form that is vulnerable to attack. (See Dodd, *Epistles*, lvi: "The simplest hypothesis, however, seems to be that the author of the Epistle was a disciple of the Evangelist and a student of his work.") Bauer ("Johannesevangelium und Johannesbriefe," 138) has a different opinion: the author of the Fourth Gospel is "the same man . . . who wrote the major Johannine letter."

23 Bultmann, "Analyse," 108, 121–23 (reconstruction of the source).

24 See the previous note, and also Bultmann, "Johannesbriefe," *RGG*[3] 3.836–39; Heinz Becker, *Die Reden des Johannesevangeliums und der Stil der gnostischen Offenbarungsrede* (FRLANT n.s. 50; Göttingen: Vandenhoeck & Ruprecht, 1956).

25 Haenchen, "Neuere Literatur," 246: "no housewife would bake a cake using nothing but raisins."

rejects the supposed source document as hypothetical. It is also important for the interpretation of 1 John to note that Bultmann's positing of a "revelatory discourse source" for the Fourth Gospel has been rejected by the majority of scholars, and for good reasons.[26]

Still more important is the fact that Bultmann also posited an "ecclesiastical redaction" for both the Gospel and 1 John. It was supposed to have contained, in particular, apocalyptic expressions (e.g., 1 John 2:28; 3:2; 4:17), as well as christological sayings about atonement (e.g., 1 John 1:7c; 2:2; 4:10), and sacramental material (5:6–9). The concluding section, which differentiates two classes of sins (deadly sins and those that do not lead to death), is also included; this is said to reflect an official church penitential praxis. But the suggestion that 1 John has been subjected to ecclesiastical redaction is more questionable than the corresponding position regarding the Fourth Gospel. No exclusive contrast between future and present eschatology can be posited for the apocalyptic statements in 1 John. Instead, in 1 John the future eschatological elements from the Johannine tradition appear to be applied to the present, while on the contrary some eschatological sayings about the present have received a future accent. This constitutes an eschatological-apocalyptic dialectic in which, in contrast to the Fourth Gospel, the future aspect is more strongly accented.[27]

As regards the idea of atonement through the blood of Christ, the expressions used in 1 John are no less traditional in origin than are those in the apocalyptic elements, and for this reason alone cannot be assigned to a secondary redactional stage without a particular argument in favor of that position. Since they occur throughout the whole of the document, they can be eliminated from it only by an artificial procedure. They belong just as much to the substance of the theology of 1 John as does the theme of "sin," which appears not only in the concluding section but elsewhere as well.

If one presupposes that 1 John is, on the whole, a literary unit, this does not mean that the author wrote the document at a single sitting. With regard to the caesura at 2:27/28, which is especially important for the analysis of the writing, Bultmann expressed the opinion that an original draft ended at 2:27 and that the following sections are nothing but variations on the themes introduced in the first part.[28] Even though one may remain skeptical of such a position, since the remarks that follow 2:28 introduce new ideas, one may still draw tradition-critical conclusions from this caesura. These suggest that the author, much like Paul in his letters, did not write without interruption, but when composing the document referred to discussions within the Johannine school. From this point of view, breaks and leaps within the body of 1 John may also be explained as the consequence of the interweaving of the results of a number of the school's discussions.

26 Cf. Schnackenburg, *John*, 1.67–68; Ernst Haenchen, "Aus der Literatur zum Johannesevangelium 1929–1956" *ThR* 23 (1955) 306–7; Ernst Käsemann, "Aus der Neutestamentlichen Arbeit der letzten Jahre," *VF* (1947/48) 195–223; Dwight Moody Smith, *The Composition and Order of the Fourth Gospel* (New Haven: Yale University Press, 1972) 110–15; Charles K. Barrett, *The Gospel According to St. John* (London: SPCK; New York: Macmillan, 1955; 2d ed.; Philadelphia: Westminster, 1978); Raymond E. Brown, *The Gospel According to John* (2 vols.; AB 29, 29A; Garden City: Doubleday, 1966, 1970) 1.xxxi xxxii; Jürgen Becker, *Das Evangelium nach Johannes* (2 vols.; ÖTK 4/1; Gütersloh: Mohn, 1979–81) 1.34–36; with some reserve also Siegfried Schulz, *Das Evangelium nach Johannes* (NTD 4; 12th ed.; Göttingen: Vandenhoeck & Ruprecht, 1972) 8. Vielhauer (*Geschichte*, 425–27) holds still another opinion.

27 The use of the verb φανεροῦν is one example of this dialectic. It has, first, a christological sense that determines the eschatological present: Christ has appeared (1 John 1:2; cf. 3:8); second, it has a future eschatological meaning, "when he is revealed" (2:28 with reference to the parousia; cf. also 3:2, "what we will be has not yet been revealed").

28 Cf. Bultmann, *Epistles*, 43.

1 Prelude: What We Have Seen, We Declare to You

1 We declare to you what was from the
beginning, what we have heard, what we
have seen with our eyes, what we have
looked at and touched with our hands,
concerning the word of life— 2/ this life
was revealed, and we have seen it and
testify to it, and declare to you the
eternal life that was with the Father and
was revealed to us— 3/ we declare to
you what we have seen and heard so that
you also may have fellowship with us;
and truly our fellowship is with the
Father and with his Son Jesus Christ. 4/
We are writing these things so that our
joy may be complete.

Like 1 John as a whole, these verses cannot be classified within the letter form. Since this is a written document, it is appropriate for the author to refer to the fact of writing (v. 4). Thus the closing phrases are only distantly reminiscent of a *salutatio,* as that form is familiar to us from NT letter prescripts.[1] Verses 1–4 are intended to introduce not a letter but rather the homily that follows. They are the prelude to the subsequent parenetic and dogmatic teaching.

The grammatical structure is confused. The introductory relative clauses that form the framework of v. 1 are missing their predicate. The connective περί cannot easily be fitted into the sentence structure. It contributes to the murkiness of the construction that v. 2 is apparently a parenthesis,[2] while v. 3 continues the series of relative clauses from v. 1 and closes them with a finite verb "we declare" (ἀπαγγέλλομεν) on which depends the following ἵνα clause. The sentence structure is further complicated by the anticipation of this verb in the parenthesis. The problems of content that result will be treated in the exegesis below. At this point it may suffice to draw the following conclusions: (1) The opaqueness of the sentence structure suggests the idea that the author did not intend a consistently developed stylistic arrangement of the individual clauses here or in what follows. He produced linguistic unevenness as a matter of course, so that one may ask whether this is a specific characteristic of this author's style. (2) Beyond this, one may also ask whether the choppiness of the style and the conscious avoidance of clear definitions allow the conclusion that the author is deliberately making a mystery of the subject being addressed. In any case one may say that neither this passage nor the logical identifications presented in the later development of the writing should be interpreted as if they were systematic definitions.[3]

■ **1** The concept of "beginning" (ἀρχή)[4] appears again in the prepositional phrase ἀπ ἀρχῆς in 2 John 5–6. Even if in the latter case it describes the beginning of the

1 On the *salutatio* in a letter's prescript, see Vielhauer, *Geschichte,* 64; I am opposing the position of Francis ("Form and Function," 122: "Verse four is a summary, transitional epistolary device alluding to the ἐχάρην in the opening of other epistles").

2 Francis differs ("Form and Function," 122): "There is no need to treat verse two as a parenthetical remark. Verse one stands in apposition to the independent sentence, verse two (especially to its subject, life), and verse three is simply a new sentence." Against this position, and in harmony with what I have said above: Bultmann, *Epistles,* 7; Schnackenburg, *Epistles,* 61; Brown, *Epistles,* 166; Stephen S. Smalley, "What about 1 John?" in Elizabeth A. Livingstone, ed., *Studia Biblica 1978,* vol. 3: *Papers on Paul and Other New Testament Authors* (JSNTSup 3; Sheffield: JSOT Press, 1980) 338.

3 See n. 11 below on περὶ τοῦ λόγου τῆς ζωῆς; cf. also the remarks on 4:8, 16.

4 On this, see *Canon Muratori,* lines 29–31, where 1 John 1:1 is combined, apparently in a free quotation, with 1:3. The combination of 1 John 1:1 with John 20:19–29 in *Epistola Apostolorum* §3 is striking: on this, see Arnold Ehrhardt, "The Gospels in the

community or (less probably) the foundation of faith through the Christ-event,[5] one cannot deny that here it reveals a close relationship to the absolute understanding of the term in the prologue to the Fourth Gospel (John 1:1). The question arises whether 1 John, in speaking of "that which was from the beginning," presumes not only the language but also the theology of the Fourth Gospel; that is, whether it is referring to the interpretation of the Christ-event in the Fourth Gospel.

If one believes that 1 John originated in dependence on the Fourth Gospel and carries the theology of that Gospel farther, the Gospel's concept of ἀρχή (as part of the "innocuous language of some passages in John concerning the beginnings of discipleship") would be "intensified" in 1 John. "The church orients itself to its origins. . . . Its eschatological self-consciousness is transposed into a reflection on the essence of Christian society."[6] This means concretely that the theology of the author of 1 John is articulated in the polemic against false teaching (2:23–24) and, having the Fourth Gospel as "a fixed authority held firmly in mind," introduces the idea of an ecclesial tradition.[7] This is an impressive construct, but it must remain open to the question whether the Gospel is not being evaluated to the detriment of 1 John. Furthermore, it provokes a counterthesis, namely, that the posited dependence must be replaced by the view that these two theologically most significant of the Johannine writings stand fundamentally in parallel to one another.

Let us begin with the Johannine use of the word ἀρχή. There can be no doubt that, in John 1:1, ἀρχή, referring to the λόγος, describes the absolute beginning. Close parallels occur in 1 John 1:1; 2:13–14. At each of these points in the text the absolute ἀρχή is used in a positive, christological sense. There is also an absolute negative meaning, both in the Gospel (John 8:44), which describes the devil as a "murderer from the beginning" (ἐκεῖνος ἀνθρωποκτόνος ἦν ἀπ᾽ ἀρχῆς), and in 1 John, which calls the devil a sinner "from the beginning" (1 John 3:8: ἀπ᾽ ἀρχῆς ὁ διάβολος ἁμαρτάνει). It is difficult to conclude from these passages that 1 John depends on the Gospel, for the decisive verse, John 1:1, is in the Logos hymn, which, according to the dominant opinion of scholars, preceded the composition of the Fourth Gospel.[8] The

---

Muratorian Fragment," in idem, *The Framework of the New Testament Stories* (Manchester: Manchester University Press; Cambridge: Harvard University Press, 1964) 28–29 (although Ehrhardt thinks that even 1 John 1:1 is answering the positions of the "Alogi": p. 34).

5 See the remarks on 2 John 5–6 and what follows. Besides these two passages, the construction appears also in 1 John 2:7, 13–14, 24; 3:8, 11, as well as John 8:44; 15:27; cf. Luke 1:2. According to Ignace de la Potterie the formulation ἐξ ἀρχῆς (John 6:64; 16:4) is materially different ("La notion de 'commencement' dans les écrits johanniques," in Rudolf Schnackenburg, Josef Ernst, and Joachim Wanke, eds., *Die Kirche des Anfangs: Festschrift für Heinz Schürmann* [Leipzig: St. Benno, 1978] 379–403, at 390ff.); but a comparison of John 16:4 with 15:27 shows that no difference is intended (cf. Brown, *Epistles*, 155: "Johannine love for variation of vocabulary").

6 Conzelmann, "Anfang," 213.

7 Ibid., 211–12.

8 Cf. Rudolf Bultmann, *The Gospel of John: A Commentary* (trans. George R. Beasley-Murray, R. W. N. Hoare, and John K. Riches; Philadelphia: Westminster; London: Blackwell, 1971) 16; Schnackenburg, *John*, 1.224–29; Brown, *John*, 1.19–21. A comparison between 1 John 1:1–4 and John 1:1–14 reveals the following picture:

1 John 1:1–4	John 1:1–14
v. 1 ἀπ᾽ ἀρχῆς	v. 1 ἐν ἀρχῇ
v. 1 ὃ ἀκηκόαμεν, ὃ ἑωράκαμεν τοῖς ὀφθαλμοῖς ἡμῶν, ὃ ἐθεασάμεθα	v. 14 ἐθεασάμεθα τὴν δόξαν αὐτοῦ
. . . τὴν ζωὴν τὴν αἰώνιον (v. 2b)	v. 4 ἐν αὐτῷ ζωὴ ἦν (= v. 1: ὁ λόγος)
v. 1 τοῦ λόγου τῆς ζωῆς	
v. 2a ἡ ζωὴ ἐφανερώθη (v. 2c + ἡμῖν)	v. 14 ὁ λόγος σὰρξ ἐγένετο καὶ ἐσκήνωσεν ἐν ἡμῖν
v. 2c ἦν πρὸς τὸν πατέρα	v. 1 (+ 2) ἦν πρὸς τὸν θεόν

The differences show that only a few concepts correspond; even the same words are used differently. Thus not only is the absolute ὁ λόγος missing from 1 John, but there is a difference of usage between ἀπ᾽ ἀρχῆς (1 John 1:1) and ἐν ἀρχῇ (John 1:1): the incarnation is predicated in 1 John not of the Logos, who "became flesh" and "tented" among us, but of ζωή. In addition, the object of seeing is not the *doxa* of the Incarnate One, but eternal life (v. 2b). Beyond this, it is clear from the comparison that not even the sequence of the Logos hymn reappears in 1 John. It follows that the author of 1 John is not referring to the prologue of John

problem at hand may be resolved by positing that the author of 1 John follows the Johannine school's understanding of ἀρχή, an understanding that is also presupposed by the prologue to the Fourth Gospel and by the fourth evangelist.

One may add to this that ἀρχή in the Fourth Gospel refers either to the work and message of Jesus (John 2:11; 16:4) or to the beginnings of discipleship (John 6:64; 15:27).[9] These two meanings may not be dismissed as "innocuous." There are correspondences in the christological and ecclesiological language of the Johannine literature. They testify to the basic structure of the Johannine idea of tradition within the church, even in the Gospel (esp. at 15:27 and 16:4). Hence in this context, despite the variation in the intention of what is being said, there is no sign of a fundamental difference among the Johannine writings. The absolute use of language emphasizes the eschatological "pre-" of the beginning, founded on the preexistent Logos and identified with it—explicitly in the Gospel, and implicitly in 1 John. This helps to underscore the tension between eschatology and history that is already present in 2 John 5–6, a tension that shaped the beginning of the Johannine community and thus the community itself.[10]

It also becomes evident at this point that the relative ὅ that appears four times in v. 1, despite its neuter form and despite the fact that it is paraphrased with the περί-expression in v. 1b,[11] in truth refers to nothing other than the Christ-event to which the author testifies. Although the concept of λόγος should be translated in the first instance as "word," so that the genitive can be understood as objective ("word of life"),[12] one still cannot exclude an epexegetical[13] or qualitative[14] sense. This indicates that the genitive ζωῆς does not necessarily reduce λόγος to an impersonal meaning ("word"),[15] but rather that the Logos can also be considered here as a person; for life-giving power belongs not only to the proclaiming word but also to Christ as the preexistent and incarnate Logos.[16] That the interpretation of λόγος as a person cannot be eliminated is suggested by the parallels to the Johannine prologue, even though this does not establish any literary dependence. Instead, what we find here is a piece of tradition from the Johannine school.[17] This conclusion is further suggested by the absolute usage τὸν ἀπ᾽ ἀρχῆς in 1 John 2:13–14. Accordingly, the author's message concerns not only the

(against Brown, *Epistles*, 178); what is cited is not even the pre-Johannine Logos hymn; rather, this author is employing the independent language and world of ideas of the Johannine school, which is also used—even though in a sharply divergent manner—in John 1:1–14. Cf. Schnelle, *Antidocetic Christology*, 53–55.

9 John 8:25 is different; here the accusative τὴν ἀρχὴν stands for ὅλως in the sense of "at all." Cf. BAGD 112.

10 The formulaic ἀπ᾽ ἀρχῆς (see n. 5 above) relieves the existing tension neither in a purely historical nor in a purely eschatological sense. Rather, it articulates the unity of eschaton and history, something that has become manifest in the Christ-event and is fulfilled in the being of the church. Cf. also Wendt ("Der 'Anfang,'" 40), who correctly disputes a dependence of our text on the prologue of the Fourth Gospel, and in v. 1 sees a statement of a "historical situation," namely, the "beginning of historical Christianity."

11 The use of the preposition περί is grammatically correct, but unusual. One would expect the accusative τὸν λόγον τῆς ζωῆς as an explication of the relative pronoun. That the author chose this other construction reveals that the "word of life" is the focal point that will define what follows. (Cf. Dodd, *Epistles*, 3: "But *prima facie* the clause 'concerning the word of life' indicates the *theme* of the announcement.")

12 Cf. BDF §163; also 1 John 1:2 (ἀπαγγέλλομεν ὑμῖν τὴν ζωὴν τὴν αἰώνιον).

13 Cf. BDF §167 (an appositive genitive), "the word that is life."

14 Cf. BDF §165 (also a descriptive or adjectival genitive), "the word that is characterized by life," the living or life-giving word. See, correspondingly, John 6:35 (bread of life); 8:12 (light of life); Rev 21:6; 22:1, 17 (water of life).

15 Tertullian already wrote in this sense (*De Anima* 17.14: "sermo vitae"; but he wrote differently in *Adv. Prax.* 15); see the corresponding v. 3 (ἀπαγγέλλομεν) and v. 5 (ἡ ἀγγελία ἣν ἀκηκόαμεν ἀπ᾽ αὐτοῦ ἀναγγέλλομεν ὑμῖν).

16 Cf. Schnackenburg, *Epistles*, 57: "The phrase 'concerning the word of life' [περὶ τοῦ λόγου τῆς ζωῆς], which disturbs the balance of the sentence, can be explained as due to the urgent need for qualification. As far as the content goes, both phrases may be making the same point, the one at the beginning and the other at the end of v. 1. The preexistent Logos, and subsequently the incarnate One, incorporates in himself the fullness of the divine life, an idea that is no more clarified here than it is in [the Gospel of John]."

17 I cannot address the religio-historical aspect of the

life and work but also the person of Jesus Christ. If to speak of the person of Jesus Christ means at the same time to speak of the work and mission, the "cause" of Jesus Christ,[18] it is equally true that the "cause" of Jesus Christ cannot be separated from his person. In the message of 1 John both the person and the "cause" of Jesus Christ are united in one.

If it is characteristic of the event involving the preexistent and incarnate Logos that it has occurred "from the beginning," one can say of the same event that it is the object of hearing, seeing, beholding, and touching. That the author uses the first person plural and combines it with aorist and perfect verbs makes clear that the reference is to an event in past time and to a perception of that event that also lies in the past. He thus distinguishes himself from the Christian community in the present that is the addressee of 1 John. The author thus counts himself among the first Christian generation. The time difference excludes the possibility that at this point he is speaking with a simple ecclesial "we." It is true that in what follows the author and the community are often combined in a "we,"[19] but in the introduction (vv. 1–4) not only is such an equation contradicted by the chronological distinction just mentioned; "we are writing" (γράφομεν ἡμεῖς, v. 4a) also sets a clear division between the author and the addressees.[20] Hence in this context "we" functions primarily as an authorial plural. It would be wrong to object, against this conclusion, that the author of 1 John ordinarily speaks of himself "in the singular,"[21] for the shift between "we" and "I" styles is also found in 2 and 3 John, and is thus to be regarded as a general expression of a claim to authority, something that is indicated as well, and by no means least, by the "witness" terminology.[22]

If this is an authorial "we," the proposal that the author is integrating himself by means of the first person

---

λόγος problem here. Even though it is advisable to be cautious in adducing the gnostic systems of the second and third centuries for an explication of the Logos concept, since a secondary Christian influence cannot be excluded (cf., e.g., the gnosis of Markos at Irenaeus *Adv. haer.* 1.15.3), it is still insufficient to refer simply to the OT (Gen 1:1) or to Jewish wisdom teaching (as early as Prov 8:1–36; Job 28:12–28; esp. Wis 18:14, 16). Alongside Hellenistic Jewish traditions (Philo *Leg. all.* 1.65: ἡ [σοφία] δέ ἐστιν ὁ θεοῦ λόγος ["Wisdom is God's Word"]) stand genuinely Greek philosophical or religious traditions that also belong to the broader environment of the Johannine Logos teaching (cf., e.g., Plotinus *Enn.* 3.2.15: ἀρχὴ οὖν λόγος καὶ πάντα λόγος ["The foundational principle is Logos and all is Logos."]). See Joachim Jeremias, "Zum Logosproblem," *ZNW* 59 (1968) 82–85 (affinity of Rev 19:11–16 to Wis 18:14–16).

18 See below on 3 John 7. Marinus de Jonge correctly sees that the movement of the language leads to v. 3, and thus to the person of Jesus Christ ("An Analysis of 1 John 1:1–4," *BT* 29 [1978] 330). J. Emmette Weir ("The Identity of the Logos in the First Epistle of John," *ExpT* 86 [1974–75] 118–20) too exclusively emphasizes the reference to the Logos Christ (with four arguments: the combination of the Logos with the idea of ἀρχή; πρός as characterizing the relationship to the Father; the Logos is source of life; and the Logos is apprehended as a real, flesh-and-blood person). But v. 2 ("we declare to you eternal life") shows that the author intends a distinction, and not an alternative between λόγος as word and as person.

19 1 John 2:1b, 2–3, 5, 18b, and frequently elsewhere; Schnackenburg distinguishes the impersonal εἴπωμεν in 1:6, 8, 10 (*Epistles*, 51 n. 7) from these passages, but it too has an ecclesiological function.

20 On v. 4b (ἡμῶν) see below (n. 59).

21 Thus Schnackenburg, *Epistles*, 51, with reference to 1 John 2:1a, 7–8, 12–14, 21, 26; 5:13; but these are contrasted with the passages cited in n. 19 above.

22 Cf. Adolf von Harnack, who writes of 1 John 1:1–5: "the author intends that his readers should take note and know that he himself, alone, has the right to speak with the same authority as a viewer, witness and proclaimer that belongs to the community of believers" ("Das 'Wir' in den Johanneischen Schriften," SPAW.PH [1923] 96–113, at 104; he writes differently on 1 John 4:6, 14, 16, saying that there "we" refers to the "community of believers" [p. 101]); similarly Bultmann, *Epistles*, 11, according to whom "the author of this Epistle is conscious of himself as having a personal authority, i.e., as being a representative of the bearers of the tradition"; cf. also Schnackenburg, *Epistles*, 51–56 (excursus 1: "The Meaning and Significance of 'Witness' in 1 John 1:1–4").

plural in a "prophetic collective"[23] is less likely, even though this would correspond to the structure of the Johannine circle, in which itinerant preachers had an important function. One could more correctly judge that the author uses "we" in order to assert membership in the "circle . . . of 'apostolic' witnesses."[24] In any case, the emphatic backward reference to the past time of salvation and the stress on the eye- and ear-witness have a "historically" accentuating function. The past tenses of ἀκηκόαμεν ("we have heard"), ἑωράκαμεν ("we have seen"), and so on were not chosen by accident. They make it clear that the saving event in the past is the object of the hearing and seeing. They testify to the reality of the Logos's becoming flesh, and not merely to the resurrection body of Christ (cf. John 20:24–29).

Not only linguistic accents but also those of content are combined with these different levels of action. The imperfect, as expression of relative time, refers back to "a time previous to the time of perception" (BDF § 330) and can point to a period of time that lies in the past and is understood in linear fashion (BDF § 324b). It is no accident that the imperfect appears where one may infer that something is being said about the preexistent basis of the saving event. In contrast, the perfect tense, which gives a solemn character to the Johannine style, expresses the "endurance of what has been accomplished," since it combines the stages of action expressed by the present and the aorist (BDF § 340). At the same time, it describes an "enduring effect on the subject," as does ἑώρακα also (cf. BDF § 342 [2], on Acts 22:15). In our passage the "hearing," by being placed first and last (vv. 1 and 3), is made as essential as the "seeing" that is mentioned three times (vv. 1 and 3; see the similar passages in John 5:37; *Ps.-Clem. Hom.* 1.9). The distinction between present and aorist is especially important: the latter reflects an action at a particular point in time, and here it designates not an ingressive but an effective content. Thus the facticity of the past event (v. 1: the seeing and touching; v. 2: the revealing) is emphasized. In contrast, the present refers to the situation of writing, which affects the author and the readers who are being addressed (vv. 2–4). One may thus conclude from the use of tenses that the author is thinking not only of the preexistent basis of the kerygma, but beyond that is looking back (perfect tense) to the words and deeds of the earthly Jesus as the object of hearing and seeing, while the statements of fact in the aorist have as their special object the appearances of the Risen One, or more generally the event of revelation. It is precisely this (vv. 1 and 3: ὅ; v. 4: ταῦτα) that the writer wishes again to proclaim to the community.[25]

Overview of the Use of Tenses in 1 John 1:1–4

	Present	Imperfect	Aorist	Perfect
v. 1		ἦν (ἀπ' ἀρχῆς)		
				ἀκηκόαμεν
				ἑωράκαμεν
			ἐθεασάμεθα	
			ἐψηλάφησαν	

23 Cf. Schnackenburg, *Epistles*, 55; Haenchen, "Neuere Literatur," 249 ("the style of a prophetic revelation").

24 Thus Schnackenburg, *Epistles*, 55. But it is characteristic of the author's self-understanding as a member of the second or third Christian generation that he does not use the concept of ἀπόστολος here or in what follows. This should be noted, even if the author's fictive claim is factually identical with that of an apostle of the first generation (see below).

25 Johannes P. Louw ("Verbal Aspect in the First Letter of John," *Neot* 9 [1975] 98–104) also emphasizes the distinction between the perfect and aorist forms, which (against James H. Moulton, et al., *A Grammar of New Testament Greek* [3 vols.; Edinburgh: Clark, 1908–63] 1.142) can be demonstrated not only in NT but also in Byzantine Greek. With reference to the development of the Russian language (!), however, he thinks that one ought to give closer attention to the function of the verbs, and that one and the same function could be expressed under different positive or negative aspects (ibid., 100). Nevertheless, the conclusion that "exegetically no distinction in meaning should be made between the perfects and aorists in 1 Joh. 1:1. They all have the semantic value of the perfect tense" (p. 101), remains undemonstrated.

v. 2			ἐφανερώθη	
				ἑωράκαμεν
	μαρτυροῦμεν			
	ἀπαγγέλλομεν			
		ἦν (πρὸς τὸν πατέρα)		
			ἐφανερώθη	
v. 3				ἑωράκαμεν
				ἀκηκόαμεν
	ἀπαγγέλλομεν			
	(ἵνα) ἔχητε			
v. 4	γράφομεν			

Is the author of 1 John who refers to this past stage of the incarnational event a contemporary of the life of Jesus? Is he a witness of the saving event, since he presents himself as a member of the apostolic generation? The emphatic backward reference to redemptive history seems to suggest this conclusion, and conservative scholars have, in fact, drawn it. Even if one does not conclude from this evidence that this author is identical with the author of the Fourth Gospel and that, in consequence, 1 John is also an eyewitness account (although the differences between the Fourth Gospel and 1 John speak too clearly against such a conclusion), the historical orientation should nevertheless be taken seriously.[26] It is not really possible to understand the terminology used in vv. 1–4 as nothing more than a transferred, spiritualistic manner of speaking.[27] Yet one

26 Dodd differs (*Epistles*, 12–14). He sees in the "we" the same meaning as in the "I" of the psalmists, which can stand both for the individual writer and also for the Israel of God. Here, according to Dodd, the author is not speaking exclusively of himself or of a group of historical eyewitnesses but of the whole Christian church. Bultmann also rejects a purely historical interpretation (*John*, 70–71 n. 3, on John 1:14). Rather, what is being emphasized is the contemporaneity of the historical and the eschatological event (cf. John 16). Indeed, the presupposed and claimed eyewitness character is in tension with John 20:24–26, where it is precisely those who do not see who are blessed (see, correctly, on this point Martin Rese, "Das Gebot der Bruderliebe in den Johannesbriefen," *TZ* 41 [1985] 53 n. 39). If the Fourth Gospel is influenced by a gnostic-docetic tendency (though this is not consistently maintained), 1 John presents a realistic perspective that cannot be understood simply as a reaction to docetic threats to the Johannine communities, but that also has an older, even apocalyptic basis.

27 Eduard Norden (*Agnostos Theos. Untersuchungen zur Formgeschichte religiöser Rede* [Leipzig/Berlin: Teubner, 1913, reprinted Darmstadt: Wissenschaftliche Buchgesellschaft, 1974] 17 n. 1) emphasizes the parallel between 1 John 1:1 and *Poimandres* (*Corp. Herm.* 1) 5.2. Here also he sees concrete sense perception being spiritualized: ἄφθονος γὰρ ὁ κύριος φαίνεται διὰ παντὸς τοῦ κόσμου. νόησιν ἰδεῖν καὶ λαβέσθαι αὐταῖς ταῖς χερσὶ δύνασαι καὶ τὴν εἰκόνα τοῦ θεοῦ θεάσασθαι ("For the Lord manifests himself unstintingly through all the universe. Can you perceive one of [his] thoughts and grasp it with your hands and behold the image of God?"). Here is a mixture of Stoic and Platonic motifs. On the one hand, there is a play on the idea of the God who is extending him- or herself through the world (on the λόγος σπερματικός, see Diogenes Laertius *Vit. phil.* 7.140; Seneca *Ben.* 4.7–8). On the other hand, this idea is combined with the Platonic notion of the incomprehensibility of God, the divine incorporeality, and the impossibility of making for oneself an image of God (cf. Eusebius *Praep. Ev.* 4.13; Plutarch *Is. et Os.* 78; *Ei Delph.* 393AB; Maximus of Tyre *Philosophumena* 11 [ed. Hermann Hobein; Leipzig: Teubner, 1910]). In a simultaneous use of ὁράω and θεάομαι, Herodotus 2.148.5 testifies to the distinction between a concrete sensible and a figurative usage: τὰ μέν νυν μετέωρα τῶν οἰκημάτων αὐτοί τε ὡρῶμεν διεξιόντες καὶ αὐτοὶ θεησάμενοι λέγομεν ("The upper chambers I myself passed through and saw, and what I say concerning them is from my own observation"). Here "saw" corresponds to the verb ὁράω, and "observation" the participle of θεάομαι. The transferred sense of ὁράω can be found in 3 John 11: Ὁ ἀγαθοποιῶν ἐκ τοῦ θεοῦ ἐστιν· ὁ κακοποιῶν οὐχ ἑώρακεν τὸν θεόν ("Whoever does good is from God; whoever does evil has not seen God"). In 1 John, "seeing" has a twofold christological interpretation. (1) In a figurative sense, it designates the object of the community's faith (1 John 3:6). This ὁρᾶν is also possible for noncontemporaries through their own decision (Braun, "Literar-Analyse," 285–86); it is thus not only an "expression of orthodoxy," and, as such, received from the author without any explanation as to its original meaning (against Conzelmann, "Anfang," 212–13 n. 20). (2) In a temporally differentiated sense, it distinguishes the generation of the eye- and ear-witnesses from the present generation (1 John 1:1–3). This chronological specification at the same time enunciates, as

must draw back from reading it as a historical statement. If John the presbyter, the author of 2 and 3 John and Papias's "teacher," is not to be counted among the historical witnesses of the life of Jesus, still less so is the author of 1 John. The tradition of the Johannine school, which this author presumes and independently edits, is already far removed from its origins.[28]

But, if the author's status as an eye- and ear-witness is thus to be regarded as improbable, why does that author appear, in terms of both the form and matter of his presentation, as a "historical" witness of the Christ-event? He appears to be activated by two motives. First, there is a theological reason: defense against the false teachers who, as will appear in 1 John 2:22–23; 4:2–3, 15, represent a docetic christology. In opposition to an ahistorical, spiritualistic christology, it is important to assert the "empirical" reality of the Christ event. This is a first and decisive reason to begin 1 John with a testimony that the Christ lived on earth as visible, audible, and tangible. The second motive could be called "pseudepigraphical," although this author does not use a pseudonym. Even though he does not use a false name, he is still writing this document under fictitious circumstances. He pretends to be an eye- and ear-witness, even though that does not correspond to historical reality. That he cannot be identical with the apostle John, although this was certainly asserted in patristic tradition,[29] should not require a separate proof. The time frame would make it difficult to attribute 1 John to a contemporary of Jesus. Moreover, the patristic tradition testifies to the early death of the apostle John, the disciple of the Lord,[30] and John 21 presupposes such a tradition. The reason for this indirectly expressed pseudepigraphical intention undoubtedly lies also in the recognition that such a fiction is appropriate to underscore the claims of this document and hence the author's intention to put the docetic teaching of the opponents in its place. The claim to apostolic authority could be understood as an element

---

something true of later generations, that they cannot see God (1 John 4:12: "No one has ever seen God"; cf. 4:20). The same idea is known to the evangelist and is given a christological foundation in the Gospel (John 1:18: "No one has ever seen God"; cf. John 5:37; 6:46). Alongside this, the Fourth Gospel is dominated by a general, historical understanding of this concept. Thus John 1:34 speaks of the seeing and witness of John the Baptizer; 1:39, 50–51; 19:35 of the disciples' seeing; 4:45; 6:2 of the Galileans' or the people's seeing; 15:24 of the world's seeing. Even Jesus' ὁρᾶν, which applies to things earthly (3:11) and heavenly (3:32; 8:38), is to be understood as historical seeing. These last several verses make clear that seeing the Father is the basis for the sending of the Son. Where the object of the seeing is Jesus, and when it leads human beings to faith, it approaches the transferred sense (cf. 6:36; 14:9, and frequently elsewhere). The same is true of seeing in its future-eschatological meaning (16:16–17, 19; 19:37) and of seeing the Risen One (20:18, 25, 29). For the connection between faith and seeing, cf. Ferdinand Hahn, "Sehen und Glauben im Johannesevangelium," in Heinrich Baltensweiler and Bo Reicke, eds., *Neues Testament und Geschichte* (Festschrift Oscar Cullmann; Zurich: Theologischer Verlag; Tübingen: Mohr [Siebeck], 1972) 125–41. The combination of verbs of seeing with ψηλαφάω is striking. This "touching" is to be found only at this point in the Johannine writings. In Luke 24:39 and Ignatius *Smyrn.* 2.2, in combination with forms of εἶδον, it appears in this concrete, sensory meaning as a proof of the bodily resurrection (cf. John 20:25). One must infer an equally concrete meaning for Heb 12:18. For the interpretation of the verb in Acts 17:27, cf. Norden, *Agnostos Theos,* 14–18.

28 Consequently, one must have doubts about regarding the author as "a disciple and representative of John bar Zebedee" (Schnackenburg, *Johannesbriefe,* 57; cf. idem, *Epistles,* 55, where the English translation has reinterpreted the sentence order to some degree); for it remains only a postulate that the author of 1 John has any historical connection to John the son of Zebedee (on this, see also n. 30 below).

29 Cf. Irenaeus *Adv. haer.* 2.22.5.

30 For testimony to the martyrdom of John the son of Zebedee, cf. the Papias fragment in a summary of church history by Philip of Sides: Παπίας ἐν τῷ δευτέρῳ λόγῳ λέγει, ὅτι Ἰωάννης ὁ θεολόγος καὶ Ἰάκωβος ὁ ἀδελφὸς αὐτοῦ ὑπὸ Ἰουδαίων ἀνῃρέθησαν (Carl von de Boor, *Neue Fragmente des Papias, Hegesippus und Pierius* [TU 5; Leipzig: Hinrichs, 1888] 170: "Papias says in the second book that John the theologian and his brother James were killed by [the] Jews"). See also the Syrian martyrology of 411, which, for 27 December, mentions "John and James, the apostles in Jerusalem." See Hans Lietzmann, *Die drei ältesten Martyrologien* (KIT 2; 2d ed.; Bonn: Marcus & Weber, 1911) 8. Clement of Alexandria gives an indirect indication. He lists the apostles who did not die as martyrs, and does not mention John among them (*Strom.* 4.9.71). On the whole question, see Bousset, *Offenbarung Johannis,* 35–38. Eduard Schwartz ("Johannes und Kerinthos" *ZNW* 15 [1914]

of so-called early catholicism, as shown by the other pseudepigraphical letters in the NT (e.g., the Pastorals, James, Jude, 1 and 2 Peter). It also remains for us to inquire whether other features of "early catholicism" occur in 1 John.[31]

The addressees, who in any case are to be sought primarily in the communities belonging to the Johannine circle, were probably already acquainted with the set of theological problems at issue here. The defense against opponents who threaten their existence allows a distinction between what the text says and what it means. According to the external, fictive statement, a historical distance is fixed between the author as a supposed eyewitness and the addressees, who must defend themselves against the Docetists. The author's "hearing," "seeing," and "touching" are thus undoubtedly impossible for them to experience, as the author says: it is part of the apostolic fiction. Nevertheless, the meaning of this historical distinction is of immediate importance to the community. Their common confrontation with docetic teaching implies *κοινωνία* between the addressees and the proclaimer (v. 3), a "community" with the Father and the Son, something that can be asserted not only of the author (v. 3b) but also of the readers (v. 6). This "community" is universal: it is true of the first generation but also of the later Christian communities; it is founded in their faith experience, which "sees" and "believes" the revelation of the love of God (1 John 4:16). This faith experience of the community has a christological foundation, since it does not permit the Logos-Christ to evaporate into a mere idea. Instead, it confesses and experiences the Christ-event as a paradoxical unification of the eschaton with the world, and the paradoxical realization of the resulting eschatological *agapē* in human history.

■ **2** The positions of the author and the community involve a variety of understandings of ζωή. If, in v. 1b, "life" (ζωή) was connected with the beginning of all things and with the λόγος,[32] in v. 2 it appears as a personified entity. Its having "appeared"[33] means that it is united

210–19, at 215–17) also rejects the identification of the author of the Fourth Gospel with John the son of Zebedee, on the basis of John 21:20. This, he says, is not a historical reminiscence but a question of salvaging the honor of the Beloved Disciple in contrast to the martyred Peter.

31 See the excursus on "Early Catholicism" below.

32 On the question of the genitive ζωῆς, the answer to which depends on the interpretation of the word λόγος, see nn. 11–15 above.

33 The verb φανερόω is relatively rare before and outside the NT. The supposition that it is gnostic in origin (so Hannelis Schulte, *Der Begriff der Offenbarung im Neuen Testament* [BEvTh 13; Munich: Kaiser, 1949] 67–84) has no basis. Etymologically it is connected with the adjective φανερός and means "to make visible what is invisible" (so Rudolf Bultmann and Dieter Lührmann, "φανερόω," *TDNT* 9 [1974] 3). It appears 49 times in the NT, seven of them in 1 John and eight in the Fourth Gospel, but not at all in 2 or 3 John. The synonym ἀποκαλύπτω, which is frequent in Paul's writings, is not used in the Johannine corpus (except for a quotation of Isa 53:1 in John 12:38). It is related to γνωρίζω (cf. John 15:15: πάντα ἃ ἤκουσα παρὰ τοῦ πατρός μου ἐγνώρισα ὑμῖν ["I have made known to you everything that I have heard from my Father"] or 17:26: καὶ ἐγνώρισα αὐτοῖς τὸ ὄνομά σου καὶ γνωρίσω ["I made your name known to them, and I will make it known"] with 17:6: Ἐφανέρωσά σου τὸ ὄνομα τοῖς ἀνθρώποις οὓς ἔδωκάς μοι ["I have made your name known to the people you gave me"], but φανεροῦν implies not merely the act of making possible a recognition that is mediated by speaking and hearing, but also a making visible, placing before the eyes what has previously been hidden. On this basis, the verb has a variety of possible uses in the Fourth Gospel. According to the evangelist, John the Baptizer baptizes in order that the Christ "might be revealed to Israel" (1:31). The Son of God himself reveals his glory through miracles (2:11), and the demand of Jesus' brothers that he reveal himself to the world (7:4) is taken up in Jesus' prayer: "I have made your name known to the world" (17:6). That this making known is at the same time an indication of an event that is taking place in the perceptible, earthly realm is evident especially from the objective phrase τὰ ἔργα (3:21; 9:3). On this basis, the reference to the appearances of the Risen One can be understood in terms of the interest of the author of the supplementary chapter (21) in depicting the reality of the Risen One as being perceived by the disciples as a visible event (21:1, 14).

In 1 John, the verb refers no less to making visible what has been hidden. The false teachers "manifest"

with the person of the Incarnate One; it manifests itself in Jesus Christ and so has become a historical event. The identification of ζωή with the Christ-event clarifies the character of the fundamental knowledge that is binding on the author and the community: the witness is to a universal meaning that is concretized in the defense against docetic teaching.[34] It is true that, at this point, the internal structure of ζωή is not more closely defined, but a particular interpretation is not excluded. It is no accident that the incarnation of the "word of life" (λόγος τῆς ζωῆς) is explained in what follows in terms of the idea of sin, which is connected with the death of Jesus.[35] From this standpoint, there is no suggestion of an opposition between a theology of the cross and an incarnational theology.[36] In any case, only a few words in this verse have to do with the incarnation; more precisely, it is said that ζωή is qualified by "being with the Father" and is thus distinct from any concept of life that is merely biological. The proper adjective for it is "eternal" (αἰώνιος): this ζωή is not exhausted in time and it has no end. What is at issue here is life pure and simple.

Excursus: Ζωή[37]

The verb ζῆν is attested 140 times in the NT: of these, seventeen are in John, and one in the Johannine Letters (1 John 4:9). The noun appears 135 times in the New Testament: 27 times in John and in ten verses of 1 John (13 occurrences); it is not found in 2 or 3 John. The combination ζωὴ αἰώνιος is frequent: 1 John 1:2; 2:25; 3:15; 5:11, 13, 20; John 3:15–16, 36; 4:14, 36; 5:24, 39; 6:27, 40, 47, 54; 10:28; 12:25; and 17:2. The adjective αἰώνιος is often silently understood when ζωή is used in an absolute sense: 1 John 1:2; 3:14; 5:11–12, 16; cf. John 1:4; 3:36; 5:24, 26, 29, 40; 6:33, 35, 48, 51, 53, 63, 68; 8:12; 10:10, and frequently elsewhere. Similarly, Mark 10:17, 30 (ζωὴ αἰώνιος) extends the absolute usage in Mark 9:43, 45.[38]

Even though the word does not appear with great frequency, it is nevertheless a key Johannine concept

the fact that "some of them do not belong to us," that is, do not belong to the community of Christ (2:19). The texts that express a future eschatological perspective speak of the revelation of things hidden in the future. The community expects that, when the judge is revealed in the parousia they will have confidence and will not be put to shame (2:28). The congregation sees itself located between the ages, since God's "beloved" are, on the one hand, "now already" "children of God," but it has "not yet" been revealed what they will be in the future (3:2). This kind of consciousness is founded on the Christ-event that, in the proper sense of the word, represents the revelation of what is hidden. In words borrowed from traditional formulae, it is said of the "appearance" of the Son that its purpose is to destroy the works of the devil (3:8), or also that the Son has "appeared" to take away sins (3:5). It corresponds to the Johannine school tradition to describe the sending of the Son as a revelation and realization of the ἀγάπη τοῦ θεοῦ, and to say that the community will live through the Son (4:9). Here ζωή is described as the ultimate goal of the revelation of Christ. The same is true of 1:2. If the eternal ζωή is revealed to believers, φανεροῦν is, by its very nature (as also in the intention of the fourth evangelist), to be understood as a christological event and its content as life-giving. See Hugo H. Huber, *Der Begriff der Offenbarung im Johannesevangelium* (Göttingen: Vandenhoeck & Ruprecht, 1934); Schulte, *Offenbarung;* Bultmann and Lührmann, "φανερόω," 3–6.

34 See below, on 1 John 2:18–29.

35 Cf. 1:7, 9. Balz ("Johannesbriefe," 163) has a different interpretation.

36 Schnackenburg (*Epistles,* 60) points correctly to Pauline christology, in which the "Golgotha event" has a commanding and central place (Rom 3:24–25; 1 Cor 1:23; 2:2; 2 Cor 5:14; Gal 3:13, and frequently elsewhere), while Johannine theology places a stronger emphasis on the Son of God's becoming human (John 1:14; 3:16; 1 John 4:9). But it is also clear that there is no conflict, since in the Johannine writings the incarnation has soteriological character from the outset. The soteriological aspect is still clearer when one considers that the widely accepted hypothesis of an ecclesiastical redaction does not touch most of these cases; instead, it can call attention to the use of traditional material in the Johannine traditions as well (see below, on 1:7, 9, and elsewhere).

37 See the older literature listed in BAGD 341; also Rudolf Bultmann, Gerhard von Rad, and Georg Bertram, "ζάω, κτλ.," *TDNT* 2 (1964) 832–75; Rudolf Schnackenburg, excursus 12: "The Idea of Life in the Fourth Gospel," *John,* 2.352–61; Luise Schottroff, "ζῶ, ζωή," *EDNT* 2 (1991) 105–9; Franz Mussner, *ZOE: Die Anschauung vom "Leben" im vierten Evangelium* (MThS 1/5; Munich: Zink, 1952).

38 The expression ζωὴ αἰώνιος is found as early as Dan 12:2 LXX; *Ps. Sol.* 3.12; 13.11; *1 Enoch* 37.4; 40.9; as well as in the Pythagorean-influenced Platonist Plutarch (*Is. et Os.* 1).

that paradigmatically reflects Johannine theology. In the Fourth Gospel, life is identified with the person of the preexistent Logos, Christ (thus in the ἐγώ εἰμί sayings: 11:25, "I am the resurrection and the life"; 14:6, "the truth and the life"; 6:35, 48, "the bread of life"; 8:12, "the light of life"). The sending of the Son of God from the Father means life for those who are his own (14:19, "because I live, you also shall live"; cf. 12:50). Hence the evangelist is writing this work with the intention "that through believing you may have life in his name" (20:31). If the life that Christ the revealer brings mediates access to the eschatological truth (14:6), it also consists in the recognition of God and Christ by the believers (17:3). It is presumed as a matter of course that such knowledge is not achieved once and for all, and that it is not restricted to the theoretical level. It demands concrete deeds from the faithful (12:25–26; cf. 13:31–35) and remains open to the future (cf. 5:29; 11:23–27). For "anyone who hears my word and believes him who sent me has eternal life, and does not come under judgment, but has passed from death to life" (5:24). In line with the basic dualistic structure of Johannine thought, ζωή thus means rescue from θάνατος.[39]

Liberation from death involves the obligation to preserve the word of the revealer and implies a challenge to discipleship (8:51–52); for the one who believes does not walk in darkness but clings to the "light of life."[40] This secular understanding of ζωή is emphatically stressed in the eucharistic section of John 6, which is subject to so much literary-critical controversy: the gift of ζωή is mediated not only through the word but also through the sacrament (6:51, 53–58).

In essence, the same structure exists in 1 John. Here also, the gift of ζωή has a christological foundation. The preexistent Son of God is revealed as life (1:1–2). He has been sent into the world "so that we might live through him" (4:9). The promise of life (2:25) is founded on being in the Son, who himself is true God and eternal life (5:20). It is only through community with him that life, as the gift of God, can be received (5:11–13). The receipt of life by believers means, as in the Fourth Gospel, that they have passed from death to life (3:14); in contrast, life is not granted to "murderers" (3:15). Sinners are confronted not only with the opportunity for pardon and the preservation of life but also with the possibility of exclusion from life (5:16). As in the Fourth Gospel, ζωή is not understood solely in an indicative sense as a gift to believers that determines their existence in the present. It is simultaneously connected with an ethical imperative. "Life" is realized in the love of brothers and sisters that is demanded of Christians (3:14–18; cf. 4:20–21). Although the word ζωή does not appear frequently, it nevertheless reflects the essential direction of the theology of 1 John. Its central position is clear when the author defines the goal of his writing: "that you [who believe in the Son of God] may know that you have eternal life."[41]

In the history of religion. In Greek mythology and philosophy ζωή is a quality belonging to the gods as immortal beings (ἀθάνατοι).[42] Sometimes, however, ζωή is synonymous with the word βίος and is predicated of human beings, to the extent that the human is a being characterized by the divine νοῦς.[43] An essential aspect of this is that human beings live out their lives in community with others.[44] If, according to the Stoic

39 Cf. Rudolf Bultmann, "θάνατος, κτλ.," *TDNT* 3 (1965) 7–25.

40 John 8:12; on this, see Josef Blank, *Krisis* (Freiburg: Lambertus, 1964) 184–86.

41 1 John 5:13. Cf. also the analysis of the context and structure of the Johannine concept of ζωή by J. C. Coetzee, "Life (Eternal Life) in John's Writings and the Qumran Scrolls," *Neot* 6 (1972) 46–62. According to this essay, the theme of 1 John is "the Christian certainty of possessing eternal life in Christ" (p. 58). This analysis of the theme does not, however, leave adequate scope for the eschatological openness of the Johannine notion of "life" (ζωή), as is clear particularly from the parenetic context.

42 Cf. Aristotle *Metaphysics* 11.7 (1072b 28–32): "We assert that God is an eternal, superior being (ζῷον ἀΐδιον ἄριστον), so that life and enduring, eternal time (ζωὴ καὶ αἰὼν συνεχὴς καὶ ἀΐδιος) belong to God; for this is God."

43 Cf. the Stoic tradition, according to which the human life (βίος) has three parts: contemplative, practical, and rational (θεωρητικός, πρακτικός, and λογικός). See *SVF* 3.173.4–5.

44 Cf. the Aristotelian definition, ἄνθρωπος φύσει ζῷον πολιτικόν ("The human being is by nature a political being," *Politics* 2.1253a 3.8–18; 6.1278b 19; *Nic. Eth.* 5.1097b 11; 1169b 18); also Menander, frg. 507 (Theodor Kock, ed., *Comicorum atticorum fragmenta* [3 vols.; Leipzig: Teubner, 1880–88] 3.145): τοῦτ' ἔστι τὸ ζῆν, οὐχ ἑαυτῷ ζῆν μόνον ("This is life: not to live for oneself alone").

idea, the duty of the human being is "life in accordance with nature" (ζωὴ κατὰ φύσιν), this means that the development of each human life must be achieved in accord with the law of nature, in which the rational world spirit realizes itself.[45]

That the Johannine ζωή is the object of revelation and of believers' knowledge and that the opposition of life and death has parallels in other dualistic ideas in Johannine theology ("light" and "darkness," "truth" and lies") would seem to suggest that the Johannine system presupposes a gnostic background, according to which life is "regarded as an absolutely otherworldly divine power"[46] and the psychic competence of life expresses itself "at root only in negations."[47] But to the extent that in gnostic dualistic systems ζωή and analogous concepts such as "light" (φῶς) are understood as "being physically alive," that is, as ontological categories associated with static nonhistoricity, such notions cannot be equated with the Johannine idea, for the latter is also understood ethically and therefore historically. Still, for the understanding of the broader horizon of Johannine concepts some texts may be cited that are gnostic or associated with gnosis, even though they belong to the post-Johannine period:

Corpus Hermeticum 1.6: the unity of the human being with God is described as ζωή. *Odes Sol.* 3.8–9: "Whoever is joined to the one that does not die, will also become immortal. And whoever takes pleasure in life will become a living one." *Odes Sol.* 6.18: "by means of the waters they lived eternal life." *Jos. Asen.* 8.10: "O Lord, the God of my father Israel, the Most High, the Mighty One, who didst quicken all things, and didst call them from darkness into light, and from error into truth, and from death into life; do thou, O Lord, thyself quicken and bless this virgin." *Gos. Thom.* 4: "The person old in days won't hesitate to ask a little child seven days old about the place of life, and that person will live." *Hyp. Arch.* 97,3: "And he will anoint them with the unction of life eternal, given him from the undominated generation."[48] The *Untitled Work* from the Bruce Codex, chap. 11 (247, 17–20): "And the word that comes from your mouth is eternal life, and the light that comes from your eyes is rest for them"; chap. 19 (261, 4–6): "He [the lord of glory] gave them the region to his right and bestowed on them eternal life and immortality" (cf. chap. 2 [227, 24], and frequently elsewhere).[49]

If life is understood in these texts as an eschatological phenomenon that human beings will experience in the present and that determines their very existence, the circumstance seems to invite one to draw parallels to the docetic opponents of the Johannine communities, even if such parallels must remain hypothetical, and although the complexity of the idea makes it impossible to confine it to a particular geographical area.

As we have seen, Johannine terminology is relatively little affected by OT language, but otherwise is open to a great variety of linguistic currents.[50] The Hellenistic Jewish field is of essential importance. Here "life" is interpreted also as an ethical quantity. Thus Philo writes: "goodness and virtue is life, evil and wickedness is death" (*Fug.* 58). It is significant that in Hellenistic Judaism future salvation is described in terms of ζωή. Thus *Ps. Sol.* 13.11: "For the life of the righteous (goes on) forever"; Wis 5:15: "The righteous live forever." The idea of life as a future eschatological phenomenon is also presumed by 1 John 5:13–17, when eternal life is contrasted with the sin that is mortal, which therefore does not lead to life. (In contrast, the fourth evangelist speaks of future life, using ἀνάστασις terminology; John 5:29; 11:24.)

How is ζωή conveyed to human beings? The author leaves no doubt that he sees it as his proper task, and

45 Cf. Alexander of Aphrodisias *De Anima* 162.32 (*SVF* 3.1.65): ἀλλὰ καὶ τὸ ζῆν κατὰ φύσιν καὶ τὸν κατὰ φύσιν βίον εὐδαιμονίαν λέγουσιν ("But they say that happiness is living according to nature and the life in accord with nature").

46 Bultmann, "ζάω," 841.

47 Ibid., 842.

48 The context of this passage undoubtedly presumes John 14:16–17, 26. (Translations of the *Odes of Solomon* are adapted from that by J. A. Emerton in H. F. D. Sparks, ed., *The Apocryphal Old Testament* [Oxford: Oxford University Press, 1984] 692, 695; *Joseph and Aseneth*, translation by D. Cook in ibid., 481; *Gospel of Thomas* in Robert J. Miller, ed., *The Complete Gospels* [Sonoma: Polebridge, 1992] 306; *Hypostasis of the Archons*, translation by Roger A. Bullard and Bentley Layton in *NHLE*, 169.)

49 For the Coptic texts with an English translation, see Carl Schmidt and Violet McDermot, *The Books of Jeu and the Untitled Text in the Bruce Codex* (NHS 13; Leiden: Brill, 1978).

50 The investigation of the concept of חי and its derivatives in the Qumran literature has yielded relatively little result. The interpretation of the few individual passages that may be applicable is disputed, and on the whole there is no emphasis on the idea of "eternal life." For this discussion, see Schnackenburg, *John*, 2.358–59; J. C. Coetzee, "Life (Eternal Life) in John's Writings and the Qumran Scrolls," *Neot* 6 (1972) 58–64.

one that he is attempting to fulfill in this writing, to mediate ζωή *by means of the word.* Hence v. 1b says that the incarnational event has to do with the "word of life"; and this is emphasized by means of the double use of ἀπαγγέλλομεν, which receives special weight because it appears as the closing finite verb.[51] The seeing and hearing of the Christ-event in its true content, and the accompanying experience of the life that has appeared in Christ, are conveyed to the hearers and readers of this document through the proclamation of the "witness."[52] In the author's proclamatory witness not only the fact but also the soteriological meaning of the Christ event[53] are made present, in order that all this may be accepted in faith (cf. 5:10).

Thus the author of 1 John differs from the Fourth Gospel in emphasizing that eschatological salvation continues to happen in the church's proclamation. Here, in the special importance that proclamation is accorded in and for the community, there lies an essential difference between 1 John and the conception of the fourth evangelist; it goes beyond the announcement of the Paraclete by the revealer (John 14–16) and corresponds to the distinction between christological (Gospel) and ecclesiological (1 John) accents. It is not really possible to define this difference by saying that in 1 John the faith decision in face of the incarnate Word is in the past, while in the Johannine prologue it is first announced; for John 1:12 already presumes the decision of faith.[54] The alternative, that the Fourth Gospel is concerned with the understanding of Jesus Christ as "the Son of God sent into the world," while the subject of 1 John is the "reliability and credibility of the Johannine message that has been handed on,"[55] undervalues 1 John's concentration on Christ in its proclamation, as well as the fact that the Fourth Gospel certainly "testifies" to the credibility of the message of Christ (cf. John 19:35; 20:31; 21:24).

■ **3** The double "you" (καὶ ὑμῖν / καὶ ὑμεῖς) emphasizes the "pre-" of the proclaimer with respect to the addressees. In both cases there is sufficient textual witness to the καί to allow one to deduce the author's intention: the readers of this document are not the only ones who are touched by this proclamation. Of course, the proclaimer is not addressing all humanity. Hence the readers can

51 Vv. 2–3. The verb ἀπαγγέλλειν appears in the Johannine Letters only here; it means "to witness [to the Christ-event]." It appears in the weakened sense of "report" in John 16:25 (and in variant readings in 4:51; 5:15; 20:18). See also the use of ἀγγελία in 1 John 1:5; 3:11; on this, see Ingo Broer, "ἀγγελία," *EDNT* 1 (1990) 12–13.

52 The combination of μαρτυρεῖν (see below on 1 John 5:6) with ὁρᾶν appears frequently in the Johannine literature. John the Baptizer testifies to what he has seen, namely, the Son of God (John 1:34). The latter in turn testifies to what he has seen (John 3:11, 32). Even the disciple under the cross proves a true eyewitness (19:35). Not only in this passage but also in 4:14 the author of 1 John underscores the unity of seeing and witnessing; the content of his testimony is the sending of the Son of God as savior of the world. Accordingly, the seeing brings testimony or preaching in its wake. This corresponds to the early Christian image of the apostle. Those are called to be apostles and proclaimers who have seen the Risen One and therefore can testify to the event of resurrection (cf. 1 Cor 9:1; 15:3–4). It is no accident that Paul identifies his conversion before Damascus, the object of which was for him the "revelation of Jesus Christ," with his calling to be an apostle among the Gentiles (Gal 1:15–16). "Appearance, witness to the resurrection, legitimation as witness, and sending forth to preach the Risen One apparently were all parts of the total concept of the appearances of the risen Lord" (Ulrich Wilckens, "Die Überlieferungsgeschichte der Auferstehung Jesu," in Willi Marxsen, et al., *Die Bedeutung der Auferstehungsbotschaft für den Glauben an Jesus Christus* [2d ed.; Gütersloh: Mohn, 1966] 49). Cf. Wilhelm Schneemelcher, "Introduction 1. Apostle and Apostolic," in *NTApoc*[1] 2.25–31; Jan-Adolf Bühner, "ἀπόστολος," *EDNT* 1 (1990) 142–46 (with bibliography).

53 On this, see Bultmann, *Epistles*, 9: "Hence what is spoken of here is not the preexistent Logos, but . . . its 'incarnation,' . . . which is . . . the origin of the ἀγγελία." But it is true of 1 John as of the Fourth Gospel that the incarnation demands the idea of preexistence (cf. v. 2b); this also gives the church's proclamation a universal scope. Cf. Giuseppe Segalla, "Preesistenza, incarnatione e divinità di Cristo in Giovanni," *RivB* 22 (1974) 155–81, esp. 170, who argues that in spite of a different set of conceptual terms, "John" emphasizes the unity of preexistence and incarnation.

54 Cf. Balz, "Johannesbriefe," 167–68.

55 Ibid., 168.

feel themselves privileged, since the author is addressing them and, through this message, is offering them fellowship with himself. The intended apostolic claim is thereby greatly strengthened, all the more since the *κοινωνία* that is offered not only unites them with the author but allows them to participate in the eschatological "fellowship" with God the Father and the Son, Jesus Christ. If in this manner a descending order is established from the Father through the Son to the proclaimer and thence to the community, at the same time what is envisioned is a comprehensive unity. The fellowship expected by the community, and which it is to bring about, bridges the undeniable differences between God and humanity as well as those between one human being and another. Hence it is not merely a matter of a community in "faith," but of a way of life that brings together faith and action in a single, harmonious whole. The relationship of believers to God as well as their relationship with their fellow human beings is founded on the incarnational event.[56] This implies an indirect judgment on the false teachers: through their docetic interpretation of the Christ-event they not only deny the reality of the incarnation but at the same time destroy the community that is meant to lead believers by way of the event of revelation to the Christian fellowship that God desires.[57]

Excursus: Κοινωνία

This word appears 19 times in the NT, four of them in the Johannine corpus (1 John 1:3, 6–7). The verb *κοινωνεῖν* also appears, in 2 John 11 (and in eight other NT passages). The majority of NT occurrences are in the Pauline and post-Pauline letters, in which the stem *κοιν-* is used in two ways: as a designation (1) for fellowship with Christ (1 Cor 1:9), especially participation in Christ's suffering (Phil 3:10; 1 Pet 4:13), in Christ's blood or body (1 Cor 10:16), and also as participation in the Spirit (2 Cor 13:13; Phil 2:1); and (2) for the community of human beings with one another (Acts 2:42: common life in the primitive community; Heb 13:16: practice of social responsibility in the Christian community; cf. also the use of the verb in Rom 12:13; 15:27). As a concrete example of Christian charitable activity, Paul's collection for Jerusalem is given the label of *κοινωνία* (2 Cor 8:4; 9:13; Rom 15:26). Correspondingly, the noun *κοινωνός* can mean a (Christian) "companion" (2 Cor 8:23; Phlm 17; cf. Luke 5:10).

This same two-dimensional usage marks the appearance of the word in 1 John. "Fellowship" with Father and Son is fundamental to the being and self-understanding of the Christian community (1:3b, 6). The fellowship of Christians with one another is a consequence of this, and the author of 1 John leaves no doubt of his conviction that the fellowship of believers founded by Christ must result in the undivided unity of the Christian community. In turn, it is a fact that no Christian *κοινωνία* is imaginable unless it is founded on participation in the Christ-event to which 1 John witnesses. This implies an indirect attack on the false teachers. Although they originally belonged to the Johannine community (1 John 2:19), they have proved themselves to be a divisive element that is destroying Christian fellowship. The dogmatic dissension between the author of 1 John and his docetic opponents has a real point of reference in this division. Pheme Perkins has attempted (although with some imaginative projections on the death of the evangelist John) to demonstrate that the opponents, on their side, claimed to represent the genuine Christian "fellowship."[58]

■ **4** Although in v. 4b the variant reading "to you" (*ὑμῖν*) would be better suited to the conclusion of a prescript, what we have here is not the opening of a letter. Not only the strong manuscript evidence but also the intention of the author support the reading *ἡμεῖς*, since what is at issue is a personal claim to community with the readers; this is the author's object in writing.[59] Such community, because it is eschatologically conditioned, is characterized by *χαρά*. As it is said in other NT letters,[60] and literally in 2 John 12, on which this passage may directly depend, "joy" (*χαρά*) is a divine gift that makes

56 Cf. 2 John 9, where fellowship with God is identified with "abiding in the teaching of Christ"; this is what it means to "have God" (cf. 1 John 2:23; 5:12–13), corresponding to "knowing God" (1 John 2:3–17; 3:6; 4:6–8) or "remaining in God" (1 John 2:6, 24, 27–28; 4:13, 15–16; 3:6, 9, 15, 17, 24). See Schnackenburg, *Epistles*, 99–103, excursus 4: "The Johannine Formulas of Immanence."

57 See the following excursus on *κοινωνία*. Joseph Cahill emphasizes the importance of this concept for our own time in a review of the German edition of this commentary in *CBQ* 53 (1991) 718–19.

58 Pheme Perkins, "Koinonia in 1 John 1:3–7," in *CBQ* 45 (1983) 631–41. See also below on 2 John 11.

59 Cf. v. 3b. On the evidence for *ἡμεῖς* (v 4a), the manuscript reading of ℵ (A) B and others is to be

eschatological salvation present to the community. What the revealer in the Fourth Gospel promises his own,[61] the author desires to convey to the readers: the coming of the eschatological χαρά. The beginning of the concluding section describes the object of this homily: "that you may know that you have eternal life" (5:13). Both goals are fundamentally identical: to have eschatological joy is to have life. But neither the one nor the other represents an accomplished state. Instead, what is described is a continual becoming of the believers' existence, for it is no accident that the author uses the verbs πληροῦσθαι and τελεῖσθαι ("to be fulfilled"). What is meant is not ending but fulfillment. Walter Bauer's translation ("joy as brought to the highest degree")[62] implies a misunderstanding, as if there must be a "decline" from that single high point. In reality, existence in joy is a progression from peak to peak. The author wishes to encourage the readers in that direction (cf. John 16:22: "No one will take your joy from you").

Excursus: Χαρά[63]

Χαρά appears 59 times in the NT, nine of those in the Fourth Gospel and three in the Johannine Letters. The verb χαίρειν occurs in eight passages in the Fourth Gospel and in 2 John 10–11 (in the technical sense, "greet"), as well as in 2 John 4 and 3 John 3.

The Greek word χαρά is sometimes used synonymously with ἡδονή, often distinguished from the latter by the subordinating of ἡδονή to χαρά (Aristotle *Nic. Eth.* 2.5, 1105b 19–23) or vice versa (4 Macc 1:22). In the NT ἡδονή appears in only five passages, not at all in the Johannine corpus. The concept of χαρά covers a wide range of meanings: from joy in heaven (Luke 15:7, 10) to joy as a mark of the Christian community (2 Cor 1:24), and as one element in a list of virtues (Gal 5:22). The Johannine Letters apply the concept to the attitude of the presbyter, who rejoices that he has received good news about the condition of his "children's" faith (3 John 4), and to the presbyter and the community whose mutual joy is to be fulfilled (2 John 12). Our passage concerns the joy of the author, the fulfillment of which is to unite him with the community. This has a parallel in the topos found in the Pauline Letters, whereby the apostle expresses his joy over the Christian behavior of his community (1 Thess 3:9; 2 Cor 2:3, 7, 13; Phil 1:4). The combination with πληρόω (active in Phil 2:2; passive in 2 John 12; 1 John 1:4; John 3:29; 15:11; 16:24; 17:13) compares joy with a measure that is to be "made full," that is, "brought to perfection" and in that sense "realized" (cf. Matt 5:17). This realization is mediated through the proclaimer's word, as is evident not only in the passage under discussion but also in 2 John 12 ("talking face to face"). A negative to χαρά, expressed by λύπη (John 16:21; 2 Cor 2:3; 6:10; 7:8–9; Phil 2:27–28; Heb 12:11; *Herm. Vis.* 3.13.2; *Herm. Sim.* 1.10; *Herm. Man.* 10.13; cf. *2 Clem.* 19.4) or θλῖψις (2 Cor 7:4; 8:2; cf. Acts 5:41), is not found in the Johannine Letters. But the idea "that the way to χαρά leads through λύπη ('sorrow' John 16:20–24)" is not excluded in 1 John simply because here the issue is not (as in the Fourth Gospel) faith versus unbelief, but the identity of false belief and wrong teaching (Bultmann, *Epistles*, 14 n. 28); for in the Fourth Gospel also the concept of "faith" cannot be separated from the true teaching proclaimed

---

regarded as better attested than that of the "majority text" and other witnesses, which read ὑμῖν. The same is true of ἡμῶν (v. 4b). The manuscript evidence shows a qualitative balance in its favor against the alternative reading ὑμῶν. Materially, in each case the preferred reading is the *lectio difficilior*, since v. 4a appears to demand an authorial "we," but v. 4b suggests an ecclesial "we." Ἡμεῖς (v. 4a) is used emphatically, something that is explained by the posited apostolic background; it implies the idea of an opposite number, namely, the community as object of the proclamation by the eye- and ear-witnesses. One may not conclude from this that the variant ὑμῖν should be preferred (against J. H. Dobson, "Emphatic Personal Pronouns in the New Testament," *BT* 22 [1971] 58–60).

60 For example, in proemia: 1 Thess 1:6; Phil 1:4.

61 See the farewell discourses: John 15:11; 16:24; 17:13, and frequently elsewhere.

62 BAGD 875. Against this, see also Hans Conzelmann: "Fulfilled . . . does not mean that joy has reached a climax but that its object has appeared" ("χαίρω, κτλ.," *TDNT* 9 [1974] 370, with a reference to Eelis Gulin, *Die Freude im NT* [2 vols.; Annales Academiae Scientarium Fennicae, 26/2, 37; Helsinki: Druckerei-A.G. der Finnischen Literatur-Gesellschaft, 1932–36] 2.34). It should be clear that what is addressed here is the "eschatological perfection" of χαρά as the goal of faith, not the object of seeing (cf. Bultmann, *John*, 506 n. 1).

63 Literature: Conzelmann, "χαίρω," 359–415; Otto Michel, "Freude," *RAC* 8 (1972) 348–418; Andries B. du Toit, "Freude I (NT)," *TRE* 11 (1982) 584–86; Klaus Berger, "χαρά," *EDNT* 3 (1993) 454–55.

by the Revealer. The fourth evangelist expresses the relationship of χαρά and λύπη in the context of the relationship between Christ and the disciples. The notion of discipleship thus described corresponds to the world of ideas in 1 John: here it is a question of preservation of χαρά in the community in the face of the threat of "darkness" and "sin" (cf. 3 John 4: "[they] are walking in the truth," and so not in accord with false teaching; cf. esp. 1 John 1:5–7: "light" and "darkness").

The religio-historical background. In the Stoa joy is reserved for the wise (Seneca *Ep.* 6.59.2: "gaudium nisi sapienti non contingere; est enim animi elatio suis bonis verisque fidentis" ["true joy can belong only to the wise; for it is the elevated temper of a soul that rests confident in its true advantages"]). The theological language of the NT corresponds in some ways to the mystery cults' understanding of joy as a fundamental religious mood (Firmicus Maternus *De errore profanarum religionum* 20.2: "Rejoice groom, rejoice, new light," χαῖρε νύμφιε· χαῖρε νέον φῶς), to the self-understanding of the human being in the Hermetic writings (*Corp. Herm.* 13.18: "I rejoice in my joy," χαίρω ἐν χαρᾷ μοῦ), or to the eschatological imagination of the Qumran community (1QS iv.17; 1QH xiii.6, and frequently elsewhere: "eternal joy"; 1QM i.9: "Peace, blessing, glory, joy and long life [for all children] of light"). Philo thinks of joy as a quality of God (*Abr.* 202) and as the τέλος of human beings (*Rer. div. her.* 315). The eschatological aspect is also found in the *Odes Sol.* 7.1–2; *1 Enoch* 5.9; 17.6 ("Joy and honor . . . for the spirits of those who have died in righteousness"), and it is reflected in the rabbinic writings: "Joy in this world is not complete, but in the future our joy will be fulfilled" (*Pesiqta de Rab. Kahana* 29, 189a, b).[64]

64 See Str-B 2.429–30, 566.

General Comment

It is frequently presumed that the section 1:5—2:27 represents a distinct unit within the structure of 1 John.[2] The exegesis, however, will show that 2:18–27 is not intended as parenesis but as dogmatic teaching (cf. 2:27), while in 1:5—2:17, the section to be treated here, ethical teachings dominate the content. The passage before us is therefore to be regarded as having been intended by its author as a parenetical unit. The following subdivisions correspond to the various objects of discussion: 1:5–10 (dualism and the problem of sin); 2:1–6 (christological foundation for the overcoming of sin: indicative and imperative);[3] 2:7–11 (old and new commandment); 2:12–17 (concrete ethical instruction, including the "table of orders in the community" in vv. 12–14).

The unit in 1:5–10 is marked by elements of Johannine style from beginning to end: an elevated prose style characterized by parallelisms and antitheses and revealing a wealth of concepts typical of the Johannine writings. The beginning (v. 5) is primarily a transition, namely, an explanation of the "message" (vv. 1–3), which here is apparently defined by the statement: "God is light." This is followed by five constructions with ἐάν, alternating negative and positive statements determined in their content by the contrast between darkness and light: fellowship with God and walking in darkness are incompatible (v. 6). In contrast, v. 7 is positive: walking in the light means fellowship with one another and cleansing from sin. This in turn forms the transition to another sequence starting from the concept of ἁμαρτία and first depicting the denial of sin negatively as error and falsehood (v. 8), then describing the acknowledgment of sin positively as precondition for pardon (v. 9). The unit concludes with another ἐάν clause, again formulated negatively and identifying the denial of sin with rejection of the word of God (v. 10).

From these parallelisms we can see that, in the Johannine style, one may not always expect the train of thought to move forward. Instead, it tends to circle around particular concepts in meditative fashion, so that one should not demand a rational or logical progression. To attempt, with Bultmann, to isolate individual verses and to apply the principle of three-member periods to trace them to a "source" or "model document" would be artificial.[4] In reality, one must concede the author some inconsistency in the construction of the parallel clauses.[5]

1 Literature: Pheme Perkins, "Koinonia in 1 John 1:3–7: The Social Context of Division in the Johannine Letters," *CBQ* 45 (1983) 631–41; Maximillian Zerwick, "'Veritatem facere' Ioh. 3,21; I Ioh. 1,6," *VD* 18 (1938) 338–42, 373–77.

2 On the structural outline, see Balz, "Johannesbriefe," 178: 1:5—2:27; Dodd, *Epistles*, xxii, 64–65: 1:5—2:28. Schnackenburg (*Epistles*, 70) has the first major part ending at 2:17, as does Wengst, *Brief*, 28–29, 45–46. According to Brown (*Epistles*, 122–25, 765), the first major break occurs at 3:10, with the following subdivisions: 1:5; 1:6—2:2; 2:3–11; 2:12–17; 2:18–27; 2:28—3:10.

3 Schnackenburg believes that 2:2 concludes the subtheme of "sin." Beginning at 2:3, "knowing God" is treated, centering on τηρεῖν τὰς ἐντολάς. It would also follow from this that 2:2/2:3 represent a change of subject (v. 2: Jesus; v. 3: God; see *Epistles*, 71–72). But that kind of shift in subject is thoroughly consistent with Johannine language and does not favor a caesura in other instances (cf. 1:6–9). Moreover, materially speaking the theme of "sin" cannot be separated from the knowledge of God and keeping the commandments (2:3–6). Cf. also Bultmann, who sees a new section in 2:3–11 (*Epistles*, 24: "The theme of fellowship with God is now replaced by the theme of knowledge of God"); also Weiss, *Briefe*, 42; Brown, *Epistles*, 276.

4 The "source" posited by Bultmann (*Epistles*, 17–23) would have contained the existing text, with the exception of v. 7c (v. 7b in Bultmann's reckoning) and v. 9 and, after the secondary verses 2:1–3, would have continued in 2:4–5, 9–11. Cf. also his "Redaktion," 189–201; and also his "Analyse," 138–58 (= *Exegetica*, 105–23). In this last article, only "v. 7b" and v. 9c are excluded and the analysis is based not on the principle of three-membered periods, but on that of "parallel members," with each pair an antithesis to the one that follows or precedes ("Analyse," 141 = *Exegetica*, 108).

5 See the discussion of structure above on 1:1–4. Bultmann had to posit this inconsistency for the "source" as well, for example, when in v. 6 the principle of three-member periods is skewed by the presence of paired finite verbs joined by καί; but in v. 8 the καί clause is understood as an independent third member.

Hence there is no formal reason to exclude the idea of atoning death (v. 7c) from the text as secondary. The same is true of v. 9, for one may scarcely conclude, simply on the basis of the plural usage of the concept of *ἁμαρτία*, that this verse is secondary.[6]

6 Against Braun, "Literar-Analyse," 213; on this subject, see n. 27 below. Hans Conzelmann is correct: "It is . . . thus as well to interpret the passage without regard to source hypotheses" ("φῶς," *TDNT* 9 [1974] 310–58, citation on p. 354).

1 **Johannine Dualism (Light and Darkness, Truth and Falsehood) and the Problem of Sin**

5 **This is the message we have heard from**
him and proclaim to you, that God is light
and in God there is no darkness at all. 6/
If we say that we have fellowship with
God while we are walking in darkness,
we lie and do not do what is true, 7/ but if
we walk in the light as God is in the light,
we have fellowship with one another,
and the blood of Jesus, God's Son,
cleanses us from all sin. 8/ If we say that
we have no sin, we deceive ourselves,
and the truth is not in us. 9/ If we confess
our sins, the one who is faithful and just
will forgive us our sins and cleanse us
from all unrighteousness. 10/ If we say
that we have not sinned, we make God a
liar, and God's word is not in us.

■ **5** As was already said in the introduction (vv. 1–4), the author understands himself to be a witness to the Christ-event. It was clear in v. 1 that this includes not only the appearance and activity, but also the message of Jesus Christ (v. 1b: "word of life"): the author has "heard" that message and "proclaims" it to others. Now, in contrast to the preceding section, this message is traced to its origin; *ἀπ' αὐτοῦ* means, in the immediate context (cf. vv. 1 and 3), "from Jesus Christ." What the Son proclaims and the witness passes on has the following content: *ὁ θεὸς φῶς ἐστιν*. This statement intends no definition of the essence, the being of God in and for Godself[1] (no more than does 1 John 4:8, 16, "God is love," or John 4:24, "God is spirit"). It is no accident that in what follows it can also be said that God is "in the light" (v. 7). The author is making use of an ancient mode of expression[2] in an attempt to describe the nature of God. As light is the source of all illumination, so God is the source of all that makes human life bright. God's being light means the fulfillment of meaning in human life, to which, in the gift of the eschaton, God gives a basis, a measure, and a goal. If God is understood as "light," this means that God

1 This is the sense of the older exegesis; Schnackenburg still counts v. 5 among the "Christian exposition[s] of the divine being" (*Epistles*, 74). Weiss (*Briefe*, 31), however, was of a different opinion: "This sentence does not contain any statement about the metaphysical nature of God, Jesus himself having made no such statement of any kind (not even John 4:24); such a statement could not be called a message, but would be a fact of salvation history. Hence it is also self-evident that the message received from Christ refers to that which has come with and in him."

2 Cf. the extensive list of literature in Conzelmann, "φῶς," 310–11; also Bultmann, *Epistles*, 16 n. 5. As early as the Pythagoreans the dualism of "light" and "darkness" occurs: *ἰσόμοιρά τ' εἶναι ἐν τῷ κόσμῳ φῶς καὶ σκότος, καὶ θερμὸν καὶ ψυχρόν, καὶ ξηρὸν καὶ ὑγρόν* "These have an equal share in the world: light, darkness, warmth, cold, dryness and moistness"; Diogenes Laertius *Vit. phil.* 8.26). Plato represents an uncompromising metaphysics of light (*Rep.* 6–7), as evidenced especially in the Hellenistic-protognostic world of ideas, for example in Philo: *καὶ τὸ φῶς ἐν οὐρανῷ μὲν ἄκρατον καὶ ἀμιγὲς σκότους ἐστίν, ἐν δὲ τοῖς ὑπὸ σελήνην ἀέρι ζοφερῷ κεκραμένον φαίνεται* ("just so the light in heaven is unmixed and free from all darkness, but in the sublunary world [on earth] it appears mixed with the dark layer of the air": *Abr.* 205; cf. *Abr.* 156–66; *Spec. leg.* 4.187, and frequently elsewhere). See further in Conzelmann, "φῶς," 310–16, 326–32. The many ancient variations are based, as Bultmann (*Epistles*, 16) correctly said, on the "notion . . . that the real meaning of light is the luminosity man needs in order to find his way in his daily as well as his spiritual life. The illumination of existence belongs of necessity to 'life' in such a way that, always and everywhere, light and life, darkness and death belong together."

is acknowledged as the giver of eschatological salvation.

Excursus: Light and Darkness

The religio-historical derivation of the Johannine dualistic opposition of light and darkness is disputed. A derivation from the OT appears probable. Here God can be compared with "light" (e.g., Ps 27:1, "The Lord is my light and my salvation"; Ps 36:9, and frequently elsewhere). But this does not lead to a corresponding light symbolism in which God is personally identified with light, nor does it suggest a dualistic contrast of light and darkness. Instead, it is characteristic that YHWH is the creator of light and of the stars (Gen 1:3–5; Isa 45:5–7).

After the discovery of the Qumran texts it was thought that the Johannine dualism could be made intelligible on the basis of those writings, and one cannot deny that the apocalyptic world of ideas of the Qumran sect, like apocalyptic in general, contains dualistic elements. Thus, for example, one can draw a distinction between the spirit of light and the spirit of darkness.[3] Light and darkness are like spheres that determine the ways of human beings; accordingly, human beings can be called "children of light" or "children of darkness" (1QS i.9–10; cf. John 12:36: "Believe in the light, so that you may become children of light"). This dualism is less ontological than ethical in nature and thus corresponds to Johannine thought. Although in both cases what is at issue is an eschatological "dualism of decision,"[4] one should not overlook the difference: an identification of God with "light" is absent from Qumran, as is the idea that at the center of theology must stand a revealer who mediates access to God.[5] For this reason alone, one may not assert any dependence of the Johannine writings on the Qumran literature.

Still another possible source is genuine (mythological) gnosis, which Bultmann posits, in his studies, as the starting point for Johannine theology. In the meantime it has been recognized that his interpretation was based on the Christian form of gnosis from the second and third centuries and cannot be read back into the NT period. This is particularly true of the idea of the *salvator salvandus*.[6] But neither is there any evidence in Johannine thought of the cosmological foundation of the gnostic doctrine of salvation that is characteristic of Christian gnosis. Hence one must be cautious about a thesis that "gnosis [forms] the basis of Johannine thought."[7] It is true that there are undeniable correspondences, and the question of the degree to which John is opposing "gnostics" or is personally influenced by "Gnosis" cannot be avoided by raising problems about a preformed concept of gnosis. Nevertheless, one is less open to misunderstanding if, instead of using the expression "gnosis,"

3 1QS iii.13—iv.26.; also 1QM xiii.10–12: "And the Prince of light Thou hast appointed from ancient times to come to our support; [all the sons of righteousness are in his hand], and all the spirits of truth are under his dominion. But Satan, the Angel of Malevolence, Thou hast created for the Pit; his [rule] is in Darkness and his purpose is to bring about wickedness and iniquity. All the spirits of his company, the Angels of destruction, walk according to the precepts of Darkness; towards them is their [inclination]." It is possible that at this point the Qumran literature is subject to Iranian influence; cf. Werner Foerster, "σαταvᾶς," *TDNT* 7 (1971) 151–54; Hans Conzelmann, "σκότος, κτλ.," *TDNT* 7 (1971) 427 n. 33, 432 n. 65.

4 Cf. Conzelmann, "φῶς," 349; Rudolf Bultmann, *Theology of the New Testament* (trans. Kendrick Grobel; 2 vols.; New York: Scribner's, 1951–55) 2.76.

5 Furthermore, the Johannine writings have no corresponding teaching about two spirits (1 John 4:6 cannot be regarded as such).

6 On this, see Luise Schottroff, *Der Glaubende und die feindliche Welt* (WMANT 37; Neukirchen-Vluyn: Neukirchener Verlag, 1970) esp. 228–45. Carsten Colpe had already expressed a fundamental critique of this thesis in his Habilitationsschrift, *Die religionsgeschichtliche Schule: Darstellung und Kritik ihres Bildes vom gnostischen Erlösermythos* (FRLANT 60; Göttingen: Vandenhoeck & Ruprecht, 1961); and Kurt Rudolph (*Gnosis* [trans. P.W. Coxon, et al.; ed. Robert McL. Wilson; San Francisco: Harper & Row] 121–31) had correctly pointed out, in opposition to Richard Reitzenstein, that the latter's strict interpretation of the figure of a "redeemed redeemer" was based only on Manichaean texts. Cf. Georg Strecker, "Judenchristentum und Gnosis," in Karl-Wolfgang Tröger, ed., *Altes Testament, Frühjudentum, Gnosis* (Gütersloh: Mohn, 1980) 266–67.

7 Schottroff, *Glaubende*, 242; Bultmann, *Theology*, 2.40–41; Ernst Käsemann, *The Testament of Jesus* (trans. Gerhard Krodel; Philadelphia: Fortress, 1968) 66–67, 70, 72–73). Of course, the image of Johannine "gnosis" has varied in scholarship. It is disputed whether the author of the Fourth Gospel is to be regarded as a critic of "gnosis" or as a "Gnostic." Cf. Schottroff, *Glaubende*, 243; Schnackenburg, *Epistles*, 30–31.

one works with the idea of "proto-gnosis" or "Hellenistic Jewish syncretism." These two terms are broad enough to incorporate the various forms of Johannine thought, and they are less apt to prejudice religio-historical judgment in a particular direction.

Among the syncretistic texts that one may adduce, the *Corpus Hermeticum* is especially important. The opposition of light and darkness is attested in the cosmogony of the *Poimandres* (*Corp. Herm.* 1) 1.4–6: "I saw an endless vision in which everything became light—clear and joyful—and in seeing the vision I came to love it. After a little while, darkness arose separately and descended—fearful and gloomy—coiling sinuously so that it looked to me like a ⟨snake⟩. . . . But from the light . . . a holy word mounted upon the ⟨watery⟩ nature, and untempered fire leapt up from the watery nature to the height above. The fire was nimble and piercing and active as well. . . . The light-giving word who comes from mind is the son of god."[8]

The antithesis of light and darkness is presumed, but receives no further reflection, in the *Odes Sol.* (21.3: "And I put off darkness, and put on light"; also 11.19; 15.2). In Mandaeanism, as in *Poimandres,* it is emphasized that the light existed before the darkness (*Ginza R.* 75–76). Ruha, the mother of darkness, is surrendered to destruction together with her son Ur, the king of darkness (*Ginza R.* 77ff.; cf. 175,10ff.). This cosmological dualism shapes humanity. Thus it is said of evil people: "The evil ones are blind and do not see. I call them to the light, but they bury themselves in darkness."[9] In *Pistis Sophia* (second half of the third century) Christian gnostic soteriology is combined in a particularly lovely way with the dualism of light and darkness. Thus the wandering Pistis Sophia says of herself: "And I went, and I came to be in the darkness, . . . And I cried out for help, and my voice did not penetrate the darkness, . . . And when I sought for light, I was given darkness. And when I sought for my power, I was given matter" (1.32,2–3, 21). The way of Pistis Sophia is a way from chaos to light; so the fallen one calls: "O Light of Lights, in whom I have believed from the beginning, hear my repentance now at this time, O Light" (1.32,1). And the rescued Pistis Sophia calls out: "I have been saved from the Chaos and released from the bonds of darkness. I have come to thee, O Light" (2.68,1). The light-darkness dualism is also found in the gnostic texts from Nag Hammadi: "Seeing that everybody, gods of the world and mankind, says that nothing existed prior to chaos, I in distinction to them shall demonstrate that they are all mistaken, because they are not acquainted with the origin of chaos, nor with its root. . . . it [chaos] comes from a shadow, which has been called by the name darkness. And the shadow comes from a product that has existed since the beginning. It is, moreover, clear that it (viz., the product) existed before chaos came into being, and that the latter is posterior to the first product" (*Orig. World* 97,24–98,5). "After the natural structure of the immortal beings had completely developed out of the infinite, a likeness then emanated from Pistis (Faith); it is called Sophia (Wisdom). It exercised volition and became a product resembling the primeval light" (ibid., 98,11–16).[10]

The contrast between "light and darkness" implies a dialectic that is formative for the Johannine community. Whereas in 1 John 1:5 this is expressed in a vertical, theocentric fashion ("God is light"), and the demand is to allow oneself in the present time to be ruled by this light and not by its negation, darkness, in 2:8 the viewpoint is horizontal. A time line is emerging: the true light has been revealed in history in Jesus Christ. This "historical" fact means that a time period has been assigned for darkness, and that time is coming to an end.[11] Does this kind of historicizing in 1

8 Translation from Brian P. Copenhaver, *Hermetica: The Greek Corpus Hermeticum and the Latin Asclepius in a New English Translation* (Cambridge: Cambridge University Press, 1992) 1–2.

9 See Mark Lidzbarski, *Ginza: Der Schatz oder das grosse Buch der Mandäer* (Göttingen: Vandenhoeck & Ruprecht, 1925); idem, *Das Johannesbuch der Mandäer* (Geissen: Töpelmann, 1915) 203, lines 19ff.

10 Carl Schmidt and Violet Macdermot, eds., *Pistis Sophia* (NHS 9; Leiden: Brill, 1989). Translation of *On the Origin of the World* by Hans-Gebhard Bethge, et al., in *NHLE,* 171–72. For an understanding of light as "God" or as "salvation," cf. also the body of Jewish apocalyptic writing: *2 Bar.* 48.50; also *1 Enoch* 38.4; 58.3–6, and frequently elsewhere. There is an informative interpretation of the text in Rudolf Bultmann, "Zur Lichtsymbolik im Altertum," *Ph* 97 (1948) 1–36 (= *Exegetica,* 323–55). On the meaning of light in classical Greece, he writes that, at first, light had for the Greeks "no 'numinous' character" (p. 332); this arose through the disintegration of perspective on life at the time of the collapse of the polis (p. 343) and in contact with sidereal religions from Asia Minor (pp. 344–46).

11 Cf. Conzelmann, "φῶς," 355 n. 381: in contrast to the Fourth Gospel, the "measure" of light in 1 John is said to be not the eschaton but the history of the church. One must ask, however, whether such an alternative is appropriate.

John represent a significant shift from the theology of the Fourth Gospel? There, differently from 1 John 1:5, it is not God but Christ who is called the light of the world. He, the Logos, appears as light in the darkness (John 1:4–5; cf. 8:12: "I am the light of the world"; also 9:5; 12:46). This kind of christological accent means that human beings are drawn by the Revealer into the choice between light and darkness (3:19). This corresponds to the ethical demand that people not allow themselves to be overtaken by darkness, but that they prove to be "children of light" (John 12:35–36). This dialectically charged self-understanding is not really different from what is said in 1 John, using the same conceptual apparatus. In both cases the situation is one of decision, and it displays not only an eschatological but also a chronological, that is, a historical, dimension. Moreover, it is clear that in both instances the victory of light over darkness is a reality that is recognized in faith.

It may well be that the contrast between light and darkness is shaped to a high degree by christology in the Fourth Gospel. But the Gospel could more easily require the label of "historicization." This is evident in the christological accent that is typical of the Fourth Gospel and that is proper to the gospel form as that of a *vita Jesu.* That 1 John identifies God, not Christ, as light may well be an indication that 1:5 reflects an older stage of tradition than that in the Fourth Gospel, one that has been secondarily Christianized both in the Gospel and in 1 John, since the equation of God with light has significant parallels in pre-Christian Hellenistic-syncretistic light symbolism.[12] In spite of the adoption of this traditional material, and despite their different accents, 1 John does not display any material difference from the Fourth Gospel in this context; for it is clear that, in the view of the author, God's being as light is manifested in the Son. This is the content of the ἀγγελία that is based on the atoning death of Jesus (1:9; 2:1–2, 12, and frequently elsewhere) and demands faith in Christ (3:23; 5:1, 5).[13] In principle, the author of 1 John, no less than the fourth evangelist, takes the revelation in Christ as the basis for the church's proclamation.

■ **6** To say that God is light is not simply a description of the divine nature but has instead, despite the ontological character of the expression, an urgent meaning that affects the community. This is clear from the use of the concept of "fellowship" (κοινωνία).[14] It presumes the unity of Father and Son (1 John 1:3; cf. John 17:21), and its intention is that the community should also be united with the Father and the Son, thus forming a comprehensive, eschatological communion. This is materially identical with the relationship to God that is expressed in 2 and 3 John, though in other terminology (3 John 11: being from God; 2 John 9; 3 John 11: seeing God). The communion that unites persons with God and that is presupposed as fundamental for all Christians implies an ethical obligation: it must lead to κοινωνία with one another (v. 7).

At this point one may already sense a conflict between the author and the opponents. Are they the ones who claim for themselves such a communion with God, and thereby their own "sinlessness" (v. 8), but whose unethical way of life does not correspond to the obligation that is necessarily connected with such a self-evaluation?[15] Whatever one's estimation of the relationship between the opponents' teaching and their manner

12 Cf. the texts cited above on the dualism of light and darkness; also Windisch and Preisker, *Die Katholischen Briefe,* 111. Philo can refer to God as the light of lights, or, to put it in Platonic terms, as the idea of light. Certainly, here is no antagonistic dualism between light and darkness, but rather (in Platonic fashion) a series of stages between heavenly and earthly light; cf. *Som.* 1.75; Conzelmann, "φῶς," 330.

13 It is no accident that both the Fourth Gospel (1:18) and the concluding section of 1 John (5:20) contain expressions of the equality of Christ and God (with Schnackenburg, *Epistles,* 263; Bultmann, *Epistles,* 87–90; Brown, *Epistles,* 625–26; against Brooke, *Epistles,* 152–53; and Dodd, *Epistles,* 140–41). The concept of ἀγγελία occurs both in 1:5 and in 3:11 (and nowhere else in the NT); in the latter case it relates to the demand to love one another (a union of the dogmatic and ethical aspects).

14 Apart from v. 6, this word occurs in the Johannine writings only at 1 John 1:3 (see above on 1:3).

15 Thus Schnackenburg, *Epistles,* 76–77; Bultmann, *Epistles,* 17; Wengst, *Brief,* 52–53, and others. One may think of Paul's opponents in Corinth as their "predecessors," people whose enthusiastic self-understanding led to unfraternal behavior (cf. 1 Cor 6:12; Hans Conzelmann, *Der erste Brief an die Korinther* (KEK 5, 12th ed.; Göttingen: Vandenhoeck & Ruprecht, 1981) 138–39; ET: *1 Corinthians: A Commentary on the First Epistle to the Corinthians* (trans. James W. Leitch; Hermeneia; Philadelphia: Fortress, 1975) 108–10.

of life, at this point the first person plural εἴπωμεν ("if *we* say") clearly demands that one believe that the author is thinking of the readers;[16] for otherwise the third person plural (subject: those who are leading people astray) would be expected. Of course, one may not conclude from this form of the verb that the "Gnostics" are part of the congregation being addressed;[17] rather, the first person corresponds to the homiletic style of the document. The author joins with the congregation because the group itself, and not simply a false docetic teaching, is in danger of failing to draw the necessary ethical consequences of being joined to God. Under these conditions, the reason for the parenesis is clear. If believers are continually in a state of becoming, the ethical demand on them is an indispensable part of the ongoing proclamation to the congregation. This leads to the negative identification: no communion with God = walking in darkness = being in falsehood = not doing the truth. Some of these expressions are specifically Johannine,[18] while others reflect the influence of Septuagint language.[19] In content, they cannot be separated from their positive presupposition, the idea of being in light and in the truth. Falsehood is, as such, discernible only in contrast to truth. Negative as well as positive ethical behavior always has a basis that transcends the realm of the merely ethical.

■ **7** This is also evident from the fact that the ethical life of the Christian community is measured by the model of God's "being in the light."[20] Although the reading μετ᾽ αὐτοῦ[21] instead of μετ᾽ ἀλλήλων recommends itself for

16 See the remarks above on 1:3 and the excursus on κοινωνία.

17 Against this supposition by Windisch and Preisker, *Die Katholischen Briefe*, 112, see (correctly) Schnackenburg, *Epistles*, 76–77; see also below at 2:19. The impersonal meaning of ὁ λέγων (2:4, 6, 9) and of ἐάν τις εἴπῃ (4:20) does not, of course, exclude the possibility of a reference to attitudes and behavior that are also known within the congregation, and not necessarily exclusive to the "false teachers." See, similarly, the rhetorical shift between ἑαυτοὺς πλανῶμεν (1:8) and μηδεὶς πλανάτω ὑμᾶς (3:7), which cannot be materially differentiated; it is otherwise with περὶ τῶν πλανώντων ὑμᾶς (2:26).

18 Cf., e.g., ἐν τῷ σκότει περιπατῶμεν: 1 John 2:11; John 8:12; 12:35b (ἐν τῇ σκοτίᾳ).

19 For ποιοῦμεν τὴν ἀλήθειαν, cf. Gen 32:10 (MT, LXX 11); 47:29; Isa 26:10; *T. Reub.* 6.9; *T. Benj.* 10.3. Further passages are noted by Schnackenburg, *Epistles*, 77–78 n. 28 (but there is no suggestion in 1 John of a reference to the Hebrew or Aramaic text).

20 Verse 7a. Cf. *Poimandres* (*Corp. Herm.* 1) 21: "You have understood rightly, my friend. But why is it (with reference to the portions of life and light that are also found in the human being) that 'those who know themselves enter into him' as the word of God says? — I answer: because the father of all things consists of light and life (ὅτι ἐκ φωτὸς καὶ ζωῆς συνέστηκεν ὁ πατὴρ τῶν ὅλων), from which comes 'the human being.' — Well said. light and life, that is (the) god and father. From him came 'the human being.' And when you have learned that you are made up of life and light and that these are the elements of your being, then you will also enter into life." This reflects the gnostic myth according to which the fallen soul, the bearer of divine particles, must recognize itself again in order to achieve the ascent into the divine sphere (cf. Karl-Wolfgang Tröger, "Hermetische Gnosis," in idem, *Gnosis und Neues Testament* (Berlin: Evangelische Verlagsanstalt; Gütersloh: Mohn, 1973) 107–8. The idea of light and life as the sphere of the divine is found in Aristotle *De caelo*, according to which the ether that moves the outermost sphere of the world is identified with God (William Keith Chambers Guthrie, "Die Entwicklung der Theologie des Aristoteles I," in Fritz-Peter Hager, ed., *Metaphysik und Theologie des Aristoteles* [Darmstadt: Wissenschaftliche Buchgesellschaft, 1969] 77; ET: W.K.C. Guthrie, "The Development of Aristotle's Theology—I," *The Classical Quarterly* 27 [1933]: 162–71); while at the same time God is the power that, by its circular movement, moves all things and holds them in being. In Plato's parable of the cave, the sphere of light is the realm of ideas; the sight of it is described as θεία θεωρία (*Rep.* 7.517D).

21 In Codex A, the Latin manuscripts, and *KJV*. Bultmann originally thought that the reading μετ᾽ αὐτοῦ belonged to the "source" (*Epistles*, 19), but he withdrew this opinion (*Epistles*, 20 n. 20) in light of Schnackenburg's arguments (*Epistles*, 78 n. 32). In favor of the relationship between communion with God and the community's κοινωνία, and therefore the reading μετ᾽ ἀλλήλων, which thus logically continues μετ᾽ αὐτοῦ (v. 6a), see Huther, *Handbuch*, 61–62; Weiss, *Briefe*, 34; Brown, *Epistles*, 201. Cf. also Ernst Käsemann, who regards the variants as corrections by an editor ("Ketzer und Zeuge," *ZThK* 48 [1951] 306 n. 2, reprinted in idem, *Exegetische Versuche und Besinnungen* [2 vols.; 6th ed.; Göttingen: Vandenhoeck & Ruprecht, 1970] 1.183 n.).

grammatical reasons, since it would agree with *αὐτός* and *τοῦ υἱοῦ αὐτοῦ*, it must be regarded as a secondary smoothing of the language that does not preserve the connection between communion with God and human community in the Christian congregation that is characteristic of Johannine theology. In reality, the author is determined to say that union with God is the foundation of Christian "walking in light," and that the community among Christians exists on that basis.

Because the union between God and the community of Christians is not perfected once and for all, it requires continual renewal. The reference to the purifying power of the blood of Jesus is intended to remind the believers of this.[22] It is probably a valid principle that one who is "born from God" does not sin (5:18), and even that a genuine communion with God makes it impossible to sin (3:9). But the author is neither utopian nor enthusiast, and does not soar beyond empirical reality. Instead, he is aware of the fact that the congregation is a *corpus mixtum* and will never realize the perfect communion of the children of God here on earth.[23] Since union with God is not a *habitus*, a continual reflection on the foundation of the Christian life is indispensable. This is expressed in similar terms in the earliest Christian creedal formulas (e.g., 1 Cor 15:3–4; Rom 3:25) and in the tradition of the Lord's Supper (Mark 14:24 par.). Behind such traditions is not only the OT and Jewish concept of sacrifice, but also the Greek and Hellenistic world of ideas, in which the shedding of blood had an atoning effect.[24]

---

22 The expression *αἷμα* (Ἰησοῦ) is found also at 5:6, 8 (in connection with the witnesses "water, blood, and spirit"), as well as in John 6:53–56 (Lord's Supper); 19:34–35 (water and blood). Bultmann regards these passages as the result of the ecclesiastical redaction. The verb *καθαρίζειν* appears only in 1 John 1:7, 9; but numerous expressions in Johannine language describe the removal of sins (cf. Brown, *Epistles*, 203); the adjective *καθαρός* is found only at John 13:10–11.

23 Thus the author of 1 John does not think that the congregation in its present form constitutes itself as a pure community by excluding sinners. Like the congregation as a whole, every individual member has a share in the *corpus mixtum*. The first evangelist illustrated this in the parable of the "weeds among the wheat" (Matt 13:24–30), according to which the separation of the good from the evil is impossible during the time of the church and must be delayed until the ultimate future. Cf. also Jean Zumstein, *La condition du croyant dans l'évangile selon Matthieu* (OBO 16; Fribourg: Éditions universitaires; Göttingen: Vandenhoeck & Ruprecht, 1977) 381–85.

24 In the pre-Christian Greek world a distinction was made between *καθαρμοί* (purifying sacrifices) and *ἱλασμοί* (atoning sacrifices). In *καθαρμοί*, the blood and other material functioned to wash away defilement (cf. Athenaeus *Deipnosophistae* 13.602C: *καθαίροντος . . . ἀνθρωπείῳ αἵματι*). For the *ἱλασμοί*, blood had a constitutive meaning: the surrender of life effects the removal of guilt and gains the favor of the gods. See Paul Stengel, *Die griechischen Kultusaltertümer* (3d ed.; HKAW 5/3; Munich: Beck, 1920) 127–28 (with source citations). On the OT and Jewish background of the idea of atoning sacrifice, see Jer 33:8 (MT) = 40:8 (LXX): "I will cleanse them from all the guilt of their sin against me, and I will forgive all the guilt of their sin and rebellion against me"; and Lev 17:11: "For the life of the flesh is in the blood; and I have given it to you for making atonement for your lives on the altar; for, as life, it is the blood that makes atonement." Cf. Heb 9:22: "Indeed, under the law almost everything is purified with blood, and without the shedding of blood there is no forgiveness of sins" (see also Heb 9:14). One should note in this connection that, in the OT conception, atonement is not a "conciliatory gesture" toward a wrathful god. On this, see Klaus Koch, "Der Spruch 'Sein Blut bleibe auf seinem Haupt' und die israelische Auffassung vom vergossenen Blut," *VT* 12 (1962) 396–416; idem, "Sühne und Sündenvergebung um die Wende von der exilischen zur nachexilischen Zeit," *EvTh* 26 (1966) 217–39; and in connection with this, for the NT, Ulrich Wilckens, *Der Brief an die Römer* (*Röm 1–5*) (EKKNT 6/1; Zurich: Einsiedeln; Cologne: Benziger; Neukirchen-Vluyn: Neukirchener Verlag, 1978), excursus "Zum Verständnis der Sühne-Vorstellung," 233–43. Here the author attempts to show that when the person sacrificing lays a hand on the sacrificial animal (Lev 1:4), that person's sinfulness is transferred to the animal. See also Hartmut Gese, "The Atonement," in idem, *Essays on Biblical Theology* (trans. Keith Crim; Minneapolis: Augsburg, 1981) 93–116; Bernd Janowski, *Sühne als Heilsgeschehen: Studien zur Sühnetheologie der Priesterschrift und zur Wurzel KPR im Alten Orient und im Alten Testament* (WMANT 55; Munich: Kaiser, 1982; 3d ed.; Tübingen: Mohr [Siebeck], 1989); Otfried Hofius, "Erwägungen zur Gestalt und Herkunft des paulinischen Versöhnungsgedankens," *ZThK* 77 (1980) 186–99; here the rite mentioned is understood (perhaps more accurately) as a ritual of

According to Bultmann (*Epistles,* 20), the saying about atoning death (v. 7c) was secondarily introduced into 1 John by the "ecclesiastical redaction." His arguments are: (1) The clause disturbs the poetic style of the context. But we have already said that the "poetry" of this context is nothing more than an elevated prose. (2) This half verse is also disturbing to the content, because the αἷμα clause follows awkwardly after "we have fellowship with one another," since both are dependent on the preceding ἐάν clause ("if we walk in the light . . . "). While "when we walk in the light" is primary, however, it is nothing more than a recapitulation of v. 6a ("we have fellowship with [God]"), and that is precisely what is elucidated, in light of its consequences, by v. 7b ("we have fellowship with one another"), and v. 7c ("the blood of Jesus . . . "). Add to this that v. 7c obviously functions as a transition to v. 8a (key word: ἁμαρτία).[25]

■ 8 The atoning event that occurs in the death of Jesus is constitutive of the believing consciousness. This is, in fact, the ἀρχή in which the absolute Logos reveals itself (v. 1). Hence, it is not possible to go behind this event and to argue about what such a revelation conveys: the realization of the forgiveness of sins. The author does not reflect on the question of whether all human beings already had an awareness of sin in the time before Christ, or whether this was first discovered through the Christ-revelation.[26] His concern at this point is only to make clear that the universality of liberation from sin through the atoning death of Jesus Christ confirms the universality of ἁμαρτία and ἀδικία (vv. 8–10). No one who has been received into the truth can deny that she or he is a sinner. The ἀλήθεια that dwells in the human being is identical with God's eschatological truth, which, as a personified entity, exercises ruling authority (cf. 2 John 1–3; 3 John 12; John 8:32). In this passage it is clear, moreover, that this sense of the word, which is transcendently applied, also implies the original meaning ("uprightness"): being in the truth (2 John 1–3) or truth's being in us (v. 8) includes an honorable, upright way of life. It is the opposite of being in falsehood, which in turn means not only an existence in error, a "misdirected self-understanding" (Bultmann, *Epistles,* 21), but also a deliberate self-deception that refuses to acknowledge what it already knows.

■ 9 Knowledge of one's own sinfulness cannot remain a

identification: the life that is actually being destroyed is restored in the ritual of sacrifice. In contrast, the idea of purification in 1 John belongs in a different religio-historical context. It is difficult to assert, as regards the author of 1 John, that in the NT passages on this subject (cf. also Eph 1:7; 1 Pet 1:2) the sacrificial blood "is simply the metaphorical garment clothing the thought of the self-offering" of Christ (Johannes Behm, "αἷμα, αἱματεκχυσία," *TDNT* 1 [1964] 175), since this author finds himself confronted with a docetic teaching that demanded, in response, an emphasis on the reality of the atoning death of Jesus as well as of the sacraments of Baptism and Eucharist.

In Hellenistic Judaism, the idea of the atoning power of representative suffering was associated with the deaths of the martyrs (cf. 2 Macc 7:37; 4 Macc 6:28–29; 17:20–23; Eduard Lohse, *Märtyrer und Gottesknecht: Untersuchungen zur urchristlichen Verkündigung vom Sühnetod Jesu Christi* [FRLANT 64; 2d ed.; Göttingen: Vandenhoeck & Ruprecht, 1963] 66–72). Even if Isaiah 53 is the earliest OT-Jewish witness to the atoning significance of representative suffering, atonement, particularly ὑπὲρ πολλῶν or ὑμῶν (Mark 14:24 par.) cannot be referred primarily to the "suffering servant of God," especially since Jewish exegesis in the pre-NT period did not rely on Isaiah 53 for a theological justification of suffering (against Joachim Jeremias, "παῖς θεοῦ," *TDNT* 5 [1967] 699; cf. also Lohse, *Märtyrer,* 104–10; Marinus de Jonge, "Jesus' Death for Others and the Death of the Maccabean Martyrs," in Tjitze Baarda, ed., *Text and Testimony: Essays on New Testament and Apocryphal Literature in Honour of A.F.J. Klijn* [Kampen: Kok, 1988] 142–51).

25 Bultmann's attempt (see n. 4 to the General Comment above) to refer v. 8a ("if we say that we have no sin") back to v. 6 ("while we are walking in darkness") has a material basis, of course; but the linking key word ἁμαρτία is missing. It not only creates the connection forward (vv. 8–10) but also backward (vv. 5–7), so that the typical Johannine sequence would be interrupted. Consequently, the statement that the "interpolator" was led by vv. 8–10 to introduce ἁμαρτία earlier, in v. 7c, is unsatisfying. See Bultmann, *Epistles,* 19, 20 n. 23; against this position also Schnackenburg, *Epistles,* 71 n. 1; and see earlier Huther, *Handbuch,* 70, according to whom v. 7 is related "as closely as possible" to vv. 8 and 9.

26 Cf. Rom 1:18–30; 7:14–25; also Weiss, *Briefe,* 36 (with reference to John 3:20).

simple act of recognition; it must lead to ὁμολογεῖν, "confession." This assertion follows so logically in v. 9 that it does not call for any distinction between a model document and an author who secondarily composed this verse and inserted it in a "source." The concept of ἁμαρτία, which here appears in the plural, does not offer much support for such a conclusion,[27] for while the plural refers to individual sins it is clear that in the context the singular πᾶσα ἁμαρτία (v. 7; also πᾶσα ἀδικία, v. 9) has the same generalizing import and applies to individual sins (cf. 5:17). The shift between singular and plural is not to be understood as a material difference and cannot be accorded literary-critical significance.

"Confession," then, refers to individual sins, which are the expression of sinful existence. Whether such a confession is meant to be public and refers to the congregation's penitential practice, or whether it refers exclusively to a confession of sins before God,[28] must remain an open question at this point. That the conclusion of 1 John distinguishes clearly between mortal sins and sins that do not lead to death, and that intercession is permitted only for the latter (5:13–17), does not suggest an alternative choice in this passage. It is clear that even public confession, if that is what is intended here, is ultimately directed to God and not to human beings, since such a confession includes the plea for God's forgiveness.[29] God, in responding to such a plea, is revealed as πιστός ("faithful") and δίκαιος ("just"), expressions drawn from liturgical tradition[30] but meant to be taken literally: God has proved God's faithfulness and righteousness in the past, in the death of Jesus as sacrifice for human sins, since in the death of Jesus God both condemned every sin and at the same time atoned for it (v. 7c; cf. Rom 3:25). If God has been shown to be the Forgiving One, those who confess their sins may expect to receive God's forgiveness; such pardon is nothing other than a "cleans[ing] from all unrighteousness."[31]

27 Against Bultmann, *Epistles*, 21; Braun, "Literar-Analyse," 213; according to them one should distinguish between the singular, which is to be assigned to the model document (1:8; 3:4, 8–9), and the plural, which is to be attributed to the author (1:9; 2:2, 12; 3:5; 4:10). But note the singular also in 1:7; 3:5; 5:16–17, and the parallel between 1:8 (singular) and 1:10 (ἡμαρτήκαμεν).

28 This is the opinion of Balz, "Johannesbriefe," 168.

29 Cf. 5:16. For the relationship between human request and divine forgiveness in Jewish exegesis, see Str-B 3.776.

30 Πιστός as an epithet for God was in use in early Greece (Pindar *Nem.* 10.54, 101) and in Hellenistic Judaism (Philo *Rer. div. her.* 93; *Sac. AC* 93; *Leg. all.* 3.204). In the OT, YHWH is called "faithful" and "trustworthy" in promises made to the people (Isa 49:7); God's faithfulness is revealed in the keeping of the covenant with Israel (Deut 7:9); in this "trustworthiness," God is revealed as ὅσιος (Ps 144[145]:17 LXX) and δίκαιος (Deut 32:4).

The Johannine writings have the word πιστός otherwise only in 3 John 5, as a predicate describing the reliability of Gaius's actions. The NT uses this adjective as a predicate for God especially to express God's faithfulness to the promises: Rom 3:3–4 (parallel to πίστις θεοῦ, together with ἀληθής); Heb 10:23 (with ἐπαγγειλάμενος); similarly in Heb 11:11; cf. 1 Cor 1:9; 10:13; 13:2; 2 Cor 1:18; 1 Thess 5:24; 2 Thess 3:3; 1 Pet 4:19; Ignatius *Trall.* 13.3.

Δίκαιος is another ancient epithet for God. In Greek inscriptions it occurs alongside ὅσιος (BAGD 195); so also in the LXX (Deut 32:4; Ps 144[145]:17), often as a description of God as judge (Ps 7:11; 2 Macc 12:6); cf. Ps 114:5 (with ἐλεήμων); 1 Sam 2:2 (with ἅγιος); Ps. 118[119]:137 (with εὐθής); Ezra 9:15; 2 Esdr 19:8; Tob 3:2; Josephus *Bell.* 7.323 (with ἀληθής); *Ant.* 11.55 (with ἀληθινός). See also the related passage in Wis 15:1–2, where God is called χρηστός, ἀληθής, and μακρόθυμος, the divine mercy and power are acknowledged, and the conclusion is drawn: "we will not sin, because we know that you acknowledge us as yours."

The NT follows this same usage: God is the "righteous judge" (2 Tim 4:8; Rom 3:26; cf. 1 Pet 2:23; Rev 16:5, with ὅσιος). The Johannine corpus calls God the Father δίκαιος (John 17:25); in 1 John δίκαιος appears as a description for Jesus Christ as the advocate (2:1) and the judge to come (2:29), who as the Son of God has already proved himself to be δίκαιος in his battle against the works of the devil (3:7). See also the other applications in 3:7 (to human beings) and 3:12 (to human deeds).

The combination of πιστός with δίκαιος occurs already in the OT (Deut 32:4), and probably came to the author of 1 John by way of liturgical tradition, as suggested by the identical formula in *1 Clem.* 27.1 and 60.1 (cf. also 56.5; Ps 140[141]:5 LXX), where πιστός refers to God's promise and δίκαιος to God's judgment. Our passage, in contrast, interprets in christological and soteriological terms: that God is trustworthy and just is evident from God's action of forgiving sins in Christ.

31 The verb ἀφιέναι expresses the same meaning as

■ **10** The confidence that forgiveness of sins can be expected from God is underscored when, paralleling v. 8, the denial of sin is once again rejected. Such a denial would not only be self-deception (v. 8) but would also make a liar of God (cf. 5:10), that is, say that God's word is untrue. In other words, those who hesitate to acknowledge their sins are rejecting God's offer of forgiveness, for this is contained in the "word" of God that was already characterized in v. 1 as "word of life" and therefore life-giving and is concretized in the Christ-event (v. 7).

In summary, the confessional statement, "the blood of Jesus his Son cleanses us from sin" (v. 7c), which is drawn from early Christian creedal formulas and appears to break formally with its context, is really the functional center of this section. The content of the author's proclamation, that God is light (vv. 5–7), is founded on the event of the cross. This event, through the medium of human preaching, in turn founds the community of believers, a communion both with God (v. 6a) and with one another (v. 7b), because forgiveness of sins is promised to every individual who acknowledges his or her own sinfulness (vv. 8–10).

The dualism of "light and darkness" (vv. 5–7) is paralleled and interpreted by the contrast of "truth and falsehood" (vv. 6, 8, 10). The accent in both instances is ethical, since *ψεύδεσθαι* ("lying") is identical with "not doing the truth" (*οὐ ποιεῖν τὴν ἀλήθειαν*) = "walking in the darkness" (*ἐν τῷ σκότει περιπατεῖν*, v. 6). Correspondingly, a subsequent distinction is drawn between the children of God and the children of the devil (3:10). This distinction, too, is ethically interpreted and equated with sinful actions or with justice (3:7–8). There is a hint of such dualism already in 2 and 3 John (esp. 3 John 11: "Whoever does good is from God"). That dualism is not only further developed in 1 John but is found at a more refined level of reflection in the Fourth Gospel (where it is characterized by a contrast between the Revealer and the world: John 14:17; 15:18–19; 17:14–19; 18:36). In these passages it is clear (and this may be said also of 3 John 11) that the description "ethical dualism of decision" is too narrow, because this contrast also represents an ontological and eschatological opposition, as shown by its being "from God" (*ἐκ τοῦ θεοῦ*, 3 John 11; cf. 1 John 3:9–10). In addition, definition by "light" and "not walking in darkness" (1 John 1:5–6) points to the underlying ethical basis, as does the idea of the spirit of truth and the spirit of error, which are related to one another in the same way as being "from God" is related to being "from the world" (4:6). Thus, if Johannine ethical dualism rests on this ontological and eschatological basis, the atoning death of Jesus in turn must be understood not only as a foundation for Christian ethical behavior, that is, as overcoming sin through God's act of forgiveness, but also as a manifestation of the bridging of ontological and eschatological opposites.

It thus becomes clear that, for this author, the problem of false teaching represents only one question among others and cannot be the key to 1 John as a whole. In essence it is a matter of orienting the community with respect to the unavoidable choice between light and darkness, between God's truth and the falsehood of the world. The Christian community itself is continually under siege, and not only because it is threatened by false prophets. It is always facing the question of assenting to God, of acknowledging God as the judging and pardoning, condemning and forgiving God and Father of Jesus Christ, and allowing God's word to be done in it, or else of closing itself to that offer. In regard to its attitude to God and fellow human beings, the community is asked whether it will acknowledge its sinfulness, confess its sins, and allow itself to be lifted up and healed through the atoning action of God in the death of Jesus Christ on the cross.[32] This immediate address to the audience, and not

καθαρίζειν: "liberation from the guilt of sin"; cf. also 1 John 2:12. It appears as a word of commissioning from the Risen One to the disciples in John 20:23 ("If you forgive the sins of any, they are forgiven them; if you retain the sins of any, they are retained.") This appears also in 1 John 5:17 ("All *ἀδικία* is *ἁμαρτία*"); in a christological context in John 7:18 ("there is nothing of *ἀδικία* in him"). It is not found elsewhere in the Johannine corpus In our passage the expression refers to "the wrong that has been done" (cf. 2 Pet 1:9: *τοῦ καθαρισμοῦ τῶν πάλαι αὐτοῦ ἁμαρτιῶν*), not to "doing wrong" (2 Cor 7:1: *καθαρίσωμεν ἑαυτοὺς ἀπὸ παντὸς μολυσμοῦ σαρκὸς καὶ πνεύματος*; Jas 4:8: *καθαρίσατε χεῖρας, ἁμαρτωλοί*; also 1 John 5:17).

32 According to Georg Eichholz ("Erwählung und

a concealed polemic against false teachers, is the author's real concern. What is said is directed immediately to the Christian community; the address to the readers as "my children" (τεκνία μου, 2:1), which introduces the rest of the work, is already implied in this first section.[33]

Eschatologie im ersten Johannesbrief," *EvTh* 5 [1938] 1–28, at 26) and Ernst Käsemann ("Ketzer und Zeuge," 306 [= *Exegetische Versuche*, 1.182]), 1 John is the first writing in the church's history to offer a thematic development of the motif of "simul justus et peccator." On this, see also Braun, "Literar-Analyse," 267: "The paradoxical, radical idea of sin and not-sin in 1:5–10 has [author's note: in 2:1b] . . . given way to a moralizing, early Catholic perspective."

33 Against Schnackenburg, *Epistles*, 85, who wants to divide this section, as an "argument with the heretics," from the following "parenesis for internal consumption." Brown also says that 1:6—2:2 should be "read against the background of a refutation of secessionist theology," and writes of 1:6: "the author is fearful that his own adherents in the Johannine Community will be misled by the secessionist interpretation of [the Fourth Gospel's] perfectionism whereby the privilege of divine indwelling makes subsequent behavior, even wicked behavior, irrelevant toward salvation" (*Epistles*, 241). In order to adopt this thesis, one must be convinced not only about the ethic of the "secessionists" as there described, but also of the chronological ordering of the Fourth Gospel before 1 John.

2 Indicative and Imperative[1]

1 **My little children, I am writing these things
to you so that you may not sin. But if
anyone does sin, we have an advocate
with the Father, Jesus Christ the
righteous; 2/ [who] is the atoning
sacrifice for our sins, and not for ours
only but also for the sins of the whole
world. 3/ Now by this we may be sure
that we know [God], if we obey [God's]
commandments. 4/ Whoever says, "I
have come to know [God]," but does not
obey [God's] commandments, is a liar,
and in such a person the truth does not
exist; 5/ but whoever obeys [God's]
word, truly in this person the love of God
has reached perfection. By this we may
be sure that we are in [God]: 6/ whoever
says, "I abide in [God]," ought to walk
just as [Jesus] walked.**

These verses reveal the (Johannine) style that is typical of 1 John: characteristic are the address (*τεκνία μου*)[2] as well as the antithetical parallel constructions: v. 1a (*ἵνα μὴ ἁμάρτητε*) is continued antithetically in v. 1b (*καὶ ἐάν τις* . . .); here *καί* is to be understood as an adversative particle ("but").[3] The christological statement in v. 2 appears to be divorced from the context but is really a clarification of and foundation for the preceding Ἰησοῦν Χριστὸν δίκαιον. The antithetical formulations resume in v. 3; here the emphasis lies on the conditional clause at the end ("if we obey [God's] commandments"), a positive resumption of the admonition in v. 1a not to sin. The clauses in vv. 4–6 are equal in length and are, for the most part, parallel in construction; they are introduced by ὁ λέγων (vv. 4 and 6) or by ὃς δ' ἂν τηρῇ (v. 5). Their relationship to one another is antithetical, just as v. 4 follows as a counterpoint after v. 3.

■ **1** The author's intention is expressed in the clause: *ἵνα μὴ ἁμάρτητε*! This refers back to 1:5–10.[4] There the

1 Literature: Stanislas Lyonnet, "The Noun *hilasmos* in the Greek Old Testament and 1 John," in Stanislas Lyonnet and Leopold Sabourin, *Sin, Redemption, and Sacrifice* (AnBib 48; Rome: Pontifical Biblical Institute, 1970) 148–55; T. C. G. Thornton, "Propitiation or Expiation? *Hilastērion* and *Hilasmos* in Romans and I John," *ExpT* 80 (1968) 53–55.

2 The word *τεκνίον* is relatively late Greek and somewhat rare (P. Lond. I 84; Epictetus *Diss.* 3.22.78; Heliodorus *Aeth.* 7.12; P. Flor. 365.15); it is not found in the LXX or in the NT outside the Johannine writings. The address (*τεκνία* [*μου*]) is found in John 13:33, but otherwise occurs in the NT only in 1 John (2:1, 12, 28; 3:7, 18; 4:4; 5:21). This usage is not only an argument for the unity of 1 John, but also underscores its difference from 2 John, since the presbyter uses only the expression *τέκνα* (2 John 1, 4, 13; 3 John 4). The diminutive "my little children" in 1 John emphasizes the distance the author sees between himself and his readers and characterizes the (fictitious) apostolic claim already raised in 1:1–4. In contrast, the address *ἀδελφοί* (*μου*) appears only in 3:13. The appearance of the word in John 13:33 cannot support the thesis of the dependence of 1 John on the Fourth Gospel; instead, both of the occurrences of *τεκνία* indicate a secondary tendency in the Johannine circle to an increased emphasis on authority. In this vein, in the Fourth Gospel Jesus is the ultimate authoritative figure, while in 1 John the author, as an eyewitness, functions as setting the norm for tradition (in response to Culpepper, *Johannine School*, 301–2). Cf. *παιδία*: 2:14, 18; John (4:49); (16:21); 21:5. It is different with the ecclesiological self-description *τέκνα* (*τοῦ*) *θεοῦ* in 1 John 3:1–2, 10; 5:2, as well as in John 1:12; 11:52; cf. also the apostolic address *τέκνα μου* in Gal 4:19 (*v.l. τεκνία μου*), which expresses Paul's spiritual fatherhood (also in 1 Cor 4:14, 17; 2 Cor 6:13; 1 Thess 2:7). According to Hirsch (*Studien*, 171), one could demonstrate the existence of an ecclesiastical redaction on the basis of the different addresses *τεκνία* and *παιδία*.

3 Cf. also BDF §442 (1); see further on 1 John 3:2.

4 This does not, of course, constitute an alternative:

possibility of distancing oneself from sin was asserted and given its foundation. Here it is a matter of the necessity of not sinning (expressly in v. 6: ὀφείλει). Of course, even when such an obligation is expressed, the fact of "sin" and the christological basis that secures the victory over sin are made clear, even in this section. Here, however, the author uses a different set of concepts than in 1:7c. As in the former passage, he anticipates the possibility of sin in the congregation (v. 1b: "if anyone does sin"), and as before he refers to the one who is the foundation of divine forgiveness. But Jesus himself is now described as "the righteous," corresponding to 1:9, where the God who demonstrates divine righteousness by forgiving sins in the Jesus-event is the δίκαιος. Here, Jesus himself is the representative of God's δικαιοσύνη; analogously, he is described at other points as ἁγνός (3:3) or as "sinless" (3:5; cf. Heb 4:15). As the representative and revealer of God's "righteousness," the sphere of holiness and sinlessness, he places on the community the obligation to be "righteous" like himself.[5] The community depends on such a mediation because it is aware of unrighteousness within its own ranks. If the sin within it is a fact not to be denied, nevertheless this should not afford any reason for it to despair or surrender its hope; rather, it can call on Jesus Christ as the Paraclete.

The word παράκλητος appears only at this point in 1 John. (Otherwise, it is found in the Paraclete sayings in John 14:16, 26; 15:26; 16:7.)[6] Luther translated the word in the Fourth Gospel with "consoler" (corresponding to the meaning of the verb παρακαλεῖν).[7]

ταῦτα γράφω refers not only to 1:5–11 but anticipates what the author will say in the rest of the text (cf. 5:13). The document is shaped from beginning to end by a parenetical field of tension that encompasses the whole community (against Bultmann, *Epistles*, 22 n. 35; cf. also Weiss, *Briefe*, 39; Brooke, *Epistles*, 23). According to Käsemann ("Ketzer und Zeuge," 306 n. 2 = *Exegetische Versuche*, 1.183 n.) 2:1–2 continues the thought in 1:8–10: "The admonition in 1:8ff., not to surrender to imaginary sinlessness, is continued in 2:1a with the warning to take seriously the struggle against sin."

5 1 John 3:7; cf. 2:29 (where it is debatable whether δίκαιος refers to God or to Christ; on this, see below).

6 The Paraclete sayings in the Fourth Gospel occur in 14:16–17, 26; 15:26–27; 16:4b–11, 12–15. On this, see Hans Windisch, "Die fünf johanneischen Parakletsprüche," in *Festgabe für Adolf Jülicher* (Tübingen: Mohr [Siebeck], 1927) 110–37. His attempt to trace the Paraclete sayings in the Fourth Gospel to a source are generally rejected today. See, in addition, BAGD 618 (with older literature); Gunther Bornkamm, "Der Paraklet im Johannes-evangelium," in idem, *Geschichte und Glaube* (2 vols.; BEvTh 48; Munich: Kaiser, 1968) 1.68–89; Felix Porsch, "παράκλητος," *EDNT* 3 (1993) 64–67; Ulrich Wilckens, "Der Paraklet und die Kirche," in Dieter Lührmann and Georg Strecker, eds., *Kirche: Festschrift für Günther Bornkamm* (Tübingen: Mohr [Siebeck], 1980) 185–203 (starting from the literary unity of the farewell discourses and the connectedness of the sayings about the Paraclete and correctly emphasizing their ecclesiological function). For literature oriented toward the history of religions, see Otto Betz, *Der Paraklet: Fürsprecher im häretischen Spätjudentum, im Johannes-Evangelium und in neu gefundenen gnostischen Schriften* (Leiden: Brill, 1963); George Johnston, *The Spirit-Paraclete in the Gospel of John* (SNTSMS 12; Cambridge: Cambridge University Press, 1970); Felix Porsch, *Pneuma und Wort* (FTS 16; Frankfurt: Knecht, 1974). Sigmund Mowinckel ("Die Vorstellungen des Spätjudentums vom heiligen Geist als Fürsprecher und der johanneische Paraklet," *ZNW* 32 [1933] 97–130), as well as Nils Johannson (*Parakletoi* [Lund: Gleerupska Universitetsbokhandeln, 1940]), and, following them, Johannes Behm, infer a connection with the Jewish notion of the advocate; cf. also Str-B 2.560–62. Betz (*Paraklet*) asserts a particular derivation from the advocate-traditions of the Qumran community; see more on this below.

7 The verb παρακαλέω does not occur in the Johannine writings. In the NT it has the ordinary meaning of "console" (2 Cor 1:4, 6; 7:6–7; Matt 2:18; Acts 20:12, and many others), but it can also mean "urge," or "encourage," or "appeal" (thus frequently: 1 Thess 4:1, 10; 5:11; 1 Cor 1:10; Matt 8:5, and many others). See also Augustine, *Tractatus In Joannis Evangelium* 94.2 (*PL* 35.1868): "Consolator ergo ille vel advocatus (utrumque enim interpretatur quod est graece paracletus), Christo abscedente fuerat necessarius" ("This consoler, then, or advocate [for the Greek 'paraclete' can mean both] became necessary because of Christ's departure"); cf. idem, *Tractatus In Epistolam Joannis ad Parthos* 1.7–8 (*PL* 35.1983–84): "Advocatum habemus ad Patrem, Jesum Christum iustum" ("We have an advocate with the Father, Jesus Christ, the Just One").

But in none of the Johannine passages is it the task of the Paraclete to do anything like "consoling" the community in its struggles. In the passage at hand it is more proper to think of the other possible translation, "advocate."[8] This corresponds to the OT and Jewish tradition about God's representatives or prophets who act as advocates (e.g., Abraham in Gen 18:23–33). In apocalyptic Judaism one also finds the idea of an angel as advocate.[9] The remaining Johannine usage must be distinguished from this. In the Paraclete sayings in the Fourth Gospel, *παράκλητος* means "helper" or "adviser"; similarly in the Mandaean writings, Manda d' Hayye or the "one sent" appears as a helping figure.[10]

These references reveal a broad religio-historical environment, proving that the idea of the Paraclete is pre-Johannine. In contrast to the older Christian tradition, in the Johannine circle the person of Christ or the Spirit has been secondarily interpreted in terms of the Paraclete. The idea that Jesus called himself "Paraclete" is quite improbable in light of the fact that there are no other instances in the NT.[11] The Johannine occurrences have a common ecclesiological function. This is true both of 1 John 2:1, where the Paraclete has a specific task in regard to the overcoming of sin in the community, as well as in the Fourth Gospel, according to which the Paraclete is to carry on the work of Jesus after his departure. In both cases there are forensic features (1 John 2:1: orientation toward the Father's judgment; John 16:8–11: accusation and judgment of the world). In both, the manner in which the Paraclete functions is derived from the Christ-event (cf. John 15:26: "[the

8 This was Luther's translation in this verse; on the linguistic background, cf. Demosthenes *Orations* 19.1 (*αἱ . . . τῶν παρακλήτων . . . δεήσεις καὶ σπουδαὶ τῶν ἰδίων πλεονεξιῶν ἕνεκα γίγνονται*); Dionysius of Halicarnassus *Antiquities of the Romans* 11.37.1 (*τῶν τὰ δίκαια λεγόντων παράκλητοι*); here *παράκλητος* also has the meaning of "advocate," without "like its Lat. equivalent *advocatus*, being used as a technical term for the professional legal adviser or defender of an accused person" (Johannes Behm, "*παράκλητος*," *TDNT* 5 [1967] 801).

9 Cf. *1 Enoch* 47.2; 104.1; *Tg. Job* 33.23; *T. Dan* 6.2. According to Otto Betz "the Johannine Paraclete [was] created in the image of the late Jewish advocate Michael and then equated with the 'spirit of truth'" (*Paraklet*, 159; cf. 207). By combining the idea of the Paraclete in 1 John 2:1 with the one in the Johannine farewell discourses, Betz comes to the conclusion that John "divided the double role of the Paraclete into two figures: the advocate on duty in heaven and the 'other Paraclete'" and in addition "united two entities who appear still to have been separated in Qumran: Michael and the 'spirit of truth'" (*Paraklet*, 156). On this, see Porsch, *Pneuma und Wort*, 315 ("Betz is compelled to propose too many transpositions in order to get back, at last, to the figure of the Johannine Paraclete").

10 Bauer's interpretation (BAGD 618) was incorrect: "in our literature the active sense 'helper,' 'intercessor' is suitable in all occurrences of the word." Nothing is said in the Fourth Gospel about an advocacy exercised by the Paraclete. Bultmann (*John*, 566–72, "Additional Note: The Paraclete") found extensive correspondences to the functions of the Johannine Paraclete as adviser and helper in the gnostic figures of revealers in the Mandaean pantheon and in the *Odes of Solomon* (sending from the world above, revelation of things past and future, teaching and leading to salvation), especially in "Jawar" (according to Wilhelm Brandt and Mark Lidzbarski a Persian loanword for "helper"; according to E. S. Drower an Aramaic pe'al participle from אור, "the shining one"), and Manda d'Hayye; both are revered in the Mandaean myths as helper, teacher, and director of souls. Thus one praying says: "Yes, I have come to love my Lord Manda d'Hayye, (and hope) that in him, there will come to be a helper for me, a helper and a sustainer, from the place of darkness to the place of light" (Lit. 212, in Bultmann, *John*, 571). The messenger addresses the believers: "Endure the world's persecutions, with genuine, believing hearts. Revere me in uprightness, that I may present myself and be to you a helper, a helper and a sustainer" (Lit. 195, in ibid.). Even though the Mandaean literature comes from a later period, and thus cannot be presumed as background for the NT authors, the significant parallels that can be demonstrated between the Mandaean texts and the NT world of ideas have some importance (in response to Raymond E. Brown, "The Paraclete in the Fourth Gospel," *NTS* 13 [1966/67] 113–32).

11 Against Behm, "*παράκλητος*," 813–14.

Paraclete] will testify on my behalf"). The Paraclete acquires a special closeness to the person of Christ in being described (in John 14:16) as *ἄλλος παράκλητος*. It appears from this that in the Fourth Gospel, as here in 1 John, the word "Paraclete" is applied to Jesus; however, this conclusion is not explicitly drawn. Nevertheless, one cannot deny that in the Fourth Gospel the Paraclete manifests to the community the work of Jesus Christ, the Revealer. This also constitutes the crucial difference between the idea in 1 John and in the Gospel. There, the figure of the Paraclete clearly represents the eschatological helper who will be active in the disciples' future lives, that is, who will be with the community after the crucifixion and resurrection of Jesus Christ. The Paraclete is the Johannine equivalent of the Spirit and has the function of bridging the time between Christ's departure and the end, securing the continuity of the church throughout its history, which means establishing the connection with the Christ-event in the past and making it continually present for the Christian community.[12] The author of 1 John, unlike the Gospel writer, distinguishes between Paraclete and Spirit; this author does not identify the Paraclete with the *pneuma* but with Jesus Christ. Although in connection with the appositional accusative *Ἰησοῦν Χριστὸν δίκαιον* only the translation "advocate" is adequate, one may not say that the author has thereby "developed further" the fourth evangelist's idea of the Paraclete.[13] The relationship is rather the reverse, inasmuch as the usage in the passage under discussion is closer to the general religio-historical background, in which "Paraclete" can be translated "advocate."[14] But the different conceptual ideas within the Johannine corpus should probably be regarded as "a further argument for different authors for the Gospel and the letter."[15] On that basis, one may draw from the use of *παράκλητος* at this point some indication of the history of the traditions of the Johannine school. 1 John 2:1 reflects the older Johannine tradition that was also taken up in the Fourth Gospel, creatively expanded, and thus established as an important foundation pillar for Johannine pneumatology.

If Jesus Christ is the Paraclete who intercedes for the community as its "advocate" or its "representative before the Father," the question arises: What christological conception does such advocacy entail? The context of our verse may suggest different intentions. If one applies the notion of the Paraclete to what has gone before, where God, as the faithful and just one, forgives sins (v. 9), one should think of the event of pardon that is present in the community now. Then Jesus Christ's role as advocate and representative belongs to him as the Exalted One who intercedes for the community before God. This idea can be related to the Hellenistic Jewish tradition as represented, for example, by Philo.[16] There

12 John 14:17; cf. Mark 13:11 par. ("for it is not you who speak [before the judge], but the Holy Spirit"); 1 John 5:7–8 ("There are three that testify: the Spirit and the water and the blood"). Paul and the theology influenced by him understand the Spirit as "guarantee" (*ἀρραβών*), that is, as a temporal phenomenon that secures the eschaton (2 Cor 1:22; 5:5; Eph 1:14). Ulrich Luck ("Kerygma, Tradition und Geschichte Jesu bei Lukas," *ZThK* 57 [1960] 51–66) points to the experience of the Spirit as the fundamental basis of the Lukan writings. For the initial and basic work on this, see Hans Conzelmann, *The Theology of St. Luke* (trans. Geoffrey Buswell; London: Faber; New York: Harper, 1960; reprinted London: SCM; Philadelphia: Fortress, 1982) 184 ("Thus the Spirit enables us to see on the one hand the individuality of Jesus, his position in the centre of redemptive history, and on the other hand the continuity between him and the Church, or in other words the positive link with the present"; cf. Acts 1:8).

13 This is the position of Balz, "Johannesbriefe," 169.

14 See n. 8 above; Brooke, *Epistles*, 23 ("The meaning 'advocate' is clearly needed in the Epistle").

15 Thus Wengst, *Brief*, 63.

16 Cf. Philo *Mos. Vit.* 2.134: *ἀναγκαῖον γὰρ ἦν τὸν ἱερωμένον τῷ τοῦ κόσμου πατρὶ παρακλήτῳ χρῆσθαι τελειοτάτῳ τὴν ἀρετὴν υἱῷ πρός τε ἀμνηστίαν ἁμαρτημάτων καὶ χορηγίαν ἀφθονωτάτων ἀγαθῶν* ("For the one who was consecrated as priest to the Father of the universe must necessarily take his Son, fully perfect in excellence, as his advocate, both for the forgiveness of sins and also to appeal for the preservation of inexhaustible happiness"). While it is disputed whether, in Philo's understanding, the "perfect Son" is identical with the "Logos" (Str-B 3.776) or with the "world" (on this, see B. Badt, in Leopold Cohn, et al., eds., *Philo von Alexandria: Die Werken in Deutscher Übersetzung* [6 vols.; 2d ed.; Berlin: de Gruyter, 1962] 1.329 n. 1), in Philo's work in general the word *παράκλητος* means "advocate" (*παραιτητής*). See also *Spec. leg.* 1.237; *Op. mun.* 23; *Flacc.* 22–23, where the verb *παρακλητεύειν* also appears; also *Leg. Gaj.* 322, and others. Similarly the Logos can also be interpreted as *ἱκέτης* (*Migr. Abr.*

are parallels in the present eschatology in 1 John, according to which Jesus Christ as the Son of God determines the present lives of the faithful (cf. 5:20: "we are in [God] who is true, [because we are] in his Son Jesus Christ. [This] is the true God and eternal life"). This is the precondition for the future eschatological expectation whose content is the return of Christ (2:28). Hence Jesus Christ, as the Exalted One, stands before God and intercedes for sinners.

Although the preceding context makes this interpretation probable, since the issue is confession of sins now and hope for present pardon, one cannot deny that the next verse could suggest another interpretation. According to v. 2, Jesus Christ is the ἱλασμός who atones not only for our sins but for those of the whole world. Thus here there is reference to the atoning death of Jesus, already known from v. 7b and to be encountered again in the subsequent text (cf. 4:10). If it is the suffering and dying Jesus who is the Paraclete, that means that Jesus' atoning suffering forms the basis for the forgiveness of sins and furnishes the assurance that sins are forgiven. Of course, the difficulty remains that the language (besides ἱλασμός ἐστιν especially the present tense, ἔχομεν) first suggests a present event. Even if the atoning suffering of Jesus is the material basis for the advocacy of the Exalted One (cf. 3:16), one should still give consideration to the first interpretation discussed above. It corresponds to a general NT outlook: the exalted Christ intercedes with God for the believing community (Rom 8:34). As the heavenly high priest, "he always lives to make intercession for them" (Heb 7:25; cf. 4:14–15; 9:24).

■ **2** Verse 2 should be seen not only as an explication of v. 1b (as, similarly, 1:10bβ interpreted the preceding clause in 1:10bα), but also as giving a reason for what is said in the preceding verse. The author uses primitive Christian concepts here. Ἱλασμός can be translated either as "expiation" or "propitiatory sacrifice."[17] The word occurs also at 4:10, but nowhere else in the NT. The idea of the ἱλαστήριον (Rom 3:25, probably a baptismal tradition) is related, as is the ἱλάσκεσθαι of the "faithful high priest" who "atones" for the sins of the people (Heb 2:17). If the author is adopting traditional concepts, the verse does not support any argument for the supposition that it has been added by an ecclesiastical redactor.[18] Rather, the author is using the same idea of atonement already introduced in 1:7c with the term αἷμα Ἰησοῦ. The advocacy that the exalted Christ exercises for the community before the Father is based on the atonement for sins accomplished in Jesus Christ's redeeming sacrifice. Christ's standing before God as δίκαιος and acting as advocate for the community is founded on his atoning death. Because he, who is sinless, has made atonement on the cross, he can stand before God's

122). In another interpretation λόγος is identical at this point with ῥῆμα, but see the translation by M. Posner in ibid., 5.184. A different interpretation is given by G. H. Whitaker, *Philo* (12 vols.; LCL; London: Heinemann, 1932) 4.200. See also Behm, "παράκλητος," 802–3.

17 On the translation, see BAGD 375. According to Henri Clavier ("Notes sur un mot-clef du johannisme et de la sotériologie biblique: ἱλασμός," *NovT* 10 [1968] 287–304), in the Hellenistic period ἱλασμός meant "God's action to remove sins." Hence in this passage the word would describe the event of reconciliation, with the reconciliation itself being identified with the Son (but see 2 Cor 5:19). In the same way, in 1 John 4:10 ἱλασμός would refer to Jesus as the living manifestation of the love of God for sinners. T. C. G. Thornton ("Propitiation or Expiation? *Hilastērion* and *Hilasmos* in Romans and I John," *ExpT* 80 [1968] 53–55) is of a different opinion. According to this author, our concept is used only in the sense of "means of atonement." Among scholars the interpretation of ἱλασμός as a *nomen actionis* (= atonement) predominates; but the concrete idea of Jesus' "propitiatory sacrifice" should not be excluded; it accords with the preceding argumentation (1:7: αἷμα Ἰησοῦ; 1:9: καθαρίσῃ ἡμᾶς) and reference can be made to LXX language (cf. Ezek 44:27: προσοίσουσιν ἱλασμόν; Num 5:8; 2 Macc 3:33); this last is also in the background of the περί constructions (e.g., ἐξιλάσκεσθαι περί at Sir 16:7; 45:16, 23). This confirms the idea that it represents traditional, primitive Christian thinking.

18 Against Bultmann, *Epistles*, 23 ("ecclesiastical redaction," as in 1:7b and 4:10); with Brown, *Epistles*, 217, and Wengst, *Brief*, 64, although the latter thinks this is a traditional "formula" adopted by the author.

throne in the present as the trustworthy Paraclete and perform effective intercession for those who are his own.[19] But this atonement is not esoterically restricted to the community; it has a universal application. Jesus' atoning act is "for the whole world" (περὶ ὅλου τοῦ κόσμου). Thus it can be said in 4:14 that the Father sent the Son as "savior of the world" (σωτῆρα τοῦ κόσμου; cf. 4:9), and even in the Fourth Gospel the world is the object of the atoning and saving action of Christ (John 1:29: the lamb of God who takes away the sin of the world; cf. John 3:16).

Like the Fourth Gospel, 1 John testifies to a tension between God's compassion toward the world in the Son and the negative qualification of the world. On the one hand, the false teachers are from the world, and the world listens to them (4:5); on the other hand, the believers are "from God" and thus separated from the world (5:4–5; cf. 3 John 11). The world's hatred pursues the community (1 John 3:1, 13; cf. 4:17), and the antichrist is in the world (4:3–4). This negative judgment culminates in the statement that "the whole world lies under the power of the evil one" (5:19). The world is thus within the realm of the evil power,[20] and the evil one is in the world. Nevertheless, these statements do not negate the truth that God's atoning action is intended precisely for the world, that is, for human beings. The message of God's forgiving action in the Christ-event promises human beings the opportunity to regard themselves either as belonging to the world or as having their human existence derived "from God," to have faith in this offer and thus to overcome the world (5:4: "Whatever is born of God conquers the world. And this is the victory that conquers the world, our faith").

■ **3** How is it possible to know that a person is responsive to God's offer, no longer interpreting oneself as from the world, but rather from God?[21] How is it evident that one "knows God"? Such terminology occurs even in 2 John 1; that verse makes clear that knowing God is simultaneously an acknowledgment of God's claim. Γινώσκειν thus describes not only a theoretical belief that something is true but a being involved with something. Those who have recognized the truth live in the truth (2 John 1–3); the truth is in them (1 John 1:8; cf. 2:4); they do what is true (1 John 1:6; cf. John 3:21). The criterion for knowing God, for being in the truth, is therefore right action. This is oriented to that which God has demanded, concretely: the divine commandments.[22]

The relationship between knowing God and human action is not understood in a synergistic sense.[23] Keeping the commandments is not a condition but rather a sign of knowing God.[24] The author is not interested at this point in making a systematic theological statement. Rather, the question of the criterion for knowing God

19 Cf. also Huther, *Handbuch*, 83; Schnackenburg, *Epistles*, 87–88; Wengst, *Brief*, 64.

20 It is characteristic that the author does not say that the world as such is evil; thus the Johannine dialectic relationship "from the world—from God" is not to be regarded as an alternative of two principles that are ontologically and physically exclusive of one another; what does seem to be presented is an opposition of two stances that are offered as choices for human beings, and these are not merely ethical in character; cf. Bultmann, *Theology*, 2.21–23.

21 The introductory καί links v. 3 with what precedes it, as the injunction not to sin (v. 1) is followed now by the positive demand to keep the commandments. While ἐν τούτῳ also points to the ἐάν clause to follow, it does not exclude the connection of the argument with what precedes it, and there is no reason to begin a new paragraph with v. 3 (against Schnackenburg, *Epistles*, 95).

22 On this subject, cf. Matt 7:15–23. The plural ἐντολαί is found, in addition to 1 John 2:3–4, also in 3:22, 24; 5:2–3 (with the definition, "the love of God is this, that we obey [God's] commandments. And [these] commandments are not burdensome"). The Fourth Gospel has the plural only in the farewell discourses as ἐντολαί μου, that is, as commands of Christ the revealer: 14:15, 21; 15:10. Singular and plural can follow one another immediately in 1 John (as in 3:22–24). Except in 2:7–8, the singular is always accompanied by an epexegetical or imperative ἵνα clause, the content of which is love of brothers and sisters. The plural as a specific concretion of the one commandment in the real life of the community occurs in verses whose subject is the actions of the disciples.

23 Against Schnackenburg, *Epistles*, 98 (according to whom it is a matter of divine and human cooperation: see his remarks on 2:5).

24 With Bultmann, *Epistles*, 24–25.

aims at parenetical counsel: urging the faithful to keep the commandments or, as v. 1 puts it in negative terms, not to sin. The imperative (vv. 1a, 3b) frames the indicative assertion, "we have an advocate" (v. 1b). Awareness of the atoning, forgiving event of salvation in Christ accompanies every phase of ethical behavior.

■ **4** If the criterion for proper knowledge of God is keeping the commandments, then, conversely, not keeping the commandments is a sign of the fact that one does not know God. This means that one has closed oneself against God's truth[25] and is a "liar." In this case, "being a liar" not only means "not telling the truth," but living in untruth, that is, in unreality.[26]

■ **5** The positive statement in v. 3 (τὰς ἐντολὰς αὐτοῦ τηρῶμεν) is resumed in v. 5, with the substitution of αὐτοῦ τὸν λόγον for ἐντολάς. The "word" is thus the same as the "commandments." At the same time it is clear that the injunction to keep God's commandments is not exhausted within the sphere of ethics, but remains open to the eschatological claim that, although it includes the ethical commandment, demands still more: it requires faith in the sending of the Son (cf. 5:4–5) and rests on the "word of life" (1:1b). In anyone who fulfills this claim, that is, by trusting in the "word of life," the ἀγάπη τοῦ θεοῦ has "truly"[27] reached its goal.

In considering the meaning of the word τελειοῦσθαι, one should keep in mind the substantive τέλος ("goal," "end"). This is an eschatological concept.[28] Similarly, in 4:17, the perfection of *agapē* is directed toward the παρρησία "that we are to have on the day of judgment."[29] While such an apocalyptic idea was certainly accessible to the author of 1 John (cf. also 3:2–3), he (differently from

---

25 On the relationship between ἀλήθεια and γνῶσις, see Schnackenburg, *Epistles*, 97 n. 116: the two are not identical; rather, "truth" is either an object (2 John 1; John 8:32) or a precondition of true knowledge (2 John 2; 1 John 2:4; John 8:44). It is true, however, that the author of 1 John does not make a conscious distinction between the "object" and "precondition" of knowledge.

26 Cf. Bultmann, *Epistles*, 25: "[ψεύστης ἐστίν] 'he is a liar' asserts (as does [ψευδόμεθα] 'we lie,' 1:6) not only that such a person says something untrue, but that [that person] is nothing, since ἀλήθεια ('truth') is reality."

27 Ἀληθῶς occurs only here in 1 John; cf. also John 1:47; 4:42; 6:14; 7:26, 40; 8:31; 17:8. The adverb can refer to ἀλήθεια, as "in [the] truth" (cf. 1 John 2:4).

28 As regards the Johannine corpus, τέλος appears only in John 13:1 (εἰς τέλος ἠγάπησεν αὐτούς), but τελειοῦν occurs four times in 1 John (besides 2:5, in 4:12, 17–18), and five times in the Fourth Gospel; the usage in the Gospel varies but is dominated by the active voice with the object τὸ ἔργον (4:34; 17:4; cf. 5:36 [plural]). One also finds the passive "to reach the goal [or end]" (with reference to the statements of Scripture) in 19:28; 17:23 expresses the union of the revealer with his disciples (ἵνα ὦσιν τετελειωμένοι εἰς ἕν). 1 John frequently uses the construction ἐν ἀγάπῃ τετελειοῦσθαι; this phrase occurs also in *1 Clem.* 49.5; 50.3 to describe the community's self-understanding; cf. the active in the meal prayer at *Did.* 10.5 (τελειῶσαι αὐτὴν ἐν τῇ ἀγάπῃ σου), as well as in Col 3:14 (*agapē* as σύνδεσμος τῆς τελειότητος). Whether lines of connection can be drawn from this to the terminology of the mysteries (Richard Reitzenstein, *Hellenistic Mystery-Religions: Their Basic Ideas and Significance* [trans. John E. Steely; Pittsburgh: Pickwick, 1978] 149–50, 431–33; BAGD 811–12 [with references]) remains in dispute. There should, however, be no doubt that the word implies an "eschatological sense" (Bultmann, *John*, 516 n. 3; Schnackenburg, *Epistles*, 98, differs). Even if, in the passage under discussion, a "perfect situation" appears to be in view, perfection in love nevertheless depends on the "fulfilling" of the commandments. The perfection demanded of the community is not completed in the present; it is open to the future and remains dependent on God's actions. On this passage, see also Ludwig Radermacher, *Neutestamentliche Grammatik* (2d ed.; Tübingen: Mohr [Siebeck], 1925) 155: "Something that one has good reason to expect will happen often is described as if it were a past event. . . . This frequently happens in general statements" (1 Cor 7:28; John 15:6; 1 John 2:5).

29 Bultmann's assignment of 4:17 to a stratum of ecclesiastical redaction (*Epistles*, 72) is consistent but not persuasive; this is true also of the evaluation of the παρρησία passages in 2:28 and 5:14 (cf. also 3:21; see Bultmann, *Epistles*, 44–45 and n. 4).

2 John) does not primarily emphasize the future aspect of the traditional apocalyptic material. Instead, apocalyptic language serves to describe the eschatological reality of salvation as it exists for the community in the present. The "perfection" of *agapē* occurs when we are "in him" (v. 5b), that is, belong to God in an eschatological and ontological sense.[30] Such an eschatological direction for Christian existence leaves no place for the idea of a moral development of the personality, step by step.[31] Instead, in the given context it is part of the general parenesis that applies to the community as a whole. The crucial goal of the ethical demand is *agapē*. Despite the perfect tense of the verb, it is not a fact to which the believer looks backward, something to boast about as a demonstrable achievement when she or he meets the coming judge. The παρρησία before the judge that it will help them to achieve (2:28) is "confidence," or "frankness," and thus not a service to be performed.

The concept of ἀγάπη τοῦ θεοῦ can have both a subjective and an objective meaning. On the one hand, if one understands it as a subjective genitive, it is "God's reality," and identical with God's love.[32] Then the obligation to love the brothers and sisters follows from the divine reality. For this interpretation one may adduce 1 John 4:9 and 4:12. On the other hand, one cannot seriously question that 1 John knows the idea of love for God, and so can understand the concept of ἀγάπη τοῦ θεοῦ as an objective genitive (4:20–21; 5:1–3). This is a crucial difference between 1 John and the Fourth Gospel where, in accordance with the evangelist's christological conception, love for God is attributed only to Jesus (14:31), and the love of the disciples, to the extent that it is an "ascending" love, is directed to Jesus (14:15, 21, 23; 21:15–16). The author of 1 John, in contrast, teaches both love for God and the love of God. Is there any grammatical term that can span these subjective and objective distinctions within the genitive? Schnackenburg suggests the idea of a genitive of quality: the genitive describes the nature of *agapē*; it is a "divine love," and τοῦ θεοῦ accordingly has the significance of an adjective.[33] What is meant is the perfection of the genuine, eschatological *agapē* that touches both God and the human being. Whether the subject of the *agapē* is presumed to be God or human beings can remain unresolved. Apparently both are possible, and indeed there can be no fundamental distinction between them, since individual passages can be classified as one or the other only with great difficulty.[34] From all this one may conclude that the love of human beings for God (objective genitive) can only be called "perfect" in the horizon of the love of God for human beings (4:18). In turn, the love of God (subjective genitive) cannot be otherwise understood than as embracing God's *agapē*-actions for human beings and requiring the love of human beings for God as a response.

If the characteristic sign of being in God is the perfection of divine *agapē*—namely, keeping God's words, God's commandments (vv. 4–5)—then the divine *agapē* must be seen in the context of the dualistic conceptions of the Johannine circle. Doing *agapē* is a criterion not only for knowing God (vv. 3, 5b) but also of "being from God" (4:6–8). That means that anyone who is formed by *agapē* knows no fear (4:17–18: "there is no fear in love," and "whoever fears has not reached perfection in love"). Such a one is separated from hatred (2:9–11: walking in light and not in darkness, thus also not in hatred for the brothers and sisters). In particular it is true that the love of the Father and love for the world are mutually exclusive; for the task of believers is to decide whether they will love the world and worldly

30 That is, in the sense of "being born of God"; cf. 3:9; 5:18 (the impossibility of sin for one who is "born of God").

31 Correctly: Schnackenburg, *Epistles*, 98 (and n. 122).

32 Bultmann, *Epistles*, 25; in a subjective sense also Balz, "Johannesbriefe," 176; Gerhard Delling, "τελειόω," *TDNT* 8 (1972) 81–82; Hans Hübner, *EDNT* 3 (1993) 826; differently Gerhard Schneider, "ἀγάπη," *EDNT* 1 (1990) 11–12; undecided Brown, *Epistles*, 257.

33 Schnackenburg, *Epistles*, 97. On this point, see BDF §165; Maximillian Zerwick, *Biblical Greek* (from 4th Latin ed.; trans. Joseph Smith; Rome: Biblical Institute Press, 1963) nos. 25–28.

34 Cf. also 2:15 ("The love of the Father is not in those who love the world"); this refers to the divine sphere that is meant to be determinative for Christians; also 3:17 ("How does God's love abide in anyone who has the world's goods and sees a brother or sister in need and yet refuses to help?"). In these passages one should most probably think of a subjective genitive.

things or will be formed by the love of the Father, whether they are "from the Father" or "from the world" (2:15–17).

If the realm of darkness receives its negative qualification because it is a denial of divine being as being in light,[35] it is true as regards the divine *agapē* that its denial occurs in the realm of hatred, sin, darkness, evil, and the devil (cf. 3:10–18). Such an opposition finds its motive in the fundamental description of the nature of God as love (ὁ θεὸς ἀγάπη ἐστίν, 4:8, 16). Although this formula, which has nothing corresponding to it in the Fourth Gospel, is no more a definition of the divine nature than the statement "God is light" (1:5), it nevertheless clarifies the being of God as an activity, namely, as the doing of *agapē* toward human beings.[36] The word ἀγάπη is, in this sense, a predicate noun: God is described as "the loving one," but the reverse is not true: love is not raised to divine status. God shows love by sending the Son. From the indicative of the Christ-event one can see that God is love; this occurs in the atoning sacrifice of Jesus (2:2; 4:10). Jesus manifests the love of God. This revelation has as its purpose "that we might live through him" (4:9). Such a manifestation of the love God has bestowed on us, expressed in the indicative, is the basis for the demand that we, on our part, should practice love (4:19: "[let us] love, because [God] first loved us").[37]

■ **6** Indicative and imperative are therefore joined to one another, analogously, as cause and effect, an offer and the acceptance of such an offer. Of course, this occurs not only to the degree that the soteriological meaning of the death of Jesus precedes the ethical imperative (as in vv. 1–2), but also in such a way that the indicative of the Christ-event itself is understood as an imperative: the way of life of Jesus, the Righteous One, is the model for the ethical behavior of believers.[38] While καθώς has both a foundational ("since") and a comparative ("just as") meaning,[39] in either case imitation is demanded. This is the moral duty of every individual who "abides in God":[40] the imitatio Jesu.[41] There is, however, no notion of earned merit associated with this idea.

---

35 See above, on 1:6.

36 See below, on 4:8.

37 The variant reading αὐτόν found its way into Luther's translation of 4:19, since it is found in the imperial text (K); but the above reading, represented by the Nestle-Aland text, is to be preferred: it makes clear that the love commandment has a general application. Cf. R. Schütz, "Die Vorgeschichte der johanneischen Formel ὁ θεὸς ἀγάπη ἐστίν" (diss., Göttingen, 1917).

38 For this "model" christology, cf. 2:1, 29; 3:7 (δίκαιος); 3:16; also John 13:15, 34; 15:10, 12 (with reference to the love commandment). See also ἁγνός ἐστίν in 1 John 3:3; ἁμαρτία ἐν αὐτῷ οὐκ ἔστιν in 3:5. The verb ὀφείλειν in the ethical sense is also in 1 John 3:16; 4:11; 3 John 8. Καθώς corresponds to the following οὕτως, although the text tradition is uncertain at that point. The absence of οὕτως in A B and other manuscripts can be regarded as the *lectio difficilior*. The word is omitted in the edition of the NT by Brooke F. Westcott and F. J. A. Hort (1881), and Nestle-Aland[26] is undecided. For the pairing of καθώς and οὕτως, cf. Rom 2:4; 2 Cor 1:5; 10:7; Col 3:13; Luke 11:30; 17:26; John 3:14; 12:50; 14:31; 15:4. On this subject, see Hans-Martin Schenke, "Determination und Ethik im ersten Johannesbrief," *ZThK* 60 (1963) 203–15, esp. 214: 1 John knows no determinism that could eliminate human responsibility. Determination and responsibility stand in a dialectical, side-by-side relationship; indicative and imperative are collapsed into one another.

39 Cf. Braun, "Literar-Analyse," 221 ("double meaning of καθώς"); BDF § 453 (1–2).

40 Jürgen Heise (*Bleiben: Menein in den johanneischen Schriften* [HUT 8; Tübingen: Mohr [Siebeck], 1967] 120–26) correctly emphasizes the connection between the theological and christological aspects in vv. 5–6, as well as the fact that "being is determined by abiding." In the view of the author of 1 John, this applies both to the relationship with God and to the relationship with Christ. In the text at hand one should think first of the former, as the shift in the personal pronouns (from αὐτός to ἐκεῖνος: vv. 5–6) makes clear.

41 Ἐκεῖνος in v. 6 refers to Jesus, as elsewhere in 1 John and in the Fourth Gospel; cf. 1 John 3:3, 5, 7, 16; 4:17; John 7:11; 9:12, 28; Bultmann, *Epistles*, 26 ("the fact that it is used here without any preparation, instead of the explicit name, shows that ἐκεῖνος was common as a designation in the circle of the author").

Excursus: Μένειν[42]

Μένειν appears here for the first time in 1 John (out of a total of 24 occurrences). It occurs 40 times in the Fourth Gospel, 3 times in 2 John: for comparison, the rest of the NT has 45 occurrences. It is applied both to the relationship of God to human beings (e.g., 3:17: "God abides in [him/her]") and to the relationship of human beings to God or Christ (e.g., 3:6: "no one who abides in [God] sins"). The construction μένειν ἐν τινί predominates (in 1 and 2 John the only exception is 1 John 2:19 [μεθ' ἡμῶν]), but the Fourth Gospel and the rest of the NT also have combinations with ἐπί τινα (John 1:32–33; 3:36), παρά τινα (John 1:39; 14:17, 25), εἰς τινά (John 6:27; 12:34), or the absolute usage (John 1:38–39; 4:40).

Although the presumptive opposites include such things as "yield," "go away," "leave the place," it would be wrong to suppose that μένειν "does not answer the question of place, of where, but rather the question, until when? how long?"[43] The literal, local meaning is certainly known to the NT (e.g., John 7:9: ἐν τῇ Γαλιλαίᾳ; 2 Tim 4:20: ἐν Κορίνθῳ); the word has a metaphorical sense as early as Plato (*Epistulae* 358C: ἐν τοῖς ἤθεσιν; *Rep.* 2.360B: ἐν τῇ δικαιοσύνῃ), and this is true also of the NT (e.g., 1 Tim 2:15: ἐν πίστει καὶ ἀγάπῃ; 2 Tim 3:14: ἐν οἷς ἔμαθες). This meaning dominates the Johannine corpus (2 John 9: ἐν τῇ διδαχῇ τοῦ Χριστοῦ; 1 John 2:24: "Let what you heard from the beginning abide ἐν ὑμῖν ['in you'], [and] . . . you will abide ἐν τῷ υἱῷ καὶ ἐν τῷ πατρί ['in the Son and in the Father']"; cf. 2:27: the χρῖσμα "abides in you"). The local usage can describe remaining in a certain realm or sphere (1 John 2:10: ἐν τῷ φωτί ["in the light"]; 3:14: ἐν τῷ θανάτῳ ["in death"]), and it can be identical with being in God or in Christ (cf. 5:20). Although this recalls the terminology of the mysteries, what is meant is not some mystical event but the personal confrontation of God and the human being. This is true also for the so-called formulas of immanence in which the relationship of God to human being and human being to God is described in reciprocal terms: thus John 6:56: "Those who eat my flesh and drink my blood abide in me, and I in them" (cf. 15:4–7). Particularly significant are 1 John 3:24 ("All who obey [God's] commandments abide in [God], and [God] abides in them"); 4:12–13 ("If we love one another, God lives in us. . . . By this we know that we abide in [God] and [God] in us"); and 4:15–16 ("God abides in those who confess that Jesus is the Son of God, and they abide in God . . . those who abide in love abide in God, and God abides in them").

The local interpretation, which has lost much of its force, has a broad background in the history of religion.[44] But it is characteristic of the Johannine corpus that no exact parallels can be shown to exist either in the OT and Jewish prayer literature or in religions outside Christianity. The community of God with humanity and of humanity with God that is expressed in the formulas of immanence has, however, a close parallel in Paul's idea of being "in Christ" (cf., on the one hand, "in Christ" in 1 Thess 1:1; 2:14; 4:16; 5:18; Gal 1:22; 3:28; 5:6, and similar passages; on the other hand, "Christ in me" in Gal 2:20; 2 Cor 11:10; "Christ in you" in 2 Cor 13:5; Rom 8:10). This may be regarded as an indication that there was some Pauline basis for the Johannine circle.

In addition to its local meaning, μένειν has a temporal dimension, discernible in εἰς- or ἕως-constructions, among others (John 8:35; 21:22; cf. 2 John 2). Because the structure of the Fourth Gospel is oriented to the past and future of the Logos-Revealer, the temporal sense is fairly frequent in that work. There μένειν can have the meaning "endure" or "persist" (John 3:36: the wrath of God on them; 14:17: the Spirit with [or among] you; 15:16: your fruit). The negative version ὁ μὴ μένων ἐν τῇ διδαχῇ τοῦ Χριστοῦ (2 John 9) refers to the "progressive" teachers who do not abide in the traditions of the Johannine circle. The author of 1 John admonishes the readers to remain "in him" in view of the coming parousia of the Son (2:28), much as the mutual relationship of people's remaining in God and God's remaining in human beings is directed to the perfection of love, which will find its final fulfillment at the day of the last judgment (4:16–17).

The presbyter confirms, in the letter "to the elect lady and her children," that the truth "abides in us and will be with us forever" (2 John 2). For the author of 1 John it is also clear that μένειν reflects the condition of the community, which is described in the indicative. If it is in possession of the χρῖσμα, it knows that it will thus be led into the truth and that it is separated from the πλανῶντες ("deceivers," 2:27). It is part of the

42 Literature: Friedrich Hauck, "μένω, κτλ.," *TDNT* 4 (1967) 574–76; B. Lammers, "Die MENEIN-Formeln der Johannesbriefe: Eine Studie zur johanneischen Anschauung der Gottesgemeinschaft" (diss., Gregoriana; Rome, 1954); Heise, *Bleiben;* Malatesta, *Interiority and Covenant;* Schnackenburg, Excursus 4, "The Johannine Formulas of Immanence," *Epistles,* 99–103; Hans Hübner, "μένω," *EDNT* 2 (1991) 407–8.

43 Bultmann, *Epistles,* 26 n. 9.

44 On this, see David L. Mealand, "The Language of Mystical Union in the Johannine Writings," *DRev* 95 (1977) 19–34, with special emphasis on "mutual indwelling."

indicative assertion that the community, if it "remains in [God]," does not sin (3:6), for God's σπέρμα endures in those who are born of God, so that they cannot sin (3:9). In contrast, the existence of nonbelievers is described as "abid[ing] in death" (3:14), just as murderers do not have life abiding in them (3:15).

Most of these passages occur in parenetical contexts, so that even here one can see a clear connection to the imperative. This is certainly true of the indicative declaratory statements that presuppose a condition or state of being. Thus the confession that Jesus is the Son of God not only characterizes adherence to the community, in opposition to false teaching. In addition, making this confession is the precondition for our remaining in God and God in us (4:15). Second, the indicative assertion that God remains in us is connected with the condition that we love one another (4:12), for the act of loving makes visible the mutual relationship of remaining in God and God's abiding in us (4:12; cf. v. 16). Similarly, "remaining in the light" presupposes that one loves one's sisters and brothers (2:10). The indicative of remaining-in-light or being-in-light (2:9) implies the indirect demand to realize this remaining-in-light in a concrete action, by avoiding hatred of the brothers and sisters and practicing love of the sisters and brothers (cf. 2:11). In addition, the promise that one will "live forever" is conditioned on fulfilling the will of God (2:17).

Still more clearly in the description of the mutual relationship of God and human beings in 3:24, μένειν expresses a condition related to the keeping of the commandments. Hence "abiding" does not describe a perfected condition of the faithful, but rather a historical event that the gift of the Spirit enables one to know (3:24b). No matter how much abiding in God characterizes the eschatological state of being of the Christian community, it is necessary to draw concrete consequences from it, such as generosity toward sisters and brothers in need; for without such an ethical consequence the love of God cannot remain in the believers (3:17). Direct imperatives are certainly rare: the neutral ὃ ἠκούσατε ἀπ' ἀρχῆς ἐν ὑμῖν μενέτω challenges the community to maintain that which has constituted it from the beginning (2:24a); for that reason it is a condition for remaining in the Son and in the Father (2:24b). Again, the imperative μένετε ἐν αὐτῷ aims at the parousia of the Son of God, for the community will be able to approach the one who is to come with confidence only if it has preserved itself through "remaining in him" (2:27–28).

First John differs from the Fourth Gospel in not describing the relationship of believers to Jesus with the concept of ἀκολουθεῖν.[45] In this, the fourth evangelist agrees with the Synoptics: discipleship ("following") describes the historical relationship of the disciples to Jesus as "followers" of the Christ working on earth. Hence ἀκολουθεῖν is not used in any of the NT letters as a description for what Christians do.[46] In the passage under discussion, the author uses the expression περιπατεῖν both for Jesus and for the members of the community in order to emphasize their mutual relationship. From this fact it is clear that one and the same attitude is demanded: it is the duty of every individual who believes in Christ to live as Jesus himself lived. Indeed, this is a description of "discipleship" in a transferred sense.[47]

It would be difficult to suppose that the author understood περιπατεῖν in harmony with gnostic thought as a "movement along a [vertical] path," so that Jesus' περιπατεῖν would be identical with "traveling the way that leads him from the Father into this world and back to the Father."[48] It is striking that the fourth evangelist does not use the verb of Jesus in a theological sense. Instead, what is characteristic is the dialectic of light and darkness, in which the disciples are represented as περιπατοῦντες (cf. 8:12). Hence the command: "Walk while you have the light, so that the darkness may not overtake you" (12:35). Thus περιπατεῖν is active human behavior in a particular realm, especially in the sphere of light or of darkness. In this, Johannine usage appears to differ from Paul's ethical teaching, in which the norm that determines human activity is expressed with περιπατεῖν combined with κατά and the accusative. But at the same time this shows that Paul also is aware of a dialectic that

45 Cf. John 1:37–38, 40, 43; 8:12; 10:4–5, 27; 12:26; 13:36–37; 21:19–20, 22. On this subject, see Gerhard Kittel, "ἀκολουθέω, κτλ.," *TDNT* 1 (1964) 210–16; C. Blendinger, "Disciple," *TBLNT (E)* 1.482–85; Georg Strecker, "Heiligung," *EKL*[3] 2 (1988) 451–54.

46 It is found in this sense, outside the NT Gospels, only in Rev 14:4. John 21:19–23 is an exception. Here the text speaks of disciples' following the risen Christ; cf. Bultmann, *John*, 714 ("a call to follow into martyrdom").

47 Cf. also John 8:12, where ἀκολουθεῖν and περιπατεῖν occur together.

48 Against Heise, *Bleiben*, 124–25; on this, cf. John 8:14; 13:3; 16:28.

can be expressed in parenetic terminology.[49] Analogously, in this passage the content of the verb is determined by a norm that bestows on it a parenetical and ethical sense. Thus as early as 2 and 3 John "walking in the truth" is associated with a commandment that determines this behavior, namely, the commandment of *agapē* (2 John 4, 6; 3 John 3–4). In addition, both in the Fourth Gospel (13:34–35) and in 1 John (1:6–7; 2:11) the dialectic of walking in light or in darkness is tied in the closest possible manner to the alternative "fulfilling the love commandment" or "bringing about hatred" toward the brothers and sisters. Jesus, too, as "the light" not only urges walking in light, but in the conception of the fourth evangelist he exemplifies such behavior by loving those who are his own (13:34; 15:9).

It is thus clear that an alternative between faith and love in the tradition of the Johannine school is impossible. It is true that *πιστεύειν* is directed toward the dogmatic statement "that Jesus is the Christ [who] has been born of God" (1 John 5:1a, 5), and eternal life is promised to those who believe (1 John 5:10–13; cf. John 3:15). To that extent *πιστεύειν* differs from *ἀγαπᾶν* in having primarily a theoretical content. But the parallel usage of *πιστεύειν* and *ἀγαπᾶν* (1 John 3:23; 5:1a, b) and of *πίστις* and *ἀγάπη* (5:3–4) shows that the two cannot be separated. Those who believe in the Son show love for God and keep the commandments, especially the commandment of *agapē* (2:5). In turn, it is unimaginable that anyone who did not stand within the eschatological context of faith in the sending of the Son could fulfill the commandment of *agapē*. While it is true that faith and love must be distinguished from one another, in the Johannine conception these two cannot be divorced.[50]

Thus far, we have begun to clarify the concept of *ἀγάπη*. The next section will take a more detailed look at the content of the *agapē* commandment.

---

49 Cf. the contrast between *κατὰ σάρκα περιπατεῖν* (2 Cor 10:2–3; Rom 8:4) or *κατὰ ἄνθρωπον περιπατεῖν* (1 Cor 3:3) and *κατὰ πνεῦμα* (Rom 8:4) or *κατὰ ἀγάπην περιπατεῖν* (Rom 14:15). The content of *περιπατεῖν* can be expressed by *ἐν* with the dative (Rom 6:4: *ἐν καινότητι*; 2 Cor 4:2: *ἐν πανουργίᾳ*; 10:3: *ἐν σαρκί*; cf. Col 4:5: *ἐν σοφίᾳ*; *1 Clem.* 3.4: *ἐν τοῖς νομίμοις . . . πορεύεσθαι*) or with a simple dative (Gal 5:16; 2 Cor 12:18: *πνεύματι*); or the characteristics of the behavior can be described by use of an adverb (1 Thess 4:12; Rom 13:13: *εὐσχημόνως*; cf. Eph 4:1: *ἀξίως*). While the contrasted usage with *πανουργία* or *ἀγάπη* expresses the ethical meaning of *περιπατεῖν*, the association with *σάρξ* or *πνεῦμα* brings out an essential contradiction. The difference between Pauline and Johannine theology is thus not so fundamental on this point as Bultmann thought (*John*, 342 n. 2; cf., in contrast, his *Theology*, 1.238, 332–33).

50 This is also clear in John 14:12 ("the one who believes in me will also do the works that I do and, in fact, will do greater works than these"). In this instance one may, like Bultmann, regard the description of the disciples' works as *μείζονα* to be "paradoxical," for "they are in fact the works of him without whom the disciples can do nothing (15:6)" (*John*, 611); cf. Brown, *John*, 2.633. The indivisible union of faith and love is also emphasized in 1 John 3:23. The objects of the *ἐντολή* are *πιστεύειν* and *ἀγαπᾶν*, or better, the unity of faith and love. Even though faith is directed to the confession of Christ and love to one's fellow believers, it is still clear that love cannot be active without faith, or faith without love (cf. below on 1 John 3:23). There is a *formal* parallel in Rom 10:9, where *ὁμολογεῖν* and *πιστεύειν* are synthetically related to one another in a couplet, and believing confession or confessing faith is described as the precondition for salvation. To attempt to use the different terms as an excuse for dividing homologies and *pistis* formulas is to ignore the *parallelismus membrorum* that exists here (Hans Conzelmann, "Was glaubte die frühe Christenheit?" in idem, *Theologie als Schriftauslegung*, 109; Vielhauer, *Geschichte*, 15, 23).

2

Old and New Commandment[1]

7 **Beloved, I am writing you no new com-**
mandment, but an old commandment
that you have had from the beginning;
the old commandment is the word that
you have heard. 8/ Yet I am writing you a
new commandment that is true in him
and in you, because the darkness is
passing away and the true light is already
shining. 9/ Whoever says, "I am in the
light," while hating a brother or sister, is
still in the darkness. 10/ Whoever loves a
brother or sister abides in the light, and in
such a person there is no cause for
stumbling. 11/ But whoever hates
another believer is in the darkness, walks
in the darkness, and does not know the
way to go, because the darkness has
brought on blindness.

The Johannine style of this section is shaped by antithetical parallelisms, although these are not so refined that one could deduce the presence of a "source."[2] One might ask whether there is a caesura between vv. 8 and 9, since only beginning with vv. 9–10 is the ἐντολή described as a command to love the brothers and sisters. But the whole passage exhibits a continuous unity. The demarcation at the beginning has to do with content. In the preceding section the subject was "love of God," which is here interpreted as "love of the brothers and sisters." In turn, the unit is set off at the end by the introduction of the list of groups in the Johannine community that begins in v. 12.

Regarding the internal outline: v. 7a–b contains an antithesis between "new" (καινή) and "old commandment" (παλαιὰ ἐντολή) established by the contrast οὐκ–ἀλλ'. This is continued with an explanation of the concept of ἐντολή (v. 7bβ: ἣν εἴχετε ἀπ' ἀρχῆς; v. 7c: ἡ ἐντολή–ἠκούσατε). If the old commandment is explained in this way, something similar is true for the ἐντολὴ καινή. The neutral relative clause in v. 8 has an interpretive function that is expanded and given its foundation in the subsequent ὅτι clause by a contrasting of σκοτία and φῶς. Verse 9 is tied to the previous verse through key words (φῶς/σκοτία), and also carries the argument forward, since prohibiting hatred of the sisters and brothers expresses a negative interpretation of the ἐντολή. Verse 10 offers a positive antithesis, since love of the brothers and sisters is clarified by ἐν τῷ φωτὶ μένει and by the absence of "stumbling." Verse 11 supplies a negative

1 Literature: Antonio Vincent Cernuda, "Engañan la oscuridad y el mondo; la luz era y manifiesta lo verdadero," *EstBib* 27 (1968) 153–75, 215–32; George D. Kilpatrick, "Two Johannine Idioms in the Johannine Epistles," *JTS* n.s. 12 (1961) 272–73; Günther Klein, "'Das wahre Licht scheint schon.' Beobachtungen zur Zeit- und Geschichtserfahrung einer urchristlichen Schule," *ZThK* 68 (1971) 261–326; Judith M. Lieu, "Blindness in the Johannine Tradition," *NTS* 34 (1988) 83–95; Martin Rese, "Gebot der Bruderliebe in den Johannesbriefen," *TZ* 41 (1985) 44–58; Heinrich Schlier, "Die Bruderliebe nach dem Evangelium und den Briefen des Johannes," in Albert Descamps and André de Halleux, eds., *Mélanges bibliques en hommage au R. P. Beda Rigaux* (Gembloux: Duculot, 1970) 235–45.

2 Against Bultmann, who under such (possible) preconditions designates v. 11b as "a homiletical expansion of the author" (*Epistles*, 29). Cf. Schnackenburg, who divides vv. 7–11 into three sections according to subject and calls vv. 7–8 an "insertion" (see *Epistles*, 110); also Bultmann, according to whom the postulated "source" is quoted in vv. 9–11a (*Epistles*, 28). Brown sees vv. 9–11 as an independent subsection (*Epistles*, 247, 288). In contrast, Weiss recognizes the unity of vv. 7–11 (*Briefe*, 46).

antithesis with hatred of the sisters and brothers, employing multiple repetition of the key word σκοτία and a concluding causal ὅτι clause.

As will be clear in the discussion of 2 John 5–6, the presbyter emphasizes the antiquity of the commandment of mutual love and contrasts it with the "newfangled people" who separate themselves from the love of Christ and thus not only question the presbyter's christological concepts but also attack the unity of the community and, thereby, the commandment of *agapē* among Christians. In opposition to such people it makes sense to emphasize that what was given from the beginning is not only the teaching of Christ but also the love commandment: both possess an unalterable validity.[3]

Excursus: Ἐντολή[4]

The noun ἐντολή is found 67 times in the NT; most occurrences are in the Pauline Letters and the Johannine writings including Revelation. In the Fourth Gospel, ἐντολή appears 10 times, in 1 John 14 times, and in 2 John 4 times.

In most cases, ἐντολή means a command promulgated by God or by Christ, but the secular meaning is also possible (John 11:57). A comparison with other writings sheds light on the specifically Johannine sense of this concept. In Hellenistic Jewish tradition ἐντολή often represents the Torah,[5] which is also called νόμος and is unfolded in the individual commandments, the ἐντολαί. This tradition is reflected in the Synoptics and in Paul.[6] In the Johannine writings, by contrast, ἐντολή is never identified with the Mosaic Torah. It is significant that the concept of νόμος never appears in the Johannine Letters. Moreover, the use of the plural ἐντολαί does not refer to the OT Jewish law; instead, the ἐντολαί are emanations of the one ἐντολή.[7]

In the Fourth Gospel this concept occurs only in Jesus' self-proclamation, as the Father's instruction to the Son (John 10:18; 12:49–50; 15:10) and as Christ's commandment to the disciples (John 13:34; 14:15, 21; 15:10, 12); keeping the ἐντολαί appears as the sign of love for Jesus. This commandment is also at the heart of the Johannine Letters. On the basis of the observation that the plural ἐντολαί is always followed by the singular ἐντολή, or vice versa (1 John 2:3–4, 7–8; 3:22–24; 4:20—5:3), one can clearly see that the love commandment is the true content of the ἐντολαί.

While in the Fourth Gospel Jesus' commandment is interpreted as the ἐντολὴ καινή (John 13:34), and in 2 John, in opposition to the false teachers, the "newness" of the love commandment is expressly denied (2 John 5–6), the author of 1 John, in a primarily intra-community effort to make this a matter of topical urgency, calls the commandment both "old" (παλαιά) and "new" (καινή).[8] The commandment of love for the sisters and brothers can also be explained by saying "that we should believe in the name of [God's] Son Jesus Christ" (1 John 3:23), for the unity of the congregation is not reflected only in deeds of love but also in creedal confession. Analogously to the

3 See below on 2 John 2–6.

4 Literature: Brown, *Epistles*, 250–52; Meinrad Limbeck, "ἐντολή," *EDNT* 1 (1990) 459–60; Schnackenburg, *Epistles*, 103–7; Gottlob Schrenk, "ἐντολή," *TDNT* 2 (1964) 545–56; Windisch and Preisker, *Die Katholischen Briefe*, 114–15.

5 In LXX, Gen 26:5; Exod 15:26; Lev 22:31. Also *T. Levi* 14.6–7; *T. Jud.* 16.3–4. Philo *Leg. all.* 1.93; *Spec. leg.* 1.300. Josephus *Ant.* 1.43, 47; 5.76, 94; 6.60, 101, and elsewhere.

6 Matt 15:4 par.; 19:16–17 par.; 22:34–40 par.; Luke 1:6; 18:20; 23:56; Rom 7:8–13; 13:9; 1 Cor 7:19; cf. Eph 2:15; 6:2.

7 Cf. John 14:15, 21; also Brown, *Epistles*, 251. According to him the shift from singular to plural is "a stylistic device."

8 1 John 2:7–8. For rabbinic parallels to the play on καινή and παλαιά, see *'Abot R. Nat.* 18 (par.); *m. Yadayim* 4.3, and elsewhere. The Babylonian Talmud also has the following: "New and old [noble fruits] have I, my dear, preserved for you [cf. *Song* 7:13; also the NT logion about the activity of the Christian scribes in Matt 13:41]. The community of Israel says to God: Lord of the world, I have imposed on myself many preventive rules [that is, the new noble fruits], more than you have imposed on me [that is, the old noble fruits], and I have kept them. Rab Chisda [† 309] said to the one among our rabbis who ordered [= recited] the haggadah before him: Have your ears perhaps heard what 'new as well as old' means? He answered him: The one are the light commandments, the other the difficult ones. He said to him: Was the Torah then given at different times [little by little] [so that some commandments are older than others]? Instead, the one speaks of the words of the Torah [= old fruits] and the other of the words of the scribes [= new fruits]" (*b. 'Erubin* 21b; see Str-B 1.677). Cf. also *Sipre Deut.* 6.6, *Waethanan* § 33: "It should be in your eyes not like a stale edict, which no one takes to heart, but like a fresh edict, which everybody runs to read" (see Jacob Neusner, *Sifre to Deuteronomy: An Analytical Translation* (2 vols.; BJS 98, 101; Atlanta: Scholars Press, 1987] 1.91).

presentation of the love commandment in the Synoptic tradition (Matt 22:37–40 par.), the author can link love for the brothers and sisters with love for God (1 John 4:21). In doing so, the author first places an accent on love for the sisters and brothers, interpreted as a proof of love for God (4:20); but "we know that we love the children of God, when we love God and obey [God's] commandments" (5:2).

As in the Fourth Gospel, so also in 1 John the christological roots of the love commandment are clear.[9] Love of the brothers and sisters is the consequence of the love of God, who "sent [God's] only Son into the world so that we might live through him" (1 John 4:9). From this statement follows the imperative: "We love [or: let us love] because [God] first loved us" (4:19). The fundamental Pauline question about the relationship between righteousness through faith or through works is not a genuine problem for the author of 1 John, "for whatever is born of God conquers the world," so that the author can say: "God's commandments are not burdensome" (5:3–4). "Keeping the commandments" is to be equated, both in the Fourth Gospel and in the Johannine Letters, with "keeping the word" or "keeping the words." Λόγος and ἐντολή are interchangeable (1 John 2:4–5), since "the old commandment is the word that you have heard" (2:7).

■ **7-8** 1 John displays a level of reflection beyond that in 2 John 4–6, presupposing a change in the composition of the Johannine circle and an interpretation of the *agapē* commandment that has been modified through discussions within the Johannine school. The "newness enthusiasts" in 2 John are now so thoroughly integrated into the Johannine circle that their teaching is no longer felt to be a divisive element.[10] Traditional and progressive thinking have joined in a dialectical unity. For the standpoint articulated here it is characteristic that the commandment can be called both "old" and "new." It is *old* because it was given to the community at its founding and because it was uttered in the preaching that called the community to life (cf. 1:1, 5). With this statement the author of 1 John takes up the thread of early Johannine tradition, which emphasized the age of what it was handing on.[11] This commandment,[12] however, is at the same time *new*, because it is derived from the revelation of the truth in the Christ-event. Here the author approaches the position of the "newness enthusiasts." The progressive attitude can be christologically founded, because with Christ the old has passed away and the new has begun (cf. 2 Cor 5:17). The commandment is not new merely because it did not exist before and because nothing analogous can be demonstrated to have existed in the history of religions before Christianity. Instead, it is new because it is the command of the revealer. As Christ brought "truth" (ἀλήθεια) into the world once and for all (John 8:32, 40), so also the commandment that comes from him is "new" and "true," for the revelation of Jesus Christ takes place in the sphere of absolute eschatological truth and must for that reason be called "true" and "new."[13]

9 Schrenk ("ἐντολή," 554–55) differs. In his opinion, in 1 John "the profound christological basis . . . is not stated here."

10 The supposition that the age of the commandment is emphasized in vv. 7–8 (as in 2 John 9) in opposition to the false teachers who do not keep the old commandment but desire to be "progressive" (Bultmann, *Epistles*, 27; Brown, *Epistles*, 264–65) is disproved by the emphasis on the newness of the commandment in what immediately follows. A clear distinction must be drawn between the different situations presupposed by the presbyter's letters on the one hand and 1 John on the other. Cf. also on 2:18–27 below (where the dogmatic position of the presbyter is seen to be no longer an object of dissension at the time when 1 John is being written).

11 A different position is taken by Konrad Weiss, "Die Gnosis im Spiegel und Hintergrund des 1. Johannesbriefes," in Karl-Wolfgang Tröger, ed., *Gnosis und Neues Testament* (Gütersloh: Mohn, 1973) 350, and by Viktor Warnach, *Agape: Die Liebe als Grundmotiv der neutestamentlichen Theologie* (Düsseldorf: Patmos, 1951) 164. According to them, παλαιά ἐντολή refers to the divine commandment in the OT. But against this position one must say that the author of 1 John otherwise shows no interest in tracing his proclamation to the OT.

12 The antithesis in v. 8 is introduced with πάλιν ("on the other hand"; cf. Luke 6:43), which can also be translated "again" (Matt 4:7; 2 Cor 10:7), because it continues the preceding line of thought. The new commandment is thus not another one that differs in its content from the old commandment.

13 In contrast, cf. the association of "old law" and "new

There is a difficulty with the reference of the neuter ὅ in v. 8b. Since it is not preceded by a neuter noun, one must decide among several possibilities. There is no real basis for suspecting an Aramaism, with ὅ in place of the Aramaic relative pronoun.[14] A reference back to the preceding sentence (v. 8a) has been suggested.[15] In fact, the neuter relative pronoun can reprise a whole sentence (Acts 2:32; Gal 2:20; Col 1:29; 1 Pet 2:8; Rev 21:8).[16] But this fact is unsatisfying, because the author does not intend to say that what he is writing to the congregation "is true in him and in you." Nor should one suppose that ὅ encompasses vv. 7b and 8a, so that the content of what is "true" is the old and new commandment. Rather, in the immediate context what is emphasized is the newness of the commandment.[17] This is made clear by the following ὅτι clause with its statement that the age of darkness has ended and the true light is already shining (v. 8c). Hence ὅ refers to the content of v. 8a: that the commandment is "new" is "true" in itself and in the community. Such truth, in which the commandment is understood as a new assurance and a new duty, has an eschatological quality.[18] That the truth occurs "in him" (ἐν αὐτῷ) most probably means, in light of what has preceded it, in Christ.[19] This points to the Christ-event as the eschatological basis for the new demand. The true newness of the commandment also exists, however, "in you" (ἐν ὑμῖν), namely, when the promised word is accepted and realized. The conclusion to draw from the antithetical negation (1:8) is thus that the truth does not become a reality in human beings who deny sin and thus make themselves guilty of self-deception.[20]

The ὅτι clause refers back to the preceding part of the verse beginning with ὅ. That the newness of the commandment is experienced as truth in Christ and in the community is founded on the fact that darkness is departing and the true light is already shining.[21] This passage differs from John 12:35 (Jesus Christ as the light of the world), because here Christ is not identified with the light. Instead, at this point comes the fundamental Johannine contrast between the two principles of "light and darkness," as already hinted in 1 John 1:5–7. This same principle will be applied to ethical problems in the following verses (2:9–11). It encompasses both Christ and the believing community. It can be said that, on the one hand, the power of darkness has been broken, on the basis of the fact that it is recognized as passing and

---

law" in Xenophon *Resp. Lac.* 10.8: "But certainly it is established that these laws are the oldest, for Lycurgus—so it is said—was born at the time of the Heraclides. Although they are so old, they are now for the other [Greeks] something quite new (οὕτω δὲ παλαιοὶ ὄντες ἔτι καὶ νῦν τοῖς ἄλλοις καινότατοί εἰσι); for what is most astonishing is that while all praise such institutions [laws, customs], they do not desire to imitate any state (πόλις)." Here, too, it is a matter of one and the same laws that at one time appear as old, and at another time as new. But the pairing in 1 John must be distinguished from this one in Xenophon, since in 1 John "new" refers to the eschatological dimension of the commandment. See also Balz, "Johannesbriefe," 171, according to whom "the one who gives life to his own has also, in the final analysis, made possible the realization of love." One should certainly note that the author of 1 John does not speak in our text of the subjective problem of enabling the realization of love; rather, what is established is an apparently objective state of things that transcends humanity.

14 Cf. Jean Héring, "Y a-t-il des Aramaismes dans la Première Epître Johannique?" *RHPhR* 36 (1956) 113–21, at 115–16; Brown, *Epistles*, 266.

15 Thus Schnackenburg, *Epistles*, 105.

16 Cf. BAGD 551–52.

17 Cf. also Brooke, *Epistles*, 36. The fact that, differently from the preceding (2:3–4), the singular ἐντολή is used means that the author is focusing on what is essential, namely, the *agapē* command, which was already seen in plural form as the central focus of God's demand; cf. also 3:23–24; 2 John 5–6 (and the excursus, " 'Εντολή," above).

18 While ἀληθές in the preceding verse had a predicative meaning (also in 2:27; 3 John 12), ἀληθινόν is construed attributively (also in 5:20). There is, however, no difference in content between the two; cf. Kilpatrick, "Two Johannine Idioms," 272.

19 The personal pronoun ἐν αὐτῷ points back to v. 6 (ἐκεῖνος). Another possibility is a reference to ὁ λόγος (v. 7: the truth manifests itself in the word of proclamation). Obviously, in the author's way of thinking both references are possible, but the following τὸ ὄνομα αὐτοῦ and τὸν ἀπ' ἀρχῆς (vv. 12–13) also suggest the christological interpretation.

20 Cf. also Heinrich Julius Holtzmann, *Evangelium, Briefe und Offenbarung des Johannes* (HKNT 4; 1891; 3d ed. Tübingen: Mohr [Siebeck], 1908) 219: καινή means "not the commandment, but its characterization as new."

21 The particle ὅτι is not recitative ("that"), but causal ("because"); what is intended here is not explication, but giving a reason for what precedes.

temporary,[22] and that, on the other hand, the power of light has already gained the victory. It is true that these two are still fighting one another, and the community is being drawn into the struggle. The two contending principles confront each other not only in a vertical, spatial dimension but also on a horizontal, temporal plane: The era of darkness will be dispelled by the era of light, and this eschatological reality is already discernible in the present time of the community. This kind of chronological thinking is also presumed by the fourth evangelist in the "light" terminology used in the Gospel, where it is said that with Jesus, light has come into the world, and that the light will be with the disciples as long as Jesus is in the world (8:12; 9:5; 12:35). While there the historical dimension of the Johannine opposition of "light and darkness" is stated retrospectively, here the view is toward the future. The author of 1 John articulates the apocalyptic hope that the era of darkness will be brought to an end once and for all, and that the victory of light will be fully accomplished.[23] The difference between the evangelist's conception and that of the author of 1 John is obvious. It is essentially to be traced to the difference between the christological accentuation of the Fourth Gospel and the ecclesiological emphasis in 1 John, but at the same time it indicates a divergence in the history of the Johannine school tradition.[24]

■ **9** Only from v. 9 onward is it clearly stated that the content of the old—and at the same time new—commandment is love of the brothers and sisters. There was an indication of this as early as vv. 5–6, in the concept of "love of God" (ἀγάπη τοῦ θεοῦ), and it is further clarified in what follows. Only 1 John speaks expressly of "love for the brothers and sisters" (besides 2:9–11, also in 3:14 and 4:21; cf. 3:10). This term does not appear either in the Fourth Gospel or in 2 and 3 John.[25] Still, the reality that is described by the expression ἀγαπᾶν τὸν (or τοὺς) ἀδελφόν (-ούς) is thoroughly Johannine. The ἀδελφός is the fellow Christian,[26] and loving the brothers and sisters means the same thing as "loving one another" (1 John 4:11–12; John 13:34;

22 The verb παράγεσθαι in the sense of "pass away" occurs also in 2:17, but nowhere else in the Johannine Letters. The active form occurs with the same meaning in 1 Cor 7:31, intransitively; it is used in a local sense in John 9:1: "pass by" (also John 8:59, *v.l.:* "go out"), and in the Synoptics (Matt 9:9, 27: "walk along"; Matt 20:30; Mark 2:14; 15:21: "pass by"). Cernuda differs: according to him this passage should be translated as "darkness seduces" or "darkness deceives" ("Engañan," 158–59); on this, see Brown, *Epistles,* 268. The verb φαίνειν appears relatively seldom in the Johannine literature, and only in the active; it always has a figurative meaning (cf. John 1:5: the light shines in the darkness; John 5:35). In 1 John it is found only in this verse; cf. 2 Pet 1:19; Rev 18:23. The opposition between light and darkness is expressed in the two verbs: as φαίνειν belongs to the nature of light (cf. also the nonfigurative use for the sun in Rev 1:16, and for the moon in *Diogn.* 7.2), so παράγεσθαι belongs to the very nature of darkness.

23 The future eschatological intent is supported by the apocalyptic tradition. Thus the author of *1 Enoch* interprets the revelation of the future "secrets of righteousness" with these words: "it has become bright as the sun upon the dry ground, and darkness has passed away" (*1 Enoch* 58.5). The same notion motivates the Pauline parenesis in Rom 13:12: "The night is far gone, the day is near. Let us then lay aside the works of darkness." Cf. 1 Thess 5:1–11; Mark 13:33–37 par.

24 Klein ("Das wahre Licht," 276–77) also points to the chronological structure of the opposition of "light and darkness" in 1 John. Schnelle (*Antidocetic Christology,* 55–56) shows that no contradiction of the Fourth Gospel can be derived from this. It is too hypothetical to try to find a polemic against gnostic ideas of light in the expression "true light" (as does Bultmann, *Epistles,* 28 n. 21).

25 The word ἀδελφός is not found in 2 and 3 John in conjunction with the stem ἀγαπ-; nor is it found in that connection in the Fourth Gospel, where ἀδελφός appears only in 20:17 and 21:23, in a theological sense, as a designation for Jesus' disciples.

26 It is clear from 1 John 5:16 that in this writing ἀδελφός describes fellow Christians; thus also in 3 John 3, 5, 10 (with Brown, *Epistles,* 270; and against Bultmann, *Epistles,* 28; Balz, "Johannesbriefe," 172). By contrast, the supposition of many commentators (including Bultmann, *Epistles,* 28; Schnackenburg, *Epistles,* 107; Brown, *Epistles,* 289–90) that hatred of the brothers and sisters in 1 John primarily reflects a polemical situation is supported by no unequivocal statement in the text (see above, on 1:6).

15:12) or "loving the children of God."[27]

What is the relationship between love of God and love of the brothers and sisters? In 1 John, differently from the Fourth Gospel, both are demanded of Christians (cf. 4:19—5:3, esp. 4:21). On the one hand, love for God requires concrete expression in love of the sisters and brothers; the latter is the "perfection" of love of God (2:5–6; 4:12). On the other hand, love for the sisters and brothers may not be understood in a purely ethical sense: its foundation and rationale is the eschatological context, that is, the love of God (4:11). Love for the brothers and sisters is neither a substitute nor a proof, but rather the characteristic mark of love for God.[28] As this is the criterion of love for God, a special parenetical emphasis rests on it. Even the statement: "we know that we have passed from death to life because we love one another [lit.: 'the brothers and sisters']" (3:14) contains an ethical challenge and is not merely an ecclesial self-affirmation. This, however, shows that the realization of love of the sisters and brothers always presupposes the contrast embodied in the Johannine dialectic: life and death, including especially light and darkness. Thus one can make the equation that loving the brothers and sisters = being in light; the negative reversal means that hating the brothers and sisters = being in darkness.[29] The expression ἕως ἄρτι should be translated "still," "to this hour." This implies the idea of a temporal orientation of human existence. There is hope for human beings, namely, that darkness will also disappear and the true light shine for them.[30] At the same time it contains a parenetical statement that urges them to reject hatred of the brothers and sisters at the present time and to open themselves to love.

■ **10** Of those who love their brothers and sisters, one can say that they "abide in the light" (ἐν τῷ φωτὶ μένει). This expression corresponds to the ἐν τῷ φωτὶ εἶναι of v. 9a, as well as to ἐν αὐτῷ μένειν in 2:6, 27–28, which at the same time refers to turning away from sin (3:6). Those who

27 Cf. 1 John 5:2; the "children of God" are described in 5:1 as "born of God." Some commentators as early as Augustine refer the expression τὸν γεγεννημένον to Jesus Christ. Windisch and Preisker differ (*Die Katholischen Briefe*, 131). Brown is also of the opinion that this description, if it applied to Jesus, would be in the singular, and that the content of 5:2 makes such a translation impossible (*Epistles*, 535–36).

28 Cf. Schlier ("Bruderliebe," 241), who emphasizes the connection between love of God and love of the brothers and sisters when he says of the latter that it is "an outflowing of love for God and for Jesus which in turn is founded on the experience of God's love and that of Jesus." He describes it as a "transition from one way of being to another" (ibid., 244). "Thus in love for the brothers and sisters the love of the Father for the Son and the love of the Son for the Father reach their goal. In love for the brothers and sisters it is, ultimately, God who is love itself" (ibid., 245). To the detriment of the positive parenetical force of this concept, Schnackenburg (*Epistles*, 107) overstresses the polemical aspect of the injunction (although that is also a possibility): "Here, in 2:9–11, he [the author of 1 John] is indulging in polemics. Love of brother and sister is the essential prerequisite for fellowship with God." In contrast, see Weiss, *Briefe*, 51; Marinus de Jonge, *De brieven van Johannes* (2d ed.; Nijkerk: Callenbach, 1973) 85: "De liefde, waarover hij spreckt, is kennelijk zo stralend, dat zij alle hoat . . . uitsluit" ("The light of which he speaks is so brilliant that it dispels all hate"). For ὁ λέγων see above (on 2:6). Cf. also H. J. Wachs, "Johanneische Ethik" (diss., Kiel, 1952) 35; according to him love of the sisters and brothers is an "integrating aspect of love for God, and ἀλλήλους ἀγαπᾶν is a structural moment of πιστεύειν."

29 In what follows, hatred for the sisters and brothers can be identified with their murder (3:15: ἀνθρωποκτόνος); cf. John 8:44 ("He [the devil] was a murderer from the beginning"). Of the 40 NT occurrences of μισεῖν, 17 are in the Johannine corpus (12 times in the Fourth Gospel and 5 times in 1 John). The verb μισεῖν in the Johannine writings means "hate" or "not love." In the Fourth Gospel it mainly means "hate" (John 7:7 [bis]; 15:18, 19; 17:14), less often "not love" (John 12:25). Both meanings are possible in John 15:23, 24, 25. In contrast, the author of 1 John uses μισεῖν primarily in the sense of "not love" or "reject" (1 John 2:9, 11; 3:15; 4:20). 1 John 3:13 is different: it refers to the world's hatred of the community.

30 1 John 2:8. In accordance with this theological conception of 1 John, one should not regard ἕως ἄρτι as "an addition of the author to his Source" (Bultmann, *Epistles*, 28 n. 23) but as an expression of a far-reaching chronological intent. Cf. John 2:10; 5:17; 16:24 ("until now"). This presupposes the idea of linear time. Thus in 16:24 past time is delimited as "until now" by the fact that the disciples have not asked anything of Jesus in his name, but at this point they are encouraged: "Ask and you will receive." Cf. also Matt 11:12; 1 Cor 4:13; 8:7; 15:6.

practice the commandment of mutual love have the assurance of God's abiding within them (so also 4:12) and of themselves abiding in God (4:13, 15–16). In turn one can say of those who do not love their sisters and brothers that they "abide in death" (*μένει ἐν τῷ θανάτῳ*; 3:14). In the words of the verse under discussion, in such a one there is *σκάνδαλον*, just as the one who loves the brothers and sisters is described by the statement *σκάνδαλον ἐν αὐτῷ οὐκ ἔστιν*. The word *σκάνδαλον* appears only here in the Johannine writings (although the verb *σκανδαλίζειν* occurs in John 6:61; 16:1). The literal sense of "trap"[31] or "stumbling block" is used only metaphorically in the NT (Rom 11:9 with *παγίς* and *θήρα*). Elsewhere the word describes the "occasion of sin," or "leading astray" (Rom 14:13; Matt 16:23; and frequently elsewhere), or, as in the present case, what is "offensive," a "blemish."[32] Thus if there is no blemish in anyone who loves the sisters and brothers, such a one is removed from the realm of sin and belongs to the realm of light.[33]

■ **11** It is crucial that this paragraph concludes with an extended negative antithesis: *ὁ δὲ μισῶν τὸν ἀδελφὸν αὐτοῦ ἐν τῇ σκοτίᾳ ἐστίν*. One who hates a brother is like a blind person who cannot find his or her way. In accordance with the author's statement that it is his intention to lead the community away from sin (2:1), the emphasis lies on the demand that they not surrender to hatred but place themselves at love's disposal. It is significant that the negative expression *ἐν τῇ σκοτίᾳ ἐστίν*, an ontological description, is placed in parallel to the designation for ethical behavior (*ἐν τῇ σκοτίᾳ περιπατεῖ*); this corresponds to the epistemological determination *ἡ σκοτία ἐτύφλωσεν*.[34] The "darkness" is total; it encompasses being, way of life, and knowledge. Hatred of the brothers and sisters therefore marks those people who, apparently without hope of recourse, have fallen prey to the realm of darkness and cannot escape their situation by their own strength. This assertion is an immediate preparation for what follows, in which the starting point is again the redeemed situation of the community, and where it is presupposed that, for this community, the power of darkness has been broken.[35]

---

31 The older Greek form *σκανδάληθρον* refers to "the crooked piece of wood in the trap on which the bait is placed, and which, when the animal touches it, springs up and causes the trap to close" (Wilhelm Pape, *Griechisch-deutsches Handwörterbuch* [3 vols.; Braunschweig: Vieweg, 1849] 2:872); the word is used metaphorically in a *scholion* on Aristophanes *Acharnenses* 687. Since this concept belongs primarily to the world of hunters and in the realm of popular speech, written examples are scarce; cf. Gustav Stählin, "*σκάνδαλον*," *TDNT* 7 (1971) 339–40.

32 Cf. Jdt 5:20; in the same sense 1 Cor 1:23 (with *μωρία*) or Gal 5:11 (*τὸ σκάνδαλον τοῦ σταυροῦ*).

33 Correctly Schnackenburg, *Epistles*, 108; against Heinz Giesen, "*σκάνδαλον*," *EDNT* 3 (1993) 249–50; cf. also Wengst, *Brief*, 83.

34 The verb *τυφλόω* appears only here in 1 John, and once in the Fourth Gospel (John 12:40, in a quotation from Isa 6:9–10). Judith M. Lieu correctly points out that the idea of "blindness" found in 1 John is distinct from the christological orientation in the Fourth Gospel and that here the behavior of believers and of the community as a whole comes into view. According to Lieu ("Blindness in the Johannine Tradition," *NTS* 34 [1988] 91), what we have here is "an independent exegesis of Isa. 6:10 within the Johannine tradition," something that is certainly not to be ascribed to the author of 1 John.

35 On *ἀγάπη* and *ἀγαπᾶν*, see the excursus at 1 John 4:8.

2 **Concrete Ethical Demands**[1]

12 I am writing to you, little children, because
your sins are forgiven on account of his
name. 13/ I am writing to you, fathers,
because you know [the one] who is from
the beginning. I am writing to you, young
people, because you have conquered the
evil one. 14/ I write to you, children,
because you know the Father. I write to
you, fathers, because you know [the one]
who is from the beginning. I write to you,
young people, because you are strong
and the word of God abides in you, and
you have overcome the evil one. 15/ Do
not love the world or the things in the
world. The love of the Father is not in
those who love the world; 16/ for all that
is in the world—the desire of the flesh,
the desire of the eyes, the pride in
riches—comes not from the Father but
from the world. 17/ And the world and its
desire are passing away, but those who
do the will of God live forever.

With apparent abruptness, the author makes a new beginning, referring again to the fact of writing. But the terminology used is an express reference to what has preceded (τεκνία also in 2:1; for γράφω, cf. 1:4; 2:1, 7–8), and as for the content, the assertion that "your sins are forgiven on account of his name" connects with the christological statements in 1:7 and 2:1–2.[2] The christologically grounded, indicatively promised forgiveness of sins is the precondition for the imperative of *agapē*, and keeping the commandments is the mark of knowing God (2:2–3, 5–6). That the forgiveness of sins is already accomplished and that the faithful can look backward to it as well as to the Christ-event are recalled by the use of the perfect ἀφέωνται. This underscores the obligation to ethical behavior. Undoubtedly the accent in this section lies on this obligation (v. 15: μὴ ἀγαπᾶτε; v. 17: θέλημα τοῦ θεοῦ); hence it should be assigned to the parenesis that begins at 1:5. That 2:15–17 correspond to the overarching parenetical movement is an argument against the assignment of these last verses to "ecclesiastical redaction."[3]

■ **12–14** The structure of the first part is marked by a

1 Literature: Thomas Barrosse, "The Relationship of Love to Faith in St. John," *TS* 18 (1957) 538–59; Cernuda, "Engañan"; P. Koutlemanis, "Exegesis of 1 Jn 2,16," *DBM* (1976) 117–32; Noel Lazure, "La convoitise de la chair en I Jean II, 16," *RB* 76 (1969) 161–205; Bent Noack, "On I John 2,12–14," *NTS* 6 (1959/60) 236–41; Schlier, "Bruderliebe"; Eduard Schweizer, "Die hellenistische Komponente im neutestamentlichen Sarx-Begriff," *ZNW* 48 (1957) 237–53; Ceslas Spicq, "La place ou le rôle des jeunes dans certaines communautés néotestamentaires," *RB* 76 (1969) 508–27.

2 Of 231 instances of ὄνομα in the NT, 30 occur in the Johannine literature (following the Lukan corpus—with 34 in Luke's Gospel and 60 in Acts—and Revelation with 37 instances). Of those 30 Johannine occurrences, 25 are in the Gospel, 3 in 1 John, and 2 in 3 John. There is a parallel in content to 1 John 2:12 ("forgiveness of sins through [or: on account of] his name") in Acts 10:43, although there διά is construed with the genitive. Ὄνομα here stands for the Lord who has been preached in the community and who works in it, through whom sins are forgiven for all who believe in him. In John 15:21, where διά is found with the accusative, the subject is persecution for Christ's sake. In 1 John 2:12, as is frequently the case, "the person of Jesus is linked with his work as the revealer of God" (Lars Hartmann, "ὄνομα," *EDNT* 2 [1991] 519–22, at 520–21).

3 Against Bultmann, *Epistles*, 30–31, 32–33 and n. 17.

threefold repetition of γράφω (vv. 12–13) followed by a threefold ἔγραψα (v. 14). In the opinion of a great many exegetes, the shift from present to aorist should be seen as an authorial variation in style that has no significance as far as the content is concerned.[4] This could be confirmed by the ὅτι clauses, on which the real emphasis is placed, for there are extensive overlaps in content among them. Nevertheless, the shift in tense is striking. Nowhere else in the NT is the aorist ἔγραψα placed alongside the present tense; and, although it often has a literary function and, for example at the end of a letter, can refer to the letter just being concluded, it also refers to actual previous letters.[5] No doubt the text makes a more powerful impression if the aorist is not merely a stylistic variant here, but refers to one or more earlier writings, possibly 2 and 3 John.

One cannot object against this position that the statements of the ὅτι clauses in v. 14 are not found word for word in the older Johannine letters. Naturally, the author does not mean to quote the earlier writings; this is simply a reference to the letters as a group. In the author's opinion, 1 John proceeds on the same basis as the other letters and is determined by the same facts as 2 and 3 John: the readers have "recognized the truth" and it abides in them. This is also the foundation for the earlier Johannine letters, which, like this writing, lay claim to an eschatological compliance because of the definitive authority of the Johannine school. The existence of literal correspondences between 1 John and 2 John makes a mutual relationship still more probable.[6]

---

4 Thus Schnackenburg, *Epistles*, 118; Bultmann, *Epistles*, 31 ("stylistic variation"); Brown, *Epistles*, 297; Balz, "Johannesbriefe," 179; Dodd, *Epistles*, 38; Wengst, *Brief*, 88–89 ("rhetorical figure").

5 The variant γράφω (in 2:14), although it is found in numerous minuscules, is to be regarded as a smoothing of the well-attested ἔγραψα. In the NT, ἔγραψα can refer to the letter in which it is contained: Rom 5:15; 1 Cor 5:11 (νῦν δέ); Phlm 19, 21; 1 Pet 5:12. In each of these cases it is an "aorist of letter style," corresponding to ἀνέπεμψα in Phlm 1; cf. Acts 23:30; Eph 6:22, and frequently elsewhere (BDF § 334). It is also letter style when this expression refers only to a particular part of the letter at hand: Gal 6:11 (Paul's writing the conclusion of the letter with his own hand). In such cases, the accusative object ταῦτα can refer to the present letter: 1 Cor 9:15. This is also the case in 1 John 2:26 and 5:13. In NT usage, however, ἔγραψα frequently refers to an earlier letter. There can be no doubt that in 1 Cor 5:9 Paul refers with this expression to an earlier missive to the Corinthian community (cf. Conzelmann, *1 Corinthians: A Commentary on the First Epistle to the Corinthians* [trans. James W. Leitch; Hermeneia; Philadelphia: Fortress, 1975] 99; Hans Lietzmann, *An die Korinther I/II* [HNT 9; 4th ed.; Tübingen: Mohr (Siebeck), 1949] 24–25). The same is certainly true of 2 Cor 2:3–4, 9; 7:12 (cf. Hans Windisch, *Der zweite Korintherbrief* [KEK 6; 9th ed.; 1924, newly edited by Georg Strecker; Göttingen: Vandenhoeck & Ruprecht, 1970] 80); and also of 3 John 9 (see below). From this standpoint, the suggestion that 1 John 2:14 does not refer to this letter (1 John) but to earlier Johannine letters seems more plausible (so, among others, Brooke, *Epistles*, 41; Brown, *Epistles*, 297). More concretely along these lines, Hans Hinrich Wendt, following other scholars, has spoken in favor of a reference at this point to 2 John ("Die Beziehungen unseres ersten Johannesbriefes auf den zweiten," *ZNW* 21 [1922] 140–46). One cannot object against this thesis that "there is no identifiable passage in 2 or 3 John to which it can refer" (Schnackenburg, *Epistles*, 118), since such a sweeping assertion cannot be maintained (cf. n. 6 below), and the very generality of the statement in v. 14 prevents any conclusions about concrete topoi. It does seem probable that the shift between present (vv. 12–13) and aorist (v. 14) can be attributed to the author's pleasure in stylistic variation. As we saw in 1:1–4, however, the author has elsewhere deliberately introduced a shift in tenses in order to express different matters of content. It is no accident that, in what has preceded, only the present tense was used in referring to this letter (1:4; 2:5, 7–8; see also 2 John 5), just as in the rest of the NT the present γράφω refers to the letter in which it is contained. Cf. Gal 1:20; 1 Cor 4:14; 14:37; 2 Cor 13:10; 1 Tim 3:14; cf. 2 Pet 3:1.

6 Cf. 1 John 2:14a (ἐγνώκατε τὸν πατέρα) with 2 John 1–3 (οἱ ἐγνωκότες τὴν ἀλήθειαν . . . εἰρήνη παρὰ θεοῦ πατρὸς) and with 2 John 9 (ὁ μένων ἐν τῇ διδαχῇ, οὗτος καὶ τὸν πατέρα); 1 John 2:14b (ἐγνώκατε τὸν ἀπ' ἀρχῆς) with 2 John 5 (ἣν εἴχομεν ἀπ' ἀρχῆς); 1 John 2:14c (ἰσχυροί ἐστε καὶ ὁ λόγος τοῦ θεοῦ ἐν ὑμῖν μένει καὶ νενικήκατε τὸν πονηρόν) with 2 John 9–11 (ὁ μένων ἐν τῇ διδαχῇ οὗτος καὶ τὸν πατέρα—τοῖς πονηροῖς); also 1 John 2:21 (ἔγραψα . . . ὅτι . . . οἴδατε τὴν ἀλήθειαν) with 2 John 1 (οἱ ἐγνωκότες τὴν ἀλήθειαν); see above on 1 John 1:4 (parallel 2 John 12: ἵνα ἡ χαρὰ ἡμῶν πεπληρωμένη ᾖ). On the relationship of 1 John to 2 and 3 John, see also the Introduction: Exegesis of 1 John above.

If the earlier Johannine letters are in the background here, one could be moved to conclude that the same author is writing, and addressing the same audience as in 2 John.[7] It is true that, for reasons of time alone, this idea cannot be developed fully. But it is certainly possible that the author of 1 John intends at this point to emphasize the connection between this writing and the older, "presbyterial" tradition of the Johannine school, and that the author is equating his authority with that of the presbyter, or tracing it to that earlier leader.[8]

The conclusion thus drawn does not say that the audience of 1 John can be assumed to be the same as the addressees of 2 and 3 John. Instead, the address *τεκνία* (2:1, 12, 28; 3:7, 18; 4:4; 5:21; cf. John 13:33), here interchangeable with *παιδία* (2:14, 18; cf. John 21:5), indicates that the Johannine circle has grown beyond the limits presumed in 2 John—a different conclusion from that to be drawn from the designation *τέκνον* in 2 John 1, 4, 13, and 3 John 4. The form of address expresses a deliberately emphasized distance between the author and the readers, appropriate to the author's unstated claim to authority, and is not restricted to readers in a single congregation. It includes all Christians who will permit themselves to be addressed by this homily.[9] Accordingly, the words *τεκνία* and *παιδία* function as summary concepts (vv. 12a, 14a), and only afterward will a distinction be drawn between two groups within the community, the *πατέρες* and the *νεανίσκοι*.[10] Here it is the men, not the women, who are the true representatives of community life, just as in 3 John only men are mentioned as conversation partners for the presbyter. The address to the members of the Christian communities as a whole, and then to the two age groups, reveals that what the author has in mind is not a catalog of status groups in the household, but a list of groups in the congregation.[11]

That the ecclesial interest dominates the community order is also evident from the six *ὅτι* clauses, some of

7 Thus Brown, *Epistles*, 19: "In this commentary, although I recognize that it cannot be proved, I shall work with the hypothesis that the same author wrote the Johannine Epistles."

8 The precondition for such an equation is that the author regards the presbyter as an eye- and ear-witness. Perhaps already here the presbyter John of Asia Minor is identified with the apostle of the same name, to which Irenaeus later testifies. See also the remarks in the Introduction, p. xxxviii.

9 The case is similar with the addresses *ἀδελφοί* (3:13) and *ἀγαπητοί* (2:7; 3:2, 21; 4:1, 7, 11).

10 Both these concepts appear uniquely at this point in the Johannine corpus. They are not rhetorical expressions covering all Christians (against Dodd, *Epistles*, 38: "The threefold arrangement is probably not much more than a rhetorical figure"). For distinctions drawn by mention of age, see Aristophanes of Byzantium. 4, *λέξεις* frg. 1. Plutarch (*De se ipsum citra invidiam laudando* 544E) gives as an example of the virtue of praising oneself the choral song of the Spartans on festival days: "Therefore in the Spartan choruses the old men (*τῶν γερόντων*) sing: 'Time was when we were valiant youths (*νεανίαι*)'; the boys (*τῶν παίδων*) sing: 'so we shall be, and braver far'; and the young men (*νεανίσκων*): 'so now we are: you need but look.'"

11 According to Windisch and Preisker (*Die Katholischen Briefe*, 115), this is "a kind of household order [*Haustafel*]"; thus also Karl Heinrich Rengstorf, *Mann und Frau im Urchristentum* (Arbeitsgemeinschaft für Forschung des Landes Nordrhein-Westfalen 12; Cologne: Westdeutscher Verlag, 1954) 24. But the "community order" here is very different from the NT household orders transmitted in Col 3:18—4:1 and Eph 5:22—6:9. These latter are parenetical listings oriented to the duties of the members of the Christian household. Their structure is determined by three pairs arranged in ascending order: women and men; children and fathers; slaves and masters. In each case, the weaker member is placed first, and the two are reciprocally related. The whole structure is determined by the purpose to admonish both sets of groups. The socially dominant position of the master of the house is presupposed. There is a parallel in 1 Pet 2:13—3:7, although that text first speaks of Christian obligations toward the state, so that it is not so much a "household order" as it is a "social-ethical primer of duties." 1 John 2:12–14 also stands within a parenetical context; even though the readers being addressed are praised for their possession of salvation, (ethical) demands placed on the Christian community furnish the overall perspective. This also emerges from the subsequent v. 15 (*μὴ ἀγαπᾶτε τὸν κόσμον*). That the language is Johannine and that the other members in the Christian household order are not mentioned make clear that this community order is entirely determined by the Johannine idea of groups within the Christian community. For literature on this point, see Karl Weidinger, *Die Haustafeln* (UNT 14; Leipzig: Hinrichs, 1928); Eduard Schweizer, *Der Brief an die Kolosser* (EKKNT 12; 2d ed.; Zurich: Benziger, 1980); Georg Strecker, "Haustafeln," *EKL*^{3} 2 (1988) 392–93; idem, "Die

which contain identical wording. They each express in the indicative the situation of having been redeemed that is presupposed for the members of the congregation. The interpretation of the particle ὅτι is disputed; it can be read either as causal or as explanatory. If one supposes an explanatory sense ("that"), the ὅτι clause describes the content of what the author is writing to the readers. This is analogous to the combination of ἀγγελία with ὅτι in 1:5, where the ὅτι clause describes the object of proclamation. Although one can thus see that this is a possible interpretation, it can scarcely be verified by positing that the author is addressing a "demoralized audience" and that, by pointing out the fact of their salvation, he is trying to protect them from falling prey to the theology of the false teachers,[12] since nothing is said in this context about false teaching.

In fact, the causal interpretation ("because") is no less likely. In that case, the writing would not be motivated so much by an acute crisis as by the fact that the readers are members of the Christian community and therefore are receptive to the author's words. In favor of this interpretation is not only that the church fathers and the Latin tradition support it,[13] but also that 2:21 (the only other passage in the NT in which the verb γράφειν precedes a ὅτι clause) requires a causal interpretation.[14] If this interpretation is correct, the author is not concerned to distinguish between a variety of individual teachings that are partly known to the readers and partly unknown. Instead, the writing is motivated by the fact that the readers are already redeemed. This is also the case in the earlier part of the text, where it is clear that both the author and the community are aware that they are shaped by a saving event, purified by the atoning effect of Jesus' death (1:7, 9), and claimed by the word of God (1:10; 2:5). Therefore for Greek readers there is no profound difference between the causal and the explanatory interpretations of ὅτι.[15] In neither case is the author referring to particular dogmatic teachings, but in general terms to the salvation that is presupposed in the Christian community; and in both cases the redeemed existence of Christians is understood as something unfinished. This is evident in our text when it is read in connection with the immediately preceding contrast between light and darkness. Christians live in a field of dialectical tension. The salvation that has been received can still be lost, namely, if darkness gains the upper hand and finds its expression in a hatred of the brothers and sisters that destroys the community. For that reason it will be necessary, in what follows, to urge the readers not to submit to the law of the world but instead to carry out the commandment of love (vv. 15–17). This is the background for the author's indirect encouragement, whether it be addressed causally to the past or as explanation to the present life of the congregation. The community should feel assured of the redeemed status that has been promised to it and that has been accomplished in Christ. It is by that very status that it should allow itself to be shaped and determined in the present. It is subject to the obligatory demand: "Be what you are!"

Given that the passage is dominated by an ecclesial orientation, the groups of readers who are addressed by it can be materially distinguished only in part. Thus it is no accident that it is said that the πατέρες know the one who is ἀπ' ἀρχῆς (vv. 13a, 14b), which probably refers to Jesus,[16] and that the transmission of the tradition appears to be entrusted to the wisdom of the "fathers"; nor that the παιδία are addressed as those who know the

neutestamentlichen Haustafeln (Kol 3,18—4,1 und Eph 5,22—6,9" in Helmut Merklein, ed., *Neues Testament und Ethik: Für Rudolf Schnackenburg* (Freiburg: Herder, 1989) 349–75.

12 Brown, *Epistles*, 301; those supporting an explanatory meaning also include Schnackenburg, *Epistles*, 116; Balz, "Johannesbriefe," 173; Malatesta, *Interiority and Covenant*, 166.

13 Augustine: "quia" (*PL* 35.1988); Vulgate: "quoniam" and "quia."

14 See below, on 2:21.

15 Cf. I. Howard Marshall, *The Epistles of John* (NICNT; reprinted, Grand Rapids: Eerdmans, 1979) 136–37: "Greek readers did not make the sharp distinction between the two uses of the conjunction which springs to the mind of the grammarian."

16 After v. 12b (τὸ ὄνομα αὐτοῦ), τὸν ἀπ' ἀρχῆς in v. 13a should probably be interpreted to mean Jesus; this corresponds to ἐκεῖνος in v. 6 and ἐν αὐτῷ in v. 8, especially in light of the Johannine idea of preexistence (cf. 1:1). In any case it is clear that the author does not wish to separate Jesus from the Father; see below.

πατήρ, so that the relationship of fathers and children is projected farther. But the parallelism of the two sentences (v. 14a, b) already reveals that, following the fundamental christological and soteriological assertion in v. 12b, which in itself has a comprehensive character, the author wishes to convince the readers that they are defined by the all-encompassing reality of the saving event. There is no playing off of a "theological" against a "christological" interpretation, for knowledge of the Father is impossible without the Son (cf. 4:15–16). The "gnosis" presupposed for these readers is not connected to any theory of the world's origins, as was characteristic of the advanced Christian gnostic systems in the second century, and it does not imply any physical-ontological meaning; what it does mean is a sharing in the event of the revelation in Christ, namely, the acceptance of the forgiveness of sins that is effected by the Father in the Son (cf. 1:7–9).

One must interpret the statement about the νεανίσκοι on this same basis. That they have conquered the "evil one" (πονηρός, v. 13b) is not only repeated in the same words in v. 14c, but more fully elaborated in the phrase "you are strong" (ἰσχυροί ἐστε). By their conquest of the evil one they have shown both their strength and the fact that the "word of God" (λόγος τοῦ θεοῦ) abides in them.[17] With this last statement, the concrete reference to the young men is dropped again and the fundamental ecclesial scope is resumed, so that the author can say of all the members of the community that the evil one has no power over them (5:18; cf. 4:4).

■ **15-16** Any division of these verses from those preceding would be artificial. They continue the parenesis, now in the form of direct admonition. The address to the community as a whole and the orientation to fundamental principles remain the same. The victory over the evil one (v. 14c) is the same thing as victory over the world (4:4–5). Both the devil[18] and the world are powers inimical to God that are overcome in faith (5:4–5). Under these circumstances, the injunction not to love the world or the things in it (μὴ ἀγαπᾶτε τὸν κόσμον μηδὲ τὰ ἐν τῷ κόσμῳ) expresses a necessary consequence that must be accepted by believers.[19] If "love of God" (ἀγάπη τοῦ θεοῦ) is God's care for human beings and the love of human beings for God, and if it implies the coming into existence of a community with ontological characteristics,[20] then love of the world (ἀγαπᾶν τὸν κόσμον) describes the orientation of human beings toward the world and at the same time a natural relationship between the world and the human. Because the world is defined by the evil one, the worldly way of being excludes community with the Father (v. 15b). This is especially apparent in human beings' unethical behavior. Anyone who lives "in the world" (ἐν τῷ κόσμῳ) and is, at the same time, "of the world" (ἐκ τοῦ κόσμου),[21] is ruled

17 Although ὁ λόγος τοῦ θεοῦ is found only at this point in the Johannine letters, the witness of Codex Vaticanus and the Sahidic translation (= ὁ λόγος) cannot claim priority; all the less so since the combination with the personal pronoun is found elsewhere in 1 John (1:10: ὁ λόγος αὐτοῦ; cf. 2:5) and presumes the same notion. According to Haenchen ("Neuere Literatur," 278), the young men have conquered the evil one "simply through their holding fast to the true confession of faith." He points to the supposed polemic against the Gnostics in this context (2:7–12) that then appears openly in 2:18–27. The case is similar with 3:14 ("we have passed from death to life"): this is said to be a contrast to the Gnostics who are leaving the community. In any case, the true mark of genuine Christianity consists in an ethical way of life *and* in the true confession of faith (cf. 2:22; 4:15–16).

18 Ὁ πονηρός (vv. 13b, 14c) is the devil, as in 3:12; 5:18; cf. 3:8, 10 (διάβολος); also John 17:15; Matt 13:19; Eph 6:16; 2 Thess 2:3.

19 That the imperative μὴ ἀγαπᾶτε means "do not love . . . in the sense of Christian ἀγάπη" is evident from its negation and from its material reference to the world. (This is said in response to Bultmann, *Epistles*, 33 n. 19, according to whom the basis here is simply the common Greek expression in the sense of "take a fancy to.")

20 Cf. "being from God" at 3 John 11; 1 John 3:9–10; 4:1–6; John 8:47, and frequently elsewhere; on the "love of God" otherwise, see the remarks on 2:5 above.

21 Of the 186 occurrences of κόσμος in the NT, 102 are in the Johannine literature (Gospel 78 times; 1 John 23 times; 3 John once). Κόσμος is understood in a positive sense in 1 John 2:2; 4:9, 14 (cf. John 3:16); here κόσμος is the object of salvation. There is a neutral meaning in 1 John 4:3, while in 1 John 2:15 the author uses the word in a negative sense. On this, cf. Schnackenburg, *Epistles*, 123: "[Ἐκ with the genitive] does not denote origin, but as often in John, nature" (cf. ibid., 125–58, excursus 6, "The 'World' in 1 John 2:15–17"); however, on p. 126 he continues, "The 'world' is *not inherently* corrupt like

by that which belongs to the world: ἐπιθυμία,[22] the state of being dominated by physical urges, no matter whether these are produced by σάρξ,[23] the human body with its desires, or through the eyes, when ἐπιθυμία is initiated by visual stimuli. Also in the realm of "the world" is ἀλαζονεία τοῦ βίου, "the pride in riches."[24] In addition, such behavior is subject to condemnation because in this situation human beings are not open to God. Rather, they interpret themselves in terms of the world: they make the world absolute and acknowledge it as the final arbiter, beyond which nothing else has any validity.

■ **17** In this verse, the contrast is given a content by way of explanation, while at the same time a rationale is offered for what has preceded.[25] Domination by physical urges is, like the world itself, transitory. In saying this, the author is not interested in proposing a philosophical thesis, motivated by the notion of creation or something on that order. Instead, this is a conclusion drawn from empirical experience that worldly existence is ephemeral.[26] It follows, then, from the alternative "from the world" (ἐκ τοῦ κόσμου) or "from the Father" (ἐκ τοῦ πατρός), that whoever belongs to God also has a share in

the evil one." Hence this applies with regard to the positive occurrences of the word, but does not preclude the numbering of the κόσμος among the powers inimical to God in 1 John (1 John 5:4–5). Cf. Philo, fragment in John Damascene, *Sacra Parallela* (Jacobus Wettstein, *Novum Testamentum Graece* [Graz: Akademische Druck- und Verlagsanstalt, 1962] 2.715, on 1 John 2:15): "It is impossible that love for the world can be present at the same time as love for God, just as it is impossible for light and darkness to be present together" (from the German translation by G. Seelig). There is a similar formulation in Philo *Decal.* 120.

22 Within the Johannine corpus, ἐπιθυμία occurs only here and in v. 17, while ἐπιθυμέω κτλ. does not occur at all. As in Eph 2:3 and 2 Pet 2:18, ἐπιθυμία has a negative meaning: desire for what is forbidden. The genitive describes the origin and location of the ἐπιθυμία (τῆς σαρκός = of the flesh; cf. also *Barn.* 10.9; *Did.* 1.4) or the general idea of belonging (τῶν ὀφθαλμῶν = of the eyes; cf. also *T. Reub.* 2.4; Philo *Decal.* 153; *2 Clem.* 17.3); BAGD 293. Dio depicts Diogenes the Cynic, in a conversation with Alexander the Great, as describing the three forms of life into which a person can fall through irrational impulse and accident. The first is submission to pleasures and immersion in all sensual enjoyments, the second is wealth and riches, and the third is honor and fame (Dio Chrysostom *Or.* 4.83–84). In Lucian *Hermot.* 22, the vices that prevent people from living a common life in peace and harmony are called gold, pleasures, and honors (similarly *Hermot.* 7).

23 The concept of σάρξ in a nonchristological sense occurs only here in the Johannine Letters; it has a different meaning than that presumed by the Pauline formula κατὰ σάρκα (but see also John 8:15). Although Paul understood it differently from the usage in the Johannine circle, as "powers" (Bultmann, *Theology,* 1.244), here "being flesh" means the human being in its createdness and mortality and describes the realm of human existence (cf. 1 John 4:2 and 2 John 7, as well as Gal 2:20; Phil 1:22; Phlm 16). Eduard Schweizer ("Die hellenistische Komponente im neutestamentlichen Sarx-Begriff," *ZNW* 48 [1957] 237–53) has attempted to discover the roots of the negative understanding of σάρξ in the Hellenistic realm. Certainly, the interpretation of "flesh" in the sense of weakness and contrast with God (Isa 40:6–8) occurs also in the OT. Noel Lazure ("La convoitise de la chair en I Jean II, 16," *RB* 76 [1969] 161–205) asserts that the background of the concept of σάρξ in 1 John 2:16 is to be sought within Judaism. On this, see also 1QH x.22–23.

24 Βίος is not restricted to food, but includes everything that is part of the necessities of life; cf. 3:17. The concept of ἀλαζονεία is found elsewhere in the NT only in Jas 4:16; the adjective ἀλαζόνες is in Rom 1:30; 2 Tim 3:2. In Wis 5:8, ἀλαζονεία also describes "boasting in riches" and characterizes (in combination with ὑπερήφανος) the attitude of pride and self-satisfaction.

25 It is questionable whether καί is to be taken as adversative ("but"), as Schnackenburg writes (*Epistles,* 115). In opposition to this it may be said that v. 17 contains an independent antithesis (transitoriness of the world vs. eternal life for those who do God's will), and that the nothingness of the world was already described in the preceding verse. Accordingly, v. 17 provides a further explanation of what has gone before, and καί should be seen as a conjunctive particle ("and").

26 For παράγεται ("it passes away," "it dies"), see also 2:8; 1 Cor 7:31 (intransitive).

God's existence and eternal life. This is illustrated in the doing of the "will of God" (θέλημα τοῦ θεοῦ), which means the works of love (v. 10). Love for the brothers and sisters effects a sharing in eternal life. No matter how much the concepts are used in formulaic fashion in this context,[27] one should not dispute that the author is concerned primarily with historical, rather than ontological, fact. The transitoriness of the world is to be understood in light of the end of the world, when the "abiding" of faith will also be revealed. The apocalyptic horizon, which 1 John does not reject (cf. 2:8, 28 and frequently elsewhere), also motivates the maintaining of a critical distance from the world. Nevertheless, the focus of the argument rests on the immediately necessary separation between God and the world, and hence on the eschatological decisions that must be made in the community today, so that it may follow the way of love. It is no accident that this statement stands at the end of a parenetical section. While the warning in v. 17 is indirect, it is still heavily emphasized.

27 The expression εἰς τὸν αἰῶνα/εἰς αἰῶνα is found in inscriptions. On this, see Wilhelm Dittenberger, *Sylloge inscriptionum graecarum* (3d ed.; 4 vols.; Leipzig: Hirzel, 1915–24; reprinted Hildesheim: Olms, 1960) 815.50 (2.508); idem, *Orientis graeci inscriptiones selectae* (2 vols.; Leipzig: Hirzel, 1903–5; reprinted Hildesheim: Olms, 1960) 194.35 (1.279); 332.33 (1.517); 515.56 (2.164). The formula occurs frequently in the Johannine writings (John 4:14; 6:51, 58; 8:35, 51, 52; 10:28; 11:26; 12:34; 13:8; 14:16; 2 John 2) and refers to an unlimited time, as characteristic for existence in God.

2 False Teaching[1]

18 **Children, it is the last hour! As you have**
heard that antichrist is coming, so now
many antichrists have come. From this
we know that it is the last hour. 19/ They
went out from us, but they did not belong
to us; for if they had belonged to us, they
would have remained with us. But by
going out they made it plain that none of
them belongs to us [RSV: that they all are
not of us]. 20/ But [or: And] you have
been anointed by the Holy One, and all of
you have knowledge. 21/ I write to you,
not because you do not know the truth,
but because you know it, and [you know
that] no lie comes from the truth. 22/
Who is the liar but the one who denies
that Jesus is the Christ? This is the
antichrist, the one who denies the Father
and the Son. 23/ No one who denies the
Son has the Father; everyone who
confesses the Son has the Father also.
24/ Let what you heard from the
beginning abide in you. If what you heard
from the beginning abides in you, then
you will abide in the Son and in the
Father. 25/ And this is what he has
promised us, eternal life. 26/ I write
these things to you concerning those
who would deceive you. 27/ As for you,
the anointing that you received from
[God] abides in you, and so you do not
need anyone to teach you. But as [God's]
anointing teaches you about all things,
and is true and is not a lie, and just as it
has taught you, abide in [him/it].

There is a clear starting point for this section: nothing has been said up to this point, *expressis verbis*, about false teaching. Moreover, the exegesis has shown that there is no probable reason to deduce any polemic posture on the author's part in the text that immediately precedes it.[2] Therefore, v. 18 is a new beginning. This is also clear from the fact that, in both form and content, the parenesis is dropped and a more dogmatic and theoretical instruction is presented. Only with the concluding μένετε (v. 27) is the parenesis resumed; this forms a

1 Literature: Wilhelm Bousset, *The Antichrist Legend: A Chapter in Christian and Jewish Folklore* (trans. with prologue on the Babylonian dragon myth by A. H. Keene; Satanism series; London: Hutchinson, 1896); Hermann Hanse, *"Gott haben" in der Antike und im frühen Christentum* (RVV 27; Berlin: Töpelmann, 1939) 104–8; Ignace de la Potterie, "L'onction du chrétien par la foi," *Bib* 40 (1959) 12–59.

2 Even Bultmann (*Epistles*, 30), who agrees with Schnackenburg and others in applying the previous section to the problem of heresy, admits that 2:15–17, as "a traditional piece of parenesis, . . . has nothing to do with the problem of the false teaching endangering the Christian congregation."

transition to what follows. The next section extends from 2:28 to 3:24 and is defined throughout by a directly or indirectly imperative address to the Christian community. This is true even of the so-called intervening section in 2:28—3:3; it not only contains a "positive presentation of the hope of salvation"[3] but also ties into the parenetic context by the challenge to abide "in him" (2:28) and to purify oneself "just as he is pure" (3:3).

This instruction is aimed against the false teaching, or more precisely, the preaching of the *ἀντίχριστοι* who are endangering the existence of the community (vv. 18–21).[4] The author describes their preaching as questioning that Jesus is "the Christ," and as a denial of the Father and the Son (vv. 22–25). There follows the concluding reference to the *χρῖσμα* the community has received, which will teach them rightly and in which they are to abide (vv. 26–27).[5] The description of the false teaching remains relatively vague. There is no detailed explanation of what is meant by denial of Jesus' being Christ, that is, his being the Anointed. Only in the course of the writing will more concrete details be added (4:2: "that Jesus Christ has come in the flesh"; cf. 4:1–6; 5:6). This matches the structure of 1 John, whose "primordial cell" is at the beginning (1:5—2:27), while the subsequent sections afford an increasing concretization—although this should not be a reason to regard them as secondary additions.[6] The same is true of other thematic fields. Thus "love of the brothers and sisters" is treated not only in 2:7–11 but also in 3:10–18 and 4:7–21. Such repetitions can be interpreted as the reflection of discussions within the Johannine school that were worked into the document by the author as additional material, or as the author's own developing meditations. Within the framework of 1 John they should be seen as a unity, since the author, as final redactor, identifies with them. Consequently, they should be taken into consideration in the treatment of each of the various themes reflected in them.[7]

■ **18** The address *παιδία*[8] ("children") formally emphasizes that this verse introduces a new section; as in v. 14, *παιδία* describes the whole community. What is substantially new in the following passage is introduced by the statement that "it is the last hour" (*ἐσχάτη ὥρα ἐστίν*). This is the only occurrence of this expression in the NT. The "last hour" describes an eschatological moment. It is not identified in terms of salvation history,[9] but is to be understood in a future eschatological sense, that is, apocalyptically. It is no accident that the next section begins with a reference to the future parousia of Christ (v. 28). Similarly, in the Fourth Gospel *ὥρα*, besides being a common reference to time,[10] and in addition to the christologically interpreted "hour" of Jesus,[11] can also have a future aspect. This applies to the biographical and to the church-historical lapse of time,[12] but also to a future apocalyptic event.[13] This is the place for the apocalyptic term "last day" (*ἐσχάτη ἡμέρα*), which in the Fourth Gospel refers to the future resurrection (John 6:39–40, 44, 54; 11:24) or to the final judgment (John 12:48).[14]

The term *ἀντίχριστος* also stems from apocalyptic tradition. The author knows it from Johannine traditions and uses it several times here. It is also found in 2 John

3 Thus Schnackenburg, *Epistles*, 130.

4 With Schnackenburg, *Epistles*, 17–19, one should distinguish the pneumatic disturbances that upset the order of community life in Corinth (1 Corinthians 12—14) from the faith-threatening views of the antichrists in 1 John, which are expressed in teaching. On the concept and imagery of the *ἀντίχριστος*, see the following discussion and that on 2 John 7 (excursus: "The Antichrist").

5 The word *χρῖσμα* appears in the NT only in this and the following verse (2:27). The use of *χρίειν* is more frequent, at least in imitation of OT usage: Luke 4:18; Acts 4:27; 10:38.

6 Cf. Bultmann, *Epistles*, 43. It can scarcely be thought accurate to say that the original writing ended with 2:27 and that the subsequent sections contain no new ideas (see only the motif of *ἐλπίς* and the problem of penance); on this, see below (on 2:28—3:24).

7 See below on 2:28; 4:1ff.

8 The use of the diminutive form *παιδία* (cf. John 16:21), like the use of *τεκνία* (see the discussion of 2:1), makes clear that the author regards himself as a "respected person," one "who feels himself on terms of fatherly intimacy with those whom he addresses" (BAGD 604); cf. 2:14; 3:7 *v.l.*; John 21:5.

9 Against Schnackenburg, *Epistles*, 132.

10 John 1:39; 4:6, 52–53; 5:35; 11:9; 19:14, 27.

11 John 2:4; 7:30; 8:20; 12:23, 27; 13:1; 17:1; cf. 5:35 (*πρὸς ὥραν*), and frequently elsewhere.

12 See the previous note, and also John 4:21, 23; 16:2, 4, 21, 25, 32.

13 Cf. 16:25; as the hour of the rising of the dead: 5:25, 28–29.

14 As a parallel term, both in language and content, see

7,[15] but not in the rest of the NT. The oldest patristic example, Polycarp *Phil.* 7.1, is dependent on 1 John 4:2–3, either on the basis of the letter itself or from oral tradition. That the antichrist will come is a piece of teaching already known to the community, as the phrase καθὼς ἠκούσατε ("as you have heard") indicates. The mythological figure of the antichrist belongs to the oldest layer of the traditions of the Johannine circle. As 2 John 7 implies, it has been demythologized at this point by being applied to a historical situation. The false teachers who are appearing in great numbers in the community at the present time are interpreted as ἀντίχριστοι. (This is the only appearance of this word in the plural.) Such an interpretation is not only a historicization of a "mythical figure,"[16] but in turn shapes people's understanding of history. The community's own story is being played out in the immediate context of apocalyptic events of the end time.[17] The appearance of the antichrists is a criterion by which the community may recognize that the end time has begun, and they must prepare themselves for the end.

■ **19** The nature of the false teachers is described in typical Johannine rhetoric. Their origin is the Christian community, probably the Johannine circle.[18] Opposition to the presbyter's realistic position could have occasioned the beginnings of a competing, docetic christology, something that is characteristic of the false teaching. This gives us a glimpse of the history of the Johannine school. At the time of the writing of 1 John and the Fourth Gospel, the core of the group had settled on a moderate "ecclesiastical" position. The competing docetic wing from which they were trying to distance themselves was probably somewhat older. These teachers had themselves emerged from the Johannine commu-

---

the Qumran expression קץ אחרון = καιρὸς ἔσχατος (1QS iv.16–17; 1QpHab vii.7, 12). The absence of the article with ἐσχάτη ὥρα in v. 18 is characteristic of definitions and presumes that the expression is understood as a *terminus technicus*, since obviously the author is thinking of "the" last hour; cf. BDF § 252. Is the religio-historically "unique" combination of ὥρα with ἐσχάτη to be regarded as a secondary expansion of the Johannine concept of the ὥρα, as Klein ("Das wahre Licht," 291–304) believes? This judgment presumes that the parallel idea of the ἐσχάτη ὥρα in the Fourth Gospel is to be attributed to the "ecclesiastical redaction" (in John 6:39–40, 44, 54; 12:48: see Bultmann, *John*, 219–20, 345 n. 6; Jürgen Becker, "Wunder und Christologie: zum literarischen und christologischen Problem der Wunder im Johannesevangelium," *NTS* 16 [1969/70] 130–48, at 145 n. 4). This claim, however, is disputed (cf. Kümmel, *Introduction*, 209; Schnackenburg, *Epistles*, 133; undecided are Luise Schottroff, "Heil als innerweltliche Entwicklung: Der gnostische Hintergrund der johanneischen Vorstellung vom Zeitpunkt der Erlosung," *NovT* 11 [1969] 294–317, at 299; Ferdinand Hahn, "Der Prozess Jesu nach dem Johannesevangelium," *EKK Vorarbeiten* 2 [1970] 23–96, at 91 n. 34). The rejection of the apocalyptic expectation of the "last day" in John 11:24 shows that this idea was not unknown to the Johannine circle. We here encounter a basic current in Johannine tradition that probably spoke, at an early stage, of both ἐσχάτη ὥρα and ἐσχάτη ἡμέρα.

15 On this, see the excursus "The Antichrist," at 2 John 7.

16 Bultmann, *Epistles*, 36. Contrary to the opinion of Büchsel (*Johannesbriefe*, 37–38) and Christian Lindskrog (*Fortolkning til første Johannesbrev* [Copenhagen: Gyldendal 1941] 49), one may not conclude from the plural ἀντίχριστοι that the opponents had described themselves as "Christs."

17 According to 4:1 "many false prophets" have come into the world. Since these are identified with "the" antichrist, these are the same opponents presumed by 2:18. An apocalyptic aspect interpreted in terms of the present can be deduced from the statement that the antichrist "is already in the world" (4:3). Obviously the expression πολλοὶ ψευδοπροφῆται does not indicate that the author is combating a great number of different false teachings. That what we have here is a common topos in early Christian parenesis is indicated by the NT occurrences of ψευδοπροφήτης: Matt 7:15; 24:21, 24; Mark 13:22; Luke 6:26; Acts 13:6; 2 Peter 2; Rev 16:13; 19:20; 20:10.

18 Cf. 1 John 4:1 (πολλοὶ ψευδοπροφῆται ἐξεληλύθασιν εἰς τὸν κόσμον) and 2 John 7 (πολλοὶ πλάνοι ἐξῆλθον εἰς τὸν κόσμον).

nity, but their true nature has now become visible; they were never really part of the community.[19] It is of the nature of the Christian community that its members remain together and maintain the unity of the group. The destruction of church unity makes the nature of the false teachers as antichrists evident; moreover, it shows that not all who count themselves as members of the community really belong to it.[20]

■ **20** In contrast, the readers of 1 John have the *χρῖσμα ἀπὸ τοῦ ἁγίου* ("anointing from the Holy One"). The genitive can be interpreted in two ways: (1) anointing by God (or Jesus).[21] This interpretation is favored by v. 27 (*ἀπ' αὐτοῦ* = God or Jesus), as well as by the fact that in John 17:11 God is called "holy" and in John 6:69 Jesus is "the holy one of God." Or (2) it may refer to anointing by the Holy Spirit. The adjective *ἅγιος* occurs with *πνεῦμα* in John 1:33; 14:26; 20:22, and the same "ecclesiastical" notion exists in 1 John, which speaks of the "Spirit of God" (4:2) or the "spirit of truth" (4:6; cf. John 14:17). Although there is a grammatical distinction, there is really no contradiction between the two possible interpretations, for the divinely effected anointing[22] has the

19 The construction in v. 19b is "present contrary to fact." It reveals a characteristic difference from the classical construction (*εἰ* with imperfect indicative, and imperfect indicative with *ἄν*). Here, by the use of the pluperfect *μεμενήκεισαν*, the principal clause is given an orientation to past time. The author apparently intends a statement about the present in the *εἰ* clause: the false teachers do not belong to the community (although their origin is within the Johannine community: v. 19a). In the principal clause he expresses a fact from the past: the false teachers did not remain with us; hence they had separated from the community even before the writing of 1 John (against Bultmann, *Epistles*, 36, according to whom the false teachers still "understand themselves as legitimate members of the congregation"; and Vielhauer, *Geschichte*, 470). Cf. BDF § 360, 4; with more nuance Radermacher, *Neutestamentliche Grammatik*, 159; esp. Raphael Kühner and Bernhard Gerth, *Ausführliche Grammatik der griechischen Sprache* (2 vols.; 4th ed.; Leverkusen: Gottschalk, 1955) 2.471 § 574 ("While the condition applies to the present, the possibility of its being fulfilled belongs to the past, since the nonfulfillment has already been determined"). One must note the distinction between *ἐξ ἡμῶν ἐξέρχεσθαι* and *ἐξ ἡμῶν εἶναι*. The first is a description of historical origin (see the use of *ἐξέρχεσθαι* in a spatial sense also in 1 John 4:1; 2 John 7; 3 John 7; differently in the statement about the nature of the revealer in John 8:42: *ἐκ τοῦ θεοῦ*; cf. 13:3; 16:27–28, 30; 17:8). This refers to the (place of) origin and is used here in contrast to the existential statement that describes their nature; this latter is expressed through such combinations as *εἶναι ἐκ θεοῦ* (1 John 3:10; 4:4, 6; 5:19; 3 John 11; John 8:47), *ἐκ τοῦ πατρός* (1 John 2:16), *ἐκ τῆς ἀληθείας* (1 John 2:21; John 18:37). In the Fourth Gospel, statements about the origin and the nature of the Revealer are identical: he is *ἐκ τῶν ἄνω* (John 8:23; cf. 3:31: *ἄνωθεν*), that is, *ἐκ τοῦ θεοῦ* (John 8:42; cf. 7:17) or *παρὰ τοῦ πατρός* (John 16:28). On the negative side of Johannine dualistic anthropology, this terminology corresponds to such phrases as *ἐκ τοῦ διαβόλου* (1 John 3:8) or *ἐκ τοῦ κόσμου* (1 John 2:16; 4:4–5; John 8:23; 15:19; 17:14). A statement of essence can also be combined with *ἔρχεσθαι ἐκ* (John 3:31: *ἐκ τοῦ οὐρανοῦ* = *ὁ ἄνωθεν ἐρχόμενος*, in contrast to *εἶναι ἐκ τῆς γῆς*). That the nature of human beings is determined by their origin is evident from the expression *ὁ γεγεννημένος ἐκ τοῦ Θεοῦ* (1 John 3:9; 5:18; cf. 2:29), which is equated with *εἶναι ἐκ τοῦ Θεοῦ* (cf. 1 John 4:7, and 4:1 with 5:1); Bultmann, *John*, 138 n. 1. The interpretation of the false teachers has a distant parallel in the Johannine depiction of Judas the betrayer, who was "one of the twelve" (John 6:71; 12:4; cf. Acts 1:17: "he was numbered among us"), of whom Satan took possession by "enter[ing] into him" (John 13:2, 27).

20 Two ideas are mixed together in the difficult *ἀλλ' ἵνα* clause: (1) "but so that it would be made plain (*φανερωθῇ*) that not all are from us," and (2) "but so that they [= the false teachers] would be revealed (*φανερωθῶσιν*) as not being from us." See the elliptical constructions with *ἀλλ' ἵνα* also in John 1:8; 9:3; 11:52; 13:18. The reading *φανερωθῇ*, represented by some minuscules, is explained by this unclarity in the text. The translation of *φανερωθῶσιν* in a passive sense, "be made known," or "become known," appears also in BAGD 853, with a reference to John 1:31; 2 Cor 3:3; 5:11; 11:6 (another possibility: "show or reveal oneself," as is said of the appearance of Christ in the world: Heb 9:26; 1 Pet 1:20; cf. 1 John 1:2a; 3:5, 8). The interpretation of Schnackenburg (*Epistles*, 140) is generalizing and optimistic. According to him, "whatever does not belong to it [the community] cannot in the long run remain within it."

21 Thus, for example, Wengst, *Brief*, 110 (with a reference to 1 Pet 1:15–16 and Rev 4:8; 6:10: God = "the holy one").

22 *Χρῖσμα* should be translated "chrism," i.e., "oil for anointing," rather than simply "anointing"

same function as that which the Fourth Gospel attributes to the Holy Spirit as the Paraclete: teaching the Christian community in order that it may know the truth, follow the way of truth,[23] and abide in God.[24] In addition, the fourth evangelist traces the spirit of truth to its divine origin (John 15:26). Thus it is already clear how the author interprets the concept of χρῖσμα. The idea of anointing has a primitive Christian basis in baptism, when the initiate was anointed with oil. This author is not thinking primarily of the sacramental significance, however, but is using the word in a figurative sense. We must presume that the false teachers had also been baptized, since they were members of the community. When it is now said of the readers of 1 John, in contrast to the false teachers, that they have been anointed, it seems that anointing is attributed only to the true community.[25] They alone possess the chrism, the oil of anointing, to the extent that they have true knowledge. What is meant is therefore the possession of the spirit of truth, which is not automatically bestowed in the sacramental action but is a gift of God requiring faith.[26] This is precisely what the author presupposes regarding all the readers, in contrast to the opponents who threaten the community.[27]

Excursus: Χρῖσμα

The word χρῖσμα appears in the NT only in 1 John 2:20, 27. The underlying verb χρίειν ("to anoint") also

(Schnackenburg, *Epistles*, 141 n. 38); nevertheless, in this text, which speaks of "having the chrism," the idea is that of anointing; cf. Bultmann, *Epistles*, 37 n. 12 ("the reception of anointing oil naturally means the act of anointing"); BAGD 886; Horst Balz, *EDNT* 3 (1993) 477.

23 Obviously, here as elsewhere in the Johannine corpus ἀλήθεια refers primarily to the eschatological reality, in contrast to ψεῦδος as eschatological nothingness; the latter becomes concrete in the denial that Jesus is the Christ (v. 22) without losing its fundamental meaning.

24 1 John 2:27; cf. the Paraclete as teacher and leader in the truth at John 14:17, 26; 16:13.

25 The distinction between true and false members of the community, between the external church and the real church, was also evident in the idea of the *corpus mixtum* (cf. above on 1:7–11, and on 2:19).

26 1 John 4:1–5, 13. Being endowed with the χρῖσμα is therefore to be paralleled with the effectiveness of proclamation, which also presupposes a decision in faith. With this limitation, we may agree with Reitzenstein's suggestion, according to which χρῖσμα is the "formulaic equivalent of the preaching associated with baptism" (*Hellenistic Mystery-Religions*, 505–6 [translation modified]). C. H. Dodd also identifies χρῖσμα with "Word of God . . . as an indwelling power" (*Epistles*, 63). Nevertheless, the pneumatological aspect deserves priority, in view of the context (cf. also 1 John 5:6; otherwise one would have to argue that 2:27 contains the empty tautology "preaching = teaching"). The connection between spirit and preaching is correctly emphasized by de la Potterie ("L'onction," 44: the word is received through the Holy Spirit) and Klaus Wengst (*Häresie und Orthodoxie im Spiegel des ersten Johannesbriefes* [Gütersloh: Mohn, 1976] 49: the chrism designates "the Spirit in its teaching function . . . in which it conveys knowledge of the truth"). There appears to be a secondary reflection of the Johannine viewpoint in the gnostic tract *Hypostasis of the Archons*, according to which the "spirit of truth" brings the χρῖσμα (= gnostic teaching) (*Hyp. Arch.* 96,35—97,1–5).

27 Haenchen ("Neuere Literatur," 277) reads the emphatic underscoring of οἴδατε πάντες as defense against the gnostic claim "that the opponents alone have gnosis." The parallels between the statements in vv. 20 and 27, however, express a different intention: the community's possession of the χρῖσμα means that no one needs to "teach" its members. According to Wengst (*Häresie und Orthodoxie*, 48) the argumentation "can best be understood if one supposes that the opponents claimed the χρῖσμα exclusively for themselves and derived from its possession a knowledge that elevated them above other members and made them teachers." One may add, in favor of this point of view, that within this context the author is debating with the opponents. It is true, however, that there is no direct statement to the effect that they regard themselves as gifted with the χρῖσμα, and the claims of the false teachers are clear even without presuming a state of knowledge founded on that basis. Hence, the further line of reasoning that deduces the opponents' anthropology from all this is no more than a suggestive proposal (in response to Wengst, *Häresie und Orthodoxie*, 50; cf. also idem, *Briefe*, 110).

has a figurative sense in 2 Cor 1:21, in parallel to ὁ σφραγισάμενος ἡμᾶς ("who has sealed us"), and refers to the bestowal of the Spirit (2 Cor 1:22).[28] Otherwise, χρίειν appears in quotations or adaptations of other passages (Luke 4:18; Acts 4:27; 10:38; Heb 1:9).

Χρῖσμα appears nine times in the LXX (Exod 29:7; 30:25 [bis]; 35:[14], 19; 38:25; 40:9, 15; Sir 38:30; Dan 9:26), ordinarily standing for Hebrew מִשְׁחָה (except in Sirach and Daniel). In combination with ἔλαιον it refers to the oil of anointing: Exod 30:25; cf. ἔλαιον τοῦ χρίσματος (Exod 29:7; 35:14, 19, and elsewhere). In later Jewish literature χρῖσμα is interpreted as the oil of life that flows from the tree of life in paradise: so in *2 Enoch* 22.8–9; 8.3, 5; *Apoc. Mos.* 9.13; *Adam and Eve* (*Vita*) 36.[29] Josephus uses the word only once, in connection with the installation of the Aaronide priesthood. The booths and the priests are purified with a sweet-smelling oil (χρῖσμα εὐωδέστατον) made up of myrrh, iris, a variety of herbs, and olive oil. With it, Moses consecrates the priests and the booths (Josephus *Ant.* 3.197). Philo (*Vit. Mos.* 2.146, 152) mentions χρῖσμα (= fragrant ointment) in connection with the installation of the priests at Sinai.

In Greek, χρῖσμα is used for all sorts of things that are applied or smeared on: (1) for a salve made of plant materials and wine (Theophrastus, frg. 4, 8); (2) for an ointment for the eyes (Theophylact *Nonnes* 46); (3) for an application of asphalt, plaster, and so on (Diodorus Siculus *Bibliotheca historica* 2.9; *Anthologia Palatina* 90 n. 19); (4) for anointing (Lucian *Anacharsis* 1; *Asinus* 54; Theophrastus *Characteres* 5.3); (5) in Xenophon, χρῖσμα is used figuratively for virtue (*Symposium* 2.4).

In a Greek magical papyrus (ca. third century CE), in a collection of formulas for concocting magical recipes for the most varied purposes, there are instructions for preparing (κατασκευή) an image and a temple for the Egyptian goddess Selene. The figure of the moon goddess is to be blessed and anointed with a moon salve (σεληνιακῷ χρίσματι). Anyone who desires to call on Selene with a plea that she will bring forth a beloved person should smear him- or herself with the salve (μετὰ τοῦ χρίσματος). Then the one summoned will love the petitioner for life (P. Lond. 7.866–913; 875, 880).

The oldest Christian example of an anointing with oil as part of a baptismal ritual is found in Tertullian *Bapt.* (*PL* 1.1206–7): "After this, when we have issued from the font, we are thoroughly anointed with blessed oil." In the Greek sphere, χρῖσμα has unmistakably been used as a designation for baptism since Gregory Nazianzus (*Theological Orations* 40.4; *PG* 36.362–63). There is a clear kinship between the expressions found here and gnostic language, for example in *Pistis Sophia* 2.86; 3.112; 3.128; 3.130; *Evang. veritatis* 36. We learn of an anointing with oil in *Act. Thom.* 27.157; *Odes Sol.* 36.6; especially in *Mandaean Liturgy*, Qolashta 22–23 and 74;[30] cf. also the anointing of the dead in gnostic communities: Irenaeus, *Adv. haer.* 1.21.3–5. In the Valentinian *Gospel of Philip* baptism, chrism, eucharist, redemption, and the bridal chamber are counted as aspects of the one "mystery" (Saying 68),[31] and the superiority of chrism to baptism is asserted (Saying 95).[32] Cf. also Hippolytus *Ref.* 5.9 (on the Naasenes) and 5.22 (application to the Christians). Ignatius of Antioch can also use the idea and concept of anointing in a figurative sense (*Eph.* 17: μύρον, ἀλείφεσθαι). The word μύρον is used in a more realistic sense in the prayer over the oil of anointing in the *Apostolic Constitutions:* "Concerning the ointment give thanks in this manner: We give Thee thanks, O God, the Creator of the whole world, both for the fragrancy of the ointment, and for the immortality which Thou has made known to us by Thy Son Jesus. For Thine is the glory and the power for ever. Amen" (*Did.* 10.8 [Coptic]; cf. *Ap. Const.* 7.27). Given its place in this context, this is probably a prayer spoken immediately after the Eucharist.[33] The oil mentioned here was used for the anointing of the sick (cf. Mark 6:13; Jas 5:14).[34] Arthur Vööbus thinks that the text in the *Didache* is an interpolation and assigns it to the baptismal liturgy.[35]

28 Cf. Hans Windisch, *Der Zweite Korintherbrief* (KEK; 2d ed.; ed. Georg Strecker; Göttingen: Vandenhoeck & Ruprecht, 1970) 71–74.

29 On this, see Franz Mussner, *Die Anschauung vom "Leben" im vierten Evangelium* (MThS 1/5; Munich: Zink, 1952) 113.

30 See Mark Lidzbarski, *Mandäische Liturgien* (Abhandlungen der Königlichen Gesellschaft der Wissenschaften zu Göttingen, Philologisch-historische Klasse, n.f. 17/1; reprinted Hildesheim: Olms, 1962) 34–35, 115–16.

31 Saying 68 = NHC 2, 3: 67,27–30; translation by Hans-Martin Schenke in *NTApoc*^{2} 1.179–208, at 196.

32 Saying 95 = NHC 2, 3: 74,12–13; translation ibid., 200.

33 Cf. also "Constitutiones ecclesiae aegyptiacae" 1.[31] 23; text in Franciscus Xaverius Funk, *Didascalia et Constitutiones Apostolorum* (2 vols. in 1; Paderborn: Schoeningh, 1905; reprinted Turin: Erasmo, 1962) 2.101; also "Euchologion of Sarapion" 17, in ibid., 178, 180.

34 On this, see Otto Böcher, *Christus Exorcista: Dämonismus und Taufe im Neuen Testament* (BWANT 16; Stuttgart: Kohlhammer, 1973) 80, 101.

■ **21** It thus appears that the readers are addressed as the true Christians. They know the truth. The presbyter in 2 John addresses the readers in the same fashion (vv. 1, 8–9). Is there a reference to this tradition in the word ἔγραψα? In any case, the aorist at this point cannot be attributed to rhetorical letter style, as is possible elsewhere in 1 John.[36] As to the verse's content, the author refers to the traditional and assured status of the community, which, as was already clear in v. 18 with its reference to the Christian tradition about the antichrist, is confronted with false teaching. The idea of tradition is also employed in service of the polemic against the false teachers.[37] The knowledge of the truth that has belonged to the community since its founding separates it from falsehood; since it knows the truth, its existence is set apart from the existence of the antichrists.[38]

■ **22–23** Only at vv. 22–23 do we begin to get an account of the content of the false teaching. The ψεύστης, the false teacher, denies the confessional statement Ἰησοῦς ὁ Χριστός ἐστιν. This is a negative quotation of the

35 Arthur Vööbus, *Liturgical Traditions in the Didache* (PETSE 16; Stockholm: Estonian Theological Society in Exile, 1968) 46–50; to the contrary Klaus Wengst, *Didache, etc.*, in idem, ed., Schriften des Urchristentums (Munich: Kösel, 1984) 2.57–59, esp. n. 200.

36 Although the expression οἴδατε τὴν ἀλήθειαν ("you know the truth") may also be part of the "tactics" of the controversy (cf. Vielhauer, *Geschichte*, 474), what one finds here is a statement that, like the idea of "sinlessness," touches the heart of Johannine self-understanding (cf. above on vv. 12–17, and below on v. 26).

The particle ὅτι, which appears three times in this verse, requires a special explanation. The suggestion that this little word should be interpreted differently in the several occurrences, the two first should be translated "because," the third "that" (Friederich Büchsel, "Zu den Johannesbriefen," *ZNW* 28 [1929] 240; Dodd, *Epistles*, 54; Huther, *Handbuch*, 137), would make the last ὅτι clause refer to the second and place it parallel to the accusative object αὐτήν. But that would be an awkward construction. It is more likely that the preceding ἔγραψα favors a parallel ordering of the three occurrences of the particle, so that one may distinguish two possible interpretations: (1) ὅτι has an explanatory meaning ("that") in each case. Then the author wishes to assure the community that he knows they know the truth. In favor of this interpretation (adopted by Schnackenburg, *Epistles*, 144; Brown, *Epistles*, 350; Balz, "Johannesbriefe," 175; Bultmann, *Epistles*, 38; de la Potterie, "L'onction," 41; and others) is that otherwise ἔγραψα would have no objective clause associated with it. But it would be easy to infer such an object (the author is, at this point, thinking of a previous writing). And is it really intended that the addressees should be assured of something they know anyway? Thus it is probable that here (as above, with regard to vv. 12–14), (2) ὅτι has a causal sense (thus also Brooke, *Epistles*, 57; Johannes Schneider, *Die Briefe des Jakobus, Petrus, Judas und Johannes: Die Katholischen Briefe* [NTD 10; 9th ed.; Göttingen: Vandenhoeck & Ruprecht, 1961] 157; Marshall, *Epistles*, 147, 156; Friederich Hauck, *Die Kirchenbriefe: Die Briefe des Jakobus, Petrus, Judas und Johannes* [NTD 10; 8th ed.; Göttingen: Vandenhoeck & Ruprecht, 1957] 125). It thus follows easily after what has preceded it. The author recognizes the actual redeemed state of the community. Through the χρῖσμα it has knowledge of the truth. That distinguishes it from the false teachers. This is the reason why the author, in turn, has written to the community, and his concern is only to strengthen it in the knowledge of the truth.

37 Cf. the similar use of ἀπ᾽ ἀρχῆς in confrontation with opponents in 2:24; also 2 John 5–6. There is unpolemical usage in 1 John 2:7; 3:11.

38 For the contrast between ψεῦδος and ἀλήθεια, between human eschatological reality and nothingness, see n. 23 above (on 2:20). This opposition (found also in v. 27) is explicable in terms of Johannine dualism of decision, which has its own ontological foundation; it corresponds to the contrasting of the "words of the devil," who tells lies and is called "the father of lies," and the words of the Revealer, who speaks the truth (John 8:44–45; the word διάβολος does not occur elsewhere in the Johannine writings). The word ψεύστης is more common: whoever asserts that he or she loves God and yet hates a brother or sister is a "liar" (2:4, 22; 4:20); cf. also 1:10; 5:10 ("[they] make [God] a liar").

community's credo[39] that is found in its positive form at the conclusion of the Fourth Gospel (John 20:31: "that Jesus is the Christ [or: Messiah], the Son of God"). Christ (or Messiah) is used as a title (as also in 1 John 5:1 and 2 John 9). Although this corresponds to the use of the name as a title of messianic honor, it is more common in the Johannine writings for Χριστός to be used as a proper name.[40] The title ὁ Χριστός and the proper name Ἰησοῦς Χριστός often occur in association with the phrase "Son of God," which clarifies them. Thus in what follows the denial of Jesus as "the Christ" is equated with the denial of "the Son."[41] From the author's point of view the false prophets thus dispute not only the application of the title "Christ" to Jesus, but also the fact that Jesus is God's Son (cf. 5:5–6). Thereby they question Jesus' sending and thus the Father who sent him; for "there is, for the author, no such thing as faith in God apart from the historical revelation."[42] Verse 23a underscores this with a generalizing (πᾶς) negative thesis that is supported by a positive antithesis in v. 23b.[43] To confess the Son is to "have" the Father, that is, to know and acknowledge the Father.[44]

■ **24** The placing of ὑμεῖς at the beginning of the verse (similar to the usage in v. 27) distinguishes the attitude of the community from that of the false teachers. The neuter ὅ refers to the content of "what you have heard from the beginning."[45] This is vaguely described; the author could have spoken more clearly of the "word of life," or of the Christ-event that is the reason for the community's origin.[46] Abiding in this, the community's foundational tradition, guarantees its abiding in the Father and in the Son. This is expressed here both in the imperative (μενέτω) and in the future (μενεῖτε). Holding fast to the tradition on which the community was established is not something that happens once for all time; it does not lead to a perfected completion of faith. The basis of the community is not some possession that has been entrusted to its administration. It must constantly recall this basis, and it requires admonition so that it will continually realize anew what has been promised to it. The Christian community is thus a historical entity inserted in time and place, subjected to changing, unforeseeable situations in which it must again and again defend itself while always remaining in harmony with its starting point.[47]

■ **25** This verse expresses openness to an eschatological future whose content cannot be anticipated. In that future, the ἐπαγγελία will reach fulfillment.[48] What has been promised to the community[49] cannot be traced to the OT or to the Fourth Gospel, in the sense of the schema of "promise and fulfillment."[50] Instead, its basis is "what you have heard from the beginning." The Christ-event has a promissory character, because it opens a redeemed future to those who believe. To that extent,

39 The negative particle οὐκ after ὁ ἀρνούμενος (as also after οὐ, οὐδείς, etc.) has the sense of an emphatic double negative that cannot be translated into German or English (cf. BDF §§ 429 [1]; 431 [1]).

40 With Ἰησοῦς in 2 John 3, 7; 1 John 1:3; 2:1; 3:23; 4:2; 5:6, 20; cf. John 1:17; 17:3 (although the titular usage is dominant in the Fourth Gospel).

41 1 John 2:22b, 23. Cf. also 2 John 3; 1 John 1:3; 3:23; 5:5–6, 20.

42 Bultmann, *Epistles*, 38.

43 The omission of the second part of the verse by the witnesses to the Koine text has no text-critical weight.

44 On "having" or "knowing" the Father, cf. above (on 2:3, 4, 5, 14).

45 See above on 1:1 (ἀπ' ἀρχῆς).

46 The conjunction οὖν occurs 194 times in the Fourth Gospel. In the Johannine Letters it is found only in 3 John 8. In 1 John 2:24, as also in 4:19, it is a secondary intrusion in the manuscript tradition. Cf. BDF § 451 (1).

47 While the older christological tradition is based on the subordination of the Son (Mark 13:32; cf. 1 Cor 15:28), here the threefold combination υἱὸς καὶ πατήρ (vv. 22–24) shows a tendency to making Father and Son equal. This is found also in 2 John 9 (against Lieu, *Epistles*, 95 n. 115, one may not suppose that this verse is only an echo of the confession of the Son in 1 John 2:23), and it is hinted in 1 John 1:3, where Christian κοινωνία is defined as communion with the Father and his son, Jesus Christ (on this, cf. Eduard Schweizer, "υἱός, κτλ.," *TDNT* 8 [1972] 387). For this author, such an ordering of Father and Son (cf. also Matt 11:27 par.; 28:19) does not exclude the use of formulas of sending (e.g., 1 John 4:14), but it does make clear, as does the use of the personal pronouns, that the Christ-event, the starting point and rationale of the community, is understood as God's revelation, and that abiding in Christ is identical with abiding in God.

48 The word ἐπαγγελία, like the verb ἐπαγγέλλεσθαι, occurs only here in the Johannine writings. It does not occur in Revelation or in Matthew. The reading ὑμῖν is weakly attested and probably came about by assimilation to the second person plural in v. 24. One

on the one hand, there is a close affinity between the content of this and the preceding v. 24. On the other hand, the demonstrative pronoun *αὕτη* points to what follows.[51] The promise, which is not only realized in the Christ-event but will continue to realize itself in the future, has as its content *ζωὴ αἰώνιος*.[52] "Eternal life" is the thing hoped for. In the expectation that the life revealed, and at the same time promised, in Christ will be bestowed on the Christian community in the future, the author comes close to primitive Christian apocalyptic. This approach will be still more clearly expressed in what follows (2:28; 3:2). This orientation preserves the continuity with v. 24. The promise of eternal life expresses the confidence that abiding in the Father and in the Son will be perfected in the future. Thus it is clear that *χρῖσμα*, in the sense of being gifted with the spirit of truth whom the community has received and who teaches them (v. 27), has "now already" inserted them into an eschatological dimension.[53] Hence it can also be said of the community that it has "passed from death to life" (3:14), and that God has "given" it eternal life (5:11–13). In the present time, such a gift separates it from falsehood and is an encouragement to "abiding" in its redeemed condition, not least in an ethical probation that consists in fending off untruth and turning toward truth; this is made concrete in the conflict with the false teachers.

Excursus: The False Teachers in 1 John (Docetism)[54]

As we have already seen, explicit information about the false teachers is found in 1 John 2:22–23 and 4:1–6. Beyond that, one can presume with a great degree of probability that the author's reference to the sacraments (5:6–8) should also be understood in terms

should, instead, read *ἡμῖν*: the author associates himself with the addressees. The whole Christian community stands within the same promise.

49 Does *αὐτός* mean God, or Christ? The application to Christ (so Schnackenburg, *Epistles*, 148 n. 72, against Büchsel, *Johannesbriefe*, 41) is not, as Schnackenburg thinks, unquestionable.

50 The texts cited by Brown (John 15:4, 7; 17:22–23) are not expressed as "promises" (*Epistles*, 357). One might rather think of the announcement of the Paraclete in John 14:16–17; 15:16; 16:7–15. In the view of the fourth evangelist, however, this is fulfilled historically, within the church.

51 This is the case also in 5:4b, 11, 14; cf. 1:5; 3:11, and frequently elsewhere. In this sense Bultmann writes: "*αὕτη* ('this') refers of course to what follows" because "the promise corresponds to the faithfulness of the believers" and "the promise is expressly formulated in v 25" (*Epistles* 40 and n. 26). So also Wengst, *Briefe*, 116; Gerd Schunack, *Die Briefe des Johannes* (ZBK 17; Zurich: Theologischer Verlag, 1982) 184; Schnackenburg, *Epistles*, 148 n. 70.

52 On this, see above (on 1:2): *ζωὴ αἰώνιος* is identical in Johannine usage with absolute *ζωή* (cf. 1:2; 3:14–15; 5:11–12).

53 This is scarcely to be regarded as a transfer of the idea of the Paraclete in the Fourth Gospel into the language of 1 John; this material is the common content of the Johannine tradition (in response to Hans Conzelmann, "*ψεῦδος, κτλ.*," *TDNT* 9 [1974] 602).

54 Literature: Walter Bauer, *Die Briefe des Ignatius von Antiochia und der Polykarpbrief* (HNT 18; 2d ed.; ed. Henning Paulsen; Tübingen: Mohr, 1985) 63–65; Josef Blank, "Die Irrlehrer des Ersten Johannesbriefes," *Kairos* 26 (1984) 166–93; Norbert Brox, "Doketismus: Eine Problemanzeige," *ZKG* 95 (1984) 301–14; John Gordon Davies, "The Origins of Docetism," *StPatr* VI (TU 81; Berlin: Akademie-Verlag 1962) 13–35; Adolf von Harnack, *Marcion: The Gospel of the Alien God* (trans. John E. Steely and Lyle Bierma; Durham: Labyrinth, 1990); Adolf Hilgenfeld, *Die Ketzergeschichte des Urchristentums* (Leipzig: Fues [Reisland] 1884; reprinted Hildesheim: Olms, 1963); Schnelle, *Antidocetic Christology;* Michael Slusser, "Docetism: A Historical Definition," *The Second Century* 1 (1981) 163–72; Karl-Wolfgang Tröger, "Doketistische Christologie in Nag-Hammadi-Texten," *Kairos* 19 (1977) 45–52; P. Weigandt, "Der Doketismus im Urchristentum und in der theologischen Entwicklung des 2. Jahrhunderts" (diss., Heidelberg, 1961); Wengst, *Häresie und Orthodoxie;* Ulrich B. Müller, *Geschichte der Christologie in der johanneischen Gemeinde* (Stuttgart: Katholisches Bibelwerk, 1975) 35ff.

of the conflict with these opponents.[55] If one distinguishes this situation from that in 2 John, which also deviates from the description in 1 John by designating the dissidents as πλάνοι (2 John 7), the false teaching can be described as docetic. In contrast, the thesis that the "false prophets" (4:1) are representatives of Judaism[56] is scarcely tenable. Rather, from 2:19 one can see that the author presumes that the false teachers originally belonged to the Johannine community, no matter how much they "did not belong to us" by their very nature. In addition, it is presumed that the opponents separated from the Johannine community before the composition of 1 John.[57] Only under these conditions can the sharp polemic of the author of 1 John be understood. Nonetheless, the influence of the Docetists on the Johannine school is not to be minimized, either before or after their separation, especially when one acknowledges that their teaching is related to the Hellenistic-syncretistic ideas transmitted within the Johannine school.

As regards the content of the docetic teaching, 1 John 2:22 shows that the opponents rejected the identification of Jesus with "the Christ." This meant, at the same time, the rejection of the Father and the Son. Moreover, a denial of the Son also involves a failure to acknowledge the Father (2:23). According to 4:2, the

55 Bultmann and Schnackenburg go quite far in presuming that polemic against gnostic false teachers is well-nigh omnipresent in 1 John. Basing his argument on the thesis that 1 John as a whole is shaped by the theme of crisis, John Painter ("The 'Opponents' in 1 John," *NTS* 32 [1986] 48–71) has attempted to deduce the position of the opponents by reversing the Johannine exposition to reveal its opposite; from the absence of specific concepts ("Paraclete," "Holy Spirit") he concludes that the false teachers claimed to possess the Spirit. Hans Hinrich Wendt (*Die Johannesbriefe und das johanneische Christentum* [Halle: Buchhandlung des Waisenhauses, 1925] 13) claims not only to have established a gnostic and docetic self-concept for the opponents in 1 John, but also an "objection to the apparently exaggerated demands of Christian fraternal love." This thesis, which has been presented in several variant versions, is questionable; equally unfounded is the suggestion that the false teachers had eulogized love (in line with 3:18) but did not wish to practice it as a "Christian" demand, that is, toward "evildoers" and "enemies," since nothing is said in the Johannine corpus about the commandment to love enemies (Matt 5:43–48; *Did.* 1.3). According to Windisch and Preisker one should suppose a fundamental gnostic-prophetic structure for the false teachers, the result of which was a rejection of a christology of atoning death as well as of the sacraments, and beyond that a libertinism in principle and an indifference toward the keeping of the moral law (*Die Katholischen Briefe,* 127–28). Following the premise that 1 John, in its literary style, presupposes the Fourth Gospel, Wengst (*Briefe,* 25) sees the conflict as "a dispute over the understanding of the common tradition." "The opponents read the Fourth Gospel under gnostic presuppositions." The result is a docetic christology and the theological irrelevance of human action (pp. 26–27). Brown (*Epistles,* 69–71) writes in a similar vein; he also deduces an intra-Johannine schism occasioned by different understandings of the Fourth Gospel as a background for 1 John. The "secessionists" propound a dualistic christology that negates the saving significance of Jesus' life and death, as well as the connection between preexistence and suffering in the existence of Jesus as the Christ (pp. 75–77). The accusation that the opponents sin against the commandment of fraternal love is said by Brown to be founded more on the fact of schism than on a gnostic understanding of God and the world (pp. (84–85; against Wengst, *Häresie und Orthodoxie,* 53–59; cf. 1 John 4:6; John 17:6, 9, 20). Cf. also Josef Blank (*Krisis: Untersuchungen zur johanneischen Christologie und Eschatologie* [Freiburg: Lambertus, 1964] 174–77), who understands the false teaching as an erroneous Jewish Christian interpretation of the Johannine *shekinah* christology and posits a connection between 1 John and Cerinthus.

56 Cf. Windisch and Preisker, *Die Katholischen Briefe,* 127; and J. C. O'Neill, *The Puzzle of 1 John: A New Examination of Origins* (London: SPCK, 1966). For O'Neill, 1 John is a combination of twelve pareneses drawn from a Jewish sect. In 1 John, a Christian redactor attempts to show that the prophecies are fulfilled in Jesus as the Messiah. According to this, the redactor's enemies are former members of the sect who do not recognize Jesus as the Messiah. On this, see also Hartwig Thyen, "Johannesbriefe," *TRE* 17 (1987) 186–200; Karl Weiss, "Die 'Gnosis' im Hintergrund und Spiegel der Johannesbriefe," in Tröger, *Gnosis und NT,* 341–56.

57 See above, on v. 19b.

false teachers do not confess that "Jesus Christ has come in the flesh" (Ἰησοῦν Χριστὸν ἐν σαρκὶ ἐληλυθότα). This is taken up in 4:3 with the statement μὴ ὁμολογεῖ τὸν Ἰησοῦν. The variant readings should be noted.[58] Insofar as the false teachers promote themselves as prophets, they are on a level with the presbyter's itinerant brothers and sisters (3 John 3–4). They participate in the basic charismatic structure of the Johannine communities.[59]

Behind the term "Docetism" is the Greek concept of δόκησις/δοκεῖν. It is applied to the earthly life of Jesus of Nazareth, his birth, his suffering, and his death. Since all this cannot be reconciled with the idea of a divinity that, as such, is impassible and removed from the coming to be and passing away of worldly things, the Christian confession of the saving significance of the person of Jesus Christ can only be understood in such a way that a sharp distinction is drawn between Christ, the Son of God (the heavenly human one, the Christ above, etc.) and the earthly human being Jesus of Nazareth. Only the latter suffered and died on the cross, while the former was united with Jesus only temporarily, "in appearance." Consequently, Docetism opposes the doctrine of the incarnation, for it is a fundamental truth that the divine cannot unite with the human, the heavenly with the earthly.[60] This christological conception, nourished by the Greek spirit,[61] could be articulated in a variety of systems. No doubt there was also a gnostic Docetism, but gnosis and Docetism should not be equated.[62] Docetism was combined with "ditheistic" or "monotheistic" ideas, even if these combinations did not always lead to clear definitions. One may also distinguish a modalistic from a subordinationist Docetism, corresponding to different conceptions of the relationship of Christ to God.[63]

58 In a marginal note of minuscule 1739, in the Vulgate, in Irenaeus, and in Lucifer, μὴ ὁμολογεῖ is replaced by λύει. According to BDF § 428 (4), ὁμολογεῖ is to be regarded, grammatically speaking, as the more difficult reading, since relative clauses in the indicative usually negate with οὐ, with but few exceptions. Because (1) λύει is weakly attested and (2) ὁμολογεῖ is a *lectio difficilior*, one should read μὴ ὁμολογεῖ at this point (against Schnackenburg, *Epistles*, 201). On the text-critical problem, see also below ad loc.

59 Communities of charismatic nature represented a widespread phenomenon in the second century; this is evident also from the expressions used by Montanists in Asia Minor. Hence this enthusiasm cannot be regarded as an argument for the Jewish-Palestinian origins of the community structure (in response to Akira Satake, *Die Gemeindeordnung in der Johannesapokalypse* [WMANT 21; Neukirchen-Vluyn: Neukirchener Verlag, 1966] 191–93).

60 The discussion surrounding the concept of "Docetism" tends in two directions. One understands "Docetism" in a very broad sense as a comprehensive, generalized summary concept for all kinds of gnostic christologies. The other interpretation restricts itself to the assertion that, from the docetic point of view, the human figure of Jesus was mere appearance. According to Norbert Brox ("Doketismus," 309), the significant element of Docetism is "that Christ was only apparently human, in the genre of δόκησις, no matter how this appearance came into existence or operated. . . . Docetism never admitted [Christ's] *becoming* human or *being* human, but always and only his *appearing to be* human." P. Weigandt, in his 1961 dissertation, upholds a narrow conception of Docetism, since the christologies labeled "docetic" are too different to be subsumed under a single heading: "Thus Docetism as a collective term *within the history of dogma* should be laid to rest, especially since, when we use the Greek stem δοκε-, we are dealing only with docetic christology" ("Doketismus," 18).

61 Cf., among others, Weigandt, "Doketismus," 29; against Brox, "Doketismus," 313–14, who attempts to derive Docetism from Jewish Christianity.

62 Going beyond the (too) narrow definition of Weigandt (see above, n. 60), one must say with N. Brox: "By all appearances, nongnostic docetic christologies were no rarity in the early second century" ("Doketismus," 313). On this, see also Karl-Wolfgang Tröger, "Doketistische Christologie in Nag-Hammadi-Texten," *Kairos* 19 (1977) 45–52.

63 One may mention Marcion as an example of a modalistic Docetism. According to Adolf von Harnack, Marcion was a modalist "like other Christian teachers, but probably more consciously so than they were" (*Marcion*, 83). Thus Marcion emphasizes that Christ raised himself from the dead. But in comparison with human bodiliness, the body of Christ was only a φάντασμα. If, according to Marcion, Christ really suffered, the appearance refers "only to the fleshly substance" (*Marcion*, 83). In contrast, Cerinthus of Asia Minor represented a subordinationist Docetism. The earthly Jesus and the heavenly Christ "always remain separate in their natures and persons" (Weigandt, "Doketismus," 17).

Three different docetic systems can be distinguished according to their description of the relationship between the heavenly Christ and the earthly Jesus:[64]

1. The one crucified was not Jesus but another human being (e.g., Simon of Cyrene). This idea is attributed, for example, to Basilides, when the latter says of the crucifixion of Jesus that the heavenly Christ "in the form of Simon" stood near the cross laughing (Irenaeus *Adv. haer.* 1.24.4).

2. The Christ above departed from Jesus before the passion. This is found in the work of Cerinthus (Irenaeus *Adv. haer.* 1.26.1), and a positive witness for this idea can be seen in the *Acts of John*. Another form of adoptionist christology, according to which the Christ above united with Jesus at his baptism, although the two natures remained separate ("enoicetic christology"), could be included under this heading.

3. There is a personal unity in Jesus Christ, who, although he was crucified, is of a pneumatic (and psychic) substance, so that he could not truly suffer (= "impassibilis"). Examples of this view include the Docetists mentioned by Ignatius of Antioch, who emphasizes in opposition to them that Jesus Christ is a "bearer of flesh" and really suffered; also Valentinus ("ouranosarkic christology": Ps.-Tertullian *Adv. haer.* 4.5). This also includes monophysite or modalistic christologies, examples of which include those of Marcion, the Gnostic Satornilius (Saturninus), Cerdon, and others.

Regarding (1): According to the account of Irenaeus,[65] Basilides taught the following doctrine at Alexandria: the "unbegotten and unnameable father sent his first-begotten Nous (he it is who is called Christ) to bestow deliverance on them that believe in him, from the power of those who made the world. He appeared, then, on earth as a man, to the nations of these powers, and wrought miracles. Wherefore he did not himself suffer death, but Simon, a certain man of Cyrene, being compelled, bore the cross in his stead; so that this latter being transfigured by him, that he might be thought to be Jesus, was crucified, through ignorance and error, while Jesus himself received the form of Simon, and, standing by, laughed at them. For since he was an incorporeal power, and the Nous (mind) of the unborn father, he transfigured himself as he pleased, and thus ascended to him who had sent him. . . . It is not incumbent on us to confess him who was crucified, but him who came in the form of a man, and was thought to be crucified, and was called Jesus, and was sent by the father" (translation in ANF 1.349). Consistently with this, Basilides (or one of his followers) taught an anthropology in which "salvation belongs to the soul alone, for the body is by nature subject to corruption" (Irenaeus *Adv. haer.* 1.24.5).

Regarding (2): Cerinthus furnishes an example of the distinction between the Christ above and the Christ below. According to the oldest and generally trustworthy report of Irenaeus, Cerinthus distinguishes between the creator of the world and the ultimate principle of the universe, who is the unknown Father of Jesus Christ. He makes a special distinction between, on the one hand, the natural son of Joseph and Mary, the crucified and risen Jesus, and, on the other hand, the Christ who, at Jesus' baptism, descended from the first principle in the form of a dove and rested on him, who proclaimed the unknown Father and performed many deeds of power.[66] This latter, since it did not participate in the bodily existence but was of a spiritual nature, returned to the Father at the end of Jesus' life (Irenaeus *Adv. haer.* 1.26.1; cf. 3.11.1).

In the conception of Cerinthus, δόκησις consists in the opinion that Christ appeared to suffer on the cross, while in reality it was only the human being, Jesus, who suffered and was crucified.[67]

While Hippolytus (*Ref.* 7.21) generally follows the description of Irenaeus, the heresiologist Epiphanius, who was later important but whose reliability in his reports has justly been criticized by scholars, apparently made a secondary connection between the teaching of Cerinthus and Judaistic elements (*Pan.* 28.2–5). This may have taken place under the influence of Cerinthus's apparently Ebionite baptismal doctrine (adoptionist christology), and was possibly

64 Cf. also the threefold division in Bauer, *Die Briefe des Ignatius;* J. Denker, "Die theologiegeschichtliche Stellung des Petrusevangeliums" (diss., Kiel, 1972); and the extensive discussion in Weigandt, "Doketismus," 4–19.

65 Cf. Irenaeus *Adv. haer.* 1.24.3–7. It is a matter of dispute whether the text of Irenaeus does not more properly apply to the followers of Basilides, since Basilides himself did not teach a docetic doctrine (cf. Wolf-Dieter Hauschild, "Christologie und Humanismus bei dem 'Gnostiker' Basilides," *ZNW* 68 [1977] 67–92, esp. 82–83; Brox, "Doketismus," 307). Most scholars favor Hippolytus's sources (*Ref.* 7.20.2–27.13) over those of Irenaeus. On this, see W. D. Hauschild, "Christologie und Humanismus," 67 n. 2; Weigandt, "Doketismus," 10–12; as well as, earlier, Hilgenfeld, *Ketzergeschichte,* 212–13; and Walter Bauer, *Das Leben Iesu im Zeitalter der neutestamentlichen Apokryphen* (Tübingen: Mohr [Siebeck], 1920) 35.

66 For the distinction between "Jesus" and "Christ," see the classic formula in Epiphanius *Pan.* 28.1.7: οὐ τὸν Ἰησοῦν εἶναι Χριστόν.

67 Against Weigandt, "Doketismus," 17, who because of

influenced by the fact that Irenaeus had placed a description of Ebionitism immediately after his account of Cerinthus (*Adv. haer.* 1.26.2). The heresiological tradition according to which Cerinthus was a chiliast is probably secondary as well, although it is witnessed as early as the end of the second or beginning of the third century. Only with great difficulty can it be reconciled with his original spiritualistic idea.[68]

Regarding (3): One of the oldest witnesses to "monophysite Docetism" is Ignatius of Antioch, who attacked docetic opponents especially in his letters to the communities at Tralles and Smyrna. He thus inaugurates the series of church fathers (Justin, Irenaeus, Hippolytus, Tertullian, Clement of Alexandria, Origen) who combated Docetism intensively; together, they constitute a testimony to the broad adherence and great significance attributed to docetic groups in the second and third centuries. Ignatius's polemic against heretics makes clear that the opponents he pictures deny that the κύριος was a σαρκοφόρος ("bearer of flesh"); see Ignatius *Smyrn.* 5.2. They assert τὸ δοκεῖν πεπονθέναι ("he suffered only in semblance"; Ignatius *Trall.* 10). Beyond that, they deny that Jesus Christ "was truly born and ate and drank, was truly persecuted under Pontius Pilate, was truly crucified and died . . . who moreover was truly raised from the dead" (Ignatius *Trall.* 9.1–2). But, says Ignatius (*Eph.* 7.2), Christ is God who has appeared in the flesh (ἐν σαρκὶ γενόμενος θεός), born of Mary and of God, at first passible (παθητός), and then after his resurrection impassible (ἀπαθής). As risen, he also appeared as "fleshly" (σαρκικός), even though, "in a spiritual way" (πνευματικῶς), he was united with the Father (Ignatius *Smyrn.* 3.1). Because the passion and death of Jesus Christ took place not only in appearance but in reality, Ignatius expresses his confidence that his own suffering and martyrdom are not in vain but will unite him with Christ (*Smyrn.* 4.2, and elsewhere). It is not only christology that is a point of controversy, but also the acknowledgment of the sacrament of the Eucharist. The opponents are consistent in absenting themselves from the Eucharist, since they "allow not that the eucharist is the flesh of our Savior Jesus Christ, which flesh suffered for our sins, and which the Father of his goodness has raised up" (Ignatius *Smyrn.* 6). In contrast, Ignatius emphasizes that the true flesh and blood of Jesus Christ contain what is necessary for salvation (Ignatius *Trall.* 8.1: σάρξ and αἷμα; Ignatius *Phld.* 4; *Eph.* 13.1; see also 1 John 4:2; cf. also Ignatius *Smyrn.* 6.1: αἷμα).

Since the Docetism Ignatius confronts is apparently not aware of any adoptionist christology, and since it says nothing about a person of Christ who stands over against the earthly Jesus, one may call this form of the doctrine "monophysite Docetism."[69] The whole event of Jesus of Nazareth is subsumed under the concept of δόκησις, and the evaluation of the sacrament of the Eucharist is also determined by this christological reality that is only appearance. This type of docetic conception can also be demonstrated, in heresiological literature, for the Gnostics Satornilius (Irenaeus *Adv. haer.* 1.24.1: "Saturninus"; Ps.-Tertullian *Adv. haer.* 1.4) and Cerdo (Irenaeus *Adv. haer.* 1.27.1). The church fathers also saw the "arch-heretic" of the second century, Marcion of Asia Minor, as a Docetist.[70] This may also be presumed by Irenaeus when he reports that, in Marcion's teaching, "Jesus . . . coming into Judea in the times of Pontius Pilate the governor, who was procurator of Tiberius Caesar, was manifested in the form of a man to those who were in Judea, abolishing the prophets and the law, and all the

---

a too-narrow definition does not count Cerinthus among the Docetists. Cf. also Schnelle, *Antidocetic Christology*, 65 n. 151.

68 "Cerinthus was a chiliast, because he was regarded as the author of Revelation" (Wengst, *Häresie und Orthodoxie*, 29; cf. also the different texts on Cerinthus's views in Hilgenfeld, *Ketzergeschichte*, 411–18). The latter sees in Cerinthus a combination of gnosis and Judaism (ibid., 420), but does not consider the question of a possible original relationship between the two (on this, see Wengst, *Häresie und Orthodoxie*, 34 n. 62). For an example of an enoicetic christology, see also the doctrine of the Ophites: Jesus was more just, more pure, and more wise than all other human beings. He served the Christ as a *vas mundum* (= pure vessel), and could do miracles. Christ left Jesus before the crucifixion (Irenaeus *Adv. haer.* 1.30.11–14).

69 With Weigandt, "Doketismus," 16, 18, 57–58; also Schnelle, *Antidocetic Christology*, 64.

70 The question whether Marcion can be called a Gnostic is disputed. Von Harnack, in his fundamental study (*Marcion*, 173 n. 1), attempted to show that Marcion should not be understood as a Gnostic. Ugo Bianchi has denied this thesis ("Marcion: Theologien biblique ou docteur gnostique," *VC* 21 [1967] 141–49). Barbara Aland takes a middle position in "Marcion: Versuch einer neuen Interpretation," *ZThK* 70 (1973) 420–47 (see 423–24 for a description of the positions of other scholars). See also Werner Foerster, in the introduction to his chapter on "Associates of Marcion," where he casts doubt on the assignment of Marcion to gnosis (in *Gnosis: A Selection of Gnostic Texts*

works of that God who made the world." Beyond this, he is said to have acknowledged only a redemption of the "souls which had learned his doctrine; while the body, as having been taken from the earth, is incapable of sharing in salvation" (*Adv. haer.* 1.27.2–3). From the time of Origen, Marcion was clearly regarded as a Docetist.[71] Tertullian reports that, according to Marcion's opinion, Christ appeared directly from heaven "in the form of a human being in the fifteenth year of Tiberius," and had "the appearance of a human substance" (*Adv. Marc.* 3.10.2); Christ was said not to have had a human body, but only a "phantasma carnis" (*Adv. Marc.* 4.42.7). This means that Christ suffered only "in appearance" (δοκήσει, Epiphanius *Pan.* 42.12.3; Hippolytus *Ref.* 19.3). It is consistent with such a docetic doctrine that, as is said, Marcion also denied the resurrection of the dead (Irenaeus *Adv. haer.* 1.27.3) and celebrated the Eucharist only with "bread and water" (Epiphanius *Pan.* 42.3.3). Of course, one may suspect that Marcion's Docetism was mislabeled as such by the church fathers. If one follows von Harnack's interpretation, Marcion was a "modalist" and did not assert that Christ's suffering and death were only a "phantasma."[72]

The most important direct evidence of "monophysite Docetism" is found in the *Acts of John*.[73] Here the content of the Christian message is said to be that Christ appeared "not like a man" (90), for "he was made [hu]man [apart from] this body" (103). The Christ has no fixed form and appears sometimes as a child, sometimes as a young man, sometimes as an old man (88–93). For human eyes, "the Lord" was crucified in Jerusalem, but in truth he has no form, just as the interpretation of the cross on Golgotha is interchangeable (98). In the *Acts of John* also, the Eucharist has no sacramental character; it is celebrated with bread, as a prayer of thanksgiving (40, 84–86, 109–10).

Against this religio-historical background, how should one judge the "false prophecy" in 1 John? Since the opponents in 1 John deny that Jesus is the Christ and Son of God, it seems likely that they made a distinction between "Jesus" and "Christ." What terminology they used, and within what system of dogmatic coordinates they were working, is not evident from the information in 1 John. But, on the one hand, their reticence regarding the Lord's Supper suggests that their teaching had docetic features (cf. below, on 1 John 5:6–8), since this was regarded by the church fathers as a mark of Docetism. One can infer such an opposing position on the basis of the Johannine traditions presupposed by the fourth evangelist; against that position, the traditions of the Johannine school asserted in a variety of ways the reality of the Logos's becoming flesh. On the other hand, the author of 1 John does not indicate what the docetic opponents taught about anthropology and ethics; there is no direct polemic here regarding those things, in contrast to the attack on the dogmatic positions just mentioned. Consequently, the reconstruction of the false teachers' anthropology and ethics remains too hypothetical for one to draw trustworthy conclusions on that score.

If the opponents distinguished between the earthly Jesus and the heavenly Christ, they may have

[2 vols.; ed. R. McL. Wilson; Oxford: Clarendon, 1972–74] 1.44).

71 "Non vere, sed visu sub specie quasi amplioris gloriae" (Origen, 5.283–84; von Harnack, *Marcion*, 159 n. 49).

72 See n. 63 above; von Harnack, *Marcion*, 83–84.

73 Cf. Weigandt, "Doketismus," 83–86; Schnelle, *Antidocetic Christology*, 67; also Kurt Schäferdiek, in the introductory remarks on the *Acts of John* in *NTApoc*[1] 2.188–259: the *Acts of John* have been known since the fourth century, and probably originated in an encratitic sect in the region of Syria or Asia Minor. Eric Junod and Jean-Daniel Kaestli contest the unity of the *Acts of John* (*Acta Iohannis* [2 vols.; CChr Series Apocryphorum; Turnhout: Brepols, 1983]). They attribute chaps. 94–102 to a tradition originating in a Valentinian sect in Syria, and think that the remaining chapters developed within a Gentile Christian environment in Egypt (similarly Brox, "Doketismus," 309–11: he denies the presence of docetic christology in the *Acts of John*). This position, in turn, is opposed by John Gordon Davies, "The Origins of Docetism," *StPatr* VI (TU 81: Berlin: Akademie-Verlag, 1962) 13–35 (esp. 34); and Kurt Schäferdiek, "Herkunft und Interesse der alten Johannesakten," *ZNW* 74 (1983) 247–67. The *Gospel of Peter* should not be mentioned in this context, despite the opinion of J. Denker (see n. 64 above). To the present time, no persuasive proof has been developed to show that this apocryphal work represents a docetic concept. The *Gospel of Truth* cannot be subsumed under the concept of "monophysite Docetism." I agree with Weigandt ("Doketismus," 93–94, 118) that the presence of "Docetism" in this writing is highly questionable (cf. also Sasagu Arai, *Die Christologie des Evangelium Veritatis* [Leiden: Brill, 1964]).

combined that notion with a dualistic concept like the one whose beginnings are discernible in the early Johannine school (cf. 3 John 11), the further development of which is reflected in 1 John's contrasting of light and darkness, life and death, God and the world. Apparently the docetic (*doxa*- or glory-) christology[74] implied a devaluation of the world as we find it, and presumed a prophetic and gnostic self-concept (in the original meaning of "gnosis" as knowledge and experience of God).[75] There is less probability in the suggestion sometimes put forward that these are spiritually motivated enthusiasts,[76] and especially the conclusion drawn from 1:8–10 that the false teachers, on the basis of their self-concept, considered themselves "sinless." Equally unfounded is the opinion that the opponents saw themselves as "libertines" and/or promoted an unethical way of life. The emphasis on love of the sisters and brothers in 1 John does not necessarily mean that the false teachers were distinguished by unethical, asocial behavior. Rather, the author interprets the split in the community brought about by those people as an offense against the commandment of *agapē*, the determining principle for the Christian life.

Docetism is comparable to the gnostic movement, which also failed to establish a set of consistent ethical principles but demonstrated tendencies both to ethical libertinism and to ethical asceticism. It is significant that the suggestion could be made that both the antidocetic and the anti-Judaistic polemic of Ignatius applied to one and the same heretical group.[77]

The geographic expansion of Docetism is attested primarily in Syria and Asia Minor but also (through the work of Cerdon and Marcion) in Rome.[78] A contemporary opposition to docetic false prophets could confirm that 1 John was written in Asia Minor. Ignatius's polemic is directed against Docetists who appeared in the communities in Asia Minor; Marcion came from Sinope in Asia Minor; and in particular, Cerinthus lived in Ephesus during the first half of the second century and was a contemporary of Polycarp and of John, the "disciple of the Lord."[79] When Irenaeus states that John wrote his Gospel against Cerinthus (*Adv. haer.* 3.11.1), this shows that even at this level of tradition John, the "disciple of the Lord," the contemporary of Papias, was being confused with the apostle and evangelist John. This makes clear that the authority of John the son of Zebedee, as the historical disciple of Jesus, had been transferred in the second century to the founder of the Johannine school.

74 Even though the concept of δόξα as characteristic of the sending and existence of Jesus Christ appears frequently in the Fourth Gospel, but never in the Johannine Letters, it would be problematic to try to draw negative conclusions from this fact about the position of the opponents in 1 John.

75 Cf. 1 John 4:1 (prophets). The word "gnosis" in this connection should be interpreted in terms of γινώσκειν τὸν θεόν (4:6); nothing can be extracted from these texts regarding a mythological gnosis as it is known in Christian systems of the second century. On the concept of "gnosis," see Strecker, "Judenchristentum und Gnosis," 265–69, and the excursus below, "Γινώσκειν," at 2 John 1. See also Karl Weiss, "Die 'Gnosis' im Hintergrund und Spiegel der Johannesbriefe," in Tröger, *Gnosis und NT*, 341–56, at 356. Weiss does not wish to describe the teaching combated in 1 John as "gnosis," because characteristic marks of a gnostic system are missing. Instead, he looks for the opponents "in association with the Greeks apostrophized by Paul in 1 Corinthians 1, . . . that is, in Hellenistic Judaism." See the critique of this by Wengst, *Häresie und Orthodoxie*, 22 n. 23.

76 Cf. the Corinthian pneumatics: 1 Cor 4:8; 6:12; 8:1; 10:23; 12:1–11; 14:1–5; and elsewhere.

77 Bauer, *Die Briefe des Ignatius*, 65. Joachim Rohde also tried to show "that the letters of Ignatius are primarily concerned with the rejection of docetic and Jewish *teachings*" ("Häresie und Schisma im Ersten Clemensbrief und in den Ignatius-Briefen," *NovT* 10 [1968] 217–33, esp. 232). In contrast, cf. Schnelle, *Antidocetic Christology*, 64 n. 147, who asserts that Docetism and Judaism are combined only in the letter to the Magnesians. One should probably take it as given that Ignatius is presupposing the existence of a number of different heretical doctrines.

78 Cf. Weigandt, "Doketismus," 155.

79 Irenaeus *Adv. haer.* 3.3.4: Καὶ εἰσὶν οἱ ἀκηκοότες αὐτοῦ (Πολυκάρπου), ὅτι Ἰωάννης ὁ τοῦ κυρίου μαθητὴς ἐν τῇ Ἐφέσῳ πορευθεὶς λούσασθαι καὶ ἰδὼν ἔσω Κήρινθον ἐξήλατο τοῦ βαλανείου μὴ λουσάμενος, ἀλλ᾽ ἐπειπών· Φύγωμεν, μὴ καὶ τὸ βαλανεῖον συμπέσῃ ἔνδον ὄντος Κηρίνθου τοῦ τῆς ἀληθείας ἐχθροῦ ("There are also those who heard from him [Polycarp] that John, the disciple of the Lord, going to bathe at Ephesus, and perceiving Cerinthus within, rushed out of the bath house without bathing, exclaiming, 'Let us fly, lest even the bath-house fall down, because Cerinthus, the enemy of the truth, is within"). Eusebius is dependent on this text: *Hist. eccl.* 3.28.6 (of the "apostle" John: *Hist. eccl.* 4.14.6; Theodoret, *Haereticorum Fabulae* 2.3).

It also suggests early connections between the Johannine circle and the Docetism of Asia Minor. It is true that the witness of 1 John is too vague, and our knowledge of the theology of Cerinthus is too spotty for us to conclude that Cerinthus influenced the Johannine tradition. Against this is also that no traces of the cosmological ideas of Cerinthus can be demonstrated in 1 John. It is certain, however, that at the time of the origin and development of the Johannine school the Docetism of Asia Minor was experienced as a threat, and that it found adherents even within the Johannine circle itself.[80]

■ **26** The aorist ἔγραψα ("I wrote") refers to the letter at hand, as is clear from the preceding ταῦτα ("these things").[81] Reference is made to the section before this one, beginning with 2:18, that spoke of these "deceivers." The participle πλανώντων, as "conative present" describes an attempted action not accomplished.[82] The readers of this document are threatened by false doctrine. The verb πλανᾶν indicates a danger that is occasioned not only by the christological heresy previously described. The community is always standing "between the battle lines" and must decide between the spirit of truth and that of falsehood (4:6). Even in 2 John 7 one can see that the πλάνοι had appeared in a different situation, against the presbyter. The verb πλανᾶν can also, in a less specific sense, represent self-deception (1:8), or call to mind the generalized danger of error (3:7: μηδεὶς πλανάτω ὑμᾶς).

■ **27** In conclusion, the author takes up the concept of χρῖσμα again. As before, in v. 24, the personal pronoun ὑμεῖς ("you") is given an emphatic position at the beginning of the verse[83] in order to strengthen the address: *you*, the members of the Christian community, who are addressed by this writing, and not the false teachers, who do not belong to us (v. 19)—it is *you* who are in possession of the "oil of anointing" that is identical with the possession of the Spirit. Since the Christian community has received the gift of the χρῖσμα,[84] it is true that οὐ χρείαν ἔχετε ἵνα τις διδάσκῃ ὑμᾶς.[85] The spirit of truth, being given to the community, leads them—like the Paraclete in the Fourth Gospel—to knowledge of the truth. Nothing is closed to such knowledge, including the identification of the opposing doctrine. On the basis of the knowledge given to it, the community knows what is ἀληθές and what is ψεῦδος (cf. v. 21), and how it is to behave in face of untruth. Beyond this, the community knows that the gift of the Spirit has been extended to it as an enduring presence (cf. also 4:13), and that this gift lays obligations upon it. The particle ὡς is resumed by καθώς. Hence the accent lies on the final clause, μένετε ἐν αὐτῷ ("abide in him"). The verb is probably not an indicative, as might appear from a comparison with μένει ἐν ὑμῖν in v. 27a,[86] but rather an imperative, as one can

80 See above, Introduction, part 4 ("The Johannine School").

81 See, in the same sense, 5:13; ἔγραψα ὑμῖν in 2:14, 21 is different (see above). As a rule, the present form of the verb refers to the letter at hand: 1:4; 2:1, 7–8, 12–13; 2 John 5.

82 Thus also the present participle in Matt 23:13 par.; indicative present in John 13:6, 27; see BDF § 319.

83 It adds to the emphasis on the καὶ ὑμεῖς that no corresponding finite verb follows this phrase; in popular language "the psychological subject . . . precedes the grammatical subject" (BDF § 466 [2]).

84 On χρῖσμα, see above at 2:20. The personal pronoun in ἀπ' αὐτοῦ is used here without definition, like ἀπὸ τοῦ ἁγίου in v. 20. God or Christ is meant: it is this one who ensures the gift. Cf. also αὐτός in v. 25. The same is true of τὸ αὐτοῦ χρῖσμα and ἐν αὐτῷ, where in each case the reference is to a person (as also in v. 28); cf. Brown, *Epistles*, 361.

85 The construction οὐ χρείαν ἔχειν is also found in John 2:25; 16:30. The verb διδάσκειν occurs only here in the Johannine Letters; it is found nine times in the Fourth Gospel: six times of Jesus, once of the Father (8:28), and once of the Paraclete (14:26); it is secondary in 8:2. In addition, διδάσκαλος occurs only in the Fourth Gospel (eight times, mainly about the Revealer). In contrast, διδαχή appears in John 7:16–17; 18:19; and 2 John 9–10. For "teaching" in the Johannine school, cf. Culpepper, *Johannine School*, 273–74.

86 Favoring an indicative are Holtzmann, *Evangelium, Briefe und Offenbarung*, 248; Brooke, *Epistles*, 63; de la Potterie, "L'onction," 41–42; Malatesta, *Interiority and Covenant*, 224; also Brown, *Epistles*, 361 (with reference to v. 28a: the imperative in v. 28a is said to favor the acceptance of an indicative at the end of v. 27—an assertion that could, of course, suggest exactly the opposite conclusion). In favor of the imperative are Bultmann, *Epistles*, 41; Marshall, *Epistles*, 162–63; Schnackenburg, *Epistles*, 150; Weiss, *Briefe*, 74–75; Windisch and Preisker, *Die Katholischen Briefe*, 119; Schneider, "Briefe," 159; Balz, "Johannesbriefe," 178; Wengst, *Briefe*, 117–18.

see from the subsequent v. 28. At this point the expression functions as a transitional link. Ἐδίδαξεν refers to the giver of the χρῖσμα, but also, of course, to the χρῖσμα itself, the Holy Spirit. The call to believers to abide "in him" (or: "it," i.e., the anointing) expresses a challenge to realize anew, at all times, the truth that is the gift of the Spirit.

Section III: 1 John 2:28–3:24

Parenesis: Whoever Keeps God's Commandments Has a Well-Founded Hope[1]

General Comment

The dogmatic statements in 2:18–27 are followed by another extensive parenetic section that can be subdivided as follows:

2:28–29: Justice before the second coming

3:1–3: Hope in the revelation of the children of God leads to renewal

3:4–10: Anyone who is from God does not sin

3:11–18: Mutual love of the sisters and brothers

3:19–24: Confidence in God is founded on keeping God's commandments and on the gift of the Spirit.

It thus appears that the division of this section cannot be derived from the differing terms of address (vv. 7, 18: τεκνία; v. 13: ἀδελφοί; v. 21: ἀγαπητοί). Instead, these addresses represent the author's customary attention to the presumed Christian readers, similar to what one finds in the other sections that are marked by parenetical features.[2]

According to Bultmann, the original document concluded with 2:27, since the parts that follow contain no new ideas, "but the same themes treated in 1:5—2:27 recur."[3] This tempts one to conjecture "that all these parts are sketches or meditations . . . [or] reports from sessions of a seminar."[4] In fact, the basic elements of the following exposition (freedom from sin, love of the brothers and sisters, the existence of the community in the world)[5] already appeared in the first section, a fact that confirms the meditative character of 1 John. One cannot really speak of a systematic development of ideas. Yet what follows is not simply an appendix to 1:5—2:27. Instead, it is significant that specific ideas from the preceding part are not taken up in this section: the figure of the Paraclete (2:1) does not appear in what follows, nor does the distinction between the new and the old commandment (2:7), nor the contrast of light and darkness (1:5–7; 2:8–11). Rather, this section introduces new words and ideas, such as the concept of "hope" (ἐλπίς, 3:3), the opposition between God and the devil (3:7–10), the example of Cain and Abel (3:11–12), the expression "to pass from death to life" (μεταβαίνειν ἐκ τοῦ θανάτου εἰς τὴν ζωήν, 3:14), and the ethical concept of "murderer" (ἀνθρωποκτόνος, 3:15). All this contributes to the independent character of this part of the text. Even if the writing was not composed at one sitting, but if, instead, its individual parts reflect ongoing discussions within the Johannine school, nevertheless the examples presented allow one to infer even here that the author was inclined to make his writing increasingly concrete and specific.

1 Literature: V. Kerry Inman, "Distinctive Johannine Vocabulary and the Interpretation of I John 3:9," *WTJ* 40 (1977) 136–44; P. P. A. Kotzé, "The meaning of 1 John 3:9 with reference to 1 John 1:8 and 10," *Neot* 13 (1979) 68–83; Sakae Kubo, "1 John 3:9: Absolute or Habitual?" *AUSS* 7 (1969) 47–56; Stanislas Lyonnet, "De natura peccati quid doceat Novum Testamentum—de scriptis Ioanneis," *VD* 35 (1957) 271–78; Franz Mussner, "Eine neutestamentliche Kurzformel für das Christentum," *TThZ* 79 (1970) 49–52; Erik Peterson, "Zur Bedeutungsgeschichte von παρρησία," in Wilhelm Koepp, ed., *Reinhold Seeberg Festschrift*, vol. 1: *Zur Theorie des Christentums* (Leipzig: Scholl, 1929) 283–97; Ignace de la Potterie, "L'impeccabilité du chrétien d'après I Joh. 3,6–9," in M. E. Boismard, ed., *L'Évangile de Jean: Études et problèmes* (RechBib 3; Bruges: Desclée de Brouwer, 1958) 161–77 (ET: "The Impeccability of the Christian According to I Jn 3, 6–9," in Stanislas Lyonnet, *The Christian Lives by the Spirit* [trans. John Morriss; Staten Island: Alba House, 1971] 175–96); Françoise Smyth-Florentin, "'Voyez quel grand amour le Père nous a donné,' 1 Jn 3.1–2," *AsSeign* 2/25 (1969) 32–38; Harry C. Swadling, "Sin and Sinlessness in I John," *SJT* 35 (1982) 205–11.

2 Cf. Schnackenburg, "[The address to the readers as τεκνία . . . need not] imply a major break in the development of the thought" (*Epistles*, 85). This does not, of course, exclude the possibility that the same author "does allow a moment's breathing space" by the use of this address (ibid.). On the translation of τεκνία, see above on 1 John 2:12.

3 Bultmann, *Epistles*, 43.

4 Ibid., 44.

5 Cf. 1 John 2:3–6, 9–11 (freedom from sin); 2:9–11 (love of the brothers and sisters); 2:15–17 (community in the world).

2 Justice before the Second Coming

28 **And now, little children, abide in him, so that when he is revealed we may have confidence and not be put to shame before him at his coming. 29/ If you know that he is righteous, you may be sure that everyone who does right has been born of him.**

■ **28** Καὶ νῦν ("and now") indicates the beginning of a new parenetical section. It has a consequent meaning, but at the same time the reference to the present (as also in 2:18; 4:3) underscores the urgency of the injunction.[1] The imperative μένετε links this verse with v. 27. "Abiding in him" was there identified as an abiding in Christ's teaching, and it will be seen at this point that the teaching is actualized by doing "right," that is, acting justly (cf. v. 29). The section ends at 3:24, for in 4:1 the author begins a new dogmatic recital concerning the discernment of spirits, the spirits of truth and error.

This matter of "abiding in him" (μένειν ἐν αὐτῷ) clearly emphasizes the necessity of a close unity between the community and Christ, and it presents Christ as a space into which the community, including all the aspects of its life, is being drawn. This is not far removed from the Pauline idea of being ἐν Χριστῷ. As with Paul, the local conception does not exclude the idea of a personal encounter in the future (cf. 1 Thess 4:16–17). Instead, the tension-filled union of present and future eschatology is especially clear at this point in 1 John: while φανεροῦν is a *terminus technicus* for the revelation of Christ in time past (1:2; 3:5, 8; 4:9), it can also refer to the unmasking of seducers in the present (2:19), and in what follows it will describe the author's expectation of the future (3:2). The fact that, here also, the future revelation of the end time is in view[2] is shown by the parallel between v. 28b and v. 28c: the revelation of Christ is equated with his "coming." The word παρουσία, which occurs only here in the Johannine writings, has a long history within Christian tradition;[3] it reflects the apocalyptic (future-eschatological) traditions that must be presumed at the beginning of the Johannine school,[4] without giving any precise time for the coming of Christ.[5] What is crucial is not the question of when and where (already at issue in the Synoptic Gospels), but *that*

1 The development of the meaning of the expression καὶ νῦν in Greek usage shows a gradual movement from a temporal "now" to a causal "for." Cf. Eduard Schwyzer, *Griechische Grammatik: Auf der Grundlage von Karl Brugmanns griechischer Grammatik* (2 vols.; ed. Albert Debrunner; 2d ed.; Munich: Beck, 1959) 2.571; Kühner-Gerth, *Grammatik*, 2.117, 2; BDR § 442 (8d) and n. 26. For NT occurrences of the temporal meaning, in addition to 1 John 2:18 and 4:3, see esp. John 11:22; 17:5; Phil 1:20, 30; for the causal or modal usage (an expanded translation of which would be "as things now stand") 2 John 5; Acts 10:5; 16:36; 23:15, and frequently elsewhere. Cf. also BACD 545; Schnackenburg, *Epistles*, 152 n. 83. This passage, like so many others, scarcely permits any choice between the two alternative meanings, the succeeding present imperative μένετε, with its view to the future that has not yet arrived, also has a temporal aspect. In some cases an influence from LXX can be demonstrated (cf. Acts 13:11; 20:22, 25, and frequently elsewhere), but it cannot be presumed in the present instance.

2 So also M. Bockmuehl, "Das Verb φανερόω im Neuen Testament," *BZ* 32 (1988) 87–99, esp. 92.

3 Cf. 1 Thess 2:19; 3:13; 4:15; 5:23; 1 Cor 15:23; 2 Thess 2:1, 8–9; Matt 24:3, 27, 37, 39; Jas 5:7–8; 2 Pet 1:16; 3:4, 12; also in an unspecific sense in 2 Cor 7:6–7; 10:10, and frequently. See Albrecht Oepke, "παρουσία, πάρειμι," *TDNT* 5 (1967) 858–71.

4 See below on 2 John 7–8. It is no accident that Bultmann felt compelled to exclude this verse as "redactional" (*Epistles*, 44 and n. 4); cf. Braun's differing opinion in "Literar-Analyse," 237.

5 This is in harmony with the tradition. The author presumes that the coming of Christ is synonymous with the coming of God: no alternative exists between God and Christ (against Weiss, *Briefe*, 76)

the future of the community and the world will be determined by the coming of the Son of God, the one who has already come (4:9–10).[6] The attitude attributed to the community that "abides in him" in the future, and at the same time demanded of it now, is described by the noun παρρησία. In accordance with the christological theme of the Fourth Gospel, this term there characterizes the appearance of Jesus as the Revealer and his public activity within the world (John 16:25, 29; 18:20, and frequently), but in 1 John it is applied exclusively in an ecclesiological context. Thus, in contrast to the usage elsewhere to refer to the attitude of one who prays to God (3:21; 5:14), it is characteristic of this passage that it is entirely future-directed. That the community is entitled to have confidence is something that can and will be demonstrated on the day of Christ's coming, that is, at the day of judgment, as will be made still clearer in 4:17. That means that they will not be put to shame on that day.[7]

Excursus: Παρρησία

The concept of παρρησία occurs in Greek from the time of Euripides and Aristophanes and was used in political, private, and moral contexts. It describes an essential feature of Greek democracy,[8] something that belonged to all full citizens, but not to foreigners and slaves.[9] In the private sphere, παρρησία was considered as part of the teaching on "friendship" or φιλία.[10] In Cynicism it was understood in a moral sense; παρρήσια was used with ἐλευθερία ("freedom") to describe "the highest good of the reflective, morally secure person who lives in full 'openness' toward his fellow citizens, friends, and enemies, and who both praises and severely reproves them."[11]

The LXX incorporates the various Greek meanings (as in Lev 26:13), but in addition the concept experiences some alteration under the influence of OT beliefs about God, especially in passages that speak of God's appearing to human beings or of the freedom and confidence of human persons before God. Thus in Job 27:9–10; 22:23–27 the word means "freedom," or "free and joyful standing before God";[12] so also in a future-eschatological sense in Wis 5:1–2, 15–16. According to LXX Pss 11:6; 93:1, God is self-revealed in the speaking of the word and in judgment.[13] The author of *1 Enoch* also recognizes a "situation of παρρησία" in an eschatological context. The word refers to "the reward of the open standing of the righteous before the throne of God or the Messiah, to the radiance given therewith, to the integration into the joy expressed in praise."[14] God creates justice for the righteous and the despised, but sinners will know pain, and darkness will grow deeper on their faces (cf. 62.3–5, 10–12). In *4 Ezra* 7.98 the Latin equivalent "fiducia" is interpreted as "boldness" expressed in eschatological rejoicing; it is equivalent to "be[ing] confident without confusion" and "be[ing] glad without fear."[15]

6 Cf. Mark 13:30–32 par.

7 Does the aorist passive subjunctive αἰσχυνθῶμεν have a reflexive meaning? Cf. the interpretation as reflexive middle in Windisch and Preisker, *Die Katholischen Briefe,* 118–19. Schnackenburg reads it otherwise, in a passive sense (*Epistles,* 151, 153 and n. 88, along the lines of "to be ruined before Christ"). The contrast between αἰσχύνη ("shame") and παρρησία ("boldness"), otherwise found in the NT only in Phil 1:20, was already current in Hellenistic Jewish apocalyptic: *4 Ezra* 7.98 (*fiducia—confundare;* the Vulgate is similar at 1 John 2:28); cf. Wis 5:1; Prov 13:5; *1 Enoch* offers content parallels, but not verbal ones (47.1–4; 61.3–13; 62.10, and frequently); cf. Heinrich Schlier, "παρρησία, παρρασιάζομαι," *TDNT* 5 (1967) 879. See also the following excursus on παρρησία.

8 Cf. Polybius *Histories* 2.38.6: "One could not find a political system and principle so favourable to equality (ἰσηγορία) and freedom of speech (παρρησία), in a word, so sincerely democratic (δημοκρατία ἀληθινή) as that of the Achaean league"; Demosthenes *Orationes* 60.26; 111.3–4.

9 Euripides *Ion* 670–75; *Phoen.* 391–92.

10 Aristotle *Nic. Eth.* 9.2, 1165a 24–31: fatherly and motherly honor (τιμήν) are due to parents. "To comrades and brothers one should allow freedom of speech (παρρήσια) and common use of all things (κοινότητα)" (translation in Richard McKeon, *The Basic Works of Aristotle* [New York: Random House, 1941] 1079).

11 Horst Balz, "παρρήσια," *EDNT* 3 (1993) 45; cf. Aristotle *Nic. Eth.* 4.3, 1124b 29; Diogenes Laertius *Vit. phil.* 6.69; also Brooke, *Epistles,* 66–67.

12 Schlier, "παρρησία," 876.

13 Cf. what Prov 1:20 says of Wisdom.

14 Schlier, "παρρησία," 879.

15 Translations in *NRSV;* cf. the version by Josef Schreiner in *Das 4. Buch Esra* (JSHRZ 5; Gütersloh: Mohn, 1983) 355.

The concept appears 31 times in the NT. Thirteen of these occurrences are in the Johannine literature (Gospel 9 times; 1 John 4 times). Five are in Acts and four are in Hebrews, but only one is in the Synoptics (Mark 8:32). Four are in Paul's writings. The verb παρρησιάζομαι (9 times in the NT) is not used in the Johannine corpus.

In the Fourth Gospel the use of παρρησία has, without exception, a christological intention. The variation in the meaning of the word between "being public" and "being open [i.e., bold, forthright]" reflects the dialectic in the appearance of the Revealer. He appears in public, in synagogues and in the temple, where all can hear him (John 18:20). If his public discourse encounters no negative response from the leaders, one may suppose that they have recognized that Jesus is the Christ (John 7:26). This public appearance is antithetically correlated to the Revealer's withdrawal into hiddenness (John 11:54; cf. 7:10: ἐν κρυπτῷ), for his work is fulfilled in the world, that is, in the realm of unbelief as represented by "the Jews" (John 7:13; cf. 10:24; 11:54; 18:20). His own brothers participate in this worldly nature when they urge him to do his works in public (John 7:4). They thus misunderstand the works, for this miraculous activity in public is not to be equated with the eschatological boldness that imbues the works, making them "signs," and whose witness in faith is grasped as truth (cf. John 7:5–8). It is obvious that it is only faith that properly comprehends the unveiled truth, and not the mere imagery in Jesus' words when the Revealer promises the disciples that he will speak to them "no longer in riddles" (οὐκέτι ἐν παροιμίαις), but will utter παρρησία of the Father (John 16:25). The disciples' response (16:29: "Yes, now you are speaking plainly [ἐν παρρησίᾳ], not in any figure of speech [παροιμίαν]") makes clear that they have not fully understood the Revealer's words, since they found their faith in his divine sending on the proof of his omniscience (16:30; cf. 16:32). Similarly, when Jesus speaks plainly of Lazarus's death the result is a misunderstanding on the part of the disciples, because they do not recognize that through the appearance of the Son of God death has been overcome (11:14). The collapsing together of empirical publicness and eschatological openness in the appearance of the Revealer corresponds to the existence of unbelief and belief, of misunderstanding and understanding side by side and even within the same individual.

First John distinguishes between a future and a present meaning of the word, although it always has an eschatological sense. While in 2:28 the future eschatological παρρησία is identical with "confidence" in salvation at the coming of the Son of God, that is, at the final judgment, the same is true in 4:17, where the perfection of love reveals itself as "boldness" on the coming day of judgment. In contrast, the present usage in 3:21 expresses the "trust" that the prayers of the faithful are heard at the present time; in 5:14, also, the concept describes the "certainty" that those who believe in the name of the Son of God and pray according to the will of God will not go unheard.

Although the OT usage adopted in the NT identifies "being put to shame" with "being disgraced" or "being excluded,"[16] such an extreme consequence is not expressed here, even though it belongs to the background of this text and is hinted in the admonition to "have no fear" (cf. 4:17). The author calls the hearers to "abide in him," with the goal[17] that such abiding will endure even in the future coming of Christ.

■ **29** The overarching thematic context that contains this expectation extends from 2:28 to 3:3, where it gives way to reflection on the ethical consequences that follow from it. The expectation of the coming parousia and the statement of the attitude demanded by this perspective also determine the content of v. 29. Hence it is insufficient to understand εἰδῆτε[18] in a merely theoretical sense

16 Isa 28:16; cf. Rom 9:33; 1 Pet 2:6; Rudolf Bultmann, "αἰσχύνω, κτλ.," *TDNT* 1 (1964) 189–91; the combination of being put to shame and being ruined also occurs in the talmudic text *b. Berakot* 46a: "May it be God's will that our host should never be ashamed in this world nor disgraced in the next world" (*The Babylonian Talmud* [12 vols. in 8; trans. Maurice Simon; ed. I. Epstein; London: Soncino, 1948] 279)

17 The particle ἵνα expresses purpose and/or consequence; for consecutive and final meanings see BDF §§ 391 (5); 456 (2).

18 The construction with ἐάν and the subjunctive does not avoid the usual construction, εἰ with the indicative (cf. BDF § 372) in order to cast doubt on the certainty that "he is righteous," but rather in order to require that the readers test themselves to see whether they have realized that he is righteous, thus also Brown, *Epistles*, 382.

("you know"). It is true that there is a reference here to the community's credo, in which Jesus Christ is confessed as Paraclete and as righteous (2:1), but such knowledge of the opportunity for salvation founded on Christ is not a merely theoretical issue. As is already shown by the consequent indicative γινώσκετε,[19] this is not a matter of an intellectual conviction that could be abstracted from one's own person and situation. The "knowledge" of Christ as the righteous one that is contained in the credo implies, rather, that the community is not and should not be excepted from such righteousness, and that it must strive for a righteous stance that would be appropriate for Christ.[20]

That Christ is "righteous" (δίκαιος) was already asserted in 2:1 in connection with the identification of Christ with the Paraclete; it may also be presumed in 3:7. Of course, the same adjective was applied to God in 1:9 (God is "just [to] forgive our sins"). Since in what follows "of him" (ἐξ αὐτοῦ) is to be understood in the sense of being begotten or born of God, the application of the adjective varies widely from one interpretation to another;[21] some interpreters also regard it as a sign of different sources in collision.[22] But despite the incorporation of fixed terms from Johannine tradition (παρουσία, δικαιοσύνη), one can again see that the author leaves the readers in a state of unclarity about the application of personal pronouns and words of attribution, because he cannot admit any alternative between christology and theology: God is in Christ! Just as there is no thought that the righteousness of Christ could exist without the divine basis that makes it possible, so the procreation of believers by God is not divorced from the reality of Christ.

When the author associates Jesus' advocacy for sinners with the key word δίκαιος (2:1), or confesses that God's righteousness is paradoxically realized in the act of forgiveness (1:9), he appears to be associating himself with Pauline tradition (cf. Rom 1:17; Gal 2:17), even though in 1 John the noun δικαιοσύνη is not predicated of God, but rather describes the object of the community's action (cf. 3:7, 10). In particular, the union of the indicative of salvation with the ethical imperative, associated with the δικ- stem, may have arisen in relationship to the traditions of Pauline thought (cf. Rom 6:1–14; Gal 5:25). The paradoxical advocacy for sinners, marked by *agapē*,[23] does not lead to libertinistic consequences;[24] on the contrary, its precondition is the overcoming of sin on the part of Jesus/God. Hence on the human side the consequence must be a life that is characterized by the doing of justice, in which the fact of being free from sin is made concrete reality.[25] Therefore, the community's doing justice not only has a christological background, namely, that Jesus' righteousness has a fundamental significance for the community (2:1), but also the anthropological precondition of being "born

19 For an understanding of γινώσκετε ("you know") in the sense of "you acknowledge," cf. Hebrew ידע (see the excursus on γινώσκειν below). There is dispute about whether this is an imperative or an indicative. Dodd favors the imperative (*Epistles*, 68: "in enforcing the ethical criterion"; similarly Windisch and Preisker, *Die Katholischen Briefe*, 119, according to whom it is "the most serious obligation to resist the temptations of the false teachers and to maintain union with 'him,' whom they are tearing apart"). Dodd rests his argument on the parenetic structure of the context. But this author combines indicative and imperative elsewhere as well (cf. vv. 27–28), and Christian existence is often expressed in the indicative with γινώσκειν (cf. 1 John 2:3–5, 13–14, 18, 29; 3:16; 4:2[?], 6–7, 16; cf. John 6:69; 2 John 1; Brown, *Epistles*, 383).

20 The conjunction καί (v. 29c) is omitted by a number of textual witnesses (B Ψ 𝔐 lat, syr., and copt.). This is undoubtedly a secondary smoothing, resulting in a tightening of the style. The translation "you know this as well" (Brown, *Epistles*, 383) wrongly attaches καί to the preceding verb; in reality it draws a parallel between Christ as the δίκαιος and the πᾶς who does justice; hence it should be translated "thus you recognize that in the same way everyone. . . . "

21 Cf. Schnackenburg: v. 29a refers to Jesus, v. 29c to God (ἐξ αὐτοῦ); the author is already anticipating 3:6, and this causes a "contamination" (*Epistles*, 154).

22 E.g., Bultmann, *Epistles*, 45; Windisch and Preisker (*Die Katholischen Briefe*, 119) wanted to trace the statement about procreation from God (v. 29b) to a source.

23 Cf. 2:1; 3:5, 8, and frequently.

24 Libertinistic conclusions were drawn from the indicative of salvation by the pneumatic opponents of Paul in Corinth (cf. 1 Cor 6:12; 10:23). I have noted above that parallels to the docetic teachers combated in 1 John should be drawn only with the greatest reservation (see the excursus on "The False Teachers in 1 John" at 2:25).

25 Cf. 3:6–10. Verse 29, following on v. 28, reflects the OT cause-effect connection (cf. Job 22:23–30; Wis 5:1, 15–16), as does the OT-Jewish traditional

of God." Christian existence is not founded on itself, but on the "wholly other." Of course, it is only when the community believes in Jesus Christ as the one who is righteous for them, and confesses him by its deeds, that it is counted among those who are born of God. For the author, the only adequate reason for this being "born of God" is found in the revelation in Christ.

Excursus: Being Born of God

Although the notion and the concept of being "born of God" is to be distinguished, both in terminology and in the history of tradition, from being "children of God" (τέκνα θεοῦ), the latter spectrum of ideas can here be identified with the former (3:9–10; 5:1–2). The verb γεννᾶν ("beget," "bear"; passive "be born") is found in the Johannine writings both in the natural sense (John 3:4, 6; 8:41; 9:2, 19–20, 32, 34; 16:21; 18:37: "beget" or [of women] "bear")[26] and in the figurative sense (John 1:13; 3:3, 5–8; 1 John 2:29; 3:9; 4:7; 5:1, 4, 18). In individual cases one may distinguish between being born of God (1 John 2:29; 3:9; 4:7), of the Spirit (John 3:6, 8; cf. 3:5: of water and spirit), or "from above" (John 3:3, 7). These statements, with a single exception,[27] are constructed not christologically but anthropologically. This makes it improbable that the notion of birth from the Spirit in the Johannine writings derives from primitive Christian christology and its OT background.[28] It is also characteristic of the Johannine writings to refer the word υἱός to Jesus alone;[29] the expression τέκνα θεοῦ is applied to the community.[30] If the "children of God" are born of God, they are "from God" (ἐκ τοῦ θεοῦ, 1 John 3:9–10). This separates them from the works of the "evil one" (5:18).

As seems probable in the light of the Fourth Gospel, Johannine theology finds the origins of the idea of being born of God in the baptismal tradition.[31] But

terminology: for ποιεῖν δικαιοσύνην (1 John 3:7, 10), cf. Isa 56:1; Jer 9:23; 2 Kgs 8:15; Ps 105:3; in the NT also in Rom 10:5; Matt 6:1; Rev 22:11; see also *1 Clem.* 13.1; *2 Clem.* 4.2; 11.7; *Ps. Sol.* 9.5. For the equivalent usage ἐργάζεσθαι δικαιοσύνην cf. Ps 14:2; Acts 10:35; Heb 11:33; Jas 1:20.

26 Typically, in reference to Jesus (18:37), γεγέννημαι is open to both meanings ("begotten of the Father" or "born of Mary"). Johannine christology and the Johannine image of God are not receptive to any male-female dualism.

27 1 John 5:18 (q.v.), like 5:1, describes two different births; this is a play on words that is not really disruptive of the basic anthropological intention of these passages. John 1:13 contains the poorly attested reading *natus est;* this can be ignored.

28 Ps 2:7 is quoted in Acts 13:33, as well as in Heb 1:5 and 5:5, but it does not appear in the Johannine writings. This is said in response to a tendency toward a "whole Bible" interpretation, as is apparent, for example, in the article by Friedrich Büchsel, "γεννάω, κτλ.," *TDNT* 1 (1964) 668–75.

29 Cf. John 3:16–17, 35–36; 5:19–23; 1 John 2:22–25; 4:14; 5:12; 2 John 9. The plural υἱοί is not attested in the Johannine literature; it occurs in Matt 5:9, 45; 8:12; 13:38; Luke 6:35; 16:8; 20:36; Rom 8:14, 19; 9:26; Gal 3:26; 4:4, 7; Heb 2:10; 12:5, 7–8.

30 Cf. John 1:12; 11:52; 1 John 3:1–2, 10; 5:2; in addition, the expression τὰ ἐμὰ τέκνα (3 John 4) refers to the members of the community (corresponding to 2 John 1, 4, 13). See Matthew Vellanickal, *The Divine Sonship of Christians in the Johannine Writings* (AnBib 72; Rome: Biblical Institute Press, 1977) 234–37.

31 It is no accident that the expression ἐν Χριστῷ, which is frequent in Paul, is also echoed in the Johannine writings (cf. 1 John 5:20, as well as μένειν ἐν αὐτῷ: 1 John 2:6, 24, 27–28; 3:6, 24; John 6:56; 15:4–10, and frequently; εἶναι ἐν αὐτῷ: 1 John 2:8; 5:11; John 1:4, and frequently; εἶναι ἐν ἐμοί: John 10:38; 14:10–11, 20; 17:21, and frequently). This allows one to suspect some continuing influence of the Pauline school on the development of Johannine theology. The pre-Pauline formula in Gal 3:26–28 testifies to ἐν Χριστῷ as part of the early baptismal tradition. From this, it is probable that there are parallels to the idea of "being born of God" as mediated by baptism; cf. Albrecht Oepke ("ἐν," *TDNT* 2 [1964] 542): "By baptism . . . believers are removed from the sphere of the first Adam, which is that of sin and death, into the sphere of the second Adam, which is that of righteousness and life. . . . This underlying spatial concept gives us the clue to the true significance of the formula ἐν Χριστῷ 'Ιησοῦ and its parallels." For the idea of "rebirth" as a consequence of baptism, cf. also Titus 3:5; 1 Pet 1:23; 2:2; also Clement of Alexandria *Exc. Theod.* 76.4; 80.1; Justin *1 Apol.* 61.4 (on this, see Georg Strecker, "Eine Evangelienharmonie bei Justin und Pseudoklemens?" *NTS* 24 [1978] 307). Vellanickal discerns "the baptismal catechetical character" of particular expressions in 1 John, and attempts to establish a basis for them by means of a synopsis with 1 Pet 1:3–23 (*Divine Sonship,*

divine origin was conceived, independently of that tradition, in connection with the acceptance of the Word or the realization of gnosis. Thus the Coptic *Gospel of Truth* says: "Therefore he who has knowledge is one who comes from above. When he is called he hears, answers and turns to him who calls him, ascends to him and knows how he is called. Since he has knowledge, he fulfills the will of him who called him. . . . He who thus shall attain knowledge knows whence he is come and whither he goes. He knows like one who was drunk and has departed from his drunkenness; he brought his own [again] into order after he had returned to himself" (NHC 1, 3: 22,2–19).[32] This suggests the docetic opponents of 1 John, in contrast to 2 and 3 John, where nothing is said about being born of God. It seems probable that the false teachers in 1 John claimed that they were born of God; for this could well be combined with a dualistic-spiritualistic notion. That the concept was taken up and incorporated in the theology of the Johannine communities in a positive sense is apparent from the passages in John and 1 John cited in the previous paragraph.

As concerns the broader religio-historical background, it is to be sought, on the whole, in the Hellenistic and syncretistic realms, for while "being born of God" and "being children of God" are identified in John and 1 John, passages in the OT and Jewish literature testify only to the latter idea.[33] As early as the hymn to Zeus by Cleanthes, the human race is derived from the divine father,[34] and in Epictetus one finds the petitioner's confession to God: *με σὺ ἐγέννησας* (*Diss.* 4.10.16: "Thou hast begotten me"). While in the Stoa the idea of divine begetting rested on a cosmological basis and can be traced to Plato, who equates the father-god with the creator of the world,[35] Greek and Stoic influences can also be detected in the Alexandrian Jew Philo, when he speaks of God as *ὁ γεννήσας* or *γεννητὴς πατήρ*, who "generated" human beings at the creation of the world.[36] Philo also distinguishes the idea of generation by God from the ethical notion of the adoption of the virtuous person as a child of God.[37] While it remains in dispute whether this idea has been influenced by the mystery religions,[38] in any case the concept of being

234–35); see also Ignace de la Potterie, *La vérité dans Saint Jean* (2 vols.; AnBib 73–74; Rome: Biblical Institute Press, 1977) 304–10.

32 Cf. Rudolph, *Gnosis,* 120. According to Irenaeus *Adv. haer.* 1.23.2, Simon Magus asserted that all angels and powers were born through the Ennoia. Cf. also the Naasenes' idea of the pneumatic birth in Hippolytus *Ref.* 5.8.23; and 5.17.6 on the Peratae: "If any of those who are here is able to comprehend that he is a character of the Father . . . brought down from above and put into a body here, . . . entirely like the Father in heaven, so will such a one ascend to that place. But he who does not receive this teaching nor recognise the necessity of becoming (i.e. the earthly world) is like an abortion born by night and will (also) perish by night" (translation in Rudolph, *Gnosis,* 115). The divine origins of the Gnostic are also echoed in the call addressed by the author of Ephesians to the Christian community: "Sleeper, awake! Rise from the dead, and Christ will shine on you" (Eph 5:14). The eschatological call to awakening in the gnostic tractate *Concept of the Great Power* (NHC 6, 4: 39,33–40, 7) reveals an instructive connection with sacramental terminology: "Still are you asleep and dreaming. Wake up, turn about, taste and eat the true food! Impart the word (*logos*) and the water of life! Cease from the evil desires and wishes and the (things) which are unlike (you)" (Rudolph, *Gnosis,* 120).

33 Cf. Schnackenburg, *Epistles,* 165–66 (against Otto Michel and Otto Betz, "Von Gott gezeugt," in *Judentum, Urchristentum, Kirche: Festschrift für Joachim Jeremias,* ed. Walter Eltester (BZNW 26; Berlin: A. Töpelmann, 1960] 3–23). The use of the verb ("to bear," "to beget") is applied in Ps 2:7 to the adoption or legitimation of the king of Israel, and remains completely in the picture in Deut 32:18 as well ("the rock that bore you," with reference to the chosen people). Something similar can be said of 1QSa ii.11–12 and 1QH ix.35–36.

34 Stobaeus *Ecl.* 1.25.7–8 (*SVF* 1.121, 37–38): *ἐκ σοῦ γὰρ γένους ἐσμέν* ("for of thy race we are").

35 Cf. Plato *Tim.* 37C (*ὁ γεννήσας πατήρ*); Richard Reitzenstein and Hans Heinrich Schaeder, *Studien zum antiken Synkretismus* (Leipzig: Teubner, 1926) 142–53; Gottlob Schrenk, "*πατήρ* A," *TDNT* 5 (1967) 945–59, at 954–55.

36 Cf. Philo *Op. mun.* 84, according to which the human being generated by God "the father" (*γεννήσας αὐτὸν ὁ πατήρ*) is made the ruler of creation; also *Spec. leg.* 2.30–31; 3.189, where God is described as "father" and "progenitor." In the same creation-theological sense Philo speaks of God as "husband and father of the universe, supplying, as He does, the germs of life" (*Det. pot. ins.* 147; cf. *Som.* 2.273; *Mut. nom.* 205).

37 Philo *Sobr.* 56: "He alone is nobly born, for he has registered God as his father and become by adoption His only son" (*γεγονὼς . . . υἱός*).

38 Cf. Friedrich Büchsel, "*γεννάω* C," *TDNT* 1 (1964) 68–72, at 669: "in the period before Christ there is certainly no reference in the Mysteries to a *γεννηθεὶς ἐκ τοῦ θεοῦ*." While Schnackenburg still wishes to acknowledge a "borrowing of terminology" between 1 John and the mystery religions (*Epistles,* 167),

"born of God," against the background thus given, must also be interpreted ontologically in 1 John, although not in terms of creation theology or in a physical sense. Since this procreation by God describes something that cannot be accounted for anthropologically, but that identifies the *extra nos* of believing existence, it is also not simply to be identified with "faith."[39]

Bultmann, referring to *Corp. Herm.* 13, asserted a material kinship between Christian and gnostic preaching (*Epistles,* 47). In opposition to this, Vellanickal (*Divine Sonship,* 234–35) and Brown (*Epistles,* 385) point out that the similarity on which Bultmann bases his argument (namely, that "the old, natural man cannot, without divine assistance, attain the salvation to which he aspires, but that he requires a renewal of his being" [*Epistles,* 46]) cannot be restricted to Christian and gnostic traditions.

39 1 John does not say that Christian faith is traceable to God's action. One must also doubt that the "existential precondition" contained in the idea of being "born of God" was asserted only by the opponents. It is valid as well for the community in 1 John, no matter how necessary it is to confirm such preexisting reality through faithful acknowledgment and righteous actions. (This is said in response to Wengst, *Brief,* 123; cf. also Schunack, *Briefe,* 53.)

3

Hope for the Revelation of the Children of God Leads to Renewal

1 **See what love the Father has given us, that**
we should be called children of God; and
that is what we are. The reason the
world does not know us is that it did not
know [God]. 2/ Beloved, we are God's
children now; what we will be has not
yet been revealed. What we do know is
this: when [he] is revealed, we will be
like [him], for we will see [him] as [he] is.
3/ And all who have this hope in [him]
purify themselves, just as [he] is pure.

■ **1** The second person of the aorist imperative "see" (*ἴδετε*) marks a new beginning, although at the same time it continues the preceding parenesis. As with verbs of knowing in general, so here it is not a matter of purely theoretical knowledge or sense apprehension (cf. 2:29). Nor is *ἴδετε* merely a formulaic expression used to focus attention.[1] The call to "see" implies the admonition to entrust oneself unconditionally to the gift of *agapē*.[2]

There is a twofold integration in the context. First, the idea of birth from God (v. 29b) is taken up in the phrase *τέκνα θεοῦ* ("children of God"), which appears here for the first time (out of five occurrences). This is peculiar to 1 John,[3] whose author never uses the phrase *υἱοὶ θεοῦ* for the Christian community; the title "son of God" is reserved for Christ.[4] Second, there is a connection with the preceding context in the relating of Christ's righteousness (v. 29a) to *ἀγάπη* (*θεοῦ*). That Christ, as the righteous one, intercedes for us and thus reveals God's justice toward us (cf. 1:9) is nothing other than the revelation of the love of God. The revelation of the Father's *agapē*,[5] however, is shown in the fact that we can be called children of God. Although one might say on

1 Against Schnackenburg, *Epistles*, 155 n. 101. In the Fourth Gospel the singular *ἴδε* often has the sense of a formulaic expression introducing a revelatory saying (John 1:29, 36, 47; 19:14, 26–27), or it is used in the expression *ἔρχου καὶ ἴδε* to express an invitation (1:46; 11:34; in the plural: 1:39 *v.l.*; 4:29). This combination makes clear that what is being described is not a distanced kind of "seeing"; rather, what is intended is an existential decision on the part of the person addressed. This is confirmed by the association of "seeing" and "acknowledging" (*θεωρεῖν* and *γινώσκειν*): 14:19–20; cf. 1 John 3:19.

2 *Ποταπός* is a late form of *ποδαπός*, the Hellenistic equivalent of *ποῖος* (BDF § 298 [3]), here made explicit by the use of *ἵνα* (cf. 5:3) in the sense of "how great." Cf. Mark 13:1; BAGD 694–95.

3 Cf. 3:1–2, 10 (alongside *τέκνα τοῦ διαβόλου*); 5:2; also John 1:12; 11:52; in each case the reference is to those who believe in Christ. There is no real material difference, since in the Fourth Gospel also the gathering of the *τέκνα τοῦ θεοῦ* is open to the future (against Haenchen, "Neuere Literatur," 280). *Τέκνον* in the NT refers first of all to biological children (Matt 2:18; 27:25), but the figurative meaning is known in literature outside the NT as well. The promise of the father-child relationship in the book of *Jubilees* is instructive: "and I will be their father, and they shall be my children. And they all shall be called children of the living God; and every angel and spirit shall know (they shall know indeed) that these are my children, and that I am truly and genuinely their father, and that I love them" (*Jub.* 1.24–25; translation by R. H. Charles, rev. by C. Rabin. In H.F.D. Sparks, ed., *The Apocryphal Old Testament* [New York: Oxford University Press, 1984], 13). One should take note of the difference from the address *τεκνία* (see at 2:1 above); cf. also Schnackenburg, *Epistles*, 156 and n. 108.

4 For Christ as *υἱὸς τοῦ θεοῦ*, see 1 John 3:8; 4:15; 5:5, 10, 12–13, 20; *υἱὸς αὐτοῦ*: 1:3, 7; 3:23; 4:9–10, 15; 5:9–12, 20; absolute use of *υἱός*: 2:22–24; 4:14; 5:12; 2 John 9; *υἱὸς τοῦ πατρός*: 2 John 3.

5 *Πατήρ* is here used absolutely, as it is frequently in 1 John (1:2–3; 2:1, 14–16, 22–24; 3:1; 4:14; cf. 2 John 3–4, 9) and in the Fourth Gospel (1:14, 18; 2:16; 3:35, and elsewhere); it is seldom found in the NT otherwise: Matt 11:27; Mark 13:32 par.

the basis of other passages that birth from God and being children of God are identical concepts (cf. 3:10; also 5:2 with 5:1), the ἵνα clause is not to be understood simply as epexegetical;[6] rather, it expresses the finality of the love of God. That love is directed toward the future in which this judgment of being children of God will be spoken over those born of God.[7] In contrast, as regards textual criticism, the overwhelmingly better attested continuation with καὶ ἐσμέν provides a counteraccent:[8] what will be true in the future is already a reality in the present. The existence of those born of God, those accepted as God's children, is not yet complete. It is open to a future reserved to God, but without ceasing to be present.

Διὰ τοῦτο refers to the preceding sentence. Because the members of the community, as present and future children of God, belong to God, the distance between them and the world is impassible. The world does not know them (οὐ γινώσκει ἡμᾶς),[9] namely, in this existence that is both promised to them and already present as a result of the promise. The lack of knowledge is at the same time a lack of acknowledgment;[10] for the author takes it as a matter of course that proper knowledge would necessarily have led to acknowledgment. But the true reason for the world's nonrecognition of the community is that it has not realized its own possible relationship to God (ὅτι οὐκ ἔγνω αὐτόν). The world neither knows nor acknowledges God.[11] That is what shapes its very being.[12] The dualism of community and world cannot be more clearly expressed.[13] The world differs from the community in that it does not believe. Correspondingly, it is true that wherever God is not acknowledged, the sphere of the world's hegemony expands.[14]

6 Against Bultmann, *Epistles*, 47 n. 15; already opposed by Weiss, *Briefe*, 80: "There is no reason at all to deny the telic meaning of ἵνα and to take it as simply an introduction to the objective clause."

7 This corresponds to 2:28. According to BAGD 399, καλεῖν "approaches closely the [meaning] 'to be,'" but Bauer leaves this to the "feeling of the interpreter." The often cited parallel passage, John 1:12, also contains a future dimension in γενέσθαι: "*become* children of God." Cf. BAGD 159 (γίνομαι 4a).

8 Even though the "majority text" supports the omission of καὶ ἐσμέν, its elimination should be regarded as secondary, since the argument of the *lectio difficilior* as well as the majority of majuscule manuscripts favor the reading here given.

9 The reading ὑμάς is fairly well attested and would correspond to the letter style; nevertheless, ἡμάς is to be preferred. It refers to the community as a whole, including the author, in contrast to the world.

10 For γινώσκειν in the sense of "acknowledge," see the excursus on 2 John 1; also Rudolf Bultmann, "γινώσκειν, κτλ.," *TDNT* 1 (1964) 689–719, esp. 698, 704–8.

11 The grammatical reference of αὐτόν is disputed; among those arguing for a christological interpretation are Dodd, *Epistles*, 69; Bultmann, *Epistles*, 48; for a "theological" interpretation are Windisch and Preisker, *Die Katholischen Briefe*, 120; Brooke, *Epistles*, 81; Schnackenburg, *Epistles*, 155–56; Balz, "Johannesbriefe," 186, and others. The preceding text (v. 1a) suggests πατήρ as the referent, but in what follows (v. 2) the passage seems to speak rather of the revelation in Christ. However, such a discussion is off the track from the author's point of view; in each case it is a matter of the personified representation of salvation.

12 The root-aorist ἔγνω appears relatively often in the Johannine writings: John 4:1, 53; 13:28; 16:19; especially close to the present passage are John 1:10 (ὁ κόσμος αὐτὸν οὐκ ἔγνω) and 17:25a (ὁ κόσμος σε οὐκ ἔγνω, ἐγὼ δέ σε ἔγνων); this last line is contrasted with the first aorist, καὶ οὗτοι ἔγνωσαν ὅτι, in 17:25b; cf. 7:26; 8:27; 10:6; 12:16; 16:3. If the contrast of the present οὐ γινώσκει ἡμᾶς with οὐκ ἔγνω αὐτόν means that the reason for the world's nonrecognition of the Christian community lies in its wrong behavior in the past, its nonacknowledgment of God or of Christ, still the world's nature is also characterized by its closing itself against the claims of truth (cf. 1 John 3:19; 4:6) and love (cf. 1 John 3:16; 4:7–8).

13 This corresponds to the opposition between Christ and the world in the Fourth Gospel. The Revealer is not recognized by the world (1:10); the Pharisees do not know where he comes from (8:10). This kind of nonrecognition leads to hatred (15:19; cf. 1 John 3:13) and persecution. the "Jews" pursue the community because they have not recognized the Father and the Son (16:3). The parallels between the relationships of community and world in 1 John and in the Fourth Gospel are obvious. It is also evident from the οὐκ ἔγνω αὐτόν in this verse that one must presume a unified structure for Johannine theology.

14 On the understading of κόσμος as "human world," cf. also what was said above at 2:2, 15–17. Friedrich

■ **2** The address "beloved" (ἀγαπητοί)[15] reinforces the element, both parenetic and paraclectic, that pervades the whole context. It is appropriate to the subject, because the addressees have experienced the love of God that was just mentioned; therefore they are "now" God's beloved children. It is, of course, clear that the "already" of their existence is in need of enhancement by the "not yet." The tension of this time in which the community finds itself, in view of the gift of divine love, is unmistakable. It is already separated from the world, and yet it is living (to speak in Pauline terms) in a state of faith and not of seeing (2 Cor 5:7). The ultimate disclosure of the members' true being is still in the future; it is reserved for the eschatological "then" (cf. 1 Cor 13:10–12; Rom 6:1–14). It is only the revelation of the coming Christ (2:28) that will make evident their future, though already anticipated, existence. In view of the apocalyptic context and the cosmic character of Christ's παρουσία, one could scarcely consider this as referring to the relationship of individual believers to the exalted Christ.[16] Instead, it is the future eschatological event, which the author conceives in terms of an apocalyptic structure.[17]

Verse 2b tells what is to be hoped for in the future. By the use of οἴδαμεν ("we know"), the author alludes to the community's existing knowledge.[18] This means that apocalyptic ideas are part of the community's traditional fund of knowledge. Such ideas would include the expectation that the eschatological future will bring with it both a likeness to God and the vision of God. This is, as Windisch rightly says,[19] an augmentation of 2:28 and would have corresponded to the apocalyptic notion of a future period of time after Christ's parousia.[20] The relationship of the ὅμοιοι clause to the following ὅτι clause is that of effect and cause:[21] the future encounter with God in the parousia[22] will include seeing God,[23] and its consequence will be likeness to God.

The ultimate goal of the community's hope is therefore to become ὅμοιοι θεῷ ("like God"). That the

Gogarten (*Die Verkündigung Jesu Christi: Grundlagen und Aufgabe* [2d ed.; Tübingen: Mohr (Siebeck), 1965]) has expounded in exemplary fashion and impressive detail the idea that no honest theological reflection can at present evade this alternative. Cf. the dust jacket for the first edition of 1948: "We are no longer pagans, and we are no longer Jews. If we are not Christians, we are necessarily and irretrievably secularists."

15 Cf. also 2:7; 3:21; 4:1, 7, 11; also ἀγαπητέ (3 John 2, 5, 11). In what follows, the current status as children of God is contrasted with the "not yet" of the final revelation. The words νῦν—οὔπω articulate this; consequently, καί is to be understood as adversative ("however").

16 This would correspond to the anthropological orientation of John 14:1–4. Bultmann gave different assessments of the origin of this verse in 1 John. At first he regarded 3:1–3 as a "digression" attributable to the author ("Analyse," 112), but later he traced ἐὰν φανερωθῇ to the "interpolator who redacted 2:28" ("Redaktion," 389). Cf. Bultmann, *Epistles*, 45, where he posits a source underlying the passage from 2:29 to 3:10 (2:29; 3:4, 6–11*).

17 See the remarks on 2:28 above. Cf. Col 3:3–4; Bultmann, *Epistles*, 48; Eduard Schweizer, *Der Brief an die Kolosser* (EKKNT 12; Zurich: Benziger, 1976) 134; Eduard Lohse, *Die Briefe an die Kolosser und an Philemon* (KEK 9/2; 2d ed.; Göttingen: Vandenhoeck & Ruprecht, 1977) 195; ET: Eduard Lohse, *Colossians and Philemon* (trans. William Poehlmann and Robert Harris; ed. Helmut Koester; Hermeneia; Philadelphia: Fortress, 1971) 133–35. Both Lohse and Schweizer maintain that there is a reference to the parousia. F. C. Synge ("1 John 3,2," *JTS* 3 [1952] 79) made the unconventional suggestion that there should be a break after the first ἐφανερώθη and again after οἴδαμεν: "Beloved, we are now God's children, and it has not yet been revealed. What we will be, we know; for when it is revealed. . . . " But against this division is the loose sequence of the postulated sentences, as well as the fact that οἴδαμεν is probably (as often elsewhere) continued by ὅτι, which therefore has not a causal but an explicatory sense; cf. Brown, *Epistles*, 393–94.

18 Cf. οἴδατε πάντες in 2:20, and the first person plural also in 5:14, 18–20. Adversative δέ (cf. BDF § 447 [1]) is attested by only one part of the manuscript tradition (esp. the "majority text"). It contrasts the statement οὔπω ἐφανερώθη with the certainty of the knowledge that the future existence of believers will make them similar to or like God. One may keep such a contrast in mind even if one agrees, in view of the important majuscule manuscripts, that the particle is secondary.

19 Windisch and Preisker, *Die Katholischen Briefe*, 120.

20 One must distinguish between the future point of the parousia and the time of salvation introduced by it. Similar is 1 Cor 15:23–28, according to which the reign of Christ, when it comes, will occupy the time between the parousia and the ultimate τέλος; cf. Strecker, "Anfänge," 35 and 44 n. 16. One may also recognize such a distinction of time in Col 3:4 (cf. n. 17 above).

believers are "children of God" and are encompassed by the love of God[24] is thus not the last word on the status of Christians. Instead, that they already have knowledge of a future salvation means that the ultimate fulfillment of the existence promised to them is still awaiting them and will be realized in their being made like God. Ὅμοιοι (θεῷ) is a strong expression to describe the final state of Christian existence; it recalls Gen 1:26 (according to which human beings were created as εἰκών and ὁμοίωσις of God) and Gen 3:5 (the serpent promises: καὶ ἔσεσθε ὡς θεοί), but there is an undeniable Hellenistic influence even in the Septuagint.[25] The background of the idea is the notion, widespread in antiquity, that like can only be understood by like.[26] The use of the adjective ὅμοιος thus does not invite speculation on the relationship of likeness to God and identity with God. Analogies to the sense here implied are found in the NT statements about the relationship between Christ and God.[27] Especially close are the sayings about Jesus' unity with his Father (e.g., John 10:30), which are also to be denied any speculative interpretation; what they defend is the difference between the earthly revealer and his father (John 14:28). In an anthropological context, the NT expresses the expectation that—since earthly existence is qualitatively different from the heavenly—Christians will undergo a change in being made sharers in the heavenly δόξα.[28] Here there are parallels to the world of Johannine thought (cf. John 17:24), even though the concept of

21 It is also possible to set the second ὅτι alongside the first and subordinate both to οἴδαμεν: "We know that . . . we will be like him (and) that we will see him . . ."; but in that case one would expect an additional καί before the second ὅτι. The sequence with an explicatory-causal ὅτι is also found in 3:14, but there, unlike the situation here, the second (causal) ὅτι refers back to οἴδαμεν (see below on 3:14).

22 The expression φανερωθῇ does not exclude the idea of the parousia of Christ (cf. more clearly 2:28); at the same time one is tempted to join many interpreters in applying the personal pronoun αὐτῷ to God. I have already said above, on this point, that for 1 John there is no alternative between God and Christ in such statements.

23 On the problem of the vision of God, cf. 3:6; 4:20; 3 John 11; John 1:18; 14:9, and the remarks below. For the phrase καθώς ἐστιν, "just as he is," see also 1 Thess 2:13; in addition, with reference to the opposite in "informal speech" 1 John 3:12; John 6:58 (BAGD 391).

24 Against Brown, *Epistles*, 423, this does not mean that "Christians are already like God as He showed Himself in His Son," even if one admits that there is a "continuity between the present and future status of God's children."

25 Cf. H. Merki, ʻΟΜΟΙΩΣΙΣ ΘΕΩι (Freiburg: Paulusverlag, 1952); Johannes Schneider, "ὅμοιος, κτλ.," *TDNT* 5 (1967) 186–99. Plato *Theaet.* 176B: ὁμοίωσις δὲ δίκαιον καὶ ὅσιον μετὰ φρονήσεως γενέσθαι ("to become like [God] is to become holy, just, and wise"); quoted in Philo *Fug.* 63, Clement of Alexandria *Strom.* 2.22.136.6. Cf. also *Corp. Herm.* 11.5.

26 Cf. the fundamental philosophical proposition ὑπὸ τοῦ ὁμοίου τὸ ὅμοιον καταλαμβάνεσθαι πέφυκεν ("Like tends to be comprehended by like": Sextus Empiricus *Adv. math.* 7.92 = *Adv. log.* 1.92). This principle can also be applied to the vision of God (see below).

27 The word ὅμοιος appears 45 times in the NT: 18 times in the Synoptics and 21 times in Revelation. In the Johannine writings, apart from the present verse, it is in John 8:55 and 9:9. It emphasizes "the agreement by which one thing is similar or equal to another" (Johannes Schneider, "ὅμοιος, κτλ.," *TDNT* 5 [1967] 187), as in Sir 13:15(19) and Tob 7:2; in a christological context, Rev 1:13 and 14:14 (ὅμοιον υἱὸν ἀνθρώπου; cf. Dan 7:13). Is it true that the word ἴσος "because of the character of exactness which clung to it as a term of quantitative equality . . . was better adapted than ὅμοιος to express what the NT has in view, the more so as it had already taken on qualitative significance as well . . . it denotes an equality which is both essential and perfect" (Gustav Stählin, "ἴσος, κτλ.," *TDNT* 3 [1965] 353)? One should, however, note that in the christological passages the accent does not lie on the positive description of the relationship of Christ to God (Phil 2:6: ἴσα θεῷ as *res rapienda* or *res rapta* of the preexistent Son of God under negative circumstances; John 5:18: ἴσον . . . θεῷ in the Jews' accusation against Jesus), even though in Johannine understanding Jesus' "equality with God" can be expressed in other terminology (John 1:18: μονογενὴς θεός). On the "varying" usage of ἴσος and ὅμοιος, see also Traugott Holtz, "ἴσος," *EDNT* 2 (1991) 201.

28 Thus the concept of δόξα describes the σῶμα of the exalted Kyrios, into which τὸ σῶμα τῆς ταπεινώσεως of Christians will be changed (Phil 3:21, a formulation not created by Paul but taken from tradition; cf. Wolfgang Schenk, *Die Philipperbriefe des Paulus* [Stuttgart: Kohlhammer, 1984] 322–27); also

δόξα does not appear in the Johannine Letters[29] and no mystical deification is expressed in either set of writings.

While the basis for such hope is the future *vision of God*,[30] this also describes a stage that leads beyond the present state of being children of God, since it is reserved to the future. Jewish eschatological expectation is also directed toward a vision of God.[31] Even though the author can say that "being in God" is a state that has a determining influence on the present existence of the Christian community, and that it is recognizable by the keeping of God's commandments (2:5), still "seeing God," here as in the rest of the NT, has a future eschatological orientation.[32] Our text not only states the future perspective but also presupposes that the vision of

1 Cor 15:49 (εἰκὼν τοῦ ἐπουρανίου); Rom 8:18–19 (τὰ παθήματα τοῦ νῦν καιροῦ πρὸς τὴν μέλλουσαν δόξαν).

29 The present eschatological use of the concept of δόξα in the Fourth Gospel (18 occurrences out of 167 in the NT) remains open to the future dimension. While "glory" is proper to the Father and to the preexistent Logos, the Revealer gives it to his own in order that they may have perfect unity in the world, and in their future community with the Son may behold his heavenly δόξα (John 17:20–24). With regard to John 11:24–25 (contrasting Martha's confession of the resurrection on the last day with the revealer's "I am" saying, "I am the resurrection and the life"), it is problematic to assert a contradiction rather than a contrast between present and future resurrection.

30 This presumes that the second ὅτι is causally related back to the first ὅτι clause (see n. 21 above). Schnackenburg's interpretation is different. He presupposes that the vision of God motivates present acknowledgment (οἴδαμεν) and is itself to be regarded as a present entity (*Epistles*, 159–60). It is true that the author of 1 John can parallel the present, redeemed situation of knowing God (2:3–6; 4:6) with that of seeing God (3:6). But this occurs only in a negative form and in a parenetical context. Beyond this, the idea of a causal relationship between the vision of God and the community's knowledge is negated by the fact that the future, ὀψόμεθα, appears in this verse. It is scarcely conceivable that such a vision of God, to be expected in the future, motivates present recognition, nor is it made more likely by the overarching theme of "nearness to God" that embraces both thoughts. Moreover, that "the idea of becoming like God through seeing him would be quite unusual in the Johannine writings" (ibid.) need not surprise us, since this is the only occurrence of the ὅμοιος idea in the whole of the Johannine corpus. According to Brown (*Epistles*, 396), the author of 1 John did not make a clear distinction between the "two future claims" (vision of God and likeness to God). Still, I must hold with the overwhelming majority of exegetes in maintaining the distinction just described; cf. Wilhelm Bousset, *Kyrios Christos: A History of the Belief in Christ from the Beginnings of Christianity to Irenaeus* (trans. John E. Steely; Nashville: Abingdon, 1970) 227–32; Reitzenstein, *Hellenistic Mystery-Religions*, 454–56; Bultmann, *Epistles*, 49; Wengst, *Häresie und Orthodoxie*, 126.

31 In *4 Ezra* the most severe future punishment, at the final judgment, is said to be that the unrighteous "shall wither with fear at seeing the glory of the Most High in whose presence they sinned while they were alive, and in whose presence they are to be judged in the last times" (7.87). In contrast, it is said of the righteous: "first of all, they shall see with great joy the glory of [the one] who receives them, for they shall have rest in seven orders" (7.91). In the book of *Jubilees*, the revelation at Sinai is crowned by a view of "the time when my sanctuary shall be built among them for all eternity, and the Lord will appear in the sight of all, and all know that I am the God of Israel" (1.27–28). Cf. also *Apoc. Abr.* 29.19 ("they will rejoice in me forever"); *Midr. Ps.* 149 §1 (270a): when the children of Israel "shall see [God] in the world to come, they will be devout." The rabbinic literature often equates the time of seeing God with the hour of death; cf. *'Abot R. Nat.* 25; *Midr. Ps.* 22 §32 (99a), and elsewhere. In a fantastic etymology, Philo interprets the name of the people Israel as "the one who sees God" and identifies the vision "of the Father and Maker of all" as it will be bestowed on "the sight of the mind" as the "dominant element in the soul" with reaching "the crowning point of happiness" (*Abr.* 57–59). Even in the OT, the vision of God is thought of as something this-worldly and is connected with the temple cult: cf. Ps 42:2: "When shall I come and behold the face of God?" On this whole subject, see Str-B 1.206–15; Wilhelm Michaelis, "ὁράω, κτλ.," *TDNT* 5 (1967) 315–82.

32 Cf. Matt 5:8; 1 Cor 13:12; Col 3:4; Rev 22:4. It is different in 2 Cor 3:18, where the vision of God and becoming like God are accomplished in the present, within a christological context; cf. Rudolf Bultmann, *Der zweite Brief an die Korinther* (KEK 6; Göttingen: Vandenhoeck & Ruprecht, 1987) 98; ET: *The Second Letter to the Corinthians* (trans. Roy A. Harrisville; Minneapolis: Augsburg, 1985) 95–96; Siegfried Schulz, "Die Decke des Mose," *ZNW* 49 (1958) 19.

God exceeds the natural capacities of human beings and represents an impossibility so long as they are bound to their earthly existence;[33] for that very reason a prior change is required (cf. Phil 3:21). It remains an open question how one should imagine the attitude of the opponents in 1 John toward this future eschatological expectation. If it entails an idea of overcoming the bonds of the flesh, its content approaches a present interpretation of salvation like that which may be posited of the "false prophets."[34]

■ **3** In a generalizing address, the author (with καὶ πᾶς, as in 2:29b) includes all readers who count themselves members of the community, and urges them to join the company of those who have this hope.[35] This verse contains the single instance of ἐλπίς ("hope") in the whole Johannine corpus. Its inclusion here[36] characterizes the future eschatological horizon. The Christian community defines itself on the basis of this hope, the content of which was described in the preceding verse. This distinguishes it from the world. While the latter is imprisoned within itself, having no knowledge of God (3:1) and being subjected to death and sin (2:17; 5:19), the community of Jesus Christ, in contrast, places its hope in that which does not come from the world, and in the one who is not of the world.[37] The future perspective (v. 2) implies an obligation. Although it is expressed in the indicative, there can be no doubt that ἁγνίζει ("purify") has an imperative meaning. While the cultic background of this word, uncommon in the Johannine writings,[38] is indisputable,[39] it is to be

33 The future vision of God (e.g., at the hour of death; see n. 31 above) is established in the rabbinic literature with reference to Exod 33.20 ("You cannot see my face; for no one shall see me and live"); according to this, a vision of God is impossible in the course of human life: cf. *Sipra Lev.* 1.1 § 2; *Sipra Num.* 12.8 §103. This corresponds to the idea (cited in n. 26 above) that like can only be recognized by like; cf. Philo *Gig.* 9: ἵνα πρὸς τῶν ὁμοίων τὸ ὅμοιον θεωρῆται ("that like may be discerned by like"); Sextus Empiricus *Adv. math.* 7.92 = *Adv. log.* 1.92–93. According to *Ps.-Clem. Hom.* 17.16, the ἄσαρκος ἰδέα ("nonfleshly figure") of the Father and the Son cannot be seen because of the excess of divine light; instead, the vision of God presumes that human flesh is changed into the nature of light, unless the οὐσία of light is changed into flesh (an allusion to the incarnation of the Son); such a vision of God is reserved for the time after the resurrection of the dead, when human bodies will become ἰσάγγελοι ("like the angels") (parallels: *Ps.-Clem. Rec.* 3.30; cf. Luke 20:36 par.). Cf. also Hans Joachim Schoeps, *Theologie und Geschichte des Judenchristentums* (Tübingen: Mohr [Siebeck], 1949) 423–24. In the *Corpus Hermeticum* the revealer Hermes explains that he cannot be seen with human eyes (*Corp. Herm.* 13.3: οὐκ ὀφθαλμοῖς τούτοις θεωροῦμαι νῦν); cf. William C. Grese, *Corpus hermeticum XIII and Early Christian Literature* (SCHNT 5; Leiden: Brill, 1979) 89–90.

34 On this, see also Françoise Smyth-Florentin, "'Voyez quel grand amour le Père nous a donné,' 1 Jn 3.1–2," *AsSeign* 2/25 (1969) 32–38.

35 The adjective πᾶς occurs more frequently from here on (vv. 4a, 6ab, 9a, 10b) and could furnish a reason for dividing the section 2:28—3:10 into four antithetical pairs in two strophes (2:28—3:6; 3:7–10; this is the suggestion of Brown, *Epistles*, 418–19). But that implies that 3:1–3 must be designated "a type of exclamatory interruption by the author." It is certain that antithetical rhetoric shapes this part of the letter also, while the supposedly chiastic construction of the two strophes in fact expresses the advancing chain of the author's ideas; cf. 2:28 (revelation of Christ) with 3:10 (the children of God and of the devil are made known): christology has anthropological consequences.

36 The verb ἐλπίζειν also appears very seldom: John 5:45 of the Jews who hope in Moses; otherwise, without theological significance, in 2 John 12 and 3 John 14.

37 It is unnecessary to decide whether ἐπ' αὐτῷ ("in him") refers to God or to Christ. Reasons can be given for either alternative (cf., on the one hand, Acts 24:15; 1 Tim 4:10; on the other hand Rom 15:12; Brown, *Epistles*, 397, who opts for the reference to "God"). In addition, when associated with a reference to analogous passages, this alternative can be misleading as regards the theological intention of this author.

38 Otherwise only in John 11:55 (of the Jewish Passover customs).

39 The verb ἁγνίζω appears frequently in LXX only in Chronicles (for קדשׁ in 1 Chr 15:12; 2 Chr 29:5, 15, and elsewhere; for טהר in 2 Chr 29.18, 30.18, and elsewhere); otherwise rarely, as in Exod 19:10–11; Num 8:21; 19:12; Josh 3:5; Isa 66:17; Jer 12:3, and others. "The word means '*to set in a state of qualification*,' and thus applies to the various measures serving this end" (Friedrich Hauck, "ἁγνός, κτλ.," *TDNT* 1 [1964] 123). In 2 Chr 31:17–18 the verb applies particularly to purification before the

understood ethically here, as elsewhere in the NT.[40] Hence one can also leave aside the question whether the background is the OT and Jewish idea that cultic purity is a precondition for access to God,[41] or a notion drawn from the mysteries, such as the cultic rule that only the initiates may see God.[42] The demand that believers "purify themselves" means that they are to "keep themselves free from sin."[43] The reason for this demand is given in the *καθώς* clause, which also has a comparative function.[44] The attitude of believers must correspond to the nature of the one in whom they believe.[45] This echoes the relationship of indicative and imperative (cf. also 3:5, 16); if "that one"[46] is *ἁγνός*—as is said in an expression that is unusual in the Johannine writings—this means that Jesus has appeared for sinners at God's command, and through his atoning death has taken away sins (cf. 1:7, 9; 2:1–2; 4:10). This lays the groundwork for correct ethical behavior, by which every believer, in light of the eschaton, shows himself or herself to be *δίκαιος*, like Christ.[47]

Passover feast. Josephus uses it in this sense for the introduction of the Passover feast at the exodus (*Ant.* 2.312), and otherwise generally for cultic purity (*Ant.* 1.341–42; 3.197–98, and elsewhere). In extrabiblical literature as well, *ἁγνίζω* is connected with the cult and the cultic purity associated with it (frequently in the tragic dramatists). Plutarch offers a possible explanation for the Roman custom that the bride must touch fire and water: "The fire purifies and the water sanctifies (*τὸ πῦρ καθαίρει καὶ τὸ ὕδωρ ἁγνίζει*); for it is necessary that the bride should always be pure and holy (*καθαρὰν καὶ ἁγνήν*)" (*Quaest. Rom.* 263E).

40 Cf. also Jas 4:8; 1 Pet 1:22.

41 Therefore it is a condition of the state of the Nazirites in the OT (Num 6:2–8; Acts 21:24, 26; 24:18); cf. also the purity requirements in connection with Israelite worship (2 Chr 30:19; 1 Macc 14:36). For the post-NT period see Justin *Dial.* 86.6: "our Christ, by being crucified on the tree, and by purifying (*ἁγνίσαι*) [us] with water, has redeemed us, though plunged in the direst offenses which we have committed, and has made [us] a house of prayer and adoration" (translation in ANF 1.242).

42 Thus Brooke, *Epistles*, 84; Windisch and Preisker, *Die Katholischen Briefe*, 120; by contrast, Schnackenburg considers this impossible because "consecration is not a precondition but an ethical requirement. That requirement arises from the certain expectation of seeing God" (*Epistles*, 161).

43 Cf. Bultmann, *Epistles*, 49.

44 *Καθώς* can have both substantiating and comparative meanings: cf. BDF § 453 (2); the construction corresponds to 3:7; 4:17; there is a material parallel in 2:29.

45 Bultmann, *Epistles*, 49; cf. 2:6, 29; 3:7, 16; 4:17. The unity of nature between Father and Son is expressed in the Fourth Gospel with the verb *ἁγιάζειν* (10:36), but applies also to the relationship of the Revealer and the community: in his life, death, and return to the Father, the Christ "sanctifies" himself for his own and prays that they also may be "sanctified" in the truth (17:17, 19). Only in the Fourth Gospel is Jesus *ὁ ἅγιος τοῦ θεοῦ*, who reveals light and life to human beings (6:69; cf. Mark 1:24; Luke 4:34).

46 With regard to *ἐκεῖνος* one may ask whether here, as in 2:6, the thought is of Christ's earthly existence; however, what was said above (n. 37) applies here.

47 The adjective *ἁγνός* is a designation for the Messiah in *Sib. Or.* 3.49. In Greek the word describes an "attribute of the divinity and everything belonging to it" (BAGD 11); it is generally used in an ethical sense in the NT: 2 Cor 7:11; 11:2; Phil 4:8; 1 Tim 5:22; Titus 2:5; Jas 3:17; 1 Pet 3:2 (cf. *1 Clem.* 38.2; 48.5), and here it is identical with *δίκαιος*: cf. 1 John 2:29; 3:7 (also Diogenes Laertius *Vit. phil.* 7.119; P. Oxy. 1.41, 29–30). Preisker correctly points to the connection between ethics and eschatology in his appendix to Windisch, *Die Katholischen Briefe*, 166; see also Christoph Münchow, *Ethik und Eschatologie: Ein Beitrag zum Verständnis der frühjüdischen Apokalyptik mit einem Ausblick auf das Neue Testament* (Berlin: Evangelische Verlagsanstalt; Göttingen: Vandenhoeck & Ruprecht, 1981) 149ff. (although without any discussion of the Johannine Letters).

3 **Anyone Who Is from God Does Not Sin**

4 **Everyone who commits sin is guilty of**
lawlessness; sin is lawlessness. 5/ You
know that he was revealed to take away
sins, and in him there is no sin. 6/ No one
who abides in him sins; no one who sins
has either seen him or known him. 7/
Little children, let no one deceive you.
Everyone who does what is right is
righteous, just as he is righteous. 8/
Everyone who commits sin is a child of
the devil; for the devil has been sinning
from the beginning. The Son of God was
revealed for this purpose, to destroy the
works of the devil. 9/ Those who have
been born of God do not sin, because
[God's] seed abides in them; they cannot
sin, because they have been born of God.
10/ The children of God and the children
of the devil are revealed in this way: all
who do not do what is right are not from
God, [nor are those] who do not love their
brothers and sisters.

■ **4** Committing sin is the opposite pole from doing justice, which was already spoken of in 2:29 and is taken up again in vv. 7 and 10. Therefore after the appeal to the readers to sanctify themselves the concept of ἁμαρτία ("sin") and its consequences is explained. Πάς has a generalizing effect and does not focus on a particular group within the community; consequently, the ethical admonition that follows does not contain any kind of specific polemic against false teaching, but has its place in the community as a whole.[1] The first thing to be noted in this section is the relationship between ἁμαρτία and ἀνομία. The latter expression is otherwise absent from the Johannine writings, nor are its derivatives present.[2] Even though one might, on the basis of these statistics, give some thought to the idea of a source that the author used,[3] the choice of words is still striking. These

1 Cf. also the remarks on v. 7 below (μηδεὶς πλανάτω ὑμᾶς).

2 The word ἀνομία occurs 15 times in the NT, but only here in the Johannine corpus. The parallel concepts ἄνομος (10 times in the NT) and ἀνόμως (2 times) are not used in the Johannine literature. The word νόμος is found in the Fourth Gospel (15 times), but not in the Johannine Letters. Hence there is no discernible struggle against nomism (Jewish law-observance) or antinomism in the Johannine Letters. The fundamental meaning of ἀνομία is already found in Matt 7:23: the Christian community is obligated to do the will of God; this is the "law" that demands its unconditional fulfillment (Strecker, *Sermon*, 174–75). Cf. also Matt 13:41; 23:28; 24:12. The expression ἁμαρτία was understood in the non-Christian realm, but not in a strictly legal fashion. Thus it appears in Aeschylus as crime (*Ag.* 1197), in Sophocles as a deed that, while punishable, is done for good and sufficient reasons (*Phil.* 1225), and in philosophy as a broad, collective concept (Ps.-Plato *Def.* 416a). Cf. also Gustav Stählin, "The Linguistic Usage, and History of ἁμαρτάνω, ἁμάρτημα, and ἁμαρτία before and in the NT," *TDNT* 1 (1964) 294–96; Ignace de la Potterie, "Sin Is Iniquity," in Stanislas Lyonnet, *The Christian Lives by the Spirit* (trans. John Morriss; Staten Island: Alba House, 1971, 37–55.

3 Thus Bultmann, *Epistles*, 49.

different terms are apparently meant to express an intensification:[4] anyone who is guilty of *ἁμαρτία* is also guilty of *ἀνομία* ("lawlessness").[5]

In chap. 5, the author distinguishes different kinds of *ἁμαρτίαι*: sins that are mortal and sins that are not mortal (5:16–17). Apparently this distinction is prepared in advance, here in chap. 3, with the generalization: no matter what appears, in individual cases, as *ἁμαρτία*, the concept of *ἀνομία*, as an overarching and summarizing expression,[6] makes visible the fundamental structure of *ἁμαρτία*;[7] therefore it can be equated with *ἀδικία* ("unrighteousness," 5:17). The relationship of sin to *ἀνομία* indicates that the divine mandate is to be fundamental for Christians' actions.[8] This is not to be understood as a Jewish or Jewish Christian nomism; rather, it is equated with the "will of God" (*θέλημα θεοῦ*, 2:17; 5:14). It is a matter of course for the author that those who are born of God should orient themselves to the will of God and do it (3:9), for it is in this way that the profound difference between the community and the world is revealed (2:17).

Here, too, one should ask how such an idea of sinlessness can be maintained in light of the concrete relationships within the community. The thesis that this is simply a matter of a delusion of sinlessness on the part of the false teachers and that the author is merely speaking against false prophets[9] was already rejected in the commentary on 1:8 above. In fact, it is presupposed that there is sin within the community (cf. 1:8 and esp. 5:17). The answer is to be derived from the parenetic sharpening that colors the present context as far as 3:10, and that emphasizes the intentionality of every sinful action as something directed against God. It is then taken up again in the following passage (3:11–18). In addition, the point is sharply made that every kind of sin is an offense against God's claims. Hence the concept of "lawlessness" (*ἀνομία*) in this section does not furnish any support for the idea that a development within Christianity[10] or a pagan Hellenistic environment[11] shaped the content of this expression. It is more significant that the word "lawlessness" appears frequently in apocalyptic writings and that in both Jewish[12] and Christian apocalyptic literature it is used to describe the activity of Satan against God immediately before the end.[13] This is the very situation of the community, which is aware that the "last hour" (*ἐσχάτη ὥρα*, 2:18) has arrived. They are

4 This is true even though the terms *ἁμαρτία* and *ἀνομία* are used synonymously in the LXX and in early Christian writings. Cf. Isa 33:15; Ps 31:1; 50:4; 58:4; Rom 4:7 (= Ps 31:1); Heb 10:17 (= Jer 38:34); *1 Clem.* 8.3; 18.3, 5, 9; 35.5; 50.6; *Herm. Vis.* 2.2.2; *Man.* 10.3.2. Schnackenburg, *Epistles,* 171; de la Potterie, "Le péché," 785–97, esp. 788; Windisch and Preisker, *Die Katholischen Briefe,* 121.

5 The "intensification" is expanded in v. 4b: *καί* contains a causal element, so that one could translate "*for* sin is lawlessness" (cf. BDR § 442 n. 18). The concepts of *ἁμαρτία* and *ἀνομία* can scarcely be contrasted as if *ἀνομία* were sin against the law of God and fellow humans, while *ἁμαρτία* would be sin against Godself, in which case the sense of the verse would be: Sin against God includes the violation of the commandment that is also obligatory as regards fellow human beings (cf. Wendt, *Johannesbriefe,* 60–61). Against this is that *ἁμαρτία* in 1 John means concrete, individual trespasses, as the plural usage indicates (1:7–9; 2:2; 4:10), and in what follows it is defined as not doing acts of justice and instead doing acts of lovelessness toward the brothers and sisters (3:9–10). For the interpretation of *ἁμαρτία* as sins of commission, see also Windisch and Preisker, *Die Katholischen Briefe,* 121.

6 According to Schnackenburg, *Epistles,* 172, v. 4b is not to be understood as a definition of sin, "for the article with the predicate noun . . . introduces *ἀνομία* not as a generic concept but as something specific, well-known, emphasized according to its own particularity." [Translation from the German, p. 187; the published English translation is not faithful to the original—Trans.]

7 Cf. 2:29; 3:7, 10. Walter Gutbrod ("*ἀνομία,*" *TDNT* 4 [1967] 1086) also understands *ἀνομία* in "a more general sense such as rebellion or revolt against God, or alienation from [God], as suggested by v. 6b, 9–10." Stanislas Lyonnet differs, equating *ἁμαρτία* and *ἀνομία* in the Johannine Letters and understanding both as rejection of and enmity toward God ("De natura peccati quid doceat Novum Testamentum—de scriptis Ioanneis," *VD* 35 [1957] 271–78).

8 Cf. Plutarch *Stoic. rep.* 16, 1041D: *τὸ ἀδικεῖν ἐστι παρανόμημα*; Euripides *Ion* 441–43: "Is it then just that you, who gave the laws (*τοὺς νόμους*) to mortals, should yourself transgress those laws? (*ἀνομίαν*)" (translation by Robert Potter in Whitney J. Oates and Eugene O'Neill, Jr., *The Complete Greek Drama* [New York: Random House, 1938] 1138). *Ps.-Clem. Rec.* 8.37.2: "omne mandatum praeterire peccatum est."

9 Thus Bultmann, *Epistles,* 49–50.

10 This thesis is advocated by Schnackenburg, *Epistles,* 171. He points to the descriptions of the evil times

warned to be aware of this hour so that when the line is drawn between the τέκνα τοῦ θεοῦ and the "children of the devil" (τέκνα τοῦ διαβόλου, 3:10), a division that is splitting the community itself, they may be counted among the children of God.

■ **5** That all this is being said in the context of a complex of problems within the community is made clear by the author's use of the word οἴδατε ("you know"), which refers to a tradition known to the community (cf. 2:20–21). According to the content of this verse, this is a christological kerygma, as suggested already by the use of the word φανεροῦν,[14] and also illustrated by an early Christian tradition known to the author regarding Jesus' advocacy on behalf of sinners (2:1–2; cf. 3:16), or his atoning sacrifice (ἱλασμός, 4:10). As the Fourth Gospel says in connection with the expression "lamb of God," such intervention is identical with the taking away of sins.[15] Thus the ἵνα clause is both grammatically and materially related to the preceding ἐφανερώθη. The revelation of the Son of God in the past had as its purpose the removal of sins. The background is the OT and Jewish idea of sacrifice, according to which the Christ-event is understood as a sacrifice of expiation (cf.

---

preceding the parousia in 2 Thess 2:3, 7, 8 and in the secondary ending of Mark in the Freer manuscript, as well as to the postcanonical writings (cf. *Did.* 16.4; *Barn.* 4.1; 14.5; 15.7; 18.2; *2 Clem.* 20.2; *Apoc. Pet.* 1.3).

11 Cf. also Schnackenburg, *Epistles*, 171: "Given the vague[ness of the concept of ἁμαρτία] which prevailed in this intellectual milieu, ἀνομία suggests lawless, wicked behavior, which arouses more disgust than [ἁμαρτία]." In Hellenistic Greek tradition, the concept of ἀνομία can refer to the idea that there is no law, or it can be directed against an existing law. The word can describe the general situation of lawlessness or (esp. in the plural) individual actions counter to law. For the sense of a general situation see, e.g., Philo *Spec. leg.* 1.188: εὐνομίᾳ καινῇ παλαιὰν ἀνομίαν ἐκνιψάμενοι ("through their new obedience they have washed away their old disobedience to the law"); it has the same meaning as ἀδικία in Philo *Conf. ling.* 108: ὀχλοκρατία . . . ἐν ᾗ ἀδικία καὶ ἀνομία καταδυναστεύουσιν ("mob rule . . . in [which] injustice and lawlessness are paramount"); also Epictetus *Diss.* 2.16.44; 3.26.32 (Heracles the expeller of injustice and lawlessness, the bringer of δικαιοσύνη [justice] and ὁσιότης [sanctity]). That, in Greek understanding, ἀνομία is simply to be equated with "chaos" is clear from Sextus Empiricus *Adv. math.* 2.33 (in a passage on the use of the law for the maintaining of the *polis*): "Hence the sensible people among the Persians also have a law [that orders them] on the death of their king to act lawlessly for [the next] five days (νόμον . . . ἀνομίαν ἄγειν); but this is not so that they may be unhappy, but in order that by this action they may learn what a great evil is lawlessness (κακόν ἐστιν ἡ ἀνομία); it brings murder, robbery, and still worse things upon them—that they may be more faithful guardians of their kings" (from the German translation by G. Seelig).

12 Cf. *T. Dan* 5.4–6; 6.1–6; 1QS iv.9, 17, 19; v.2, and elsewhere; esp. 1QS iii.20–24: "but all the children of falsehood are ruled by the Angel of Darkness and walk in the ways of darkness. The Angel of Darkness leads all the children of righteousness astray, and until his end, all their sin, iniquities, wickedness, and all their unlawful deeds are caused by his dominion in accordance with the mysteries of God. Every one of their chastisements, and every one of the seasons of their distress, shall be under the sway of his persecution; for all his allotted spirits seek the overthrow of the Sons of Light."

13 Cf. esp. 2 Thess 2:3–4: the ἀντικείμενος as ἄνθρωπος τῆς ἀνομίας; 2:7–8: μυστήριον τῆς ἀνομίας; the ἄνομος will be destroyed at Jesus' parousia; see also 2 Cor 6:14; Matt 24:12; Luke 13:27 *v.l.*; Mark 16:14 (Freer); *Did.* 16.3–4; *Barn.* 4.1–4; 14.5; 15.7; 18.2; also the excursus "The Antichrist" (below).

14 Cf. 2:28; John 2:11 is different (in connection with Jesus' σημεῖα the preexistence and incarnation of the Logos are presupposed).

15 The reading ἡμῶν (א C Ψ 𝔐, also in the Latin, Syriac, and Sahidic traditions) accords with the context in referring τὰς ἁμαρτίας to the community; but the author's concern, in harmony with the Johannine tradition, is with the universal task of the Son of God on behalf of the whole world (cf. 2:2; John 1:29). On αἴρειν, cf. Joachim Jeremias, *TDNT* 1 (1964) 185–86, where he rightly rejects the possible translation of John 1:29 in the sense of Isa. 53:12 LXX as "bear," in favor of a translation in the evangelist's own sense as "take away," "remove." Thus also Walter Radl, "αἴρω," *EDNT* 1 (1990) 41; Bultmann, *Epistles*, 51 n. 29; Schnackenburg, *Epistles*, 172.

Mark 10:45 and elsewhere). This is indicated also by the last clause, *καὶ ἁμαρτία ἐν αὐτῷ οὐκ ἔστιν*. As the sacrificial animal must be unblemished, so also for Christ as the sacrificial lamb the necessary precondition of his atoning efficacy is sinlessness.[16] As sin has no power over the Son of God, it is fundamentally true for the community that as those who are born of God and freed from sin by Christ, Christians are separated from sin. Christ's atonement applies not only to sins committed in the past, as the early Christian baptismal tradition said (cf. Rom 3:25), but also to the sins of the community at the present time.[17] This appears to contradict 1:7c, according to which purification from sins through the blood of Jesus could refer to "former sins," while here the Revealer "has brought the possibility of freedom from sinning."[18] But this is not a real contradiction: while the author may at one point rest his argument more strongly on the traditional content of the Christ-kerygma,[19] and elsewhere express himself in more Johannine language, nevertheless his theological conception forms a unity. The traditional world of ideas furnishes the background for his particular theological statement. The "cleans[ing] from every sin" effected in the Son of God (1:7) is nothing other than "tak[ing] away sins" (3:5), and the "Son of God" (1:7) is no one other than the sinless Revealer (3:5).[20] By removing sins, he has created a new situation for humanity, once and for all.

■ **6** If, through Christ, sin has been abolished *sub specie aeternitatis*,[21] this means for Christians that they, like Christ, do not sin. As the generalizing *πᾶς* reveals an imperative intention,[22] so is this particularly true for the indicative *οὐχ ἁμαρτάνει* ("does not sin"): this is not the statement of an objectively discernible fact, but rather, in the parenetical context, it is a warning to the community to draw the necessary conclusions from the liberating indicative of the Christ-event. There is thus no intention on the part of the author to establish a theology of sinlessness in contrast to 1:8–10.[23] On the contrary, the connection between "not sinning" and "abiding in him" is of fundamental importance: while one could, in ontological perspective, understand *μένειν ἐν αὐτῷ* as "the condition of [*μὴ ἁμαρτάνειν*],"[24] in the framework of the parenesis it is more proper to interpret this expression as the prelude to the admonition not to sin (cf. 2:6). Anyone who belongs to Christ, that is, who abides in him, anyone who is born of God (2:29; 3:9) is subject to the demand to refrain from sinning. In 1 John, *μένειν* (*ἐν αὐτῷ*) can in itself be understood as part of the parenesis (2:24, 27c, 28; indirectly also in 2:27a; 3:24; 4:15c). It does not describe a *habitus* that would be at Christians' disposal, but is characteristic of Christian life as, in the face of continual danger, it must continually renew its awareness of its origins and thus of its own identity.[25]

Verse 6 represents an antithetical parallelism. The first

16 Cf. John 8:46; 9:16; Isa 53:9; 2 Cor 5:21; 1 Pet 2:22.

17 Walter Grundmann, "ἁμαρτία," *TDNT* 1 (1964) 307–8 (on 1 John 2:1–2).

18 Thus Bultmann, *Epistles*, 50.

19 See above on 1:7c (*αἷμα*).

20 When Bultmann (*Epistles*, 50) inquires whether v. 5 "as in the case of 1:7b" has been interpolated by the ecclesiastical redaction or written by the author and opts for the latter interpretation, he at the same time admits that the author of 1 John adapted traditional ("ecclesiastical") christological tradition. Does the author intend a differentiation of singular and plural in the use of *ἁμαρτία*? This is the opinion of Brown (*Epistles*, 402), according to whom the singular expresses the possibility of being freed from sinning, while the plural emphasizes that the individual sins of one's life are a manifestation of *the* sin and are opposed to Jesus Christ. However, this is questionable (to speak with Wengst, *Brief*, 134: "equivalent in meaning"), because the singular is also combined with *πᾶσα* (1:7), thus anticipating and incorporating the plural (1:9); or it may simply alternate with the simple singular (1:8).

21 Cf. Bultmann, *John*, 96 n. 1. Martin Luther wrote: "Ubi est Christus tollit peccatum; ergo manet in eo negotio, quod est 'tollit peccatum'" (WA 20.702, 17–18) ["He who is in . . . Christ, does not sin; for when Christ is present, sin is conquered"].

22 The combination of *πᾶς* with a participial noun is typical of Johannine language (cf. Wilbert Francis Howard, *The Fourth Gospel in Recent Criticism and Interpretation* [London: Epworth, 1955] 278). It is "[a] construction used by the author to divide the human race into two all-inclusive groups" (Brown, *Epistles*, 402).

23 Against Windisch and Preisker, *Die Katholischen Briefe*, according to whom those who have been cleansed of sin "are lastingly preserved from sin, if they hold to what they have seen and recognized in him" (121).

24 Thus Bultmann, *Epistles*, 51.

25 Bultmann consequently translates the word *μένειν* as "be faithful" (*Epistles*, 26 n. 9). Schnackenburg (*Epistles*, 103, 259) emphasizes that in 1 John the *εἶναι*

part of the sentence is negatively constructed, while the second is positive. Since this is Johannine language, there can scarcely be any doubt that this antithesis is to be traced to the author of 1 John.[26] Of course, the parenetic meaning is also dominant here: if anyone in the community sins (the present tense indicates that this is not simply a matter of former sins), this permits the conclusion that such a sinner has neither seen nor acknowledged "him."[27] On the one hand, whereas the word ἑώρακεν could cause one to think of the witnesses' "seeing" (1:1–3), or of a polemic rejecting the false teachers' claim to spiritual sight,[28] the parallelism makes clear that the reference is to ὁ ἐν αὐτῷ μένων: both the "seeing" and the "recognizing" or "acknowledging" are made concrete in "abiding,"[29] which simply means "keeping his commandments" (2:3–4). On the other hand, "sinning" is not only identical with "not seeing" and "not recognizing" or "not acknowledging," but also with ἀνομία (3:4) or with "being a liar" or "being in darkness" (2:4, 9). In what follows, sinning will be described as service to the devil (v. 8).

■ **7** The beginning of the verse with "little children" (τεκνία) should not lead one to suppose that the author intends to begin a new topic. On the contrary, this will be a continuation of the community parenesis, now effectively underscored by addressing the readers again.[30] One group of manuscripts has παιδία, which also corresponds to Johannine usage (cf. 2:14, 18), but it has not been able to suppress the accepted text. This address expresses the authority asserted by the author toward the readers.

The third appearance of πλανᾶν in 1 John at this point (after 1:8 and 2:26; nowhere else in 1 John) has led to the supposition that the author is again (as in 2:26) turning to the problem of docetic opponents.[31] However, what the author is dealing with here is not a false christology, but a false mind-set that fails to recognize the necessary connection between knowledge of God and ethical behavior. In 1:8, as well, the verb is to be understood as applying not to false teaching but to the community's own self-deception.[32] Hence there is no connection between the content of this verse and 2:26, where the opponents are being combated.[33] Instead,

ἐν that is commonly part of the formulas of immanence is frequently replaced by μένειν ("The [indicatives] always point back to the blessed state of salvation expressed in the immanence formulas. But they are accompanied by the imperative, which makes clear the preliminary character and the threatened state of our union with God in this world" [103]).

26 Bultmann wavers on whether, in light of the unmistakably Johannine vocabulary, this verse should be assigned to the source; of course, this requires him to speculate further that the author of 1 John had replaced an original ὁ γεγεννημένος ἐκ τοῦ θεοῦ with the expression ὁ ἐν αὐτῷ μένων (*Epistles*, 45 n. 5).

27 Although christological elements dominate the preceding passage, one cannot be sure whether the personal pronoun (αὐτῷ / αὐτὸν) refers to Christ or to God. On the basis of 3:2, one would think of Christ in connection with ἑώρακεν (cf. 1:1–3), and of θεός with ἔγνωκεν (cf. 2:3–4, 13–14; 3:1; 4:6–8; 5:20 [*v.l.*]). But here again an alternative is inadmissible. With regard to the interchangeability of God and Christ, Brown (*Epistles*, 403) refers to John 14:9: "Whoever has seen me has seen the Father."

28 Thus Wengst, *Brief*, 135.

29 See v. 6a above; and the remarks on 2:6. In any event one could ask whether the author intends an order of consequences: seeing—recognizing (acknowledging)—abiding—not sinning.

30 On τεκνία and παιδία, see above on 1 John 2:12–13. Cf. also 2:1, 28; 3:18; 4:4; 5:21.

31 Thus Pierre Bonnard, *Les épîtres johanniques* (CNT 2/13c; Geneva: Labor et Fides, 1983) 71, who dubs the whole section 2:28—3:10 "polemical" and "antignostic." It is also incorrect to posit two opposing groups (a christological and a libertinistic heresy). Brown differs (*Epistles*, 429), believing that v. 7a is about "inroads of propagandists and not just about some weak Christians." Wengst (*Brief*, 135) sees in v. 7a a reference to 2:26. Cf. also Schnackenburg, *Epistles*, 173.

32 The expression ἑαυτοὺς πλανῶμεν (1:8) represents an ecclesial "we," not the "we" of the opponents; see above on 1:8.

33 This is true if one sets aside the fact that false christology can also be thought of as an offense against the unity of the community and thus against love of the sisters and brothers and against justice.

what is at issue here is a set of problems within the community that need not originate with an opposing position. The pronoun *μηδείς* (occurring only here in the Johannine writings) should thus be understood literally: "no one," without restriction! "Leading astray" is a well-known topos in the history of ideas and of religions, appearing both in the Hellenistic Greek[34] and in the OT-Jewish realms.[35] In this passage it relates to the author's usage: in what follows he will treat temptation dualistically and associate it with being a child of the devil (vv. 8, 10).

Similarly, the expression "who does what is right" (*ὁ ποιῶν τὴν δικαιοσύνην*) should not be restricted to a particular religio-historical sphere (cf. 2:29; 3:10). In Judaism the Torah encourages "doing justice,"[36] but in ancient Greece it was also taken, as a matter of course, to be the goal of ethical behavior.[37] Since this seems to be a matter of an ethical demand expressed in ethical vocabulary, the author appears to be very distant from Paul's teaching on justification according to which it is not one's own righteous action but the revelation and bestowal of God's righteousness that makes sinful human beings righteous (Rom 1:17; 3:21–26; Phil 3:9). In fact, the parenetic address to the community causes the author to formulate an uncompromising ethical statement, namely, that the only one who is *δίκαιος* is the one who does *δικαιοσύνη*.[38] This statement does not, however, stand in isolation but receives an additional clarification in the last clause, "as he is righteous" (*καθὼς ἐκεῖνος δίκαιός ἐστιν*). This presupposes that Christ is the Just One (cf. 2:29a). It thus corresponds to the parallel construction of clauses in v. 3b (Christ = *ἁγνός*). This comparative, or rather causal, clause[39] has two aspects. First, the indicative of the preceding, liberating Christ-event conveys the understanding that the revelation through the Son of God is an atoning sacrifice[40] and that the righteous, sinless Christ intercedes for the community (2:1; cf. 3:5b). Second, the imperative presupposes

34 In the Stoic diatribe, *πλανάω* is understood as "wavering" and "going astray," within the framework of theory of knowledge or that of practical ethics. A negative evaluation is not necessarily implied. Thus Epictetus (*Diss.* 1.18.3, 6) understands *πλανάω* as being in error regarding good and evil (cf. also *Diss.* 1.28.9–10). In 4.6.23 he appeals to the readers not to be misled by their own thinking into misunderstanding the sage's desire to be free from all desires, but instead to acknowledge it for what it is (on this, cf. Herbert Braun, "*πλανάω, κτλ.*," *TDNT* 6 [1968] 231). Stoic parallels are very suggestive for NT usage in 1 Cor 6:9; 15:33; Gal 6:7; Jas 1:16. Christians are warned "against the dangerous error of not recognizing the penal severity of God" (ibid., 244).

35 In the OT, *πλανάω* seldom describes a worldly error; its primary reference is to people's being led astray to serve idols (cf. Deut 13:6; 2 Kgs 21:9; Jer 23:13, 32; Hos 8:6; Amos 2:4, and frequently). YHWH appears as the subject of this leading astray (cf. Isa 63:17; Job 12:23–24; Ezek 14:9). In the extracanonical literature of ancient Judaism, leading astray is ascribed to demonic powers; in the process, OT monotheistic ideas are replaced by dualistic thinking (cf. *1 Enoch* 6—11; 15.3–12; 19.1; *Jub.* 5.1–10; 10.5–11; *T. Reub.* 4.6; 5.3, 5–7; *T. Levi* 10.2; *T. Jos.* 1.13, and frequently). The primary weight lies on warnings against idol worship and sexual immorality. According to *T. Levi* 10.2; 16.1 the end time will be characterized by *πλανᾶν* and *πλανᾶσθαι* (cf. Otto Böcher, *EDNT* 3 [1993] 99).

36 The human activity that corresponds to God's will is contrasted, in LXX, to *ἀνομία*: *ἐποίησεν ἀνομίαν καὶ οὐ δικαιοσύνην* (Isa 5:7). The concept of צדקה is restricted in the rabbinic literature to such things as almsgiving and charity (cf. Matt 6:1 *v.l.*). Regarding 2 Sam 8:15 ("So David reigned over all Israel; and David administered justice and equity to all his people") it is said that David "used to acquit the guiltless and condemn the guilty; but when he saw that the condemned man was poor, he helped him out of his own purse [to pay the required sum], thus executing judgment and charity (צדקה)—justice to the one by awarding him his dues, and charity to the other by assisting him out of his own pocket" (Tosephta *Sanhedrin* 1.2ff.; see Str-B 3.210; cf. Gottlob Schrenk, "*δικαιοσύνη* C: Righteousness in the Synagogue," *TDNT* 2 [1964] 196–98).

37 Cf. Plato *Gorgias* 460b 8: *ὁ δίκαιος δίκαια πράττει* ("he who is just may be supposed to do what is just"); Xenophon *Mem.* 4.6.6: *οὐκοῦν οἵ γε τὰ δίκαια ποιοῦντες δίκαιοί εἰσι* ("are not they who do what is just, just men?"); Aristotle *Nic. Eth.* 2.4, 1105b 9–10: *ἐκ τοῦ τὰ δίκαια πράττειν ὁ δίκαιος γίνεται* ("it is by doing just acts that the just man is produced").

38 According to Windisch and Preisker, *Die Katholischen Briefe*, 121, this is a "misuse or misunderstanding of Pauline teaching on justification."

39 On the twofold meaning of *καθώς*, see above at v. 3.

40 See above at 2:1–2 (and at 3:16 below).

that, in Christ's righteousness, being and doing are identical. This means for the community that the righteous Son of God is its model and that it must allow itself to be measured by his righteousness.[41] Hence the reference to "the righteous one" contains not only a backward look at the liberating action of the Revealer, but also a demand directed to the community that it adapt itself to the manner of his appearance and avoid sin (cf. 3:9).

■ **8** In a movement of thought typical of Johannine style, the positive statement about doing δικαιοσύνη is followed, in v. 8, by a negative, antithetical statement. The expression "who commits sin" (ὁ ποιῶν τὴν ἁμαρτίαν) formally takes up the preceding ὁ ποιῶν τὴν δικαιοσύνην, so that there is a content parallel as well: the one who commits sin is not righteous, but a sinner. Instead of the designation ἁμαρτωλός, which one might expect (although this word does not appear in the Johannine Letters; it is, however, found in John 9:16, 24–25, 31), it is the connection with the διάβολος that, in a sharp, personified (Bultmann: "mythological") expression, characterizes the sinful human being. The condemnation of the sinner is brusque; the dualism could scarcely be more complete. Whoever sins is ἐκ τοῦ διαβόλου. The opposition between being a child of God or a child of the devil (v. 10) is anticipated here.[42] The parallel in John 8:44 is striking. There "the Jews" are accused of being the devil's children: "You are from (your) father the devil, and you choose to do your father's desires. He was a murderer from the beginning and does not stand in the truth, because there is no truth in him." Truth and falsehood are placed in opposition to one another and, accordingly, "the Jews," as Jesus' opponents, are stereotypically assigned to the realm of lies. When in the present passage it is not truth and falsehood but righteousness and sin that characterize the children of God and of the devil and separate them from one another, it is not because there is a secondary application here of the anti-Jewish polemic in the Fourth Gospel.[43] Rather this author, independently of the evangelist, is drawing on the same Johannine tradition, to which belongs the distinction between devilish and divine origin.[44] In the service of community parenesis he applies this tradition in order, by describing the alternative to Christian life, to appeal to the community to act righteously (cf. v. 7).

The διάβολος ("devil") is named only here and in v. 10 as God's opponent,[45] although the word πονηρός (the

41 It is difficult, however, to derive even from the antiheretical and christological expositions in 1 John that the author was concerned "to put emphasis on the way Jesus lived and died" (Brown, *Epistles*, 404); no matter how much the incarnate Son of God is confessed as δίκαιος and, to that extent, the earthly facticity of the revelation of Jesus Christ is not neglected, the author has no thought of a life-of-Jesus theology; in this respect he also distinguishes himself from the christological intent of the fourth evangelist.

42 Cf., besides εἶναι ἐκ (vv. 8, 10: "stem from"), which is factually identical with γεννᾶσθαι ἐκ (v. 9), εἶναι ἐν as well (1:8; 2:4; John 1:47; 2:25, and elsewhere). On this, see Bultmann, *John*, 321 n. 1: the expression εἶναι ἐν describes "the determination of a person's being by the thing which 'is' or 'remains' in him." Wengst (*Brief*, 139) restricts this: it is not said "that the sinner is born of the devil. . . . The devil does not, like God, possess creative power." In light of the expression τέκνα τοῦ διαβόλου, however, this insight should not be given too much weight. It is true that the author does not say "whoever comes from the devil sins," but knows only the reverse idea: "whoever sins is from the devil." This indicates the historicity of being handed over to the satanic power and corresponds to the parenetic intention of 1 John.

43 Cf. Brown, *Epistles*, 405. The fourth evangelist knows that Jesus, as the lamb of God, takes away the sins of the world (1:29) and that the Paraclete will prove the world wrong about sin and righteousness (16:8–10).

44 It is also characteristic that the opposition of "truth and falsehood" typifies even the early Johannine tradition: 2 John 1–4, 3 John 1, 3, 12; cf., in addition, 1 John 2:21, 27 (ψεῦδος) and 1 John 1:10; 2:4; 4:20, and frequently (ψεύστης).

45 Cf. also John 6:70; 8:44; 13:2.

"evil one") is used as a personification in the same sense (2:13–14; cf. 3:12; 5:18–19). This concept rests on a broad Jewish tradition[46] but, in addition, the distinction between children of the devil and children of God has a Jewish background that is especially evident in apocalyptic literature.[47] The author does not, however, intend to describe a future eschatological situation, especially since he makes a clear distinction between the devil and the antichrist.[48] Instead, he is interested in illuminating present existence, and he employs a vocabulary found also in gnostic writings.[49] Christian existence is not divorced from sin once for all; it remains subject to the attacks of the satanic power that exists *ἀπ' ἀρχῆς*. In saying this, the author is probably not thinking of the beginning of the world, for that would presume an absolute dualism between God and Satan, an idea that can, of course, be demonstrated in the case of Marcion and in some gnostic literature.[50] The reference is more probably to the story of paradise or the opposition between Cain and Abel; at that time, according to OT and Jewish tradition, the power of the evil one intervened in the course of history for the first time.[51] The expression, however, need not be precisely explained at this point, because what is being described is the devil's sinful nature and activity, which extend throughout time and unalterably influence the present: this is made obvious by the present tense of *ἁμαρτάνει* ("he sins from the beginning," i.e., always).

To the activity of the devil, which permeates the whole course of history and causes sin, is opposed the revelation

46 In the LXX *διάβολος* (Hebrew שטן) is the "accuser" (Ps 109:6); in Esth 7:4; 8:1 the word is used in the sense of "opponent," "enemy." The concept appears in 1 Chr 21:1 and Job 1:6 as "adversary." In all the passages, it is the task of the *διάβολος* "to separate God and [the human being]" (Werner Foerster, "*διάβολος*," *TDNT* 2 [1964] 73). The idea of an opponent of God appears in Hellenistic Judaism from the second century BCE onward; such a one intends to destroy the relationship between God and the human being. The *διάβολος* attempts to tempt human beings to sin (*Apoc. Mos.* 2; *Jub.* 11.5, and elsewhere), accuses them before God (*1 Enoch* 40.7; *Jub.* 1.20; 48.15, 18; *Apoc. Zeph.* 4.2; 10.5, and elsewhere), and tries to interfere in God's plan of salvation (*Jub.* 48.2, 10). In the NT *διάβολος* appears 34 times with the meaning "adversary" (cf. LXX); 7 instances are in the Johannine literature (Gospel 3 times; 1 John 4 times), 5 in Revelation, 6 in Matthew, and 5 each in Luke and the Deutero-Pauline letters (cf. also Otto Böcher, "*διάβολος*," *EDNT* 1 [1990] 297–98).

47 *Jub.* 15.26–32; *T. Dan* 4.7; *Apoc. Abr.* 13—14.

48 See below on 2 John 7; 1 John 2:18, 22; also 4:3; excursus, "The Antichrist."

49 Cf. *Act. Thom.* 143 (p. 250,15–16, ed. Lipsius-Bonnet) on the *ἄρχων* (*τοῦ κόσμου*): *τὸ ἀληθὲς οὐκ ἔγνω, ἐπειδήπερ ἀληθείας ἐστὶν ἀλλότριος* ("he does not recognize the truth, because he is a stranger to truth"); Porphry *Abst.* 2.42 (p. 171, 22) on the evil demons: *τὸ γὰρ ψεῦδος τούτοις οἰκεῖον* ("for they are familiar with lies"); Lidzbarski, *Ginza* 1.22, 22–23: Satan is "full of all magic, deception and seduction"). Cf. Walter Bauer, *Das Johannesevangelium* (HNT 6; 3d ed.; Tübingen: Mohr [Siebeck], 1933) on John 8:44; Bultmann, *John*, 320 n. 4.

50 Cf. Clement of Alexandria *Strom.* 3.3.12: *οἱ ἀπὸ Μαρκίωνος κακὴν τὴν γένεσιν ὑπειλήφεσαν . . . φύσιν κακὴν ἔκ τε ὕλης κακῆς καὶ ἐκ δικαίου γενομένην δημιουργοῦ* ("the followers of Marcion regard birth as something evil . . . nature is regarded as evil because it was created out of evil matter and by a just Creator"). *Ginza R.* 12.6: "Its own evil nature exists from the beginning and to all eternity. . . . From the black water the King of Darkness was fashioned through his own evil nature and came forth. He waxed strong, mighty, and powerful, he called forth and spread abroad a thousand thousand evil generations without number and ten thousand times ten thousand ugly creations beyond count" (translation from Foerster, *Gnosis*, 2.160).

51 So also Brown, *Epistles*, 429: "the devil, who is the one who sins from the beginning (3:8b), as illustrated in the stories of Adam and Eve and of Cain"; similarly Schnackenburg, *Epistles*, 174; Stephen S. Smalley, *1, 2, 3 John* (WBC 51; Waco: Word, 1984) 168. Bultmann differs (*Epistles*, 52 n. 35): "*ἀπ' ἀρχῆς*" . . . intends the primordial beginning since the nature of the devil is being characterized." Wengst, *Brief*, 136: "It is instead important that he does not begin with the idea of an absolute existence and nature of the devil, but rather defines the devil in terms of the *deeds* he has been doing from the beginning." On the other hand, one may ask whether the author really distinguishes between the devil's nature and his deeds. On this subject, see Origen *Homily on Ezekiel* 9.1: "Omnis enim qui facit peccatum, ex diabolo natus est" ("for everyone who commits sin is born of the devil").

of the Son of God.[52] While the devil is a sinner from the beginning, the Son of God, in contrast, has no part in sin; he is sinless (3:5; cf. John 8:46), righteous (1 John 2:29; 3:7), and holy (3:3). The purpose of his appearance in history[53] is the destruction of the works of the devil. Λύσῃ is fundamentally equivalent to ἄρῃ.[54] However, this verse clarifies and makes concrete what was said in v. 5. That the ἔργα of the devil are the equivalent of his sinful activity, that is, that the doers are identical with their deeds, is the conclusion to be drawn from what has preceded (cf. also 3:12; John 8:41, 44). Thus when the "works" are destroyed, not only the effects of satanic power but the power itself are overthrown.[55] Although this may be the purpose of the revelation, it does not mean that such a divine intention has already been accomplished in the present time. On the contrary, the community is called to unite itself with this action, to allow it to be accomplished in and for the community itself, and to make it real within its own ranks, for the opposition between Satan and Christ is not understood as an unalterable dualistic "given,"[56] but as the opposition of two mutually challenging historical powers that demand action on the part of believers and call for a decision in favor of the one and a turning away from the other side.

■ **9** A third antithesis (after vv. 6 and 7b–8a) describes the contrast between the children of the devil and the children of God. The generalizing πᾶς ("everyone") reappears.[57] This means that the community is being addressed as a whole; consequently, an argument against opponents is not intended here.[58] There appears to be some material difference between v. 6, which says that

52 The verb φανεροῦσθαι can be actively translated with "make known," "reveal" (cf. John 7:4, of the Revealer over against the world; 17:6, the Son has revealed the name of the Father to human beings); in 1 John the verb appears only in the passive, "be made known," "be revealed," "be made visible," "appear;" thus generally of Christ: 1:2; 2:28; 3:5; of the love of God: 4:9; neutrally: 3:2; of the false teachers: 2:19. The reflexive meaning "reveal oneself" is not excluded. This could be the assumed meaning in the present verse: "the Son of God has revealed himself for this purpose." The verb is so construed by Brown (*Epistles*, 406), who has the Son's self-revelation begin with the appearance of John the Baptizer (John 1:31). However, the author offers no reflection on the beginning of the revelation.

53 Εἰς τοῦτο points to the following ἵνα clause; 3:5 is similar (so also Brown, *Epistles*, 406; Smalley, *1, 2, 3 John*, 169; cf. BDF §§ 290 (3); 394.

54 Cf. 3:5 (αἴρειν: "abolish," "remove"); on λύσῃ (only here in 1 John), see the variant reading in 4:3 (below); λύειν in the sense of "destroy," "eliminate," also in John 2:19, and frequently elsewhere.

55 That is Ignatius's understanding of the effects of the Eucharist (Ignatius *Eph.* 13.1–2): "For when you meet with frequency, Satan's powers are overthrown (καθαιροῦνται αἱ δυνάμεις τοῦ Σατανᾶ), and his destructiveness (ὄλεθρος) is undone by the unanimity of your faith. There is nothing better than peace, by which all strife in heaven and earth is done away (πόλεμος . . . ἐπουρανίων καὶ ἐπιγείων)."

56 Hence the dualistic two-spirits teaching in the *Community Rule* (1QS iii.13—iv.26), associated with expressions that have a flavor of predestination: "He has created (human beings) to govern the world, and has appointed for (them) two spirits in which to walk until the time of His visitation: the spirits of truth and of falsehood" (translation by Geza Vermes, adapted). Cf. also Werner Foerster, "σατανᾶ," *TDNT* 7 (1971) 151–63.

57 See above at 2:29; 3:3–4, 6.

58 Wengst (*Brief*, 138) differs, arguing that the author at this point has taken up a "crucial saying of his opponents" in a positive way. This would mean that the false prophets had asserted their superiority to every sin and that, consequently, they led a sinless life. In opposition, the author would be asserting that the content of being "born of God" is the ethical obligation not to sin, and therefore to distance oneself from every form of libertinism. Harry C. Swadling ("Sin and Sinlessness in I John," *SJT* 35 [1982] 207) writes in a similar vein, interpreting the statements in 3:6, 9 as "actually slogans used by the heretics." But his attempt to demonstrate the grammatical and logical independence of these verses is questionable, in light of the indisputable lines of connection to the context. It is true that the unique appearance of the word σπέρμα (only here in 1 John; otherwise in the Johannine writings only at John 7:42) is striking, but there is a material connection between this word and the Johannine idea of being "born of God."

"no one who *abides in him* sins," where "abiding" reflects the length of human existence, and v. 9a, where we read: "those who have been *born of God* do not sin," so that here the text "speaks quite objectively of that, and that alone, which God has done."[59] But what immediately follows will make clear that being born of God does not simply mark a mathematical point in Christian life, but indicates the moment in time at which Christian life begins.

This is suggested by v. 9b: ὅτι σπέρμα αὐτοῦ ἐν αὐτῷ μένει ("because [God's] seed abides in [them]"). The personal pronoun αὐτοῦ (lit.: "his") declares that this σπέρμα is not human sperm. The anthropological context is, rather, expressed by ἐν αὐτῷ (lit.: "in him"). Instead, αὐτοῦ refers the noun to God, as fits the context. Those who are born of God possess the divine seed, and the effect of this is that they do not commit sin. The author's intention in using the expression σπέρμα (θεοῦ) is disputed. According to a widespread opinion, it refers to the "word" of God that is accepted by the hearers.[60] This interpretation is supported by 1:10, which, in formal parallel to this text, speaks of the sinlessness of Christians ("If we say that we have not sinned, we make him a liar, and *his word* is not in us"). But there it is a question of the admission of sin, while here the issue is an assertion that those born of God do not sin. Moreover, in 1:10 λόγος is contrasted to "lie," and thus has a close relationship to "truthful speech."[61] No less likely is the interpretation of the concept of σπέρμα as the "Spirit" of God, understood as a divine gift to the community.[62] The Spirit is given to believers at baptism as χρῖσμα ("anointing") and "abides in them" (2:27; cf. 2:20). Hence it is an idea handed down from earliest Christianity that Christians may also be described as πνευματικοί ("those gifted with the Spirit of God").[63] In any case, the author is referring to that which joins Christians to God and takes up residence within them.[64] This could also be understood in a christological sense, especially since the concept of σπέρμα (descendant, progeny) is applicable to Christ as the "Son of God" (1 John 1:3, 7; 3:8, and frequently);[65] the teaching about the λόγος σπερματικός was not alien to the second century.[66] Moreover, in the anthropology of the Hermetic literature,[67] in gnostic systems, and in the mystery religions the idea is widespread that the human being is possessed by an ontologically understood divine "fullness."[68]

This *non posse peccare* applied to Christians (v. 9c) is an

59 Wengst, *Brief*, 138.

60 Thus Martin Luther, WA 20.705, 20f–706,1: "quoniam semen dei, i.e. verbum . . . verbum dei manet, est aeternum semen" ("Now the seed of God, that is, the Word [of God] . . . the word of God remains; it is eternal seed").

61 Cf. 2:4 (ἀλήθεια), as well as 2 John 2 ("because of the truth that abides in us"). That the word of God can be compared with "seed" is evident from the interpretation of the parable of the sower (Luke 8:11); the word has a figurative sense in 1 Pet 1:23 (where the word of God is compared to imperishable seed). James 1:18 says that the "word of truth" has "[given] us birth" (ἀπεκύησεν). On the word of God "abiding," cf. John 5:38 (15:7 in the plural); see also 1 Cor 4:15; Justin *1 Apol.* 32.8–10.

62 1 John 3:24; 4:13. This is Schnackenburg's interpretation (*Epistles*, 175); also Windisch and Preisker, *Die Katholischen Briefe*, 122; Wengst, *Brief*, 140.

63 Cf. Titus 3:5; Mark 1:10; esp. John 3:5–8. Cf. also Valentinus's teaching about the divine seed in good souls (Irenaeus *Adv. haer.* 1.5.6; 1.7.2; Clement of Alexandria *Exc. Theod.* 53.2).

64 J. du Preez ("'Sperma autou' in I John 3:9," *Neot* 9 [1975] 105–12) defines the concept as "new life of being pure and doing right" (p. 111).

65 For Christ as σπέρμα, see also Gal 3:16, 19; Acts 3:25; Rev 12:17. For Christ's abiding in Christians, see John 6:56; 15:4, 5.

66 The concept of λόγος σπερματικός was known even in the early Stoa: Zeno (4th/3d century BCE) *SVF* 1.28.26. Cf. also the Neoplatonic *logos* doctrine: Plotinus (204–270 CE) *Enn.* 3.2.15: Ἀρχὴ οὖν λόγος καὶ πάντα λόγος καὶ τὰ γινόμενα κατ' αὐτὸν καὶ συντταττόμενα ἐπὶ τῇ γενέσει πάντως οὕτως ("The rational principle, then, is the origin, and all things are reason, both those which are brought into being according to the principle and those which, in their coming to birth, are altogether ranged in this common order." The idea of creation as being born of God was quite familiar to Philo; cf. *Ebr.* 30; *Virt.* 204–5; *Conf. ling.* 63; *Cher.* 43–44; *Vit. Mos.* 1.279; *Mut. nom.* 138; *Leg. all.* 3.180–81, 219; *Migr. Abr.* 31; *Poster. C.* 135; on this, see Windisch and Preisker, *Die Katholischen Briefe*, 122–23. On the whole subject, see Hermann Kleinknecht, "λέγω B: The Logos in Greece and in Hellenism," *TDNT* 4 (1967) 77–91. In the longer Coptic version of the *Apocryphon of John* (NHC 2, 1) the resurrected and exalted Christ appears in a shifting form to John the son of Zebedee and says to him (30,11–16): "I, therefore, the perfect Pronoia of the all, changed myself into my seed, for I existed first, going on every road. For I am the

intensification of *non peccare* (3:6, 9a) and appears to stand in an absolute opposition to 1:8 ("If we say that we have no sin, we deceive ourselves, and the truth is not in us") and also to 3:4, which presumes the existence of sinful acts in the Johannine community.[69] There can be no doubt that this is determined by a parenetic framework, and that it is an especially powerful form of expression aimed at warning the community not to sin.

In fact, anyone who is born of God and therefore is of one nature with God lives in irreconcilable opposition to every kind of sinful action.[70] The community should

---

richness of the light; I am the remembrance of the pleroma." Cf. Theophilus of Antioch 2.10, 22: *λόγος ἐνδιάθητος, προφορικός.*

67 Cf. Porphry in Eusebius *Praep. Ev.* 3.11.42: *Ὁ δὲ ἐντεταμένος Ἑρμῆς δηλοῖ τὴν εὐτονίαν, δείκνυσι δὲ καὶ τὸν σπερματικὸν λόγον τὸν διήκοντα διὰ πάντων* ("The phallic Hermes represents vigour, but also indicates the generative law that pervades all things"). See Edwin H. Gifford, trans., *Eusebius, Preparation for the Gospel* (2 vols.; 1903; reprinted Grand Rapids: Baker Book House, 1981) 1.125; *Corp. Herm.* 13.2: *Ὦ τέκνον, σοφία νοερὰ ἐν σιγῇ καὶ ἡ σπορὰ τὸ ἀληθινὸν ἀγαθόν. — τίνος σπείραντος, ὦ πάτερ . . . τὸ γὰρ σύνολον ἀπορῶ. — τοῦ θελήματος τοῦ θεοῦ, ὦ τέκνον* ("'My child, [the womb] is the wisdom of understanding in silence, and the seed is the true good.' 'Who sows the seed, father? I am entirely at a loss.' 'The will of god, my child'").

68 In the mystery religions a necessary aspect of the highest consecration is "a sexual union through which the human being imbibes the most intimate nature and power of a god, his seed" (Reitzenstein, *Hellenistic Mystery-Religions,* 34; cf. 310–19; also Albrecht Dieterich, *Eine Mithrasliturgie* [3d ed.; Leipzig: Teubner, 1923, reprinted Teheran: Pahlavi Commemorative Reprints, 1976] 121–22). This is witnessed by Hippolytus *Ref.* 5.3: "For this, he says, is the gate of heaven; and this a house of God, where the Good Deity dwells alone. And into this (gate), he says, no unclean person shall enter, nor one that is natural or carnal; but it is reserved for the spiritual only. And those who come hither ought to cast off their garments, and become all of them bridegrooms, emasculated through the virginal spirit. For this is the virgin who carries in her womb and conceives and brings forth a son, not animal, not corporeal, but blessed forevermore" (translation in ANF 5.56). Cf. also Philo, on the chosen people Israel: "Who has made accurate discovery of how the sowing of their generation was first made? Their bodies have been moulded from human seeds, but their souls are sprung from divine seeds, therefore their stock is akin to God" (*Vit. Mos.* 1.279). Cf. also Clement of Alexandria *Exc. Theod.* 1, 2, 38, 40, 49, 53, etc. Cf. Irenaeus *Adv. haer.* 1.2.6: "the whole Pleroma of the Æons, with one design and desire, . . . produced . . . a being of most perfect beauty, the very star of the Pleroma . . . namely Jesus. Him they also speak of under the name of Saviour" (ANF 1.318). Cf. Gerhard Delling, "*πλήρωμα, κτλ.*," *TDNT* 6 (1968) 298–311.

69 Cf. also 2:1–2; 5:16, 18. According to Nigel Turner (*Grammatical Insights into the New Testament* [Edinburgh: Clark, 1965] 151), the aorist subjunctive at 2:1 (*ἐάν τις ἁμάρτῃ*) is to be taken as ingressive: "If anyone began to be a sinner," or "if one committed a sinful act." In contrast, *οὐ δύναται ἁμαρτάνειν* in 3:9 would mean "he or she cannot be a sinner," the present description of a situation, not an action. Turner attempts a corresponding comparison between 2:1 and 3:9: it is true that a Christian can begin to be a sinner, but such a one will not enter into the condition of being a sinner. In 1:10, however, the perfect *ἡμαρτήκαμεν* concedes that a Christian may recall a sinful action. In the same way, the aorist subjunctive in 2:1 can be understood not as ingressive but as effective ("if anyone sins" or "if anyone has sinned"); cf. BDF § 318 (1). For the author, there is no contradiction to the statement in 3:9, which instead speaks of the eschatological dimension of the human being, the fact of being born of God; in that dimension it is true that "they cannot sin." Hence there is also no distinction drawn between individual sins (2:1) and an ongoing situation of sinlessness (3:4–10) for Christians (against Dodd, *Epistles,* 78–79). Similarly, the formal difference between *ποιεῖν ἁμαρτίαν* (3:4, 8) and *ἁμαρτάνειν* (3:6, 8–9; 5:18) does not offer persuasive support for the conclusion that sinlessness is habitual (in response to V. Kerry Inman, "Distinctive Johannine Vocabulary and the Interpretation of I John 3:9," *WTJ* 40 [1977] 136–44, esp. 141).

70 It is the achievement of Hans Windisch to have made a clear exposition of this point. However, his distinction (*Die Katholischen Briefe,* 136) between sinfulness in the community and sinlessness, which is said to come from a later literary stratum in 1 John, is not persuasive. Equally unsuccessful is the attempt to assign responsibility for this discrepancy to polemic against opposing views. Bultmann also engages in harmonizing, since he speaks only of a "possibility of not sinning," although admitting at the same time

return to this, its beginning point. "Being incapable of sin" represents the eschatological reality[71] out of which the community has lived from its beginning; it is a fundamental and appropriate description of that reality.[72] However, it does not eliminate the earthly reality within which sin remains a threatening force that must be repeatedly overcome, until the end of the world.[73]

■ **10** The expression ἐν τούτῳ ("in this") refers to what follows.[74] Hence v. 10 is not merely a conclusion from what has gone before but carries the discussion further. If it is true that sinners come from the devil (v. 8), and that those born of God cannot sin (v. 9), it is easy to understand what the mark of distinction is, the thing that separates those who belong to God from those others who come from the devil. The adjective φανερά, which occurs only here in the Johannine writings, refers to this kind of recognizability. The children of God and of the devil are "revealed" or "made visible" by what they do. Does this mean that here—as is the case in Matt 7:16–20—a conclusion is drawn from people's deeds to their nature? In fact, what is at issue for the author, here as in what precedes, is not a statement of essence but rather that the community should behave in the right way. That means that they should appear as τέκνα θεοῦ. Since they already bear that designation, and because Christians in eschatological perspective are already "children of God,"[75] the operative principle here (not, of course, from an idealistic point of view) is: "be what you are."[76] The indicative, by its own inner logic, demands the imperative. Those who are born of God, all who belong to God, must present themselves as what they truly (although not yet in earthly reality) already are. They must make a reality of the condition of sinlessness that has been promised to them (v. 9) and practice justice and love (v. 10b).

Τέκνα τοῦ διαβόλου is a parallel construction to τέκνα τοῦ θεοῦ and appears only here in the NT.[77] While the

that "the gift of a possibility always includes a demand" (*Epistles*, 53). Wengst (*Brief*, 140) correctly speaks "not only of a fundamental possibility or an ideal, but of a reality."

71 The Stoic notion of the perfection of the wise person appears closely related to this. Cf. Velleius Paterculus (1st century CE) 2.35: "He never acts rightly for the sole purpose of creating the impression of acting thus, but because he could not have acted otherwise." Also Seneca *Ep.* 72.6: "The wise . . . cannot slip back, or slip into any more illness at all." Similarly *Ep.* 120.10; *Ben.* 6.21.2. Seneca refers to an immanent condition of moral perfection for the sage, while Johannine anthropology is concerned with an eschatological reality. In this latter sense, see also Ignatius *Eph.* 8.2: "Carnal people cannot act spiritually, or spiritual people carnally, just as faith cannot act like unbelief, or unbelief like faith. But even what you do in the flesh you do spiritually. For you do everything under Christ's control." The author of 1 John is thus not speaking in an "idealizing vision"; at this point the connection with the theology of Paul seems especially close (cf. also Schnackenburg, *Epistles*, 176).

72 Ignace de la Potterie, "The Impeccability of the Christian," explains "not being able to sin" on the basis of two aspects of Johannine eschatology: "(a) . . . that the eschatological realities are *present* realities for John . . . (b) . . . eschatological dualism" (*The Christian Lives by the Spirit*, 186). The connection with the dualism in Johannine eschatology is also emphasized by P. P. A. Kotzé: "The Christian existence is thus secure and at the same time insecure" (*Neot* 13 [1979] 81).

73 Jewish apocalyptic expectation also includes hope for an eon liberated from sin; cf. *1 Enoch* 5.8–9; *Jub.* 5.12; *T. Levi* 18.9; 1QS iv.21–23, and frequently. Sakae Kubo ("I John 3:9: Absolute or Habitual?" *AUSS* 7 [1969] 47–56) differs, attempting to understand v. 9 as an "idealistic context" and on the basis of an opposition between Christians and heretics (p. 50).

74 An alternate possibility is a reference to what has preceded (so Brown, *Epistles*, 416, who refers it back as far as 2:18), but that would mean that the caesura between 2:27 and 2:28 would have to be denied. For Schnackenburg (*Epistles*, 176 n. 181) instead ἐν τούτῳ points both backward and forward. Nevertheless, the intended answer is to be discovered only in v. 10b; in contrast to 2:5, the expression at this point is not constructed personally but is to be understood as neuter ("by this" or "in this way"). Cf. BAGD 596–97ba on 3:19 (and see below on 3:19).

75 For the distinction between this phrase and τεκνία, see above, at v. 7.

76 An idea of development or growth should not be introduced into the text, as it is by Brown, *Epistles*, 431, who speaks of a "growth in God's children. The divine seed abides and continues to transform the child of God into the image of God's Son which is the image of God Himself, until at the final revelation we are like God Himself. The more that this divine seed transforms the Christian, the more impossible it is for the Christian to sin."

origin of this expression is the distinction between the "children of light" and the "children of darkness"[78] expressed in Jewish apocalyptic literature in a number of different terms, a similar contrast, even independent of a future eschatological perspective, occurs in such documents as the Letter to the Ephesians.[79] This is not a description of the future; instead, two possible kinds of human existence within history are described as presented in an eschatological perspective: the revelation of life (1:2) results in the separation of human beings into "children of God"[80] and "children of the devil." It is characteristic that the author does not speak of the children of God and the children of the devil in the same way. It is not possible to speak of being born of the devil, apparently because, differently from the case of being a child of God, adherence to the devil is not the result of an (un)saving event or a sacramental action, but depends instead on human acts.[81]

On this basis one must also give a negative answer to the question whether the author at this point is distinguishing between those who are "dividing" the community (cf. 2:19) and his Christian sisters and brothers.[82] It is true that the opponents belong among the children of the devil, because their existence in resistance to God is manifested in their leaving the community and can be evaluated as an offense against justice and love, but the author's fundamental opinion is that "all (πᾶς) who do not do right are not from God." The criterion of being a child of God or of the devil is an ethical one.[83] The noun δικαιοσύνη appears only in an ethical sense in 1 John (in a construction with ποιεῖν also in 2:29; 3:7). If it refers to the righteousness of God, which is equated with forgiveness of sins (cf. 1:9; 2:1, 29; 3:7), this means that being from God and "abiding in God" (2:28) must be concretely expressed as an existence in righteousness.[84] By contrast, not acting righteously makes people recognizable as not belonging to God. The author adds, apparently without a break, *καὶ ὁ μὴ ἀγαπῶν τὸν ἀδελφὸν αὐτοῦ*. This phrase has been interpreted as an added gloss,[85] but it is significant not only as a transition to what follows (vv. 11–12) but also as an interpretation of the concept of δικαιοσύνη. Καί has the meaning "that is" or "namely."[86] The righteousness demanded of Christians is evident in their love for one another.[87] As

77 However, the idea itself is in the NT (also in John 8:44; Acts 13:10; Matt 13:38) and in Jewish apocalyptic literature (cf. 2QFlor i.8).

78 Cf. 1QS i.10; 1QH vi.29–30; *Jub.* 15.26–32; *Apoc. Abr.* 13—14; *T. Dan* 4.7.

79 Eph 2:2–3: children of disobedience, children of wrath; 2:19: members of the household of God.

80 That the idea of "being children of God" in the NT had its preparation in the Greek and Hellenistic world is evident from the traditions about divine heroes and emperors. Thus Diogenes the Cynic, also with ethical purpose, addresses Alexander the Great (who thought himself to be a son of Zeus): "if you are self-controlled and know the royal art of Zeus, nothing prevents your being a son of Zeus (τοῦ Διὸς .. υἱόν); for this is what they claim Homer says: that Zeus is the father, not only of gods but of men as well, though not of slaves nor of any mean and ignoble man. If, however, you are cowardly and love luxury and have a servile nature, then you are in no way related to the gods or to good men. Why, methinks of old the 'Sown men,' as they were called, of Thebes had what seemed a spear mark on their bodies as a sign of their origin, and he who did not have this mark was not regarded as one of the 'Sown men.' And do you not think that in the souls of the offspring of Zeus also a sign is to be found by which those who have the power to judge will know whether they are of his seed or not?" (Dio Chrysostom *Or.* 4.21–23).

81 Cf. Wengst, *Brief*, 142; Schnackenburg, *Epistles*, 176. See also n. 51 above.

82 Brown (*Epistles*, 416) thinks that he is doing so.

83 On the question whether the author's opponents are guilty of an unethical way of life, see above.

84 The variant reading ὢν δίκαιος (Ψ vg. sy^{hmg}(sa); Tertullian, Origen, Cyprian) preferred by Adolf von Harnack ("Zur Textkritik," 534–73) corresponds materially to ποιῶν δικαιοσύνην (cf. v. 7); the latter reading, despite differences in the placement of the article, is on the whole well attested. Smalley also considers ὢν δίκαιος a secondary reading "since the context demands a reference to the practice (rather than the character) of righteousness" (*1, 2, 3 John*, 177 n. a).

85 This possibility is also considered by Windisch and Preisker, *Die Katholischen Briefe*, 123.

86 Cf. John 1:16; BDR § 442 (6a); thus Bultmann, *Epistles*, 54; Brown, *Epistles*, 417 ("namely").

87 Cf. Augustine *De natura et gratia* 49 (CSEL 60.270): "ipsa [= caritas] est enim verissima, plenissima, perfectissimaque iustitia" ("for nothing short of this [= love of God] amounts to a most true, pleasing, and perfect righteousness").

elsewhere in 1 John, ἀδελφός is to be understood primarily as referring to fellow Christians,[88] even though the ethic of 1 John does not exclude a universal application; in fact, its fundamental orientation points beyond the community circle.

88 Thus also Bonnard, *Les épitres johanniques*, 72–73; and Brown, *Epistles*, 417; Bultmann (*Epistles*, 54) differs (understanding ἀδελφός in analogy to 2:10 as "neighbor").

3 Love of the Brothers and Sisters

11 For this is the message you have heard
from the beginning, that we should love
one another. 12/ [We must not be] like
Cain who was from the evil one and
murdered his brother. And why did he
murder him? Because his own deeds
were evil and his brother's righteous. 13/
[And] do not be astonished, brothers and
sisters, that the world hates you. 14/ We
know that we have passed from death to
life because we love one another.
Whoever does not love abides in death.
15/ All who hate a brother or sister are
murderers, and you know that murderers
do not have eternal life abiding in them.
16/ We know love by this, that he laid
down his life for us—and we ought to lay
down our lives for one another. 17/ How
does God's love abide in anyone who has
the world's goods and sees a brother or
sister in need and yet refuses help? 18/
Little children, let us love, not in word or
speech, but in truth and action.

■ **11** While keeping God's commandments (2:3) is interpreted as avoiding sin and doing justice (2:28—3:10), the relationship between δικαιοσύνη and love of the brothers and sisters was already obvious in v. 10. The criterion of being a child of God is "righteousness," and therefore fraternal/sororal love. The following subsection, connected with the preceding verse through a causal ὅτι, is devoted entirely to the meaning of such love of the brothers and sisters. It ends with v. 18.[1] When the author resumes "those who do not love their brothers or sisters" (ὁ μὴ ἀγαπῶν τὸν ἀδελφὸν αὐτοῦ, v. 10) with the contrasting expression "that we should love one another" (ἵνα ἀγαπῶμεν ἀλλήλους, v. 11b), this indicates that for him there is no real difference: love of the brothers and sisters exists as mutual love, the *agapē* exercised in the community and by its members.

From a structural point of view, v. 11 recalls 1:5, where the concept of ἡ ἀγγελία ("the message") also appears. However, the author speaks there in the first person and presents himself as a witness to the message, a message he has received "directly." It is no accident that ἀπ' ἀρχῆς ("from the beginning") is introduced at this point, and not in the earlier passage: the proclamation the community has heard from the beginning, and that has therefore served a foundational function for them, is the preaching of the apostolic witnesses.[2] He is handing on the message he has received. Although ἀγγελία should be translated "message" in 1 John,[3] there is still

1 Cf. Windisch and Preisker, *Die Katholischen Briefe*, 123 (vv. 11–18: an "initial discussion of fraternal love"). Wengst differs (*Brief*, 155–56), beginning a new section with v. 18. For Brown (*Epistles*, 123–29) 3:11 begins the second part of 1 John, extending to 5:12 (with a subsection 3:11–24 in which 3:13–17 and 3:18–24 represent two strophes of equal length, separated by the addresses ἀδελφοί in v. 13, τεκνία in v. 18, and framed by 3:11–12 and 3:23–24). Ernst von Dobschütz has a completely different solution ("Johanneische Studien I," *ZNW* 8 [1907] 1–8). He sees 2:28—3:12 as a unit intended to admonish to a Christian moral life.

2 On ἀπ' ἀρχῆς ("from the beginning" [of the community]), cf. 1:1; 2:7, 13–14, 24; 3:8; 2 John 5–6.

3 Thus also in 1:5; nowhere else in the NT. The variant ἐπαγγελία in v. 11 has rather good attestation, but from the point of view of content it is inappropriate, since this word should be translated "promise" (as also in 2:25; cf. Schnackenburg, *Epistles*, 178 n. 187); against Bultmann, *Epistles*, 54 n. 42, who sees no difference in meaning. Alexander Sand ("ἐπαγγελία," *EDNT* 2 [1991] 14) emphasizes

another reason why one should not overlook the difference between 3:11 and 1:5. In 1:5 the issue is the message that God is light. The emphasis is on the christological context, namely, that this message was established through the revelation of life in Jesus Christ (1:2). Only in what follows is it apparent that this message has ethical implications, since it separates truth from lies (1:6–7) and implies freedom from sin (1:7–10). In 3:11, on the contrary, the interpretation of the "message" is clarified by the *ἵνα* clause that follows; its function is not so much explicatory as imperative.[4] The meaning of the word thus approaches the concept of *ἐντολή* ("commandment"). The "message" contains an obligation, just as a commandment does.[5] At this point the christological foundation of the obligation is not expressed, even though it is clear in what follows that ethics and christology cannot be separated from one another (3:16).

The author has also said in the second part of his writing that the community stands under the love commandment, and that it represents a central and immediate demand on them (2:7–11). Even at that point, the old and new commandment of love was understood as foundational for the community (2:7: *ἀπ' ἀρχῆς*). Moreover, "to love brothers and sisters" (*ἀγαπᾶν τὸν ἀδελφόν*) was identified with "living in the light" (2:9). While this expresses a specifically Johannine world of ideas,[6] at the same time one cannot overlook the differences between this and the tradition of the love commandment in the Fourth Gospel (13:34–35; 15:12). It is significant, for example, that the following *καθώς* clause (v. 12) refers not to Christ but to Cain, and that in the Fourth Gospel the issue is the word of the Revealer to his disciples, while here it is the teaching of the witnesses to the community. Since one cannot presume a literary dependency of 1 John on the Fourth Gospel,[7] here are two independent expressions of the Johannine school that, without reference to one another, emphasize the special importance of the commandment of love for Johannine theology.

This passage is dominated by the idea of the community as a closed unit separated from the world. What is expressly spoken of is love for one another; nothing is said about love for neighbors or fellow human beings. That the demand of mutual love is emphatically brought home to the readers (cf. v. 10) underscores the character of 1 John as an ecclesial writing. Even though *agapē,* in principle, extends beyond the Christian community, the truth that the love of Christians, like the love of God, must encompass nonbelievers as well (cf. 2:2; 4:14) is not expressed here. On the contrary, the example of Cain is applied *expressis verbis* to the first interfamilial murder reported in the Bible.

■ **12** This example is introduced with *οὐ καθώς* ("not like"), a negative conjunction found in the NT only here and in John 6:58. In the Fourth Gospel it is used to introduce a reference to an OT parallel, the miracle of the manna, and in the present instance the ultimate background is also OT tradition (Gen 4:14). This is the only possible allusion to the OT in 1 John; however, one should not assume that the author made direct use of the OT.[8] On the contrary, the figure of Cain is depicted in a

that, although the word group is still used in the LXX in a secular Greek sense as "announcement," and no difference can be established there between *ἀγγελία* and *ἐπαγγελία*, the meaning "promise of salvation" had developed within Judaism; as in *2 Bar.* 57.2; 59.2.

4 The same is true of *ἵνα* in John 13:34; cf. BDF § 389 (*ἵνα* as recapitulation of an imperative infinitive) and BDR § 394 n. 3 (circumscription of an explicatory infinitive).

5 Thus *ἐντολή* also occurs in combination with *ἵνα* in 3:23a ("that we should believe . . . and love one another"); 4:21 ("[that] those who love God must love their brothers and sisters also"); 2 John 5–6 ("let us love one another. And this is love, that we walk according to his commandments").

6 Cf. 1:5, 7; John 1:4–9; 3:19–21, and frequently.

7 Against Wengst (*Brief,* 145), who sees here, as in 2:7, a backward reference to John 13:34–35. Windisch and Preisker (*Die Katholischen Briefe,* 123) and Bultmann (*Epistles,* 54 n. 44) also refer to John 13:34, although without expressly asserting a relation of dependence between the passages.

8 The reference to Cain is not a direct citation of Gen 4:3–16 (against Windisch and Preisker, *Die Katholischen Briefe,* 123–24; Schnackenburg, *Epistles,* 179), but a borrowing from Jewish tradition by Christian interpreters. T. C. de Kruijf ("Nicht wie Kain [der] vom Bösen war . . . [1 Joh 3,13]," *Bijdragen* 41 [1980] 47–63) suggests the possibility "that the author of 1 John was acquainted with the Cain motif in the background of John 8 and inserted it in his letter after his own fashion, namely, as a powerful warning to the community" (p. 62).

developed manner that goes beyond the OT story. He is ἐκ τοῦ πονηροῦ which, as in 2:13–14; 5:18 (cf. 3:8) is interpreted as a masculine figure. That Cain is "from the evil one" designates him as a τέκνον τοῦ διαβόλου ("child of the devil," v. 10). While this qualifies not only the deeds but the very existence of Cain as evil,[9] the author does not engage in further reflection on the connection between being and doing. He simply states that Cain, who belongs to the evil one, murdered his brother. The verb σφάζειν is a strong expression for "killing" and appears elsewhere in the NT only in the book of Revelation.[10] It is also used for "murdering" or "slaughtering" in the Septuagint.[11] That the name of Abel is not mentioned here shows that the focus of the argumentation lies on the negative side of the opposition between good and evil and that the parenetic purpose shapes the thought. This presupposes that Abel, in distinction from Cain, is "from the good one," that is, ἐκ τοῦ θεοῦ ("from God"; cf. v. 10).

The second half of the verse presents the reason for Cain's evil deed.[12] The question of the reason for the evil action is not directly answered. That Cain's ἔργα ("deeds") were πονηρά ("evil"), while those of his brother were δίκαια, is not explained, but one may suppose that the author sees the evil action as motivated by Cain's hatred, since this key word will play a significant role in what follows (vv. 13 and 15).

Although the motive for Cain's action is not specified in the OT, it is hinted in the LXX translation (Gen. 4:7) and is treated in Jewish and Christian exegesis. The fundamental presupposition, as in our verse, is that Abel is a just person. Thus Josephus (*Ant.* 1.53) describes Abel as δίκαιος ("righteous") and Cain as πονηρός ("wicked"). Philo interprets the brothers in terms of Greek Stoic ideas: Cain is considered a representative of κακία ("vice"), while Abel is an embodiment of ἀρετή ("virtue," *Sac. AC* 14; *Det. pot. ins.* passim). The reason why Cain's offering was not accepted is given in *Apocalypse of Abraham* with the statement that Cain was guided by satanic power. Hebrews 11:4 takes Abel as a witness to faith who brought a greater sacrifice than Cain and thus was approved as righteous; Matt 23:35: the evil strand in OT Jewish history begins with the blood of righteous Abel; Jude 11: Cain is the prototype of the false teachers who follow his path. In patristic tradition, the *Pseudo-Clementines* give extended attention to Cain and Abel. Abel is considered on the positive side, as δίκαιος, while Cain is assigned to the negative side of the series of syzygies (*Ps.-Clem. Hom.* 2.16.3; 3.26.1; 19.9.5; *Rec.* 3.61.1). Cain is regarded as φονεύς ("murderer") and ψεύστης ("liar," *Hom.* 3.25.2). He is ἄδικος ("unrighteous," *Hom.* 2.16.3; 19.9.5); his name can be rendered either as κτῆσις ("possession") or as ζῆλος ("greed, envy") (*Hom.* 3.25.1; 42. 7).[13]

9 Wengst (*Brief,* 146) rejects this connection, although he admits that there is a "slippery slope" from the "power that causes evil deeds, to location within the history of sin, to actual evil deeds."

10 It is active in Rev 6:4, passive in 5:6, 9, 12; 6:9; 13:3, 8; 18:24. The idea of bloody slaughter is connected with ritual sacrifice. Thus in 5:6, 9, 12; 13:8 Christ is the slain lamb, and in 6:9 the death of the martyrs is compared with the slaughtering of sacrificial animals (cf. Otto Michel, "σφάζω, σφαγή," *TDNT* 7 [1971] 934–35). Schnackenburg (*Epistles,* 179 n. 191) emphasizes that the concept of sacrifice is not present in this passage. Brown (*Epistles,* 442) explains that the verb does not necessarily have a cultic significance here: "it catches the brutality of one brother's action toward the other."

11 It is used both for the cultic (Gen 22:10; Isa 57:5; Ezek 16:21; 23:39) and the profane (Num 14:16; Judg 12:6; 1 Kgs 18:40; 2 Kgs 10:7, 14; 25:7; Jer 39:6; 41:7; 52:10) slaughter of human beings, as well as for the cultic (1 Sam 1:24–25; Ezek 44:11, and frequently) and profane (Deut 28:31; Gen 37:31, and frequently) killing of animals (cf. Josephus *Ap.* 1.76).

12 The expression χάριν τίνος is unique in the NT. In the introduction of a question, the preposition is ordinarily placed second; cf. Luke 7:47: οὗ χάριν; Eph 3:1, 14: τούτου χάριν; *1 Clem.* 31.2: τίνος χάριν; BDF § 216 (2).

13 Cf. Josephus *Ant.* 1.52, 60–61. According to Karl Georg Kuhn (""Ἄβελ-Κάιν," *TDNT* 1 [1964] 7), in contrast to Matt 23:35 par. and Jude 11, where the opposition between Cain and Abel is "regarded purely from an ethical point of view," in 1 John 3:12 there is an absolute metaphysical dualism. Cain and

■ **13** As already said, the contrasting of the evil works of Cain with the righteous deeds of his brother has no independent function in this context, even though one may suspect that this topic is not confined to v. 12, but is echoed in what follows (esp. vv. 15 and 22). That Abel's name is not mentioned, even though one would expect it after *τοῦ ἀδελφοῦ* ("his brother," v. 12), indicates that the author is not interested in reflecting on the past history of Cain and Abel, but rather on the brotherhood and sisterhood that exist in the present. This is also evident from the address, *ἀδελφοί* ("brothers and sisters"), attested only in this verse, with which the author speaks directly to the readers,[14] takes up the injunction to love the brothers and sisters (vv. 10–11), and characterizes the congregation as a community in contrast to the world. What happened to Abel is, *sub specie aeternitatis,* nothing unusual: *μὴ θαυμάζετε* ("do not be astonished") has a rhetorical significance, introducing (as in John 3:7) a central theological statement.[15] This points to an essential feature of the Christian community and marks the offense that the community evokes in the world.[16] Their relationship to the world is characterized by their being the object of its hatred. The verb *μισεῖν* is here to be understood not merely as "not to love,"[17] but is identical with a hatred that can lead even to murder and deadly violence (cf. v. 15). It is not said that the world's enmity toward the community is caused by Christians' acts of love for one another.[18] Instead, what is fundamental is the contrast between being from God and being from the devil (v. 10). Wherever people like Cain live "from the evil one," there is no place for love; instead, hatred and deadly violence are in control. One should not infer on the basis of the text that the author is thinking of a concrete persecution of the Christian community, such as the one under Domitian.[19] Bultmann correctly observes that in 1 John (differently from John 15:20; Matt 5:10–12) nothing is said about *διώκειν* ("persecuting").[20] It is thus a matter of the

Abel are "simply expressions of their individual ways of being." A similarly absolute opposition is said to be attested in Heb 11:4. According to Windisch and Preisker (*Die Katholischen Briefe,* 124), this passage takes up the idea that the "opposition between the righteous and sinners . . . is thus not initially established by the appearance of Christ," but instead exists "from the beginning of the world." They refer for their reasoning to Philo *Praem. poen.* 68, where it is said of Cain: *οὗτος ἐστιν ὁ πρῶτος ἐναγής, ὁ πρῶτος καθαρευούσῃ τῇ γῇ μίασμα προσβαλὼν ἄηθες ἀνθρωπείου αἵματος* ("He it was who first fell under a curse, who first brought the monstrous pollution of human blood upon the still pure earth"), and to *T. Benj.* 7.5: "For through all times those who are like Cain in envy and hatred of their brothers and sisters will be punished with the same plague." Correctly also Chaine, *Les épîtres catholiques,* 188: "the story of Cain continues" (with reference to Matt 5:11–12; 24:9; John 15:18–19; 17:14). For the interpretation of Cain in ancient Jewish and early Christian times, see also Brown, *Epistles,* 442–43.

14 The personal pronoun *μου* is probably a secondary addition, as one may conclude from the overwhelmingly negative manuscript evidence. The same is true of the explanatory *ἡμῶν* with *τοὺς ἀδελφούς* (v. 14). On this subject, see above at 2:9–11. The beginning with *καί* (v. 15) corresponds to Johannine style (cf. 2:28; 3:23–24, and frequently), but for that very reason it is probably not original (similarly in v. 19). An ascription on the basis of homoioteleuton (as with the preceding *δίκαια*), as Brown (*Epistles,* 444) suggests, is improbable, since the *α* at the end of *δίκαια* is against it.

15 The word *θαυμάζειν* appears only at this point in 1 John (6 times in the Fourth Gospel). The construction with *εἰ* (in the sense of *ὅτι*, "that") is also in Mark 15:44; *Diogn.* 10.4; *Mart. Pol.* 16.1; Josephus *Ap.* 1.68 (BAGD 219, 352).

16 Thus also in the Fourth Gospel, with reference to Jesus' work in the world: 3:7; 4:27; 5:20, 28; 7:15, 21. More powerfully than in the Synoptic Gospels, it is not so much the miracles (cf. Matt 8:27; 15:31; 21:20, and frequently) as the word of Jesus that creates offense in the Fourth Gospel (5:20; 6:21). Jesus' attitude also occasions misunderstanding among the disciples (4:27, 33), but it is they who receive the admonition not to be astonished (3:7; 5:28). Cf. Georg Bertram, "*θαῦμα, κτλ.*," *TDNT* 3 (1965) 27–42, esp. 40.

17 As, for example, in Matt 6:24; Luke 14:26 (par. Matt 10:37); John 12:25; cf. Otto Michel, "*μισέω*," *TDNT* 4 (1967) 690–93.

18 Against Heinz Giesen, "*μισέω*," *EDNT* 2 (1991) 431; similarly Büchsel, *Johannesbriefe,* 55; and Wengst, *Häresie und Orthodoxie,* 148, who explains that the author here "really [understands] fraternal love as the originating cause of the hatred." Schnackenburg (*Epistles,* 180) differs, regarding hatred as a characteristic of the world that is at enmity with God.

19 Schnackenburg (*Epistles,* 179) suggests the possibility that, in particular, the crass expression *ἔσφαξεν* (v. 12) could refer to "the brutal killing of Christians in the earliest persecutions under Domitian"; cf. also

fundamental contrast, more precisely characterized in ontological terms, between community and world,[21] as it is also addressed in the Fourth Gospel, although there in an independent, christological exposition.[22] The world's hatred is expressed in its rejection of the community. It is an essential characteristic of the world, and it has a material relationship to the fact that the world is subjected to death (cf. v. 14), and thus is not in a position to effect love or life. This distinguishes the world from the congregation of Christians that, as the community of those born of God, shares life and effects love.

■ **14** As ἡμεῖς ("we") shows, the author locates himself within the community, after having written the preceding verse still in the second person plural. He refers to their common knowledge (οἴδαμεν, "we know"), something that can be assumed for Christians in general and confirms that they have "passed from death to life." The perfect μεταβεβήκαμεν ("we have passed") describes the past event. To the extent that the congregation really is a community founded in baptism and abiding in faith, it can refer its existence to this event. Death as a destroying power has been abolished, so far as the community is concerned.[23] Just as it does not belong to the world but is exposed to its hatred, it has no share in the nature of the world, which is characterized by θάνατος ("death").[24] It acknowledges that it has exchanged the realm of death's power for the rule of life.[25] The dualistic opposition of death and life is not

---

Büchsel, *Johannesbriefe*, 55, who sees v. 13 as the consequence drawn from v. 12, namely, that the world's hatred of Christians is natural if "the evil one cannot even contemplate the doing of good works by his brother without being inflamed to commit murder."

20 Bultmann, *Epistles*, 54 n. 47.

21 On κόσμος, cf. 2:15–17 and 5:4b.

22 John 15:18–19; 17:14–16. The cause of the contrast between community and world cannot simply be derived from external circumstances. It is true that such hatred can be awakened by social differences or political opposition: "The congregation, as the community of those whom love makes equals, challenges the world by calling into question all domination and privilege that obstruct human solidarity. Thus it will necessarily encounter the hatred of those who possess positions of power and privilege. The hatred of the world is, in the first instance, the hatred of the powerful. A community that encounters the hatred of the powerless must ask itself whether it is not united with the powerful in an unholy alliance and sharing in its domination and privileges" (Wengst, *Brief*, 148). Even though 1 John does not neglect concrete relationships (cf. 2:12–17; 3:16–18), however, these do not correspond one to one with the eschatological dimension of his message. The hatred in question is one that is rooted in the very nature of the world, and that divides the community from the world *sub specie aeternitatis*. Against all appearances, it documents the powerlessness of the world.

23 Cf. John 5:24; 6:50; 11:25–26; 15:19; 17:16; Rudolf Bultmann, "θάνατος," *TDNT* 3 (1965) 18–21.

24 Cf. also 1 John 2:15–17; 4:3; Rom 5:12; 1 Cor 7:31; Hermann Sasse, "κόσμος," *TDNT* 3 (1965) 883–95.

25 The verb μεταβαίνειν occurs 12 times in the NT, mainly in a local sense ("go away"; cf. John 7:3). The christological interpretation is attested in John 13.1, "his hour had come to depart from this world and go to the Father." The figurative, anthropological sense is also found in John 5:24. Josef Blank ("Der Mensch vor der radikalen Alternative," *Kairos* 22 [1980] 146–56) sees an analogy between John 5:24 and 1 John 3:13–14. In both cases it is a matter of "a 'transition' from the realm of death into a new dimension of life." This transition is said to be connected in the first instance with faith, in the second with love, "where faith and love appear as the two existential-dynamic attitudes of human beings who have accomplished this transition. Anyone who lives in this way realizes exactly what, according to the Johannines, constitutes the essence of believing existence" (156). In addition, Schlier ("Bruderliebe," 244) draws a parallel to John 5:24 when he emphasizes that, for those who practice it, love of the brothers and sisters is not only a moral but also an ontological event: "It is a transition from one state of being to another, from being 'in death' . . . to being in life." But in spite of the internal connection, one may not speak of any literary dependence; instead, the author is drawing on the tradition of the Johannine community that he has in common with the fourth evangelist.

simply peculiar to the Johannine writings; it was widespread in the NT and its environment.[26] It fits an esoteric position, although it need not be thought that in this passage there is a clear polemic against gnostic opponents or that here the praxis of brotherly and sisterly love as practiced in the community is being set up in opposition to a gnostic, dualistically framed self-understanding.[27]

Structurally, the sentence is organized around two ὅτι clauses. The first ὅτι should be translated "that,"[28] and refers to the nature of the community. The second has a causal sense and is open to two basic interpretive possibilities; it can apply both to the preceding ὅτι clause and to οἴδαμεν ("we know"). In the first case, it would mean that the overcoming of death is founded on the community's mutual love. Paul would reject such a theological position in terms of the concept of "righteousness through works of the law." For him the deed of love is the precondition and foundation of life. While such an idea is attested within the environment surrounding the NT,[29] it cannot be demonstrated within Johannine theology. Instead, the primary idea is that the gift of life revealed in Christ is realized in love. Hence one should suppose that the second ὅτι clause, like the first, is dependent on οἴδαμεν.[30] The community's confessional stance is strengthened by its genuine practice of love toward the brothers and sisters.[31] Love for the sisters and brothers is a sign that gives certainty to the believing knowledge of the community. Hence the real basis of that love and the basis on which it can be recognized should not be set up in opposition to one another.[32] It is true that in this passage the author is addressing a parenesis to the community with the intention that love for the brothers and sisters should replace love for the world as a concrete reality in the community (cf. 2:15–16; 3:16, 18).

The antithetical statement in v. 14c gives a negative exposition to underscore what has already been said.

---

26 In addition to John 5:24, cf. esp. 3:15; 1 John 2:9–11; Rom 5:17; 8:2; 2 Tim 1:10; Col 2:13; Eph 2:1, 5; *Corp. Herm.* 1.21. In *Corp. Herm.* 1.32 the recipient of revelation confesses: "Thus I believe and I bear witness; I advance to life and light" (*Hermetica: The Greek Corpus Hermeticum and the Latin Asclepius in a New English Translation*, trans. B. P. Copenhaver [Cambridge: Cambridge University Press, 1992]).

27 Hartwig Thyen ("' . . . denn wir lieben die Brüder' (1 Joh 3,14)," in Johannes Friedrich, Wolfgang Pöhlmann, and Peter Stuhlmacher, eds., *Rechtfertigung: Festschrift für Ernst Käsemann* [Tübingen: Mohr (Siebeck), 1976] 527–42, esp. 536) also emphasizes that one could scarcely understand love of the sisters and brothers as a restriction of the required love of neighbor to an esoteric circle. Schlier's opinion ("Bruderliebe," 243) is similar, "where the discussion concerns love and hatred of the brothers and sisters, the concepts of 'brother and sister' are inevitably transformed into that of the neighbor."

28 Thus frequently in the NT in place of the accusative with infinitive after verbs of knowing; cf. 1 John 3:2; 5:18–20 (οἴδαμεν ὅτι); also John 3:2; 9:31; Matt 6:32; 22:16, and frequently; BAGD 556, 1e; BDR § 397 n. 3.

29 Cf. *T. Gad* 4.6–7: "For just as love would bring back the dead to life and revoke a death sentence, so hatred would kill those who are alive . . . but the spirit of love cooperates with the law of God by long-suffering, and the result is men's salvation"; *T. Benj.* 3.4: "for [whoever] fears God and loves his neighbour cannot be struck down by the spirit of . . . Beliar, because he is protected by the fear of God" (translation by Marinus de Jonge in Sparks, *Apocryphal OT*, 595; cf. also Str-B 4.562, § 3).

30 Cf. also the twofold ὅτι in 3:2—(1) "that"; (2) "for"—and John 13:35, where in place of the second ὅτι clause there is a conditional clause, also with a parenetical intent. On the Johannine use of ὅτι, Christian Gottlob Wilke remarks that frequently in the Johannine writings a concept just enunciated is reintroduced with ὅτι (*Die neutestamentliche Rhetorik* [Dresden: Arnold, 1843] 186). For this, he refers to John 1:17; 8:44; 10:13; 14:28; 1 John 4:18; 5:6; cf. also Edwin A. Abbott, *Johannine Grammar* (London: Black, 1906; reprinted Farnborough: Gregg International, 1968) §§ 2174–76 and 2757.

31 The reading ἡμῶν clarifies the concept τοὺς ἀδελφούς without changing its content. It is still more weakly attested than the additional μου, also secondary, in 3:13 (see above on 3:13).

32 On this point, Wengst (*Brief*, 149) emphasizes that there is no alternative between "basis for recognition" and "real basis," for on the one hand fraternal/sororal love is more than simply a characteristic of life, since it both qualifies it and makes it what it is. On the other hand the issue is not the gaining of "life" by means of "fraternal/sororal love," but the perfection of fraternal/sororal love is itself life. Life is more than love for the sisters and brothers, but to the extent that "we participate in it here, it happens in no other way than in love for the sisters and brothers." Schnackenburg (*Epistles*, 180)

Whoever does not love[33] abides in death. The dualistic concept is crassly stated. *Μένει* is stronger than *ἐστίν* (cf. also 2:9–10); it describes not only the present situation but its continuing existence. The unloving person is subjected to death and cannot escape that fate. No matter how little the author desires to reflect on the problem of theodicy at this point, or to discuss the question of how such a state of "captivity" could come about, he nevertheless underscores, with this statement, the absolute necessity of mutual love within the community. No one can escape this demand because its content is the division between death and life.

■ **15** Πᾶς ("all") at the beginning of the verse again makes clear that the address is to the whole community.[34] Hatred, which is an attitude typical of the world, can have no place in the Christian congregation. This is explained by the word *ἀνθρωποκτόνος* ("murderer"),[35] which echoes the example of Cain and Abel (v. 12), since Cain is the prototype of the "fratricide." In this verse, however, the general term for "murderer" is deliberately chosen; it recalls the Noachic law (Gen 9:6: "Whoever sheds the blood of a human, by a human shall that person's blood be shed"). The equation of hatred with murder derives from a broad ethical tradition.[36] In the rule of law as generally practiced, murderers had forfeited their physical life,[37] and so in the apocalyptic tradition one finds connected with this fact the idea that murderers were threatened with eternal death.[38] It is

differs, arguing that, as in 3:2, the second *ὅτι* clause gives the reason for recognition. Love can only be a sign by which those born of God can be recognized, for otherwise "it would suggest that one can attain to life through love, an idea not found in John." Bultmann's opinion (*Epistles,* 55) is similar: *ὅτι ἀγαπῶμεν τοὺς ἀδελφούς* must be understood as "a characteristic of the congregation as a community of those who love." This characteristic poses the question to each individual "whether he [or she] belongs to the Christian congregation."

33 The addition *τὸν ἀδελφόν* after *ἀγαπῶν* can be interpreted, with Brown (*Epistles,* 446) as an "imitation of the standard Johannine phrase." Undoubtedly this addition is weakly attested and appears to restrict "the absolute claim of the assertion" (Schnackenburg, *Epistles,* 181 n. 196). However, it is appropriate in the context of 3:11–18 (cf. below on v. 16).

34 See above at 2:23.

35 The concept of *ἀνθρωποκτόνος* is rare in secular Greek usage (e.g., Euripides *Cycl.* 127; *Iph. T.* 389); cf. BAGD 68. In the NT this concept occurs otherwise only in John 8:44, where the *διάβολος*, as the *ἀνθρωποκτόνος . . . ἀπ᾽ ἀρχῆς* is God's opponent. Cf. Bultmann, *John,* 318 n. 3, and what follows.

36 Cf. Matt 5:21–22; *Derek 'Ereṣ* 10: "Rabbi Eliezer said: Whoever hates his [or her] neighbor belongs among the shedders of blood" (Str-B 1.282); *'Abot R. Nat.* 12 (on Hillel's saying in *m. 'Abot* 1.12: "[Be thou] one who loveth [one's fellow-] creatures"): "Teach this, that one should love [human beings] and not hate them; for so we find it among the people of the generation of the dispersion: because they loved one another, God did not wish to destroy them out of the world, but scattered them to the four winds of the world. But the people of Sodom, because they hated one another, God rooted out of both this world and the world to come." Also *Sipre Deut.* 19.11 §§186–87 (108[b]) and frequently elsewhere (Str-B 1.364–65).

37 Exod 21:12; Lev 21:17. Cf. Philo *Praem. poen.* 70, where we read of the punishment of a murderer: *ζῆν ἀποθνήσκοντα ἀεὶ καὶ τρόπον τινὰ θάνατον ἀθάνατον ὑπομένειν καὶ ἀτελεύτητον* ("That he should live for ever in a state of dying and so to speak suffer death which is deathless and unending").

38 In the OT, death is understood as the temporal limit of life: it is "the end. The idea that life and death can be regarded in a dialectical unity . . . is quite alien," but in later Judaism an idea developed that death was a punishment for sin (cf. Bultmann, "*ζάω*," 849, 856), and destruction or eternal damnation was threatened as retribution for sin. *Ps. Sol.* 3.10–12a: "He has added sins to sins in his lifetime. He fell—how grievous his fall! And he shall not rise up. The destruction of the sinner is for ever, And *God* will not remember him when he visits the righteous. This is the portion of sinners for ever"; 13.11: "For the life of the just *is* for ever, but sinners shall be taken away into destruction" (Sebastian P. Brock in Sparks, *Apocryphal OT,* 659, 672). The notion of an *ἀίδιος θάνατος* is also found in Philo *Poster. C.* 39, on the life of the godless: *τοὺς δὲ ἐκείνως ζῶντας ὁ ἀίδιος θάνατος* ("but awaiting those who live in that way there will be eternal death"; cf. *Migr. Abr.* 189, and frequently. The idea of a retribution after death occurs in the Synoptics, e.g., Matt 10:28; 11:20–24; 13:40–43. The destruction of the godless is especially emphasized in Revelation, e.g., 11:18; 14:8, 10, 19; 15:1—18:24; 21:8; 22:15; see also *Apoc. Pet.* 25, and cf. the previous footnote.

noteworthy, as regards Johannine usage, that the same expression occurs also in John 8:44. It is true that this does not reflect any literary dependence,[39] because in that verse the devil is identified as "murderer," while 1 John 3:15, in contrast, suggests that the murderous human being comes from the devil (cf. 3:8, 10). What is important is that the community should not participate in the murderous nature of the world. Therefore, they are forbidden to hate and commanded to love. Such an indirect warning can be connected to the state of the community's knowledge (for *οἴδατε*, cf. v. 14), according to which hatred and murder on the one hand, and Christian existence on the other, are mutually exclusive. The latter is described as *ζωὴ αἰώνιος* ("eternal life"), and thus the absolute concept of "life" from v. 14 is carried forward. As already noted in 1:2 and 2:25, and as will be explained especially in 5:11–12, this life is an eschatological gift founded on Christ and present in the community. *Οὐκ ἐν αὐτῷ μένουσαν* ("not abiding in them"), placed at the end of the verse, emphasizes that life is not something to be possessed.[40] For that very reason, this statement does not contradict v. 14,[41] but sharply reminds the community that hatred is a mortal danger.[42]

■ **16** The demonstrative pronoun *ἐν τούτῳ* ("by this") is resumed in the next clause with *ὅτι*.[43] The intention is to say that knowledge of love is founded in Christ's self-sacrifice. Such knowledge or recognition is presupposed, as far as the Christian community is concerned (perfect tense: *ἐγνώκαμεν*; cf. also the combination of present and

39 Against Wengst, *Brief,* 149, who supposes the word has been adopted from John 8:44 because the term *ἀνθρωποκτόνος* is otherwise used for "murderer" only there. So also Dodd, *Epistles,* 83, who wishes to see parallels between the dominant ideas in both passages: if, in John 8:44, the Son of God stands in opposition to the children of the evil one, this corresponds to the Christians' love for the Son of God as a sign of their being children of God and, on the other side, the deadly hatred of their opponents is a sign that they are children of the evil one. In opposition, Schnackenburg correctly emphasizes the material difference: "There is no reference here to Satan, . . . [because] [t]he author would hardly have wanted to say of [that hater of God and envier of human beings]: 'who hates his brothers or sisters'" (*Epistles,* 181). [The published English translation has been altered to reproduce the German more exactly.—Trans.]

40 The verb *μένειν* occurs as a late-positioned participle also in John 5:38 and 2 John 2. According to Friedrich Hauck ("*μένω, κτλ.,*" *TDNT* 4 [1967] 576) the expression *μένειν ἐν* in the present tense in Johannine usage turns an eschatological promise of salvation into an immediately experienced possession of salvation. At the same time he sees this as avoiding the statements of identity characteristic of Hellenistic mysticism (e.g., *Corp. Herm.* 5.11). Bultmann makes a sharper distinction (*John,* 535–36, esp. 535 n. 1). According to him *μένειν ἐν* in John describes (1) human beings' abiding in that which one has or is; in other words, the loyalty that, in the present, holds fast for the future to what has been given in the past; (2) the eternal validity of the divine act of salvation for believers. "The language used about the word 'abiding' in the believer is different; for here (apart from 1 Jn. 2.14) the stress is not on the word as the blessing of salvation, but as command, and its 'abiding' in the believer denotes his loyalty (5.38), as in 15.7; I Jn. 2.24." Cf. also Hermann Hanse, *Gott haben in der Antike und im frühen Christentum* (RVV 27; Berlin: Töpelmann, 1939) 132, who describes the relationship between the Johannine *μένειν* and *ἔχειν* (John 5:38; 1 John 3:15) and points to the "aura of meaning surrounding the word *μονή*: 'dwell,' 'remain.'" Thus the human being is said to be "a dwelling place" for the one God.

41 Against Schnackenburg, *Epistles,* 181, according to whom the author is not thinking of his Christian readers but of the community's opponents. In contrast, cf. also Windisch and Preisker, *Die Katholischen Briefe,* who weigh the possibility that this is a statement about Christian brothers and sisters who "are falling back into the sphere of death" (p. 125).

42 Büchsel (*Johannesbriefe,* 56) observes correctly that the author has in view "Christians who hate." He sees a moral difference between Christians and non-Christians. It is precisely the hatred that the world holds toward Christians that shows that the works of the world are evil, while those of Christians are good. A Christianity that no longer lives out this moral difference is no longer Christianity. To that extent a "Christian who hates . . . is, indeed, a self-contradiction," yet for the author it is "by no means a matter of course that Christians will abide in love; he also finds occasion to issue a warning."

43 This is a typical quirk of Johannine usage, found also in 2:5c; 3:19; 4:9, 10, 13, (17), and John 4:37; 9:30; 16:30; *ἐν τούτῳ* is found in combination with *ἐάν* in John 13:35; 1 John 2:3; with *ἵνα* in John 15:8; 1 John 4:17; with *ὅταν* in 1 John 5:2; with *ἐκ* in 1 John 3:24.

perfect in 2:3). It has come to know *agapē* by accepting as its own the revelation of God's love in the Christ-event and acknowledging that love as fundamental to its existence. The pronoun ἐκεῖνος ("he") should be referred first of all to the Son of God: it is he who "laid down his life for us." The aorist ἔθηκεν ("laid down") looks back to the death of Jesus on the cross at Golgotha and elevates this past event out of the stream of history. The expression θεῖναι τὴν ψυχήν does not mean merely "to set one's life at hazard"[44] or to "risk"[45] one's life, nor is it simply a circumlocution for the readiness to sacrifice oneself. Instead, like the parallel δοῦναι τὴν ψυχήν (Mark 10:45 par. Matt 20:28), it means "to surrender one's life (ψυχή = נפש)." This expression appears rather frequently in the Fourth Gospel (John 10:11, 15, 17–18; 13:37–38; 15:13) and, in combination with the preposition ὑπέρ, is to be understood as reflecting a sacrificial action.[46] The Son of God, by presenting himself as a "means of atonement" or "atoning sacrifice" (1 John 2:2: ἱλασμός; Rom 3:25: ἱλαστήριον) has offered himself. Such a sacrifice means not only liberation from sin;[47] it includes an unconditional obligation. As frequently attested in the NT tradition, the model of Christ must lead to *imitatio.*[48] The indicative of the Christ-event founds the imperative of Christian life (cf. 1 John 4:11; 5:12–13). The community is faced with a "you must." The verb ὀφείλειν is found in the sense of an ethical obligation also in 1 John 2:6; 4:11; 3 John 8; John 13:14. Those who are touched by the love of God may not withdraw from their obligation to make the love they themselves have experienced a reality for others. Such a self-sacrifice is owed first of all to the brothers and sisters, and thus is an intracommunity phenomenon. At this point one may raise the question whether the author presumes a concrete situation of persecution in which members of the community may face martyrdom, and if he is therefore demanding of his addressees that they be prepared to be martyrs.[49] In any case what he has in view are the most extreme ethical consequences that this letter draws on the basis of the christological indicative.[50]

Cf. Brown, *Epistles,* 248–49.

44 Bultmann, *John,* 370 n. 5 (on John 10:11).

45 Eduard Schweizer, "ψυχή, D: The New Testament," *TDNT* 9 (1974) 638 (also in v. 16b).

46 On this, see Christian Maurer, "τίθημι, κτλ.," *TDNT* 8 (1972) 155–56. The Johannine expression τίθημι τὴν ψυχήν μου ὑπέρ τινος weaves together two linguistic strands. The author takes up the Greek expression τίθημι τὴν ψυχήν ("put one's life at hazard"), but uses it in the sense of δίδωμι τὴν ψυχήν, which expresses the actual surrender of life (Euripides *Phoen.* 998; Josephus *Bell.* 2.201). The corresponding rabbinic Hebrew expression would be נתן נפשו. The author thus gives the Greek expression he is using a new meaning in analogy to the Synoptic δίδωμι τὴν ψυχὴν αὐτοῦ λύτρον (Mark 10:45 par.), going back "directly to the Hebrew of Isa 53:10." However, the conclusion just cited underestimates the internal Christian tradition to which the author had access within Greek-speaking circles. On the construction with ὑπέρ, see Rom 5:8; 1 Thess 5:10; 2 Cor 5:15; Mark 14:24; also 1 John 2:2 (περί; also a weakly attested reading in this verse). Since the difference between ὑπέρ and περί faded in the Hellenistic period (Ernst Harald Riesenfeld, "περί," *TDNT* 6 [1968] 54), the distinction between ὑπέρ as referring to the atoning death of Christ and περί as influenced by OT texts (Brown, *Epistles,* 448) is problematic, even though περί can be found in the sacrificial terminology of the LXX (e.g., Ps 39:7; Lev 6:23; 14:19), and in the text before us the parallelism between christology (ὑπὲρ ἡμῶν) and discipleship (ὑπὲρ τῶν ἀδελφῶν) is intentional; cf. Ernst Harald Riesenfeld, "ὑπέρ," *TDNT* 8 (1972) 514; Strecker, *Weg,* 222 n. 1.

47 Cf. 2:2, and the remarks on it above.

48 Cf. 2 Cor 5:15; Phil 2:5–11; 1 Tim 6:12–13; 1 Pet 2:21–24; Heb 13:13–14; also Schnackenburg, *Epistles,* 182.

49 The theology of the martyred bishop Ignatius of Antioch offers a highly suggestive example here, even though a literary dependence on this verse cannot be persuasively maintained: "Ransom for you all (ἀντίψυχον ὑμων) are my spirit and my chains" (Ignatius *Smyrn.* 10.2; cf. *Eph.* 21.1; *Pol.* 2.3; 6.1). The legend of John related by Eusebius tells of a conversation between the apostle and a bandit chief: "I will account to Christ for you (ὑπὲρ σοῦ). If it must be, I will willingly suffer your death, as the Lord suffered for us; for your life I will give my own (ὑπὲρ σοῦ τὴν ψυχὴν ἀντιδώσω τὴν ἐμήν)" (Eusebius *Hist. eccl.* 3.23.17). Cf. Col 1:24.

50 Cf. also Wengst, *Brief,* 152.

■ **17** The relative pronoun ὅς in combination with (ἐ)άν describes something that is regular and repeated. The author intends to express a principle of general validity. Although the following δέ can have either an adversative (2:5; John 4:14) or a copulative (additive) meaning,[51] the latter is the case in this instance. The fundamental statement about the community's obligation to self-surrender is again followed by an example: the material needs of a brother or sister. The relationship between poor and rich is a regular part of Christian parenesis in general. In particular, the wealthy Christians are called upon not to close their eyes to the plight of their fellow Christians.[52] This follows a long-standing tradition documented in the OT and in Judaism.[53] The high value placed on giving "alms" (ἐλεημοσύνη) persisted in the Christian sphere also.[54]

Βίος means "material goods" (i.e., that which sustains life) (so also in Mark 12:44) or "property" (cf. Luke 8:43 *v.l.;* 15:12, 30). The qualification with the qualitative genitive τοῦ κόσμου ("of the world") makes clear that riches belong to this passing world and must vanish along with it (cf. 1 John 2:16). This very fact should make it easy for the Christian to bear in mind the obligation that accompanies property and to share with suffering brothers and sisters.[55] Although the expression κλείειν τὰ σπλάγχνα has no genuine parallel either in Greek or in Jewish literature, it is clear that here the noun is roughly the equivalent of "heart,"[56] and that "closing one's heart" can be equated with "having no pity."[57]

The rhetorical question, so abruptly introduced,

51 Cf. BDF § 447.

52 Cf. Mark 10:2; Luke 3:11; 6:38; 12:33; Jas 2:15–16.

53 Gen 43:30; Deut 15:7–8; Jer 31:20; *T. Zeb.* 7.3–4; 8.1–3.

54 Matt 6:2–4 par.; Acts 3:2–3, and frequently elsewhere. Cf. CD xiv.13–16a: "They shall place the earnings of at least two days out of every month into the hands of the Guardian and the Judges, and from it they shall give to the fatherless, and from it they shall succour the poor and the needy, the aged sick and the homeless, the captive taken by a foreign people, the virgin with no near kin, and the ma[id for] whom no man cares." Str-B 4.537–58 emphasizes that the giving of alms was common in the rabbinic period in Judaism and that it was a regular practice. There are non-Jewish parallels, for example, in the Mandaean *Book of John* 101, 10, where in addition to mildness, modesty, and reverence for Sunday there is a demand for "prayer [and] alms, of greater value than wife and child" (translation by Mark Lidzbarski, *Das Johannesbuch der Mandäer.* 2 vols. in 1 [Giessen: Alfred Töpelmann, 1915], vol. 2, p. 101, section 29, ll. 23–24); also *Ginza R.* 5.187, where the "great" and the "braggarts" are described as those who "thrust the poor and suffering from their gates and give no alms" (Lidzbarski, *Ginza,* 188); cf. *Ginza R.* 13.286.

55 In the matter of responsibility toward sisters and brothers in need, early Christian ethics could connect with the OT tradition: cf. the demand that consideration be shown to the poor members of the community of Israel (Deut 15:7–8). In the NT, Luke in particular is considered the evangelist of the poor; the logion in Luke 16:9 ("make friends for yourselves by means of dishonest wealth") is characteristic of this attitude. On this point, see Friedrich Wilhelm Horn, *Glaube und Handeln in der Theologie des Lukas* (GThA 26; 2d ed.; Göttingen: Vandenhoeck & Ruprecht, 1986) 75–80. (See also n. 52 above.) Parallels occur in 1 John, esp. at 2:16 and 4:20 (juxtaposition of not seeing God with seeing the sister or brother, which is the foundation for the admonition to love them). The word χρεία in the sense of "material want" occurs in Mark 2:25; Acts 2:45; 4:35; Eph 4:28; cf. also Phil 2:25; 4:16, 19. The warning not to cling to wealth because of its temporal nature is also found in Pseudo-Phocylides 109–10: "Do not cling to money, you cannot take it with you to Hades" (Gerhard Delling, "πλεονέκτης," *TDNT* 6 [1968] 270). Philo can also challenge people to apply their own wealth to assist others: περιουσιάζεις μεταδίδου· πλούτου γὰρ τὸ κάλλος οὐκ ἐν βαλαντίοις, ἀλλ᾽ ἐν τῇ τῶν χρῃζόντων ἐπικουρίᾳ (*Jos.* 144: "You have abundance of wealth, give a share to others, for the excellence of wealth consists not in a full purse, but in succouring the needy").

56 The notion of σπλάγχνα as the locus of feeling is found, for example, in 2 Macc 9:5–6; Prov 12:10; Sir 30:7; it is parallel to καρδία in *T. Zeb.* 2.4–5; cf. also *T. Naph.* 7.4. Paul uses σπλάγχνα similarly at 2 Cor 6:12; 7:15 and Phlm 7, 12, 20. It is different in *Herm. Sim.* 9.24.2, where the Shepherd of Hermas writes of believers: "[They were] clothed in the holy spirit of these maidens, and were ever merciful (σπλάγχνα) to every[one], and helped every[one] from the fruit of their labours, without upbraiding or doubting."

57 The meaning "mercy" or "pity" for σπλάγχνα is found especially in the *Testaments of the Twelve Patriarchs,* where this word takes the place of οἰκτιρμοί: cf. *T. Zeb.* 5.3–4; 7.3–4 (*v.l.*); Helmut Koester, "σπλάγχνον, κτλ.," *TDNT* 7 (1971) 552. It is disputed whether such an identification is also found

shatters the train of thought (instead of the statement that might be expected here: "the love of God abides in the one who . . . "). It leaves the judgment to the reader and does not disrupt the parenetic context, since it is obvious that ἡ ἀγάπη τοῦ θεοῦ ("the love of God") cannot be at home where meanness and lack of pity reign.[58] The genitive τοῦ θεοῦ is often interpreted as a qualitative genitive,[59] so that, with reference also to Acts 17:29; 2 Pet 1:3–4, it would have the same meaning as the adjective θεῖος. Accordingly, the "divine life-style of love expresses itself in human beings as a love for God and for brothers and sisters."[60] Although such an interpretation of the concept may possibly be attested in 2:5 and 2:15 as well, it does not answer the question of what constitutes the love of God so understood. More often, the genitive is understood as objective: in those who close their hearts to their sisters and brothers, the "love of [i.e., directed toward] God" has no permanent abode.[61] The parallels in 2:5, 15; 5:3; John 5:42 could also be understood in this sense. But since in the context human activity is directed toward fellow human beings, this meaning is also unlikely. Hence the third possibility seems most probable: that the idea should be interpreted primarily as a subjective genitive.[62] God's love for human beings has

in Paul (Phil 2:1). While Koester denies this (pp. 555–56), defining σπλάγχνα as "love from the heart" and οἰκτιρμοί as "personal sympathy," Martin Dibelius wished to bring the two concepts as closely into agreement as possible (*An die Thessalonicher I, II. An die Philipper* [HNT 11; Tübingen: Mohr (Siebeck), 1925] 60). In Col 3:12 (σπλάγχνα οἰκτιρμοῦ = "compassionate kindness") the two ideas mutually interpret one another; cf. also Nikolaus Walter, "σπλάγχνον," *EDNT* 3 (1993) 265–66.

58 For the construction with πῶς, see Johannes Bauer, "ΠΩΣ in der Griechischen Bibel," *NovT* 2 (1958) 81–91. Bauer explains that πῶς here, as elsewhere with few exceptions, does not ask "how," but "rather, in general terms, introduces a (rhetorical) question as a way of denying a possibility." When it is constructed with the present, a fact, an assertion, a demand, or an action is denied its internal justification; when it accompanies the future tense, the thing itself is called into question (pp. 82–83). Although this author reads the sentence, with several manuscripts, as future (μενεῖ), and although that possibility is also suggested in BDR § 366 (4), because the present indicative is rarely used in a deliberative sense (John 11:47; Matt 7:4; 11:3), nevertheless the quantitative and qualitative weight of the manuscript witnesses favors the present, μένει. For the interpretation of μένει ἐν, see above, n. 40.

59 Thus Schnackenburg, *Epistles*, 183, with a reference to *T. Gad* 5.2: "I tell you this from my own experience, my children, so that you may turn your backs on hatred and hold fast to the love of the Lord." Joseph Bonsirven's interpretation is similar: "La charité est un attribut divin, l'amour de Dieu: Dieu se montre pour toutes ses créatures patient et secourable; quiconque pratique la charité possède, immanente en lui-même comme une force vivante et comme un principe d'action, cet amour de Dieu: il demeure en lui" ("Charity is a divine attribute, the love of God: God shows patience and helpfulness toward all creatures; those who practice love have the love of God dwelling in their hearts as a living power and a principle of action; it abides in them") (*Épîtres de Saint Jean* [VS 9; 2d ed.; Paris: Beauchesne, 1954] 172). See also the following notes.

60 Schnackenburg, *Epistles*, 183.

61 Thus Brooke, *Epistles*, 97, who believes it possible to establish this meaning from the context. Similarly, Weiss emphasizes that neglecting to come to the aid of others indicates a deliberate closing of one's heart and turning away from one's sister or brother: "The question with πῶς . . . involves the thought of how impossible it is that the love of God should abide in such a person" (*Briefe*, 101). The question introduced by πῶς disrupts the surrounding structure and stands for a negated statement; cf. Chaine, *Les épîtres catholiques*, 191; also Alfred Plummer, "The Epistle of St. John," in Arthur J. Mason, Alfred Plummer, and William MacDonald Sinclair, *The Epistles of St. Peter, St. John and St. Jude* (Ellicott's Bible Commentary 11; 2d ed.; London/New York: Hodder & Stoughton, 1903) 85–86.

62 Thus Büchsel, *Johannesbriefe*, 57: "ἡ ἀγάπη τοῦ θεοῦ is here . . . the love of God as experienced by human beings, so that it is within them as a living and active power." Wengst (*Brief*, 154) writes similarly of "God's love for us . . . demonstrated in the total gift of Jesus." Bultmann (*Epistles*, 56) sees τοῦ θεοῦ as a genitive of the author, "since the love of God given to us is the presupposition of brotherly love." Similarly Brown, who, while he alludes to the ambiguity of the construction in his remarks on 2:5, here understands

been demonstrated in the sacrifice of God's Son, as v. 16, with its absolute use of ἀγάπη, had stated. This kind of indicative of salvation encompasses the whole life of believers, for brotherly and sisterly love is also "from God." Anyone who practices such love is born of God (4:7; cf. 3:10).

The gift of being a child of God is bestowed by the loving God; however, it can be lost if one loses sight of one's duty and does not actualize the ethical imperative as an abiding obligation of Christian life. Even though the author speaks of such a threatened event only obliquely, in the form of a question, there can be no doubt that the idea of apocalyptic judgment is implied. It was already hinted in 2:28, and in early Christian tradition this threat was hurled at those who closed themselves to the appeal for love and mercy (cf. Matt 25:40, 45). A loveless attitude is not only a rejection of the offer of divine love, but also a retrogression beyond the movement from death to life, and thus is a renewed subjection of oneself to the rule of the world and of death (3:14–15).

■ **18** The address τεκνία ("little children")[63] was deliberately chosen by the author to underscore the distance between himself and the readers. He seeks to use his authority to give emphasis to the apostolic claim he has already advanced. His renewed address to the readers does not mean that a new section begins at this point, but rather that the whole of what has been said up to now will be summarized in this verse. The subjunctive ἀγαπῶμεν ("let us love") has an imperative force, and accords with the parenetic thrust of the context. The community is admonished to practice love not in a false manner (in word), but in the right way (in deed). This also indicates that the author is not thinking of a particular group,[64] but intends to proclaim an ethical teaching of comprehensive scope.

The two sets of paired concepts are arranged antithetically. The familiar complementary pairing of λόγος ("word") and ἔργον ("deed, action") offers a starting point.[65] Here it is expanded with the concepts of γλῶσσα ("tongue, speech") and ἀλήθεια ("truth"), without setting up a hendiadys in either case, since obviously the tongue, as the human organ of speech, implies a more concrete idea than "word," and since the relationship between action and truth cannot be readily summarized in a single concept.[66] One could more easily suppose that the second concept in each pair is meant to express the reason for the one preceding it.[67] The author, however, makes obvious only the association of the two sets of parallel concepts and the contrast between the two pairs of ideas. The love that is called for is not fulfilled if it is restricted to the formulation of friendly words; it must be realized in action.

As a result, the simple dative has an instrumental

love as something coming from God; God's love is said to have been described just before, in v. 16 (*Epistles*, 450). Schlier deliberates whether the genitive may be a *genitivus auctoris*, but writes that one could also read it "as a subjective genitive. Ultimately, love for God is also a mode of God's love for us" ("Bruderliebe," 239).

63 Also in 1 John 2:1, 12, 28; 3:7; 4:4; 5:21; the word is occasionally translated "little children," as in Wengst, *Brief*, 154; Brown, *Epistles*, 451. On the use of τεκνία and παιδία, see above at 2:12.

64 Against Schnackenburg, *Epistles*, 184, according to whom "the author is apparently hitting out at the gnostics."

65 Also in Rom 15:18; 2 Cor 10:11; Col 3:17; Luke 24:19; Acts 7:22; 2 Thess 2:17; Sir 3:8; 16:12; 4 Macc. 5:38, and frequently; see BAGD 307–8 and 477–78. Closer to this text is Theognis 1.978: μή μοι ἀνὴρ εἴη γλώσσῃ φίλος, ἀλλὰ καὶ ἔργῳ ("Not [only] with the tongue shall a man be my friend, but also in deed").

66 Against Bultmann, *Epistles*, 56, who understands both λόγῳ—γλώσσῃ and ἔργῳ καὶ ἀληθείᾳ as hendiadys; similarly Wengst, *Brief*, 156, who wishes to understand action and truth as a "single combined concept."

67 Thus Ignace de la Potterie emphasizes that in Greek literature τὸ ἔργον describes "facts, events" and ἡ ἀλήθεια is "reality." Thus it is said to be possible that the second expression explains the first: "the truth (= the reality) of the facts" (*La vérité*, 2.666); regarding the combination of λόγος with γλῶσσα he says that in Greek thought λόγος is not found directly connected to γλῶσσα (cf. Thorlief Boman, *Hebrew Thought Compared with Greek* (trans. Jules L. Moreau; Library of History and Doctrine; Philadelphia: Westminster; London: SCM, 1960) 67: "It is striking that *logos* originally had nothing to do with the function of speaking," but that in biblical thought it is indeed possible to establish a progression from the heart to the tongue, from the tongue to the word, from the word to action; cf. Ps 139:4; Sir 4:24; 51:5; Ezek 36:3; Matt 12:34 (de la Potterie, *La vérité* 2.668–69).

meaning; the same is true of the construction with ἐν. That this last is attached only to ἔργῳ emphasizes the weight laid on the final pair of ideas.[68] It tells us that the action that is demanded cannot be properly performed if it is dissociated from truth, and that love must be associated not only with "objective reality,"[69] but with "genuine reality," that is, with God's eschatological truth,[70] if human beings want to be able to present themselves before God. Thus the author does not wish to distinguish between "concrete actions" and "deeds of truth,"[71] but rather urges that the eschatological truth that is believed should become concrete action. This corresponds to a broad NT tradition (e.g., Jas 1:25; 2:12–18) that does not deny its Jewish and Hellenistic ethical background, but appears here in a typically Johannine shape in conjunction with the idea of truth.

68 The simple instrumental dative and ἐν with the dative can be interchanged in NT Greek. The tendency within the development of the language is toward the construction with ἐν and the dative (corresponding to modern Greek εἰς with the accusative); cf. BDF § 220 (1). The idea that the paired concepts "word and action" are meant to encompass the "unity of human conduct" (Roman Heiligenthal, "ἐργασία," *EDNT* 2 [1991] 49) is quite contrary to the emphasis of the text at hand.

69 Thus Bultmann, *Epistles,* 56 n. 55, who sees here a formal sense of ἀλήθεια ("objective reality"), differently from 1:8 and 2:4 (= the reality of God). The translation of ἀλήθεια as "sincerity in our willingness to love," as suggested by Büchsel, *Johannesbriefe,* 58, is not especially appropriate in this context; see below at v. 19.

70 Thus, besides v. 19, also in 1:8; 2:4; 5:6.

71 Against de la Potterie (*La vérité,* 2.667), who explains that the Johannine formula ἐν ἔργῳ καὶ ἀληθείᾳ is to be understood in different ways: sometimes it is used as a "Jewish formula" (τὰ ἔργα τῆς ἀληθείας) in the sense of "works of truth," and sometimes as a "Greek formula" (ἡ ἀλήθεια τῶν ἔργων) in the sense of "the *reality* of the *facts.*"

3 **Confidence in God Is Founded on Keeping God's Commandments and on the Gift of the Spirit**

19 And by this we will know that we are from
the truth and will reassure our hearts
before [God] 20/ whenever our hearts
condemn us; for God is greater than our
hearts, and knows everything [or: that,
when our hearts condemn us, God is
greater than our hearts, and knows
everything]. 21/ Beloved, if our hearts do
not condemn us, we have boldness
before God; 22/ and we receive from
[God] whatever we ask, because we
obey [God's] commandments and do
what pleases [God]. 23/ And this is
[God's] commandment, that we should
believe in the name of [God's] Son Jesus
Christ and love one another, just as [God]
has commanded us. 24/ All who obey
[God's] commandments abide in [God],
and [God] abides in them. And by this we
know that [God] abides in us, by the
Spirit that [God] has given us.

■ **19–20** The interpretation of vv. 19–20 presents great difficulties for exegesis, because the textual tradition and grammatical structure are in dispute. It is clear that the two problems are connected: the construction is difficult to understand, and this alone has led to quite a number of conjectural readings. Thus Bultmann suggested that an οὐ had dropped out before πείσομεν ("we will reassure"),[1] and in v. 20 he inserts an οἴδαμεν ("we know") before the second ὅτι.[2] Although these suggestions have no basis in the textual tradition, one could show a weak manuscript support for the insertion of μή and the omission of the second ὅτι (v. 20).[3] However, both of these variants represent smoothings of the difficult text, so that it is not possible to claim that they are original. It is different with the suggestion that the first ὅτι (v. 20) was mistakenly written as one word and should be read correctly as ὅ τι. This intervention does not really change the written text and has substantial arguments in its favor.[4]

The introductory ἐν τούτῳ (here preceded in most of the manuscript witnesses by καί) occurs frequently in 1 John in combination with a subsequent ὅτι, but this

1 This is based on the negative understanding in v. 21 (ἡ καρδία [ἡμῶν] μὴ καταγινώσκῃ); this would mean that the content here makes the same statement: "If our hearts condemn us, we *cannot* reassure them before God" (vv. 19–20). We can only have boldness before God if our hearts do not condemn us (v. 21). But it is also possible that v. 20 and v. 21 are deliberately made to indicate two contraries: "if our hearts condemn us" (v. 20) and "if our hearts do not condemn us" (v. 21). (Rudolf Bultmann, "πείθω, κτλ.," *TDNT* 6 [1968] 3). Windisch and Preisker (*Die Katholischen Briefe,* 125) are also willing to allow for the possibility of a corrupted text.

2 Bultmann, *Epistles,* 57.

3 This reading is in A 33 pc latt; in that case the first ὅτι is to be understood as explicative ("that").

4 Thus Dodd, *Epistles,* 88; Schnackenburg, *Epistles,* 185. If one understands ὅτι ἐάν as ὅ τι ἄν (cf. John 2:5; 14:13; 15:16), the expression stands as a second accusative alongside τὴν καρδίαν and is, like the latter, dependent on πείσομεν; it then means "with respect to everything," "whenever." On this basis, the second ὅτι clause should be translated causally ("for God is greater . . . "). However, the translation "that if" is also not improbable; then the second ὅτι (v. 20) has the function of a resumption of the first ὅτι, with the same meaning and content and an explanatory function. Cf. also Brown, *Epistles,* 456 ("'that if' emerges as the most plausible of the three translations of *hoti ean*").

should not predetermine one's reading of its content. The demonstrative pronoun can refer either to what has preceded it (as in 2:5) or to what follows.[5] In the latter case, it would be difficult to see ἐν τούτῳ in this verse as being clarified by the succeeding ὅτι clause, since the latter instead explains the verb γνωσόμεθα ("we will know").[6] Instead, ἐν τούτῳ finds its explanation in v. 20, something that corresponds to the clarification with an ἐάν clause in 2:3 and in John 13:35. Thus, the knowledge that we are from the truth is based on the believing conviction that God proves to be greater than the accusation of our hearts against us. However, such a construction would be confused and not very satisfying. A smoother interpretation can be derived by reading ἐν τούτῳ as referring to what has preceded. Verse 18 has spoken of the necessity to make love concrete in action; now it is said that such a demonstration in action represents the basis on which we can recognize that we are from the truth.[7]

The language in these two verses is partly un-Johannine, causing Preisker to posit a pre-Johannine "eschatological" source.[8] Even if one dissociates oneself from attempts to reconstruct a written source, it should be admitted that the whole statement is difficult to understand without some kind of tradition-historical reference to the idea of the final judgment, when the judge of the world will render a verdict. The expression ἔμπροσθεν αὐτοῦ ("before him") suggests the image of a human being standing before the judgment seat of God or Christ.[9] No matter how πείσομεν is translated,[10] in any case it implies the idea that the human conscience[11] is disturbed and suffering doubts. Therefore, it requires a "consolation" legitimated by God. Obviously, such a "soothing" will not occur only at the last day through God's assurance of grace that grants acquittal. It is also a

5 For example, in 2:3; 3:24. The content to which ἐν τούτῳ points is then given in a clause with ἐάν or ἐκ τοῦ, while the following ὅτι clause explains a preceding γνωσόμεθα (or something similar). Verse 3:16 is different, since there the ὅτι clause interprets the preceding ἐν τούτῳ ἐγνώκαμεν τὴν ἀγάπην (see above on 3:16).

6 I read γνωσόμεθα with the majority of witnesses, instead of the present γινώσκομεν (K L 049, 623, 2464, 𝔐 lat.).

7 Thus also Büchsel, *Johannesbriefe*, 59; Schnackenburg, *Epistles*, 185; Brown, *Epistles*, 454. For "being from the truth," cf. 2:21 and John 18:37.

8 It is supposed to have contained the words πείσομεν τὴν καρδίαν, παρρησία, and others; cf. Windisch and Preisker, *Die Katholischen Briefe*, 167; Bultmann, *Epistles*, 56–57.

9 Cf. Matt 25:32 par. Luke 21:36; Matt 10:32–33; 1 Thess 2:19; 3:13; 2 Cor 5:10.

10 Gustav Wohlenberg has chosen the translation "we will convince," so that the word here would mean "either persuade that something is happening, or convince that something is true" ("Glossen zum ersten Johannesbrief," *NKZ* 13 [1902] 636). BAGD 639 offers a different interpretation: "conciliate," "pacify," with reference to Matt 28:14 ("satisfy"), also *Mart. Pol.* 10.2 (τὴν καρδίαν ἡμῶν) and Xenophon *Hell.* 1.7.7 (τὸν δῆμον).

11 The word καρδία appears in the Johannine Letters only in 1 John 3:19–21 (but 7 times in the Fourth Gospel). In the OT, καρδία is not only the "heart" as an essential bodily organ (Hos 13:8); it also describes the deepest interior of the human being (1 Sam 16:7). The word (Hebrew לב) is also used for the locus of human spiritual or intellectual powers and abilities, such as courage (2 Sam 7:27) and reason (Deut 29:3). This is reflected in the LXX, which uses such synonyms as διάνοια, ψυχή, νοῦς, and so on. In secular Greek literature as well, the word has a double meaning, both physiological (Homer *Il.* 10.94: "But my heart is leaping from my breast"; also in the botanical field, e.g., Theophrastus *Historia plantarum* 1.2.6: "heart of the tree") and figurative; for the latter, cf. Homer *Il.* 9.646: the heart as the organ of wrath; *Corp. Herm.* 7.1–2: contrast between καρδία and νοῦς: the former the organ of spiritual vision, the latter the human eye; Johannes Behm, "καρδία, κτλ.," *TDNT* 3 (1965) 611–14. In our text the word applies to the innermost part of the human being, representing the human person, the "I"; so also in John 13:2; 14:1, 27; 16:6, 22; Col 2:2; 1 Pet 3:4. In the NT it is also used more specifically as the locus of feeling (2 Cor 7:3; Phil 1:7), of the will (Matt 5:8), or of understanding (Acts 1:26). The usage in our text also suggests the translation "conscience"; cf. Acts 2:37; *T. Gad* 5.3; John M. Court, "Blessed Assurance?" *JTS* 33 (1982) 513; Balz, "Johannesbriefe," 192–93; Brown, *Epistles*, 456.

reality for the community throughout its history, as on the one hand it by no means thinks of itself as free from sin (cf. 1:8), and yet at the same time hopes for Christ's intervention as an advocate on its behalf even now (2:1). The author, as we already saw in 2:28, sustains the tension between the "not yet" and the "already," so that even the future forms of the verbs should not be attributed solely to an apocalyptic perspective; they can also have a gnomic sense.[12] This accords with the application of the following passage to the present, where the community is promised παρρησία now, as well as the certainty that their prayers are heard (vv. 21–22).

However, the forensic idea already demonstrated has an important background function, as is clear from v. 20, which enunciates not only a further point of reference (v. 20a) but also the specific content of the "consolation."[13] The community can have its doubtful conscience soothed if it practices love toward the sisters and brothers and therefore knows that it is from the truth (vv. 18–19). This kind of consolation is directed against the "accusation" that the human conscience raises against itself. The verb καταγινώσκειν appears in the NT only here and in Gal 2:11, meaning "to condemn."[14] That it can be applied to God's rejecting, destroying verdict of condemnation[15] is evident from the eschatological aspect of the judgment that is given by the verdict of one's own conscience. Hence, it is understandable that Augustine, with powerful influence on the medieval and Reformation church, interpreted this verse as referring to God's wrath and universal knowledge (γινωσκει πάντα, "knows everything") in the sense of knowledge that discovers human beings in their wicked deeds and destroys them.[16] It cannot be objected against this interpretation that elsewhere in 1 John God's final judgment is only mentioned when the purpose is to encourage the readers,[17] for it is precisely in the passages in which the community is reminded of the future judgment and where the ethical teaching is motivated by such a reminder that judgment and grace are inseparably united (cf. 2:1–2, 28; 4:17–18: φόβος). Nevertheless, in v. 20 the author's confidence that God's mercy will have the deciding word is of primary importance. This is clear from the context, which presupposes that the community has traveled from death to life and lives in and from the truth (vv. 14, 19), and which will next speak of its confidence in being heard (v. 22). Thus the clause ὅτι

12 BDF § 349 (1).

13 For the explicative sense of the ὅτι clause, see n. 4 above.

14 Also in *Diogn.* 10.7; Sir 14:2; especially close is *T. Gad* 5.3: οὐχ ὑπ' ἄλλου καταγιθινωσκόμενος ἀλλ' ὑπὸ τῆς ἰδίας καρδίας ("being rebuked, not by someone else, but by [one's] own conscience [the humble is ashamed to do what is unrighteous])."

15 Josephus *Bell.* 7.327: γινώσκειν, ὅτι τὸ πάλαι φίλον αὐτῷ φῦλον 'Ιουδαίων κατέγνωστο ("We ought, I say, to have read God's purpose and to have recognized that the Jewish race, once beloved of Him, had been doomed to perdition").

16 Cf. Augustine *In epistolam* 6.3, in: Paul Agaësse, S.J., *Saint Augustin, Commentaire de la première Epître de S. Jean* (SC 75; Paris: Cerf, 1961) 282: "Quia si male sentiat cor nostrum, id est, accuset nos intus, quia non eo animo facimus quo faciendum sit; major est Deus corde nostro, et novit omnia. Cur tuum abscondis ab homine; a Deo abscondi si potes" ("For if our hearts condemn us—if they accuse us from within, because we don't act with the intention we ought to have—God is greater than our hearts, and . . . knows everything. You hide your heart from human beings. Hide it from God if you can!" Translation by John Leinweber, *Love One Another My Friends: Saint Augustine's Homilies on the First Letter of John* [San Francisco: Harper & Row, 1989] 56). Cf. also Bede *In Epistolam S. Joannis* III (*PL* 93.104) and Pseudo-Oecumenius *Comment. in Epistolam 1. Joannis* IV (*PG* 119.657). John Calvin (*The Gospel According to St. John 11–21 and The First Epistle of John* (in Calvin's Commentaries; trans. T. H. L. Parker; ed. D. W. and T. F. Torrance. [Edinburgh: St. Andrew Press, 1961] 278) also applies this passage to God's judgment: "He calls God *greater than our heart* with reference to judgment, inasmuch as [God] sees far more keenly than we do and investigates more searchingly and judges more severely."

17 Thus Brown, *Epistles*, 460; also Schnackenburg, *Epistles*, 186 ("Every attempt to understand this statement [in terms of] the terrifying greatness and judicial strictness of God introduces an uncharacteristic trend into the epistle, concerned as it is to heighten the Christian's consciousness of salvation"). [Schnackenburg's intention in this sentence differs somewhat from the interpretation implied by the published English translation; the brackets represent my interpretation.—Trans.]

μείζων ἐστὶν ὁ θεὸς τῆς καρδίας ἡμῶν ("that God is greater than our hearts") means that God overcomes the accusations leveled by our consciences against ourselves, and in fact has already overcome them.[18] When the text here speaks of God's "knowing everything," this is simply another way of speaking of God's all-encompassing love,[19] for the epexegetical καί joins v. 20b and 20c into a single statement that God is superior to the accusing conscience and is ready to forgive.[20]

■ **21** The address Ἀγαπητοί ("beloved")[21] does not function as a caesura at this point, but represents an emphatic turning toward the readers. This further clarifies, as did the preceding verses, the connection between the *agapē* of God that is the foundation of Christian life (2:15; 3:1, 17), and the commandment of love for the brothers and sisters (2:7; cf. esp. 4:11). Where such love rules, conscience has no occasion to accuse any human being.[22] That the author understands Christian existence as something dynamic and hence does not deny the existence of sin in Christian life was already clear at 1:8. But when what is in view is not the fragile figure of the Christian community but the promise of salvation founded on Christ (cf. 2:2), the existence of believers "from the truth," whose essential characteristic and sign are love for the sisters and brothers, can accordingly be stated in the indicative.[23] A signal feature of Christian existence that knows itself to be in accord with the love of God is παρρησία. This word, found also in Demosthenes, referred originally to the freedom of speech that belongs to citizens of the *polis*,[24]

18 Verse 16. Ceslas Spicq is correct in saying that "μείζων évoque un changement de catégorie, le passage à un autre ordre" ("μείζων suggests a change in category, the movement to a different level") ("La Justification du Charitable: 1 Jo 3, 19–21," *Bib* 40 [1959] 915–27, at 923), since this is concerned with the divine order of love (cf. 1 John 4:4). Haenchen, in contrast, draws the following conclusion from this verse: "The author really means that when our sins lie heavy on our hearts we can console ourselves with the thought that God also sees our good works (if we have done any!). Our hearts should by no means always condemn us." 1 John "in fact is much more thoroughly a part of early catholicism than are the Pauline Pastorals" (Ernst Haenchen, *Gesammelte Aufsätze* [Tübingen: Mohr [Siebeck], 1968] 277).

19 A comparison with John 21:17 (πάντα σὺ οἶδας) is deceptive, insofar as that verse speaks of Christ's knowledge and not, as here, of God's. Simon Peter trusts Christ's knowledge to recognize his love (in response to Büchsel, *Johannesbriefe*, 59). In v. 20, by contrast, γινώσκει is an antithesis to καταγινώσκῃ: judgment is set in opposition to God's recognition, which really amounts to "choice" (cf. 1 Cor 8:3; Gal 4:9), although one should not speak in terms of "predestination" in this passage; the context has to do with the accusing consciences of the members of the community. For God's or Christ's knowledge as a form of testing, cf. also Ps 7:10; John 2:24.

20 Martin Luther interpreted the clause in this sense (WA 20.716–17): "Deus tamen maior est corde nostro" ("God is greater than our heart"): "Against an evil conscience you should say: you are a tiny drop, and God is an endless fire that devours such things. No sin is greater than that of unbelief. . . . Only unbelief receives no forgiveness; for it struggles against the forgiveness of sins, all of which receive forgiveness. Wonderfully it is said and it is the sweetest of all promises: if (our heart) accuses us, and so on. Does your evil somehow surpass God's goodness, do your sins outweigh God's kindness? This honor must one give to God, that God is greater without limit" (translation by Büchsel, *Johannesbriefe*, 59). John M. Court ("Blessed Assurance?" *JTS* 33 [1982] 516) differs, setting up a connection to vv. 16–18 and seeing this context as determining, on the basis of the "Jewish Tradition," "the radical nature of this demand" in this verse, namely, the warning against self-satisfaction.

21 Also in 2:7; 3:2; 4:1, 7, 11; in the singular 3 John 2, 5, 11; cf. 3 John 1 (address to Gaius, a fellow Christian).

22 Ceslas Spicq ("La Justification du Charitable: 1 Jo 3, 19–21," *Bib* 40 [1959] 924) impermissibly restricts the meaning of this statement when he translates μή with "ne plus" ("no longer"). It would also unjustifiably eliminate the alternative implied in the text and shift the line of argumentation to express the opposite idea from that intended if one were to interpret it to say that "the supreme fruit of love for the sisters and brothers is the guarantee of a peaceful conscience" (ibid., 919).

23 Cf. v. 19. In this connection, it is not particularly helpful to think of the covenant people, or of "the disciple whom Jesus loved" (Brown, *Epistles*, 264).

24 Demosthenes *Or.* 3.3–4; cf. Eric Peterson, "Zur Bedeutungsgeschichte von παρρησία," in W. Koepp, ed., *Reinhold Seeberg Festschrift*, vol. 1: *Zur Theorie des Christentums* (Leipzig: Scholl, 1929) 283–97; Horst Balz, "παρρησία," *EDNT* 3 (1993) 45. Cf. the excursus on παρρησία, above at 2:28.

and in Jewish texts means "confidence [or: boldness] before God."[25] God also behaves "boldly" toward the despised and brings them help (LXX Pss 11:6; 93:1), and the righteous person possesses "confidence" in face of oppressors.[26] In contrast to the christological understanding in the Fourth Gospel, the word is used ecclesially in 1 John; here the future-eschatological aspect of judgment plays no small role (cf. above, at 2:28). As the vocabulary in the context suggests,[27] such a perspective is also in the background here, but at this point it is understood in the sense of a confident certainty, implying that between believers and God there is no dividing wall, but rather that access to the Father of Jesus Christ lies open to them. This is shown by their possession of the Spirit, through whom the community lives (3:24), and on that basis it can speak "with boldness" (Acts 4:29–31). In v. 21, *παρρησία* is the equivalent of confidence in being heard; the community's prayer, addressed to God,[28] will find a hearing (cf. 5:14; Matt 7:7–11).

■ **22** The continuation with *καί*[29] indicates that v. 21b is to be clarified by v. 22a. The freedom of believers before God is made concrete in confident prayer. The particle *ὃ ἐάν* ("whatever") does not introduce a conditional clause,[30] but designates what is ordinary and regular, so that it is almost impossible to distinguish between an iterative and a future statement.[31] The indicative *λαμβάνομεν* ("we receive") expresses, even more strongly than the future (which is also a possible reading), the certainty that these prayers, the content of which is not restricted and which therefore can address the fulfillment of every possible kind of concrete wish, will find a hearing. This resumes the preceding *παρρησίαν ἔχομεν*: "boldness" and the certainty of being heard constitute the attitude of Christians who possess clear consciences (v. 21).

The *ὅτι* clause should be understood in a causal sense. Thus confidence and the certainty of being heard do not arise (as might be inferred from the preceding context) from the indicative state of believers, founded on Christ, but from doing God's commandments. Does such reasoning mean that the author intends to enunciate a condition, saying more or less that only someone who observes God's commandments can have confidence and the certainty of being heard? In that case he could be accused of falling back into a kind of nomistic piety.[32] It would appear that 2:3 could be adduced in support of this. There a correct knowledge of God is associated with the condition of keeping the commandments (*ἐὰν τὰς ἐντολὰς αὐτοῦ τηρῶμεν*; cf. 2:24 and 5:2). Yet it is clear that the author is not rationalistically reflecting on the relationship between God and the human being. Rather, he begins with the union between the Father of Jesus Christ and believers, into which he wishes to incorporate

25 Cf. Josephus *Ant.* 2.52: *πολλὴν τὴν ἀπὸ τοῦ συνειδότος, καὶ πρὸς τὸν θεὸν παρρησίαν καὶ πρὸς τοὺς ἀνθρώπους* ("great boldness from a good conscience, both before God and before [other people]"); also Job 22:26; 27:9–10, and frequently.

26 Wis 5:1. Cf. *1 Enoch* 61.4; 62.16; 69.26; *4 Ezra* 7.98; however, the examples in the Jewish apocalyptic writings are not available in Greek, and the original versions are disputed. Consequently, inferences on that basis about the concept of *παρρησία* are questionable. See below, at 4:17.

27 See above on *καταγινώσκειν*; also Windisch and Preisker, *Die Katholischen Briefe*, 167; Schnackenburg, *Epistles*, 187; Brown, *Epistles*, 259.

28 For *πρὸς τὸν θεόν*, cf. also Josephus *Ant.* 2.52; 1 John 2:1 (*πρὸς τὸν πατέρα*); 5:14 (*πρὸς αὐτόν*).

29 The particle *καί* is epexegetical; cf. BDR § 442 (6).

30 Against Büchsel, *Johannesbriefe*, 61.

31 Cf. BDR § 380 (1b) and n. 2; Brown correctly translates the expression with "whatever" (*Epistles*, 460).

32 Windisch and Preisker, *Die Katholischen Briefe*, 125–26 ("Being heard depends not only on calling on the name of Jesus [John 16:23], . . . but also on an obedient way of life pleasing to God"), with reference to Job 22:26; Philo *Praem. poen.* 84; John 9:31; *2 Clem.* 15.3; *Herm. Mand.* 9.1–4; cf. the OT-Jewish schema of action and result: Exod 15:26; *b. Berakot* 6b (R. Helbo [ca. 300] in the tradition of R. Huna [died 297]): כל אדם שיש בו יראת שמים דבריו נשמעין ("If one is filled with the fear of God his words are listened to"); also the Greek, Hellenistic and Roman traditions: Homer *Il.* 1.218: *ὅς κε θεοῖς ἐπιπείθηται, μάλα τ' ἔκλυον αὐτοῦ* ("Whoever obeys the gods, to him they gladly hearken"); Plato *Leg.* 4.8; Iamblichus *Vita Pythagori* 11; Philostratus *Vita Apollonii* 1.12; Plautus *Rudens* Prologue 26: "Facilius si qui pius est a dis supplicans, quam qui scelestus inveniet veniam sibi" ("It is easier for a pious person who asks help from the gods to find forgiveness than for a criminal").

his readers. Corresponding to the christological unity that exists in the Fourth Gospel between the Father and the Son (John 8:29; 10:30; 17:11, 21–23), 1 John can assert the existence of such a union between believers, the will of God, and the very being of God (2:12–17; 3:14), and yet at the same time he can emphasize that the Christian community is confronted with the demand to love God and other human beings (5:1–2). The connection between faith and works, the indicative foundation of the ethical demand and the ethical imperative, may not be dissolved.[33] This connection can appropriately be described as "paradoxical,"[34] for without any rationalizing equalization the author can still make such contrary statements as: God is love, but also we can be put to shame by God (4:8, 16 and 2:28); we have passed from death to life, but also our conscience accuses us (3:14 and 20). Similarly, in what follows, *πιστεύειν* ("to believe") can appear as the content of the *ἐντολή* ("command," v. 23), whereas according to John 6:29 faith is an *ἔργον τοῦ θεοῦ* ("work of God").

If, then, such tensions are possible within the theological argumentation of 1 John, and in the Johannine writings as a whole, and if it is precisely such things that characterize the unique, post-Pauline shape of Johannine thought, one should not overlook the real situation in which these words are addressed to the community. It is not primarily a polemic context, in which the necessity of fulfilling the commandments would be asserted against particular (gnostic) teachers;[35] instead, the author here addresses problems within the community as well. As in the broader context, the parenetic intention is of decisive importance for the interpretation. The community is admonished—and this does not require any sidelong glance at gnostic teaching—to comprehend what it fundamentally already has and is. What is demanded is unity between the certainty of faith and keeping the commandments, not as a demonstration for those outside, and not even as the expression of an "untrammeled Christian self-consciousness,"[36] but as a warning to each individual Christian in order that the union between God and the community may become the reality that is already anticipated in Christ.

That such a union is concretely imaginable is shown by the plural form of *τὰς ἐντολάς* ("the commandments"). These commandments are, of course, not defined, nor does the parallelism with the following *τὰ ἀρεστά* ("what pleases") make it any more obvious what they are.[37] Still,

---

33 Wengst (*Brief*, 160) differs. He places too one-sided an emphasis on the fact that the "confidence of fulfillment" is not founded on one's own action, but on the fact that human desire and prayer accord with what God wills and what pleases God.

34 Thus Bultmann, *Epistles*, 59 n. 77; against Brown, *Epistles*, 481.

35 Schnackenburg differs (*Epistles*, 188): "in contrast to the perverse attitude of the gnostics. . . . "

36 Schnackenburg, *Epistles*, 188; however, he correctly states that "the indicative in v. 22 implies an imperative." Cf. also Brown, *Epistles*, 479 ("Beyond the general covenant love between God and His people, there is a special Christian family relationship as the Father responds in love to His children who live 'just as' His Son")—although nothing is said about a "covenant" either in the narrower or in the broader context; on the contrary, the idea of a divine covenant is something foreign to the Johannine writings.

37 The word *ἀρεστός* is attested both in Greek Hellenistic literature (cf. the examples in BAGD 105) and in Jewish Hellenism. The secular usage (= "good," Acts 6:2; 12:3) has an OT parallel in the use of Hebrew טוֹב (cf. 2 Sam 18:27; Prov 12:2; 13:22, and often) and is frequently attested in the LXX; here *ἀρεστός* "denotes what God (or a [human being]) accepts as pleasing, and it can thus be an expression of full freedom" (Werner Foerster, "*ἀρέσκω, κτλ.*," *TDNT* 1 [1964] 456; thus in an anthropological-ethical sense: Tob 4:3; Neh 9:37; Josephus *Ant.* 16.135; applied to God: Isa 38:3 (*τὰ ἀρεστὰ ἐνώπιόν σου ἐποίησα*); Exod 15:26; Sir 48:22; singular *τὸ ἀρεστόν*: Dan 4:37a; Tob 3:6; 4:21; also *Barn.* 19.2; *Did.* 4.12. Our text offers the only instance in 1 John. The theological significance appears in the NT otherwise only in John 8:29 (*ἐγὼ τὰ ἀρεστὰ αὐτῷ ποιῶ πάντοτε*) and is materially connected with "doing the will of God" (cf. John 7:17; 9:31, and frequently). More frequent in the NT is the synonym *εὐάρεστος*: Heb 13:21; Rom 12:1–2; Eph 5:10, and frequently. For the expression *ἐνώπιον αὐτοῦ*, stemming from Jewish or Koine Greek usage (only one instance in the Johannine writings; but cf. 3 John 6 and John

it is clear that the author is thinking of responsible performance of human actions, that is, the fulfillment of concrete commandments. This is expressed in the same way elsewhere in 1 John, in spite of its more general rather than specifically ethical tendency (cf. 3:17; also the direct address to young men and fathers in 2:12–14). The resumption of the plural with the singular ἐντολή in v. 23 is very helpful for our understanding. The fulfillment of individual commandments culminates in fulfilling the commandment of love for the brothers and sisters. Thus the admonition "to keep his commandments"[38] is specified by the old and new commandment of love for the sisters and brothers (2:7–8). In turn, the demand "to obey his commandments" (5:2) refers back to the commandment to love God and the sisters and brothers (4:21); for the essence of love for God consists in this, that "we obey his commandments" (5:3).

■ **23** In a typical Johannine expression, καὶ αὕτη ἐστίν ("and this is") connects the following, summary statement, which can also be regarded as the high point and conclusion of the parenesis, with what has preceded it.[39] The fundamental character of this statement is emphasized by the fact that the author does not identify ἐντολή with the love commandment, but instead describes the essence of the Christian commandment in two strophes (v. 23b/c); the controlling particle ἵνα lends an imperative sense to what follows.[40] In a short formula, the essence of Christianity is at the same time brought home to the hearers as a demand placed on them. They are to believe in the name of Jesus Christ, the Son of God, and they are to exercise love toward the brothers and sisters. It is unusual for faith in Christ[41] to appear as the content of the ἐντολή, especially if one concedes that in Johannine (and Pauline) thought, "faith" is not identified with any work or achievement. Yet this passage shows that people are called to believe because belief must be understood as a responsible human deed—the single human "condition" of salvation, but not to be interpreted as something done by the human being in advance, since it is nothing other than the person's own self-surrender.[42] Faith is directed toward the "name," an idea that is expressed here by the verb πιστεύειν with a dative.[43] Since, in Semitic thinking, ὄνομα ("name") is an equivalent description of the person,[44] and Jesus Christ bears the name υἱὸς θεοῦ ("son of God"),[45] the first, dogmatic-foundational part of this formula demands

---

20:30), see BDR § 4 n. 8 and § 214 (5, 6); Schnackenburg, *Epistles,* 188 n. 232; Helmut Krämer, "ἐνώπιον," *EDNT* 1 (1990) 462.

38 1 John 2:3–4; the expression τὰς ἐντολὰς τηρεῖν occurs also in 3:24; 5:3.

39 Cf. also 1:5, *v.l.;* 3:11; 5:11, 14; also John 1:19; 3:19; 6:29; 17:3.

40 Cf. BDR § 389, 2; § 392, 1c.

41 There are 243 examples of πιστεύειν in the NT, of which 73 are in the Synoptic Gospels and Acts, 42 in Paul, and 107 in the Johannine literature (Gospel 98 times; 1 John 9 times). By contrast, πίστις is absent from the Fourth Gospel and is used only once in 1 John (5:4). It is also striking that, within the NT, the only documents that lack both πίστις and πιστεύειν are 2 and 3 John.

42 The reading πιστεύωμεν (א A C Ψ et al.) may be an accommodation to the following ἀγαπῶμεν. Materially speaking, the aorist subjunctive πιστεύωμεν can emphasize not so much the endurance as the beginning of faith; cf. BDF § 318. The combination of ἵνα with the aorist subjunctive is attested overwhelmingly in the NT, but the construction with the present is also "not unusual" (Radermacher, *Neutestamentliche Grammatik,* 177–78).

43 Besides this construction, both Johannine (1 John 5:10, 13; John 1:12; 2:23; 3:18, and frequently) and extra-Johannine writings use the combination πιστεύειν εἰς, and no change in meaning is discernible. This disagrees with Ignace de la Potterie, "L'Emploi dynamique d'εἰς dans Saint Jean et ses incidences théologiques," *Bib* 43 (1962) 366–87, at 375–76; cf. also Acts 10:43; 14:23; Matt 18:6; Rom 10:14; Gal 2:16, and frequently. The Semitic distinction between בְּ and לְ may, in any case, be important for our text, by way of the medium of the language of the LXX; on this, see BDR §187 n. 2.

44 Cf. as early as 1 Sam 25:25; Gen 3:20; 4:1; 5:29; 28:17, 19, and elsewhere. "The name denotes the person, establishes its identity, and is a part of it" (Hans Bietenhard, "ὄνομα, κτλ.," *TDNT* 5 [1967] 242–83, at 254). Cf. also above at 1 John 2:12; πιστεύειν εἰς τὸ ὄνομα, besides 1 John 5:13, also in John 1:12; 2:23; 3:18.

45 On the concept of υἱὸς θεοῦ, see above at 1 John 1:3.

faith in the saving event in Jesus Christ. The Johannine tradition, not only here but elsewhere, tells us that Christian faith is not without content but is christological in orientation (John 6:29; 20:31). In all this, *πιστεύειν* is not used in the intellectual sense of merely "holding something to be true," but has the meaning of "acknowledging," implying also a "realization" or "fulfillment," and to that extent is close to the Johannine *γινώσκειν* ("to know").[46] Nonetheless, a parallel or even an identity with *ὁμολογεῖν* ("to confess") is improbable in this verse,[47] because it is not simply a question of the external action of speaking the name, as a "confession" (as in 4:2–3, 15; cf. 2:23; John 9:22), even if, in most cases, "faith" precedes "confession." Instead, the verb *πιστεύειν* describes the total self-surrender of the human being who acknowledges the person of Jesus Christ as eschatological event.

Such a perspective on Christian faith is not simply vertical in its orientation. It also includes the historical past in which the "Christus incarnatus" appeared (cf. 1:1–3). That it cannot be restricted to the dogmatic sphere is evident from the second part of the formula, joined to the first by a paratactic *καί*: *καὶ ἀγαπῶμεν ἀλλήλους* ("love one another"). The commandment to which every Christian is subject includes both the saving acknowledgment in faith of the Son of God and action toward one's fellow human beings. In what follows the author will also recall the love commandment for the readers, again and again; that is, the commandment of mutual love[48] or of love for the sisters and brothers.[49] Faith in Christ demands actualization through loving deeds. The two are not to be seen as alternatives; instead, one cannot exist without the other. As faith is commanded and is an act of obedience, so it is true also of love for the sisters and brothers that it must be practiced in obedience to the eschatological demand. The more the community is conscious of the invisibility, even the absence, of God, the more is it challenged to allow the true nature of the loving God to be concretely manifest in mutual love.[50]

What is obligatory for Christians in this short formula is underscored by the final clause. The particle *καθώς* serves the function of giving a reason for something ("because," "since") and connects the phrase back to v. 23a. While v. 23d confirms that this has the character of a commandment, it also affirms that the *ἐντολή* is a gift to the community. Is "Jesus Christ" the implied subject? This could be inferred from the immediately preceding text,[51] but in v. 24 *ἔδωκεν* ("he has given") unmistakably refers to "God," and *ἐντολὴ αὐτοῦ* ("his commandment," v. 23a) is also more probably connected to the preceding *θεόν* ("God," v. 21). Hence there is no real distinction to be made in the present passage either. It is sufficient to assert that the commandment expresses an eschatological obligation, demanding of Christians both faith and action.

■ **24** This verse shares the summary function of v. 23. Confidence in face of divine judgment is founded on Christian belief and action. Thus the shift from the singular *ἐντολή* (v. 23) to the plural *ἐντολάς* (v. 24) does not express anything fundamentally new. In any event, the plural emphasizes the multiplicity of concrete (individual) commandments (cf. earlier in v. 22) whose observance is demanded of Christians.

Although the author again fails to say precisely whether he is thinking of "abiding" in God or in Christ, in any case his expression *ἐν αὐτῷ μένειν* refers to "abiding relationship."[52] It conveys the idea of a reciprocal relationship between believers and the

46 Cf. 4:16: parallel to *πιστεύειν*, which also appears in 4:1 (q.v.) and 5:10, 13 in the sense of "acknowledge"; cf. also the noun *πίστις* in 5:4.

47 Bultmann differs (*Epistles*, 59 n. 78), as does Schnackenburg (*Epistles*, 189); they see scarcely any difference from *ὁμολογεῖν* in 2:23; 4:2–3, 15.

48 For *ἀγαπᾶν ἀλλήλους*, cf. 3:11; 4:7, 12; 2 John 5; John 13:34; 15:12, 17.

49 For *ἀδελφούς*, accusative plural, see 3:15; singular: 2:10, 11; 3:10; 4:20–21.

50 Franz Mussner ("Eine neutestamentliche Kurzformel für das Christentum," *TThZ* 79 [1970] 49–52) writes correctly that "the 'absent' God is present in our brothers and sisters, in our fellow human beings, and anyone who practices love toward them 'knows God' (4:16)" (p. 51).

51 So Schnackenburg, *Epistles*, 190 n. 239.

52 Bultmann, *Epistles*, 59; cf. also above at 2:6.

eschatological basis of their belief.[53] On the one hand, where ethical behavior is the rule, in accord with the will of God (cf. 2:17), there faith is abidingly fixed in the eschatological reality of salvation as in a space or sphere[54] that utterly surrounds and preserves it. On the other hand, it is also true that salvation (*αὐτός*) takes up its abode in the believer, who is thereby entirely saturated and possessed by it.[55]

Such statements about the mutual relationship between gods and belief are nothing foreign to ancient religion.[56] They are found in the NT, especially in the letters of Paul, wherever the reality of salvation is conceived spatially (e.g., 1 Thess 2:13–14: God's word "is also *at work in* you believers. For you . . . became imitators of the churches of God *in Christ Jesus* that are in Judea"; Rom 8:9: "But you are not in the flesh; you are *in the Spirit,* since the Spirit of God dwells *in you*"; also 2 Cor 11:10 and 17; 13:5; Gal 2:20). The Johannine writings are also familiar with the exchange between the redeemer and the redeemed. This exchange occurs in the probably original verse John 6:56, which should not be degraded into a redactional gloss ("Those who eat my flesh and drink my blood abide in me, and I in them"), an expression of the sacramental indwelling of the Revealer in believers and, in turn, of believers in the Revealer. It is similarly true of the relationship between Jesus and his disciples, independent of the sacramental context, a relationship constituted by the word: "I am the vine, you are the branches. Those who abide in me and I in them bear much fruit" (John 15:5; cf. 15:7, 10). This affirmation is founded on the unity that exists between the Revealer and his Father (John 14:10).

The author of 1 John testifies to a sacramentally grounded exchange between God and the community, an exchange that is established by the *χρῖσμα* ("anointing," 2:27–28). Beyond this, the combination

53 Martin Luther spoke, in different words, of the "joyful exchange" in his essay "On the Freedom of a Christian": "Auß wilcher ehe folget, wie S. Paulus sagt, das Christus und die seel eyn leyb werden, ßo werden auch beyder gutter fall, unfall und alle ding gemeyn, das was Christus hatt, das ist eygen der glaubigen seele, was die Seele hatt, wirt eygen Christi. So hatt Christus alle gutter und seligkeit, die seyn der seelen eygen. So hat die seel alle Untugent und sunt auff yhr, die werden Christi eygen. Hie hebt sich nu der frohlich wechßel und streytt" ("By this mystery, as the Apostle teaches, Christ and the soul become one flesh. . . . it follows that everything they have they hold in common, the good as well as the evil. Accordingly the believing soul can boast of and glory in whatever Christ has as though it were its own, and whatever the soul has Christ claims as his own. . . . Christ is full of grace, life, and salvation. The soul is full of sins, death, and damnation. Now let faith come between them and sins, death, and damnation will be Christ's, while grace, life, and salvation will be the soul's. . . . Here we have a most pleasing vision not only of communion but of a blessed struggle and victory and salvation and redemption"). WA 7.25, 28–34; translation from Timothy F. Lull, ed., *Martin Luther's Basic Theological Writings* (Minneapolis: Fortress, 1989) 603.

54 Cf. also Heise (*Bleiben,* 173): "The new existence is a new space and a new time by which a new quality is given to human existence. . . . This change of place is due to the fact of the presence of God in Jesus Christ."

55 C. Lindskrog (*Fortolkning til første Johannesbrev* [Copenhagen: Gyldendal, 1941] 16) indicates that in 1 John commandments, word, and promise are used in an identical sense. Whether it follows that, with that kind of understanding of its faith, Christianity is at the point of being shaped by a "nova lex" (so Haenchen, "Neuere Literatur," 278) is a question we need not address here.

56 Rather than *μένειν*, Philo uses the verbs *ἐνοικεῖν* and *ἐμπεριπατεῖν* in a similar sense. Thus on Num 14:9 ("their protection is removed from them, but the Lord is with us [*ὁ δὲ κύριος ἐν ἡμῖν*]"), he writes: "that the Divine word dwells and walks (*λόγος θεῖος ἐνοικεῖ καὶ ἐμπεριπατεῖ*) among those for whom the soul's life is an object of honor, while those who value the life given to its pleasures, experience good times that are transient and fictitious" (*Poster. C.* 122). On the prophet as a speaker whose utterance does not come from himself, Philo says, "when knowing not what he does he is filled with inspiration, as the reason withdraws and surrenders the citadel of the soul to a new visitor and tenant, the Divine Spirit . . . plays upon the vocal organism and dictates words which clearly express its prophetic message" (*Spec. leg.* 4.49).

with μένειν ἐν ("to abide in") expresses the enduring unity between God/Christ and believers (cf. also 2:6; 3:9, 15; 4:13, 15–16). It thus corresponds to the union with God that is appropriate to the notion of being born of God or being children of God.[57] In the present passage it is interpreted in relation to keeping the commandments; this means that believers' community with God, as an abiding in the love of the Father, must be concretely expressed in ethical behavior, namely, love for the sisters and brothers (cf. 2:5–6; 4:11–12; John 15:10).

Without any apparent transition, the indirect warning to keep the commandments and the promise of "abiding" (v. 24a–b) is joined, with a paratactic καί, to the statement of a criterion of recognition that will indicate the condition of the abiding, namely, the gift of the Spirit (v. 24c–d). However, μένει ἐν ἡμῖν ("abides in us") constitutes a link to the latter half of the preceding sentence, since it is also presupposed by v. 24b (αὐτὸς ἐν αὐτῷ). It thus becomes clear that even the singular τηρῶν ("obey," v. 24a) has an ecclesiological import. Beyond this, the present tense of γινώσκομεν is to be understood as the end of a chain of criteria for recognition beginning with the perfect ἐγνώκαμεν in v. 16a. Accordingly, Christ's sacrificial surrender represents the criterion of *agapē* relating to the past. Then follows, with the future γνωσόμεθα in v. 19a, the criterion for discerning the truth about the future, which will reveal the believers' triumph in the final judgment. In v. 24 the criterion of recognition relates to the present of believers; if it is to be described as μένει ἐν αὐτῷ, it is determined by the gift of the Spirit.[58]

What is unique to this verse, which concludes the parenetic section, is the recapitulation of ἐν τούτῳ with an ἐκ construction in which the concept of πνεῦμα ("Spirit")[59] appears for the first time in 1 John. The author uses a ponderous construction with the emphasis on the last part of the verse to say: Christian awareness of the reality of salvation is brought about by the Spirit! Here ἐκ is not partitive, as might be suggested by the parallel construction in 4:13,[60] but should be understood as causal.[61] The believers' knowledge is effected by the Spirit, who is also its source (cf. John 3:6: ἐκ τοῦ πνεύματος, in contrast to ἐκ τῆς σαρκός). This means nothing other than that Christians possess the Spirit. Hence, the *pneuma* is a universal characteristic of the Christian community. This results from the fact that they are all baptized and have received the χρῖσμα (2:20, 27). Not only are the church's beginnings characterized by this efficacious working of the Spirit, but Christians will also continue to be guided by the Spirit in the realm of truth.[62]

Thus the author reminds his readers of Christian origins and of the gifts of the Spirit, and he can presume that all this is acknowledged in every congregation. As a result, the sacramental accent involved in the possession of the Spirit cannot be ignored in this passage,[63] the more so since 1 John 5:6 will make the sacramental role of the Spirit abundantly clear. It can correctly be said of 1 John that "πνεῦμα is first used along primitive Christian lines for the distinguishing mark of the great turning-point."[64] In the passages cited it is evident that the Spirit does not bring about a magical change in the situation,

57 See above at 3:11, and frequently elsewhere.

58 See v. 24c; cf. 5:2: ἐν τούτῳ γινώσκομεν (the criterion for recognizing love of the sisters and brothers is loving God and keeping the commandments).

59 The word πνεῦμα occurs 12 times in 1 John; cf. also 4:1 (bis), 3, 6 (bis), 13; 5:6 (bis), 8. The concept does not appear in 2 or 3 John.

60 Cf. BDF §164; also Bultmann, *Epistles*, 59. This is said in opposition to the position of Brown, *Epistles*, 466: he wishes to identify the construction with a partitive genitive, and adduces as a comparison John 3:34 (ἐκ μέτρου). In that passage, however, a "measured" gift of the Spirit is expressly denied, and a fundamental distinction between the Spirit of God and the Spirit of Jesus (in which case the latter would have to represent a part of the Spirit of God) is not Johannine.

61 Cf. BDF § 212.

62 1 John 2:21–27. Given all this, it is an inadmissible reduction to conclude on the basis of 4:11–13 "that the gift of the spirit consists in loving one another" (Bultmann, *Epistles*, 59).

63 Bultmann denies this, on the basis of a preconception that "sacramental thinking is foreign to 1 John (as also to the Gospel of John)" (cf. *Epistles*, 60 n. 84). His additional reasoning, that otherwise "the community would not need to be warned against false πνεύματα . . . which are at work through the false teachers (4:1ff). For the false teachers are also baptized" (ibid.), is equally unpersuasive, since apparently baptism cannot prevent a later falling away; cf. also Brown, *Epistles*, 483.

64 Eduard Schweizer, "πνεῦμα, κτλ.," *TDNT* 6 (1968) 448. However, there is an unsurpassable contra-

but rather is unceasingly united with the word and faith.[65] In what follows, it will be said that the Spirit, as the guarantor of truth, has an important function in the conflict with opposing teaching. Then it will also be clear that the spirit of truth is opposed by the spirit of error, and that the *pneuma* is not handed over to the community as a fixed possession, but rather enters into a historical process in which the danger of losing the right path is, in fact, realized in a variety of ways. Thus v. 24 is not only to be understood as the conclusion of the parenesis, but at the same time—with its emphasis on the common possession of the Spirit—as a transition to the next section, which will treat of the discernment of spirits.[66]

diction to this statement in the same author's saying, with regard to John 6:51–58, that "for Jn. the function of baptism and the Lord's Supper is to bear witness [*sic*] to the incarnation" (ibid., 441), or in his attempt effectively to narrow the meaning of the sacraments by saying that they are important "because the prophetic πνεῦμα preaches the real life and death of Jesus through them too" (ibid., 448 n. 811). To the contrary, and correctly, Schnackenburg, *Epistles*, 195.

65 See below, at 5:6.

66 Regarding the relationship between 3:24 and 4:13: the correspondences are so strong that Schnackenburg could suggest that we are here faced with "something in the nature of a catechetical formula" (*Epistles*, 191). The question whether the causal (3:24) or the partitive ἐκ (4:13) comes first in the history of the tradition can remain unresolved at this point.

4 On Discernment of Spirits (Truth and Error)

1 Beloved, do not believe every spirit, but
test the spirits to see whether they are
from God; for many false prophets have
gone out into the world. 2/ By this you
know the Spirit of God: every spirit that
confesses that Jesus Christ has come in
the flesh is from God, 3/ and every spirit
that does not confess Jesus is not from
God. And this is the (spirit) of the
antichrist, of which you have heard that
it is coming; and now it is already in the
world. 4/ Little children, you are from
God, and have conquered them; for the
one who is in you is greater than the one
who is in the world. 5/ They are from the
world; therefore what they say is from
the world, and the world listens to them.
6/ We are from God. Whoever knows
God listens to us, and whoever is not
from God does not listen to us. From this
we know the spirit of truth and the spirit
of error.

After the parenesis calling for the keeping of the commandments, especially that of love for the sisters and brothers (most recently at 3:23–24) and supported by an apocalyptic vision (esp. in 2:28–29), this new thematic unit deals with the concept of "spirits" (*πνεύματα*). This section is also conceived as an address to the community, as the imperatives *μὴ πιστεύετε* ("do not believe") and *δοκιμάζετε* ("test") make clear. In what follows, however, the imperatives will be replaced by an indicative description of the various spirits. The end of the section is marked by a renewed address to the community (*'Αγαπητοί*) and by another set of remarks on the topic of love of God and love of one another (v. 7).

The unit can be subdivided.[1] Verses 1–3 are particularly concerned with the discernment of different spirits; vv. 4–6 refer to the relationship of the spirits to the world, and the community is set in opposition to false teaching, within the framework of a God-world dualism. However, what is decisive for understanding the passage is the material unity it possesses, based on the key words *πνεύματα / πνεῦμα*. We have already seen that the author can interpret the life of Christians as something shaped

1 The commentaries incline to a different division: 4:1—5:12 = third major section (Wengst, *Brief*, 29, 163–64; Schnackenburg, *Epistles*, 196–98; Balz, "Johannesbriefe," 166, 194–96; Schunack, *Briefe*, 5, 71–73). Against this division, however, is the parallelism between this section and 2:18–27 and 5:4b–12, each of which addresses the dogmatic-christological controversy. According to Brown, *Epistles*, 467 (cf. also his introduction), the section is constituted by 3:11—5:12 (following the first major section, 1:5—3:10). His reasoning: both sections begin with "This is the *ἀγγελία*"; both sections are of equal length and are concerned with "fraternal love." However, 3:11 is different from 1:5: it begins with *ὅτι αὕτη ἐστίν*; nor can *ἀγγελία* have such a wide-ranging superordinate function, as its interpretation in each case depends on the narrower context.

by the Spirit.[2] The verbal link to the end of v. 24 should not, however, lead one to suppose that the concept of πνεῦμα is used without differentiation. Our text differs from what has gone before in speaking not about the Holy Spirit but about human beings who are guided by different spirits.[3]

■ **1** The author takes for granted the existence of a variety of spirits (implicit in "every," παντί). In what follows it will be apparent that this multiplicity of *pneumata* is at work especially in the preaching of the false prophets (vv. 1b–6). The warning against them is "do not believe" (μὴ πιστεύετε). It is doubtful whether at this point one may translate the verb πιστεύειν in the sense of "trust,"[4] thus contrasting it with the fundamental meaning of πιστεύειν in 3:23. Even though the dative object distinguishes this from the christological context in 3:23, the principal meaning, "believe," or "acknowledge" can be applied in both verses, especially since this is characteristic of 1 John as a whole.[5] Thus the community is warned not to submit itself to the various spirits, but to maintain a critical distance from them, that is, to "test" them.[6] The purpose of this testing is to determine "whether they are from God" (εἰ ἐκ τοῦ θεοῦ ἐστιν; also in v. 3; cf. 3:10). Since ἐκ describes origin,[7] this means that the condition of belonging to God and truth, in contrast to the world and lies (cf. also 2:22) or to the devil (3:8, 12), is the thing to be tested. This was the common attitude of the primitive Christian church, in its earliest days, toward "heresy." Even Paul called on believers not to quench the Spirit but to "test everything" (1 Thess 5:19–21). The

2 Cf. above at 3:24.

3 According to Schnackenburg, πνεύματα means "the human spirit . . . , insofar as it is inspired either by God or the devil" (*Epistles*, 193). This is denied by Wengst (*Brief*, 168), who understands the spirits as "the very spirit of God" or as "that of the devil or the antichrist, but in the way in which it appears as given to each individual human being." Brown's definition tends in the same direction: "combination of . . . the Holy Spirit and the Evil Spirit" (*Epistles*, 486). Also in a confrontation with the spirit of the false prophets, we read in *Herm. Man.* 11.5: πᾶν γὰρ πνεῦμα ἀπὸ θεοῦ δοθὲν οὐκ ἐπερωτᾶται, ἀλλὰ ἔχον τὴν δύναμιν τῆς θεότητος ἀφ' ἑαυτοῦ λαλεῖ πάντα, ὅτι ἄνωθέν ἐστιν ἀπὸ τῆς δυνάμεως τοῦ θείου πνεύματος ("For every spirit which is given from God is not asked questions, but has the power of the Godhead and speaks all things of itself, because it is from above, from the power of the Divine spirit").

4 Thus Schnackenburg, *Epistles*, 200, with reference to John 4:21 ("believe me!").

5 So also Bultmann, *Epistles*, 61. He prefers to understand πιστεύειν "as faith in the sense of acknowledgment: 'do not come into the power of every spirit.'" See above on 3:23.

6 The verb δοκιμάζειν occurs only here in the Johannine writings. It was current throughout the Greek-speaking world in its secular meaning of "testing," "putting to the proof" (cf. Xenophon *Mem.* 1.2.42; 1.4.1; 3.5.20; Plato *Leg.* 6.754a ff.; Job 34:3 LXX; Luke 14:19). In the LXX the verb appears as a synonym for בחן and is understood primarily in a religious sense; in most cases it assumes YHWH as its subject (cf. Jer 9:6; 11:20; Pss 17:3; 26:2.; Wis 11:10, and frequently). In the NT, in contrast, people often appear as subjects of the verb. In Gerd Schunack's formulation ("δοχιμάζω," *EDNT* 1 [1990] 342), one should "also not proceed in an unreflective way with the formal-neutral meaning examine/authenticate"; instead, the word indicates "the thought and action" corresponding to an existence "which consists in its fundamental referent, in knowledge and understanding. It is expressed as critical discernment (examination) and in practical testing of the experience of knowing or of being known in relation to oneself and to others." While for Paul it is essentially a matter of "the critical-practical understanding and response of faith" (cf. 1 Cor 9:27; 2 Cor 13:3; Rom 5:3–4, and frequently), δοκιμάζειν in post-Pauline writings "takes on a certain fixed meaning in the sense that the testing and accreditation can, so to speak, be delegated according to general, ecclesiastical-ethical criteria" (ibid., 343); cf. 1 Tim 3:10; 2 Tim 2:15; Jas 1:12; *Did.* 11.11; 12.1; 15.1; *1 Clem.* 42.4; 44.2; 47.4, and frequently.

7 This phrasing is found in a dualistic sense in 2:16 (in contrast to ἐκ τοῦ κόσμου); εἶναι ἐκ is a typical Johannine expression. It appears 55 times in the Johannine writings: 28 times in the Fourth Gospel, 19 times in 1 John, and once in 3 John. In the rest of the NT, εἶναι ἐκ appears only 28 times. The expression describes descent or origin in a secular sense (cf. John 1:44; 3:1; 7:42), but especially from a theological point of view, in order to describe, within the dualistic world of ideas, the state of belonging to or descent from one of the two sides (cf. 2:21; 3:8, 12, 19; 4:5; John 3:31; 6:32; 8:23, 44; Acts 5:39; 1 Cor 11:12).

preacher of the Sermon on the Mount also demands a fundamental distance toward all phenomena that might be characterized as false teaching, in warning the hearers to distinguish false prophets by their fruits.[8] "False prophets"—the word ψευδοπροφῆται appears only here in the Johannine literature—are, in the opinion of the earliest Christians, a phenomenon of the end time. It is especially in apocalyptic texts that they are named among the future dangers threatening the communities.[9] But even in OT times they were already a familiar phenomenon, disrupting the community of Israel (cf. Luke 6:26; 2 Pet 2:1). They also appear in the era of the church, as our text shows.[10] In similar fashion, the presbyter warns against the πλάνοι as opponents of his preaching and identifies them with the antichrist (2 John 7). Not only the Johannine but the Pauline school as well[11] found itself in acute conflict with "false spirits" and in this way participated in the beginnings of early catholic thinking, in which "true" teaching is clearly defined in contrast to "false" teaching. Whereas the false teachers spread "teachings of demons" (1 Tim 4:1), they are branded in 1 John as the embodiment of the "spirit of error" (4:6). When the author says of them that they "have gone out into the world," the perfect ἐξεληλύθασιν appears to express not a unique act, but the duration of their appearance in the world.[12] In contrast to the first reference to false teachers (2:19), here the author appears concerned to make clear that the false prophecy his community is encountering is not an isolated phenomenon and cannot be limited to a particular historical period; it will accompany the church in the future as well. When he says that the teachers of error and corruption have gone out into the world, his primary purpose is not to describe their cosmic origins in contrast to ἐκ τοῦ θεοῦ (as later in v. 5), but rather to illustrate the universality of their appearance and their worldwide activity.[13] They are an enduring and pervasive danger that constantly accompanies the Christian community on its journey through the ages.

■ **2** Although Christians' fund of knowledge is not closed, but remains open to the future,[14] even at the present

8 Matt 7:15–20; cf. esp. Matt 7:16, 20 (ἐπιγνώσεσθε) with 1 John 4:2 (γινώσκετε); on this, see below.

9 Mark 13:22 par.; Rev 16:13; 19:20; 20:10 (each time in the singular). The "Teaching of the Apostles" presents a future-eschatological proclamation of the existence of false prophecy, in a tradition dependent on the Synoptic Gospels and approximately contemporary with the Johannine literature: "For in the final days multitudes of false prophets (ψευδοπροφῆται) and seducers will appear. Sheep will turn into wolves, and love into hatred. For with the increase of iniquity people will hate, persecute, and betray each other. And then the world deceiver (κοσμοπλάνος) will appear in the guise of God's Son. He will work 'signs and wonders' and the earth will fall into his hands and he will commit outrages such as have never occurred before. Then humankind will come to the fiery trial, 'and many will fall away' and perish, 'but those who persevere' in their faith 'will be saved'" (*Did.* 16.3–5; translation adapted from Richardson, *Early Christian Fathers*, 178–79).

10 For the appearance of lying prophets in the OT, cf. Jer 23:13–40; 28; 29:21–23; Mic 3:5–7. In the NT this designation is also found in Acts 13:6, where the Jewish magician Bar-Jesus is called a "false prophet." In *Did.* 11.5–6, suspect itinerant apostles are designated false prophets, and *Herm. Man.* 11 speaks of the problem of distinguishing true from false prophets (see n. 3 above). Similar ideas are found, couched in a variety of expressions, in the Qumran texts (cf. 1QpHab ii.1–2; v.11: "the Liar"; 1QH ii.31; iv.20: "lying interpreters") and in the related Damascus document (cf. CD i.14–15; viii.13; xx.15).

11 Cf. 1 Thess 5:21; 1 Cor 2:12; 12:3, 10; 14:29; as well as the deutero-Pauline literature (cf. 2 Thess 2:2; 2 Tim 1:7; Eph 2:2), although no tradition-historical connection with 1 John 4:1 may be derived from these passages. Cf. also Schnackenburg, *Epistles*, 199–200.

12 BDF § 340 (continuance of completed action); also Brown, *Epistles*, 490. 2 John 7 is different (aorist ἐξῆλθον; *v.l.*: ἐξῆλθαν, cf. 1 John 2:19), expressing the uniqueness of the past action. Neither here nor, for example, in 1:1ff. should one consider this to be merely a rhetorical variation in the Johannine style; in 1:1ff. the temporal shift clearly distinguishes between past and future (see above, at 1:1ff.); against Brown, *Epistles*, 161; Bultmann, *Epistles*, 8 n. 8; Schnackenburg, *Epistles*, 58.

13 So Schnackenburg, *Epistles*, 199, Bultmann, *Epistles*, 62 n. 2. Brown differs (*Epistles*, 490): "he wishes to underline their choice of the world, theologically understood as the enemy of Christ."

14 Cf., on the one hand, the future γνωσόμεθα (3:19),

time they possess a knowledge that they are actualizing in accord with the new situation. This is established by the indicative γινώσκετε ("you know"). Believers have at all times an ability to distinguish spirits and to recognize what rightly presents itself as the Spirit of God.[15] The connection to what has gone before has been deliberately created by the author. The congregation, as a community of those who have been born of God, have the Spirit of God, and the Spirit in turn has the function of shaping the community and bringing it to insight (3:24). However, the relationship between the Spirit and the community is not a one-way path, as though the Spirit were some sort of magical power that made use of human beings; the relationship can only be rightly understood in historical terms. Even though the community understands itself as being shaped by the Spirit of God, it is still in a position to take an apparently detached position and to propose and answer the question whether that which presents itself as the Spirit of God, through the preaching of the Christian prophets, has a right to make that claim.

The criterion that aids discernment of spirits is confession.[16] In what follows, this will be expressed in an antithetical parallelism (vv. 2b–3a), in which a positive phrase is followed by its negative counterpart. The parallel placement of these phrases reveals that both members are related to one another and can be interpreted together. The divine origins of the prophetic spirit can be recognized, according to this, by whether that spirit is able to accept the confession that "Jesus Christ has come in the flesh" (Ἰησοῦν Χριστὸν ἐν σαρκὶ ἐληλυθότα).[17] This formula recalls 2 John 7, but by using the perfect tense it expresses the "endurance of what has been accomplished."[18] It does not refer to the future but to an event in the past whose effects continue even to the present time. There can be no doubt that the author is thinking at this point of the incarnation of Jesus Christ,[19] which occurred "in the flesh"—in other words, the entry

and, on the other hand, the reference to the past in 3:16.

15 The finite verb γινώσκετε can also be interpreted as an imperative; however, the textual variants γινώσκεται and γινώσκομεν show that the manuscript tradition also presumes an indicative meaning. Beyond this, one may point to 3:16 (not so much to 3:20; thus Bultmann, *Epistles*, 62), where the readers are reminded of the knowledge they possess.

16 Cf. the function of confession, alongside office and canon, as *notae ecclesiae* in early catholic theology; it appears clearly for the first time in Ps.-Tertullian *Adv. haer.* 21; 32; 36; cf. Adolf von Harnack, *Lehrbuch der Dogmengeschichte* (3 vols.; 5th ed.; Tübingen: Mohr [Siebeck], 1931; 1909 ed. reprinted Darmstadt: Wissenschaftliche Buchgesellschaft, 1964) 1.353–54. ET: *History of Dogma*. Translated from the 3d German edition by Neil Buchanan. 7 vols. bound as 4 (New York: Dover Publications, 1961 [reprint of 1900 edition]) 2.18–19. The early stages of this kind of "apostolic teaching" are brief kerygmatic confessions; on this, see Hans Conzelmann, "Was glaubte die frühe Christenheit?" in idem, *Theologie als Schriftauslegung* (Munich: Kaiser, 1974) 106–19; also the excursus below on "Early Catholicism."

17 In contrast to v. 3, this text has been transmitted more or less without blemish; the transposition, Χριστὸν Ἰησοῦν, in C is secondary.

18 See the remarks on v. 1 above (ἐξεληλύθασιν). Brown also understands the perfect participle as "emphasizing the enduring result of a past coming" (*Epistles*, 493) but denies the consequences of this insight by refusing to differentiate this from the present participle in 2 John 7 and the aorist in 1 John 5:6.

19 Thus also Schnackenburg (*Epistles*, 200–201), who, in addition, correctly reflects the difference between the position of the fourth evangelist and that of the author of 1 John: "The perspective of [the one] making the confession is not that of the evangelist, who is giving a historical overview of the saving event (John 1:14), [but that of a believer, for whom] Jesus Christ is the living Son of God enthroned at the right hand of the Father (1 John 2:1)." Paul S. Minear improperly confuses the christological and ecclesiological aspects by choosing to understand the expression ἐν σαρκί as parallel to ἐν ὑμῖν (1 John 4:4) and arguing that: "The coming of Christ in the flesh is one way of saying that within the authentic Christian fellowship, there abides or dwells Christ's life" ("The Idea of Incarnation in First John," *Int* 24 [1970] 291–302, at 292). Brown has still another opinion. He upholds the point of view that the "opponents" taught "an overly high christology (exaggerating the christology of [the Gospel of John])," and "stressing the importance of preexistence to the point of neglecting the flesh or humanity of Jesus" (*Epistles*, 53–54); in opposition to this, according to Brown, the author of 1 John emphasizes that there is no separation between "Jesus and Christ," and that the person of Christ must be understood "in terms of his career in the flesh. . . . the author says 'come in the flesh,' not 'come into the flesh'"; therefore "the act of incarnation is not the

of the Son of God into the sphere of the tangible and mutable, just as the word "flesh" (σάρξ) was already used in a negative sense in 2:16 ("the desire of the flesh," ἡ ἐπιθυμία τῆς σαρκός). In such usage the author of 1 John is on the same plane as the fourth evangelist, who can use σάρξ as a concept in opposition to πνεῦμα.[20] Thus power "over all flesh" is attributed to the Revealer (John 17:2), but before everything else it is acknowledged that the Logos has become flesh (1:14), a central affirmation of Johannine theology whose ultimate consequence is found in the sacramental assertion that the Revealer has given "his flesh" for the life of the world and has left it to his own as true food.[21] While this idea, as found in the Fourth Gospel, is partly derived from tradition, and while at the level of the fourth evangelist it scarcely reflects any further confrontation with a concrete opposing thesis, 1 John is still in an acute phase of struggle with a different interpretation of the Christ-confession. From the point of view of the history of tradition, 1 John has a position prior to the Fourth Gospel, and inquiry about the polemical context within which the Johannine school arrived at its own christology should more properly be conducted on this basis and in connection with 2 John than on the basis of the Fourth Gospel.[22] It is certain that the author's opponents are not merely concerned with contesting a "chiliastic," realistic anticipation of the future, the parousia of Christ ἐν σαρκί, as one may observe in 2 John 7.[23] Because the false teachers instead contest Christ's having come in the flesh, they deny Jesus' fleshly existence and hence the "paradoxical identity of the historical and the eschatological figure of Jesus Christ."[24]

■ **3** The second, negative part of the parallel expresses the same thing, even though, if one accepts the reading τὸν Ἰησοῦν, v. 3a appears to differ significantly from the preceding phrase.

On the text-critical problem: τὸν Ἰησοῦν is supported by codices A and B, a number of minuscules (945, 1241, 1739, and others), the Latin tradition, and the church fathers. The "majority text" (primarily minuscules) reads τὸν Ἰησοῦν Χριστὸν ἐν σαρκὶ ἐληλυθότα and thus repeats the statement in v. 2b—an obvious sign of its secondary nature. This secondary reading is also represented by Codex ℵ, which replaces Χριστόν with the word Κύριον (cf. Rom 10:9). In this connection

point" (*Epistles*, 493). But however much one may wish to avoid overemphasizing the difference between this verse and John 1:14 (ὁ λόγος σὰρξ ἐγένετο, "the Word became flesh"), to the extent that the "opponents" represent an exaggerated pre-existence christology, it cannot be separated from their understanding of σάρξ, that is, the incarnation of Christ. As regards the expression ἐν σαρκί (v. 2), it may be influenced by 2 John 7. Greek often fails to distinguish clearly between ἐν and εἰς: cf. Homer *Il.* 16.437; further examples in BAGD 230 and (for the NT), BDF § 218.

20 John 3:6; 6:63; cf. also 8:15: κατὰ τὴν σάρκα. At this point one may inquire whether a Pauline influence should be assumed: cf. Rom 8:4–5, 12–13; 2 Cor 1:17; 5:16; 10:2–3; 11:18, and frequently elsewhere.

21 John 6:51ff.; in addition, cf. the whole of the Johannine concept of atoning death: John 10:11, 15, 17–18; 15:13; 6:53–56; 19:34–35; 1 John 1:7; 3:16; 5:6, 8.

22 The question of tradition history is different within the context of 1 John. With regard to 2:22, one may ask with Haenchen whether it is based on an older formula, "Jesus is the Christ," which in the verse now under consideration has experienced "a transformation directed against Gnosis" ("Neuere Literatur," 274). In any case, there can be no doubt that, in combination, 1 John 2:22 and 4:2–3 maintain the same trajectory of assertion, and that it relates to the same opposing christological doctrine.

23 See below at 2 John 7.

24 Bultmann, *Epistles*, 62. Similarly, Wengst (*Brief*, 169) points out that, for the opponents, it was probably true that a "bearer of salvation" had come, but "what is offensive and unacceptable is that he is supposed to have come 'in the flesh.'" Dodd (*Epistles*, 99) also holds the opinion that "whatever else the heretics affirm of Christ, they would not confess the reality of Incarnation." The idea that these are Jews, who deny the messianic quality of the figure of Jesus (thus J. C. O'Neill, *The Puzzle of 1 John: A New Examination of Origins* [London: SPCK, 1966]; also Hartwig Thyen, "Johannesbriefe," *TRE* 17 [1987] 186–200) is improbable on the basis of ἐν σαρκί, which presupposes a differently defined controversy within the Johannine tradition itself.

one also finds the transposition of the words: τὸν Χριστὸν ᾿Ιησοῦν (614, 2412) or the expansion of τὸν ᾿Ιησοῦν by the addition of Χριστόν (629*[?] it$^{\text{ar. dem}}$).

Although these readings cannot shake the priority of τὸν ᾿Ιησοῦν, since they can be explained as secondary accommodations to v. 2b or as interpretive additions, the reading λύει seems to be more significant. It appears in the tradition of the church fathers (Irenaeus, Clement, Origen, Lucifer, Priscillian, Augustine, Fulgentius), as well as in manuscripts of the Itala and the Vulgate (and in 1739^{mg}) in place of μὴ ὁμολογεῖ. This reading is also preferred by a number of newer commentaries.[25] The verb λύειν can scarcely support the meaning "divide,"[26] but should be translated in agreement with 3:8 as "annul" or "destroy." What is meant is that the false teachers "destroy faith in Jesus as the Son of God made man, whom God sent to save the world" and "do away with him as the indispensable Mediator of salvation."[27] This statement can be explained as an interpretation of the better-attested μὴ ὁμολογεῖ and has no claim to priority. It may have entered the text rather late, under the influence of the christological conflicts.[28] As far as the content is concerned, scarcely any difference can be discerned, since not confessing means at the same time closing oneself to the salvific significance of Jesus Christ and thus annulling his meaning for oneself.

If the object of the opponents' nonconfessing is Jesus, this would mean, in agreement with v. 2b, that they deny not only the act of becoming flesh but also the Son of God's being-in-the-flesh.[29] This kind of denial of the Son of God is a trenchant criterion for the accuracy of the perception that the Spirit of God does not speak through them and that they themselves are not from God. By their heretical christology they have separated themselves from the community out of which they have gone forth (2:19).

The demonstrative "and this" (καὶ τοῦτο) refers back to "every spirit" (πᾶν πνεῦμα, v. 3a), so that the word πνεῦμα should be understood after the following article τὸ. The author thus identifies the spirit of those who deny Jesus with the spirit of the antichrist. The assertion that they have become representatives of the spirit of the antichrist can be linked with the primitive Christian apocalyptic expectation, according to which the antichrist will appear as the opponent of Christ before the end of the present age.[30] This is known to the community from oral tradition,[31] as was apparent at 2:18. While the antichrist also remains a future figure associated with the events of the end time, he is present "now already" as a historical figure within the scope of teaching. In contrast to the idea of history as a linear time sequence, the end has already become a dangerous present in the persons of the false teachers. The dialectic of "already—not yet," which also marks the appearance of the Revealer in the Fourth Gospel,[32] can thus be experienced in negative form within the life of the community. The apocalyptic phenomenon of the antichrist has become a historical fact through the appearance of the false prophets.[33]

■ **4** Making a renewed beginning (with respect to v. 1) with "you" (῾Υμεῖς), the author turns directly to the

25 For example, Schnackenburg, *Epistles*, 201; Bultmann, *Epistles*, 62; Wengst, *Brief*, 171; Brown, *Epistles*, 496.

26 Brown sees this correctly (*Epistles*, 495).

27 Cf. Schnackenburg, *Epistles*, 202.

28 Cf. Origen: "cum sit scriptum apud Joannem: omnis spiritus, qui solvit Jesum, non est ex deo" (*Comm. In Matt., PG* 13.883). Smalley writes: "This variant is almost certainly a later scribal gloss, attempting to explain the exact way in which Jesus was being denied by heretics" (*1, 2, 3 John*, 215). On this problem, see also Bart D. Ehrmann, "1 Joh 4:3 and the Orthodox Corruption of Scripture," *ZNW* 79 (1988) 221–43.

29 On this, see the excursus above, "The False Teachers in 1 John."

30 Cf. the excursus below, "The Antichrist." This is a Christian concept.

31 The perfect ἀκηκόατε points to the community's past; cf. also ἀκηκόαμεν (1:1) as the beginning of the line of tradition. (BDF § 340: "The perfect combines in itself, so to speak, the present and the aorist.")

32 Cf. esp. 4:23; 5:25 ("The hour is coming and is now here"); also 12:31; 13:31; for ἤδη see 1 John 2:8; John 15:3; 19:28.

33 Cf. 2:18c; Bultmann, *Epistles*, 63: "The mythological figure of the antichrist is thereby demythologized and historicized."

readers again,[34] now describing the opposition between the community and the false teaching against the background of a dualism of God and world.[35] Christians are "from God" (ἐκ τοῦ θεοῦ; cf. 4:1, 3). Their belonging to God indicates that they have already achieved victory over the false teachers.[36] Similarly, it could be said of the "young men" that they have "conquered the evil one."[37] This presumes that the power of evil reveals itself as active in false teaching.[38] The community is preserved from such a power, and reassurance of this is again given[39] with a special justification. "The one who is in you is greater" (μείζων ἐστὶν ὁ ἐν ὑμῖν) recalls 3:20b, where, in the contrast between the merciful judge of the world and the accusation of our own hearts, God is described as "greater." There is no reason to doubt that in this passage as well, θεός should be understood as the subject, especially since the readers are addressed as those who are from God.[40] At the same time, it is clear that being from God, or God's being "in you," is materially congruent with the christological basis of the community. It can also be said of the Son of God that we are "in him" (καὶ ἐσμὲν . . . ἐν τῷ υἱῷ αὐτοῦ Ἰησοῦ Χριστῷ).[41] The community, insofar as it is in Christ, belongs entirely within the sphere of God and Christ. This not only separates it from the being of the world, but gives it assurance that the hoped-for victory over the opponents,[42] already experienced in the present, has its basis in the superiority of the Father of Jesus Christ over the one "who is in the world." That this latter phrase refers to the antichrist requires no demonstration, because with this description the author repeats word for word what was said of the appearance of the antichrist in v. 3b. Even though, according to Johannine interpretation, the world has not totally succumbed to the power of the evil one but remains the object of God's love,[43] being

34 The second person (cf. earlier at 2:28; 3:1, 11, 13) alternates, as in the preceding parts (cf. 3:19, 21ff.) and in what follows (v. 6), with "we." The address to the readers is underscored by the use of τεκνία (see above, at 2:12).

35 This contrast is signaled by (a) ἐκ τοῦ θεοῦ, ἐν ὑμῖν (v. 4), πνεῦμα τῆς ἀληθείας (v. 6); and (b) αὐτούς, ἐν τῷ κόσμῳ (v. 4), ἐκ τοῦ κόσμου (v. 5), πνεῦμα τῆς πλάνης (v. 6).

36 The pronoun αὐτούς refers back to ψευδοπροφῆται (v. 1).

37 1 John 2:13–14; for the victory of the community over the cosmos, see below at 5:4–5.

38 Cf. also the identification with the antichrist (v. 3); see above on 4:3.

39 The secure state of salvation of the Christian community, which is something to be described in the indicative, has already been expressed in a variety of concepts in what has gone before; cf. "being born of God" (2:29; 3:9) or the χρῖσμα, the divinely effected anointing that preserves the community in the truth (2:20, 27).

40 Verses 4a, 6; cf., in this sense, also Bultmann, *Epistles*, 63; Schnackenburg, *Epistles*, 203 4; Wengst, *Brief*, 173. According to Brown (*Epistles*, 497), one should not insert "God" as the subject, since εἶναι ἐν cannot be said of the Father, but at most μένειν ἐν (3:24; 4:12–13, 15–16). This is not, however, a weighty argument, since "remaining" presupposes "being," and the parallel to the christological statements of equivalence cannot be denied. If Brown wishes to understand this passage as a continuation of the contrasting of spirits (vv. 2–3) and an anticipation of the opposition between the "spirit of truth" and the "spirit of error" (v. 6), his interpretation can refer to 3:24 ("by the Spirit that he has given us"), but it is in opposition to the nearer context; and it certainly cannot rest on the idea of the Paraclete in the Fourth Gospel, who as the spirit of truth "will be in you" (John 14:16–17), for the author of 1 John differs from the author of the Fourth Gospel in identifying the Paraclete not with the Spirit but with Christ (2:1).

41 Cf. 5:20 (on its presence as part of 1 John, see below); cf. also above, at 3:24.

42 The author presumes that the community as such will not allow itself to be led astray by the false prophets (cf. 2:19; Büchsel, *Johannesbriefe*, 65). But this does not exclude the possibility that its existence is repeatedly placed in jeopardy and that the demand to provide access for the spirit of truth must continually be heard and realized anew.

43 Bultmann has persuasively demonstrated that the concept of "world" is primarily anthropological in its scope within the Fourth Gospel; this includes an understanding of the world as "creation." See Rudolf Bultmann, "Die Eschatologie des Johannes-Evangeliums," *Glauben und Verstehen: Gesammelte Aufsätze* 1.134–52. ET: "The Eschatology of the Gospel of John," in Bultmann's *Faith and Understanding* 1. Ed. and with an introduction by Robert W. Funk. Trans. Louise Pettibone Smith (New York and Evanston: Harper & Row, 1969), 165–83, esp. 166–68. Josef Blank emphasizes that a creation-theological and anthropological definition of the

in the world is not something neutral, a state abstracted from the struggle between good and evil. Instead, it is in the world that the decisions are made[44] that will be presented before the judge at his parousia (2:28), and that even now allow a distinction to be drawn between the children of God and the children of the devil (3:10). Even though the antichrist is thus designated as a cosmic being, it is clear that this apocalyptic figure represents the root of the danger threatening the community in the world.[45] It is true that the author does not set aside the future aspect, but he is not concerned with painting a mythological picture of the end of the world; rather, his interest is in historicizing the antichrist. In any case it is not said, as one would expect in parallel to *ὁ ἐν ὑμῖν*, that the antichrist appears in the false prophets (= *ὁ ἐν αὐτοῖς*). While the author can say that God, Christ, and the Spirit dwell in Christians, one may ask whether he deliberately avoids using this expression with regard to the relationship of the antichrist to the false teachers.[46] However, he makes an even stronger emphasis elsewhere when he identifies the false teachers with the antichrist (2:18). So here as well one may presume that the antichrist appears in the world as a false prophet. The people who place themselves at his disposal are thoroughly saturated with his evil essence.

■ **5** This is evident also in the relationship of the false prophets to the "world" (*κόσμος*). In contrast to the Christians, who are born of God (cf. 2:29; 3:9; 5:1, and frequently), the origin of these people is derived from the world. They thus stand on the negative side of the dualistic system characterized by the antichrist, who is "the one who is in the world" (*ὁ ἐν τῷ κόσμῳ*, v. 4), and by the spirit of error (v. 6). Because their origin is worldly, they are prisoners of cosmic existence and subject to mortality (cf. 2:15–17). Like other cosmic powers,[47] they represent a desire for destruction that is directed against the community (3:13). Their worldly origin corresponds to their appearance as preachers.[48] Their message belongs to the sphere of the world, and their successors are also part of the world.[49] This kind of dualistic categorization of the opposing teachers and their adherents appears to imply an idea of predestination according to which being from the world is an irrevocable decree of God, permitting no exit from the prison of the world.[50] But in Johannine thought destiny and ethics are telescoped into one another,[51] and the mode

Johannine understanding of the world must be expanded christologically, i.e., in connection with the Johannine interpretation of the revelatory event. See Josef Blank, *Krisis: Untersuchungen zur johanneischen Christologie und Eschatologie* (Freiburg: Lambertus, 1964) 186–93.

44 Cf. 2:18 ("it is the last hour").

45 Correspondingly, in the Fourth Gospel the devil can be described as ὁ ἄρχων τοῦ κόσμου τούτου (12:31).

46 Thus Schnackenburg, *Epistles*, 204: ("The author does not dare to credit Satan with [the same] direct influence, or with the same kind of real indwelling as God has"); similarly Wengst, *Brief*, 173.

47 In the Fourth Gospel, the unbelieving Ἰουδαῖοι are regarded as representatives of the world or cosmos (John 8:23: ὑμεῖς ἐκ τούτου τοῦ κόσμου ἐστέ; cf. 3:31; 18:37); cf. also John 15:19; 17:14–16 (the world's hatred of Jesus and his disciples). In apocalyptic conceptions the earth is the place of eschatological struggle between God and Satan (Ezek 38:1–23; Rev 20:7–9).

48 Bultmann (*Epistles*, 63) emphasizes that the *κόσμος* is not the space in which the false teachers (like all human beings) are to be found, but their nature. However, this kind of theological qualification does not exclude the spatial notion of the world as a place of eschatological struggle (cf. v. 4).

49 Wengst (*Brief*, 174) correctly describes their "speaking from the world" as "a [speaking] that is conformed to the world, . . . it does not challenge the unjust world, is not a goad or an annoyance to it, and offers no opposition to it."

50 Schnackenburg (*Epistles*, 203) speaks against an interpretation that claims to find here a *praedestinatio ad infidelitatem:* "People's characters are judged by their practical behavior, speaking, and hearing, but not vice versa. They are not predestined to faith or unbelief." Similarly Wengst, *Brief*, 175–76.

51 The tension-filled coupling of destiny and ethics is explained, according to Schenke ("Determination," 215), by the reality that surrounds the author and compels him "to formulate such contradictory statements. This reality is Christian existence with its heavenly and earthly aspects." In this view, ethics is rooted in the earthly and destiny in the heavenly trajectory of existence.

of existence of the false teachers is something historical, subject to their own decision—in contrast to that of the Christians born of God, who are delivered from the works of the devil[52] and yet are not removed once and for all out of the reach of the seducer's plotting. Hence they are warned not to set themselves on a par with the "world [that] listens to them."[53] The supposition that v. 5 suggests the conclusion that "the false teachers are having considerable success in the world" and that the early church is using this observation as a way of coming to terms "with the outward success of their opponents,"[54] so that the author is expressing a pessimistic view,[55] overvalues the possibility of deriving historical, sociological, or psychological data from our text. Instead, what is in the foreground is the dualistic theological statement that wherever the messengers of the world appear they find a hearing among worldly people. This is true no matter what the statistical measure of their success; in turn, it means that wherever God's messengers appear they will also find hearers, namely, those who belong to God.

■ **6** This consolation is expressed in v. 6, with a shift from the second person (v. 4: ὑμεῖς) to the first (ἡμεῖς). The apostolic author thus joins with the community, although he need not "be thinking exclusively and directly of the special circle of witnesses who were called to proclaim the faith,"[56] because the whole community leads a missionary life (cf. 4:11–12). Thus the author speaks at this point with an ecclesial "we."[57] The Christian community, through its origin ἐκ τοῦ θεοῦ, possesses a unique quality and can be certain that, just as it knows God (2:3–6, 13–14; 3:1, 6), it will find a hearing among those who also "know" God.[58] By contrast, those who are not born of God will give no hearing to the preaching, and this conclusion is drawn in the antithetical second clause.[59]

The conclusion is drawn with a causal phrase "from this" (ἐκ τούτου):[60] what has just been said furnishes, in

52 See above at 3:9.

53 In contrast to ἀκούειν, "to listen" (14 times in 1 John, and in 2 John 6; 3 John 4; 58 times in the Fourth Gospel), λαλεῖν ("to speak") appears only here in 1 John (as well as 2 John 12; 3 John 14; 59 times in the Fourth Gospel). The "speaking" of the false teachers and the world's "hearing" in response has a contrasting positive parallel in the appearance of Jesus as described in the Fourth Gospel: the Revealer "speaks" and his disciples "hear" and follow him (1:37; cf. 18:21). That all speaking seeks agreement is also evident from 12:19; on the other hand, the Revealer speaks what he has heard from his Father (8:26, 40); in this, the unity of his will and nature with the will and nature of the Father is presupposed (10:30; 14:20; 17:21); similarly, it is true of the Paraclete that "he will speak whatever he hears" (16:13). While in the Fourth Gospel the correspondence of speaking and hearing is thoroughly shaped by the christological, saving revelation, in 1 John it is characterized by the anti-redemptive reality of the false teachers.

54 Thus Schnackenburg, *Epistles*, 204; Bonnard also suspects a major success of the false teachers, especially in sophisticated circles (*Les épîtres johanniques*, 88).

55 Brown, according to whom the world would have found the opponents' ethical perfectionism "attractive" (*Epistles*, 508).

56 Schnackenburg, *Epistles*, 204.

57 So also in 3:13–14 in alternation with the second person plural; in addition, 2:24–25, 28, 29–30; 5:13–14, 20–21. This is the position also of Bultmann, *Epistles*, 64; Brown, *Epistles*, 499 ("non-distinctive use of 'we'"); Dodd (*Epistles*, 100) represents a middle position: he also thinks immediately of the church as a whole, but sees it as represented by its "responsible teachers who embody the authentic apostolic tradition." Bonnard (*Les épîtres johanniques*, 88) thinks differently, understanding ἡμεῖς (as did Calvin) in a more exclusive sense. Wengst (*Brief*, 175) thus also refers "we" to "the circle of original witnesses."

58 For γινώσκειν as "knowing," see the excursus below on 2 John 1: ὁ γινώσκων τὸν θεόν ("the one who knows God") makes essentially the same statement as ἡμεῖς ἐκ τοῦ θεοῦ ἐσμεν ("we are from God") thus it follows from v. 6b (ὃς οὐκ ἔστιν . . .) that both being from God and knowing God describe what it is to be Christian; cf. 2:4, where accordingly one should not automatically suspect the presence of an opponents' slogan, as Schnackenburg maintains (*Epistles*, 205).

59 The omission of v. 6b (ὃς — ἡμῶν) in codices A and L and a few other late manuscripts is explained by the homoioteleuton ἡμῶν.

60 Ἐκ τούτου occurs only here in 1 John, but also in John 6:66; 19:12. It furnishes a stronger substantiation than ἐν τούτῳ γινώσκομεν (also causal in 1 John 2:3, 5; 3:24; 4:2, 9, 13; 5:2; similarly 3:16, 19; John 16:30; Acts 24:16).

itself, the proper criterion of knowledge. The referent of ἐκ τούτου is disputed. According to Brown the reference point is to be found in 3:24c (ἐν τούτῳ).[61] This would allow one to interpret vv. 1–6 as a unit: the confession and nonconfession of the different spirits (vv. 2–3) is followed by the description of the relationship of those spirits to the world (vv. 4–6). The contrast of the two spirits (v. 6c), however, takes us beyond the foundation so confidently given to the parenesis in 3:24, according to which the Spirit is a divine gift to the community. Even if in the last analysis it is a matter of a single certitude, namely, of having the Spirit (3:24d) and being from God (4:6a), in that case ἐκ τούτου more properly refers to what has immediately preceded (v. 5). Hearing or not hearing the message is the proper criterion of recognition by which the spirits are to be distinguished.[62] That the word is accepted or rejected makes clear where the border between the territories of the spirit of truth and the spirit of error runs. Hence it can be applied to the relationship between the community and false teaching. Where the community of Jesus Christ is, there the spirit of truth reigns.[63] But where the community is divided by false teachers, the reign of the "spirit of error" (πνεῦμα τῆς πλάνης)[64] is expanding, for the false prophets, who do not confess Jesus Christ in the same sense as the community does (vv. 2–3) and who do not abide in the teaching of Jesus Christ (2 John 9), are nothing other than representatives of the spirit of error.

The distinction between the spirit of truth and the spirit of error, found only here in the Johannine writings, is the climax and conclusion of this section (vv. 1–6), and therefore an essential part of the author's polemic against false teachers. It provides a fundamental perspective from which to view the preceding warning to test the spirits (v. 1) and places it within the context of Johannine dualism. While the false prophets are regarded as representatives of the antichrist (2:18, 22; 2 John 7), and while they appear, according to primitive Christian ideas, as signs of the end time (cf. 2 John 7; Matt 24:11 par.), they were not originally identical with Satan.[65] It is true that Satan can also be called "the deceiver" (Rev 12:9; *Did.* 16.4) or "the tempter" (Mark 1:13 par.), but his appearance is not limited to the time immediately before the end. The author of 1 John distinguishes between antichrist and διάβολος since, although the latter is assigned sin as his realm (3:8, 10) and works within sin as "the evil one" (2:13–14), he is not connected with false teaching as its originator.

The notion of "being deceived" into sin by demons (*1 Enoch* 10.7–16; 64.2) or into idolatry and apostasy (*1 Enoch* 8.1–3; 19.1) belongs to the world of apocalyptic Judaism. In the Qumran literature it took shape in a way that is analogous to the text under consideration,[66] because there the contrast of the

61 Brown, *Epistles*, 500.

62 Thus also Schnackenburg, *Epistles*, 205; and Wengst, *Brief*, 176. Obviously, hearing is here identical with confessing (see above, on v. 2).

63 Cf. 3:24; on ἀλήθεια, see above (on 1:6, 8; 2:4; and 2:21). For de la Potterie the true function of the πνεῦμα τῆς ἀληθείας consists in awakening faith in Christ. Thus the author insists particularly on the ecclesial manifestation of faith: the witness of disciples, confession of faith, submission to apostolic authority (*La vérité*, 1.281–328, esp. 309).

64 The word πλάνη ("error") appears 10 times in the NT, but only once in the Johannine writings; the verb πλανᾶν is more common; cf. 1:8, 2:26; 3:7; John 7:12, 47; on this, see Otto Böcher, *EDNT* 3 (1993) 100 ("this reflects both intramural Jewish polemic against heretics and the process of Christian separation from Judaism"). While one might put counterquestions to such a historical arrangement, in any case this passage is to be interpreted within the framework of the underlying Johannine dualism; cf. also Herbert Braun, "πλανάω," *TDNT* 6 (1968) 246–47: "πλανᾶν and πλάνη are not of the ἀλήθεια (1:8; 4:6). They take place in the sphere of ἀλήθεια and ψεῦδος (2:21f., 27), of φῶς and σκοτία (1:5–7; 2:11), of θάνατος and ζωή (3:14) and do not belong intrinsically to the community (2:19). Error is the opposite of ἀλήθεια, the divine reality . . . these false teachers are metaphysical figures."

65 See the excursus below, "The Antichrist."

66 The suggestion that the teaching on the two spirits in the Qumran writings has an Iranian background has been disputed with renewed vigor in recent years: cf. P. Wernberg-Møller, "A reconsideration of the two spirits in the rule of the community (1 Q Serek III, 13–IV, 26)," *RQ* 3 (1961) 413–41; Marco Treves, "The two spirits of the rule of the community," *RevQ* 3 (1961) 449–52. Peter von den Osten-Sacken (*Gott und Belial* [SUNT 6; Göttingen: Vandenhoeck & Ruprecht, 1969] 139–41) points to the intimate kinship between 1QS iii.13—iv.14 and the most closely related passage in the *Gatha* (*Yasna* 30.3: "Yes, there are two fundamental spirits, twins which are renowned to be in conflict. In thought and in word,

children of light and of darkness (1QS iii.20–21) is traced to the difference between the "spirits of truth and falsehood" (1QS iii.18–19). The seduction of the children of righteousness is the work of the latter, and it is the cause of their sins and iniquities (1QS iii.21–22; 1QH vii.11–12). The parallel to our text is quite evident, since here also the spirits of truth and of falsehood are understood as phenomena of the end time. It is true that the Qumran sect affirmed that God was the creator of both spirits and thus asserted a limited predestinarianism (1QS iii.25), while in 1 John the mythological powers are interpreted historically. Moreover, in the Qumran literature the two angelic beings, Michael and Belial, are engaged in an eschatological struggle with one another and represent an ethical dualism that finds its place "in human hearts."[67] In contrast, the author of 1 John interprets the battle of the two spirits not in an ethical sense but in terms of the contrast between the teaching of the false prophets and the confession of the community.[68]

The *Testaments of the Twelve Patriarchs* includes a teaching about two spirits that, like those in the Qumran texts, appear against one another in an eschatological battle and, as forces of destiny, rule over human beings: the spirit of truth and the spirit of error, between which the human spirit of understanding must decide (*T. Jud.* 20.1). Beliar, as the spirit of error, leads humans astray, causing them to act against the Law and to fall into sin (*T. Jud.* 14.8; 19.4; 23.1; *T. Sim.* 3.1). He will be destroyed at the end of time when the salvation of the people is accomplished (*T. Jud.* 25.3). Similarly, the contrast in 1 John 4:6 is not to be explained in terms of a polemical, antignostic situation,[69] no matter how much it reflects something like that. Its background is the world of apocalyptic ideas as found in the Qumran literature and in the Christian-edited *Testaments of the Twelve Patriarchs* and here incorporated into the polemic against the false prophets.[70]

---

in action, they are two: the good and the bad" [S. Insler, *The Gāthrās of Zarathustra* (Acta Iranica 8; Textes et Mémoires 1; Paris: Édition Bibliothèque Pahlavi; Leiden: Brill, 1975) 33]); however, he excludes any direct dependency, especially since it would present "difficulties" for a Jew "to incorporate the idea of a dualistic separation of creation" (idem, 139). For a recent and exhaustive discussion of 1QS iii.13—iv.26, see Hermann Lichtenberger, *Studien zum Menschenbild in Texten der Qumrangemeinde* (SUNT 15; Göttingen: Vandenhoeck & Ruprecht, 1980) 123–42 (with bibliography).

67 1QS iv.23; possibly a secondary addition: so Osten-Sacken, *Gott und Belial*, 170–84.

68 1 John 4:1–6. On the question whether the opponents in 1 John represented a libertinistic concept, see above, p. 75. In the broader religio-historical horizon (cf. also Windisch and Preisker, *Die Katholischen Briefe*, on 1 John 4:3) one should also consider the Pauline eschatological contrast of *σάρξ* and *πνεῦμα*; it is close to the statements in 1QS iv.20–21, 23, where, however, "flesh" is not set in opposition to the "Holy Spirit" of God and is not understood as a power of the evil one; cf. Georg Strecker, "Befreiung und Rechtfertigung," in *Eschaton und Historie* (Göttingen: Vandenhoeck & Ruprecht, 1979) 24; Robert Jewett, *Paul's Anthropological Terms* (AGSU 10; Leiden: Brill, 1971) 82ff.

69 This is said against Schnackenburg, *Epistles*, 205. According to him, 1 John 2:4 ("I have come to know him") is a gnostic slogan opposed by the author under a moral aspect (accusation of lying), while in the present verse he turns to the "question of faith."

70 In addition to the text passages and secondary literature mentioned in the previous notes, cf. also *T. Reub.* 2.1: "And now listen to me, children, [and I will tell you] what I saw concerning the seven spirits of error when I repented. Seven spirits were appointed by Beliar against [humanity], and they are responsible for what [they do] when young." See, in contrast, *T. Naph.* (from the Hebrew chronicle of Jerahmeel XXXVIII, 15): "Blessed is the man who does not defile the Divine spirit which hath been put and breathed into him, and blessed is he who returns it as pure as it was on the day when it was entrusted to (him by his) Creator" (translation by Moses Gaster, *The Chronicles of Jerahmeel, or, The Hebrew Bible Historiale* [Oriental Translation Fund, n.s. 4; London: Royal Asiatic Society, 1899] 93–94); also *T. Dan* 5.5; *Adam and Eve (Vita)* 12; Jas 4:5; *Herm. Vis.* 3.7.1, 3; Herbert Braun, *Qumran und das Neue Testament* (2 vols.; Tübingen: Mohr [Siebeck], 1966) 1.131, 297–300; 2.123–24.

Section V: 1 John 4:7–5:4a	Parenesis: The Love of God Revealed in the Son Obliges Us to Love Our Brothers and Sisters[1]

General Comment

In this section the theme of love for the brothers and sisters, already treated in 2:7–11; 3:10–18, 23, is taken up again and extended.[2] At the same time, the relationship of this section to what has gone before should not be defined in such a way as to indicate that everything essential had already been said in 2:7–11 and what follows is only an echo.[3] Instead, one may say that 2:7–11 is the prelude, announcing the basic theme by speaking of the old and simultaneously new commandment of love for the sisters and brothers, and this is next made concrete in 3:10–18, 23 when that love is clarified through the negative example of Cain (v. 12) and then interpreted as having been realized in Christ's surrender of his own life and in human readiness to do the same (v. 17), and as simultaneously a social obligation (v. 17), hence as a human action (v. 18). In a third movement, then, the present passage represents the melding of love for God and for the brothers and sisters. The outline also indicates that this section carries the theme beyond where it previously stood: the author begins with the absolute concept of ἀγάπη, referring it to mutual love (vv. 7–8), then speaks of God's love for us as revealed in the Christ event (vv. 9–10), and by a combination of "indicative and imperative" focuses on the connection between love of God and love of the sisters and brothers (vv. 11–12). Here the indicative has a pneumatological (v. 13), a christological (vv. 14–15), and an anthropological (v. 16) application. In the present, *agapē* is subject to an eschatological restriction and looks toward final fulfillment at the end (vv. 17–18). It is therefore all the more to be understood as an obligation resulting from God's *agapē*-actions, an obligation owed both to God and to Christian sisters and brothers (vv. 19–21). This kind of conjoining of the two loves finds its place within the field of tension whose poles are *pistis* and *agapē* (5:1); its goal is a proper attitude toward the τέκνα τοῦ θεοῦ. It is in this particular way that love reveals itself as the appropriate response to God's commandments (5:2–4a).

1 Literature: N. H. Cassem, "A Grammatical and Contextual Inventory of the Use of κόσμος in the Johannine Corpus with Some Implications for a Johannine Cosmic Theology," *NTS* 19 (1972/73) 81–91; John V. Dahms, "The Johannine Use of Monogenēs Reconsidered," *NTS* 29 (1983) 222–32; André Feuillet, "Dieu est Amour," *EeV* 81 (1971) 534–48; P. W. van der Horst, "A Wordplay in 1 Joh 4:12?" *ZNW* 63 (1972) 280–82; Marinus de Jonge, "Beloved, let us love one another, for love is of God (1 Jn 4,7)," *NedThT* 22 (1968) 352–67; Rudolf Kittler, "Erweis der Bruderliebe an der Bruderliebe? Versuch der Auslegung eines 'fast unverständlichen' Satzes im 1. Johannesbrief," *KD* 16 (1970) 223–28; Eduard Schweizer, "Zum religionsgeschichtlichen Hintergrund der 'Sendungsformel.' Gal 4,4f, Röm 8,3f, Joh 3,16f, 1 Joh 4,9," *ZNW* 57 (1966) 199–210; Ceslas Spicq, "Notes d'exégèse johannique: La charité est amour manifeste," *RB* 65 (1958) 358–70.

2 Cf. Schnackenburg, *Epistles*, 207 ("The initial challenge . . . is not meant to open up a discussion of the special theme of mutual love. For the heart of what the author is about to deal with comes out only in the ensuing *hoti*-clause. This places love (*hē agapē*) in the center, though in quite general terms"). In what follows, I will show that ordinary *agapē* is expressed in love for God and the brothers and sisters, and that the emphasis in this section lies on the latter (v. 21).

3 Against Bultmann, *Epistles*, 2–3, where he says that 1:5—2:27 was originally an independent writing to which, at a later time, individual units were secondarily added (see the remarks on 1:5 above).

4 Love of the Brothers and Sisters and Love of God

7 Beloved, let us love one another, because love is from God; everyone who loves is born of God and knows God. 8/ Whoever does not love does not know God, for God is love. 9/ God's love was revealed among us in this way: God sent [God's] only Son into the world so that we might live through him. 10/ In this is love, not that we loved God but that God loved us and sent [God's] Son to be the atoning sacrifice for our sins.

■ **7** The following section reveals a meditative progression of thought, but no clearly defined subsections;[1] hence there is no reason to describe vv. 7–10 as a hymnic unit.[2] The address ἀγαπητοί ("beloved") resumes the address at 4:1 and is therefore the expression of deliberate attention to Christian readers, corresponding to ὑμεῖς ("you") in 4:4. This is not contradicted by the fact that, in the following section, the presentation is in the first person plural, for ἡμεῖς (vv. 9–10, 11, and frequently) describes the ecclesial "we," expressed also in the verb forms associated with it. The parenetic character of the section is underscored by admonitions couched in wisdom language. The expressions with πᾶς (4:7; 5:1, 4a) or ὅς (4:15), as well as the participial constructions (4:8a, 18b, 20b) recall similar linguistic forms in the wisdom literature.[3] These show that the author is not interested in continuing a "discussion with the false teachers,"[4] but instead wishes to describe the realization of the spirit of truth in the community's *agapē* as a goal worth striving for. Accordingly, ἀγαπῶμεν should not be read as an indicative, "we do love" (although that is grammatically possible), but as an imperative, "let us love."[5] The injunction to love one another is nothing other than a repetition of the commandment of love of the sisters and brothers as enunciated in 3:10–11.[6] On this basis, one cannot easily deny that this section truly begins with the injunction to love the sisters and brothers.[7] It is true that the following ὅτι clause does not take up this admonition, which first reappears expressly at 4:10–11. Instead, it speaks only of the ἀγάπη that is from God, adding the absolute "the one who loves" (ὁ ἀγαπῶν),[8] so that *agapē* first appears in its ordinary sense.[9] Here, by preceding "love" with "from God" (ἐκ τοῦ θεοῦ), the author establishes a link with v. 6: being from God determines the nature of the community, as does *agapē.* Only by denying its point of origin could the community depart from *agapē.* "The real Christian is one who loves."[10] This is

1 The same is true of vv. 17–18, where Bultmann (*Epistles,* 72–73) sees redactional interventions; however, in spite of their specific terminology these verses correspond quite consistently with their context. On this, see below on 4:17–18.

2 Contrary to the division of the text in Nestle-Aland[26], there are no real parallelisms; the positing of three lines in vv. 9–10 is also unfounded, as is the blank space in the text at the end of v. 14 and the paragraph break before v. 16b.

3 For this wisdom language see, e.g., Prov 8:36. For the construction with πᾶς cf. also 1 John 2:23, 29; 3:3–5; 5:18, analogous constructions with ὅς are also found in 2:5; 3:17.

4 Bultmann, *Epistles,* 65.

5 It thus corresponds not only to what follows (v. 11), but also to the preceding parenetical section (3:23); on this problem, see also the remarks on 4:19.

6 Cf. 2:10; 3:14 and (for ἀλλήλους) 3:23; 4:11–12; 2 John 5.

7 See n. 2 above; in opposition, Smalley (*1, 2, 3 John,* 237) emphasizes the absolute character of *agapē.* But see also Bultmann, *Epistles,* 66 ("There is certainly no love without a vis-à-vis"). Brown (*Epistles,* 514) draws love's boundaries at the limits of the Christian community.

8 Codex A inserts the accusative object τὸν θεὸν—undoubtedly a secondary clarification which reveals that the copyist applied the word to the love of God.

9 The absolute use of ἀγάπη had already appeared in 3:1, 16; cf. also in the following text 4:8, 10, 16–18; see, in addition, 2 John 6.

10 Schnackenburg, *Epistles,* 207.

true without reservation. Love of the brothers and sisters is part of the comprehensive love that is the mark of Christian existence. This is expressed by the generalizing πᾶς. "Everyone" who loves (whether the love be directed to God or to fellow human beings) is one of those who are born of God, just as, in turn, "being born of God"—as the parallel in v. 7b (ἐκ τοῦ θεοῦ ἐστιν) makes clear[11] —is identical with "being from God" and expresses itself as *agapē*.

The ontological descriptions ("being from God" and "being born of God") could invite one to ascribe an objectifiable nature to *agapē*. However, the sphere of *agapē*[12] is not a magical phenomenon. Instead, so far as it includes human beings, it presupposes that human actions are marked by accountability. This is clear from the last clause of the verse: καὶ γινώσκει τὸν θεόν does not refer to a theoretical "knowing" or "understanding" (thus 4:2; 5:2), but to "acknowledging God." Christians who make love a reality recognize or acknowledge God by that very fact (2:13–14; cf. 5:20), while the world demonstrates its denial of God by its lovelessness (3:1, 6, 13). That the Christian is addressed as one who is responsible for his or her own actions is evident from the combination of "knowing" (γινώσκειν) with "keeping the commandments" (τὰς ἐντολὰς αὐτοῦ τηρεῖν). Whoever acknowledges God keeps God's commandments (2:3–6), and before all others the commandment of *agapē* (2:7–11).

■ **8** The author takes up the end of v. 7 with an antithesis: ὁ μὴ ἀγαπῶν οὐκ ἔγνω τὸν θεόν.[13] While this is not a chiastic construction,[14] it is closely tied to the preceding verse by the verb γινώσκειν. As the one who loves is the one who knows and acknowledges God, so "the one who does not love" is the one who does not "know" or "acknowledge" God. The aorist οὐκ ἔγνω may be intended to articulate the particularly strong negation in the statement that one who does not love has not arrived at such knowledge.[15] The sequence of present and aorist verb forms is also found at 3:1 (cf. 1 Cor 8:2). That Codex A has the present οὐ γινώσκει is not sufficient reason for an absolute rejection of the possibility that here is something rare in the NT, namely, a gnomic aorist. In any case the author intends to make a statement of general validity: on the one hand, lovelessness characterizes the human being in relation to God, while on the other hand (and the tendency of this statement corresponds to the immediate parenetical context), the one who acknowledges God is one who loves and must behave in the way that is appropriate for one who loves. A similar statement was made in 3:6 with reference to sin: sin and knowledge of God are mutually exclusive. Just as there the line of division between the children of God and the children of the devil was clearly drawn (cf. 3:1, 10), here also it is true that the one who does not love belongs to the world and has no community with God.

The clause "God is love" (ὁ θεὸς ἀγάπη ἐστίν) is joined to the preceding by a causal ὅτι, thereby giving the basis and rationale for v. 8a. The statement that "whoever does not love does not know God" is founded on the assertion that God is love. That loveless people do not acknowledge God, and consequently have no community with God (cf. 2:5), follows from the consideration that being from God is determined by *agapē*. Thus at this point the author allows himself to be led into making a statement about the being of God, a statement that is often taken as an abbreviated summary of Christian theology. In fact, a religio-historical investigation shows that the religions that existed in the environment of primitive Christianity did not speak of God in this way.

Excursus: ʼΑγάπη

The word ἀγάπη is not a Christian creation, nor are its derivatives. Even though its origins in Greek are not absolutely clear,[16] it can occasionally be demonstrated in prebiblical Greek. The verb ἀγαπᾶν is particularly well-attested, as describing the relationship of

11 Parallel placement represents a statement of identity in 3:9–10 as well; cf. also 2:29 (ἐξ αὐτοῦ γεγέννηται) with 3:1 (τέκνα θεοῦ . . . ἐσμέν) and 3:9 (σπέρμα αὐτοῦ ἐν αὐτῷ μένει).

12 On this, see 4:16.

13 The variant readings (οὐ γινώσκει τὸν θεὸν: A 33. 81. 623. 2464 al sy^h; οὐκ ἔγνωκεν τὸν θεόν: Ψ* [69]; οὐκ ἔγνωκεν: $ℵ^2$) are presumably secondary smoothings.

14 Against Brown, *Epistles*, 548: v. 8ab cannot be coupled with v. 7cd to form a chiasm, since nothing in v. 7c corresponds to v. 8b ("God is love").

15 Cf. Schnackenburg, *Epistles*, 207–8; Brown, *Epistles*, 515; Smalley, *1, 2, 3 John*, 239.

16 Another opinion is expressed by Eric Peterson ("ʼΑγάπη," *BZ* 20 [1932] 378–82), who regarded the instances adduced by Hans Lietzmann (*An die*

superiors to inferiors.[17] This kind of "descending" love is also predicated of the deity with respect to mortal human beings.[18] It is especially significant that the word *agapē* is attested apparently as a cultic name for the fertility goddess Isis. This divinity of the Egyptian mysteries is celebrated as the foundress of love.[19] The

Korinther I, II [HNT 9; 3d ed.; Tübingen: Mohr (Siebeck), 1931] 68), Ethelbert Stauffer ("ἀγαπάω," *TDNT* 1 [1964] 37–38), and Walter Bauer (BAGD 4–5) as utterly uncertain and held it to be "quite improbable . . . that the word ἀγάπη was created or used outside Christian-Jewish circles" ("'Αγάπη," 382); however, the noun has since been demonstrated to occur, without any doubt, in pagan Greek, on the basis of texts that at that time had not yet been studied, and from newer findings (see the examples in BAGD 5). Cf. esp. Oda Wischmeyer, "Vorkommen und Bedeutung von Agape in der ausserchristlichen Antike," *ZNW* 69 (1978) 212–38; according to this article the oldest instances are nonliterary attestations of the woman's name 'Αγάπη from the sixth and fifth centuries BCE. Like Στοργή and Φιλία, 'Αγάπη is said to be an "abstract name" whose origin presupposes the existence of the noun ἀγάπη (pp. 226–27). From the fact that one of these oldest instances reflects the name of a *hetaera* one could conclude that ἀγάπη "as 'love' in a similarly generalized, erotically conceived sense as in the parallel names Στοργή and Φιλία lay behind it" (p. 237).

17 Thus, for example, with respect to foreigners: Homer *Od.* 8.33; ἀγαπητός refers to the (only) beloved son of his parents: Homer *Il.* 6.409; *Od.* 2.365, and frequently.

18 Thus the god demonstrates love for mortals by honoring them with a visitation: Homer *Il.* 24.464; also *CIG* 5119; Dio Chrysostom *Or.* 33.21.

19 It is true that the passages here adduced from P. Oxy. 1380, a text that has become known as the "Isis Litany," stemming from the second century CE, are controversial. According to the edition of Bernard Pyne Grenfell and Arthur Surridge Hunt (*The Oxyrhynchus Papyri XI* [London: Egypt Exploration Fund, 1915] 196, 198) one should read ἐν Θῶνι ἀγάπ[ην . . .] in lines 27–28, and ἐν 'Ιταλίᾳ ἀ[γά]πην θεῶν in lines 109–10. This would mean that the goddess Isis was addressed in Thonis as ἀγάπη, and in Italy as ἀγάπη θεῶν. But this reading has been disputed, since only three letters in each of the words completed by the editors can be clearly identified. The sharpest critic of the interpretation of these passages as evidence for the extra-Christian occurrence of ἀγάπη is Eric Peterson; however, in his criticism he proceeded on the no longer tenable assumption that the word is not to be found anywhere in extrabiblical literature ("'Αγάπη," 382). Even among scholars who acknowledge P. Oxy. 1380 as an instance of the extra-Christian appearance of ἀγάπη there is great uncertainty in detail: Ethelbert Stauffer ("ἀγαπάω," *TDNT* 1 [1964] 38) accepts G. Manteuffel's conjecture for line 109, reading ἐν 'Ιταλίᾳ ἀ[γα]θὴν ἄθολον (*Revue de philologie* 54 [1928] 163), but thinks "there can be little doubt" about ἀγάπην in line 28 on the basis of the parallel with φιλίαν in line 94. Colin H. Roberts came to the opposite conclusion (*JEA* 39 [1953] 114) on the basis of a personal examination of the originals. While regarding ἀγάπην in line 28 as doubtful and considering the readings ἀγάπησιν or ἀγαθήν more probable, he believes one should follow Grenfell and Hunt's reconstruction of line 109; the initial ἀ in the word read as ἀγάπην does not even deserve to be marked as doubtful. Most of the more recent scholars have followed him, so that the controversy carried on in the pages of *JTS* over a period of years between Stephanie West and R. E. Witt (*JTS* 18 [1967] 142–43; 19 [1968] 209–11; 20 [1969] 228–30; summarized by J. Gwyn Griffiths, *JTS* 29 [1978] 147–51) revolved around line 109, especially the religio-historical possibilities of the readings ἀγάπη θεῶν or ἀγαθὴ θεός as titles for Isis. Isis was venerated in late antiquity as a universal deity, as "una quae es omnia dea Isis" (*ILS* 4362), and was equated with various Eastern and Greek divinities; she could be described as the "one with a thousand names" (μυρόνυμα). Cf. Johannes Leipoldt and Walter Grundmann, *Umwelt des Urchristenums* (3 vols.; Berlin: Evangelische Verlagsanstalt, 1965–67) 1.123–24. She was identified with Demeter (= "Bona Dea") and also with Aphrodite, so that "there are connections both to a title such as ἀγάπη θεῶν and to ἀγαθὴ θεός" (Wischmeyer, "Vorkommen und Bedeutung," 220–21). It is true, however, that in both cases we are dealing with a single occurrence. Even if one were not to describe line 109 as a definite instance, "because of the unsatisfactory tradition and because of the additional difficulty of translating ἀγάπην θεῶν in a meaningful way" (Wischmeyer, "Vorkommen und Bedeutung," 220–21), such a title is not improbable, in view of other predications: φιλία in line 94 and φιλόστοργος in lines 12 and 131, as well as the instances in which Isis appears as the subject of ἐρᾶν (*CIG* 5119 and Ludwig Mitteis and Ulrich Wilcken, *Grundzüge und Chrestomathie der Papyruskunde* [Berlin/Leipzig: Teubner, 1912] 109, 112). This also corresponds to the use of στέργειν with regard to Isis in the aretalogy of Cyme, 19–20, 27 (published by Werner Peek, "Hymnus in Isim

semantic field as a whole is certainly not widely attested. It is less frequent than the equivalent terms ἐρᾶν, φιλεῖν, and στέργειν. There is in it none of the natural drive of "ascending" Eros, which in the Dionysian religion brings human beings to an ecstatic union with the deity, while in Platonic and post-Platonic philosophy it withdraws from the world of the senses and becomes a measure of the truly Beautiful and Good.[20] In contrast, ἀγαπᾶν had a rather narrow significance in Greek culture. It can be translated by the relatively colorless expressions "to be satisfied with something" or "to honor someone."[21] The NT usage is far removed from such a pale type of expression. Hence, to understand the background of the NT concept of *agapē*, it is necessary to look to the non-Greek world of ideas.

The Septuagint translates Hebrew אהב with the verb ἀγαπᾶν.[22] Here, unlike in Greek literature, "love" has a distinctive, exclusive meaning, and the concept often achieves a specific keenness by its opposition to "hatred": as the king of Israel "love[s] righteousness and hate[s] wickedness" (MT Ps 45:8[ET 7] = LXX 44:8), so also the Lord "love[s] justice . . . hate[s] robbery and wrongdoing" (Isa 61:8). Here it is already evident that in the LXX ἀγαπᾶν is universally applied to the actions of God and human beings and that no field of divine or human affection is excluded. Thus sexual love is described by the word ἀγαπᾶν (Hos 3:1; 4:18; Jer 2:25; Ezek 16:37), but so is the love of friends in a nonsexual sense. For example, the friendship between Jonathan and David can be characterized by the word ἀγάπησις.[23] Not least is this true of ethical consideration for fellow human beings, as expressed in the fundamental ethical demand, "you shall love your neighbor as yourself" (Lev 19:18).

The OT doctrine of God is not shaped by the idea of "love," but rather by the idea of YHWH-God's choosing of the people of Israel. That choosing can, however, be interpreted as an act of God's love toward God's people: "It was because the Lord loved you and kept the oath that he swore to your ancestors, that the Lord has brought you out with a mighty hand, and redeemed you from the house of slavery, from the hand of Pharaoh king of Egypt" (Deut 7:8). As YHWH has been revealed as a lover through the saving deliverance of the people from their captivity in Egypt, the prophet Hosea is able to describe YHWH's relationship to the people in a marital image (2:16–20). This same picture was taken up by the later prophets (Jer 2:2; Isa 62:4–5). In Deuteronomy it is combined with ethical teaching: the people Israel is to act lovingly toward its God (Deut 6:5) and to keep God's commandments (Deut 20:12; cf. Exod 20:6). This anticipates the fundamental structures of the NT understanding of *agapē*. In the OT, however, "love" does not yet—as will be the case later in Judaism and in the NT—function as a summary principle comprehending all the commandments. Instead, the OT love commandment is on a level with a great many other admonitions. A further step in the direction of the NT is taken by the literature of Hellenistic Judaism outside the Septuagint. Here one may distinguish a threefold development of meaning:[24]

1. Love of one human being for another: described, for example, in the *Letter of Aristeas*, written in the second century BCE, as "the gift of God" and as "the strength (τὸ δυνατόν) of devotion (εὐσέβεια)."[25] Alongside the love of one human for another stands

2. the love of human beings for God. According to Philo of Alexandria, this is a turning toward God as the "Existent One"; through it a human being overcomes all fear and receives access to true life.[26] Finally, *agapē* appears

3. as the love of God for human beings, whereby the

Andrius" [diss., Berlin, 1929] 18–20; ET in Ross S. Kraemer, ed., *Maenads, Martyrs, Matrons, Monastics: A Sourcebook on Women's Religions in the Greco-Roman World* [Philadelphia: Fortress, 1988] 367–68), and the general characteristics of the goddess (on this, cf. Franz Cumont, *The Oriental Religions in Roman Paganism* [1911; reprinted New York: Dover, 1956] 72–102, esp. 89).

20 Cf. Ethelbert Stauffer, "ἀγαπάω," *TDNT* 1 (1964) 36 (with reference to the later humanistic cultivation of the concept of *eros* in Maximus and its mystical sublimation by Plotinus).

21 Ibid., 36.

22 The verb ἀγαπάω and related terms appear as follows in the LXX: ἀγαπάω 258 times (167 times for אהב); ἀγάπη 19 times (6 times for אהבה); ἀγάπησις 10 times (6 times for אהבה); ἀγαπητός 22 times (once for אהב).

23 2 Sam 1:26 (surpassing ἀγάπησις γυναικῶν).

24 Corresponding to this, in Greek culture touched by Stoicism the concept of φιλέω means (1) love of one human being for another in a "descending" sense (*Anthologia Graeca* 7.378.2: spouse; Pindar *Pyth.* 10.66: friends; Homer *Od.* 14.146; 15.370: masters and servants); (2) the love of the gods for human beings (Homer *Il.* 2.197; 16.94; *Od.* 15.245–46). In contrast, humans' love for God is not described as φιλέω.

25 *Ep. Arist.* 229 (ἀγάπη).

26 Philo *Deus imm.* 69; cf. *Migr. Abr.* 169; Wis 3:9; Philo *Fragments* (in John of Damascus), cited by Jacobus Wettstein, *Novum Testamentum Graecum* (2 vols.; 1751–52; reprinted Graz: Akademische Druck und Verlagsanstalt, 1962) 2.715, on 1 John 2:15 (= Thomas Mangey, ed., *Philonis Judae Opera* [4 vols.;

original character of *agapē* as a "descending love" comes to expression, because God bows down in love to God's people and promises them the advent of God's anointed, the Messiah (*Ps. Sol.* 18.4–9). God's love is shown also in the gift of the Torah, which reveals God's wisdom; it was created before the world and is promised not only to the chosen people of Israel but to all humanity (Prov 8:22). Hence God's love is identical with the mercy God shows toward "the whole earth" (*Ps. Sol.* 18.3).

This divine gift is expressed in a multitude of individual admonitions, for all of which rational explanations are given. Jewish wisdom literature in particular, revealing even in its initial phases some Greek influences,[27] is marked by an ethical, rationalist vocabulary. Its teachings are motivated by reasoned considerations, such as the idea of a reward for righteous persons even in this world. Here one finds the commandment to do good to one's enemies, which anticipates the NT teaching. The reason given is not only the idea of reward but also the statement: "you will heap coals of fire on their heads," that is, you will make a friend of your enemy (Prov 25:22). Paul adopted this saying in the parenesis in Romans (Rom 12:20). In the *Letter of Aristeas*, also, the recommendation to the Egyptian king that he willingly show favor to his enemies has a utilitarian dimension, for in this way the ruler will be able to lead his subordinates back to their duty and win them to his own service (*Ep. Arist.* 227).

As in Judaism and in Greek culture, so especially in the NT writings we are familiar with the motif of the "descending love" of God.[28] This love manifests itself in the death of Jesus Christ on the cross. Paul attests this, in harmony with older Christian tradition, when he writes: "God proves his love for us in that while we still were sinners Christ died for us" (Rom 5:8). God's love is not merely an abstract idea, something conceivable, nor is it to be attained through a mystical indwelling. It happens in a historical event, in the crucifixion and death of Jesus of Nazareth. A historical fact creates the relationship between God and human beings, the relationship that opens for humanity the fullness of God and the goal of life. At the end of the believers' journey stands that which has been promised to them, which they will experience: that God will be all in all.[29] In the immediately preceding text, Paul indicates that Christians, through faith in the word that has been proclaimed and in the effectiveness of baptism, have received the Spirit of God, and that the gift of the Spirit means an outpouring of the love of God in human hearts.[30] Therefore the members of the Christian communities in the early days of the church could be given the common title ἀγαπητοί, those "beloved" of God (1 Thess 1:4; cf. Col 3:12). They are loved by God because God has revealed the divine love in the Son, and because this love is handed on in baptism and appropriated by a faith-filled listening to the word of God.

Eschatological salvation is experienced not only in the Christian community's believing acceptance of the love of God in Jesus Christ, but by no means least in the way in which it responds to the gift of divine love by its own love for God. Paul describes this relationship of believers to God with the words, "We know that all things work together for good for those who love God, who are called according to God's purpose" (Rom 8:28). The love of God for human persons is identical with "God's purpose." It points backward to a divine decision, before all time, for the salvation of humanity. This election, already given to human beings and furnishing the reason for their existence, must have a determining influence on human lives: the electing love of God causes human beings to turn to God in

London: Bowyer, 1742] 2.649).

27 For example, Proverbs 1—9; Artur Weiser, *Einleitung*. ET: *The Old Testament: Its Formation and Development*. Trans. Dorothea M. Barton (New York: Association Press, 1961), 296–97.

28 Central examples of "descending love" in the NT are Rom 5:5–11; 8:32, 39; John 3:16; cf. also below.

29 Cf. 1 Cor 15:28. In spite of this apparently pantheistic formulation, Paul stands within the current of Jewish eschatological tradition, in which one expects to find not an identification of God with the universe at the end of time, but rather the future, final exercise of God's sovereign power, as Conzelmann correctly emphasized (*1 Corinthians*, 274–75). This distinguishes NT thought from the ideas of Zen Buddhism, according to which perfection consists in recognizing "one in all and all in one" (cf. the brief but penetrating description by Helmut Thielicke, *Zu Gast*. ET: *Notes from a Wayfarer: The Autobiography of Helmut Thielicke* (New York: Paragon House, 1995).

30 Rom 5:5 ("because God's love has been poured into our hearts through the Holy Spirit that has been given to us"); cf. also John 3:16 ("for God so loved the world . . . "); 1 John 4:9 ("God's love was revealed among us in this way: God sent his only Son into the world so that we might live through him").

love and, in that turning to God, to experience assurance and confidence.[31]

If the Christian community is the communion of those who, as beloved of God, reciprocate that love, their attitude can also express itself as love for Jesus Christ. For what is offered to the Son of God is also directed to his Father, something that is attested especially in the Johannine writings: "Jesus said to them, 'If God were your Father, you would love me; for I came from God'" (John 8:42; cf. 1 Pet 1:8). Love of God is, at the same time, love of Jesus Christ. The believer acknowledges the unity of Father and Son (John 10:30: "The Father and I are one"). If believers manifest ascending *agapē* as the response to the descending love of God bestowed on them, that *agapē* is extended at one and the same time to the Father and the Son.

This is a sketch of the fundamental dogmatic content of ἀγάπη in the NT, where it applies both to the relationship of God to human beings and to the relationship of human beings to God. It is evident that this relationship cannot be adequately described in mystical categories, for the revelation of God in Jesus Christ is a personal event. The consequence of this is that human beings who, through faith in God's revelation in Jesus Christ, understand themselves as those who are beloved of God, at the same time understand that they are personal beings who are responsible in and for God's world.

The statement "God is love" is something special to Johannine theology.[32] The closest correspondence to it occurs in ontological statements such as "God is light" (1 John 1:5) or "God is spirit" (John 4:24). The *egō eimi* ("I am") sayings of the Johannine Christ constitute a further christological parallel.[33] These statements of identity are not to be understood as definitions in the philosophical sense. They are not an attempt to speak objectively about God, but must be interpreted from their material and literary context. Nonetheless, our text should not be explained purely from the perspective of v. 7b ("Love is from God").[34] Instead, v. 8b takes us beyond the statement that all love that is found in the world ultimately comes from God. Here, surpassing v. 7, in an abstract, theocentric formula that apparently implies no anthropological statement, the being that is fundamental to all things and all natures is described with the word *agapē*. That which precedes and transcends humanity and its history is love!

This statement thus by no means presents a definition of the concept of "God" that would assign that concept its appropriate place in a philosophical or theological system. Yet it is equally true that the statement cannot be understood to represent a tautology in which the subject, ὁ θεός, would be identical with the predicate, ἀγάπη ἐστίν. That would contradict the author's intention, which is to demonstrate what is obligatory for human beings, as well as the fact that the word ἀγάπη existed in the NT environment, and is not a creation of the Johannine school or of primitive Christianity. In adopting a concept from the linguistic environment, the author indicates the proper location of the God of whom he speaks. He immediately clarifies this in what follows, by attesting to the revelation of the love of God (v. 9). Since this is not a tautological statement, it is not reversible. It cannot be paraphrased by saying "Love is God," or "Where love is, there is God."[35] The author did not intend to say that God, as a "kind of human fellowship," is simply an object for theological anthropology and ethics. Instead, Christians' ethical actions presuppose the reality of God's *agapē*. It is all-embracing and bestowed on human beings from the outset, but it is not solipsistically related to itself. This text has no intention of describing an inner-trinitarian relationship.[36] What is

31 Cf. 2 Cor 3:4; Eph 3:12, and below at 4:9–10.

32 Cf. also André Feuillet ("Dieu est Amour," *EeV* 81 [1971] 536), according to whom the formula "God is love" is the high point of NT revelation. That it represents the "synthesis" of Johannine thought is said to be shown (but this is not unproblematic) especially in the division of the Fourth Gospel into two parts: chaps. 1—12 = the love of the Father for the Son; chaps. 13—21 = the love of Christ for human beings. The formula "God is love" does not reduce God to an abstract principle, but is to be understood dynamically. Every activity of God is inspired by love (543). This is the foundation for love of neighbor; for the same love that unites Father and Son will also unite human beings with the Father and Son and with one another, making them one (545).

33 Cf. John 6:35; 8:12; 11:25; 15:1.

34 This is said against Wengst, *Brief*, 179.

35 With Balz, "Johannesbriefe," 197–98; cf. also Smalley, *1, 2, 3 John*, 240; Marinus de Jonge, "Beloved, let us love one another, for love is of God (1 Jn 4,7)," *NedThT* 22 (1968) 352–67.

36 Brown (*Epistles*, 549) points out that according to the fourth evangelist's statement "God is love in himself"

important is, rather, that God has appeared as one who loves.[37]

■ **9** In v. 8, a general statement was made about the relationship between God and *agapē*. In what follows, that statement is anchored in earthly reality; a christological excursus will show that the fact that God is the one who loves can be experienced in the Son.[38] Ἐν τούτῳ ("in this way") appears four more times in the rest of the letter (4:10, 13, 17; 5:2) and here, as frequently elsewhere, relates to the following, explanatory ὅτι.[39] The verb φανεροῦν was already found at 1:2 and is used primarily as a christological term (also in 3:5, 8).[40] One could translate: the love of God has "appeared" or "been revealed." In any case the meaning is that the ἀγάπη τοῦ θεοῦ[41] is not an abstract idea but has accommodated itself to the human capacity to experience it. Love has entered history in the Son.

The author attests, with the expression ἐν ἡμῖν, that the love of God has become an object of human experience. The phrase can be interpreted as a dative ("to us" or "for us").[42] So in John 9:3 we read: "so that God's works might be revealed in him [the blind man]," or in 2 Cor 4:10: "so that the life of Jesus may also be made visible in our bodies." In each case the addressee of the revelation is described by ἐν with the dative.[43] The other possibility is a local usage ("among us"). This corresponds to the usual meaning of ἐν, which can also have a spatial meaning in regard to persons (cf. Gal 1:16: "among the Gentiles," as well as Matt 2:6; 1 Cor 2:6; 11:19b; 2 Cor 4:3). While the first possibility is not to be excluded, the

(cf. John 17:24: "because you loved me [the Son] before the foundation of the world"). But the Fourth Gospel has no statement that is identical with that in 1 John 4:8; and it leads one into unbiblical speculations if, with reference to the Johannine writings, one says that "God loves . . . Godself," or combines the statement "God loves Godself" with the thesis that God loves by nature (Eberhard Jüngel, *God as the Mystery of the World* [trans. Darrell L. Guder; Edinburgh: Clark; Grand Rapids: Eerdmans, 1983] 327, 368).

37 The tension between anthropocentric and theocentric exposition is evident in the dictum of Ludwig Feuerbach: "if we do not sacrifice God to love, we sacrifice love to God" (*The Essence of Christianity* [trans. George Eliot; New York: Harper, 1957] 53). For Feuerbach, the statement "God is love" represents the "clearest, most irrefragable proof that man in religion contemplates himself as the object of the Divine Being, as the end of the divine activity, that thus in religion he has relation only to his own nature, only to himself" (57). Cf. also Georg Wilhelm Friedrich Hegel, *Vorlesungen I: Die absolute Religion*, 75. ET: G.W.F. Hegel, *Lectures on the Philosophy of Religion I: Introduction and the Concepts of Religion*, ed. Peter C. Hodgson. Trans. R. F. Brown, P. C. Hodgson, and J. M. Stewart, with the assistance of J. P. Fitzer and H. S. Harris (Berkeley, Los Angeles, and London: University of California Press [1984]) 2 vols. 2:183–84.

38 Heinrich Schlier suspects here a fending off of gnostic ideas. In contrast to the docetic dissolution of the figure of the historical Jesus, it is emphasized that life has appeared in Christ and that in Jesus Christ it has become possible to experience God as love (*Ende der Zeit* [Freiburg: Herder, 1971] 125: "The Son is the life of love").

39 By contrast, in 3:10 ἐν τούτῳ relates to the preceding text (see above on 3:10).

40 Φανερόω: see above, 1:2; 2:19, 28; 3:2, 5, 8. In the Johannine literature γνωρίζω is used as a synonym (cf. John 17:6 with 17:26). It is a question of becoming visible to all eyes (John 7:4), or of Jesus' revealing the divine reality: God's name (17:6) or God's works (3:21; 9:3). Jesus' activity is described as revelation. Correspondingly, in 1 John Jesus' sending is understood as the revelation of the love of God (1 John 4:9; John 3:16). Its goal is that we may have life (ibid.), and the concept of ζωή can summarize the whole revelation (John 1:2). 1 John uses the same verb also for revelation that is still in the future (2:28; 3:2). Cf. Bultmann and Lührmann, "φανερόω," 5.

41 Ἀγάπη τοῦ θεοῦ is to be understood as a subjective genitive; cf. also 2:5 (q.v.).

42 Cf. ποιεῖν ἐν τινί: Matt 17:12; ἐργάζομαι ἐν τινί: Mark 14:6; also γένηται ἐν ἐμοί: 1 Cor 9:15; cf. Albrecht Oepke, "ἐν," *TDNT* 2 (1964) 538–40: with expressions of coming to know or making known, ἐν describes either the person who knows or the one who provides the knowledge. In the former case it is translated with the simple dative. Thus in Rom 1:19: φανερόν ἐστιν ἐν αὐτοῖς; Gal 1:16: ἀποκαλύψαι τὸν υἱὸν αὐτοῦ ἐν ἐμοί. Also in the vernacular usage in *Act. Thom.* 20 (by M. R. James, ed., *Texts and Studies* 5/1 [London: Thyateira House, 1987] 32, 17–18): εἰσῆλθεν πρὸς τὴν γυναῖκα τοῦ ἄρχοντος καὶ ἀνέγνω ἐν αὐτῇ τὸ εὐαγγέλιον τοῦ θεοῦ ("he read the gospel of God *to her*"); Herman Ljungvik, *Studien zur Sprache der apokryphen Apostelgeschichten* (Uppsala: Lundequistska Bokhandeln, 1926) 32; Winfred Elliger, "ἐν," *EDNT* 1 (1990) 447–49.

43 BDF § 220 (2); see also below, at 4:16a.

second appears to approximate the Johannine world of ideas more closely, since the revelation in the Son is similarly conceived in the Fourth Gospel as well (John 1:14: ἐσκήνωσεν ἐν ἡμῖν, "dwelt among us"). Furthermore, in v. 17 the demand of *agapē* can be expressed by μεθ ἡμῶν ("among us"), that is, in a spatial-personal sense. Such a sense is particularly evident in John 13:35: "By this everyone will know that you are my disciples, if you have love for one another (ἐν ἀλλήλοις)."

In connection with this question, which in the Johannine view by no means represents an absolute alternative, there arises the problem whether the author's use of the personal pronoun in the first person plural refers to the Christian community or to the world as object or place of revelation. That in any case the world cannot be excluded as the comprehensive horizon of revelation is evident from the statement that God sent his Son "into the world" (εἰς τὸν κόσμον, v. 9b), an expression closely paralleled in John 3:16 ("For God so loved the world . . . "). The sending of the Son happens in and for the world, that is, for all humanity. Therefore the Son of God can be called σωτὴρ τοῦ κόσμου ("savior of the world").[44] An expression like this is certainly not only universal in scope, setting forth the cosmic demand of revelation. It applies to the Christian community in a twofold fashion. First, it is formulated out of the community's confession of faith. Therefore, it is not an objective statement that can be separated from the person of the one who speaks it but presupposes the faith of the community in the saving significance of the Christ-event. In other words, it is "witness." Further (and second), the following passage makes clear that the demand of revelation is addressed not only to the world but continually, again and again, to the Christian community. The very expression "so that we might live through him" (ἵνα ζήσωμεν δι᾽ αὐτοῦ, v. 9c) raises the question whether the primary intent is to express the universal purpose of revelation (the life of all human beings), or the goal of the community (the eternal life of believers). What is certain is that the context addresses the members of the community directly and with renewed force (e.g., in the address ᾽Αγαπητοί, "beloved," in v. 11, and earlier, in ἡμᾶς in v. 10), so that v. 9a also presumes the horizon of the believing community. It is the Christian community that says, in its confession of faith, that God's love has been revealed "among us" (cf. 1:2).

A fixed tradition of the "formula of mission," demonstrably pre-Pauline, stands behind the clause ὅτι υἱὸν αὐτοῦ τὸν μονογενῆ ἀπέσταλκεν ὁ θεὸς εἰς τὸν κόσμον. The idea of the "sending of the Son of God" forms part of its structure.[45] There is a close parallel to this in John 3:16–17, which, in contrast to other mission formulas, agrees with the present passage in its cosmic aspect, in its use of the motif of the love of God, and in its expression of the meaning for salvation as well. This scarcely indicates any dependence of 1 John on the Fourth Gospel, but rather points to a common early Johannine tradition available both to the author of 1 John and to the evangelist. In addition, the concept of ἀποστέλλειν appears also in 1 John 4:14 in combination with the idea of the Son and his saving activity (cf. also John 5:36, 38; 6:29, and frequently).

The sending of the Son is specifically characterized by the adjective μονογενής, which appears only here in 1 John but is found five times in the Fourth Gospel.[46] While in secular language μονογενής describes the "only one,"[47] in the LXX this word is used to translate יָחִיד, which, however, in that case refers to the human ψυχή.[48] Ancient religious literature also makes use of this

44 See below, at 4:14.

45 Gal 4:4; cf. Rom 1:3–4; 8:3; Werner Kramer, *Christ, Lord, Son of God* (SBT 1/50; trans. Brian Hardy; Naperville: Allenson, 1966) 111–15, who finds a pre-Pauline formula in Gal 4:4–5. "The closest parallels to this are found in the Johannine writings: John 3.17; 1 John 4.9, 10, 14. They show a definite pattern, for the first clause speaks of the sending, the next unfolds its saving significance, sometimes by means of a ἵνα-clause, sometimes by a phrase of apposition" (p. 113). For the religio-historical background of the sending of the (preexistent) Son of God, cf. Schweizer, "Zum religionsgeschichtlichen Hintergrund," 199–210. The construction ἀποστέλλειν with εἰς is found in John 3:17; 10:36; 17:18 (sending of the Son) and 17:18 (sending of the disciples into the world). Cf. N. H. Cassem, "A Grammatical and Contextual Inventory of the Use of κόσμος in the Johannine Corpus with Some Implications for a Johannine Cosmic Theology," *NTS* 19 (1972/73) 83–84.

46 It occurs in four passages: John 1:14, 18 (bis); 3:16, 18; otherwise it appears in the NT only in a nonchristological sense. For Greek examples (since

expression.[49] Thus the god addressed in the magical papyri is called μονογενής (with the addition of εἷς), as a way of emphasizing the god's uniqueness.[50] The OT יָחִיד can also be rendered with ἀγαπητός in the LXX.[51] In the same way, the language of the NT can say that Jesus is not only the "only Son" but also the "beloved Son" (Mark 1:11 par.; 9:5 par.; 12:6; 2 Pet 1:17). While in the NT Jesus Christ is also "only son" (υἱὸς ἴδιος, Rom 8:32) or "firstborn" (πρωτότοκος, Rom 8:29; Col 1:15, 18), in the Johannine writings in contrast to the Synoptic Gospels μονογενής is used christologically as a "further step . . . to describe Jesus."[52] As in John 3:16, so also in the present verse the uniqueness of the Son of God is linked as closely as possible to the revelation of the ἀγάπη τοῦ θεοῦ. The Son is "unique" because only in him is God's *agapē* manifest; only he represents the δόξα θεοῦ to the world (John 1:14) and reveals to humanity an offer of life that it cannot accomplish in and of itself.

The revelation of the love of God in the sending of the Son is directed "to the world" (εἰς τὸν κόσμον). That scarcely refers to the world merely as a "scene of action" or field where the struggle between God and Satan, the children of God and the children of the devil, takes place.[53] Instead, the world is the object of the mission of the Son of God, because, as the "world of humanity," it is subjected to the domination of sin and is governed by nothingness and enmity toward God (1 John 2:2, 15–17; 3:1; 4:4–5, 14). That the revelation of the love of God represents an unmistakable alternative to existence within the domain of the world is indicated by the attached ἵνα clause.[54] The purpose of the sending of the Son is ζῆν, which means the eschatological notion of "eternal life."[55] This is a term common to the Fourth

Hesiod), cf. Walter Bauer, *Johannesevangelium* (HNT 6; 3d ed.; Tübingen: Mohr [Siebeck], 1933) on 1:14; and BAGD 527.

47 Cf. also Plato *Tim.* 31B (μονογενής as an intensification of εἷς); similarly of the cosmos, Cornutus *Theologiae Graecae compendium* 27; Clement of Alexandria *Strom.* 5.74. See also Friedrich Büchsel, "μονογενής," *TDNT* 4 (1967) 737–39. Thus the word does not mean "firstborn"; cf. Joseph A. Fitzmyer, "*unique* is the actual meaning of μονογενής" ("μονογενής," *EDNT* 2 [1991] 439–40, with bibliography), with reference to Heb 11:17; in early Christian literature the idea may be either "the only one of its kind" (*1 Clem.* 25.2), or "the only one born/begotten" (cf. Luke 7:12; 8:42; 9:38). According to John V. Dahms ("The Johannine Use of Monogenēs Reconsidered," *NTS* 29 [1983] 231), the word should be translated in the Johannine writings as "only begotten" (with references to Philo *Abr.* 194; Justin *Dial.* 105, and *1 Apol.* 23; Tertullian *Adv. Prax.* 7). In this sense, cf. also *Mart. Pol.* 20.2; *Diogn.* 10.2; also Josephus *Ant.* 1.222 (of Isaac, the only son of Abraham).

48 Ps 21:21; 24:16; 34:17 (LXX numbering); Judg 11:34; cf. also Tob 3:15; 8:17. Gen 22:12 (LXX: ἀγαπητός) is translated μονογενής in Aquila and Symmachus.

49 Cf. Bultmann, *John*, 71–72 (on John 1:14). The word was not used by Philo, although he can call the Logos πρωτόγονος υἱὸς (θεοῦ) (*Agric.* 51) and attribute to it sinlessness and creative functions (*Som.* 1.215; *Conf. ling.* 67).

50 Cf. Büchsel, "μονογενής," 738 n. 5, a reference to a love spell: ἐν τῷ οὐρανῷ θεός, ὁ μονογενής (Friedrich Preisigke, *Sammelbuch griechischer Urkunden aus Ägypten* [18 vols. in 13; Strassburg: Trübner, 1915–93] vol. 2, no. 4324, 15); εἰσάκουσόν μου, ὁ εἷς, μονογενής (*PGM* 1.124). Richard Wunsch, *Antike Fluchtafeln* (2d ed.; Bonn: Marcus & Weber, 1912) 4, 34: ὁρκίζωσε τὸν θεὸν . . . τὸν μονογενῆ τὸν ἐξ αὐτοῦ ἀναφανέντα. Of πνεῦμα it is said in Wis 7:22 that she is νοερὸν ἅγιον μονογενές ("intelligent, holy, unique"). In the old Roman creed Jesus Christ, the Son of God, is called μονογενή (Latin *unicus*); Hans Lietzmann, "Symbolstudien [cont.]," *ZNW* 22 (1923) 257–79, at 277–78.

51 Gen 22:2, 12, 16; Jer 6:26, and frequently.

52 Büchsel, "μονογενής," 739.

53 Differently Schottroff (*Glaubende*, 286–87), who sees a sharp distinction between the Fourth Gospel and 1 John with regard to κόσμος, so that in 1 John 4:9, 14 it refers not to the whole world but to the salvation of "believers," with the result that the world, while the scene of the event of salvation, is not an object of divine affection. Cf. also Smalley, *1, 2, 3 John*, 242, according to whom κόσμος at this point has a neutral meaning. In contrast, see the examples mentioned above (esp. 2:15–17).

54 On ἵνα, see below at 4:17.

55 The verb ζῆν occurs only here in 1 John; it appears more frequently as a theological term in the Fourth Gospel (4:10–11; 5:25; 6:51, 57–58; 11:25–26; 14:19). That at this point the author is thinking of "eternal life" is evident from the uses of the noun

Gospel and 1 John. One should not try to define it in such a way as to say that the Gospel addresses only Jesus' promise of life to the disciples, while in 1 John "we see the promise realized."[56] On the contrary, in the mind of the evangelist the fullness of life appears with the coming of the Revealer (cf. John 4:10–11; 5:24, 26; 6:35, 63; 10:10, and frequently), while both in the Gospel (John 3:15–16; 12:25, and frequently) and in 1 John (1 John 2:25; 5:16) the ζωή manifested in Christ is primarily an object of hope.

■ **10** Parallel to v. 9a, v. 10 begins with a connecting ἐν τούτῳ, which also refers to what follows and is continued by οὐχ ὅτι and ἀλλ' ὅτι ("not that . . . but that").[57] This describes what it is that constitutes the love of God. Even if one reads the absolute ἡ ἀγάπη,[58] the author is not thinking here of absolute *agapē,* but of God's loving, as will be immediately evident from what follows. The antithesis is marked by the contrasting of human and divine love. One should read, with numerous manuscripts: οὐχ ὅτι ἡμεῖς ἠγαπήκαμεν τὸν θεόν.[59] This probably represents, in the mind of the author, a deliberate variation, not merely a rhetorical stylization. The perfect expresses the endurance of love, the aorist its unique occurrence, its relation to the unique Christ-event in the past;[60] in English translation: "it is not we who have loved God, but God loved us." This fits the context, in which an antithesis contrasts human failure to love with the revelation of the love of God. The two members of the antithesis are not of equal weight, as the subsequent explanation indicates: there God's loving action is interpreted as the sending of God's Son. Human failure to love is at the same time the background against which the statement about the love of God is validated. Such contrasts are frequent in the Johannine writings (cf. 2 John 5; John 6:38; 12:6). So also John 15:16 ("You did not choose me, but I chose you") has the sense of emphasizing God's action in contrast to that of human beings. This contrast recalls the Pauline doctrine of justification, according to which it is not the righteous deeds of human beings but only God's gracious action that justifies anyone (Rom 3:21–26; Gal 2:15–21). An echo occurs in the deutero-Pauline letter to Titus (Titus 3:5: "[God] saved us, not because of any works of righteousness that we had done, but according to his mercy").

The author does not speculate about human capacity or incapacity for the love of God, hence not about a *gratia infusa,* grace poured into human beings, or a *gratia praeveniens,* grace given in advance of human action, that would make such love possible. No developed scholastic system should be introduced here, nor even remotely suggested.[61] All that is said is that God's *agapē* has been revealed without human cooperation. It is not stated that this is directed against some opposing position.[62] Moreover, it can scarcely be derived from any principle of "sinlessness" claimed by the false teachers for themselves and consequently expressed as "love of God" (1:8), since it otherwise appears that the false prophets were rather reproached for having a deficiency of love.[63]

In the OT, especially in the Psalms, one finds the idea of the all-embracing and steadfast love of God (חסד) to which the petitioner refers when asking for the

---

elsewhere (ζωὴ αἰώνιος: 1 John 1:2; 2:25; 3:15; 5:11, 13, 20; cf. John 3:15–16, 36, and frequently).

56 Thus Brown, *Epistles,* 518.

57 Büchsel disagrees, seeing a reference to the preceding v. 9: "On this basis there is love" (*Johannesbriefe,* 70, with reference to John 16:30: ἐν τούτῳ πιστεύομεν ὅτι).

58 With the overwhelming majority of manuscripts; in contrast, ℵ, some Vulgate manuscripts, and the Sahidic translation add τοῦ θεοῦ.

59 The perfect is the *lectio difficilior;* in contrast, the aorist ἠγαπήσαμεν, while widely attested in the manuscripts (ℵ, A, 048[vid], 𝔐) is to be explained as an accommodation to the following ἠγάπησεν.

60 That the perfect is negated need not speak against the differentiation here described (in response to Brown, *Epistles,* 518). Again, the shift from the perfect ἀπέσταλκεν (v. 9) to the aorist ἀπέστειλεν (overwhelmingly attested in v. 10) can scarcely be ascribed to "narrative style" (Schnackenburg, *Epistles,* 209 n. 33 [published English translation differs]). Instead, it draws a deliberate contrast between the sending of the Son of God into the world, which has brought forth life even to the present day (v. 9), and the unique atonement accomplished in the Christ-event (v. 10).

61 In response to Schnackenburg, *Epistles,* 209: "The true power of love has entered the world solely through God's initiative. The human race stood in *need* of God's merciful love but was quite incapable of producing it."

62 This is said against Bultmann, *Epistles,* 68.

63 Thus Schnackenburg, *Epistles,* 209; cf. the connection of 4:6 (recognition of the spirit of truth)

forgiveness of sin or for help.[64] It is connected with the idea of the election of the nation and the notion of covenant (e.g., the covenant with Noah at Gen 9:9–17). While this is stated in theocentric terms, so that God's action anticipates and is revealed to human beings within the history of God's people, in the Greco-Hellenistic sphere the πρόνοια θεοῦ ("providence of God") can also be thought of as a gracious provision of God that conditions human actions; this takes place against a cosmic background (Seneca *Prov.* 1.1–2; Epictetus *Diss.* 1.12.1–6). The syncretistic *Odes of Solomon,* often called "gnostic," speak with particular emphasis of the anticipating love of God that determines the existence of the pious (3.3: "For I should not have known how to love the Lord, if he had not loved me"; also 7.1–2; 8.13, 22; 42.7). Similar things are found in the Mandaean *Ginza:* "[The great life] entrusted me with love to be given to my friends."[65] When 1 John speaks of the anticipating love of God, the thought is not of the present experience, such as belongs to pious Gnostics or Hellenistic Christians, but of the Christ-event in the past, in which the love of God was made manifest. On the other hand, this statement clearly differs from the Jewish or Hellenistic-syncretistic idea that the love of God is subordinated to the love of human beings: *Corp. Herm.* 1.22 ("they propitiate the father lovingly"); Philo *Abr.* 50 ("their affection for the true God was returned by him"); *T. Naph.* 8.4 ("If you do what is good, my children, both [people] and angels will bless you, . . . and the Lord will love you, and the angels will keep close to you"). This relationship between the (preceding) love of human beings and the love of God is especially well attested in Christian tradition within parenetic contexts (cf. Matt 6:14–15) and is found even in the Johannine writings as "ascending *agapē*" (John 14:21: "They who have my commandments and keep them are those who love me; and those who love me will be loved by my Father, and I will love them and reveal myself to them"). In contrast, the present passage expresses the descending love of God that was revealed in the Son.

The unique revelation was already described in v. 9 as the sending of the Son, and its purpose as the life of human beings. The content of this revelation is now given a new concreteness: the Son is ἱλασμὸς περὶ τῶν ἁμαρτιῶν ἡμῶν. The word ἱλασμός was already encountered in 2:2 as a synonym for the soteriological action of Jesus Christ. It is not found elsewhere in the NT.[66] Its meaning can frequently approach that of "atoning sacrifice."[67] In general, it refers to God's act of forgiving. Accordingly, Jesus Christ is represented here not as a means or result of the divine forgiveness of sins. Instead, the sending of the Son, an action proceeding from the Father, is the act that creates reconciliation between God and humanity.[68] When Paul speaks of God's reconciling action in Christ he uses the verb καταλλάσσειν (2 Cor 5:19). The author of 1 John has clearly equated this reconciliation with the person of Jesus Christ. While in the conception of the Fourth Gospel the Revealer is identified with resurrection and life (John 11:25), here he is identical with God's forgiveness. This kind of atoning event removes sins:

with 4:7 ("everyone who loves, . . . knows God"); also 2:21; 5:2. For what follows, see also Schnackenburg's excursus 10: "Love as the Nature of God."

64 Pss 25:6; 40:12[11]; 51:3; 69:14[13], 17[16]; 86:5; Mic 7:18; Isa 54:7–8; Jer 31:3, and frequently.

65 *Ginza*, book 15, parts 10–17. See Lidzbarski, *Ginza*, 333, lines 31–32.

66 But cf. ἱλάσκεσθαι in Luke 18:13; Heb 2:17; ἱλαστήριον in Rom 3:25; Heb 9:5; ἵλεως in Matt 16:22; Heb 8:12.

67 Thus in the LXX: Ezek 44:7; cf. Num 5:8; 2 Macc 3:33.

68 Cf. Henri Clavier, "Notes sur un mot-clef du johannisme et de la sotériologie biblique: 'Ἱλασμός,'" *NovT* 10 (1968) 287–304. When ἱλασμός occurs in 2:2 in the context of the appearance of the Exalted One as "paraclete" for the community (2:1), the "atonement" is already applied to the whole world at that point. This corresponds to the conclusion drawn by our text in 4:14. Cf. also Friedrich Büchsel, "ἱλασμός," *TDNT* 3 (1965) 318 ("For John the ἱλασμός is much more than a concept of Christian doctrine; it is the reality by which he lives").

although περί is ordinarily translated "concerning" or "about" (1:1; 2:26–27; in combination with *μαρτυρία*: 5:9), here it means much the same as ὑπέρ ("for").[69] The plural ἁμαρτίαι describes individual "sins" that are the object of atoning action.[70] In distinction from OT-Jewish or Greek-Hellenistic ideas, according to which human priests were to soothe God's anger through sacrificial actions, the author emphasizes that it is not human action but only the deed of God in sending the Son that has effected atonement. Thus it is motivated by the love of God, which has become visible in the Son.

69 Thus also in 2:2 and 3:16. Cf. BDR § 229 n. 4. While ὑπέρ is the usual expression (cf. Mark 14:24; Luke 22:19–20; 1 Cor 1:13; 11:24; Gal 1:4; Acts 21:26; 1 Tim 2:6, and frequently), the preposition περί (possibly influenced by the LXX) has the same meaning also in 1 John 2:2a; so also Brown, *Epistles*, 519. Cf. Matt 26:28; Heb 5:3; 1 Pet 3:18.

70 Cf. 1 John 1:9; 2:2, 12; 3:15; thus also the singular πάσης ἁμαρτίας (1:7).

4 Love of God and Love of the Brothers and Sisters

**11 Beloved, since God loved us so much, we
also ought to love one another. 12/ No
one has ever seen God; if we love one
another, God lives in us, and [God's] love
is perfected in us. 13/ By this we know
that we abide in [God] and [God] in us,
because [God] has given us of the Spirit.
14/ And we have seen and do testify that
the Father has sent the Son as the Savior
of the world. 15/ God abides in those
who confess that Jesus is the Son of
God, and they abide in God. 16/ So we
have known and believe the love that
God has for us. God is love, and those
who abide in love abide in God, and God
abides in them.**

■ **11** For the last time (of six occurrences) the word ἀγαπητοί ("beloved") appears at this point in 1 John. If one understands this address as a reference to v. 7, it seems appropriate to refer οὕτως to all four of the preceding verses, 7–10.[1] This does not, however, exclude the possibility of a close connection to v. 10. Thus it is in the sending of the Son to atone for sins that God's love "for us" is manifest. The little word οὕτως occurs in 1 John only at 2:6[2] and here. While in the first occurrence it is connected with a comparative or foundational καθώς, it retains a qualitative sense. In the present instance one can ask whether it also has a qualitative meaning ("in this way")[3] or whether it is meant to express intensity or effectiveness ("so much").[4] Both readings are possible and presuppose an interpretation of the content of the love of God like that presented above.

The indicative, whose object is the revelation of the love of God in the Christ-event, is followed by the imperative, to a great extent identical in its formulation with 3:16 (cf. also John 13:14). Thus the community is obligated to behave in accordance with God's action; its being and acting must be analogous to the love of God. This kind of ethical obligation was already expressed in 2:6 with the verb ὀφείλειν. The obligation is a direct result of the experience of the love of God. This is evident from the added καί, which, in addition to its comparative meaning ("also")[5] can have a causal and consequent sense ("for," "therefore").[6] The deliberate and emphatic insertion of the personal pronoun ἡμεῖς ("we") contrasts the action of God and that of human beings. Because human action is motivated by the indicative of the Christ-event, it is not subject to law. The "law," once it has appeared, is instead the revelation of the love of God. This means freedom to do what is necessary, namely, to practice mutual love. The sequence ἀλλήλους ἀγαπᾶν ("to love one another") appears only here in the Johannine writings.[7] The placement of

1 Thus Wengst, *Brief*, 184; Brown, *Epistles*, 519.
2 However, the tradition is text-critically uncertain; see the commentary on 1 John 2:6.
3 Thus, for example, in Sophocles *Phil.* 104: οὕτως ἔχει τι δεινὸν ἰσχύος θράσος ("What makes him so much to be feared—his arrogant strength?"); Herodotus 4.28: οὕτω μὲν δὴ τοὺς ὀκτὼ μῆνας διατελέει χειμὼν ἐών ("So it is ever winter for eight months"; 4.52: ἐκδιδοῖ γὰρ ἐς αὐτόν κρήνη πικρή, οὕτω δή τι ἐοῦσα πικρή, ἣ μεγάθεϊ σμικρὴ ἐοῦσα κρινᾷ τὸν Ὕπανιν ἐόντα ποταμὸν ἐν ὀλίγοισι μέγαν ("for a spring issues into it which is so bitter that although its volume is small its admixture taints the Hypanis, one of the few great rivers of the world").
4 Thus John 3:16; 7:46; cf. Isa 54:10 LXX; 1 Macc 3:60; Matt 9:33.
5 1 John 2:6; cf. Rom 5:15, 18; 6:11, and frequently.
6 Cf. John 12:18; 15:8; Matt 5:15; Jas 4:7; BDF § 442.
7 Cf. also Rom 13:8; 1 Pet 1:22; elsewhere ἀγαπᾶν ἀλλήλους: 1 John 3:11, 23; 4:7, 12; 2 John 5; John 13:34; 15:12, 17; 1 Thess 4:9; also Polycarp *Phil.* 10.1; *2 Clem.* 4.3; earlier in Plato *Leg.* 3.678; Epictetus *Diss.* 4.1.126.

ἀλλήλους before the verb is evidently meant to underscore the mutuality of human beings and thus the Christian obligation to love; for mutual love is obviously nothing other than love for the sisters and brothers. Such love involves consideration and care, as these are now practiced among Christians in community and are to be practiced in future.

■ **12** The general statement *θεὸν οὐδεὶς πώποτε τεθέαται* ("no one has ever seen God") is a piece of proverbial wisdom in harmony with the currents both of OT-Jewish and Hellenistic Greek tradition.[8] On the one hand, it is true that the OT cannot make a dispassionate statement about YHWH's invisibility. Rather, this hiddenness from human eyes is attributed to YHWH's own will (Exod 33:20: "You cannot see my face; for no one shall see me and live"). But in exceptional situations this condition of hiddenness can be set aside.[9] On the human side, this corresponds to a fear of seeing YHWH (Gen 17:1–3; Exod 3:6; 1 Kgs 19:13). In Greek tradition, on the other hand, there is an ontological statement as early as Homer that invisibility is proper to the deity.[10] Here the adjective *ἀόρατος* ("invisible"), unknown in the OT, is applied to the world of the gods.[11] Philo of Alexandria documents the union of Greek and Jewish thought when he asserts the invisibility of God.[12] Hence, the author is under the influence of the Hellenistic Greek imaginative world when he speaks of God's invisibility. The use of the verb *θεᾶσθαι* ("to see, behold") is probably to be explained not only as alliteration[13] or as a play on the word *θεόν*;[14] apparently *θεᾶσθαι* has a spiritual, contemplative tone,[15] while *ὁρᾶν*, despite its frequent use as a synonym in the Johannine writings,[16] often expresses a more realistic note.[17] If the author is really thinking again of the false prophets who threaten the truth of Christian teaching, he presupposes that they assert not only knowledge of God (cf. 4:7–8) but also a vision of God (cf. 4:20).[18] This presupposition could correspond to the opponents' docetic ideas. However (even apart

8 On the tradition behind this proverbial wisdom, cf. Rudolf Bultmann, "Untersuchungen zum Johannesevangelium," *ZNW* 29 (1930) 169–92 (= *Exegetica*, 174–92); Eduard Lohse, *Colossians and Philemon* (Hermeneia; trans. William R. Poehlmann and Robert Karris; ed. Helmut Koester; Philadelphia: Fortress, 1971) 47–49.

9 Gen 17:1–22: Abraham; Deut 34:10 (also Josephus *Ant.* 3.5.3): Moses; Judg 6:22–23: Gideon; Judg 13:21: Manoah.

10 Homer *Od.* 16.161; 10.573; *Il.* 20.131; Empedocles *frg.* 133; Wilhelm Michaelis, "*ὁράω, κτλ.*," *TDNT* 5 (1967) 315–82, at 320–21. The Stoic tradition differs by asserting the knowability of God on the basis of the universe's regulation by laws; cf. Aristotle *De mundo* 6 (399b22–23): it is said of God, the perfect being, that *πάσῃ θνητῇ φύσει γενόμενος ἀθεώρητος ἀπ' αὐτῶν τῶν ἔργων θεωρεῖται* ("Though he is invisible to every mortal thing, he is seen through all his deeds").

11 In the NT only in Rom 1:20; Col 1:15–16; 1 Tim 1:17; Heb 11:27; cf. John 1:18; *2 Clem.* 20.5; *Diogn.* 7.2; Ignatius *Pol.* 3.2.

12 Although Philo in some places appears to speak of seeing God, without restriction (*Q. in Exod.* 2.39–40; *Leg. all.* 2.81), in principle he presupposes that God is invisible; cf. *Poster. C.* 15: *ἰδεῖν ὅτι ἐστὶν* (= God) *ἀόρατος* ("that which is beyond matter and beyond sight"); *Leg. all.* 3.103; *Rer. div. her.* 262; *Vit. Mos.* 1.66; *Spec. leg.* 1.18, 20, and frequently elsewhere. Cf. also *Corp. Herm.* 11.22; 14.3.

13 Thus Brown, *Epistles*, 520 (together with the other alliteration in the context: *ἀγαπᾶν ἀλλήλους*).

14 P. W. van der Horst, "A Wordplay in 1 Joh 4:12?" *ZNW* 63 (1972) 280–82 (suggesting that the etymological wordplay originates with Diogenes, in the 2d century BCE; cf. Philodemus *De musica* 1.23; 4.4–5).

15 Thus also Carl-Heinz Peisker, "*θεάομαι*," *EDNT* 2 (1991) 136 ("intensive, thorough, lingering, astonished, reflective, comprehending observation").

16 In the view of Wilhelm Michaelis ("*ὁράω*," *TDNT* 5 [1967] 345), "throughout 1 Jn. *θεάομαι* is like *ἑώρακα*"; cf. 1 John 4:12 with John 1:14, 18, and 1 John 4:14 with John 1:34. Jacob Kremer also ("*ὁράω*," *EDNT* 2 [1991] 527) emphasizes the synonymity of *ὁράω* and *βλέπω*, *θεωρέω* and *θεάομαι* (with reference to the LXX).

17 Cf. 1:1 in combination with *τοῖς ὀφθαλμοῖς* (see the commentary on 1 John 1:1); that there is a distinct tendency in the use of tenses (*θεᾶσθαι* in the aorist, *ὁρᾶν* in the perfect and future) does not really explain the difference; cf. also the "exception" in 4:12, 14, where *θεᾶσθαι* appears in perfect and future forms (Brown, *Epistles*, 162).

18 Cf. Schnackenburg, *Epistles*, 217–18; Wengst, *Brief*, 185 ("ecstatic vision of God"). Religio-historical parallels include Rev 4:1–11; *b. Ḥagiga* 14b (four rabbis are transported to paradise); Apuleius *Metamorphoses* 11.23; *Mithras Liturgy* 6.9–20 (see Marvin W. Meyer, ed., *The "Mithras Liturgy"* [SBL Texts and Translations 10; Missoula: Scholars Press, 1976] 13); *Poimandres* (*Corp. Herm.* 1) 24–26.

from the possibility of such a confrontation) the readers of 1 John know that they are being addressed directly by "apostolic" authority, which has "seen" and "touched" the earthly reality of the "word of life" (1:1–2). On the basis of this witness, the vision of God is promised to the community in the future (3:2: ὀψόμεθα, "we will see"). In expectation of the eschatological future the community can itself confess that it has seen and known God (cf. 3:6; 3 John 11), just as it can assert, in anticipation, that it is free from sin. This confession cannot be detached from the assertion that God has appeared in Christ (1:2; 3:5, 8; 4:9) and that the basis for the present vision of God is the divine revelation in Jesus Christ.[19]

Since God, as the invisible one, is unapproachable, escape into a direct vision of God is closed to the Christian community. The encounter with God that is promised to them takes place, instead, here and now in love for one another. The actualization of mutual love in relationships within the Christian community is given an exalted title. It is nothing other than God's "abiding" (*μένειν*) in the community.[20] The enduring presence of God is described in the phrase *ἡ ἀγάπη αὐτοῦ ἐν ὑμῖν τετελειωμένη ἐστίν* ("his love has been perfected in you"). Since the context speaks of the love of God for human beings (vv. 9–11, 19–21), it is clear that the disputed question of the meaning of *αὐτοῦ* must be answered primarily in the sense of a subjective genitive.[21] As already said above, the sending of the Son reveals God as the subject of the *agapē* that is bestowed on human beings (vv. 9–10). But it is also clear that wherever God abides, mutual human love is characterized by the loving presence of God.[22] The love of the brothers and sisters that is now and is to be practiced in the future by the Christian community is the love demanded by God, the love that is in accordance with God's nature. The author wishes to say that in the love of the sisters and brothers achieved by human beings, God's *agapē* reaches its goal. It is not because human love is superior to divine love—for the indicative of the event of the love of God in Jesus Christ precedes all human reality (cf. vv. 10–11 and v. 19)—but because the love of God for human beings intends, by its very nature, to actualize itself in the Christian community in the form of mutual love of human beings for one another.

■ **13** The assurance that, through mutual love, God personally dwells in Christians and that God's love is perfected in brotherly and sisterly service (v. 12) has a pneumatic aspect; for the community knows that it possesses the Spirit, who has been given them through the *χρῖσμα* ("anointing").[23] Thus this verse is not merely "an addition *ad vocem μένειν*"[24] but a proper continuation of the train of thought. The *ἐν τούτῳ* construction with the double *ὅτι* following gives it a succinct structure. Both of the *ὅτι* clauses refer to *ἐν τούτῳ* and relate back to the governing verb *γινώσκομεν*.[25] The first, explanatory *ὅτι* clarifies the content of our knowledge ("that"). Thus abiding in community with God, that is, belonging

19 Cf. 4:14. That such a vision of God is scarcely to be interpreted as ecstatic is clear from the parallels in the Fourth Gospel, where Jesus the Revealer's vision of God is not ecstatic, either. The contrast with not seeing God (cf. 1 John 4:20) is found three times in the Fourth Gospel, always governed by the christological premise that the Son of God has seen the Father (*ἑώρακεν*: 1:18; 5:37; 6:46). The author of the Gospel, unlike the author of 1 John, does not orient the "fusion of horizons" of the "historical reality of life" and the "perfection of salvation" that is manifest in "seeing" ecclesiologically, but christologically (14:9: "Whoever has seen me has seen the Father"). Cf. Ferdinand Hahn, "Sehen und Glauben im Johannesevangelium," in Hans Baltensweiler and Bo Reicke, eds., *Neues Testament und Geschichte: Historisches Geschehen und Deutung im Neuen Testament: Oscar Cullmann zum 70. Geburtstag* (Zurich: Theologischer Verlag; Tübingen: Mohr [Siebeck], 1972) 125–41 (esp. 140).

20 Cf. 2:14, 24, 27; 3:9, 17, 24, and frequently.

21 Thus Bultmann, *Epistles*, 68; Wengst, *Brief*, 185; Brown, *Epistles*, 521. Dodd differs (*Epistles*, 113), seeing here an objective genitive.

22 For this reason, Schnackenburg opts here for a qualitative genitive (*Epistles*, 218; on this, see BDF §165).

23 Cf. 3:24; 2:20, 27 (see the commentary on those verses).

24 Windisch and Preisker, *Die Katholischen Briefe*, 129.

25 For this type of construction, see also 2:3 and 2:5.

to God,[26] which is actualized in mutual love (v. 12), is the object of knowledge. The sense of the second ὅτι clause is not epexegetical[27] but causal.[28] As we saw already at 3:24, so here the *πνεῦμα* ("Spirit") is the true basis for Christian knowledge. Even if this formulation stems from "the church catechism,"[29] for the author it also means that believers live in the realm of the Spirit who proceeds from God and who determines their very being, hence also their knowing. This kind of "knowing" (*γινώσκειν*) cannot be separated from "believing," "acknowledging," and "realizing," for it is the eschatological reality in which and from which Christians know themselves to be abidingly united with God and acting toward their sisters and brothers as persons who love must act. Thus it is significant that (differently from 3:24) the Spirit as such is not the gift, but instead that *δέδωκεν ἡμῖν* ("he has given us") is combined with *ἐκ πνεύματος* ("of his spirit"). Accordingly, it is not the Spirit in its fullness that is the object touched by the action of "giving."[30] The Spirit is not exhausted in the gift that is the foundation of believers' knowledge. The spirit of right knowledge is, instead, an aspect of the spirit of truth who speaks through the one who testifies[31] and bears witness for the "children of God" (cf. Rom 8:16).

■ **14** Even if the author rejects the idea of a direct vision of God and ties knowledge of God as tightly as possible to the actualization of love for the sisters and brothers, he can still say that "we have seen." *Τεθεάμεθα* has, as was evident earlier,[32] a tendency toward a contemplative, spiritual vision in contrast to the realistic seeing that the author claims for himself as an apostolic witness (1:1–2). This "seeing of faith"[33] issues in a proclamatory witness. That the Spirit speaks through the proclaimer and witness[34] is presumed in the wake of v. 13. The content of the testimony is stated in the epexegetical ὅτι clause: *ὅτι ὁ πατὴρ ἀπέσταλκεν τὸν υἱὸν σωτῆρα τοῦ κόσμου*. The traditional formula of mission[35] designates the "Son of God" as "Savior of the world." The noun *σωτήρ*, which appears fourteen times in the NT, is attested in the Johannine writings only here and at John 4:42.[36] That the purpose of the Son's mission is the salvation of the world (cf. John 3:16–17; 1 John 4:9, 17) may be an early conviction of the Johannine school. It is possible, but cannot be proved, that the author employs this terminology in a polemic contest with the docetic opponents.[37] The title *σωτήρ* is, however, widely attested in the religious-historical environment. It has parallels in Hellenistic worship of heroes and in the Roman cult of the emperor,[38] as well as in the worship of healing gods in the late Hellenistic period.[39] It is found in the LXX as a divine title,[40] and it appears in the Lukan language of the NT, under the influence of the Greek Bible (Luke 1:47; cf. Hab 3:18). In this context, the salvation of the world is not explained in detail. It is clear, however, that,

26 Eduard Schweizer differs ("*πνεῦμα*," *TDNT* 6 [1968] 448). According to him, one should think of "the abiding of Christ in believers" (similarly at 3:24); but in the present passage the emphasis clearly lies on *θεός* (v. 12), and this cannot be excluded in 3:24, either.

27 Against Brown, *Epistles*, 521.

28 In this sense also Bultmann, *Epistles*, 70 (with reference to 3:24, where the clause *ἐκ τοῦ πνεύματος οὗ ἡμῖν ἔδωκεν* states the basis for the same knowledge, namely, that "God abides in us").

29 Thus Schnackenburg, *Epistles*, 219.

30 BDF §169 (2).

31 1 John 5:6–7; cf. 4:2, 6.

32 See above, at v. 12.

33 Bultmann, *Epistles*, 71.

34 Cf. also John 15:26.

35 On this, see above at v. 9.

36 By way of comparison, *σῴζειν* is not in the Johannine Letters, but appears 6 times in the Fourth Gospel; *σωτηρία* is only at John 4:22.

37 Cf. Schnackenburg, *Epistles*, 220: In 1 John 4:14 "the emphasis lies on the *fact* of the world's redemption. This is because the gnostics thought they had no need of salvation by the blood of Jesus."

38 According to Pausanius 1.8.6 Ptolemy I (383–285 BCE) was called "savior" by the grateful people of Rhodes. Cf. also Phylarchos of Athens, *Historiae* . . . 6.66 (255A): at their feasts, the Athenians of Lemnos called the third cup "Seleucos savior" instead of "Zeus savior." Even Philip of Macedon is supposed to have been honored as *φίλος*, *εὐεργέτης*, and *σωτήρ* (Demosthenes *Orations* 18.43). Among the Ptolemies, *θεὸς σωτήρ* was part of the official name of the king. See the additional texts cited by Werner Foerster, "*σωτήρ*," *TDNT* 7 (1971) 1009–10. Examples of the use of the title *σωτήρ* in Roman emperor worship are found in Philo *Flacc.* 74 (Augustus), Josephus *Bell.* 3.459 (Vespasian), and frequently elsewhere. Cf. Bousset, *Kyrios Christos*, 310–17 (although, according to the witnesses adduced by Bousset himself, it is too narrow a reading of the present text to call it "a title which in particular is explained, both as to content and as to form, in terms of the Caesar cult").

in the author's conception and in harmony with his tradition, the sending of the Son means liberation from sin (cf. 2:2), brings human beings salvation from the nothingness of the world (2:15) and from death (3:14; cf. John 5:24), and gives them the gift of life (1 John 1:1–2; 3:14; 5:11–12; cf. John 1:4; 3:15–16, 36; 4:14, and frequently). Hence, the Son of God is the foundation and source not only of life but also of *agapē*, which is revealed in him and is the model of love for others (1 John 3:16).

■ **15** The salvation of the world, which Jesus Christ brings, is inseparable from his person. When believers—in contrast to the docetic opponents[41] —confess that Jesus is the Son of God, salvation happens for them. This confession, however, is more than a simple theoretical declaration. It is the existential act of turning toward the Son of God and the acceptance of the eschatological gift that he has made possible. In this sense ὁμολογεῖν is used also in 2:23 ("everyone who confesses the Son has the Father also"), just as, in turn, the confession of sins implies acknowledgment of one's own guilt, and trust in forgiveness (1:9). Therefore ὃς ἐὰν ὁμολογήσῃ should be understood as an aorist subjunctive used in a conditional relative clause and expressing the moment of confession, its taking place at a particular point in time.[42] The confession addresses the fact that Ἰησοῦς[43] is the Son of God. Jesus' being Son of God also incorporates his mission as the one sent to save the world (cf. v. 14). Believers' confession of this saving deed has as its consequence[44] that ὁ θεὸς ἐν αὐτῷ μένει καὶ αὐτὸς ἐν τῷ θεῷ. The reciprocity of God's abiding in believers and believers in God does not refer to any mystical indwelling. What is expressed is a close, personal relationship between believers and God.[45] That community with God cannot be perfected without the actualization of *agapē* follows from what has been said previously and will be treated immediately in the next verse.[46]

39 Thus as early as the second century BCE Asclepius was called σωτὴρ τῶν ὅλων (Aristides *Orations* 42.521; Wilhelm Dittenberger, *Orientis graeci inscriptiones selectae* [1903–5, reprinted Hildesheim: Olms, 1960, 2 vols.] 332.9, 1.514); his cult is contrasted by Celsus, the opponent of the Christians, to the Christian church's worship of the savior Jesus Christ (Origen *C. Cels.* 3.3). The mystery deities Isis and Sarapis were also honored with this title; cf. the references in Bousset, *Kyrios Christos*, 312; BAGD 800–801, with additional literature.

40 Judg 3:9, 15; 1 Sam 10:19; Isa 12:2; 17:10; 45:15, 21; Ps 24:5; 26:1; 61:3, 7; Wis 16:7; 1 Macc 4:30. Behind each of these is the Hebrew root ישע; cf. Büchsel, *Johannesbriefe*, 72; Georg Fohrer, "σωτήρ in the Old Testament," *TDNT* 7 (1971) 1012–13.

41 Cf. the excursus above, "The False Teachers in 1 John."

42 The present subjunctive (Codex A pc), by contrast, emphasizes the endurance of the confession, while the future indicative without ἄν (Ψ) yields no materially different reading (BDF § 380 [2]). The vacillation between ἐάν and ἄν in the manuscripts is of no practical importance, cf. BDF §107.

43 This is the correct reading; the addition of Χριστός (B vg^{ms}) is secondary, although appropriate in the context. The full title is also found in 4:2 (differently from 4:3 and 5:5: "Jesus"). When 5:1 says, corresponding to this, that Jesus is the Christ, it underscores that the name and title belong together. The question that one may raise is whether this presumes an opposing position that distinguished between "Jesus" and "Christ."

44 Since v. 15a is a conditional relative clause, the dependent and independent clauses are related to one another as condition and consequence (cf. BDF § 380), without requiring that this ordering be explicated schematically. Obviously, "confessing" is not the only condition for "abiding," and it is not impossible that the reverse is true: that "abiding" leads to "confessing." However, there is no reason to reduce the confession to a mere "sign" (Weiss, *Briefe*, 127: "For that very reason this adherence to the confession becomes . . . a sign of the fact that God abides in the one confessing"), because the author intends to describe not merely a theoretical but an eschatological and ontological connection: where there is true confession, there also is genuine community with God.

45 Cf. above at 3:24; 4:13; also below at 4:16b. It is irrelevant that in this text God's abiding is mentioned first, while in 3:24; 4:13, 16 the believers' abiding comes first. So also Brown, *Epistles*, 524: "The reversed order here suggests that there is no set priority."

46 The relationship of the verses to one another is a matter of dispute. According to Marshall (*Epistles*, 221), v. 16 is parallel to v. 14, because in v. 16 "another basic Christian conviction" is expressed. This is not without foundation, since τεθεάμεθα is taken up and interpreted by ἐγνώκαμεν, and μαρτυροῦμεν by πεπιστεύκαμεν, whereby a connection is established between the level of the author, as apostolic witness, and that of the community he is

■ **16** The perfect construction ἐγνώκαμεν καὶ πεπιστεύκαμεν[47] appears in a similar form, though in reverse order, in the Fourth Gospel, when Simon Peter, representing the disciples, says: "We have come to believe and know that you are the Holy One of God" (John 6:69). This is almost a hendiadys, in which one expression complements the other in order to clarify the believing knowledge that at the same time is an actualizing acknowledgment on the part of believers. Here, differently from the Gospel, the words are not applied to the relationship between the disciples and the Revealer, but to the community- and Christ-event. The community has accepted in faith the content of their confession of Christ: the salvation of the universe by the Son of God (vv. 14–15), that is, the forgiveness of sins (v. 10). In this, God's *agapē* has been revealed; in this event it has "preceded" human beings (v. 19). But it did not happen "in and for itself," but "in us" (ἐν ἡμῖν). In what went before, the text spoke of the spatial presence of God "in us" and the abiding of believers "in God" (v. 13; cf. 3:24), which suggests a local meaning here as well. One might think of the combination of the verb ἔχειν with ἐν in 3:15 and 5:10, where the literal translation "in" should be preferred;[48] but there the subject of ἔχειν is in both cases identical with the personal pronoun, while here θεός ("God") and ἡμεῖς ("we") are clearly distinct. Moreover, since there is no genuine parallel to 4:9,[49] in this verse ἐν should be translated in a dative sense as "for" or "toward."[50] This accords with the indicative description of the event of salvation. In Christ, God's love for human beings has become real (2:2; 4:14). Thus it was accepted, in faith, by the community, and thus it is made real through faith.

This experience motivates the repetition of the statement that ὁ θεὸς ἀγάπη ἐστίν.[51] Even though this is a literal replication of v. 8b, the context is different. The idea that God's nature can be described with the word ἀγάπη is here not an object of christological but of

addressing. However, v. 15 is not an insertion; it gives a concrete statement of the confession already expressed in v. 14b. Consequently, for the immediate explanation of v. 16 one need not look far beyond vv. 14–15. Schnackenburg differs (*Epistles*, 221), writing of v. 16a that it "deliberately harks back to v. 11 and perhaps to vv. 9–10."

47 The reading of Codex A and others has πιστεύομεν, apparently a secondary accommodation to μαρτυροῦμεν (v. 14). Smalley (*1, 2, 3 John*, 234) emphasizes that "the perfect tense in itself contains a 'continuous' and thus present reference." Marshall (*Epistles*, 221 n. 9) writes similarly of ἐγνώκαμεν, "Perfect tense: We have come to know and still know." The combination of πιστεύειν with the accusative (of the thing; cf. John 11:26; 1 Cor 13:7; BAGD 660: "be convinced") is rare; it is explained by the preceding ἐγνώκαμεν; the combination of "believing" and "knowing" is peculiar to Johannine language: whereas in the Fourth Gospel πιστεύειν precedes γινώσκειν (6:69; 8:31–32; 10:38), thus designating "belief" as the first movement toward the Revealer, the reverse order (as in the present case) also occurs (17:8; cf. 16:30), so that πιστεύειν (corresponding to the position of μαρτυρεῖν in v. 14) appears to describe the consequence of γινώσκειν. In any case it is clear from the ordering that not only is "knowing" a constitutive element of "believing" (thus Bultmann, "πιστεύω," *TDNT* 6 [1968] 226–27; Gerhard Barth, *EDNT* 3 [1993] 96), but "believing" is also a structural element of "knowing" in Johannine understanding. (On the relationship of γινώσκειν and ידע, see the excursus below on γινώσκειν.)

48 Thus Edward Malatesta, "Τὴν ἀγάπην ἣν ἔχει ὁ θεὸς ἐν ἡμῖν: A Note on 1 John 4:16a," in William C. Weinreich, ed., *The New Testament Age: Essays in Honor of Bo Reicke* (2 vols.; Macon: Mercer University Press, 1984) 2.301–11, at 306; also Büchsel, *Johannesbriefe*, 72; Brown, *Epistles*, 525–26.

49 Cf. ἐν ἡμῖν (4:9) in a spatial context ("among us"); possibly also at 2:5 and 3:17.

50 The particle ἐν instead of the dative is found also in Gal 1:16; Luke 2:14; Acts 4:12, and frequently; cf. BAGD 261. Thus also Wengst, *Brief*, 190; Schnackenburg, *Epistles*, 221 n. 75; similarly Dodd, *Epistles*, 116 ("the love God has for us"); Bonnard, *Les épîtres johanniques*, 98.

51 Some exegetes begin a new paragraph with v. 16b (thus Nestle-Aland[26]; Brooke Foss Westcott, *The Epistles of St. John* [2d ed.; London: Macmillan, 1886; new ed. with introduction by Frederick F. Bruce; Abingdon: Marcham Manor; Grand Rapids: Eerdmans, 1966] 156; Brooke, *Epistles*, 122; Windisch and Preisker, *Die Katholischen Briefe*, 130); contrast C. Haas, M. de Jonge, and J. L. Swellengrebel, *A Translator's Handbook on the Letters of John* (HeTr 13; London: United Bible Societies, 1972) 111: the repetition of the formula about "abiding" unites v. 16b with vv. 13 and 15. It would be more accurate to posit a caesura between vv. 16 and 17. However, it will appear that the subsequent development is materially connected and consistent with what went before.

ecclesiological reflection. The Christian community knows through faith that, in the Christ-event, God has expressed love for it; for only in this context can it be said that God is love, precisely because God is experienced in Christ as one who loves. Moreover, the love of God is the foundation of believers' community with God. This is expressed, as it was already in 3:24 and 4:13, 15, in a "joyful alternation" (Luther). The twofold καί produces a consequent meaning: if God's nature can now be expressed in the word *agapē*, it is true that everyone who really practices such love also has communion with God.[52] In turn, this last, namely, abiding in God, implies the consequence that God dwells in the loving person. The absolute use of ἀγάπη[53] indicates that the author is speaking of love in an unlimited sense. He is thinking not only of God's love for human beings or that of humans for God but also of the love of human beings for one another. In the context of 1 John this means love of the sisters and brothers. None of the three modes of appearance of *agapē* can be isolated from the others, although the starting point remains that God is love.[54] This fusion of the three manifestations of *agapē* makes impossible: (1) any objectifying reflection centered on God's aseity, that is, God's love as existing in and for itself; (2) any anthropocentric explanation of *agapē* that would separate the love that is to be shown to one's brothers and sisters from the love of God that precedes it (cf. 4:10, 19); (3) any mystical interpretation that solipsistically limits love to the relationship between God and the self, which would exclude the fulfillment of the commandment of love for others.[55]

52 The omission of the second μένει in Codex A, some minuscules, Old Latin manuscripts, and the Vulgate is probably a smoothing intended to avoid the repetition of the verb. It is also possible that the scribe was accommodating to vv. 13b and 15b, where the verb appears only once (thus Brown, *Epistles*, 526). For the consequent sense of καί cf. BDF § 442 (2). Dodd (*Epistles*, 118) warns against a falsely sentimental interpretation: "It does not mean that anyone who feels for another person any sort of liking, affection or passion, which we loosely include under the term 'love,' is *ipso facto* in union with God."

53 On this, see above at 4:7–10.

54 Cf. also Stott, *Epistles*, 168; Marshall, *Epistles*, 221–22.

55 Dodd (*Epistles*, 117) illustrates the fusion of the three manifestations of *agapē* with the image of a triangle "whose points are God, self and neighbour."

4 Eschatological Reservation and Present Perfection in *Agapē*

17 Love has been perfected among us in this: that we may have boldness on the day of judgment, because as he is, [so] are we in this world. 18/ There is no fear in love, but perfect love casts out fear; for fear has to do with punishment, and whoever fears has not reached perfection in love. 19/ We love because [God] first loved us. 20/ Those who say, "I love God," and hate their brothers or sisters, are liars; for those who do not love a brother or sister whom they have seen, cannot love God whom they have not seen. 21/ The commandment we have from [God] is this: those who love God must love their brothers and sisters also.

■ **17** The theme of *agapē* does not recede into the background in what follows, even though the appearance of ἐν τούτῳ indicates a new beginning, in which the historical aspect will be addressed anew. This demonstrative is a stylistic feature of this author; its reference is disputed.[1] It is often connected with the ἵνα clause that follows it.[2] This would mean that the perfection of love consists in our having boldness in the future, and that in turn would correspond to the Johannine assertion that abiding in love describes an incomplete condition. The combination of a demonstrative with a following ἵνα clause is found elsewhere in 1 John;[3] moreover, a resumption with ὅτι is also frequently attested.[4] However, this interpretation leaves us with the difficulty that the perfection of love refers to something that has not yet occurred.[5] It is consistent with this position to suspect here again that the future-eschatological perspective represents "an addition by the ecclesiastical redactor."[6] One may more correctly refer ἐν τούτῳ to the preceding verse.[7] That in the Johannine writings the demonstrative can be linked not only with what follows but also with what precedes it is shown by John 16:30; 1 John 2:5;

1 Brown (*Epistles*, 526–27) summarizes the discussion. According to him, one may distinguish three possibilities: (1) ἐν τούτῳ is explained by the following ἵνα clause; (2) ἐν τούτῳ is explained by the ὅτι clause in v. 17c (this, however, would make v. 17b parenthetical, which would be a harsh and even "unnatural" construction; cf. also Westcott, *Epistles*, 157. Brown writes: "If the author meant to say this, he should have reversed the order of 17b and 17c"); (3) ἐν τούτῳ takes up what has been said in v. 16d. In what follows, I will defend this third interpretation.

2 Bultmann, *Epistles*, 72; thus also Brooke, *Epistles*, 123–24; Schnackenburg, *Epistles*, 222; Schneider, "Briefe," 177–78; Friedrich Hauck, *Die Kirchenbriefe: Die Briefe des Jakobus, Petrus, Judas und Johannes* (NTD 10; 8th ed.; Göttingen: Vandenhoeck & Ruprecht, 1957) 141.

3 1:4; 3:8, 11, 23; 4:21; 5:3; cf. 2 John 6, and frequently.

4 1:5; 3:16; 4:9–10, 13; 5:9, 11, 14.

5 Thus correctly Brown, *Epistles*, 526 ("Love has reached perfection in something that has not yet happened").

6 Bultmann, *Epistles*, 72.

7 Thus also Neil Alexander, *The Epistles of John* (TBC; London: SCM, 1962) 111–12; Alfred Plummer, *The Epistles of St. John* (CBSC; Cambridge: Cambridge University Press, 1889) 105; Westcott, *Epistles*, 157; Brown, *Epistles*, 527; Marshall, *Epistles*, 223 (with reference to 2:5); Weiss, *Briefe*, 129 (with reference to 2:5; 3:10, 19); Vellanickal, *Divine Sonship*, 347: "The phrase 'ἐν τούτῳ' refers to the preceding affirmation of communion with God." He refers to John 15:8. On ἐν τούτῳ see also above at 1 John 3:10 and 3:19.

3:19. What is meant is that the perfection of love is achieved when the exchange between the divine and human lovers takes place. Only in the interpenetration of the loving divine and human existence is love itself perfected (cf. v. 12).

The verb τελειοῦν ("to perfect") appears in 1 John only in the passive voice.[8] It includes the idea of wholeness and undividedness, but without losing its concrete reference.[9] Hence the subject ἀγάπη, as well, is not limited to the spiritual; it is provided with a concrete goal. It is a question of the love of God in the community (μεθ' ἡμῶν) that must be realized *here and now* as "mutual love."[10]

The actualization of Christian *agapē* includes the certainty of having "boldness in the day of judgment" (ἵνα παρρησίαν ἔχωμεν ἐν τῇ ἡμέρᾳ τῆς κρίσεως). No matter how much the love of God and of human beings abounds in the community (as was also made clear in v. 12), it needs a future-eschatological goal. It contains within itself an intention (ἵνα) that points to an event that has not yet happened. Here, as elsewhere in Hellenistic Greek, no exact distinction is drawn between intention and consequence, particularly when an outcome is implied that is thus far only imagined.[11] The apocalyptic background of the Johannine school tradition is evident in the tension that characterizes the orientation of Christian *agapē* to both the present and the future. Behind the word παρρησία is a future eschatological sense.[12] This future aspect is also familiar to Hellenistic Jewish wisdom literature: "Then [at the final judgment] the righteous will stand with great confidence (ἐν παρρησίᾳ πολλῇ) in the presence of those who have oppressed them" (Wis 5:1). By contrast, the older proverbial literature testifies that the godless are marked by their lack of παρρησία (Prov 13:5; 20:9; cf. *T. Reub.* 4.2–3). This situation corresponds to 1 John 2:28, according to which the righteous (unlike sinners) need not be ashamed on the day of judgment.[13] In this verse,

8 Cf. 2:5; 4:12, 17–18; also John 17:23; 19:28; the active in the Fourth Gospel always has the accusative object τὸ ἔργον (John 4:34; 5:36; 17:4 in the sense of "finish." Hans Hübner differs (*EDNT* 3 [1993] 344), preferring to translate the active voice in the Fourth Gospel with "carry out," so as to distinguish it, as does Bultmann (*John*, 194 n. 3), from "bringing something to a finish which has already been begun." Cf. also Gerhard Delling, "τελειόω," *TDNT* 8 (1972) 81–82.

9 Hübner (*EDNT* 3 [1993] 345) emphasizes that in all four passages in which τελειόω appears in 1 John, it stands in the context of *agapē*. On this, see also Delling, "τελειόω," 81–82. The verb τελειόω is said to describe, in the perfect passive form used in 1 John, "the completeness or perfection of the love of God or of the Christian in love." He indicates that the choice of the verbal form instead of the adjective emphasizes that it is only "in brotherly love, in obedience . . . [that] the love of God achieve[s] totality in the lives of Christians." On this, cf. Georg Strecker, *The Sermon on the Mount: An Exegetical Commentary* (trans. O. C. Dean, Jr.; Nashville: Abingdon, 1988) 92–97 (on Matt 5:48): "In spite of the absolute divine claim, perfection does not stand in opposition to the concrete demand. It is also not a human super-achievement that stands at the pinnacle of an ethical scale of values; it is rather the human realization of the totality of Jesus' instructions and hence identical with the demanded 'righteousness' (5:20)."

10 1 John 3:11, 23; 4:7, 12; cf. 2 John 5.

11 On the "mixture of intention and consequence" in the NT use of ἵνα, cf. BDR § 391 (10); Radermacher, *Neutestamentliche Grammatik*, 191–92; Zerwick, *Biblical Greek* nos. 406–15. Ethelbert Stauffer ("ἵνα," *TDNT* 3 [1965] 323–33) explains that Pauline and non-Pauline final clauses can speak not only of the "*purpose of the divine work of salvation*," but also of the "*goals* which God has set for human action" (p. 332). Certainly, in the Koine ἵνα can "take on consecutive and even causal significance," but it is said that in the NT this shift of meaning is "less common, and it is of no theological importance" (p. 323). In contrast, Peter Lampe ("ἵνα," *EDNT* 2 [1991] 189–90) emphasizes that frequently, in Johannine usage, a consecutive or imperative understanding of ἵνα is possible as an alternative to a "final" interpretation. Balz ("Johannesbriefe," 200) sees the "point" of the statement in 4:17 in the idea "that believers already know the heavenly Lord and Judge before the parousia." This is said to make the thought of judgment still more intense; for the church's "historical reality in conflict with the unholy world calls for the complete, final revelation of God, in which the division between good and evil, now already present, will be brought to its ultimate realization."

12 So also in 2:28; differently in 3:21 and 5:14 (q.v.).

13 On this, see Schlier, "παρρησία," 876–79; παρρησία appears frequently in *1 Enoch* in eschatological contexts: 62.10, 15; 63.1–12; 69.26, and often; cf. also *4 Ezra* 7.87; *1 Enoch* 62.3–5 (sinners must feel shame on the day of judgment).

παρρησία means freedom from fear. There is an important apocalyptic parallel in *4 Ezra* 7.98–101: "The seventh [joy of the righteous, . . . is that] they shall rejoice with boldness, and shall be confident without confusion, and shall be glad without fear."[14] Those who have this freedom will not be ashamed before the coming judge of the world; nor need they fear punishment; "for παρρησία is simply a reflection of the fulness of the love of God for us in which we abide. Abiding in the love of God, which knows no fear because it keeps the commandments, is brought to light in the future judgment in the fact that we have access and openness, i.e., *parrhesia*, to God."[15]

The expression ἡμέρα τῆς κρίσεως ("day of judgment"), found only at this point in the Johannine writings, is still more strongly marked by apocalypticism.[16] While its background is the OT idea of the "day of YHWH" (Joel 3:4 LXX; cf. Acts 2:20), it was interpreted in Jewish apocalyptic as the great day of judgment: this is the day of the revelation of wrath and of judgment on sinners.[17] Corresponding to this in early Christian literature is the expectation of the end, connected with the idea of the coming of Christ for judgment.[18] The expression "the day of judgment" appears with especial frequency in this sense, with reference to Christ.[19] Instructive for the development of the Johannine tradition is the comparison between Matt 10:15 ("day of judgment") and the parallel in Luke 10:12 ("on that day"). Like Luke (and Matthew), the Fourth Gospel presupposes the older Christian apocalyptic tradition of the "last day" as the day of resurrection and judgment and, in spite of the strongest kind of emphasis on a present eschatological perspective, allows it to show through in a great variety of expressions.[20] For the author of 1 John there can be no doubt that the traditional idea of a future judgment applies also to him and his community.[21] It is true that this community has been drawn into the perfection of love that is happening here and now.[22] The realization

14 *NRSV;* cf. Schlier, "παρρησία," 879.

15 Ibid., 882.

16 The reading ἀγάπη in place of ἡμέρα, attested by ℵ pc, is probably traceable to a displacement (cf. v. 17a: ἀγάπη).

17 Cf. *1 Enoch* 10.12: "When all their sons kill each other, and when they see the destruction of their beloved ones, (then) bind them for seventy generations under the hills of the earth until the day of their judgement and of their consummation, until the judgement which is for all eternity is accomplished." (According to Siegbert Uhlig, *Das Äthiopische Henochbuch* [JSHRZ 5/6; Gütersloh: Mohn, 1983] 551, "day of the [great] judgement" is "an expression found in almost every part of *1 Enoch*": 10.6; 19.1; 22.4, 13; 45.6; 94.9; 96.8; 97.3; 98.8, 10; 99.15; 100.4; 104.5, and elsewhere.) The idea appears frequently in other parts of Jewish apocalyptic literature, e.g., *4 Ezra* 7.113–14: "But the day of judgment will be the end of this age and the beginning of the immortal age to come, in which corruption has passed away, sinful indulgence has come to an end, unbelief has been cut off, and righteousness has increased and truth has appeared." Cf. also *Ps. Sol.* 15.12; Wis 3:13–18; *Jub.* 5.10; 24.30. According to Wilhelm Bousset and Hugo Gressmann (*Die Religion des Judentums in späthellenistischen Zeitalter* [HNT 21; 4th ed.; Tübingen: Mohr [Siebeck], 1966] 257), the formulas "the great judgment" and "the last day" are of central importance in Jewish apocalyptic; they stem from the idea of a judgment on Israel's enemies by the "heroic captain, YHWH, fighting with the sword," and are spiritualized into the notion of a genuine act of judgment, when God will sit on the throne with the books of judgment open before him and surrounded by his court (as in Dan 7:9–12). See further references in ibid., 257 nn. 1 and 3.

18 The influence of Jewish apocalyptic is especially noticeable in the concepts of "the day of God" (2 Pet 3:12; Rev 16:14) and "the day of the Lord" (Acts 2:20; 2 Pet 3:10). Even Paul makes no distinction in meaning among "the day of [Jesus] Christ" (Phil 1:6, 10; 2:16), "the day of the Lord" (1 Thess 5:2; 1 Cor 5:5; cf. 2 Cor 1:14: "the day of our Lord Jesus"), and "the day" (1 Thess 5:4; 1 Cor 3:13). However little it may be disputed that the different terminology reveals a variety of influences from OT and Jewish contexts, in early Christian literature "the day of the manifestation of the glory of Christ is very closely linked with the day of world judgment" (Gerhard Delling, "ἡμέρα," *TDNT* 2 [1964] 952).

19 Thus Matt 10:15; 11:22, 24; 13:36–43 (cf. 12:40–41 par.; Luke 11:31–32); 2 Pet 2:9; 3:7; *Barn.* 19.10; 21:6; *2 Clem.* 16.3 (cf. also Jude 6; *2 Clem.* 17.6). With reference to this, cf. 2 Esdr 13:52: "Just as no one can explore or know what is in the depths of the sea, so no one on earth can see my Son or those who are with him, except in the time of his day." See also *1 Enoch* 61.9.

20 Cf. "on the last day," John 6:39–40; 11:24; 12:48; "my day," John 8:56; "on that day," John 14:20; 16:23, 26; as well as the "authority of the Son of Man to execute judgment," John 5:27–29.

of such love among Christians is sufficient reason for certainty that on the day of judgment the Christian congregation, as a community of those who love, will have confidence, that is, that they will be able to stand firm before the judge of the world.[23]

The ὅτι clause refers back to v. 17a and gives its foundation: the reason why love is perfected among us is that we, "like him," are in the world. The existence of the community in the world is an existence in *agapē*. What is the referent of the comparative (and at the same time explanatory) clause: καθὼς ἐκεῖνός ἐστιν ("as he is")? According to the grammatical sequence, it would be speaking of God as ἐκεῖνος; then the subject would remain the same from v. 16 through v. 17 to v. 19 ("[God] first loved us"). This would also agree with the content of the preceding statement, namely, that God's existence is characterized by *agapē* (vv. 8, 16). Nevertheless, commentators, with scarcely an exception, refer this demonstrative pronoun to Christ. This is suggested by the parallel passages (2:6; 3:3, 7, and others), which use a similar explanatory and comparative construction to refer to Christ as example.[24] In the present passage, as in those others, there is no intention to create an alternative between the past, present (cf. 2:1), and future of Christ. Even though the reading attested by minuscule 2138 emphasizes the past of the incarnate one,[25] the present tense of ἐστίν shows that the model existence of Christ transcends time and space and is meant to be determinative for the community in all ages. Accordingly, as early as 2:2 the universal atonement by Christ was stated in the present tense (ἱλασμός ἐστιν). Christ is the manifestation of God's *agapē*.[26] The community's task is derived from

21 Against Bultmann, *Epistles*, 72, according to whom ἐν τῇ ἡμέρᾳ τῆς κρίσεως is "an addition by the ecclesiastical redactor," because the following ὅτι clause is not intelligible; it is also said to be evident from the manuscript variants that the traditional text "does not make unambiguous sense" (ibid., n. 5); cf. idem, "Analyse," 153–54. In contrast, Smalley (*1, 2, 3 John*, 258) correctly points to the future eschatology in 1 John (2:18, 28; 3:2). Schunack writes similarly (*Briefe*, 84): "There is no compelling reason for attributing the traditional . . . presentation to an intervention by an ecclesial redactor."

22 According to Bultmann, *Epistles*, 73, ἀγάπη in v. 17a is "God's [ἀγάπη μεθ' ἡμῶν], and must therefore be the love of God given to us." Wengst writes similarly (*Brief*, 192): "the love mentioned in v. 17 [means] first and primarily God's own love." But the author speaks in absolute terms of the perfection of *agapē* among us, and not of the love of God, even though the one can scarcely be separated from the other. Even in v. 17a the idea of the *agapē* that is to be practiced by human beings is included. Only in this interpretation is there a seamless transition to v. 17c (ὅτι).

23 In v. 17b some minuscule manuscripts insert πρὸς τὸν ἐνανθρωπήσαντα, identifying the judge of the world with the incarnate Christ. As to its content this is not without foundation, since in what follows ἐκεῖνος is identical with Christ and 1 John makes no distinction between God who judges and Christ as judge of the world (cf. above at 2:28); however, this is a secondary expansion and is essentially significant only for the history of interpretation.

24 See above at 3:3. The demonstrative pronoun ἐκεῖνος is occasionally used of Jesus in the Fourth Gospel as well, but in a distancing manner (7:11; 9:12, 28; the interpretation of 19:35 is disputed). Erasmus already interpreted ἐκεῖνος as referring to Jesus (cf. *Paraphrasis in Evangelium Johannis, Opera Omnia* [10 vols.; Leiden: Vander Aa, 1703; reprinted London: Gregg, 1962] 7.641); however, the reference to the eyewitnesses in v. 35a is not improbable (cf. BDR § 291 [8]). In interpreting ἐκεῖνος in John 19:35 as referring to Jesus, Bultmann (*John*, 678 n. 6) explicitly cites 1 John 4:17. BAGD 239 explains that ἐκεῖνος in John frequently refers back to an immediately preceding word (John 5:37; 8:44; 10:6, 11, 29; 12:48; 14:21, 26; 16:14, and often elsewhere); this occurs in 1 John only at 5:16, where the demonstrative pronoun refers to the immediately preceding concept of ἁμαρτία πρὸς θάνατον, whereas elsewhere it always refers to Jesus Christ: 2:6; 3:3, 5, 7, 16. Cf. also Horst Balz, "ἐκεῖνος," *EDNT* 1 (1990) 409–10.

25 In place of ἐστίν, minuscule 2138 pc read ἦν ἐν τῷ κόσμῳ ἄμωμος καὶ καθαρός, οὕτως . . . ("As he was in the world pure and without reproach, so . . . ").

26 Cf. 4:9–10. From this point of view, Bultmann's suggested reconstruction (*Epistles*, 73) appears to have foundation (καθὼς ἐκεῖνός ἐστιν ἐν τῇ ἀγάπῃ τοῦ πατρός), although from a literary-critical perspective it certainly lacks probability. Windisch (*Die Katholischen Briefe*, 130) also believes, with reference to 4:16, that "something must be added, such as ἐν θεῷ or ἐν τῇ ἀγάπῃ." Cf. Philo *Poster. C.* 69: τὸ μὲν οὖν

this: it must present itself in the world in the same way as Christ did;[27] for it has already become obvious that in 1 John the indicative description of the Christian community's existence can often be understood as an indirect demand.[28] This community lives ἐν τῷ κόσμῳ τούτῳ. The demonstrative has a devaluative intent and emphasizes—in a way that is found only here in 1 John—the distance between the community and the world.[29] Elsewhere the author also sees the cosmos as the threatening opposite to the community (2:15–17; 3:1), for the "world" in its hatred persecutes the believers (3:13). In the "world" the false prophets are fomenting trouble (4:1–3) and the antichrist rules (4:3–4). It is therefore only consistent that at the end of this writing it should be said: "The whole world lies under the power of the evil one" (5:19). Nonetheless, the salvific mission of the Son is directed to the world (4:9, 14). Whoever takes the existence and activity of the Son as a model must, in the same way, actualize love in and for the world. This happens everywhere when love reaches its perfection (v. 17a) and believers can look to the future with confidence (v. 17b). So it must be when the Christian community accepts its responsibility and understands its existence as *agapē* in the world to be a binding obligation.[30]

The contrary attitude, also found in the community, is fear. Just as *parrhēsia* in face of the final judgment by definition excludes all anxiety and fear (v. 17b), it is also true of existence in *agapē* that it is separated from fear. The word φόβος is found only here in 1 John.[31] Since the community feels itself threatened "in this world," it is only natural that fear is not unknown to Christians. But it is of the nature of community with God (cf. vv. 13, 16) that it prepares a space in which there is room for nothing but *agapē*. It is a matter of either-or: love or fear! Just as believers cannot at the same time be children of God and of the devil (3:10), so they cannot be moved at the same time by fear and by love (cf. Rom 8:15: either the spirit of slavery to fall back into fear, or the spirit of adoption as sons and daughters). Such a description of the situation contains the demand to overcome the fear and anxiety that are present.

■ **18** This verse states specifically that *agapē* is the opposite of fear.[32] The absolute usage (like that in v. 17) indicates that it is not legitimate to set up an alternative between the love of God and that of human beings, or to ask whether the author is thinking only of one or the other.

κατὰ θεὸν ζῆν ἐν τῷ ἀγαπᾶν αὐτὸν ὁρίζεται Μωυσῆς ("Now Moses defines living in accordance with God as consisting in loving Him"). However, the necessity for such an addition is disputed by Preisker, *Die Katholischen Briefe*, 167: "The one born again, in his divine way, that is, his ἀγάπη, which he now has for God and exercises towards his brethren, is full of confidence on the day of judgment. . . . In the practice of ἀγάπη Christians follow the model that the historical Christ represents for them, and that supports their παρρησία."

27 Καθὼς . . . καί = "just as." Brown (*Epistles*, 332) points out that the construction καθὼς . . . καί is used in the Fourth Gospel when the Father's action on behalf of Jesus is compared with Jesus' action on behalf of the disciples (cf. John 15:9; 20:21). The plane of comparison is different in 1 John: "Just as Jesus was or did for the disciple, so must his disciples be or do." On the use of καθώς, cf. also above at 1 John 2:6 and 3:3.

28 Cf. above at 2:12–14.

29 Cf. also John 12:31b; 16:11: "This world" is subject to the devil's rule. For Jewish apocalyptic teaching on the eons, see *1 Enoch* 48.7 ("this world of iniquity"); 71.15 ("the world which is to come"); esp. *4 Ezra* 7.112–15: "This present world is not the end. . . . But the day of judgment will be the end of this age and the beginning of the immortal age to come, in which corruption has passed away, . . . and truth has appeared." Cf. also 7.50; 6.9; 9.19; *2 Bar.* 51.8–16; Hermann Sasse, "αἰών," *TDNT* 1 (1964) 206–7; Str-B 4.799–976: excursus, "This World, the Days of the Messiah, and the Future World."

30 The secondary reading ἐσόμεθα (ℵ 2138 pc) does not have a future but an imperative sense ("thus should we also be in this world!"); it makes explicit the text's indirect demand for love.

31 In the Johannine Letters, φόβος is found only at 4:17–18; φοβέομαι only at 4:18. The Fourth Gospel has the verb 5 times (John 6:19–20; 9:22; 12:15; 19:8), the noun 3 times (7:13; 19:38; 20:19). The fourth evangelist uses φόβος almost exclusively to describe fear of human beings (esp. the "Jews" as prototypes of unbelievers). The verb φοβέομαι, like the noun, indicates fear in face of the representatives of the Jewish order (9:22; 19:8) or the fear of the Jews (cf. the quotation in 12:15). Theological weight is given to φοβέομαι in the "epiphany fear" of the disciples, as a reaction of human beings toward miraculous revelation (6:19–20); cf. Horst Balz, *EDNT* 3 (1993) 430, 433.

32 This is evident already from the οὐκ . . . ἀλλά construction in vv. 17d–18a, which in the Johannine writings frequently expresses a fundamental

Instead, the subject is the all-embracing *agapē* that unites God and human beings. This is "perfect love" (ἡ τελεία ἀγάπη), love that has been perfected,[33] and that corresponds entirely to the will of God. It guarantees unity between God and human beings, as well as the unity of the congregation, embracing all its members.

Where *agapē* is found, fear has no right to exist: ἔξω βάλλει τὸν φόβον. The word ἀγάπη is personified, as the subject of the action of casting out. With sovereign power, love triumphs over fear.[34] There is an echo of the forensic-eschatological aspect, whereby the division at the judgment, between believers and unbelievers, righteous and unrighteous will be expressed by the unrighteous being "cast into the outer darkness."[35] In the Fourth Gospel, the ultimate division between Christ and Satan is similarly expressed,[36] and in contrast the community between Christ and his own has its negative paraphrase in the words: "I shall not cast them out" (οὐ μὴ ἐκβάλω ἔξω, John 6:37).

The incompatibility of love and fear is also evident from the fact that fear is associated with κόλασις. The original Greek understanding of this word is not so much related to "punishment" as to "discipline" or "physical training."[37] In Hellenism it takes on the meaning of "punishment" and later becomes a technical term for the "eternal punishment" that will be imposed at the final judgment. Thus it does not yet appear in Jewish apocalyptic literature, but evidently surfaces in Christian or Christian-redacted apocalyptic traditions.[38] The

opposition: cf. 1 John 2:16; 4:10; 5:18; John 5:30; 6:38; 7:16, and often elsewhere; see also Walter Radl, "ἀλλά," *EDNT* 1 (1990) 61.

33 The adjective τέλειος occurs only here in the Johannine writings (cf. Matt 5:48; 19:21; Jas 1:4, 17, 25, and frequently). For τελειόω, cf. 1 John 2:5; 4:12, 17 (each time, as here, in connection with ἀγάπη). The context is different in the Fourth Gospel (John 4:34; 5:36; 17:4). There, what is to be perfected is τὰ ἔργα or τὸ ἔργον; in contrast, John 17:23 speaks of the perfection of unity; John 19:28 of the fulfillment of Scripture. If the aorist with the accusative is understood in the sense of "actualize," "carry out," the passive perfect forms in 1 John express "wholeness," "completeness"; this understanding is also found in the Gospel (John 17:23; 19:28). Cf. Delling, "τελειόω," 81–82.

34 For the contrast between fear and love, cf. the epigram of Palladas in *Anthologia Graeca* 11.385: Πλαστὸν ἔχεις τὸν ἔρωτα, φόβῳ δὲ φιλεῖς καὶ ἀνάγκῃ· τοῦ δὲ φιλεῖν οὕτως οὐδὲν ἀπιστότερον ("Thy love is counterfeit and thou lovest from fear and by force. But nothing is more treacherous than such love"). On the meaning of love in contrast to fear, cf. Cicero *De officiis* 2.7: "Omnium autem rerum nec aptius est quicquam ad opes tuendas ac tenendas quam diligi nec alienius quam timeri" ("The most suitable means to achieve and assert power is love, while the least suitable is fear").

35 Thus Matt 22:13: ἐκβάλετε αὐτὸν εἰς τὸ σκότος τὸ ἐξώτερον; cf. Matt 25:30; ἔξω βάλλειν is also found at Matt 5:13; 13:48; Luke 14:35; John 15:6; like the more frequent ἔξω ἐκβάλλειν (Matt 21:39 par.; Luke 4:29; John 6:37; 9:34–35, and often) it implies an intensification of ἐκβάλλειν, which in the NT is used primarily in connection with the driving out of demons: Mark 1:34 par., and frequently; 3:15, 22–23 par.; 7:26, 29–30; 9:18, 28, 38 par.; Matt 7:22; 8:31; 9:33; 12:27, and frequently. In the Fourth Gospel it is found also at 2:15; 6:37; 9:34–35; 10:4; 12:31. In the Johannine Letters, ἐκβάλλειν is otherwise found only at 3 John 10 in the sense of "excommunicate" (q.v.).

36 Thus in John 12:31: ὁ ἄρχων τοῦ κόσμου τούτου ἐκβληθήσεται ἔξω ("the ruler of this world will be driven out").

37 The word κόλασις was not yet used by Homer; in the Platonic writings it is used to mean "discipline," "punishment," "reprimand" (Plato *Prot.* 323; *Leg.* 11.932); Aristotle (*Rhet.* 1.10) distinguishes between κόλασις and τιμωρία ("punishment"); Theophrastus (372–287 BCE) uses κόλασις for the pruning of trees (*De causis plantarum* [2.4.4] 3.18.2).

38 Philo already emphasizes that the thought of punishment (κόλασις) causes terror (δέος) (*Spec. leg.* 4.6), and he is acquainted with the pedagogical connection between fear and punishment; cf. *Agric.* 40: fear (φόβος) is seen as the "corrector" (σωφρονιστής), insofar as "punishment" (κόλασις) is prescribed as a "boon" for the ignorant. *Abr.* 129: God receives in friendly fashion the one "who [out of fear] (φόβῳ) propitiates the dominance and authority of the master to avoid chastisement (εἰς ἀποτροπὴν κολάσεως)." Cf. also *Vit. Mos.* 1.96 (where κόλασις means the same as τιμωρία and is used of the ten punishments inflicted on the Egyptians before Israel's exodus); *Conf. ling.* 171 ("chastisement is not a thing of harm or mischief, but a preventive and correction of sin"). According to Josephus *Ant.* 1.60, the "punishment" (κόλασις) was intended to serve as a "warning" (νουθεσία) for Cain. The meaning of divine punishment was frequently discussed in Hellenistic

apocalyptic terminology that precedes it here (esp. v. 17b: ἡμέρα τῆς κρίσεως) indicates that the future-eschatological horizon is also to be taken into account, so that we could think of ἔχει as also meaning "has in view."[39] This corresponds to the idea that Christians' future posture in face of the judge of the world will be characterized by confidence, and not by fear (v. 17b). This kind of expectation includes an assertion about the present.[40] Of course, it is not a question of closing off the future-eschatological perspective and referring the concept of φόβος only to the present.[41] The author's thinking is really dialectic: Fear looks (in one sense) toward the future punishment at the final judgment. As such fear is an impossible eventuality for Christians, because perfected love includes openness and confidence before the judge of the world. Nonetheless, fear can be understood as "punishment" even in the present;[42] for those who are fearful not only before God but also before human beings[43] demonstrate thereby that they have not achieved perfect love and are not yet really living in community with God. Fear anticipates what will be accomplished at the final judgment in the form of a division between the children of God and of Satan, that is, expulsion from the community of those who love. Hence it can be understood as a punishment already effective in the present. In the true community this is an unreal possibility, for where love is genuine there is a complete separation from fear. But because the fulfillment of this true existence of the Christian community, wholly determined by *agapē,* is still in the future, it

---

(Stoic) theodicy debates: cf. Plutarch *Stoic. rep.* 35 (1050E: Chrysippus); idem, *De sera numinis vindicta* (553–54, 555D); Johannes Schneider, "κολάζω," *TDNT* 3 (1965) 816–17. The LXX uses the idea primarily in Ezek 14:3, 4, 7; 18:30; and Wis 19:4 in speaking of divine punishments; also 2 Macc 4:38; in the NT it appears, apart from the present verse, also in Matt 25:46 (εἰς κόλασιν αἰώνιον). The concept of κόλασις αἰώνιος is also found in *T. Reub.* 5.5; *T. Gad* 7.5; Origen *C. Cels.* 8.48; also *Mart. Pol.* 2.3; *2 Clem.* 6.7; *1 Clem.* 11.1; the absolute κόλασις has the same meaning: *Diog.* 9.2; *Herm. Sim.* 9.18.1; *T. Levi* 4.1. Since the Byzantine era, κόλασις has simply meant "hell"; in *Apoc. Pet.* 21 it is called τόπος κολάσεως (Schneider, "κολάζω," *TDNT* 3 [1965] 816).

39 Thus Windisch and Preisker, *Die Katholischen Briefe,* 130.

40 Cf. also the Zurich Bible: "Denn die furcht hat pein [For fear has its own agony]"; so also Martin Luther, WA (*Deutsche Bibel*) 7.336 (cf. idem, revised text of 1984: "Denn die Furcht muss vor der Strafe zittern [For fear must tremble before punishment]"). On this, see Luther's sermon on 1 John 4:18 (28 July 1532, WA 36.471–72): "*Ideo* kan mich die Welt nicht verzagt machen, wie wol ich nicht drauff fusse ut Paulus 1. Cor. 'Nihil mihi,' 'sed per hoc.' Item 1. Thess. 2. 'ut pater' sc. das ist ein ruhm et fiducia etiam ad extremum diem, 'sed per hoc non iustificatus.' Quando hoc habes, so hastu dich entledight der Furcht der Welt" ("Therefore, the world cannot cause me to fail, so long as I do not rely on it, as Paul says in 1 Corinthians '[I am not aware of] anything against myself' 'but through this [I am not justified, 1 Cor 4:4],' and again in 1 Thessalonians 'like a father [with his children we exhorted you, 1 Thess 2:11],' that is a source of pride, and of confidence for the last day, 'but [one is] not thereby justified [1 Cor 4:4].' When you have this [attitude], then you have put off the fear of the world").

41 Thus Bultmann, *Epistles,* 74, who in this context thinks an appropriate interpretation is "fear contains its own punishment." In that event, "the concept of the eschatological κόλασις ('punishment') is historicized like the concept κρίσις ('judgment') in John 3:19." Horst Balz's opinion is similar (*EDNT* 3 [1993] 432, on 1 John 4:18): "The traditional OT Jewish rhetoric concerning fear of God is jettisoned here; the redeemed now also know the God of judgment only as the God of love, before whom they are already living, focused on Christ, in unlimited παρρησία (4:17)." Schnackenburg (*Epistles,* 225) differs: "Fear is not a punishment in itself, but a kind of mesmerized contemplation of the prospect of future judgment."

42 Thus Westcott, *Epistles,* 160: "Fear . . . must include suffering. And the suffering . . . is divine punishment . . . such punishment is not future only but present."

43 Against Bultmann, *Epistles,* 73, according to whom it is only a question of "fear before God." But absolute φόβος cannot be understood one-dimensionally, any more than absolute ἀγάπη; they also refer to the relationship between human beings. Cf. also Horst Balz, "φοβέω," *TDNT* 9 (1974) 214–17: "Fear as Exhortation"; and Strecker, *Weg,* 234: expression of the "helplessness of human existence."

remains the task of believers to allow themselves to be shaped by *agapē* ever anew, to overcome fear, and to approach the goal where love, freedom, and truth will be joined in harmony (cf. 2 John 3; 3 John 1), and therefore will have achieved their ultimate fulfillment.[44]

The particle δέ does not refer to the immediately preceding ὅτι clause but concludes the main clause of v. 18a with an antithesis. If love excludes all fear, it can be said in turn that no one who is dominated by fear truly loves. The perfect τετελείωται resumes the adjective τελεία (v. 18a) and says that the love of one who fears has not been perfected. This can scarcely be said to presuppose a scale of various forms of realization of *agapē*;[45] rather, the author could also have said that someone who fears is not living in love,[46] for he is thinking of absolute *agapē* as it is described in v. 16 and as it is to be actualized in the world by the Christian community.

■ **19** The personal pronoun ἡμεῖς takes up the first person plurals from vv. 16 and 17 (μεθ' ἡμῶν),[47] confirming that, in spite of the shifts between adhortative and descriptive presentation, the author never loses sight of the community being addressed; instead, the intracommunity parenesis continues. The continuity of the train of thought cannot be disputed, either, by interpreting ἀγαπῶμεν in the sense of "love of the sisters and brothers," whereby the theme of vv. 7–12 would be resumed at this point;[48] the absolute use of the verb here continues the absolute ἀγάπη of vv. 16–18, and the author has deliberately refused to specify either of these concepts.[49] The question whether the finite verb is to be

44 A psychological interpretation of v. 18b, as suggested by Windisch and Preisker (*Die Katholischen Briefe*, 130), is false: "18 offers a sensitive commentary on the psychology of faith"; similarly Oskar Pfister, *Das Christentum und die Angst* (Zurich: Artemis, 1944; ET *Christianity and Fear* [trans. W. H. Johnston; London: Allen & Unwin; New York: Macmillan, 1948]) 18–19, who sees 1 John 4:18 as formulating an almost "neurological doctrine" and draws the conclusion, "Thus according to 1 John 4:18 fear results from disordered love." However, the author of 1 John does not intend to write a psychogram of believers, but to describe an eschatological and ontological fact in order to draw parenetic conclusions from it.

45 Against Windisch and Preisker, *Die Katholischen Briefe*, 130 ("The author apparently knows of an imperfect early stage, at which love has not yet been able to cast out fear"). Brown (*Epistles*, 532) rightly disputes this. Of the suggestion that this represents "a parallel to the Pauline idea of gradation among Christians so that only some are perfect or mature," he says: "This is dubious, however, for in Johannine dualism the opposite to perfect love may not be imperfect love but hate."

46 Thus also *1 Clem.* 49.5: "By love all God's elect were made perfect (ἐν τῇ ἀγάπῃ ἐτελειώθησαν)," followed by the significant statement: "Without love nothing can please God"; cf. *1 Clem.* 50.3.

47 According to Brown (*Epistles*, 532), the placement of ἡμεῖς at the beginning of the sentence is for emphasis; thus it could be further strengthened by the addition of οὖν (as in the secondary variants in A 048^vid, 33, 69, 623, 2464 *al* r vg). However, the primary placement of the personal pronoun is a common rhetorical feature of Johannine letter style (cf. also [καὶ] ἡμεῖς in 3:14, 16; 4:16–17 and [καὶ] ὑμεῖς in 1:3; 2:20, 24, 27; 4:4). Distinct from this is the author's literary "we," by means of which he locates himself in relation to his audience (1:4; 4:6, 14; on this, see the commentary above). This allows no inference of a polemical situation, for it is difficult to suppose, with Bultmann (*Epistles*, 75), that vv. 20–21 are "evidently directed against the gnosticizing notion that human love can be aimed directly at God."

48 Thus Bultmann, *Epistles*, 75–76.

49 This first appears in secondary readings in which either τὸν θεόν (thus ℵ and others) or αὐτόν (Ψ 𝔐) is introduced as the object of ἀγαπῶμεν. According to Bultmann, *Epistles*, 76, the "leading question" to be presupposed here is "the question of the [ἀγαπᾶν τὸν θεόν]." Then on the basis of v. 20 one could demonstrate why those people who say they love God but stand in a relationship of hatred to their brothers and sisters are rejected. However, this very continuation of the thought says that the love of God and of the sisters and brothers are intertwined in the most intimate manner possible. The author has deliberately avoided giving an object for ἀγαπῶμεν in order to preserve the general and comprehensive character of the expression. Schnackenburg differs (*Epistles*, 225): according to him, "the author already has the subject of mutual (human) love in mind, and not . . . love toward God."

understood as indicative or imperative[50] should be decided in favor of the latter.[51] This corresponds to 4:7, 11, while the contrast of indicative and imperative in this verse is also closely paralleled in 4:10–11.[52]

The demand for *agapē* addressed by the author to his hearers is founded on the statement that God first loved us (αὐτὸς πρῶτος ἠγάπησεν ἡμᾶς). The reading ὁ θεός in place of the personal pronoun produces a clarification[53] without changing the meaning, for it is clear from what has preceded that one should think of ὁ θεός as the subject (cf. vv. 9–10, 20). God's love is temporally prior to human love;[54] it has made itself known in Jesus Christ. The revelation of divine love in Jesus Christ represents the ἀρχή of the community.[55] But as regards its real implications also, divine love precedes the human, because it opens up the possibility for a new existence in which love for God and for one's sisters and brothers becomes a reality.[56] It implies an obligation for the Christian community to make this loving existence concrete (3:16b; 4:11). It is thus realized in the overcoming of fear. The demand of *agapē* points out a way that is determined not by fear, lies, hatred, and death, but by confidence, truth, love, and life.

■ **20** Now for the first time we find a definite assertion that love of God and love of one's sister or brother cannot be separated. This is additional confirmation that the absolute ἀγάπη and ἀγαπᾶν in vv. 17–19 do not refer to love for God.[57] The initial ἐάν τις εἴπῃ (lit.: "if anyone says") does not necessarily introduce the proposition of a false teacher, which would suggest here an opposing

---

50 When interpreting ἀγαπῶμεν in an imperative sense one should think of a hortatory subjunctive; cf. BDF § 364.

51 Against Weiss, *Briefe*, 132; Windisch and Preisker, *Die Katholischen Briefe*, 131; Wengst, *Brief*, 196; Brown, *Epistles*, 532. Brown points to the indicative statements in vv. 14a and 16a, but emphasizes that while no definite decision is possible, "the tone of confidence throughout this subsection favors the indicative." In favor of my interpretation is the fact that the indicatives in the immediately preceding and following verses also have an imperative intention.

52 However, one may not say with Bultmann (*Epistles*, 75) that the section 4:19—5:4 "does not contain any new and developing thoughts [with respect to 4:7–12], but repeats, with slight variations, what had already been said." No matter how much one may see here "a combination of individual meditations or discussions of the Johannine 'school'" (ibid.), one will see in what follows that, in the course of his writing, the author produces increasingly concrete statements.

53 The reading ὁ θεὸς πρῶτος is found in A 33, 81^vid *al* lat; ὁ θεὸς πρῶτον in 623, 2464 pc; ὁ θεὸς αὐτὸς πρῶτον in 1505, 2495 pc.

54 Πρῶτος occurs only here in 1 John. In the Fourth Gospel the concept appears 15 times (including the variant readings in 5:4 and 8:7), in both anthropological (2:10; 20:4, 8) and christological (1:15; 8:30) contexts; cf. also 15:18: the disciples of the Revealer know that the world has hated Christ "before you." Brown (*Epistles*, 532) and Schnackenburg (*Epistles*, 225 n. 91) point out that πρῶτος can have a comparative meaning (πρότερος); cf., e.g., John 1:15, 30 or 2:10; 20:4, 8; on this, see BDF § 62.

55 See above at 1:1 (ἀπ' ἀρχῆς).

56 Cf. 3:16; it is characteristic that in this connection the author does not mention the law and human enslavement under the demands of the law; he is not living in an environment of Jewish thought. Consequently, it is false to the Johannine worldview to suspect that this passage (or 4:10) implies an aversion to works-righteousness (against Schneider, "Briefe," 179, according to whom the author rejects the idea "that the love that leads to the overcoming of fear is our own work"). On this subject, cf. Dietrich Bonhoeffer, *Ethics* (ed. Eberhard Bethge; trans. Neville Horton Smith; London: SCM; New York: Macmillan, 1955) 175–76: "The relation between the divine love and human love is wrongly understood if we say that the divine love precedes the human love, but solely for the purpose of setting human love in motion as a love which, in relation to the divine love is an independent, free and autonomous activity of man. On the contrary, everything which is to be said of human love, too, is governed by the principle that God is love. The love with which man loves God and his neighbor is the love of God and no other; for there is no other love; there is no love which is free or independent from the love of God. In this, then, the love of men remains purely passive. Loving God is simply the other aspect of being loved by God. Being loved by God implies loving God; the two do not stand separately side by side."

57 Since v. 20 makes the absolute ἀγαπῶμεν (v. 19) concrete, as love for God and the brothers and sisters, one could join Brown (*Epistles*, 563) in regarding the passage from 4:20 to 5:4a as an independent subsection. However, even here the author's meditative style allows one to discern no definitive caesura, especially since the preceding passage spoke of the commandment of mutual love

thesis to the effect that the false teachers laid claim to possessing the love of God;[58] for *τις* has a general significance elsewhere in 1 John as well, and cannot be limited to the emergence of opponents.[59] In the same way, in NT usage the verb *εἰπεῖν* often appears at the beginning of a rhetorical expression,[60] or it expresses a possibility that can be generally realized in the Christian church.[61] Even though one can imagine, in principle, that the docetic teachers within the environment of 1 John acknowledged only the dimension of love for God, and deliberately ignored the question of relationships with fellow human beings, this is not a conclusion that can be clearly drawn from the text. According to the structure of the document and the intention of the author, it is primarily the audience, that is, the Christian community *in toto* that is being addressed, and so it has been understood throughout the many centuries of the letter's reception. The Christian community in every age is constantly in danger of neglecting the ethical consequences of its confession of Christ (vv. 9–10) and of the saving indicative of the love of God (v. 19), and thereby being unfaithful to the "law" that constitutes it.

Those who do not make the connection, who fail to understand the urgent consequences that the event of salvation imposes on them but instead are consumed by hatred toward their fellow human beings,[62] fall out of the realm of communion with God. They separate themselves from the sphere of truth and love and become *ψεύστης* ("liars"). They not only speak falsehood but are divorced from the only genuine reality, that of God.[63] They belong to the world, whose ruler is the *διάβολος*.[64] Such behavior is on the same level with that

(vv. 11–12; cf. v. 21). Cf. also Bultmann, *Epistles*, 76; and Schnackenburg, *Epistles*, 225, both of whom treat v. 19 as a transition to 4:20—5:4.

58 Thus Wengst, *Brief*, 196: the author "quotes a thesis of the opponents (love for God—20a), contrasts it with a type of behavior that contradicts it (hatred of the brethren—20b), and draws the conclusion that the one who utters this thesis is a liar (20c)." Schnackenburg also emphasizes (*Epistles*, 226) "that the author has returned to his polemic against the gnostics." However, he "unmasks them with all their specious words, with which they pretend to fellowship with God but fail in showing mutual love."

59 Ἐάν τις appears in 1 John also at 2:1, 15; 5:16; εἴ τις at 2 John 10; τις at 1 John 2:27. Cf. the rhetorical ὁ λέγων: 2:4, 6, 9; 5:16, alternating with πᾶς ὁ: 2:23, 29; 3:3, 4, 6 (bis), 9, 10, 15; 4:7; 5:1 (bis), 18; also the generalizing ὃς ἐάν: 4:15. In the same way, the preceding ὁ φοβούμενος (v. 18) has a general meaning, referring to the Christian community as a whole. Cf. BDF § 301; Zerwick, *Biblical Greek*, 9; Klaus Beyer, *Semitische Syntax im Neuen Testament* 1/1 (2d ed.; Göttingen: Vandenhoeck & Ruprecht, 1968) 226 20.

60 Cf. ἐρεῖ τις in 1 Cor 15:35; Jas 2:18; ἐρεῖς οὖν in Rom 9:19; 11:19; BAGD 226 (at 2b).

61 Cf. the first person plural ἐὰν εἴπωμεν in 1:6, 8, 10. As stated above, this does not reflect opposing teachers and their claims but is instead a matter of the church's self-understanding. This is said against Brown, *Epistles*, 533.

62 Ἀδελφός is, in the first instance, the designation for fellow Christians; with this meaning it occurs frequently in Paul's writings (Rom 8:29; 1 Cor 15:58; Phil 4:1, and often), and is also known to the Fourth Gospel: John 21:23 (cf. also 13:34–35; 15:12, 17). For the corresponding usage in 1 John, cf. 2:9–11; 3:10–17; 4:20–21; 5:16; cf. also 3 John 3, 5, 10. However, the word is also used in the NT in the sense of "neighbor," "fellow human": Matt 7:3–6 par.; 18:15 par. (cf. πλησίον in Matt 22:39 = Lev 19:18); Johannes Beutler, "ἀδελφός" *EDNT* 1 (1990) 28–30. The construction μισεῖν τὸν ἀδελφὸν αὐτοῦ is contrasted only here with ἀγαπᾶν τὸν ἀδελφὸν αὐτοῦ. It is identical with "being in darkness" (1 John 2:9, 11) or "being a murderer" (3:15). Μισεῖν corresponds to the behavior of the world, which pours its hatred on the Christian community (3:13). Thus it is also found in the Fourth Gospel (John 3:20; 7:7; 15:18–19; 17:14). Accordingly, such "hating" describes an active, negative deed that goes far beyond "not loving" one's brother or sister (cf. 1 John 3:17). There is little probability in Schnackenburg's restriction (*Epistles*, 226), according to which hatred concretely designates "the hatred of the gnostics and their secret enmity toward the true believers."

63 Cf. Bultmann, *Epistles*, 76; above at 1:6: "lying" (ψεύδεσθαι occurs only here in the Johannine writings) is identical with "not doing the truth" and "living in darkness." See also Hans Conzelmann, "ψεῦδος," *TDNT* 9 (1974) 602: the lie, in the Johannine sense, is not just "error but an active contesting of the truth, i.e., unbelief."

64 Cf. ἄρχων τοῦ κόσμου: John 12:31; 16:11; 14:30;

of the false prophets, who are also called "liars," because they close themselves against the truth of the Christ-confession (2:22). In this way the author has taken up anew the statement of 2:4 ("Whoever says, 'I have come to know him,' but does not obey his commandments, is a liar"). But here the connection between acknowledging and loving God is made more specific, because now the relationship between "loving" (*ἀγαπᾶν*) and "seeing" (*ὁρᾶν*) is brought into view.[65] After it had been said in 3 John 11 that "whoever does evil has not seen God," thus equating not loving God with not seeing God (cf. also 1 John 3:6), here the relationship between seeing and loving is described in a more reflective fashion and with greater clarity about its ethical relevance.[66] The author presupposes the idea, common not only in Hellenistic Judaism[67] but also in antiquity as a whole, that God is invisible.[68] This is also presumed by the Fourth Gospel when the invisibility and thus general unknowability of God is stated and it is said that only the Revealer has seen this God.[69] The idea that is pointedly expressed in a christological context there is here articulated in an ecclesiological and ethical sense. The statement takes the form of an aphorism: anyone who does not love the sister or brother who stands visibly before his or her eyes cannot love the invisible God.[70] This does not mean that love of the sisters and brothers is a first stage leading to love of God and therefore the immediate precondition of it.[71] Instead, the author wishes to say that love of sisters and brothers and love of God belong inseparably together, and together they constitute the reality of the one *agapē* given and demanded by God in the behavior of individual Christians and of the Christian community as a whole.

The parenetic intention is undeniable: the community's attention is directed to the existing reality, the needs of their brothers and sisters (cf. 3:17). This implies a rejection not only of Docetism but of every form of mystical adoration and vision of God that employs religion as a pretext for withdrawing from the demands of the social situation. As this danger is commonly present in Christian communities, and therefore to be presumed among the readers of 1 John, it is understandable that this passage impresses on them the unbreakable connection between love of God and love of the sisters and brothers. This occurs in a negative formulation in v. 20 (*μὴ*, *οὐχ*), and takes a positive form

διάβολος: 6:70; 8:44; 13:2. In 1 John it is said of the *διάβολος*: "the devil has been sinning from the beginning" (3:8).

65 This is the only place in the Johannine writings where this happens. The Fourth Gospel knows only the positive (20:8) or negative (20:25, 29) concept of the relationship between *ὁρᾶν* and *πιστεύειν*; it refers to the seeing and believing of the miracle; so also 11:45 (*θεᾶσθαι/πιστεύειν*).

66 A related argument, touching the relationship of children to their parents and making "reverence" an obligation of children, occurs in Philo *Decal.* 120: *ἀμήχανον δ' εὐσεβεῖσθαι τὸν ἀόρατον ὑπὸ τῶν εἰς τοὺς ἐμφανεῖς καὶ ἐγγὺς ὄντας ἀσεβούντων* ("and how can reverence be rendered to the invisible God by those who show irreverence to the gods who are near at hand and seen by the eye?").

67 Thus Jacob Kremer, "*ὁράω*," *EDNT* 2 (1991) 529.

68 Cf. also Wilhelm Michaelis, "*ὁράω*," *TDNT* 5 (1967) 315–67, at 320–21; also Empedocles, *frg.* 133: *οὐκ ἔστιν πελάσασθαι ἐν ὀφθαλμοῖσιν ἐφικτὸν ἡμετέροις ἢ χερσὶ λαβεῖν* ("one cannot bring the deity near to oneself as accessible to our eyes, or touch it with the hands").

69 John 1:18; 5:37; 6:46; 14:9; cf. 12:45.

70 This is not a rhetorical question (unlike 3:17), even though this might be suggested by the addition of the interrogative particle *πῶς* (A 048 𝔐 latt sy^p bo). Brown rightly emphasizes (*Epistles*, 533) that the conclusion *a minori ad maius* (Schnackenburg, *Epistles*, 226) in v. 20de is constructed chiastically: "[A] The one not loving [B] the brother whom he has seen, [B] the God whom he has not seen [A] he is not able to love." The perfect *ἑώρακεν* (v. 20de) expresses the "endurance of what has been perfected" (cf. BDF § 340). Since "seeing" the sister or brother, as well as "not seeing" God, endures to the present time, this is frequently translated in the present tense; Martin Luther, "den er sihet [whom he seeth]" (*Deutsche Bibel* 7:336); Zurich Bible: "den er von Angesicht kennt [whose countenance he knows]." The English translation "whom he has seen" (*NEB, RSV*) or "whom they have seen" (*NRSV*) is more accurate.

71 Against Windisch and Preisker, *Die Katholischen Briefe*, 131 ("While, according to [4:]7, 11, love of the brethren flows from the experience of the love of God, here one ascends from the former to the latter").

in the following verse.

■ **21** The copulative *καί* has not only a connective but also an epexegetical function.[72] It indicates that the following sentence draws a conclusion from what has gone before, reaching back at least to v. 19, where the imperative "We [must] love" illustrates the parenetical intention of the section. Were there any doubt about the author's intention to issue a warning, it is eliminated by the expression *ἐντολὴ καινή*. Thus what was said above about love of God and the brothers and sisters, and will be clarified in what follows, is the content of the Johannine "new commandment." It is "new" because it has been truly (2:8) given, namely, by God (*ἀπ' αὐτοῦ*) through Jesus Christ.[73] The difference between this and John 13:34, according to which Christ the Revealer teaches the new commandment to his disciples (cf. also John 15:12, 17), as well as our statement that the new commandment is God's gift to the community (also in 2 John 4–5: the commandment "[from] the Father, . . . one we have had from the beginning"), can be explained by the christological aim of the Fourth Gospel; it therefore indicates no discrepancy in the matter itself. Differently from what has gone before, the commandment of *agapē* is not only identified with the demand for love of the brothers and sisters, or for mutual love,[74] but refers to the connection between love of God and of the sisters and brothers. It thus represents a valuable early Christian "commentary on the double commandment of love as preached by Jesus,"[75] even though 1 John never quotes the Synoptic Gospels and, by its use of the expression "love of the *brothers and sisters*" creates an essential distinction between its own usage and the problem of love of God and *neighbor* as handed down by Mark 12:29–31 and parallels. The dense interweaving of love of God and of the sisters and brothers, as presented in the *ἵνα* clause's[76] connection of subject (*ὁ ἀγαπῶν τὸν θεὸν*) and predicate (*ἀγαπᾷ καὶ τὸν ἀδελφὸν αὐτοῦ*), constitutes the climax of the author's authoritative teaching to the Christian community. The community with God that presents itself as love of God is not an abstraction; it happens where it takes form in the praxis of love for the Christian sisters and brothers.

72 On this, see BDR § 442, 6 (even though there only examples of a *καί* within the clause are given). Cf. also Schnackenburg, *Epistles*, 227: "[*καί*] forms a close connection with v. 20," and Brown, *Epistles*, 534: "The 'and' tightly connects v. 21 to the preceding verse, upon which it is a commentary."

73 Instead of *ἀπ' αὐτοῦ*, some manuscript witnesses read *ἀπὸ τοῦ θεοῦ* (A 048^{vid} r vg^{cl}); this is clearly a secondary reading, but it correctly interprets the text as given.

74 Cf. also 3:23: "his commandment" has the twofold content of believing in Christ and loving one another, esp. at 2:7–11: the old and new commandment to love the sister or brother; on this, see the commentary on those verses.

75 Schnackenburg, *Epistles*, 227.

76 "*Ἱνα* in combinaton with a preceding demonstrative has an explicative meaning; cf. above at 4:17–18. On this, see Peter Lampe, "*ἵνα*," *EDNT* 2 (1991) 190 (with reference to John 6:39, 40; 15:12; 1 John 3:11, 23; 4:21; 5:3; 2 John 6a, and elsewhere).

5 The Actions of Those Who Are Born of God: Loving God's Children and Keeping the Commandments

1 Everyone who believes that Jesus is the Christ has been born of God, and everyone who loves the parent loves the child. 2/ By this we know that we love the children of God, when we love God and obey [God's] commandments. 3/ For the love of God is this, that we obey [God's] commandments. And [these] commandments are not burdensome, 4/ for whatever is born of God conquers the world.

■ **1** The generalized character of the address is evident not only from the initial πᾶς but also from the content: in what follows, the author intends to connect the universal Christian phenomenon of faith with the theme of *agapē*. The address is to every Christian, for it is true of all of them that they believe that Jesus is the Christ. Hence nothing is said here directly against any opponents.[1] They are only indirectly in view, to the extent that they deny that Jesus is the Christ (2:22; cf. Acts 9:22). That what is formulated at this point is not their denial but rather its "positive counterpart"[2] strengthens its primary direction to the listening community, which is meant to recognize itself in this form of address.[3] It confesses Jesus as the Christ[4] and articulates its credo, that is, the *fides quae creditur* ("that which is believed") (cf. 4:15). It is true that in the Johannine writings Christian faith is essentially a *fides specialis* ("special faith"), the *fides qua creditur* ("the way of believing"), which amounts to an *assentiri promissioni Dei* ("acceptance of God's promises").[5] This attitude of trust is founded on the fact of being born of God, which is the sign by which Christians are known,[6] and which as early as 4:7 was equated with love and with knowing God.[7] Faith and love overlap and coincide, as is clear from the second half of the verse, where the participial noun ὁ ἀγαπῶν is parallel to ὁ πιστεύων in the first half. In the Johannine writings, dogmatics and ethics cannot be played off against one another; instead, every faith statement has an ethical quality. In turn, Johannine *agapē* is only valid within the eschatological horizon expressed by the expressions "love of God" and

1 Against Wengst, *Brief*, 201, according to whom πᾶς expresses a "polemic intention."

2 Cf. Schnackenburg, *Epistles*, 227. He emphasizes correctly that the author "is clearly addressing his readers."

3 Thus also in the subsequent presentation of the Christ-confession and its consequences: 5:5, 10, 13.

4 The absolute Χριστός is found also at 2:22; 2 John 9; elsewhere Ἰησοῦς Χριστός: 1 John 1:3; 2:1; 4:2; 5:6; 2 John 3, 7.

5 As distinguished from the *fides generalis*, which Melanchthon (*Apologia Confessionis Augustanae* 4.48) equated with *notitia historiae:* "Sed illa fides, quae iustificat, non est tantum notitia historiae, sed est assentiri promissioni Dei" ("the faith that justifies is not merely [faith in] a historical concept, but a trusting in the promises of God").

6 The perfect γεγέννηται occurs 9 times in the Johannine corpus. This use does not present a reflection on the "priority" of being born of God over faith, so that faith would be understood as a result of being born of God. That, however, is the opinion of John R. W. Stott, *The Epistles of John* (TNTC 19; Grand Rapids: Eerdmans, 1964) 172. In contrast, Chaine (*Les épîtres catholiques*, 210) places faith prior to being born of God. Differently, and correctly, Brown, *Epistles*, 535; according to him it is probable that "the Johannine writers think of believing and begetting as belonging together and simultaneous." It is not apparent from our text that the author is here referring to John 1:12–13 (against Wengst, *Brief*, 201). See the excursus above, "Being Born of God."

7 Cf. also 4:16 ("We have known and believe . . . "); also the identification of being born of God with "doing right" (2:29), "not being able to sin" (3:9), "conquering the world" (5:4), and with "protection" (5:18; see below).

"love for God."

The interpretation of *τὸν γεννήσαντα* and the subsequent *τὸν γεγεννημένον* is disputed. An ordinary reference to human parents in the sense of an aphorism comparable to that in John 5:19–20[8] is as little likely as an interpretation that would make the expression a reference to one's own parents.[9] Instead, one may gather from the context that, after the reference to being born of God (v. 1a), from this point on God is spoken of as the parent; this accords with the interlacing of love for God and love for the sisters and brothers (4:21). This kind of commingling is also envisioned in the rhetorical expression[10] that answers the question whether "the child" might mean Jesus.[11] From the connection to what has preceded and the resumption by means of the phrase *τέκνα τοῦ θεοῦ* (v. 2) it seems highly probable that the author is thinking of the sisters and brothers who are born of God, that is, of other Christians. He intends to say that being Christian is something that is realized in faith and love; this Christian love must be directed to God and fellow Christians.[12] It is in the nature of a demand, and corresponds to the character of this section as commandment (cf. 4:21) and to the jussive subjunctive *ἀγαπᾷ*.[13] The *καί* ("so also"), probably secondary,

---

8 Thus Brown, *Epistles*, 536; cf. in this sense Plutarch *De fraterno amore* 480D–F: "For he that hates his own brother and is angry with him cannot refrain from blaming the father that begat and the mother that bore such a brother (*ὁ γὰρ μισῶν τὸν ἀδελφὸν αὑτοῦ καὶ βαρυνόμενος οὐ δύναται μὴ τὸν γεννήσαντα μέμφεσθαι καὶ τὴν τεκοῦσαν*). . . . Excellent and just [offspring] will not only love each other the more because of their parents (*διὰ τοὺς γονεῖς ἀγαπήσουσι μᾶλλον ἀλλήλους*), but will also love their parents the more because of each other (*τοὺς γονεῖς δι' ἀλλήλους*) . . . as regards parents, brotherly love (*φιλαδελφία*) is of such a sort that to love one's brother is forthwith a proof of love (*ἀπόδειξιν . . . τοῦ φιλεῖν*) for both mother and father." Also Plotinus *Enn.* 2.9.16: "where we love (*ὁ γὰρ τὸ φιλεῖν ἔχων*), our hearts are warm also to the kin of the beloved (*τὸ συγγενὲς πᾶν οὗ φιλεῖ*); we are not indifferent to the children of our friend (*ἀγαπᾷ*). Now every soul is a child of that Father (*ψυχὴ δὲ πᾶσα πατρὸς ἐκείνου*); . . . where there is contempt for the kin of the Supreme the knowledge of the Supreme itself (*μηδὲ ἐκεῖνα ἴσασιν*) is merely verbal" (Plotinus, *The Enneads* [trans. Stephen MacKenna; 2d ed.; ed. B. S. Page; London: Faber and Faber, 1956] 148). Against the interpretation of this passage in terms of the relationship to human parents is the fact that even related texts like John 5:19–20 and Matt 11:27–28 are not to be understood in this ordinary sense, but contain clear statements about the relationship between God as father and Christ as son.

9 Brooke, *Epistles*, 127; C. Haas, M. de Jonge, and J. L. Swellengrebel, *A Translator's Handbook on the Letters of John* (HeTr 13; London: United Bible Societies, 1972) 115.

10 Thus correctly Bultmann, *Epistles*, 76; Westcott, *Epistles*, 177; Wengst, *Brief*, 200, and elsewhere.

11 Thus Windisch and Preisker, *Die Katholischen Briefe*, 131.

12 That here, differently from 4:20–21, the author speaks not of love for the sisters and brothers but of love for "the one born of [God]" seems to suggest the parallel pairing of creator and creation, and to hint that the circle of "children of God" whom the Christians are obligated to love (5:2) reaches beyond the borders of the community. This would be supported by the reading attested by Codex Sinaiticus and other manuscripts, whereby v. 1b would have *καὶ τὸ γεγεννημένον* ("and the thing begotten/born") instead of *καὶ τὸν γεγεννημένον* ("and the one who is begotten/born"); however, this variant is probably secondary (see below, n. 14). In addition, the Johannine doctrine of creation is, in its fundamentals, incorporated in the doctrine of election: "being born of God" is the same as "being loved by God," and that in turn is indissolubly bound to "believing" and "loving God." Of course, in Johannine understanding Christian love is certainly not limited to love for fellow Christians, because *agapē*, since it is an action that accords with the nature of God and is something done by God, is by definition a love that is boundless. In this sense also, according to Bultmann, *Epistles*, 28, "brother or sister" (*ἀδελφός*) means "not especially the Christian comrade in the faith, but one's fellow [human being], the 'neighbor.'"

13 The finite verb *ἀγαπᾷ* can be read either as present indicative or present subjunctive. In fact, an imperative meaning is clearly attested only for the third person aorist subjunctive (e.g., *Barn.* 19.1; Edwin Mayser, *Grammatik der griechischen Papyri aus der Ptolemäerzeit* [2 vols. in 6; Berlin: de Gruyter,

underscores the fundamentally parenetic intention of the author.[14]

■ **2** The sentence construction is difficult. To begin with, the question whether *ἐν τούτῳ* refers to what precedes or what follows has received different answers. If one refers the demonstrative pronoun to the preceding sentence, v. 2 would simply be "an application of the rule in v. 1b."[15] But against this is not only that the relationship of v. 2 to v. 1b is not so much an "application" as an explanation, but also that this would make the following *ὅταν* clause impossible to explain.[16] Since *ἐν τούτῳ* in 1 John often refers to what follows,[17] the same can be presumed here. The demonstrative pronoun is taken up not only by the *ὅτι* clause but by the *ὅταν* clause as well. The latter has an epexegetical function and takes the place of a second *ὅτι*.[18] Thus one can also translate: "By this we know that we love the children of God, because we love God and keep God's commandments." In combination with the present subjunctive *ἀγαπῶμεν*, *ὅταν* describes an action that is thought of as constantly recurring. Thus the expression is not far removed from the idea of a condition that accompanies recognition of love for the brothers and sisters.[19] Hence it is true that there is no knowledge of love for the sisters and brothers that does not, as such, include *ἀγαπᾶν τὸν θεόν* and *τὰς ἐντολὰς ποιεῖν*. When the author uses the concept of *τέκνα τοῦ θεοῦ* here in place of *τοὺς ἀδελφούς*, he is applying an expression that described Christians as early as 3:1–2, 10, that is, all those who believe in the name of Christ (cf. John 1:12; 11:52). The conclusion to draw from v. 1, then, is that the love that is (indirectly) demanded is directed toward those who are born of God, the members of the Christian community.

It is striking that the author does not begin with the criterion for recognizing love for the sisters and brothers, on the basis of which the reality of love for God could be discerned (cf. 3:14–15, 17–19; 4:20). Instead, the order is reversed. Love for God and keeping God's commandments become the basis for recognizing love for the brothers and sisters. Of course, this is not a question of theoretical knowledge. Rather—as is true for the verb *γινώσκειν* in 1 John generally and particularly in connection with *agapē*[20] —it is a matter of the reality of love of God. That reality allows no distinction between theory and practice but assumes love for the sisters and brothers as its necessary consequence. Nonetheless, the author is able to derive assurance about love for God from the fact of the mutual love that is practiced in and through the community.[21] This "circular reasoning"[22] indicates that love for the brothers and sisters and love for God cannot become reality in isolation from one another. The author is not polemicizing against false prophets at this point,[23] and has equally little interest in speculating on a possible basis for recognition or making

1926] 2/1.229); but the imperative (jussive) meaning for the first person present subjunctive is frequently found; cf. BDF § 364; Kühner-Gerth, *Grammatik*, 1.219ff.

14 The adverbial *καί*, used for emphasis (attested by A P 𝔐 and others), seems to have intruded from 4:21b (thus Brown, *Epistles*, 535); it underscores the parallel between love of God and love of the sisters and brothers. In the same way, the reading *καὶ τό* (ℵ 69 pc) is secondary.

15 Schnackenburg, *Epistles*, 228; cf. Dodd, *Epistles*, 125; Weiss, *Briefe*, 136 (with reference to 2:5; 3:10, 19; 4:17).

16 In that case one would have to suppose that the *ὅταν* clause (found only here in the Johannine Letters) was placed afterward by mistake, and reverse the two clauses (Schnackenburg, *Epistles*, 227–28); the awkward placement is then explained by the author's effort to create a connection with the following verse (so Marshall, *Epistles*, 227–28).

17 Cf., e.g., 4:2, 9–10; also 3:10; Bultmann, *Epistles*, 77.

18 Thus BDF § 394 (*ὅταν* replaces *ὅτι* "if the fact is only assumed").

19 Cf. BAGD 588 (on *ὅταν*). Bultmann (*Epistles*, 25) wishes to make a distinction in vv. 2–3: he thinks that *τηρεῖν τὰς ἐντολάς* describes "not the condition, but rather the characteristic of the knowledge of God." It is, however, difficult to conceive the one without the other.

20 On this, see the excursus below on "*γινώσκειν*."

21 Rudolf Kittler ("Erweis der Bruderliebe an der Bruderliebe? Versuch der Auslegung eines 'fast unverständlichen' Satzes im 1. Johannesbrief," *KD* 16 [1970] 223–28) sees a problem in the concept of "children of God," and paraphrases v. 2a as follows: "This is the way in which we know that we in such a case also love the true children of God: whenever and as often as we, in true love for God, really keep his commandment (that is, his commandment of love)." Thus fellow human beings become "true" sisters and brothers "whenever they really practice this love of the brothers and sisters" (pp. 223–28). However, the concept of *τέκνα τοῦ θεοῦ* as well as their acknowledgment as "brothers and sisters" is

abstract reflections on the relationship between love of God and love of the sisters and brothers.[24] It is not a question of theoretical analysis, but of a call to concrete action. This is expressed also by the seeming afterthought in the clause *καὶ τὰς ἐντολὰς αὐτοῦ ποιῶμεν*.[25] It is true that the verbs *τηρεῖν* and *ποιεῖν* can alternate in the NT, and can refer to one and the same thing, but *ποιεῖν* seems more strongly dynamic than *τηρεῖν*.[26] Doing the commandments of God is identical with "doing the will of God" (cf. 2:17). The plural *ἐντολαί* points beyond what is commanded in the immediate context (vv. 1–2: "faith and love"; cf. 3:23: the commandment to believe and to love). What is demanded is a clear and unmistakable action on the part of those who believe, which is to be understood not only as a component part of love for God[27] but also as addressed to real conditions in the world. This is expressed in the following verse: the Christian demand to love the sisters and brothers is fulfilled when love for God is made a reality in the concrete situations of life.

■ **3** The demonstrative *αὕτη*, like *ἐν τούτῳ* in v. 2, refers to what is to follow and is continued by the *ἵνα* clause. The author presents a new "definition" of *agapē* by expanding the thought of v. 2:[28] love for God becomes a reality only when God's concrete commandments are kept. Even though it is not always possible to distinguish clearly among the different possible interpretations of the expression *ἀγάπη τοῦ θεοῦ*, and although in this verse the subjective sense may also be in the background,[29] there can be no doubt, in light of the parallel with v. 2, that this is primarily an objective genitive. The relationship of *agapē* that human beings have toward God cannot be

---

already established by the context of *ἐκκλησία* (cf. 3:1–2).

22 Thus correctly Wengst, *Brief*, 203 ("the love brought about by God has no basis for recognition outside itself"); although it is not sufficient to say that God "does not [bring forth] an exclusive group of enlightened spirits, but [places them] in a community of needy brethren," since "love for the sisters and brothers" is not restricted to the social dimension in 1 John; it includes, for example, cooperation in maintaining the unity of the congregation. Theodor Häring (*Die Johannesbriefe* [Stuttgart: Calwer, 1927] 67) had already indicated that the section 4:7–21 proceeded on the pattern of "love, faith, love" (vv. 7–12, 13–16, 17–21), while the section 5:1–12 was patterned as "faith, love, faith" (vv. 1a, 1b–4, 5–12); however, this arrangement can hardly correspond to any deliberate plan (Windisch and Preisker, *Die Katholischen Briefe*, 131).

23 Against Brown, *Epistles*, 538, according to whom the author is speaking against the false teachers who think they love their sisters and brothers but do not love God (see also above, at 4:10).

24 But see Braun, "Literar-Analyse," 275–76, who points to a "circle of statements in which, contrary to the schema previously observed, participation in salvation now yields the basis for recognizing the right kind of love. . . . Thus love for God, and the keeping of God's commandments which is identical with it, can also be called a basis for recognition of love for the brethren (5:2)."

25 The phrase *τὰς ἐντολὰς ποιεῖν* appears only here in the NT (cf. Ignatius *Eph.* 9.2; *2 Clem.* 4.5; 17.6, and frequently). Related to it is *τὸν νόμον ποιεῖν* (John 7:19; Gal 5:3) or *τὸ θέλημα τοῦ θεοῦ ποιεῖν* (1 John 2:17; John 4:34; 6:38, and frequently; Acts 13:22). The reading *τηρῶμεν* (א P [048] 𝔐 vg^{mss}) is a secondary accommodation to Johannine usage; cf. 2:3–5; 3:22, 24; 5:3; John 14:15, 21; 15:10 (alternating with *τὸν λόγον τηρεῖν*: 14:23–24; 15:20, and frequently); *τηρεῖν τὰς ἐντολάς* also Matt 19:17.

26 Thus Brown, *Epistles*, 539. Differently Herbert Braun, "*ποιέω*," *TDNT* 6 (1968) 478, according to whom the context indicates that it is synonymous with *τηρεῖν* (cf. 1 John 5:3; Matt 23:3), *πράσσειν* (John 5:29; Rom 1:32, and frequently), or *ἐργάζεσθαι* (Col 3:23).

27 Against Bultmann, *Epistles*, 77, who interprets v. 2b as hendiadys. Thus also Joseph Bonsirven, *Épîtres de Saint Jean* (VS 9; 1936; 2d ed.; Paris: Beauchesne, 1954) 221: "To love God is to carry out his commandments."

28 The relatively infrequent introductory *γάρ* (also in 4:20; 2 John 11; 3 John 3, 7) where one would expect a *καί* (as in 2:25; 3:23; 5:4, 11, 14; 2 John 6) does not mark a new beginning (as Schnackenburg writes: *Epistles*, 228). It indicates, rather, the causal connection with v. 2. For the interpretation of *agapē*, cf. 4:10; 2 John 6 (on which see below).

29 As, for example, in 2:5; 3:17; 4:9–10; cf. 3:1; John 15:9–10, and frequently; Brown, *Epistles*, 254–57, 540.

understood one-dimensionally. As v. 2 already said, it is tied to the carrying out of the ἐντολαί that God has given. In the other Johannine writings the plural can be interchanged with the singular ἐντολή;[30] but in 1 John a distinction is drawn between the new and old love commandment (singular: 2:7–8) or between the one commandment of faith and love (3:23) and God's commandments, which are not to be limited to the demand for *agapē*, even though it is obviously a background to all of them.[31] The "commandments" are not defined with any more precision; plurality is characteristic of them. The commandment to love God is not a fetter that chains human actions in bondage. It implies from the beginning the undefined duty to act always and in every constantly changing historical situation, as a Christian and as Christ's community, in a way that corresponds to the will of God (cf. 2:17; John 4:34). Such a demand is understandable in itself. Its interpretation does not require the positing of any "anti-gnostic tendency"[32] within it. It is addressed to the Christian community as a whole, which is called upon "to obey his word," so that λόγον αὐτοῦ τηρεῖν is identical with τὰς ἐντολὰς αὐτοῦ τηρεῖν (2:4–5; cf. John 14:23–24).

The concluding clause in this verse, καὶ αἱ ἐντολαὶ αὐτοῦ βαρεῖαι οὐκ εἰσίν, only appears to be related to the rabbinic distinction between easy and difficult commandments.[33] In reality, the author is not distinguishing between different classes of commandments in the way that is familiar to the OT and Jewish tradition. Nor does he refer elsewhere to the OT and its Jewish interpretation. On this basis, it does not seem proper to suppose that this passage is taking a position on the question of justification by works, because the whole problem of law and justification is not under discussion. The adjective βαρύς, found only here in the whole Johannine corpus, means "difficult to fulfil."[34] The question why God's commandments are not difficult is neither asked nor answered. The comforting thought that God gives us the power to keep the commandments[35] has no basis in this text, no matter how much support it finds in Pauline theology.[36] Nor is it a matter of contrast, as if to say that, on the one hand, God did not make the commandments difficult, and therefore they are easily managed;[37] on the other hand, human beings are equipped with adequate strength and therefore must not fail in what is demanded of them.[38] Instead, this statement is to be located within

30 Cf. 2 John 6; John 10:18; 12:49–50 with 15:10. For the shift from singular to plural in the use of the word ἐντολή, see the excursus above on "ἐντολή."

31 Thus in 2 John 5–6 keeping the commandment of mutual love is interpreted as "walking according to God's commandments"; cf. also the connection between the *agapē* commandment and "keeping the commandments" in the Fourth Gospel (see n. 25 above).

32 Thus Schnackenburg, *Epistles*, 228; cf. his interpretation of 2:3–5, where he contrasts the "clarity and simplicity of the Christian ethic" with the gnostic "perversion of moral sensitivity" (p. 96).

33 On the distinction between easy and difficult commandments in the rabbinic tradition, cf. Str-B 1.901–2: "They called 'easy commandments' in particular those that placed only minor demands on the strength or property of human beings" (e.g., Deut 12:23; 22:7; Lev 23:42; Gen 2:17); "while those were difficult that required a lot of money or might even be connected with mortal danger" (e.g., Exod 20:12; Gen 17:10). It followed from this distinction that difficult commandments were seen as important (Matt 22:36), easy commandments as rather less important or slight (Matt 5:19). Cf. *y. Qiddušin* 1.7 (61b [1.61b, 5f]): Rabbi Abba bar Kahana (ca. 310) said: "The Scripture has compared the easiest of all the religious duties to the most difficult of them all. The easiest of them all is sending forth the dam from the fledglings [Deut 22:7]. The most difficult of them all is honoring father and mother. Yet in regard to both of them, the same reward is specified: 'that your days may be long'" (*The Talmud of the Land of Israel*, vol. 26: *Qiddushin* [trans. Jacob Neusner; Chicago Studies in the History of Judaism; Chicago: University of Chicago Press, 1984] 106).

34 It occurs in this sense only here in the NT; cf. Philo *Spec. leg.* 1.299 (αἰτεῖται . . . ὁ θεὸς οὐδὲν βαρύ: "God asks nothing . . . that is heavy"); differently Matt 23:23 ("weighty"); 23:4 ("heavy")—in contrast to 11:30 (ἐλαφρόν = "easy to bear"); cf. also Acts 25:7 and 2 Cor 10:10 ("weighty"); Acts 20:29 ("savage").

35 Thus Brown, *Epistles*, 541; Dodd, *Epistles*, 126; Windisch and Preisker, *Die Katholischen Briefe*, 131. Cf. 1QM xi.4–5; *Herm. Man.* 12.4.3–5; *1 Clem.* 50.2.

36 Cf. Phil 4:13.

37 Cf. Deut 30:11–14; Matt 11:30; 23:4; *Herm. Man.* 12.4.3–5; Philo *Spec. leg.* 1.299, 301–2; *Abr.* 5; *Praem. poen.* 80.

38 Thus Windisch and Preisker, *Die Katholischen Briefe* 131, with reference to 1 John 2:13–14, 29; 3:9; 4:4; *Herm. Man.* 12.3.4–6; but the passages mentioned for 1 John are not persuasive; not even 3:9 (οὐ δύναται ἁμαρτάνειν) can be adduced to support this thesis,

the context of the train of thought already established: the existence of those born of God is expressed—as was said in vv. 1–2—in love for God and for the sisters and brothers. This location presumes existence and abiding "in God"; Christians live in and from their community with God.[39] As the Matthean Jesus can recommend his yoke to his disciples as something easy and light because it leads them on the way of righteousness and not on the path of error and hypocrisy (Matt 11:30), so in the opinion of this author the commandments given by God should not be seen as "difficult," because in the life that is lived in community with God they are *eo ipso* fulfilled. Such a statement does not intend to provoke some kind of "Christian" quietism; it means that keeping God's commandments is the Christian's ongoing duty.[40]

■ **4a** This clause, which forms the first half of v. 4, also asserts that the fact of belonging to God has created a new situation. The causal ὅτι emphasizes the connection: the keeping of the commandments, which characterizes the community and is presented to it as its duty, has its basis in Christians' being born of God.[41] The neutral πᾶν underscores still more sharply than would the masculine πᾶς[42] (which would also be possible here) the general nature of this statement. Wherever human beings love God, the ethical demand will be not only theoretically acknowledged but fulfilled in practice. This is possible because believers, as such, are withdrawn from the world's sphere of domination. It is true that everyone who belongs to those γεγεννημένον ἐκ τοῦ θεοῦ (that is, every believer, as the parallel in v. 1 makes clear) exists within the world. It is to the world as a whole, and not only to the believing community, that the Son was sent (2:2). But being in the world is an existence that places believers in jeopardy; it constantly puts them to the test and contains within itself the danger of apostasy and loss of their condition of belonging to God (2:16–17). In face of this situation, the author can make the assertion and promise to the community that overcoming the world is an essential element of faith.

The word νικᾶν has already occurred, in 2:13–14 (with reference to the young men who have overcome the evil one), and in 4:4 (speaking of the community, of whom it is said that they have conquered the false teachers). At this point, the most extensive occurrence in 1 John, the verb describes the relationship of believers to the world. There is a parallel passage in the Fourth Gospel, a unique usage by that evangelist. The Revealer consoles his disciples about the persecution they face in the world, saying: "I have conquered the world" (John 16:33). Here, in 1 John 5:4a, the author says the same thing, in the present tense, about believers. Verse 5 will show that the christological background is also in view. As indicated by the mutually independent traditions in the Fourth Gospel and in 1 John, the Johannine circle gave ongoing testimony to the overcoming of the power of the universe through the appearance of Jesus Christ, the Son of God.

One can still discern hints of the apocalyptic component, according to which the future final event will be characterized by the victory of the Christians who overcome the ruinous and corrupt powers of the universe,[43] at least to the extent that the world is of its

because what is at issue there is not a statement about human ability (see above on 3:9).

39 Cf. 2:9 ("being in the light"); 2:10 ("living in the light"); 2:6, 27–28; 4:13, 15, and frequently ("abiding in [him = God]"); 2.5, 5:20 ("being in God").

40 Cf. also Wengst, *Brief*, 203, according to whom v. 3 is to be understood as a challenge to the readers "to involve themselves in the praxis of love for the sisters and brothers"; of course, it should be said that the expression "the commandments" points beyond the realm of love of the sisters and brothers (see above).

41 Bultmann (*Epistles*, 77) also rightly rejects every form of "ethical idealism or optimism" and emphasizes "that the sentence is conceived on the presupposition of faith: ὅτι πᾶν τὸ γεγεννημένον ἐκ τοῦ θεοῦ νικᾷ τὸν κόσμον."

42 BDF §138 n. 1; cf. also Brown, *Epistles*, 541–42. Schnackenburg (*Epistles*, 229 n. 99) refers to ὃ ἦν ἀπ' ἀρχῆς (1:1), which "perhaps" is kept [not "must be regarded as" as in the published ET—Trans.] "intentionally general" (p. 56).

43 Rev 2:26; 21:17, because of the victory of the Lamb, already accomplished, it can also be said of the Christian martyrs that through their death they have conquered the "accuser" (12:11).

very essence transitory (cf. 2:17). What is important for the author is that the victory over the world is not something that will appear only in the future, but that it is happening everywhere that people are "born of God." There is no detailed inquiry about the nature of the cosmic rule from which believers have escaped. Whether it is a matter of the ἐπιθυμίαι of the world that threaten Christians (2:17), or of the evil one (2:13–14), or of the antichrist as embodied in the false teachers (4:4)—what is crucial is that, by means of believers' belonging to God, whatever is at enmity with God, however it expresses itself within the world and however it is represented by the world, is condemned to nothingness, and it can no longer exercise its power over believers.[44]

44 Thus also Brown, *Epistles,* 305: "but since the Johannine Christians in *koinonia* with the author belong to God, he can say to them: 'You have conquered these people, for he who is in you is greater than he who is in the world' (4:4)."

5 Faith Founded on the Testimony of Water, Blood, and Spirit[1]

**4b And this is the victory that conquers the
world, our faith. 5/ Who is it that
conquers the world but the one who
believes that Jesus is the Son of God? 6/
This is the one who came by water and
blood, Jesus Christ, not with the water
only but with the water and the blood.
And the Spirit is the one that testifies, for
the Spirit is the truth. 7/ There are three
that testify: 8/ the Spirit and the water
and the blood, and these three agree [or:
are one]. 9/ If we receive human testi-
mony, the testimony of God is greater; for
this is the testimony of God that [God]
has testified to [God's] Son. 10/ Those
who believe in the Son of God have the
testimony in their hearts. Those who do
not believe in God have made [God] a liar
by not believing in the testimony that
God has given concerning [God's] Son.
11/ And this is the testimony: God gave
us eternal life, and this life is in [God's]
Son. 12/ Whoever has the Son has life;
whoever does not have the Son of God
does not have life.**

■ **4b** We begin with v. 4b. It was preceded by a parenetic section expressing the obligation to love the sisters and brothers (4:7—5:4a). The condition of this love of the brothers and sisters is given on an eschatological level:

1 Literature: Markus Barth, *Die Taufe—ein Sakrament?* (Zurich: Evangelischer Verlag, 1951); M. C. de Boer, "Jesus the Baptizer: 1 John 5:5–8 and the Gospel of John," *JBL* 107 (1988) 87–106; François-Marie Braun, "L'Eau et l'Esprit," *RThom* 49 (1949) 5–30, esp. 20–22, on 1 John 5:6; Oscar S. Brooks, "The Johannine Eucharist: Another Interpretation," *JBL* 82 (1963) 293–300; James Denney, "He That Came by Water and Blood (I John 5,6)," *Exp.* 7th series, 5 (1908) 416–28; A. Greiff, "Die drei Zeugen im 1 Joh 5,7ff," *ThQ* 114 (1933) 465–80; Annie Jaubert, "O Espírito, e Agua e o Sangue (1 Jo 5,7–8)," in S. Voigt and F. Vier, eds., *Actualidades Bíblicas* (Festschrift for J. J. Edreira de Castro; Petropolis, Brazil: Vozes, 1971) 616–20; P. W. Keppler, "Geist, Wasser und Blut. Zur Erklärung von 1 Joh 5,6–13," *ThQ* 68 (1886) 3–25; Albert Klöpper, "1 Joh 5,6–12," *ZWTh* 43 (1900) 378–400, 585–602; Thomas W. Manson, "Entry into Membership of the Early Church," *JTS* 48 (1947) 25–32; Manuel Miguens, "Tres testigos: Espiritu, agua, sangre," *SBFLA* 22 (1972) 74–94; Nauck, *Tradition,* 147–82; Ignace de la Potterie, "La notion de Témoignage dans Saint Jean," *Sacra Pagina* (2 vols.; BEThL 12–13; Louvain/Paris: Librairie Lecoffre, 1959) 2.193–208; Georg Richter, "Blut und Wasser aus der durchbohrten Seite Jesu (Joh 19,34b)," *MThZ* 21 (1970) 1–21, reprinted in idem, *Studien zum Johannesevangelium* (ed. Josef Hainz; BU 13; Regensburg: Pustet, 1977) 120–42; Eduard Schweizer, "Das johanneische Zeugnis vom Herrenmahl," *EvTh* 12 (1952/53) 341–63; Wilhelm Thüsing, *Die Erhöhung und Verherrlichung Jesu im Johannesevangelium* (Münster: Aschendorff, 1960); Hermann-Josef Venetz, "Zeuge des Erhöhten: Ein exegetischer Beitrag zu Joh 19,31–37," *FZPhTh* 23 (1976) 81–111; idem, "'Durch Wasser und Blut gekommen': Exegetische Überlegungen zu 1 Joh 5,6," in Ulrich Luz and Hans Weder, eds., *Die Mitte des Neuen Testaments: Einheit und Vielfalt neutestamentlicher Theologie: Festschrift für Eduard Schweizer zum siebzigsten Geburtstag* (Göttingen: Vandenhoeck & Ruprecht, 1983) 345–61; R. Winterbotham, "The Spirit and the Water and the Blood," *Exp.* 8th series, 2 (1911) 62–71.

faith in Jesus and being born of God,[2] as well as love of God. The ethical intention of this eschatological exposition is indicated by the fact that ἀγάπη τοῦ θεοῦ is paralleled by the keeping of the commandments (v. 3). All these features separate the preceding section from the text at hand. On the one hand, that the former ends with v. 4a is indicated by the key expression γεννᾶσθαι ἐκ τοῦ θεοῦ (v. 4a), which refers not to 5:1 but back to the beginning of the section at 4:7b, and appears again only at 5:18. Consequently, it does not determine what immediately follows. On the other hand, the concept of πίστις as an interpretation of the νικᾷ τὸν κόσμον (v. 4a) sounds the opening note of the new section (cf. v. 5), which will present a theoretical teaching about the content of faith and the three witnesses. The section ends with v. 12, as the new beginning at v. 13 shows; there ἔγραψα functions as a summary of what has gone before. The language of the preceding part of the verse (v. 4a) refers to the contrast between being born of God and life from the world, while in its content it presumes the Johannine dualism. With these two features it serves to summarize the preceding parenesis. As was already said with regard to 2:15, an orientation to the world signifies that one has submitted to the world's criteria and is, at the same time, separated from the love of the Father. In contrast, their origin in God means for believers that they keep the commandments and overcome the world (cf. 4:4–6).

■ **5** Thus the Christian community's overcoming of the world is not based on an ethical-individualistic or secular-optimistic attitude. Instead, its distance from the world is to be interpreted in an exclusively eschatological mode. The noun πίστις, whose only occurrence in the Johannine writings is in v. 4b, plays on this eschatological state of salvation. There is obviously no opposition here between "faith" and "works" in a Pauline sense. Instead, the word πίστις must be interpreted to correspond with the verb πιστεύειν. "Faith" in the Johannine writings is not a theoretical assessment of the truth of something, but an acknowledgment, that is, the acceptance of the sending of Jesus (see the association with γινώσκειν in 1 John 4:16). This acceptance and surrender is expressed in confession of faith (see the association with ὁμολογεῖν in 4:15–16). The noun πίστις in this verse therefore implies an acknowledgment, a "confession."[3] The reference is to a real, current situation: the background is apparently the teaching of the opponents who deny that Jesus Christ is the Son of God and cast doubt on the interpretation of the person of the historical Jesus as an eschatological promise of salvation (cf. 2:18–25 and the excursus on false teachers at 1 John 2:25).

■ **6** In opposition to false teaching, v. 5 pointed to the content of the confession of faith and to Jesus as Son of God. Now, with the words ὕδωρ and αἷμα (vv. 6 and 8), concrete assertions are made against the opposing teaching. "Water" and "blood" are characterized by their relationship to πνεῦμα, so that in what follows the author can speak of "three witnesses" (vv. 7–8).

The history of research on this verse offers a picture of disparate conclusions. The interpretation of the words "water" and "blood" is particularly diverse. The church fathers saw here a reference to the sacraments of Baptism and Eucharist,[4] an interpretation that is maintained by scarcely anyone at present[5] because it does not fit the christological context: Ἰησοῦς Χριστός is the one of whom is said ὁ ἐλθὼν δι' ὕδατος καὶ αἵματος. The aorist participle reflects a past event and refers to a punctual, completed fact, in contrast to the perfect ἐληλυθότα, which describes a situation resulting from a past action.[6] This means that the author is thinking of the two christological "saving realities," the baptism and sacrificial death of Jesus Christ. While it is true that Jesus' baptism is not specifically described in the Fourth Gospel, it is presupposed, in accord with the Synoptic tradition, that Jesus was baptized by John the Baptizer.[7] It was evident earlier (at 1:7; 2:1–2; 3:16; 4:10) that in 1 John the death of Jesus is interpreted as an atoning sacrifice to wipe out the guilt of sin. If an opposing,

2 Cf. 5:1. On γεννάω, see Friedrich Büchsel, "γεννάω," *TDNT* 1 (1964) 665–66, 671–72; BAGD 155.

3 Cf. above at 4:15–16. It appears that the combination of faith and confession indicates an early Catholic notion of a creed; but this kind of parallel can be attested even in Paul (Rom 10:8–9). Cf. the excursus below on "Early Catholicism." For the concept of νίκη/νικᾶν see above at 5:4a.

4 Thus Ambrose, Augustine, John Chrysostom, Cyril of Alexandria; Tertullian differs (*Bapt.* 16).

5 But see Ernst Günther, Μαρτυς: *Die Geschichte eines Wortes* (Gütersloh: Bertelsmann, 1941), according to whom v. 6a ("by water and blood") conceals a sacramental formula (p. 137 n. 2).

6 Cf. 4:2; BDF § 318.

7 John 1:6–8, 15, 19–37; 3:22–36. No connection can

docetic teaching is in view, the reference back to the baptism and death of Jesus, the beginning and end of Jesus' life, emphasizes that these are to be understood as real, historical events, and that eschatological salvation cannot be separated from the empirical person of the earthly Jesus. It is possible, but cannot be proved, that in addition one should understand from the expression οὐκ ἐν τῷ ὕδατι μόνον that the author sees himself confronted by a heretical adoptionist christology, according to which the heavenly Christ was joined to the earthly Jesus at the time of his baptism, since the presumption of 4:2 seems to be only that the opponents disputed the fact of the incarnation.[8] What is more important is that, apparently, the shift of the διά construction to one with ἐν also introduces a change in the system of theological coordinates, and that in the phrase ἐν τῷ ὕδατι καὶ ἐν τῷ αἵματι it is no longer simply the baptism and death of Jesus (including its atoning effect), but also the two community sacraments of Baptism and the Lord's Supper that are the object of the instruction.[9] Even though both particles can have an instrumental meaning, ἐν is more likely to indicate "the ongoing effectiveness" of the Christ-event in the sacraments.[10] This means that the opponents, who

be drawn between our text and John 4:14, according to which the water given by Jesus the Revealer bestows eternal life; in the latter ὕδωρ is used as a symbol for the Revealer's word, and not for the sacrament. John 3:5 is more important: the new birth from water and spirit occurs, according to Johannine understanding, in baptism. Venetz differs: he disputes both the reference to the baptism of Jesus and to the sacrament, favoring instead a soteriological interpretation ("Durch Wasser und Blut," 347–48, 357). But it remains an open question how v. 6 (with its reference to ὕδωρ and αἷμα) can address "a soteriological error," unless Jesus' baptism is presupposed. (This is said in response to idem, "Durch Wasser und Blut," 347.) The suggestion of de la Potterie (*Sacra Pagina*, 2.203–5) is also improbable. He wishes to refer the aorist soteriologically to the overall purpose of the sending of the Son of God, while the perfect applies to a particular aspect of Christ's having come. But in the mind of the author of 1 John it is impossible to play off the soteriological against the christological meaning: the fact that Jesus Christ has come by water and blood, that is, in his baptism and death on the cross, and therefore "in the flesh" (4:2), is understood, as our text shows, as the crucial saving event and the foundation of the victory of Christian faith over the world. It is this very reality that is grasped by faith and made concrete in the community through the sacraments of Baptism and the Lord's Supper.

8 In response to Bultmann, *Epistles*, 80; on this, cf. the excursus above on the false teachers at 2:25.

9 An interpretation in terms of the sacraments is found also in Günther Bornkamm, "Zum Verständnis des Gottesdienstes," in idem, *Das Ende des Gesetzes: Gesammelte Aufsätze* (BEvTh 16; 1966) 113–32. ET: "On the Understanding of Worship," in Bornkamm, *Early Christian Experience: A Selection of Articles Translated by Paul L. Hammer from the German* (London: SCM, 1969), 161–79. According to this essay the reference to the water is not about baptism, certainly, but instead to a "gnostic water-eucharist" that, in accord with Mandaean tradition and in a manner similar to Christian baptism, signifies the reception of the heavenly water of life. A combination of eucharistic liturgy and warning against false teachers is posited from the earliest period (idem, 128–30, with reference to Rom 16:16; 1 Cor 11:27–32; 16:22; Heb 6:4–6; 13:9–10; Rev 22:15; *1 Clem.* 34; *Did.* 10.6). But one cannot conclude from the evidence at hand that the "false teachers" in 1 John celebrated a water-eucharist. For ὕδωρ as the water of baptism, cf. also Acts 8:36–39; 10:47; Eph 5:26; Heb 10:22; 1 Pet 3:20; *Did.* 7.1–3. Regarding the textual tradition: on the one hand, it appears that a reminiscence of John 3:5 lies behind the reading of v. 6 attested by minuscules 954, 1241, and others, whereby the word αἵματος has been replaced by πνεύματος; on the other hand, the addition of πνεύματος as a third member (ℵ A 614, 1505, 1739[c], 2495) or in the second place (P 69, 323, 945, 1241, 1739) is to be regarded as an anticipation of the following triplet (vv. 7–8). This addition acknowledges that the author is here concerned with "the characterization of the historical reality of the Son of God having come in the flesh" (Bultmann, *Epistles*, 80 n. 2).

10 Thus Heinrich J. Holtzmann, *Evangelium, Briefe und Offenbarung des Johannes* (HKNT 4; 2d ed.; Freiburg im Breisgau and Leipzig: Mohr, 1893) ad loc. Ἐν with the dative in the NT often represents the *dativus sociativus*, describing the accompanying circum-

presumably are baptized,[11] did not reject water baptism, but took a critical posture toward the Eucharist, as can be established for other docetic groups as well.[12]

A reference to the sacraments is also favored by the consideration that in 1 John 1:7 the word *αἷμα* describes the death of Jesus, interpreted in the sense of an atoning sacrifice as the cause of sins being forgiven, but in the Fourth Gospel the same word, taken together with *σάρξ*, refers to the eucharistic elements,[13] and John 19:34b ("and at once blood and water came out") seems also to suggest a double meaning: both the confirmation of the historical fact of Jesus' death and the basis for the community's sacramental actions in Baptism and Eucharist.[14] When in v. 6a the facticity of Jesus' baptism

---

stances, the manner and kind of an event (BDF §198). It is, of course, also possible that the preposition *διά* in combination with *ἔρχεσθαι* implies a local meaning (cf. BAGD 179; Albert Klöpper, "1. Joh. 5,6–12," *ZWTh* 43 (1900) 378–400; Chaine, *Les épîtres catholiques*, 213: the way by which Jesus came), so that this would certainly be part of the thought contained in the following *ἐν*: the Son of God has come in water and blood and is present in his community. This interpretation would approach that of the church fathers, according to whom the text speaks of the sacraments as early as v. 6a-b. However, the participle *ἐλθών* suggests that v. 6a is to be interpreted christologically; nonetheless, it is uncertain whether the same participle can be supposed to apply to v. 6b. It is also possible that a present participle may be implied, corresponding to v. 6c, so that the reference to the community's sacrament is anticipated as early as v. 6b (against Schnackenburg, *Epistles*, 233–34; Norbert Brox, *Zeuge und Märtyrer: Untersuchungen zur frühchristlichen Zeugnis-Terminologie* [SANT 5; Munich: Köstel, 1961] 86–88, also differs: in addition, he rejects a sacramental interpretation for v. 8, because he does not consider a change of meaning from *ὕδωρ* to *αἷμα* possible).

11 Cf. above at 2:19. The expression *οὐκ ἐν τῷ ὕδατι μόνον* apparently implies an opposing assertion. One can conclude from John 3:5 that baptism was generally practiced in the Johannine communities (see n. 7 above). It is improbable that the author is speaking in opposition to Jews and disciples of John the Baptizer who accept only a cleansing with water and a baptism in water (Windisch and Preisker, *Die Katholischen Briefe*, 132); that kind of confrontation cannot be presumed for the proximate environment of our text. It is also difficult to accommodate to the author's perspective the idea that only Jesus' atoning death on the cross is emphasized here, and not the event of his baptism; cf. Herbert Klos, *Die Sakramente im Johannesevangelium* (SBS 46; Stuttgart: Katholisches Bibelwerk, 1970) 78–79; similarly Schnackenburg, *Epistles*, 233: "But it is in his [bloody] death on the cross that the redemption is really fulfilled"; Brown (*Epistles*, 577–78) regards this last as the most probable of four possible solutions. However, the association of "water and blood" is characteristic and makes clear, in contrast to the opposing teaching, that Jesus' earthly existence as Son of God is the basis of Christian faith and hope; the sacrificial death of Jesus makes a significant, but not the only, contribution to it.

12 Cf. Ignatius *Smyrn.* 1.1; 6.1; 7.1; *Phld.* 4; *Eph.* 13.1; Epiphanius *Pan.* 30.16.1; G. Gentz, "Aquarii," *RAC* 1.574–75.

13 John 6:53–56; so also Ignatius *Phld.* 4 (" . . . a single eucharist. For there is one flesh of our Lord Jesus Christ, and one cup of his blood, that makes *us* one, and one altar"); cf. 1 Cor 10:16–17 (cup of blessing = blood of Christ, breaking of bread = communion in the body of Christ; for the eucharistic "cup," see also Mark 14:23 par.). The words *αἷμα* and *σάρξ* have another meaning in the prologue to the Fourth Gospel; here they are ordered to the dualistic concept of the fourth evangelist (John 1:13). Ernst Käsemann differs (*The Testament of Jesus: A Study of the Gospel of John in the Light of Chapter 17* [trans. Gerhard Krodel; London: SCM; Philadelphia: Fortress, 1968] 27–28), as does Vielhauer (*Geschichte*, 452), according to whom the fourth evangelist is opposing the church of his own time by showing reserve toward the sacrament, and also toward apostolic office and the church as institution; cf. also Günther Bornkamm, "Die eucharistische Rede im Johannesevangelium," *ZNW* 47 (1956) 161–69; here John 6:51c–58 is attributed to the ecclesiastical redaction rather than to the evangelist, because vv. 60–71 continue the imagery of vv. 26–51b. In opposition to this, however, see Klos, *Sakramente*, 61–62, who correctly points out the controlling concept "Son of Man" in John 6:27, 53, 62; also Wilhelm Thüsing, *Die Erhöhung und Verherrlichung Jesu im Johannes-evangelium* (NTAbh n.f. 21, 1/2; 2d ed.; Münster: Aschendorff, 1970) 258ff.; Hartwig Thyen, *Studien zur Sündenvergebung im Neuen Testament und seinen alttestamentlichen und jüdischen Voraussetzungen* (FRLANT 96; Göttingen: Vandenhoeck & Ruprecht, 1970) 127; Ulrich Wilckens, "Der eucharistische Abschnitt der johanneischen Rede vom Lebensbrot (Joh 6,51c–58)," in Helmut Merklein and Joachim Lange, eds., *Biblische Randbemerkungen: Schülerfestschrift für Rudolf*

as well as his death is stated, in opposition to the docetic objection to the reality of the earthly existence of Jesus Christ, one may suppose that the emphasis on the sacraments of Baptism and Eucharist (v. 6b) is appropriate to this kind of antidocetic purpose, and that the twofold mention of "water and blood" in v. 6a-b is attributable to the text's two-layered usage of those words.[15]

The author of 1 John is not teaching sacramentalism, even though he emphasizes the paradoxical fusion of the eschaton with history not only in the earthly existence of Jesus Christ but also in the sacraments. It is not yet clear that the elements "water and blood" have a soteriological effect in and of themselves. The sacraments do not work *ex opere operato,* and have nothing in common with magic. Rather, they are characterized by their connection with the *pneuma,* to whom the function of *μαρτυρεῖν* is expressly attributed. The copula *καί* refers back to the beginning of v. 6. Thus the coming, in the past, of Jesus Christ as Son of God and the witness of the Spirit are placed in parallel. It is not only the fact of the Son of God's having come but also the presence of the Spirit that attests the truth for the community. The present participle *μαρτυροῦν* expresses the fact that the Christian community is not dependent solely on eye- and ear-witnesses who bring the past event of Christ near to them (cf. 1:1–4), because the truth of Christian faith is also guaranteed for it by the Spirit.[16]

Schnackenburg (2d ed.; Wurzburg: Echter, 1974) 220–65; cf. esp. 264–65; Schnelle, *Antidocetic Christology*, 208–10; Peder Borgen, *Bread from Heaven* (NovTSup 10; Leiden: Brill, 1965) 86–88, 185–86, 191. In patristic tradition, John 6 was interpreted not only in terms of the Eucharist (John Chrysostom *Hom. in Joh.* 46; Cyprian *Testimonia* 1.22), but also in an allegorical sense (Eusebius *Hist. eccl.* 1.3.12: Christ is speaking not of his flesh, but of his words; Augustine *Tractatus* 26.15.18–19; 27.6: Body and blood of Christ mean the community of his body and its members, i.e., the holy church). That the text speaks of the *σάρξ* of Christ, rather than of his *σῶμα* ("body") as in the Synoptic Last Supper texts, says nothing against a eucharistic interpretation; cf., rather, Ignatius *Rom.* 7.3; *Phld.* 4.1; 11.2; *Smyrn.* 7.1; Justin *1 Apol.* 1.66.

14 Contrary to what Bultmann says, John 19:34 is not to be attributed to the "ecclesiastical redaction," but is compatible with the evangelist's ideas; cf. Klos, *Sakramente*, 75; Schnelle, *Antidocetic Christology*, 208–10. Schnackenburg (*John*, 3.291) emphasizes that one should think of a symbolic meaning and therefore of the sacraments. For the acceptance of a two-layered meaning in the Johannine statement, see also Hermann Strathmann, "*μάρτυς*," *TDNT* 4 (1967) 497–502; cf. in addition Walter Bauer, *Das Johannesevangelium* (HNT 6; 3d ed.; Tübingen: Mohr [Siebeck], 1933) 226, who rests his sacramental interpretation on John Chrysostom *Hom. in Joh.* 85.3 (*PG* 59.463). The close relationship to 1 John 5:6 is obvious. That John 19:34b mentions *αἷμα* first is in accord with the given situation of Jesus' bloody death on the cross, while 1 John 5:6, in placing "water" first, also argues in harmony with its situation, namely, by first mentioning what the author and his opponents have in common and then referring to the blood, in opposition to the docetic position (against Bultmann, *John*, 678 n. 1, on 1 John 5:6: "this concept has nothing to do with Jn. 19.34; for here the paradoxical thing is not the blood but the water").

15 The church fathers of the fourth and fifth centuries (Ambrose, Augustine, John Chrysostom, Cyril) advocated a sacramental interpretation, while Tertullian *Bapt.* 16.1–2 referred the water to Jesus' own baptism. For an interpretation in terms of the incarnation, see Wengst, *Häresie und Orthodoxie*, 19–20. Wengst is of the opinion that the opponents of the author of 1 John made a sharp distinction between the earthly Jesus and the heavenly Son of God as the Spirit. Then the Spirit would have descended on Jesus "through water," or "in water" (at his baptism), and left him again before his death. The author of 1 John would, in contrast, be assigning only the function of witness to the Spirit, and emphasizing the identity of Jesus and the Son of God, as was done already in 4:2 by the assertion of his having come in water and blood (with reference to Ignatius *Eph* 18.2; Irenaeus *Adv. haer.* 3.11.3).

16 According to Venetz ("Durch Wasser und Blut," 356) not only v. 6a but also v. 6b-c and v. 8 refer to the experience that "Jesus Christ is the true giver of life . . . and that this life is to be had nowhere but in the crucified." What is correct in this more dogmatic than exegetical statement is that the Spirit's witnessing (v. 8) resumes the thought of v. 6b-c. But precisely the fact that the Spirit is understood by the community as a life-giving reality makes the conclusion inescapable that according to v. 6b-c the testimony of the "three witnesses" (vv. 7–8) concerns

Just as Christians from of old have regarded the Spirit as the gift given in baptism (Mark 1:10 par.; Heb 6:4), so the Johannine circle presumes that the community possesses the Spirit of God. Thus the Fourth Gospel knows that Jesus received the Spirit at baptism (John 1:32–33), and this is true also of believers, whose new birth is "of water and spirit" (3:5–6). Existence "in spirit and truth" is the condition for genuine worship (4:23–24). A corresponding attitude is guaranteed by the Paraclete, who is identified with the Holy Spirit, interprets the Christ-event, and accompanies the community on its journey through time (14:17, 26; 15:26; 16:13; cf. 20:22: the Spirit as the Risen One's gift to the disciples).

In 1 John the gift of the Spirit is given to the community in the *χρῖσμα* (2:20, 27). Through this gift, the sacramental actions are made effective. The Spirit's *μαρτυρεῖν*, which takes place in conjunction with the sacraments, is not automatic; it requires believing acceptance. The sacrament thereby escapes a sacramentalistic interpretation; the "witnessing" interprets both the Christ-event and the sacramental event. The Spirit leads to knowledge of the truth of God and is itself "true" (2:27), even "the truth" itself (5:6). Those who are possessed by the Spirit understand not only that the Spirit's testimony is true, but also that the eschatological truth is revealed through the Spirit.[17] Such testimony is critically opposed to false teaching and at the same time points the Christian community of the present time (*ἐστίν*) to the foundation and content of its faith. It is maintained by the Spirit in true knowledge (2:27; 4:13), and also in its confession that Jesus is the Son sent by God into our earthly reality (4:1–3).[18]

Excursus: Μαρτυρεῖν[19]

The words *μαρτυρεῖν* and *μαρτυρία* are Johannine favorites. The verb appears in the Fourth Gospel 33 times, in 1–3 John 10 times (33 times in the rest of the NT). The noun is found 14 times in the Fourth Gospel, 7 times in 1–3 John (16 times in the rest of the NT). By contrast, the related words *μάρτυς*, *μαρτύρεσθαι*, and *μαρτύριον*, which are quite frequent in the remaining NT, are not found in the Johannine writings. While the verb *μαρτυρεῖν* also has a secular meaning (in the Fourth Gospel especially in combination with rhetorical expressions: 3:28; 12:17; 18:23) the transition to a religious significance is subtle (cf. 3 John 12). The same is true of the noun, which can be used actively ("bearing witness") and passively ("testimony") (active: John 1:7; Rev 11:7; passive: Mark 14:56, 59; Luke 22:71; John 8:17; 19:35; 21:24; 3 John 12), and which has both secular (testimony before the court: Mark 14:55–56, 59; Luke 22:71; John 8:17) and theological (1 John 5:9, 10, 11; John 1:19; 3:11, 32–33; 8:14; Rev 1:2, 9; 6:9; 12:11; 19:10; 20:4) applications.

not only the saving events of the past but also the present bestowal of salvation through the sacramental elements.

17 Cf. Bultmann, *Epistles*, 81: "The matter can therefore be formulated: the revelation bears witness for itself."

18 Regarding *ὅτι* (v. 6c): the particle after *μαρτυρεῖν* can be interpreted epexegetically ("that"), as also in John 1:34; 3:28; 4:39, 44; Gal 4:15; Rom 10:2; Col 4:13; Matt 23:21. In the context, however, the thought cannot be that the Spirit testifies concerning itself that it is the truth (correctly Brown, *Epistles*, 580). Therefore the causal interpretation "since" (attested also in combination with *μαρτυρεῖν* in John 8:14; 15:27) is preferable: the Spirit can be an effective witness because it speaks nothing false, but rather is the truth. The Fourth Gospel also enunciates the identity of Spirit and truth. Thus the Revealer attests that genuine worship of the Father must occur "in spirit and in truth" (4:23). Here the combination of *πνεῦμα* and *ἀλήθεια* is not to be understood merely as a mutual clarification but has become a hendiadys describing the one eschatological truth of salvation. This is the reason why the Paraclete is described as *πνεῦμα τῆς ἀληθείας*, whom the world cannot receive but who will abide with the disciples (John 14:17). Obviously *ἀλήθεια* is not only "correctness," such as might be attributed to a human statement, but is the eschatological truth revealed in the Christ-event and conveyed to believers through word and sacraments.

19 Literature: Johannes Beutler, *Martyria* (FThSt 10; Frankfurt: Knecht, 1972); idem, "*μαρτυρέω, κτλ.*," *EDNT* 2 (1991) 389–91; idem, "*μαρτυρία*," *EDNT* 2 (1991) 391–93; Brox, *Zeuge;* Hans von Campenhausen, *Die Idee des Martyriums in der alten Kirche* (2d ed.; Göttingen: Vandenhoeck & Ruprecht, 1964); Theo Preiss, *Das innere Zeugnis des Heiligen Geistes* (ThSt 21; Zurich: Evangelischer Verlag, 1947); Hermann Strathmann, "*μάρτυς, κτλ.*," *TDNT* 4 (1967) 474–514; Schnackenburg, *Epistles*, 51–56, 242–45.

In the Fourth Gospel the word has a primarily christological orientation. It describes the relationship of the Son to the Father (5:32: "there is another who testifies on my behalf"; 8:18: "I testify on my own behalf, and the Father who sent me testifies on my behalf"). Here the testimony of the Revealer, because it is the testimony of his Father in its reference to the truth (18:37), and because it has him as its object, is located within the time line of a preceding and following testimony. Thus the Scriptures have already borne witness to him (5:39), and in the prologue to the Fourth Gospel the figure of John the Baptizer appears as that of a "man" who "testified to the light" (1:6–8; cf. 1:15). The Baptizer's testimony is developed in 1:19–34: as "the voice of one crying out in the wilderness," John the Baptizer testifies to Jesus as the "Lamb of God," and as the Son of God on whom the Spirit has been bestowed (cf. also 3:26). In this way the Baptizer is recognized as the forerunner who "testified to the truth" (5:33).

The testimony of the Son of God is greater than that of John, for that which he does bears witness to him (10:25) and at the same time to the Father who sent him (5:36). In his speech, Jesus testifies to himself: his testimony is true (8:13–14). His testimony points to the Father who sent him and testifies on his behalf (8:18). This testimony is continued in the sending of the Paraclete, "the Spirit of truth who comes from the Father," and "will testify on my behalf" (15:26). But the disciples also, as those who accompany the Revealer, are to be witnesses (15:27). This is made concrete in the testimony of the (beloved) disciple beneath the cross, who sees water and blood emerging from the side of the Crucified, and whose testimony is true (19:35). This statement is taken up in the post-Johannine conclusion and applied to the evangelist (21:24).

While the witness terminology in the Fourth Gospel is applied to the content but also to the temporal context of the Christ-event, and thus characterized as both eschatological and historical, there is no corresponding chronology in the Johannine Letters, which are independent of the Gospel. It appears, instead, that in the letters the root has a clearly eschatological orientation. Thus according to 3 John 12 everyone, including the presbyter, testifies (favorably) about Demetrius. This testimony is at the same time the attestation of the eschatological truth.[20] The remaining instances in 3 John (vv. 3 and 6) also show that this is a question of testimony within the Christian community whose content is the truth and love that are made a reality by the sisters and brothers.

Differently from the situation in the Johannine writings just mentioned, μαρτυρεῖν in 1 John is oriented to the presupposed apostolic situation. The author conceives himself to be an eye- and ear-witness to the Christ-event who "testifies" to his readers about what he has seen (1:2), that is, "declares" it to them in order to create a community between himself and his hearers (1:3). The combination of seeing and testifying creates the basis for the community's confession of the Son of God.[21] The Father's testimony bears witness to him (1 John 5:9–10; John 5:37), and is united with the testimony of the three witnesses, "Spirit, water, and blood" (1 John 5:6–8); it is received in faith as testimony to eternal life (5:10–11).[22]

■ **7** The subsequent verses are, according to Rudolf Bultmann, a "redactional gloss" that should be marked off from the original context.[23] Indeed, v. 10 can, if

20 Brox (*Zeuge*, 90–91) correctly points out that the connection between testimony and truth oversteps the boundaries of the secular use of the word; however, his supposition that the author is thus adopting "formulaic language" is problematic.

21 Cf. 4:14; John 1:34; 3:11, 32; 19:35—without sense-knowledge the witness's ability to testify is invalidated. Of course, this seeing is not separable from believing, for the ζωή that God gives in the Son is revealed only to those who believe (1 John 5:9–12). Nonetheless, especially in view of the Fourth Gospel and 1 John 1:1–4, it is true that "Christian faith . . . has to do with a concrete act of seeing, because it is a matter of God's concrete salvation, made manifest in the earthly realm and therefore visible as well" (Ferdinand Hahn, "Sehen und Glauben im Johannesevangelium," in Hans Baltensweiler and Bo Reicke, eds., *Neues Testament und Geschichte: Historisches Geschehen und Deutung im Neuen Testament: Oscar Cullmann zum 70. Geburtstag* [Zurich: Theologischer Verlag; Tübingen: Mohr [Siebeck], 1972] 129).

22 That 1 John 5:9 speaks in the perfect passive of God's testimony to God's son recalls the perfect construction in 1:1–3; the reference is to the Christ-event, which can be spoken of in the Fourth Gospel in present-tense witness terminology as well (5:32; 8:18); but since the Fourth Gospel also uses the perfect in this connection (cf. John 1:32, 34; 3:26; 5:33, 37; 19:35), it would be difficult to suppose that 1 John 5:9 is "referring back" to the Fourth Gospel (in response to Johannes Beutler, "μαρτυρία," *EDNT* 2 (1991) 392.

23 Cf. Bultmann, *Epistles*, 80.

necessary, be interpreted as a continuation of v. 6 (with the key words being μαρτυροῦν and μαρτυρία), so that vv. 7–9 would represent a secondary insertion. However, the transition from v. 9 to v. 10 presents no problem, especially since not only the key word indicated but also the expression "Son of God" appears in both verses. Moreover, the trio of "water, blood, and Spirit" (v. 6) reappears in vv. 7–8. In distinction from the preceding v. 6, here water and blood are described as "witnesses." Thus these two verses must be understood as an appropriate continuation and interpretation of what has preceded: as the Spirit reveals the eschatological meaning of water and blood (v. 6), this epiphanic reality is to be found in the stages of Jesus' earthly journey, that is, in his baptism and sacrificial death, as well as in the sacraments. Even though the witnessing cannot take place without the Spirit, the sacraments themselves, and not only the Spirit, are "witnesses." Thus v. 7 continues the idea of "giving testimony" that was already expressed in v. 6. The particle ὅτι has this function of continuation and can be translated by an indefinite "for."[24] This meaning is not fundamentally altered if one supposes that ὅτι stands elliptically for εἰς ἐκεῖνο ὅτι and should be translated "in consideration of the fact that."[25]

Excursus: The Textual Tradition of the "Comma Johanneum"[26]

1. Basis

The textual tradition contains an addition to 1 John 5:7–8, called the *Comma Johanneum* or "Johannine

24 Similarly Brown, *Epistles*, 581, according to whom it is not a question of additional reasons being given, but of "further specification," and the word ὅτι should be translated "indeed."

25 BAGD 589; BDF § 457; Kühner-Gerth, *Grammatik*, 2.371–72.

26 Literature: Ezra Abbot, "I John 5, v. 7 and Martin Luther's German Bible," in idem, *The Authorship of the Fourth Gospel and Other Critical Essays* (Boston: Ellis, 1888) 458–63; Mateo del Alamo, "El 'Comma Joaneo,'" *EstBib* 2 (1943) 75–105; idem, "Los tres testificantes de la 1. Ep. de Juán," *CuBi* 4 (1947) 11–14; Aland and Aland, *Text*, 249, 311; Teofilo Ayuso Marazuela, "Nuevo estudio sobre el 'Comma Ioanneum,'" *Bib* 28 (1947) 83–112, 216–35; 29 (1948) 52–76; Anton Baumstark, "Ein syrisches Citat des 'Comma Johanneum,'" *Oriens Christianus* 2 (1902) 438–41; August Bludau, "Das Comma Johanneum bei den Griechen," *BZ* 13 (1915) 26–50, 130–62, 222–43; idem, "Das 'Comma Johanneum' bei Tertullian und Cyprian," *ThQ* 101 (1920) 1–28; idem, "Das Comma Johanneum (1 Joh 5,7) im 16. Jahrhundert," *BZ* 1 (1903) 280–302, 378–407; idem, "Das Comma Johanneum (1 Joh 5,7) in dem Glaubensbekenntnis von Karthago vom Jahre 484," Tijdschrift voor geschiedenis 11 (1919) 9–15; idem, "Das Comma Johanneum (1 Joh 5,7) in den orientalischen Übersetzungen und Bibeldrucken," *Oriens Christianus* 3 (1903) 126–47; idem, "Das Comma Johanneum (1 Joh 5,7) in den Schriften der Antitrinitarier und Socinianer des 16. und 17. Jahrhunderts," *BZ* 2 (1904) 275–300; idem, "Der hl. Augustinus und 1 Joh 5,7–8," Tijdschrift voor geschiedenis 11 (1919) 379–86; idem, "Der Prolog des Pseudo-Hieronymus zu den katholischen Briefen," *BZ* 15 (1918–21) 15–34, 125–38; idem, "Richard Simon und das Comma Johanneum," *Der Katholik* 84 (1904) 29–42, 114–22; idem, "The Comma Johanneum in the Writings of English Critics of the Eighteenth Century," *ITQ* 17 (1922) 66–67; Riekele Borger, "Das Comma Johanneum in der Peschitta," *NovT* 29 (1987) 280–84; Norbert Fickermann, "St. Augustinus gegen das 'Comma Johanneum'?" *BZ* 22 (1934) 350–58; Balthasar Fischer, "Der Bibeltext in den pseudo-augustinischen 'Solutiones diversarium quaestionum ab haereticis objectarum,'" *Bib* 23 (1942) 139–64, 241–67; Claude Jenkins, "A Newly Discovered Reference to the 'Heavenly Witnesses' (I John v. 7,8) in a Manuscript of Bede," *JTS* 43 (1942) 42–45; Henk Jan de Jonge, "Erasmus and the Comma Johanneum," *EThL* 56 (1980) 381–89; Karl Künstle, *Das Comma Johanneum auf seine Herkunft untersucht* (Freiburg: Herder, 1905); Jules Lebreton, *Histoire du dogme de la Trinité* I (2d ed.; Paris: Beauchesne, 1927); A. Lemmonyer, "'Comma Johannique,'" *DBSup* 2 (1934) 67–73; Jean Pierre Paulin Martin, *Introduction à la critique textuelle du Nouveau Testament, Partie Pratique*, 5 (Paris: Maisonneuve frères et C. Leclerc, 1884–86); Metzger, *Text*, 101–2; Eberhard Nestle and Ernst von Dobschütz, *Einführung in das griechische NT* (4th ed.; Göttingen: Vandenhoeck & Ruprecht, 1923) 131; Eduard Riggenbach, *Das Comma Johanneum* (BFCTh 31/4; Gütersloh: Bertelsmann, 1928) 367–405; Jean Rivière, "Sur l'authenticité du verset des trois témoins," *Revue Apologétique* 46 (1928) 303–9; Walter Thiele, "Beobachtungen zum Comma Johanneum (1 Joh 5,7f)," *ZNW* 50 (1959) 61–73; idem, "Untersuchungen zu den altlateinischen Texten der drei Johannesbriefe" (diss., Tübingen, 1956).

Comma" (*comma* = sentence or clause), which made its way almost exclusively into the Latin texts of the Bible. In 1592 the *Comma Johanneum* was incorporated into the official Catholic edition of the Vulgate, the Sixto-Clementine, where it reads as follows (italicized):

7 Quoniam tres sunt, qui testimonium dant
in caelo: Pater, Verbum, et Spiritus Sanctus,
et hi tres unum sunt.
8 *Et tres sunt, qui testimonium dant in terra:*
Spiritus et aqua et sanguis,
et hi tres unum sunt.

2. Attestation

Greek manuscripts: The *Comma Johanneum* is absent from almost the whole of the Greek textual tradition, including the quotations in the church fathers. It is transmitted by only eight Greek minuscules, where it probably entered via the Latin textual witnesses. None of these examples can be dated before 1400, and only four of them appear in the text; the others are marginal additions.

The following minuscules contain the *Comma Johanneum:*

Gregory	61	Codex Montfortianus, early 16th century
Gregory	629	Codex Vatic. Ottobonianus, 14th/15th century or later
Gregory	918	Spanish 16th-century manuscript (Escorial)
Gregory	2318	Rumanian 18th-century manuscript (Bucharest)
Gregory	88vl	Later marginal note, 16th century, in Codex Regius (12th century), Naples
Gregory	221vl	Addition to a 10th-century manuscript, Oxford
Gregory	429vl	Addition to a 16th-century manuscript, Wolfenbüttel
Gregory	636vl	Addition to a 15th-century manuscript, Naples[27]

On the basis of this weak attestation, it is probable that the *Comma Johanneum* was never included in an older Greek text.

Latin manuscripts: The *Comma Johanneum* is also absent from the manuscripts of the Vetus Latina before 600 and the Vulgate before 750: a stronger Latin attestation is found beginning only with the ninth century. But even then, until the end of the millennium, the *Comma Johanneum* appears only in Spanish or Spanish-influenced texts. The most important witnesses are:

a palimpsest from Léon, 7th century
the Freising fragments (q or r), 7th century
Codex Cavensis, 9th century
Codex Complutensis, 10th century
Codex Toletanus, 10th century
Codex Theodulphianus, 8th/9th century (Franco-Spanish)
a few St. Gallen manuscripts, 8th/9th century (Franco-Spanish)

Other manuscripts: The *Comma Johanneum* is absent from all Coptic, Ethiopian, Arabic, and Slavic translations up to 1500. It entered a few late Syrian manuscripts by way of the Vulgate. In the first editions of the Syriac NT by Widmanstadt (1555) it was not accepted, but in the edition of 1569, edited by Tremellius, it appears as a marginal note. In the following century it was included in the text, owing to the impression that it had originally been part of it and had been excised by the Arians. The *Comma Johanneum* is also found in a few late Armenian witnesses and in the Armenian edition of Oskan (1662), which originated after the Vulgate.

Attestation in other authors prior to 650: Although the oldest textual witnesses of the *Comma Johanneum* occur in Latin manuscripts of the seventh century, it had already been cited by a number of Christian authors at an earlier period, so that one may pursue its traces farther back in time.

The oldest undoubted instance is in Priscillian *Liber apologeticus* 1.4 (CSEL 18.6).[28] Priscillian was probably a Sabellianist or Modalist, whose principal interest would have been in the closing statement about the heavenly witnesses ("and these three, the Father, the Word, and the Holy Spirit, are one"). Here he found his theological opinions confirmed: that the three persons of the Trinity are only modes or manners of appearance of the one God. This observation caused some interpreters to suppose that Priscillian himself created the *Comma Johanneum.* However, there are signs of the *Comma Johanneum*, although no certain

27 Codex Ravianus sive Berolinensis (16th century), a copy of the Complutensian printing, should simply be mentioned here.

28 Priscillian founded an ascetic, fervently enthusiastic conventicle in southern Spain in 375. Its purpose was church renewal, but it ended in sectarianism. In about 386 the usurper Maximus had him executed at Trier for heresy and magical arts. Persecution of his successors continued after his death; the *Comma Johanneum* is sometimes attributed to one of them, the bishop Instantius.

attestations, even before Priscillian, and they lead to the vicinity of North Africa.

An initial echo of the *Comma Johanneum* occurs as early as Tertullian *Adv. Prax.* 25.1 (CChr 2.1195; written ca. 215). In his commentary on John 16:14 he writes that the Father, Son, and Paraclete are one (*unum*), but not one person (*unus*). However, this passage cannot be regarded as a certain attestation of the *Comma Johanneum.*

More important is the evidence in Cyprian († 258). He writes in *De ecclesiae catholicae unitate* 6 (CChr 3.254): "Dicit dominus: ego et pater unum sumus (Joh 10:30) et iterum de patre et filio et spiritu sancto scriptum est: et tres unum sunt" ("The Lord says: I and the Father are one [John 10:30] and again it is written of the Father and Son and Holy Spirit: and the three are one").

If the *Comma Johanneum* is behind this, it would already have been a part of the oldest Latin Bible.[29] But it is possible that it is merely a reflection on the Trinity by Cyprian, similar to Tertullian's (or perhaps even occasioned by the latter). An African witness contemporary to Cyprian, commonly called Pseudo-Cyprian, in his tract *De rebaptismate,* does not attest the *Comma Johanneum,* even though he twice cites the text of 1 John 5:7–8 (15 and 19; CSEL 3/3.88 and 92). In addition, Facundus of Hermiane, in the sixth century, does not know the *Comma Johanneum,* but in his work *Pro defensione trium capitulorum ad Iustinianum* (1.3.9–14; CChr 90A.12–14) he interprets the usual text allegorically in reference to the Trinity. Except for a brief remark in *De civitate Dei* (5.11; CChr 47.141), where he says of Father, Word, and Spirit that the three are one, Augustine († 430) does not cite the *Comma Johanneum.* But it is certain on the basis of the work *Contra Maximum* 2.22.3 (*PL* 42.794–95) that he interpreted 1 John 5:7–8 in trinitarian terms.[30] The *Comma Johanneum* is unknown to other Latin church authors of this period, for example, Hilary of Poitiers († 367), Ambrose († 397), Leo the Great († 461), and Gregory the Great († 604). Thus, although there is no clear attestation of the *Comma Johanneum* in the time before Priscillian, after him the addition is cited more frequently, most often in order to adduce a proof for the Trinity—contrary to Priscillian's own ideas. As examples one may cite the twelve books *De Trinitate* and three books *Contra Varimadum.* Their authors and time of composition are unknown, but a date in the fifth century is probable. In addition one should mention the *Historia persecutionis Africanae Provinciae* by Victor, the bishop of Vita in North Africa (ca. 485),[31] as well as the *Responsio contra Arianos* by Fulgentius (10; CChr 91.93); and finally a prologue to the Catholic Letters from the period before 550.

---

29 Thus Walter Thiele, "Untersuchungen zu den altlateinischen Texten der drei Johannesbriefe" (diss., Tübingen, 1956), who adduces the following reasons: On the one hand, (1) the old form of the Latin Bible (Cyprian and Pseudo-Cyprian) has a great many additions; the subsequent development shows that when the text was accommodated to the Greek, these additions were no longer attested. If the *Comma Johanneum* had not been part of the old Latin Bible, this addition would be an utterly unique instance. (2) An examination of Cyprian's quotations of 1 John shows that Cyprian's Bible text for 1 John contained a considerable number of additions, beyond what is found in the Greek text (cf. 1 John 1:9; 2:16–17, 23; 4:4; 2 John 11). On the other hand, (3) the reasons to suppose the *Comma Johanneum* was not attested in Cyprian's text of the Bible are, in Thiele's opinion, not compelling. The principal argument adduced is that in Cyprian "filius" replaces "verbum" as the second person among the heavenly witnesses. But an overview of the whole of the material shows that "filius" is a reading of the *Comma Johanneum,* just as is "verbum"; "filius" is the reading of the manuscript witnesses 67, Θ, Ω^c. With reference to other Latin expansions of 1 John, which might represent lost translations of the Greek original, Thiele also considers it possible that a translation of a Greek text is behind the *Comma Johanneum* as found in Cyprian.

30 Brown discusses and opposes Norbert Fickermann's thesis ("St. Augustinus gegen das 'Comma Johanneum'?" *BZ* 22 [1934] 350–58), according to which Augustine knew the *Comma Johanneum* but rejected it. Fickermann refers in this connection to a previously unpublished text from the eleventh century, in which it is asserted that Jerome had regarded the *Comma Johanneum* as a genuine part of 1 John. But this thesis is derived from the "Prologue" of Pseudo-Jerome and is supported by no text of Augustine. Walter Thiele ("Beobachtungen zum Comma Johanneum [1 Joh 5,7f]," *ZNW* 50 [1959] 71–72) calls attention to the fact that Augustine's use of the text is not characteristic of his time, because Augustine prepared his own biblical text of 1 John by making revisions of the Latin text known to him in light of the Greek. The rejection of the *Comma Johanneum* could have been his personal decision.

31 2.82; CSEL 7.60; 3.11: *PL* 58.227C.

3. History of Influence

In the sixteenth century, after the *Comma Johanneum* had found entry into a number of Latin manuscripts, it again became the subject of controversy. In the first two editions of his Greek NT (1516 and 1519), Erasmus did not reproduce the *Comma Johanneum*. The Complutensis Polyglot by the Spanish Cardinal Primate Ximenes, previously printed (1514) but not published until 1522, contained it, but the Greek text of the *Comma Johanneum* was translated from the Vulgate. After Erasmus had been criticized by D. Lopez de Zuñiga ("Stunica"), the editor of the Complutensis, and by the Englishman E. Lee for omitting the *Comma Johanneum*, he decided against his better judgment to include the text in the third edition of his NT (1522). The most persuasive argument for him was that the *Comma Johanneum* was found in Codex Montfortianus (= minuscule 61). Erasmus's authority was used to support the acceptance of the *Comma Johanneum* in the third edition of the Paris edition of the Greek NT (1530). It also found entry into the Textus Receptus (Elzevir, 1633), the standard Greek text for the next several centuries.

Beginning in 1581, the *Comma Johanneum* was included by the Frankfurt printers, and after 1596 in the Wittenberg edition as well. It was even in Martin Luther's German edition of the NT, although he himself had expressed criticism regarding the genuineness of the *Comma Johanneum*.[32] Zwingli rejected it[33] but Calvin reluctantly included it.[34]

The inclusion of the *Comma Johanneum* in the Catholic church's official edition of the Vulgate, the Sixto-Clementine of 1592, was highly important. From that time, its genuineness was considered indisputable, and it was also printed in the English translations of the NT (*KJV* and Rheims). Johann Salomo Semler was the first who again questioned its originality (in 1764). From that time its secondary character has been considered proved.

The Sacred Congregation of the Inquisition issued a decretal on 13 January 1897, forbidding anyone to question the authenticity of the *Comma Johanneum:* its genuineness could neither be denied nor doubted. Pope Leo XIII confirmed this judgment two days later. On 2 June 1927, however, a new official declaration by the Holy Office, as the successor institution to the Sacred Congregation of the Inquisition, made Roman Catholic exegetes again free to discuss the question of the *Comma Johanneum*. From that time it has been generally recognized in Roman Catholic scholarship also that the *Comma Johanneum* is neither original nor authentic.[35]

■ **8** The objective weight of the three witnesses, "Spirit, water, and blood," cannot be evaluated as if all three were on the same plane. The parallel between v. 6c and v. 6a already indicated a special emphasis on τὸ πνεῦμα. This is also clear from the relatively extensive explication in v. 6c and from the listing of the Spirit as first among the three witnesses.[36] The number three is usually seen as derived from Deut 17:6; 19:15.[37] According to those passages, no judgment should be given on the basis of the statement of a single witness. The determination of a misdeed must be based on the statement of "two or three witnesses." Paul refers to this OT-Jewish background when he uses this citation to justify his intention to make a third visit to Corinth in order to reinforce his apostolic claims in relation to the Corinthian community (2 Cor 13:1). The evangelist Matthew also cites Deut 19:15 in

32 Cf. WA 20.780, 21–781, 2.; WA, *Deutsche Bibel*, 7.628–29.

33 Ulrich Zwingli, *Opera* (8 vols. in 6; ed. Melchior Schuler et Johannes Schulthess; Turici: Schultess, 1829–42) 6.2, 338.

34 Jean Calvin, *Opera quae supersunt omnia* (59 vols. in 58; CR 29–87; ed. Wilhelm Baum, Eduard Cunitz, and Eduard Reuss; Braunschweig: Schwetschke, 1863–1900, reprinted New York: Johnson, 1964) 54 (CR 83).364–65.

35 Cf. Brown, *Epistles*, 781. With this, both text-critical authenticity and theological recognition have been rejected by Roman Catholic exegesis, although the Holy Office, in its declaration of 2 June 1927, still maintained the position that the church alone could decide the question whether the *Comma Johanneum* is really part of Scripture.

36 According to Nauck (*Tradition*, 147–82), πνεῦμα is a third sacramental ritual alongside Baptism and the Lord's Supper, and is identical with the "anointing" that precedes baptism as part of the rite of Christian initiation; cf. Schnackenburg's persuasive arguments to the contrary (*Epistles*, 237–38), as well as his review article in *BZ* 4 (1960) 292–307, at 297.

37 Cf. Schnackenburg, *Epistles*, 235; Schunack, *Briefe*, 95; Wengst, *Brief*, 210.

connection with his instructions for carrying out disciplinary procedures, in the second stage of which the calling of "two or three witnesses" is advised, so that the unrepentant sinner may not be brought to the third stage, the deliberation within the community assembly, without the presence of an adequate number of witnesses (Matt 18:16). Similarly, the author of 1 Timothy instructs that no accusation is to be brought against an elder unless "two or three witnesses" are available (1 Tim 5:19). The Fourth Gospel also knows the OT ruling that the testimony of a witness must be confirmed "by two persons" (John 8:17; cf. also Heb 10:28). In spite of the witness terminology, however, the background of our text is not the idea of a court proceeding. Neither here nor elsewhere in 1 John is there any suggestion of OT influence. For that reason the number three is more probably due to the principle of round numbers, which is employed in a number of different forms in the NT tradition as a whole.[38] The testimony of the "three" expresses the divine plenitude that always characterizes God's revelation in and to the community (John 1:16; Eph 1:23; 4:10). This is also evident in the post-NT tradition where, in similar contexts, other (round) numbers of witnesses can be mentioned.[39]

The phrase *καὶ οἱ τρεῖς εἰς τὸ ἕν εἰσιν* is unique in the NT. It can scarcely be interpreted as a Semitism, although the closest NT parallels have the OT as their background and suggest the translation "become" for *εἶναι εἰς*; this is the case with Matt 19:5 (*καὶ ἔσονται οἱ δύο εἰς σάρκα μίαν*; cf. Gen 2:24) or Luke 3:5 (cf. Isa 40:4).[40] However, no OT text can be found corresponding to the phrase in this verse. The classical *εἶναι εἰς* ("serves to") occurs occasionally in the NT (1 Cor 14:22, and elsewhere), and also in the Priene inscription,[41] but that affords no meaning in the present instance. Philo is relatively close when he says that the trio "reason, clearness of speech, truth" are virtually one.[42] Of course, when Latin translators render this phrase with "hi tres unum sunt," the move to a trinitarian idea is already accomplished, but that is not (yet) implied here. Spirit, water, and blood are instead directed "to the one." In the context of Johannine witness terminology this probably means not only that their testimony agrees but primarily that it corresponds to the one truth. Through this coinciding testimony to the truth they are joined in unity.[43] This agrees with the preceding assertion that the Spirit is truth (v. 6c), and with the understanding of the *χρῖσμα*, which is "true" and "is not a lie" (2:27). When, in the Fourth Gospel, the Revealer makes the claim that his testimony is true (8:14), he stands within a series of witnesses to the truth extending from John the Baptizer (5:32) to the disciple beneath the cross (19:35) and to the evangelist (21:24). This kind of concurring testimony has its center in the twofold self-attestation of the Revealer: "I am the truth" (14:6) and "I and the Father are one."[44]

■ **9** Verse 9 follows seamlessly. The conclusion *a minori ad maius* interprets the testimony of the three: if human testimony is accepted within society[45] and must be accepted, since without trust among human beings any kind of order within this world would come apart at the seams, this is all the more the case with the *μαρτυρία* that is the subject here.[46] The testimony of the three is the

38 Cf., with a variety of meanings, Mark 5:37; Matt 1:17; 5:7–9, 21–22; Acts 5:7; 7:20; 9:9; 10:16; 1 Cor 13:13; 2 Cor 11:20; Rev 6:6; 8:13; 9:18, and elsewhere.

39 E.g., the disciples of Elchasai called on seven witnesses; cf. Hippolytus *Ref.* 9.15. 2, 5; Epiphanius *Pan.* 19.1.6, and frequently.

40 Also 2 Cor 6:18 (Jer 31:1); Heb 1:5 (2 Sam 7:14); the corresponding construction *γίνεσθαι εἰς*: Matt 21:42 (Ps 117:22), and frequently; BAGD 230; BDF §145 (1); Horst Balz, "*εἰμί*," *EDNT* 1 (1990) 393; cf. also the parallel in 1QS v.2: להיות ליחד = "to belong to the community."

41 50.39; cf. Gustav Adolf Deissmann, *Light from the Ancient East* (trans. Lionel R. M. Strachan; 1927; reprinted Grand Rapids: Baker, 1978) 120–21. There is a purely formal parallel in Ignatius *Magn.* 7.2 (*εἰς ἕνα ὄντα*), since here *εἰς* is used in the sense of a local *ἐν* (with *χωρήσαντα*).

42 Philo *Leg. all.* 3.124: *ἕν γάρ ἐστιν δύναμει*; cf. also *Quaest. in Gen.* 4.2. The alchemical text from the "Teaching of Queen Cleopatra" mentioned by Reitzenstein (*Hellenistic Mystery-Religions,* 398) emphasizes that the human being made up of the trio of "body, soul, and spirit" is a unity (*γεγόνασιν ἕν*); cf. R. Reitzenstein, "Zur Geschichte der Alchemie und des Mystizismus," Göttingen: Akademie der Wissenschaften, 1919) 1–37. Reprint of an article originally published in Akademie der Wissenschaften, Göttingen, Philologisch-Historische Klasse, vol. 1 (1919).

43 Cf. Appian *Romanae Historiae* 6: *De rebus hispaniensibus* 66 § 280: *ἐς ἕν* = "together, as a unity" (BAGD 230).

testimony of God. It is superior to all human affirmations, even when these latter are supported by the testimony of many witnesses (cf. at v. 8 above), and therefore is more worthy of trust.[47] However indispensable human testimonies may be—the author emphasized at another point that the Christ revelation was transmitted by authoritative eye- and ear-witnesses[48] — they can at most only be pointers and proclamations of the Christ-event in which God has given testimony. That testimony is made present by the three witnesses. As God's testimony is made concrete in them, they point back to the Christ-event in the past and testify to the Son (v. 6). Thus their testimony is the object of the community's creedal confession, whose antidocetic thrust must be kept in mind at this point also, as the goal of the sacramental testimony: the Spirit's testimony is bound to the historical fact of Jesus of Nazareth and his sacramental "action." That God has borne witness to God's own self in the divine Son and that this testimony is a present reality for believers in Baptism and the Lord's Supper make a purely spiritual understanding and appropriation of the Christ-event impossible.

■ **10** The previous verse, with its chiastic juxtaposition of human and divine witness and its high point attained in describing the latter, reached a climax from which v. 10 now draws an antithetical parallelism that carries the thought just expressed a step farther: God's witness to the Son demands faith. In those who show faith in the Son, the divine witness becomes reality; for it is defined by the truth that God has given. The movement of the thought is thus shaped by the key word πιστεύειν. The construction with εἰς and the accusative[49] refers to the object "Son of God" (cf. 1:3, 7; 3:8; 4:15, and frequently). The "faith" to which the author summons his community was already interpreted, above, in the confessional statement "Jesus is the Christ" (5:1, 5). This does not suggest the common distinction between *fides qua creditur* and *fides quae creditur*. The confession of the

44 John 10:30. The idea of sacramentally unified testimony corresponds to the Johannine idea of the unity of the Son with the Father (cf. also John 17:11, 21–33); it can be seen in 1 John in the interchangeability of the personal pronouns; cf. 1 John 1:5, 6, 7, 10; 2:3–6, 25, 27–28; 3:24; 4:13, 19, 21; 5:6, 14, 15, 20.

45 Εἰ with the indicative introduces an indefinite conditional clause and could be replaced by a causal particle. What is said in the subordinate clause is presumed as really existing ("real conditional clause"); cf. Adolf Kaegi, *Griechische Schulgrammatik* (1884; 62d ed.; Dublin: Weidman, 1974) §179; BDF §371.

46 For the concept of μαρτυρία (in 1 John only at 5:9–11), see the excursus above.

47 The word μείζων is Johannine (cf. John 5:36; 19:11); the comparison with John 5:36–37 is especially suggestive (the testimony of the Son is "greater" than that of the Baptizer); Dodd, *Epistles*, 131–32. However, it is characteristic of the present text that there is no reference to the testimony of Scripture (unlike John 5:39). Otherwise there is scarcely any difference; this, at least, is the opinion of Schnackenburg, *Epistles*, 238 n. 124 (John 5:36 refers to the higher degree of credibility, 1 John 5:9 to the stronger binding force of God's testimony). Regarding the reconstruction of v. 9c-d: αὕτη ("this itself") refers back to μαρτυρία (corresponding to οὗτος in 5:6; the reference to what follows in vv. 11, 14 is different). The first ὅτι has a causal function: the preceding clause, according to which the testimony of God is greater, is given a foundation through the remark that its object is the Son. From this it follows that the second ὅτι has an explanatory sense ("that"). This is also evident from the secondary reading (P 𝔐): the relative pronoun ἥν refers to ἡ μαρτυρία and makes clear that the subordinate clause that follows explains this very concept (corresponding to the end of v. 10: "the testimony that God has given concerning his Son").

48 Cf. at 1:3 above. This corresponds to the Latin expansion found in some manuscripts of the Spanish Vulgate (as well as in the Armenian tradition): "Whom [the Son] he [God] sent to earth as savior, and the Son gave testimony on earth, by fulfilling Scripture. And we give testimony that we have seen him, and we proclaim to you, so that you may believe"—undoubtedly a secondary recapitulation of the prologue (1:2) and of John 20:31.

49 Apart from two occurrences in v. 10, this is also found in v. 13 (see below); cf. John 2:11; 3:16; 9:35, and frequently; more often the connection is with the following ὅτι (1 John 5:1, 5; John 6:64, 69; 8:24; 9:18, and frequently) and the dative (apart from v. 10b, also in 1 John 3:13; 4:1; John 2:22; 4:21, and frequently).

Son is not contrasted with the act of believing trust. Rather, the eschatological truth attested in the creedal confession is recognized only in believing acceptance.[50] Nonetheless, "faith" is directed to this same creedal confession and cannot be isolated from it. One may also conclude from the expression ἔχει τὴν μαρτυρίαν ἐν ἑαυτῷ that the community's faith is characterized by its relationship to what is *extra nos.*[51] This can scarcely mean that there is an alternative between external confession of God and internal confession within the human heart.[52] Instead, what is meant is that the testimony of God, which goes before us and which has become concrete in the Christ-event, is to be acknowledged by human beings and made their own possession through faith. The author means to describe this acceptance by asserting, in the indicative, that believers have this testimony "in their hearts." Thus one may say that the proof that the Christ-event opens access to eschatological truth is produced by faith itself. It is not to be shifted to some event external to the human being. This is not, however, to say that "the event of faith is the witness."[53] Rather, faith is only faith when it refers to an event that precedes it, the event of the incarnate and crucified Christ, and is constituted by it; for it is not a human idea but the testimony given by God in Jesus Christ whose truth is verified in faith. Christian faith is thus not something that stands in isolation within history. It is founded on an *extra nos* evoked by the attesting word, the "three witnesses" (v. 8), and the Christ-event, to which word and sacrament point (1:1). It can neither be separated from the Christ-event nor from the word or the sacraments that mediate between Christ and believers.

Verse 10b completes the antithesis: whoever refuses to believe in this testimony rejects God's claim, remains closed to divine truth, and perverts it into falsehood.[54] Such people place themselves on the side of the false teachers and are, like them, governed by lies (cf. 2:21–22, 27).[55] The author draws the following parallel: confession of the Son in faith (v. 10a) is identical with faith in God (v. 10b) and believing in God's testimony (v. 10c). In turn, failure to believe in God (v. 10b) is the same thing as failing to believe in God's testimony (v. 10c) and denying the truth of the Christ-confession (cf. 2:22).[56]

■ **11** The introductory καὶ αὕτη indicates the beginning of

50 Cf. the mutual orientation of πιστεύειν and γινώσκειν at 1 John 4:16; also John 6:69; 10:38; 17:8.

51 As regards the text itself, the attestation of the genitive τοῦ θεοῦ is relatively weak, and in light of the repetition of the expression ἡ μαρτυρία τοῦ θεοῦ (v. 9) it should be regarded as nothing but an expansion that, while materially correct, is nevertheless secondary. Αὐτῷ is an important alternative reading for ἑαυτῷ; it adds no new content to the thought of the latter, so long as one presupposes that the reference of the pronoun is to ὁ πιστεύων ("in oneself" = "in the believer"). It is different if αὐτῳ is referred to the preceding αὐτῷ. It could then be translated, "[They have] the testimony through him [= through God]"; but in fact that would be a repetition of v. 9b. Hence the reading ἐν ἑαυτῷ, as the *lectio difficilior,* is to be preferred.

52 Thus Weiss, *Briefe,* 145: "It is a question here of a testimony that the believer has within him- or herself, and that thus is given not by God, but by one's own internal experience"; cf. also Albert Klöpper, "Zur Lehre," *ZWTh* 43 (1900) 585–602.

53 Bultmann, *Epistles,* 82; cf. idem, *John,* 163, on John 3:33: "[whoever] believes in the Son . . . , does not need to look any further for something to confirm the testimony, for he already possesses it in the testimony itself" (with a reference to John 7:17: "Anyone who resolves to do the will of God will know whether the teaching is from God").

54 Literally, "makes God a liar," by failing to recognize and acknowledge the offer of divine testimony to the truth for what it is. The construction ψεύστην ποιεῖν αὐτόν appears also in 1 John 1:10 (= "his word is not in us"); ψεύστης occurs also in 2:4, 22; 4:20; cf. John 8:44, 55.

55 The variant τῷ υἱῷ is presumably an accommodation to v. 10a (εἰς τὸν υἱὸν τοῦ θεοῦ). The present participle ὁ μὴ πιστεύων emphasizes the general application; it is resumed by the perfect πεποίηκεν. The reality of the course of events is thus regarded as certain, since it is represented as something that has already happened (cf. also 1 John 2:5; Rom 14:23; Jas 2:10; BDF § 344).

56 The negative particle shifts, without any change in meaning, from μή (v. 10b) to οὐ (v. 10c); whereas οὐ is seldom used with the participle, e.g., once each in John (10:12) and Matthew (22:11; cf. also Luke 6:42; 1 Pet 1:8; the negation is strongly emphasized: see Radermacher, *Neutestamentliche Grammatik,* 212; BDF § 430; BAGD 590–91), μή, in harmony with later Greek usage, predominates in the NT, especially with the participial noun (1 John 3:10; 2 John 9; John 20:29); cf. also John 3:18: "whoever does not believe (ὁ μὴ πιστεύων) is already condemned, because he or she has not believed in the name of the only Son of

something new, going beyond what was said previously. The demonstrative αὕτη points toward the following ὅτι clause, which thus acquires an explanatory function.[57] The μαρτυρία, the divine witness described in vv. 9–10, does not refer to something that happens within the Trinity; it has, instead, an anthropological intent. God's self-witness in Jesus Christ has a soteriological meaning. It contains the offer of ζωὴ αἰώνιος for all human beings. This introduces the key word that will govern the author's exposition from this point until the conclusion of the work. The word ζωή occurs thirteen times in 1 John, six of them in absolute usage,[58] alternating with a use in combination with the adjective αἰώνιος.[59] This means that everywhere it appears in 1 John, this expression refers to "eternal life" as the content of eschatological salvation. In what follows, it will be contrasted with "not having life" (v. 12) and with θάνατος (vv. 16–17). Whereas the divine witness testifies to the Son (v. 10), this idea is now interpreted by the statement that God has given us eternal life in the Son. The aorist ἔδωκεν is effective in meaning and (in contrast to the preceding perfect μεμαρτύρηκεν) describes the uniqueness of the past Christ-event. It is this event, proclaimed by the author as one who has seen and heard it (cf. 1:1–5), that is the basis for the life of salvation that is present in the community now. It is accomplished through faith in the word that is proclaimed and the saving efficacy of the sacraments; for it can be said of believers that they have passed from death to life (3:14).[60] The possession of ζωή is not a *habitus,* an unchangeable condition. Instead, life must be grasped continually anew in love for the sisters and brothers. This is illustrated by the negative example of Cain, the fratricide, whose misdeed was born of hatred and represents "abiding in death" (3:15). In contrast, Jesus' self-surrender is a fundamental example of love for the sisters and brothers as it is to be practiced in the community (3:16).

As indicated by the second αὕτη, which takes up the first (v. 11a), the content of the μαρτυρία is not only the divine gift of eternal life but also the revelation of the truth: ἡ ζωὴ ἐν τῷ υἱῷ ἐστιν. The author does not say that the Son is life, but "life is in the Son [of God]." This echoes the NT formula ἐν Χριστῷ and may indicate a Pauline background for the Johannine school.[61] This suggests that the meaning of the preposition ἐν ("in") is local rather than instrumental.[62] For the community, the place that is ordained for them is "existence-within" the present Christ-event. Wherever the divine witness that consists in the gift of life is accepted, there is community between believers and the Son. The Christ-event is not a thing of the past to which one may look back with an

God." Regarding the text: the relative clause (similar to the variant reading in v. 9b) has been eliminated in the manuscript tradition as superfluous (048) or else shortened (1881, vg[mss]); it is a matter of a (pleonastic) repetition of v. 9b. The *figura etymologica* εἰς τὴν μαρτυρίαν ἣν μεμαρτύρηκεν is not simply the language of the LXX nor is it a Semitism. It was also used in classical Greek (Kühner-Gerth, *Grammatik,* 1.303–4). In the NT it occurs also in John 7:24; 1 John 5:16; with the relative pronoun in Luke 1:73; John 17:26; Eph 2:4; cf. BDF §153.

57 Thus, in an epexegetical sense, also 1 John 1:5; 5:14; John 3:19, and frequently (see below, at v. 14).

58 1 John 1:1–2; 2:25; 3:14–15; 5:11–13, 16, 20.

59 Cf. 1 John 1:2; 3:14–15; 5:11–12.

60 The first person pronoun ἡμῖν here (as earlier in 1:6–8) has an ecclesial sense. It is emphatically placed at the beginning and is the dative object of ἔδωκεν (differently from the reading ὁ θεὸς ἡμῖν attested by B and minuscules, which, however, yields no meaning); the prior placement of ὑμῖν (1241) is very weakly attested, and so has no significance that would require an alteration of the text.

61 In this regard, see Rom 3:24; 6:11, 23; 8:2; 1 Cor 1:2; 15:22; Gal 3:14, 28; 5:6; Eph 2:14; 4:10–11; 5:23, 27; Phil 2:1, 5; 1 Thess 4:16; cf. D. Zeller, "Paulus und Johannes," *BZ* n.s. 27 (1983) 167–82; Schnackenburg describes this relationship between Pauline and Johannine christology with somewhat greater nuance: see his *Das Johannesevangelium* (4 vols.; HThKNT 4/1–3; Freiburg: Herder, 1965–86) 4.102–18 ("Ein Vergleich . . ."). There is a close parallel in John 1:4: ἐν αὐτῷ ζωὴ ἦν (*v.l.* ἐστίν); also John 20:31: ἵνα πιστεύοντες ζωὴν ἔχητε ἐν τῷ ὀνόματι αὐτοῦ.

62 Cf. also 1 John 3:24 ("he abides *in them*"); 4:13, 15–16; or 2:24 ("you will abide *in* the Son and *in* the Father"); 5:20 ("And we are *in* [the one] who is true, *in* his Son Jesus Christ"); also John 14:20; 15:4; Gal 2:20.

objectifying glance. Instead, its christological statement has a soteriological intention that draws human beings into and holds them within its way of life and point of view. It occurs *hic et nunc* in the community, as a reconciling, life-giving reality. Christian life before God is life in the Son.

■ **12** This is confirmed by a concluding antithetical parallelism. "Having" the Son means possessing life, just as, in turn, "not having" the Son includes loss of life. The use of the verb ἔχειν makes clear that the author is not merely interested in a theoretical apprehension of the Christ-event, but that the christological statement implies a soteriological content. This is bound up with a call to have faith in what is being offered. "Having" the Son is to be equated with "accepting in faith," rather than with "possessing," and the phrase τὸν υἱόν[63] stands for the Christ-event as such. It is no accident that the author can speak of the "Son of God"[64] or "his Son"[65] and mean the same thing, or that in this verse the absolute τὸν υἱόν (v. 12a) can be taken up by τὸν υἱὸν τοῦ θεοῦ (v. 12b). The present participle ἔχων indicates that life is not merely something promised in an unapproachable future,[66] but is that which determines the present existence of the believing community. In turn, not accepting the Son "even now" means not having life. This recalls 2:18, according to which the antichrists, who deny that Jesus is the Christ, also do not have the Father. The christological controversy is echoed in the present passage as well; this was especially evident in 5:6–10. The opponents' denial of Christ does not simply mean, in the abstract, that they reject the application of christological titles of honor to Jesus. In the mind of the author they are calling into question the saving significance of the "Christus incarnatus." They deny the reality of the suffering and death of the Son of God and thereby represent a different view of history and of the world from that adopted by the author. For him, the community's consciousness of being incorporated into ζωή as the reality of the divine gift of salvation presupposes a concrete acceptance of humanity and world in the Son of God. This is expressed most clearly in the realistic interpretation of the sacraments of Baptism and the Lord's Supper, and in the witness of the Spirit that accompanies them: an appropriation in faith of the Christ-event rests on the testimony to the truth borne by the three witnesses.

63 See the absolute "the Son" also in 2:22–24; 4:14; 2 John 9.

64 See 3:8; 4:15; 5:5, 10a, 12b, 13, 20; cf. 2 John 3 ("the Father's Son").

65 See 1:3, 7; 3:23; 4:9–10; 5:9–11.

66 For the future eschatology of 1 John, cf. 4:17, and frequently elsewhere. For absolute ζωή (1:1–2, and frequently), as well as the equivalent ζωὴ αἰώνιος (1:2b; 2:25, and frequently), see above (at v. 11).

Section VII: 1 John 5:13-21 | **Final Parenetic Remarks**

5

The Power of Prayer[1]

13 **I write these things to you who believe in**
the name of the Son of God, so that you
may know that you have eternal life. 14/
And this is the boldness we have in
[God], that if we ask anything according
to [God's] will, God hears us. 15/ And if
we know that God hears us in whatever
we ask, we know that we have
(obtained) the requests made of God. 16/
If you see your brother or sister
committing what is not a mortal sin, you
will ask, and God will give life to such a
one—to those whose sin is not mortal.
There is sin that is mortal; I do not say
that you should pray about that. 17/ All
wrongdoing is sin, but there is sin that is
not mortal. 18/ We know that those who
are born of God do not sin, but the one
who was born of God protects them, and
the evil one does not touch them. 19/ We
know that we are God's children, and
that the whole world lies under the
power of the evil one. 20/ [But] we know
that the Son of God has come and has
given us understanding so that we may
know [the one] who is true, in [God's]
Son Jesus Christ. [This] is the true God
and eternal life. 21/ Little children, keep
yourselves from idols.

■ **13** The introductory phrase "I write these things" (ταῦτα ἔγραψα) refers back to what has preceded. The readers are to recognize what has already been promised them, that which they possess through faith in the Son of God, namely, eternal life. The key words linking this section to the preceding one show that this verse follows seamlessly

1 Literature: Horst Balz, "Johanneische Theologie und Ethik im Licht der 'letzten Stunde,'" in Wolfgang Schrage, ed., *Studien zum Text und zur Ethik des Neuen Testaments: Festschrift zum 80. Geburtstag von Heinrich Greeven* (BZNW 47; Berlin: de Gruyter, 1986) 35–56; Otto Bauernfeind, "Die Fürbitte angesichts der 'Sünde zum Tode,'" in *Von der Antike zum Christentum: Festgabe für Victor Schultze* (Stettin: Fischer & Schmidt, 1931) 43–54; A. H. Dammers, "Hard Sayings II: I John 5,16ff.," *Theology* 66 (1963) 370–72; Francis, "Form and Function"; Josef Herkenrath, "Sünde zum Tode," in Theodor Steinbüchel and Theodor Müncker, eds., *Aus Theologie und Philosophie: Festschrift für Fritz Tillmann zu seinem 75. Geburtstag* (Düsseldorf: Patmos, 1950) 119–38; Julian Hills, "'Little Children, Keep Yourselves from Idols.' 1 John 5:21 Reconsidered," *CBQ* 51 (1989) 285–310; G. D. Kilpatrick, "Two Johannine Idioms" (on 5:20); Albert Klöpper, "Zur Lehre von der Sünde im 1. Johannesbrief, Erläuterung von 5,16 fin," *ZWTh* 43 (1900) 585–602; Nauck, "Das Problem der Redaktion," in idem, *Tradition*, 133–46; S. M. Reynolds, "The Sin unto Death and Prayers for the Dead," *RefR* 20 (1973) 130–39; David M. Scholer, "Sins Within and Sins Without: An Interpretation of 1 John 5:16–17," in Gerald F. Hawthorne, ed., *Current Issues in Biblical Interpretation: Studies in Honor of Merrill C. Tenney* (Grand Rapids: Eerdmans, 1975) 230–46; Albert Segond, "1re Epître de Jean, chap. 5,18–20," *RHPhR* 45 (1965) 349–51; J. L. Ska, "'Petits enfants, prenez garde aux idoles,' 1 Jn 5,21," *NRTh* 101 (1979) 860–74; Ekkehard Stegemann, "'Kindlein hütet euch vor den Götterbildern!' Erwägungen zum Schluss des 1. Johannesbriefes," *TZ*

after what has just been said.[2] However, the author is referring not only to the immediately preceding section but to the whole document up to this point. In spite of its theoretical passages, as a whole it is a parenetical writing expressing an intention to strengthen "knowledge" of the community's status with regard to salvation.

The author of the Fourth Gospel presents a similar formulation at the conclusion of that work (20:31). This does not prove that 1 John is dependent on the Fourth Gospel.[3] Instead, what one finds here are common elements in the world of ideas and basic intentions of the different authors within the Johannine school. There is no material contradiction in the fact that the author of John 20:31 refers to "faith" and the text before us to "knowledge," for the fourth evangelist is not writing a missionary tract either. The Gospel is primarily addressed to readers who are part of the community, and that author presupposes the readers' "faith." The same is true for the author of this section; beyond that, he could point to the possession of the *χρῖσμα*, which confirms the community in its knowledge of the truth (2:20, 27). It is also presumed that the readers of 1 John have the knowledge of faith. The author's purpose is to strengthen that knowledge. In accordance with the Johannine understanding of *εἰδέναι* (and *γινώσκειν*), this is not merely a matter of a broadening and deepening of Christian knowledge, but of the complete fulfillment of Christian existence.[4]

According to Rudolf Bultmann, v. 13 is the original conclusion of 1 John. The following verses, 14–21, are to be assigned to a "later redaction," especially because they lack unity as a group.[5] Moreover, these verses have a number of hapax legomena and theological ideas that appear to give this section an un-Johannine character: *κατὰ τὸ θέλημα* (v. 14; but cf. the reference to the "will of God" in 2:17; also John 4:34; 7:17; 9:31); *διάνοια* (v. 20; see below); absolute *ὁ ἀληθινός* (v. 20; also John 7:28; on this, see below at

41 (1985) 284–94; J. N. Suggit, "I John 5:21: ΤΕΚΝΙΑ, ΦΥΛΑΞΑΤΕ ΕΑΥΤΑ ΑΠΟ ΤΩΝ ΕΙΔΩΛΩΝ," *JTS* 36 (1985) 386–90.

2 Cf. vv. 11–12 and v. 13 (*ζωὴ αἰώνιος*); vv. 1, 5, 10 (*ὁ πιστεύων*) and v. 13 (*τοῖς πιστεύουσιν*); vv. 5, 9–11 with vv. 13 and 20 (*υἱὸς τοῦ θεοῦ*).

3 Against Brown, *Epistles*, 125 ("The epistolary author has reflected at length on the original conclusion of [the Gospel of John]"); also Balz, "Johanneische Theologie," 36 n. 8. The correspondences cannot be denied: an initial *ταῦτα*, address in the second person plural, construction with *ἵνα* and a *ὅτι* clause dependent on it, the expressions *ζωὴν ἔχειν*, *υἱὸς τοῦ θεοῦ*, the use of *γράφειν*, *πιστεύειν*, *ὄνομα*. Nevertheless, these should be contrasted with the differences in construction and vocabulary:

1 John 5:13	John 20:31
ἔγραψα	*γέγραπται*
εἰδῆτε	*πιστεύσητε*
—	*Ἰησοῦς ἐστιν ὁ Χριστὸς ὁ υἱὸς τοῦ θεοῦ*
ζωὴν αἰώνιον	*ζωήν* (with a different variant)
τοῖς πιστεύουσιν (*εἰς*)	*πιστεύοντες* (absolute)
εἰς τὸ ὄνομα τοῦ υἱοῦ τοῦ θεοῦ	*ἐν τῷ ὀνόματι αὐτοῦ*

Here, as elsewhere, the differences do not suggest literary dependency of 1 John on the Fourth Gospel. This is also true of the more restricted position that it was not the Fourth Gospel, but the conclusion of the *sēmeia* source (John 20:30–31) that was used (but see the important arguments of Schnelle against the hypothesis of a *sēmeia* source in his *Antidocetic Christology*, 135–39, 150–64). One could more easily suppose that the extended confession of "Jesus as the Christ, the Son of God," might be a later reflection of the antidocetic controversies, demonstrable elsewhere in the Fourth Gospel as well; these controversies in the Johannine school find unmediated attestation in 1 John. However, an attempt to demonstrate a literary dependence of the Fourth Gospel on 1 John is equally unpersuasive.

4 Schnackenburg (*Epistles*, 246) is correct in drawing attention to the frequency of *οἴδαμεν* in what follows (vv. 15, 18–20); together with *εἰδῆτε* it produces a "basso continuo" for the whole passage. As early as 2:20 a fundamental significance was assigned to the community's "knowledge," which has reference to the truth and is the reason for this writing.

5 Bultmann, *Epistles*, 2; see also his "Analyse," 156, and "Redaktion," 191. Critical positions against Bultmann are taken by Nauck, *Tradition*, 136–46; Schnackenburg, *Epistles*, 15–17. The concluding section is considered secondary also by Dodd, Vielhauer, Wengst, and Schunack; favoring its integrity are Balz, Brown, Stegemann, Kümmel (*Introduction*, 438–40), Francis ("Form and Function," 124). Marinus de Jonge (*De brieven van Johannes* [Nijkerk: Callenbach, 1968] 223–24) also comes down on the side of literary unity; according to him v. 13 is a typical transitional verse; as in 1:4; 2:1; 2:12–14; 2:21, 26, the author wishes to emphasize in a particular way that the addressees are to take to heart what he is saying.

5:20); the distinction between two classes of sins (vv. 16–17); and the warning "keep yourselves from idols" (v. 21).

However, such arguments are not sufficiently weighty to allow one to impute this section to a secondary redaction. Hapax legomena are also known in other parts of 1 John, without provoking literary-critical conclusions.[6] The oral tradition of the Johannine school may be responsible for the uniqueness of some formulations and ideas, in this passage as well as elsewhere (thus the distinction between "mortal sins" and "sins that are not mortal" would rest on existing practices in the community).[7] It must be denied that, as a whole, this last section of 1 John, with its impeccable textual tradition, gives the impression of disorder. The exegesis will show that the thought pattern develops in a logical manner. Even if one were to label the content of these verses as "assorted additional remarks,"[8] it is not out of the question that the additions are deliberately placed at the end of 1 John in connection with the concrete question of the forgiveness of sins within the community. In concluding, the author makes the parenetic orientation of his writing evident, as is also clear from the summary final saying, which apparently echoes pre-Johannine tradition (v. 21). The outline of the passage includes: the author's eschatological declaration (v. 13), confidence that prayer is heard (vv. 14–15), appeal for prayers with reference to the two classes of sins (vv. 16–17), the sinless condition of those who are born of God (vv. 18–20), and concluding admonition (v. 21).[9]

Although in v. 13 the author refers back to the whole of 1 John,[10] this does not mean that the writing origi-

6 Some central concepts occur as hapax legomena: *πίστις* (5:4), *ἐλπίς* (3:3), *νίκη* (5:4), *παρουσία* (2:28), *πλάνη* (4:6), *σκάνδαλον* (2:10), among others.

7 Bultmann introduces as an argument against the unity of this passage the fact that vv. 14–21 cannot be arranged within the alternations of dogmatic and ethical discourse ("Redaktion," 192), but one should question this assertion as well. Contrary to what he says, the fact that a dogmatic section (vv. 4b–12) precedes this raises the possibility that the parenetic passage (vv. 13–21) was deliberately conceived by the author as a concluding admonition to the readers. Elsewhere the christological-dogmatic discourses are placed before those that are parenetical and ethical, as is evident when 2:28 (*καὶ νῦν*) follows 2:18–27, or also in the attachment of 4:7–21 to 4:1–6. On the other hand, parenesis dominates the whole document; this is evident from the introductory section 1:5—2:17, just as 4:7–21 leads toward the dogmatic passage 5:4b–12. For this reason there is no point to Schnackenburg's objection that 3:23–24 "clearly forms a conclusion" (*Epistles*, 12). At the same time, one must acknowledge that christological and parenetic statements are also connected within the christological sections.

8 Thus Bultmann, "Redaktion," 190, 194–96; according to this the section represented by vv. 18–20 would be a secondary construction separate from vv. 16–17 (cf. Bultmann, *Epistles*, 86–89).

9 Francis ("Form and Function," 124–26) makes a similar division: eschatological injunction (v. 13), prayer and the sinner (vv. 14–17), thematic reprise (vv. 18–20), final injunction (v. 21).

10 That the aorist *ἔγραψα* refers to something in the past was clear already at 2:14, 21, 26—in contrast to the present usage in 1:4 (first person plural) and 2:1, 7–8, 12 (first person singular; cf. the present participle in 2 John 5). In 5:13 the author of 1 John is speaking (as in the instances just cited). The shift from singular to plural normally has no special meaning. However, the subsequent resumption of the first person singular with the first person plural (*οἴδαμεν*) is transitional to the ecclesial "we." The combination of *γράφειν* with a following *ἵνα* clause, indicating the intention of the writing, occurs also in 1:4 and John 20:31. Codex P and the Koine text insert between *ὑμῖν* and *ἵνα*: *τοῖς πιστεύουσιν εἰς τὸ ὄνομα τοῦ υἱοῦ τοῦ θεοῦ*; this is to be regarded as a secondary assimilation to v. 13c. Similarly, the manuscript tradition in v. 13a forms a parallel by inserting *καὶ ἵνα πιστεύητε* (in place of the participial construction in the dative plural). If one accepts the text of ℵ* B vg sy[h] and others as a basis, the dative plural *τοῖς πιστεύουσιν* in v. 13ca is parallel to the introductory *ὑμῖν*, and its purpose is to interpret this personal pronoun. The construction *πιστεύειν εἰς τὸ ὄνομα* is found also in the Fourth Gospel (John 1:2; 2:23; 3:18), where the "name" always stands for the person in whom one has faith (cf. also "in my Father's name" in John 5:43; 10:25; similarly 17:11–12). In the present verse *πιστεύειν* is combined with *εἰς* (with the accusative); in 1 John 3:23 it is used with the dative (*ἵνα πιστεύσωμεν τῷ ὀνόματι τοῦ υἱοῦ αὐτοῦ Ἰησοῦ Χριστοῦ*). Both constructions alternate in the

nally ended with v. 13. Since 1 John is not a real letter, but rather a written homily,[11] the present verse cannot have been part of an original epistolary conclusion, all the more since essential elements of a literary conclusion to a letter, for example the greetings and benediction, are missing. The function of v. 13 is not to conclude the writing but to introduce the final section. It anticipates what is to follow, in both form and content, since the parenetic orientation characteristic of this closing section is already evident in this verse. Here, that is, it is evident that the Christians addressed are enjoined to realize the salvation promised them through concrete deeds. It is scarcely accidental that v. 13 expresses in positive terms what the saying in v. 21 will repeat in negative form. The injunction to be careful to avoid "idols" is translated into action when people have correct knowledge and turn to Jesus Christ in faith—that is, when they share in eternal life.[12]

■ **14-15** The "knowledge" of eternal life in which the author wishes to encourage renewed confidence is identical with a complete acceptance of God's testimony (v. 9), an acceptance that is to be realized both in theory and in practice. This includes the fulfillment of *παρρησία*, of boldness and confidence, such as will be characteristic of Christian believers at the parousia (2:28; 4:17). This boldness is founded on the certainty of already sharing in eternal life (v. 13; cf. 3:22), and is made concrete in the confidence that believers' prayers will be heard.[13] The prayer is addressed to God.[14] The supplementary "according to [God's] will" (*κατὰ τὸ θέλημα αὐτοῦ*) is not to be read as a restrictive condition placed on prayer or as a limitation on the confidence of being heard. Instead, it makes clear that every proper prayer is directed toward the fulfillment of God's will.[15] That the one who prays can confidently hope to be heard[16] is expressed by the phrase *ἔχομεν τὰ αἰτήματα*.[17] The author does not say which prayer he has in mind. There is no reason in the matter itself to restrict the object of proper prayer. The

---

Fourth Gospel as well (John 3:36: *ὁ πιστεύων εἰς τὸν υἱόν*; 5:24: *πιστεύων τῷ πέμψαντι*). There is no difference in meaning, as was clear also at 1 John 5:10 (*πιστεύειν εἰς* twice; *πιστεύειν* with the dative once). In any case what is meant is a total surrender in faith. The attempt to postulate a Semitic background for this construction is unpersuasive. *Πιστεύειν* with the dative of the thing or person is ordinary Greek (BAGD 660–61; it is also LXX Greek: Rudolf Bultmann, "*πιστεύω*," *TDNT* 6 (1968) 197 n. 149, 203. In addition, *πιστεύειν εἰς* does not really correspond to Hebrew הֶאֱמִין לְ or בְּ, but is an "original NT construction" (Ethelbert Stauffer, "*εἰς*," *TDNT* 2 [1964] 432), which, however, has early parallels outside the NT (cf. BAGD 661–62).

11 See above (Introduction to 1 John).

12 See, in addition, what is said with regard to v. 21 below. Beyond this, it is not appropriate to point to the correspondence between *οἴδαμεν* (vv. 15, 18–20) and *εἰδῆτε* (v. 13) in support of the original unity of the final section (as do Schnackenburg, *Epistles*, 246; and Balz, "Johannesbriefe," 207). Instead, one should look especially to the concepts of *ζωή* and *υἱὸς τοῦ θεοῦ* (see n. 2 above).

13 The demonstrative pronoun with a following *ὅτι* clause is also found at 5:9, 11, and refers here, as there (and earlier in 3:16) to what follows; *ὅτι* accordingly has an epexegetical function ("that"). Regarding *ὅτι ἐάν τι*: *ἐάν* is occasionally used, in NT language, in place of *ἄν* after a relative pronoun. This usage emphasizes the conditional character of the clause (cf. v. 15aβ and the close parallel in 3:22: *ὃ ἐὰν αἰτῶμεν*; also 3 John 5; John 15:7; BDF § 107 [1]). Such an emphasis is indicated also by the variant readings for the present text: *ὅτι ὃ (ἐ)άν* (33 81; latt) or *ὅ τί* (or *ὅτι*) *(ἐ)άν* (A 049 69* pc). But the reading mentioned above, as the *lectio difficilior*, is to be preferred. While a condition may be presumed (cf. John 5:31; 8:16; 15:14; Luke 6:33; Rom 2:25, and frequently), one should also consider that *ἐάν* can sometimes have the meaning of *ὅταν* ("as often as"): 1 John 2:28 *v.l.*; John 12:32; 14:3; BAGD 211. Hence, the certainty of being heard has already been expressed in v. 14bα, not first at v. 14bβ. The construction in v. 14, *ἐάν* with the present indicative, is unusual; however, in the NT *ἐάν* does appear, though very rarely, in place of *εἰ* or *ἐπεί* (1 Thess 3:8; perhaps also at John 5:31). The information in BDR § 373, 3 n. 12, that Greek examples are found only from the second century CE and later, is incorrect (cf., in contrast, BAGD 211).

14 Regarding *πρὸς αὐτόν*: it seems likely, at first glance, that the personal pronoun refers to the preceding *τοῦ υἱοῦ τοῦ θεοῦ* (v. 13). In line with 3:21, however, it is more proper to refer the concept of *παρρησία* to God, who judges and pardons; this applies also to what follows (v. 18: "being born of God"); the application of the *αὐτόν* to Jesus is thus less appealing, although here as elsewhere the author is deliberately unspecific.

15 Cf. Matt 7:7; 26:42 par. (on this, see Brown, *Epistles*, 609: "a Johannine echo of the Synoptic account of Jesus' own prayer"). Dodd (*Epistles*, 134) interprets the expression *κατὰ τὸ θέλημα αὐτοῦ* in terms of

boldness and confidence of the one praying are without limit because such a person is conscious of being supported by God's saving care in Christ.

The certainty that believers' prayers are heard is also expressed in the Fourth Gospel in the word of the Revealer (14:13; 15:7; 16:23–24, 26). Of course the present verse, with its observation that prayer must be spoken "according to God's will," calls attention to the fact that proper prayer should not place human will and desire in the foreground, but should open itself without reservation to God's demand. It is no accident that the assurance of prayer's being heard was previously given a foundation with the statement that "we obey his commandments and do what pleases him" (3:22). It was a matter of general conviction in primitive Christianity that one who does not meet God's ethical demands is also incapable of praying properly. This is illustrated in the Sermon on the Mount with the bad examples of the Pharisees and scribes, as well as those of the Gentiles (Matt 6:5–8; cf. 6:14–15), and in the Letter of James with the observation that contentious members of the community will not have their prayers heard, because they pray *κακῶς* ("wrongly"): Jas 4:3.

If v. 15 is a parallelism in which the first part expresses that which conditions, and the second part that which is

---

"limiting conditions" that must determine the prayer, so that the human wishes presented in prayer can be "redirected." This interpretation is not without its problems. Certainly, he thinks of these "limiting conditions" as obedience to God (3:22), abiding in Christ (John 15:7), and prayer in the name of Christ (John 14:14). But in the mind of the author this means that proper prayer, because it opens itself without restriction to the will of God, represents an "unconditional" turning of the human being toward God. It is different with the expression *ποιεῖν τὸ θέλημα τοῦ θεοῦ*, which in the Johannine writings asserts a correspondence between human behavior and the will of God and thereby describes a "condition" that is to determine the relationship of human beings to God (1 John 2:17; John 7:17; 9:31; for the relationship of the Revealer to God: John 4:34).

16 The verb *ἀκούειν* is constructed with the genitive here: "to listen to someone," "to pay attention to someone" (apart from vv. 14–15, also 4:5–6; cf. John 9:31; 11:41–42, and frequently); otherwise it is used with the accusative (1:1, 3, 5; 2:7, 24; 3:11) or with a following *ὅτι* (2:18; 4:3). Cf. Gerhard Kittel, "*ἀκούω*," *TDNT* 1 (1964) 216: "The class[ical] rule of the gen[itive] . . . for the persons whom we hear, and the acc[usative] for the persons or things about whom or which we hear, is applied even more systematically in the NT."

17 BAGD 333: "to have been granted the requests"; also = "enjoy" (what was asked for). *Αἴτημα* is found in the NT otherwise only in Luke 23:24 (*γενέσθαι τὸ αἴτημα*: to grant a request) and Phil 4:6 (*αἰτήματα* = "prayers"); close to our text is *Herm. Sim.* 4.6 (*λαμβάνεσθαι τὰ αἰτήματα* = "to receive what is asked"); cf. Jas 4:3 (*ἔχειν* parallel to *λαμβάνειν* in contrast to *αἰτεῖσθαι*). *Ἔχειν* appears frequently in the Johannine corpus (88 times in the Fourth Gospel; 28 times in 1 John; 4 times in 2 John, 2 times in 3 John) and refers both to God (2 John 9; 1 John 2:23; cf. 1:6–7: "have fellowship with God") and to Christ (2:1: the advocate; also 2:23) as the source of eschatological salvation; it can also refer to eschatological salvation itself (*ζωή*: 5:12; *παρρησία*: 3:21; 4:17; 5:14; *μαρτυρία*: 5:10). Different objects represent eschatological salvation (*φῶς*: John 8:12; 12:35; *ἀγάπη*: 13:35; *εἰρήνη*: 16:33; *χαρά*: 17:13; also *τὰς ἐντολάς*: 14:21). The verb thus belongs completely in the context of present eschatology. This is also clear from the combination with *μένειν*: "having" the Father and the Son means nothing other than "abiding in the Son and in the Father" (1 John 2:23–24; cf. 3:21 with 3:24). The presbyter also recognizes that "abiding in the teaching of Christ" is identical with "having God" (2 John 9). This consciousness of salvation describes the present condition of the community, so that one may speak in the sense of the Johannine writings of a "religion of having as distinct from other religions of seeking and expecting" (Hermann Hanse, "*ἔχω*," *TDNT* 2 [1964] 826). However, this "having" does not refer to a possession at one's disposal; it is open to the future, dependent on the advocacy of the Paraclete (1 John 2:1), and implies the demand not to lose what has once been attained (cf. the imperative *μένετε*: 1 John 2:28; 2:24, 27).

conditioned, it would appear from the double οἴδαμεν as well as from the parallelism of the other expressions that this is a tautology intended to underscore only one point, that the community knows that God hears its prayers.[18] But there is a distinction already in the fact that, in contrast to the preceding clause, v. 15b, with ἀπ' αὐτοῦ, places its emphatic focus on the *divine* answer to prayer. Moreover, it is perhaps not accidental that the perfect ᾐτήκαμεν follows the present αἰτώμεθα (v. 15b).[19] Even though this might represent a mere stylistic variation, one may note that the certainty of prayer's being heard is underscored by the assertion that the community can remember concrete experiences of such response to their prayer. This kind of faith experience is reflected also in Mark 11:24 ("whatever you ask for in prayer, believe that you have received it, and it will be yours").[20] Verse 15 is not to be interpreted as a tautology; instead, it expresses an escalation of the assurance of being heard. This prepares for the following verses, which will address themselves to a particular prayer intention.

■ **16–17** It follows that there is a logical development of the thought in vv. 13–15. The section begins with the author's expression of his intention to promote the knowledge of eternal life among the readers. It leads then to an indirect demand that they realize παρρησία through proper prayer. It ends with a reference to the community's concrete experience of prayer. Verses 16–17 follow logically. An individual instance of such prayer, and one that the author thinks important, is now addressed. In this connection, the key word αἰτεῖν serves the purpose of clarification.[21] While in the preceding verses there was a general discussion of prayer, here it is a matter of prayers of petition on behalf of a fellow Christian as ἀδελφός.[22] The community situation already echoed in 1:6–7 is presupposed. The Christian community—as is generally the case in the NT (cf. Matt 13:24–30, 36–43)—is not an empirically sinless body but a communion continually threatened by sin, a union of good and evil people, a *corpus mixtum* to whom forgiveness of sins is promised through the Christ-event and that is constantly striving not to sin (2:1).

Thus the present text is to be understood as community parenesis, but without reference to any opposing teaching. The future αἰτήσει has an imperative force. The Christian brother or sister's failing is to be the occasion for the community's petitionary prayer. It opens the way to life.[23] As elsewhere in 1 John (cf. 2:25; 5:20, and frequently), ζωή refers to "eternal life." Consequently, θάνατος refers to "eternal death" (cf. 3:14; John 5:24; 8:51), and "mortal sin" means the offense that subjects the doer to God's unrelenting judgment, and on behalf of which no petition is allowed.[24] The thought is logically carried through. After the encouragement to pray for the sinful sister or brother who has committed a

18 This is given as an argument for the redactional hypothesis in Bultmann, "Redaktion," 193.

19 Regarding the variants: instead of ἀπ', A P Ψ and 𝔐 read παρ', which, however, does not really change the statement. A substantial number of minuscules have the aorist ᾐτήσαμεν in place of the perfect ᾐτήκαμεν, but the distinction between this and the preceding present indicative is maintained.

20 In this connection, Dodd (*Epistles*, 135) speaks of the "paradox" of the mystery of prayer: "To the extent that it is really a prayer, it contains its own answer."

21 The middle voice, αἰτεῖσθαι (vv. 14–15), is here replaced by the active αἰτεῖν (v. 16). That the latter also appears at 3:22 makes clear that the shift is not to be evaluated in literary-critical terms; there is no difference in meaning. The word is reflected again at the conclusion of the verse by the synonym ἐρωτήσῃ.

22 In the OT one already finds instances of someone petitioning on behalf of another, e.g., Moses for the people Israel (Exod 32:11–13, 34–35, and frequently); these show that OT Israel, like the Christian community, saw human existence not as something isolated but as a life supported by community. Cf. also the prayer of Jesus for his own (John 17:9), as well as the general encouragement to pray (John 14:13–14; 1 John 3:22).

23 One could think of θεός as the subject of δώσει (so Schnackenburg, *Epistles*, 249, with reference to 5:11); however, it is also possible that τις (v. 16) is assumed to be the subject. This construal is most likely from the point of view of the grammar, since otherwise one would have to suppose another shift in the subject before ἐρωτήσῃ. That prayer, in NT understanding, can be thought of as a life-giving power is shown by Jas 5:15, 20.

24 Regarding ἐρωτήσῃ: the variant reading τις (minuscules 15, 26, 36, 43, 98, 614, sy^{p}, and others) is secondary. It is also understandable, even without it, that the same subject (τις) as in v. 16a is presumed. The verb ἐρωτᾶν as "ask," "pray," also occurs in John 14:16; 16:26; 17:9, 15.

"sin that is not mortal" (v. 16a, b) comes a prohibition against praying for "mortal sins" (v. 16c, d). Then the author returns to the beginning: all ἀδικία ("wrongdoing") is sin. But[25] a distinction must be made. Only in the case of the "sin that is not mortal" is the community's prayer allowed.[26] This is the only passage in which 1 John distinguishes between "mortal sins" and "sins that are not mortal." Only in the latter case may prayers of petition be offered. In contrast, "mortal sins" are judged to be such serious offenses that they separate one from Christian fellowship, subject the sinner to final, eschatological judgment, and do not permit a return to the community. The concept of ἁμαρτία πρὸς θάνατον, unique in primitive Christian writings, recalls the OT-Jewish idea of the sin unto death, referring to an unforgivable, serious, deliberate offense (cf. Num 18:22: ἁμαρτίαν θανατηφόρον), the consequence of which was physical death.[27] However, the author uses this expression in a spiritualized sense, in terms of "eternal death," definitive exclusion from eschatological existence. Even though individual offenses are not precisely stated, and though a strict casuistry is still foreign to 1 John, this idea of "mortal sin" has its place in the dualistic and eschatological context of this homily and is to be understood as the radical opposite to the highest good of salvation, eternal life.

Excursus: Second Repentance

Primitive Christian penitential practice is reflected in this passage at a relatively advanced state of development. In the pre-Johannine period and alongside the Johannine communities there was not yet any similar differentiation. Instead, decisions regarding sinners were made in individual cases, and there existed no institutional basis with its corresponding system of norms.[28]

25 Καί (v. 17b) has an adversative meaning, presupposing the reading οὐ (see the following footnote); cf. also 3:2; BDF § 442 (1).

26 In v. 17, οὐ is relatively well attested; if it were omitted (so Windisch and Preisker, *Die Katholischen Briefe*, 135) v. 17 would express a climax concluding with the indirect warning against "mortal sin."

27 Num 15:30–31 LXX (ἐξολεθρευθήσεται ἡ ψυχὴ ἐκείνη ἐκ τοῦ λαοῦ αὐτῆς, . . . ἐκτρίψει ἐκτριβήσεται ἡ ψυχὴ ἐκείνη, ἡ ἁμαρτία αὐτῆς ἐν αὐτῇ, "That person shall be cut off from among his people . . . that person shall be utterly cut off; his iniquity shall be upon him"); Isa 22:14; also the distinctions in *T. 12 Patr.* (*T. Iss.* 7.1; *T. Gad* 6.3–7); 1QS viii.17, 21—ix.2; *Jub.* 21.22; 26.34, and frequently.

28 For what follows, cf. Ingrid Goldhahn-Müller, *Die Grenze der Gemeinde: Studien zum Problem der Zweite Busse im Neuen Testament unter Berücksichtigung der Entwicklung im zweiten Jahrhundert bis Tertullian* (GThA 39; Göttingen: Vandenhoeck & Ruprecht, 1989), with extensive bibliography; see in particular W. R. Cook, "Harmatiological Problems in First John," *BSac* 123 (1966) 249–60; Bernhard Poschmann, *Paenitentia secunda: Die kirchliche Busse im ältesten Christentum bis Cyprian und Origenes* (Theoph 1; Bonn: Hanstein, 1940; reprinted 1964), P. Trudinger, "Concerning Sins, Mortal and Otherwise: A Note on 1 John 5,16–17," *Bib* 52 (1971) 541–42. Cf. also above, at 5:13–15. It is often the case that a harmonizing interpretation of vv. 16 and 17 takes the sting out of them. Reference is made to the author's subjective formulation (οὐ . . . λέγω = "I do not command" in the sense of someone giving personal advice). This approach is found as early as Ambrose *De poenitentia* 1.10.44–47; also Walter Doskocil, *Der Bann in der Urkirche* (MThS, canonical section 11; Munich: Zink, 1958) 97; Bauernfeind, "Fürbitte," 51; K. Wennemer, "Der Christ und die Sünde nach der Lehre des ersten Johannesbriefes," *GuL* 33 (1960) 370–76, esp. 372; cf. A. H. Dammers, "Hard Sayings II: I John 5,16ff.," *Theology* 66 (1963) 370–72, esp. 372. Others presume that the verbs λέγειν and ἐρωτᾶν are used intransitively and understand "ask" as "asking a question" (a Christian is not meant to reflect on the question of what is pardonable and what is unpardonable): Cook, *BSac* 123 (1966) 259; Trudinger, *Bib* 52 (1972) 542. Another harmonizing interpretation limits the concept of "mortal sin" to sinners unwilling to repent (Poschmann, *Paenitentia*, § 78, and the majority of Catholic exegetes), to non-Christians (Stott, *Epistles*, 188–90), or, most frequently, to the false teachers opposed by 1 John (beginning with Augustine *De sermone Domini* 1.22.73 [CChr 35; Turnhout: Brepols, 1967] 81–83; Klöpper, Bonsirven, Chaine, Scholer, Houlden, and Brown). The dominant idea in this concluding section of the letter is, however, its disciplinary intention, the purpose being to achieve a complete separation from gross sinners for the sake of the community's purity.

Thus in a specific instance Paul recognizes the community's right, as well as the necessity, to separate from a sinful member (1 Cor 5:1–13). Characteristic of this early disciplinary advice is the charismatic and pneumatic nature of judgment within the community, the connection between law and spirit, the orientation of the means adopted to the last day, and their radical character, which may even aim at the physical death of the sinner and leaves no opportunity for repentance.

In contrast, the evangelist Matthew already testifies to a more developed stage of institutionalization, in light of the vanishing hope of the immanent end of things. Adopting a halakic rule of his community, he hands on a fully formulated series of steps with a unified description of the procedure. According to this, a sinner is to be definitively excluded from the community only after three attempts to move him or her to repentance have failed.[29] Both these cases (in the Pauline letter and the Gospel of Matthew) are to be assigned to the middle or end of the first century, and there is as yet no distinction drawn between light and serious sins. In each case the participation of the whole community in the disciplinary process is presumed.[30]

On the other hand, a differentiation within the category of sin is suggested by the Letter to the Hebrews, in a manner somewhat analogous to that in 1 John, when the author categorically denies the possibility of a second repentance for apostates (6:8: They are, like a briar patch, "nigh unto a curse, whose end is burning," κατάρας ἐγγύς, ἧς τὸ τέλος εἰς καῦσιν) and those who willfully persist in sin (6:6: they "have fallen away, since on their own they are crucifying again the Son of God and holding him up to contempt," παραπεσόντας, πάλιν ἀνακαινίζειν εἰς μετάνοιαν, ἀνασταυροῦντας . . . παραδειγματίζοντας) in 6:4–6; 10:26–31; 12:16–17. As in 1 John, this rigoristic view is founded on the knowledge of the "already" of the glory of eschatological existence and the resulting obligation ("vertical eschatology"), but also, at the same time, on the establishment of Christian existence through the past Christ-event (9:26) and the expectation of the "future day" that will bring the second coming of Christ, which necessitates mutual admonition and ethical behavior in the present (9:28; 10:25; 12:26: "horizontal eschatology"). There is special emphasis placed on the importance of baptism for Christian life, on the uniqueness of Christ's sacrifice, which permits no repeated pardon,[31] and on the OT and Jewish teaching on τόπος μετανοίας, according to which the sinner needs divine empowerment to be able to repent.[32] With this rigorous limitation the author attempts to master the problem of increasing weakness of faith and apostasy in the postapostolic period. Around the turn of the third century the Montanists, and in the third century Novatian and his adherents, refused to accept the return of those who had fallen away.[33] That such a rigorous position had to collide not only with the Christian commandment of *agapē*, but also with the factual situation of the communities is clear from the case of the Jewish Christian sectarian Elchasai (Syria, ca. 110), who preached that there was one opportunity for repentance of mortal sins.[34] In a different way, the Roman author of the *Shepherd of Hermas*, writing

29 Matt 18:15–18; the other passages on unforgivable sins in Matthew's Gospel (12:28, 31–32) are primarily directed to the person of Jesus and at best permit nothing more than speculation about the praxis of the community (cf. Strecker, *Weg*, 190 n. 3). The saying about the unforgivable sin against the Holy Spirit (Mark 3:28 par.) is not connected with the institution of penance, either in Mark or in the Q version (Luke 12:10 par. Matt 12:31–32).

30 In a general sense, the demand of John the visionary is that the communities in Asia Minor should "repent" (μετανόησον), that is, overcome the temptation to fall away and place themselves entirely in the service of the exalted Christ (Rev 2:5, 16, 21; 3:3, 19). No distinction is made between various grades of offenses. Instead, the necessity of repentance is urged on the whole community.

31 Poschmann interprets differently (*Paenitentia*, § 42): Hebrews presupposes an "ecclesial" penitential practice and intends to restrict the impossibility of repentance to a concrete, temporary situation in the community (with reference to 6:3: ἐπιτρέπῃ, and 6:8: κατάρας ἐγγύς). However, this is a misunderstanding of Hebrews, under apologetic colors. On this subject, cf. Schnackenburg, *Epistles*, 249–51; also 1QS x.19–21 (the deliberate sinner is surrendered to God's merciless wrath).

32 Cf. Wis 12:10, 19; *1 Clem.* 7.5; Otto Michel, *Der Brief an die Hebräer* (KEK 13; Göttingen: Vandenhoeck & Ruprecht, 1955) 151; and Harold W. Attridge, *The Epistle to the Hebrews* (Hermeneia; Philadelphia: Fortress, 1989) 166–77.

33 Cf. Tertullian *Pud.* 21.7 (a quotation from the original Montanism, according to which the Paraclete will permit no further pardon); cf. also *Pud.* 5.20. Among the texts that foresee a permanent loss of salvation as the consequence of apostasy are *Acts of John* 107; *Act. Thom.* 35; *Pass. Andr.* 13; in the Nag Hammadi texts *Gos. Thom.* 44; *Ap. John* 70,9–71,2; *Gos. Phil.* 79,13–18; *2 Apoc. Jas.* 59,16–17; also Novatian *Ep.* 55.28.

34 Hippolytus *Ref.* 9.15.1–2, 3; cf. 13.3–4; Eusebius *Hist. eccl.* 6.38; cf. Georg Strecker, "Elkesai," in idem, *Eschaton und Historie* (Göttingen: Vandenhoeck &

around 140, offered the possibility of a second repentance, asserting that because of "the weakness of [human beings] and the subtlety of the devil" God offers this possibility to all sinners, except for the newly baptized and catechumens in the Christian community. This author, however, agrees in principle with the author of Hebrews in believing that baptism is the only means by which forgiveness of sins is offered to Christians, because although its pardon is applied to previous sins, it at the same time implies an obligation not to sin any more.[35] Both these offers of repentance have an eschatological motivation; it is a question of a last, unusual "hour of grace" before the end comes. In contrast, Poschmann's statement that the *Shepherd of Hermas* presents no special offer of grace that would modify a general rigor, but rather a pastoral announcement of a final repentance in preparation for the rapidly approaching parousia, is not very persuasive. The reference to rigorist teachers, the modes of revelation through a letter from heaven and an angel of repentance, which underscore the unusual character of the *metanoia*, and the joyful relief with which Hermas cries, as in *Man.* 4.3.7 ("I attained life when I heard these things"), cannot be explained in this way.

Of course, the prophetic messages of Elchasai and the *Shepherd of Hermas* concerning a unique exception to rigorous practice in the expectation of the approaching end of the world could be nothing more than a provisional solution. The more the immediate future-eschatological expectation gave way to a linear conception of history or was combined with it, the more intense was the consciousness of general sinfulness as something not to be overcome, and of the daily need for forgiveness. Awareness of the reality of community life forced the question of the law of *metanoia* to recede before the emphasis on its absolute necessity, until finally, with the development of a clearly dominant clerical order, a claim could be made for the forgiveness of sins now and at all times, no matter what kind they might be. This progress toward a "catholic" penitential system is already echoed in the Pastoral Letters,[36] is solidified in the Apostolic Fathers,[37] and is found in a fully developed form in Dionysus of Corinth, about 170 (Eusebius *Hist. eccl.* 4.23.6), in Irenaeus, bishop of Lyons, 180–200 (*Adv. haer.* 1.6.3; 13.5.7), and finally in the Catholic Tertullian in his tract *De paenitentia*, from the first years after 200. Here one finds testimony to the church's practice of one-time repentance as a fixed institution. It is called a second *planca salutis*, which reestablishes the state of grace given in baptism. It is an opus with the power of satisfaction; for sinners must publicly humiliate themselves in sackcloth and ashes, with prayer, fasting, and tears, before the clerics, the martyrs, and the whole community, in order to present *satisfactio* to God and the church. This practice was confirmed in the third century by the Roman bishop Callistus († 222) and Cyprian, bishop of Carthage († 258), and not least by Cornelius, the episcopal opponent of Novatian in Rome (ca. 251).

The development of second repentance in the early Christian church can be represented schematically as follows:

Ruprecht, 1979) 320–33 (at 328– 29); Johannes Irmscher, "The Book of Elchasai," in *NTApoc*[1] 2.745–50; L. Cirillo, *Elchasai e gli Elchasaiti. Un contributo alla storia delle comunità giudeo-cristiane* (Cosenza, 1984); Gerard P. Luttikhuizen, *The Revelation of Elchasai* (Texte und Studien zum Antiken Judentum; Tübingen: Mohr [Siebeck], 1985) (and on this, see F. Stanley Jones's review, JAC 30 [1987] 200–209).

35 *Herm. Man.* 4.3.1–7; *Vis.* 2.2.5; *Sim.* 6.2; 9.18, and frequently; cf. Martin Dibelius, *Der Hirt des Hermas* (HNT Ergänzungsband 4; Tübingen: Mohr [Siebeck], 1923) 510–13.

36 Cf. 1 Tim 1:20; 5:19–20; Titus 3:10–11.

37 Cf., e.g., Ignatius *Phld.* 8.1: πᾶσιν οὖν μετανοοῦσιν ἀφίει ὁ κυρίος, ἐὰν μετανοήσωσιν εἰς ἑνότητα θεοῦ καὶ συνέδριον τοῦ ἐπισκόπου ("The Lord forgives all who repent—if, that is, their repentance brings them into God's unity and to the bishop's council"); *2 Clem.* 8.3: only death limits the possibility for confession of sins and repentance. *Herm. Vis.* 3.7.5–6: apostate Christians have the opportunity for repentance "after they have been tormented and fulfilled the days of their sins." That Hermas here allows for a "post-mortal opportunity for repentance" (so Klaus Wengst on *2 Clem.* 8.3: *Schriften des Urchristentums* [Munich: Kösel, 1984] 2.249 n. 62) is debatable (cf. Dibelius, *Hirt des Hermas*, 470–71).

Paul (charismatic law)
Matthew (fixed process in three stages)

		One-time, final offer of repentance	Rigorism
Right of repentance not viewed as problem	Pastorals/ 2 Thessalonians		Hebrews
	Apostolic Fathers (except *Hermas*)	Elchasai (ca. 110)	1 John
		Shepherd of Hermas (ca. 140)	Apocryphal Acts (*John, Thomas*)
	Dionysius of Corinth (ca. 170)		Nag Hammadi Texts *Gos. Thom./ Ap. John/Gos. Phil./Ap. Jas.*
Church penance	Irenaeus (180–200)		Early Montanism
	Catholic Tertullian (before 203)		Montanist Tertullian (after 203)
	Callistus († 222) Cyprian († 258) Cornelius (251)		Novatian (251)

Our text distinguishes itself from the other two central passages in 1 John that also speak thematically of the subject of ἁμαρτία (1:7—2:2 and 3:4–10) by its introduction of two classes of sins. In 1:8–10 the universality of ἁμαρτία and ἀδικία is confirmed by the universality of the Christ-event that frees us from sins. In that instance, the author is concerned with individual sins. On the one hand, the existence of offenses allows one to conclude to the offenders' not being in the truth (v. 8); on the other hand, existence in the truth also means being free from sin. This is not only true of the single action of baptism. The community in the course of its history, like the individual Christian, is placed under a demand not to sin. They must continually realize anew the "cleansing" from sin given them in the Christ-event.[38]

Whereas this section describes the fundamental link between Christ's atoning sacrifice and Christians' freedom from sin and emphasizes the ethical consequences of this situation, 3:4–10 also stands within a parenetic context. Here there is also reference to the Christ-event (v. 5: Jesus as the sinless one), but this time a dualistic contrast is derived from it: (1) Sinlessness is predicated of the one who abides in Christ (v. 6). This is escalated to a statement that one who is born of God cannot sin (v. 9: οὐ δύναται ἁμαρτάνειν); instead, the one born of God "does what is right" (v. 7). (2) Anyone who sins has not known Christ (v. 6). Such a person is "from the devil," and the devil is the one who "has been sinning from the beginning" (v. 8). Obviously, the author does not refer to any physically based distinction between sinners and righteous. Within the context of parenesis he wishes to emphasize that Christians must make a decision in favor of doing what is right, namely, loving the sisters and brothers (v. 10). The assertion of *non posse peccare*[39] is not a statement of an unchangeable situation but is connected with the condition of being born of God. Being born of God, in turn, is a historical possibility, namely, an eschatological reality actualized through faith. The section at 3:4–10 therefore offers a parenesis directed to fundamental principles, not an abstract reflection on the difference between the mode of existence of the children of God and the children of the devil (v. 10a).

The author thus does not minimize sin. It is as all-encompassing as ἀδικία, which is also equated with ἁμαρτία in 1:9.[40] In the passage now under discussion, however, he distinguishes two kinds of sins. Is this the expression of a different standpoint from what is found elsewhere in 1 John, and should one conclude from it that this section is secondary? In this line Rudolf Bultmann, on behalf of his theory that the concluding section should be attributed to the "ecclesiastical

38 1 John 2:1–2; cf. above, ad loc.

39 1 John 3:9; on this problem, see Augustine's conflict with Pelagius: the latter taught that, in principle, every human being is capable of living a sinless life, because if this were not so, freedom of the will and individual responsibility would not exist. Primarily in the interest of an ascetic and moral theory, he rejected the idea of an original sin and interpreted Adam's sin as merely a bad example. In response, Augustine interpreted sin as a wrong basic inclination of the entirety of human existence, from which not the free human will but only God's undeserved and irresistibly working grace can free us (Augustine, "On the Grace of Christ, and On Original Sin," 1.4, 5, in many editions, e.g., Marcus Dods, ed., *The Works of Aurelius Augustinus* [Edinburgh: Clark, 1895], vol. 12: *The Anti-Pelagian Works of St. Augustine*, vol. 2; or Philip Schaff, ed., *Nicene and Post-Nicene Fathers* [reprinted, Grand Rapids: Eerdmans, 1956] 5.213– 55).

40 Cf. 1:7. This also clarifies the concept of ἀνομία (3:4; otherwise not found in the Johannine writings): sin is an offense against what is commanded by God (the word νόμος does not appear in the Johannine Letters;

redaction," postulated an irreconcilable contradiction to 1:5–7 and 3:4–6. While those passages presume a dialectical interpretation of Christian existence, namely, that being a Christian is determined by the gift of forgiveness of sins, this dialectic is said to be abandoned in 5:16–17. The either-or between the gift of sinlessness on the one hand and the call to decision and admonition to do what is right on the other hand is completely destroyed by the distinction between pardonable and unpardonable sins.[41] One must ask, however, whether that kind of unrestricted dialectic can be posited as representing the author's conception, and whether it is not true instead that not only are 5:16–17 to be interpreted on the basis of 1:5–7 and 3:4–6, but that the two latter passages are to be read in light of 5:16–17. It is certainly true that the distinction of two classes of sins contradicts an unrestricted dialectic of Christian existence, and it appears that as a result the universality of the revelation of the *agapē* of God is narrowed. But the eschatological demand that is part and parcel of the mission of the Son of God would be impermissibly neutralized if it did not also leave room for the risk of an irreversible failure to meet the demand.[42] And the dialectic between sin and righteousness within which the Christian is placed would lose its proper force, would even be eliminated in principle, if it were not determined by the two fundamental elements: hope in an ultimate passage to an all-embracing life and the expectation of a judgment that effectively demonstrates that death is the payment for sin.[43] From the fact that the concept of "mortal sin" is not defined it is evident how little the conception of 1 John in this regard has been institutionalized, and how strongly it preserves the freedom of human decision founded on the Christ-event.[44] The line between pardonable and unpardonable sins cannot be drawn once and for all. This leaves room for the

---

in the Fourth Gospel its meaning is restricted to the "law of Moses": 1:17, 45; 7:19, and frequently). This definition in 3:4 can scarcely be directed against false teachers (cf. above on 3:4).

41 Bultmann, *Epistles*, 86–87.

42 This also happens, in the thinking of the fourth evangelist, with regard to the mission of the Son; John 7:12 is significant in this regard: the crowd's judgment on Jesus is divided; some say: "he is deceiving the crowd." Cf. also John 1:11 and the function of the διάβολος (6:70; 8:44; 13:2), the world's "hatred" (17:14–15), and the "son of destruction" ("the one destined to be lost") who appears "that the scripture might be fulfilled" (17:12).

43 Cf. Rom 6:23. Origen's idea of the ἀποκατάστασις πάντων ("restoration of all things") is not taught by the NT (the expression itself occurs only in Acts 3:21), for this concept would unjustly vitiate Christians' obligation to ethical behavior. Therefore Dodd's reflection (*Epistles*, 137; similarly Smalley, *1, 2, 3 John*, 298–99) that, in light of Mark 10:27, even in the case of mortal sin divine pardon cannot be excluded is beside the point, as far as the intention of this text is concerned.

44 Cf. also Bultmann, *Epistles*, 87–88; Balz, "Johannesbriefe," 202, Schnackenburg, *Epistles*, 251; Windisch and Preisker, *Die Katholischen Briefe*, 134; Nauck, *Tradition*, 144; Wengst, *Brief*, 219; Brown, *Epistles*, 615–17. S. M. Reynolds interprets differently: according to this author, the expression ἁμαρτία πρὸς θάνατον refers to physical death ("The Sin unto Death and Prayers for the Dead," *RefR* 20 [1973] 130–39). Scholer ("Sins Within and Sins Without: An Interpretation of 1 John 5:16–17," in Hawthorne, ed., *Current Issues in Biblical Interpretation*, 230–46) distinguishes "mortal sin," as the sin of unbelievers, from "sins that are not mortal," as those predicated of the community. This is not very useful, since the commandment itself, i.e., the prohibiting of prayers, indicates that this is a problem within the community itself. Bauernfeind ("Fürbitte," 43–54) is more correct in emphasizing that the prayer is to be understood pneumatologically, even though his thesis goes far beyond the text itself, to the point of positing that the author of 1 John thought that, even in the case of the worst sins, there was still hope that a Spirit-inspired prayer could be successful. Herkenrath ("Sünde zum Tode") sees a relationship between the two classes of sins and the community of life with God, Christ, and the sisters and brothers. He takes his stance on the basis of classical Catholic theology in asserting that, on the one hand, "in being born of God the Christian [has] the opportunity and the power to preserve him- or herself from sin" (127), and that, on the other hand, "the sin that is not mortal" could be a "'mortal sin' in the ecclesial-theological sense, destructive of the life of grace, but not at the same time proceeding to a complete destruction of life in communion with Christ" (137).

self-knowledge that is demanded of the community, which sees itself as a unified whole confronted by God's claim, and also for love's action on behalf of the sisters and brothers who are falling into error.[45]

■ **18** The introduction of each of the first three verses of this concluding part (vv. 18–21) with *οἴδαμεν* is an effective rhetorical device. The "knowledge" of the community, with which the author expresses his own solidarity (using the first person plural), so that he and they appear as a unified whole, presupposes the condition of salvation that has been attributed to the readers throughout this document and that has been accepted by the community as the gift of God (cf. 2:12–14; 5:11, and frequently elsewhere). This knowledge includes the conviction that the one born of God does not sin (5:1–2) and thus the indirectly expressed warning not to sin (cf. 2:1). These verses therefore follow seamlessly after the previous reflections on the problem of sin in the community. The necessary distinction between forgivable and unforgivable sins also acknowledges the fundamental assertion and warning that a Christian is set apart from sin, that is, that she or he cannot sin (3:9). That this "sinlessness" is not a matter of human worth but must ultimately be acknowledged as the gift of a gracious God is asserted by the following *ὁ γεννηθεὶς ἐκ τοῦ θεοῦ*, the exegetical meaning of which is not easily clarified.[46]

There are two possible interpretations: (1) The one "born of God" is the human being. The individual who is "born of God" (*ὁ γεννηθεὶς ἐκ τοῦ θεοῦ*) would then be identical with the one referred to in the previous clause as *ὁ γεγεννημένος ἐκ τοῦ θεοῦ*. But in that case one would expect *τηρεῖ ἑαυτόν*,[47] because a reference to Semitic forms is too hypothetical.[48] Moreover, if one adopts this interpretation the shift from perfect participle to aorist participle would be an inexplicable puzzle. (2) Thus a reference to Christ is more probable. In Johannine

---

45 Dodd correctly points out that a precise classification of mortal sins was reserved for the moral theology of the later church. Even though the opposing teaching combated by the author could fall under the classification of "mortal sin" because it included a denial of the Christ-confession and was traced to the antichrists (thus Dodd, *Epistles*, 136), it is no accident that this conclusion is not expressly drawn. One would be jumping to conclusions to think only of the false teachers in 1 John at this point. Instead, what is prohibited is prayer for any Christian who does not show him- or herself to be a member of the community, a "sister" or "brother." The OT and Jewish texts adduced to provide an explanation in terms of the history of religions (Lev 18:29; 19:8; 20:1–9; *Jub.* 21.22; 26.34; 33.13; cf. *Jub.* 33.18; *T. Iss.* 7.1: "deadly sin") can be applied only with reservations, since in them death is understood as a physical, not an eschatological consequence of sin, nor is the prayer of petition mentioned in those texts (cf. Smalley, *1, 2, 3 John*, 297–98).

46 The textual variants have relatively poor attestation (33: *ἐγεννήθη ὁ δὲ γεννηθεὶς ἐκ*; some minuscules, all the Old Latin manuscripts, and the Bohairic translation read: *ἡ γέννησις*) and can lay no claim to priority.

47 This is the reading of 𝔐, as well as ℵ A P Ψ and others; in spite of this considerable attestation, however, this reading must be seen as a secondary smoothing (with Nestle-Aland^{26}), especially since a predicate expansion (such as *ἁγνόν*) would have been expected (cf. also Schnackenburg, *Epistles*, 252–53).

48 This is said in response to Klaus Beyer, *Semitische Syntax im Neuen Testament* 1/1 (1962; 2d ed.; Göttingen: Vandenhoeck & Ruprecht, 1968) 216–27, according to whom this expression is a Semitism combined with a conditional participle (the reference to John 17:2, *πᾶν ὃ . . . αὐτῷ*, is inappropriate, since that text has neither a participle nor a shift from nominative to accusative; instead, the accusative object *ζωὴν αἰώνιον* is simply anticipated by *πᾶν ὅ*). If one presupposed a Semitic usage, one could join Albert Segond ("1re Epître," 350) in augmenting *τηρεῖ* with the nominative subject *θεός*: "The one who is born of God, (God) guards him or her and the Evil One does not touch him or her." Thus also Schnackenburg, *Epistles*, 253; Schunack, *Briefe*, 105. For the nominative aorist passive *ὁ γεννηθείς* in the rest of the NT, cf. only Heb 11:23; the genitive singular only at Matt 2:1; genitive plural in Rom 9:11. A christological interpretation is represented by, for example, Gustav Wohlenberg, "Glossen zum ersten Johannesbrief," *NKZ* 13 (1902) 240 (art. IV, on 5:18); Windisch, *Die Katholischen Briefe*, 135 (undecided); Preisker in Windisch and Preisker, *Die Katholischen Briefe*, 168; Nauck, *Tradition*, 139.

understanding he is not only the "Son of God" but also bears the title μονογενής (4:9; John 1:14, 18; 3:16, 18) and is also apostrophized in 1 John as ὁ Χριστὸς ἐκ τοῦ θεοῦ γεγέννηται (5:1). While Jesus is generally represented as the object of God's sending and of the faith of human beings, he can certainly be the subject as well (1 John 3:8; cf. 1:7), and the Fourth Gospel can describe the activity of Jesus Christ, the Revealer, with the verbs τηρεῖν and φυλάσσειν (17:12).

If Jesus Christ is ὁ γεννηθεὶς ἐκ τοῦ θεοῦ, and if he protects the people who are born of God, the complete thought would be: what is primary for those born of God is their relationship to God. They are "protected" from the evil one by Christ (v. 18). They are thereby separated from the world (v. 19) and have knowledge of the "true God" (v. 20). When Christians know that they are secure under the rule of Christ, they are withdrawn from the sphere of the devil's power. The "evil one" cannot touch them to stain them with sin.[49]

■ **19** It is on the basis of "being from God" that humans can be preserved from the power of the evil one, for such existence is at the same time a matter of being defined by the one who was born of God, that is, Christ. The second οἴδαμεν thus makes an interpretive connection with the first (v. 18). In v. 19 the dualistic contrast contained in the preceding verse is taken up and interpreted. The difference between God and the devil here corresponds to the alternative between God and the world. When believers are grounded in God[50] they are separated from the world, which "lies under the power of the evil one."[51] This separation is then recognized through faith, with a knowledge that can only be achieved in faith. It would be a mistake to attempt to read this statement as the expression of the arrogant self-confidence of an esoteric community, for Christ's saving work is not accomplished simply for the ἐκκλησία, but universally on behalf of the whole κόσμος (2:2; 4:14). There is an indirect expression here of the warning not to allow oneself to be overcome by the power of the world and the evil one (cf. 2:15).

■ **20** The third object of knowledge in faith (after vv. 18 and 19) is recognition of God. In accordance with the fundamental statement of Johannine theology, however, this cannot be had without an understanding of the Christ-kerygma. Therefore the author first looks back to the Son's having come[52] as gift.[53] This makes the christological statement in v. 18b concrete. While that passage spoke of Christ's protective function, here it is

49 Compare this with 1:7. Ὁ πονηρός is also in 2:13–14; 5:20; John 17:15; in addition, there is the expression ὁ διάβολος (1 John 3:8, 10; John 6:70; 8:44; 13:2); by contrast, the Semitic σατανᾶς is not found in the Johannine corpus. Ἅπτεσθαι ("touch," "hold on to") is also in John 20:17, with reference to bodily touch; it does not occur elsewhere in our literature. On this subject, cf. *1 Clem.* 56.8 (Job 5:19): οὐ μὴ ἅψηταί σου κακόν ("no harm shall touch you").

50 For the parallel between ἐκ θεοῦ εἶναι and εἶναι ἐν τῷ θεῷ, cf. below at v. 20.

51 Thus also BAGD 427, with an alternative translation "be dependent on someone" (with reference to Sophocles *Oedipus Rex* 247–48; Polybius 6.15.6); less likely is the translation "the whole world lies in malice," that is, it is thoroughly evil; this would be founded on κεῖσθαι ἐν = "be in a certain condition" (2 Macc 3:11; 4:31, 34; 3 Macc 5:26); but in that case the article τῷ would be superfluous.

52 Ἥκει refers to Jesus' earthly existence; the verb is also used in this sense—corresponding to the "biographical" outline of the Fourth Gospel—in John 2:4; 4:47; 8:42; in the rest of the NT it refers especially to future (apocalyptic) events (Matt 8:11 par.; Luke 19:43; Rev 3:9; 15:4, and frequently), particularly the parousia of Christ (Matt 24:50 par.; 2 Pet 3:10; Rev 2:25; 3:3), and also in quotations (Rom 11:26; Heb 10:7, 37). The christological and kerygmatic aspect was expanded by Latin scribes: "et carnem induit nostri causa et passus est et resurrexit a mortuis adsumpsit nos" (t vg^{mss} etc.). According to Adolf von Harnack, this formula goes back to Greek antignostic creedal traditions from the third or second century ("Zur Textkritik," 570–71; Brown, *Epistles*, 623).

53 While the present ἥκει expresses "the situation arising from the action" (Kühner-Gerth, *Grammatik*, 1.136), namely, the appearance of Jesus, the perfect δέδωκεν describes the duration of what has been accomplished (as a combination of present and aorist; BDF § 340) and refers (like the aorist of the variant reading ἔδωκεν) to the present situation of the community; it is now defined by the gift of insight.

clear that such protection consists in his bestowing the insight or "understanding" that comes from faith.[54] This insight leads to knowledge and is therefore directed to "the one who is true."

Even though Codex A and other manuscripts signal, by the addition of *θεόν*, that in the opinion of later copyists ἀληθινόν is intended to refer to God, the absolute adjectival noun must be recognized as the original reading. Since this usage is unique in the Johannine literature, the question whether the author intends to designate God or Jesus Christ as "the one who is true" is initially to be regarded as open. The Johannine corpus knows God as the representative and giver of truth (John 17:17), just as untruth belongs to the sphere of the evil one, the realm of God's enemies (John 8:44; cf. 1 John 1:8; 2:4). Thus the adjective ἀληθινός in the Fourth Gospel (John 7:28; 17:3), as elsewhere in the NT and its environment (1 Thess 1:9; *1 Clem.* 43.6) can refer to God. There is a more distant background for this usage in the OT, according to which God is regarded as faithful and true (Exod 34:6; cf. 2 Chr 15:3; Ps 86:15). In addition, especially in the Jewish Hellenistic context, God is accorded the title "real," "genuine," as opposed to the false divinities of the gentile world.[55] It is true that the OT parallels are not the genetic point of origin for Johannine usage.[56] Greek religion also used ἀληθινός as a divine predicate (e.g., Athenaeus *Deipnosophistae* 6.62.28, together with μόνος θεός). However, the history of such attribution does not suggest that in this passage it is exclusively God who is called "the one who is true,"

54 A distinction must be drawn between the gift of διάνοια and its goal and point of completion, which is γινώσκειν: διάνοια is not to be identified with γνῶσις and should therefore not be translated "knowledge." It means something like "power of thought" or "thinking consciousness" (cf. Johannes Behm, "διάνοια," *TDNT* 4 [1967] 963; BAGD 187). This is confirmed by its negative use in the deutero-Pauline letters (Col 1:21; Eph 4:18: the pre-Christian, pagan way of thinking is equated with a perverted διάνοια). This concept appears only here in the Johannine writings; for an understanding of its use in 1 John a look at the long Greek and Hellenistic history of the word is not without importance. Adolf Schlatter ("Herz und Gehirn in 1 Joh," in *Studien zur Systematischen Theologie: Festschrift für Theodor von Haering zum siebzigsten Geburtstag*, ed. Friedrich Traub [Tübingen: Mohr (Siebeck), 1918]) described the expression in this passage "as a somewhat hellenized formula" in comparison with the Semitic thinking of "ἔδωκεν εἰς τὰς καρδίας with the infinitive" (Rev 17:17). From this point of view it is impossible that in the present text the διάνοια clause forms a pleonastic unity with the following ἵνα clause. There is also no material identity with the statement that the χρῖσμα has been given to believers and with it knowledge (2:20–21, 27), since that has to do with the sacrament of Baptism, which occurs at the beginning of the Christian life and mediates the possession of the truth and complete knowledge (in response to Bultmann, *Epistles*, 89); the gift of διάνοια is not necessarily connected with the sacrament. One may identify it temporally with the beginning of Christian life of the readers of 1 John (Brown, *Epistles*, 639, with reference to 1 Pet 1:13; 2 Pet 3:1). The interpretation of its content is found in the subsequent ἵνα clause: the object of a Christian consciousness is knowledge of "the truth."

For an understanding of this verse, cf. also the well-attested textual variant that reads the indicative present γινώσκομεν in place of the subjunctive γινώσκωμεν. It is true that the construction with ἵνα and the indicative present is unique in the Johannine corpus. It appears in the NT only in passages where the subjunctive is also attested. However, not a few examples show that such a construction is possible within the field of NT and contemporary Greek (cf. BAGD 377). The statement that this always represents a "corruption of the text" (ibid., cf. also BDF § 369 [6]) is not very persuasive. One would be more inclined to join Brooke (*Epistles*, 151) in thinking that it reflects the impact of popular usage. However, this textual variant is not primary, even if it entered the text at an early stage; although well attested and favored by the argument of the *lectio difficilior*, that it is unique in the usage of 1 John means that it cannot be acknowledged as original. Consequently, καὶ ἐσμέν cannot be understood as a continuation of the ἵνα clause; instead, it introduces a new, independent statement.

55 3 Macc 6:18; Philo *Spec. leg.* 1.332; cf. earlier Isa 65:16; further examples may be found in Rudolf Bultmann, "ἀληθινός," *TDNT* 1 (1964) 250.

56 This is said against Brown, *Epistles*, 639–40, who suggests that the OT and Jewish covenant tradition may be the background.

because in the Revelation of John the adjective is applied not only to God (Rev 6:10) but also to Christ (3:7, 14; 19:11). Since the author's use of language is flexible in applying personal pronouns either to God or to Christ, one should not think of the absolute τὸν ἀληθινόν as presenting an either/or: "God" or "Christ." Even though αὐτοῦ (with reference to ἐν τῷ υἱῷ) suggests that θεῷ should be added to the preceding ἐν τῷ ἀληθινῷ, the subsequent ὁ ἀληθινὸς θεός, predicated of Christ, shows that the adjective ἀληθινός can be attributed not only to the Father but also to the Son. Existence in the true God is existence in the Son of God, and in turn the existence of the true God can be known only through the Son. Just as elsewhere the object of Christian knowledge can shift from God (2:3–5) to Christ (2:6, 13–14), so also here the attention of Christians is directed to knowledge of God *and* Christ. As the Father revealed himself in the Son (4:9), knowledge of the Father is also possible only through the Son (cf. 4:16; John 10:38; 14:7; 17:7, 25). Truth, which is unconcealed, genuine, real existence, belongs to the Father and the Son.[57] The community shares in it through the Spirit; its existence in the truth is a pneumatic state of being (5:6; cf. 4:6; John 14:17; 15:26; 16:13). In the Spirit, it is separated from the realm of lies and of the devil.[58]

If the community's life is shaped by eschatological truth, its existence in "the one who is true" is an existence within the realm of God's power "through his Son Jesus Christ." But if believers cannot encounter the divine reality in any other way than through Christ, the equation of Jesus Christ with "true God and eternal life" is correct. As the Son of God is identified with eternal life in the Fourth Gospel (John 11:25; 14:6; cf. 1 John 1:2; 5:11–12) and can even be called "God" (John 1:18; 20:28), the same is true in 1 John. Here one finds an expression of the Johannine idea of the unity of Son and Father (John 10:30; 17:11, 21–23; cf. 1 John 1:3; 4:15, and frequently) that is unmistakable in its language and unsurpassable in its significance.

In the conclusion of his writing, the author turns again to the central focus of faith. It is no accident that there is a parallel here to John 20:28. As the fourth evangelist sees the culminating point of the Gospel in the disciple Thomas's confession of the true godhead and lordship of Jesus Christ, so the author of 1 John makes clear that it is his real intention to demonstrate the reality of God's revelation in Jesus Christ and its meaning for the Christian community. This means not only—as must certainly be acknowledged here as well, keeping in mind the conflict with the opponents—that the divine revelation is bound up with the earthly reality of Jesus Christ, the Son of God (2:22; 4:2: ἐν σαρκί), but also that faith in the incarnate Son of God, sent by the Father (3:8; 4:9; 5:9–10), includes the confession of the earthly and heavenly existence of the Christ and the acknowl-

57 Cf. John 17:17; for the Son: 14:6; 18:37. Even in Hellenistic Judaism τὸ ἀληθινόν was used in a philosophical and religious sense for the Eternal as the only one who genuinely exists. Cf. Philo *Leg. all.* 1.32. "But this earthlike mind [νοῦς: the human spirit] is in reality also corruptible, were not God to breathe into it a power of real life (δύναμιν ἀληθινῆς ζωῆς); when he does so, it . . . becomes a soul . . . one endowed with mind and actually alive (εἰς νοερὰν καὶ ζῶσαν ὄντως [ψυχήν])"—true life is, in Philo's understanding of it, a life in the proper state of knowledge; see the further examples in Bultmann's article, "ἀληθινός," *TDNT* 1 (1964) 250; cf. also Heb 8:2 (σκηνὴ ἀληθινή, the "true tabernacle"); correspondingly, φῶς ἀληθινόν: 1 John 2:8; John 1:9. This meaning also finds an echo in the present passage, since ἐσμέν expresses the relationship to its grounding in divine existence, which is made possible by the right kind of knowledge (so also Schnackenburg, *Epistles*, 262). If "being in the truth" (v. 20) is the same thing as "being born of God" (v. 19; on this, see Bultmann, *Epistles*, 89–90), this is also true of the relationship of believers to Christ as the Son of God. On the question whether in the Fourth Gospel truth is identified with God, or only with Christ and the Spirit (thus de la Potterie, *La vérité*, 2.1009), cf. Hans Hübner, "ἀλήθεια," *EDNT* 1 (1990) 60.

58 1 John 2:22; cf. 3:5, 8; John 8:44; the present passage can scarcely be set apart from these others in its content, so that nothing would be present here but an "apparently resigned . . . and inward-looking . . . acknowledgment of the existence of this sphere of power (that of the evil one)" (in response to Wengst, *Brief*, 223).

edgment of Jesus Christ as preexistent (cf. 1:2–3) and as the mediator of divine life (5:11–12). Therefore in conclusion, and going beyond all the other christological statements in his writing, the author can triumphantly say: *οὗτός ἐστιν ὁ ἀληθινὸς θεὸς καὶ ζωὴ αἰώνιος*.[59]

This confession does not anticipate the rational conceptuality of the later confessional formula, such as is expressed in the Athanasian Creed ("perfectus deus, perfectus homo"),[60] even though the seeds of such a development seem to exist here. Our text does not envision a christological speculation about the relationship between the divine and human person or nature, nor is the Son identical with the Father.[61] Instead, what is crucial is that Jesus Christ, as the true God, is eternal life.[62] He does not "preserve" life as if it were a possession;[63] rather, in the encounter with him in faith, life is revealed in its unrestricted fullness and elusiveness.[64]

■ **21** From this point of view it is probable that the concluding verse as well is not to be applied solely to the "false teaching" presupposed by this writing, but that—corresponding to the style of the final section—it expresses an intention to present an admonition to all readers of the document. This is evident from the address, *τεκνία*, directed to the whole audience of the writing, that is, having a general ecclesial scope.[65] The sentence *φυλάξατε ἑαυτὰ ἀπὸ τῶν εἰδώλων* ("to keep yourselves from idols") employs a traditional form of expression and is ultimately traceable to a Jewish Hellenistic basis.[66] However, the author would have found this meaning of *εἴδωλον* handed on in

59 One cannot object against the application of *οὗτος* to the immediately preceding *Ἰησοῦ Χριστῷ* that on the basis of 2:22 and 2 John 7 the referent could also be found earlier in the text, because there the construction as a whole is unblemished; the positing of a "clumsy marginal note" describes the problem, but is not very persuasive (in response to Segond, "1re Epître," 351; cf. n. 64 below).

60 Cf. *Bekenntnisschriften der evangelisch-lutherischen Kirche* (Göttingen: Vandenhoeck & Ruprecht, 1930) 29; different is the so-called Nicene-Constantinopolitan Creed, which is closer to our text because the Son of God is called "deus verus de deo vero," but which lacks an exact parallel statement about his humanity, even though it is clearly enunciated: "et incarnatus est de spiritu sancto ex Maria virgine et homo factus est" (ibid., 26).

61 Brown (*Epistles*, 640) sees this correctly.

62 On the relationship of Father and Son see also John Calvin, *In Ioannis epistolam primam*, 376: "Vitae quidem origo est Pater: sed fons ex quo haurire licet, Christus est" ("The Father is the origin of life, but the fountain from which we must draw it is Christ").

63 Thus the textual variant in Codex Ψ (*παρέχων*).

64 According to von Harnack's conjecture, *ὄντες* should be inserted after *Χριστῷ*, having been accidentally omitted because of the following *ὄντος* ("Zur Textkritik," 538–39 n. 1). This would corroborate the interpretation, advocated by others as well, according to which *ἐν τῷ υἱῷ αὐτοῦ Ἰησοῦ Χριστῷ* (v. 20b) should be attached to *ἐσμέν* as a prepositional specification, so that one could translate: "We are in the one who is true, in that [= to the extent that] we are in his son, Jesus Christ." This would undoubtedly be in line with the author's conception. However, probably v. 20bβ was deliberately placed after v. 20ba without a distinct connection in order to emphasize the unity between the "one who is true" and the Son of God, Jesus Christ, so that it is more proper to translate: "We are in the one who is true, namely, his son, Jesus Christ." Bousset considers the expression *ἐν τῷ υἱῷ αὐτοῦ Ἰησοῦ Χριστῷ* a gloss, so that the assertion of Jesus' divinity as expressed in v. 20c would be a secondary result of the insertion; according to this, the original text would have spoken solely of the true God who is identified with life (*Kyrios Christos*, 238–39). This hypothesis destroys the tension-filled combination of concurrence and difference between the true God and Jesus Christ that is the outstanding structural feature of this text; given its position, *οὗτος* can relate only to the preceding *Ἰησοῦ Χριστῷ*.

65 The address *τεκνία* is a diminutive of *τέκνα* (1 John 3:1–2, 10; 5:2; 2 John 1, 4, 13; 3 John 4) and is often translated "little children" or "little ones." The word is part of the vocabulary of 1 John (cf. 2:1, 12, 28; 3:7, 18; 4:4; also John 13:33) and shows that the author of 1 John deliberately placed v. 21 at the end of his work (cf. also above, at 2:12–13).

66 The construction *φυλάσσειν τινὰ ἀπό τινος* ("to guard someone from something") is occasionally traced to the influence of Semitic usage (cf. Moulton, *Grammar*, 2.460). But the use of the middle voice is found as early as the LXX (Deut 23:10; also *T. Sim.* 4.5; 5.3; P. Lond. 1349, 35; Luke 12:15), and the active *φυλάσσειν τινὰ ἀπό τινος* is attested in Xenophon and Menander (cf. also 2 Thess 3:3; Sir 22:26; *PGM* 4.2699); the construction *φυλάσσειν ἑαυτὸν ἀπό τινος* is also in Horapollo 2.94; *Corp. Herm.* excerpt from Stobaeus *Ecl.* 13 (in Walter Scott, ed. and trans., *Hermetica* [4 vols.; Oxford: Clarendon, 1924–36] 1.434, 13); *T. Reub.* 4.8 (cf. BAGD 868).

Christian tradition.[67]

There have been a great number of suggested interpretations (Brown, *Epistles,* 627–28, counts ten, all different). The expression is frequently applied to images of gods in pagan cults.[68] In a more specialized sense, some think of apostasy in situations of persecution, accomplished by sacrificing to idols as prescribed by law.[69] Here Wengst and Schunack presuppose the situation of a *status confessionis* before Roman officials and see this as an argument in support of the thesis that the conclusion of the letter is to be attributed to a later redactor. Stegemann questions the antiheretical interpretation of 1 John. Since 1 John is not shaped by a conflict with false teachings within the church, the document as a whole must be understood as a reaction to a crisis originating with a persecution of Christians by the Roman authorities. In support of this position he cites the (supposedly) forensic terms in 1 John (ὁμολογεῖν, ἀρνεῖσθαι), the statements about atonement, the terminology of martyrdom, as well as "mortal sin," love for the sisters and brothers, and "abiding" (2:18–29; 5:15–17), and the comparison with Josephus *Bell.* 7.46–53; Pliny *Ep.* 10.96. Finally, the contrast between εἴδωλα (v. 21) and "true God and eternal life" (v. 20) appears to reflect the antithesis between the gods of the Gentiles and the true God of Israel. However, this must not compel the conclusion that this passage refers to official persecution. Moreover, the Johannine concept of truth certainly has a general ecclesiological meaning applicable beyond any particular, concrete situation. The application to false teachers is also quite common.[70] In support of this it is asserted that the aorist imperative φυλάξατε introduces a new situation, namely, one of polemicizing against false teachers. J. N. Suggit thinks that the translation "phantom, spirit, unreal thing" for εἴδωλον would fit well in the context of opposition to a docetic false teaching.[71] By contrast, Nauck (*Tradition,* 137) and Schnackenburg (*Epistles,* 264) read this passage as a metaphor for "sin" in a comprehensive sense.[72]

There is no genuine parallel in the passage sometimes cited in this connection from *T. Reub.* 4.5–6, since there φυλάξατε πάντα must be translated "observe all" (not: "keep yourselves from all"); on this, see also Schnackenburg, *Epistles,* 264 n. 201.

67 Εἴδωλον occurs only here in the Johannine writings; the word was freely used in Greek for the "image of a god," which of course was not thought of even by gentile authors as something living, although it was often the object of cultic veneration (Artemidorus *Oneirocritica* 4.36; cf. Acts 7:41; Rev 9:20). In the OT and in Hellenistic Judaism it was regarded as a characteristic of paganism and equated with "idols" (cf. Isa 30:22; 2 Chr 23:17; 1 Macc 1:43; 3 Macc 4:16). It was then adopted by the NT authors (Acts 15:20; Rom 2:22; 1 Cor 8:4, 7; 10:19; 12:2; 1 Thess 1:9); in line with this, a clear choice between God and idols is demanded (2 Cor 6:16). For the Hellenistic Jewish background, see also Traugott Holtz, who, however, reaches the following conclusion in his analysis of 1 Thess 1:9b–10: "The individual formulations in this sentence, in spite of their clearly traditional character, do not justify us in assigning them to a tradition that reached Paul in an already fixed form" (*Der erste Brief an die Thessalonicher* [EKK 13; Zurich: Benzinger; Neukirchen-Vluyn: Neukirchener Verlag, 1986] 60).

68 See Windisch, *Die Katholischen Briefe,* 136; Dodd, *Epistles,* 141; Herkenrath, "Sünde zum Tode," 136.

69 See Wengst, *Briefe,* 225–26; Schunack, *Briefe,* 106; Stegemann, *TZ* 41 (1985) 284–94.

70 See Bultmann, *Epistles,* 90–91; Balz, "Johannesbriefe," 204; Brown, *Epistles,* 629; Ska, *NRTh* 101 (1979) 860–74.

71 Suggit, *JTS* 36 (1985) 386–90.

72 Reference is made to texts from Qumran in which the word גלולים appears for "false gods": 1QS ii.11, 17; iv.5; 1QH iv.15, 18–19; CD xx.9–10; this expression is said to be used in a metaphorical sense, as shown by the parallel with "sin" (cf. esp. 1QH iv.15 with 18–19). From this, one could translate the final verse, "Children, keep yourselves from sin" (thus Nauck, *Tradition,* 137). The preceding context also, "being in the one who is true" (v. 20) and the separation from the world, as the realm of the evil one, that is presumed for "those who are born of God" (v. 19), is said to suggest a fundamental and generalized interpretation of εἴδωλα. It cannot be persuasively inferred from our text, either directly or indirectly, that there is special reference to the sin of apostasy (Brown, *Epistles,* 628–29).

If one chooses the translation "false god,"[73] the contrast with the truth and genuineness of Christian faith (v. 20) is obvious, although no antiheretical point can be deduced from it. The warning here should more probably be related to the earlier admonition about "mortal sin," with apostasy to false gods now given as a specific example. But since the distinction between different classes of sins that was connected with the earlier warning is not suggested here, it is more proper to consider this as a matter of general encouragement to keep oneself at a distance from everything that could take the place of God, not least from all that poses an obstacle to the exercise of *agapē* toward God and the sisters and brothers (2:7–11; 3:17), and to be in communion with the Father and the Son, Jesus Christ, in the unity of brotherly and sisterly love.[74]

73 This is the interpretation of εἴδωλον in Josephus *Ant.* 9.273; 10.50; *T. Reub.* 4.6; cf. BAGD 221.

74 Cf. 1:3. While the concluding ἀμήν is attested by 𝔐 and a few other manuscript witnesses, it is a secondary addition; it is intended to set a clear mark at the conclusion of the letter (cf. Gal 6:18; 2 Pet 3:18 *v.l.*).

2 John

The document called 2 John gives the impression of being a genuine letter and probably was one, for it has the usual letter form. The prescript (vv. 1–3) is followed by the body of the letter expressing the writer's particular interest. The two major thematic clusters are (1) vv. 4–6: an admonition to mutual love, and (2) vv. 7–11: a warning against deceivers. The document ends with an epistolary conclusion (vv. 12–13) promising the writer's coming and sending greetings.

The idea that 2 John is a fictive letter was suggested by Martin Dibelius[1] and Hirsch.[2] Since Bultmann[3] it has been upheld with particular energy by Heise.[4] According to Heise the unspecific address κυρίᾳ (2 John 1), the greeting from the τέκνα τῆς ἀδελφῆς σου ("children of your sister," 2 John 13), and the vague designation ἐκ τῶν τέκνων σου ("from your children," 2 John 4) are indications that "the author wished to write in such a way that his letter could be read at any time in any community." However, such generalized indications are more probably a sign of the uncertain relationship between the presbyter and the community to which he writes (presumably that of Diotrephes). The other arguments adduced in this context scarcely demonstrate "that the second letter was written by someone who attempted, in the name of the presbyter, to correct the third letter, and Johannine theology as a whole, in the direction of the thinking of the official church."[5] On the contrary, this argumentation partly presumes the expected result as already given, for example, the assertion that the prescript of 2 John is dependent on that of 3 John.[6] The case is similar with the epistolary conclusion[7] and with the supposed dependence of 2 John on 1 John.[8] But this line of argument can be used to underscore the independence of 2 and 3 John from the Fourth Gospel. Thus Heise has correctly emphasized the special character of 2 John 7 (ἐρχόμενον) in contrast to 1 John 4:2, or that of 2 John 8 (μισθόν) in contrast to John 4:35–36; 5:17; 6:28–29.[9]

1 Dibelius, *RGG*² 3.348.
2 Hirsch, *Studien*, 177.
3 Bultmann, *Epistles*, 107; also Vielhauer, *Geschichte*, 481.
4 Heise, *Bleiben*, 165; cf. also Windisch and Preisker, *Die Katholischen Briefe*, 137.
5 Heise, *Bleiben*, 170.
6 Ibid., 166: "expansion of 3 John 1."
7 Ibid., 167: literal agreement with 3 John, together with expansion.
8 Ibid., 168: 2 John 5 is said to be a "shortened summary of 1 John 2:17 and 3:11"; 2 John 6 rests on 1 John 5:3.
9 Ibid., 168.

Beginning of the Letter

1 **The elder to the elect lady and her children, whom I love in (the) truth, and not only I but also all who know the truth, 2/ because of the truth that abides in us and will be with us forever: 3/ Grace, mercy, and peace will be with us from God the Father and from Jesus Christ, the Father's Son, in truth and love.**

■ **1-2** The prescript follows the form found at the beginning of a genuine letter. Verse 1 indicates the sender (the presbyter, or elder), the receiver (with two datives, "to the elect lady and her children"), and is expanded through two relative clauses in vv. 1b–2; v. 3, then, is a *salutatio* or greeting, in which the writer of the letter blesses the receivers.

The three-part structure of the prescript has parallels in other NT letters. One may distinguish the so-called Greek form combining the three basic elements of the prescript in a single sentence (sender, addressee, blessing; cf. Acts 15:23; 23:26; Jas 1:1; 3 John; 1 John), and the so-called oriental form with two sentences (sender, receiver/blessing, as found in the Letters of Paul, 1 and 2 Peter, and the letter of Jude). This oriental style of beginning is also found in 2 John. While it thus agrees with the majority of NT letters, on the whole it is like 3 John in possessing the form and structure of an ordinary Hellenistic and Roman letter.[1] Much as the codices from Nag Hammadi interpret Synoptic texts in a "gnosticizing" manner, so here the tradition has been supplied with specifically Johannine meaning. Particular concepts and expressions (e.g., "know the truth," "abide in the truth," the word *agapē*) constitute the "Johannine character" of the prescript and at the same time represent key theological terms that can offer a clue to the whole basic Johannine theological structure.

The sender of this letter is described in 2 John 1 (and 3 John 1) as ὁ πρεσβύτερος. The word can mean two things: (1) an older person, who has a special position of authority based on his long experience; (2) a (community) elder, a presbyter. Such an elder would be a community functionary who—as long as the monarchical episcopate has not yet been established—is acknowledged as having an important share of authority in the community based on an official position, an authority that is, however, not limited to the "office" as such.[2] This analysis does not necessarily mean that the "presbyter" has come into conflict with his "bishop," Diotrephes, and been excommunicated as a result;[3] for nothing is said in 3 John of a "bishop" Diotrephes. It is scarcely likely that the designation "presbyter" refers to a local community official who is set over against a fixed hierarchy of offices.

We do not know whether it was office or age that brought the "presbyter" his special title. But we can probably conclude from the fact of the title itself, which

1 Cf. Robert W. Funk, "Form and Structure," *JBL* 86 (1967) 424–30; according to Funk, ἐχάρην λίαν (2 John 4; 3 John 3) and ἐρωτῶ σε (2 John 5), etc., are specifically Hellenistic conceptual terms.

2 Thus Haenchen ("Neuere Literatur," 308–11) attempts to establish a connection with the *praeses presbyterii,* the presider in a college of presbyters; this person is said to have been on a level corresponding to the episcopal station of Diotrephes. However, the reference to the prescript of Polycarp's letter is not persuasive, since Polycarp places himself—apparently as bishop—alongside the other presbyters without claiming the title of presbyter for himself. See, correctly, Vielhauer, *Geschichte,* 481 n. 9.

3 Käsemann ("Ketzer und Zeuge," 168–87) constructs here a classical case of conflict between orthodoxy and heresy: the orthodox bishop Diotrephes has turned the heretical presbyter out of the church. This reverses the thesis of Walter Bauer, according to whom the presbyter, as representative of the orthodox church, has collided with the heretical chief Diotrephes, the representative of a majority of Christians. Cf. Walter Bauer, *Orthodoxy and Heresy in Earliest Christianity* (trans. by a team from the Philadelphia Seminar on Christian Origins; ed. Robert A. Kraft and Gerhard Krodel; Philadelphia: Fortress, 1971) 93. On this, see below.

is presumed to be known and acknowledged without further explanation, that its meaning was not exhausted either by its community function or by its description of the bearers' age. It seems, instead, to have represented a fixed title of honor, so that the presbyter must have been a high-ranking authority. This is evident from the letters,[4] where the claims of the writer (not, of course, unchallenged) are acknowledged beyond the boundaries of the presbyter's own community. Even if the assertion that the presbyter "with his wishes and works is outside any ecclesiastical constitution"[5] need not be chronologically accurate, his claims and importance in the communities he addresses were not limited by any constitutional order. Had his authority not been so dominant one could scarcely explain the fact that these two letters, which are the shortest in the NT, and which in their subject matter are scarcely to be placed alongside the other NT letters, found entry into the canon. All the evidence indicates that the presbyter was the principal authority in the Johannine circle, and that the preservation of 2 and 3 John is due to that fact. These are original documents handed down from the founder of the Johannine school. But in that case, 2 and 3 John are of fundamental significance for understanding the beginnings of Johannine theology.[6]

The historical background of the figure of the presbyter is clarified by the testimony of Papias. In his work "The Sayings of the Lord Explained," he attests that there were different meanings for the concept of "presbyter."[7] According to him, the "presbyters" (= the elders) were those entrusted with the oral tradition, that is, that which was superior to the written tradition because temporally prior to it. Papias thus testifies to a series of stages in the history of the tradition: (1) The first Christian generation includes the apostles, that is, the eyewitnesses; they are the "disciples of the Lord." (2) From them, other πρεσβύτεροι received the corpus of tradition. They are also called "disciples of the Lord," but are members of the second generation, not the first generation of eyewitnesses. (3) What Papias writes in "The Sayings of the Lord Explained" refers to what has gone before. He does not count himself among the presbyters, but is one of their pupils and is making an effort to hand on their tradition, and thus the apostolic tradition preserved by them, as exactly as possible.

Names are given to two of the second generation of presbyters, Aristion (one of Papias's sources, otherwise unknown) and John, who is expressly described as ὁ πρεσβύτερος. Eusebius, using what is probably a later inference by the church, identifies the latter with John, the author of the book of Revelation.[8] Is it accidental that Papias only gives the name of one person from the generation of presbyters, this John, and that the title "presbyter" appears in 2 and 3 John? Both letters were called "Johannine" in the patristic tradition.[9] Hence it is certainly possible that the presbyter John whom Papias mentions is identical with the "presbyter" of 2 and 3 John. It is true that the few fragments of Papias's work permit no certain conclusions, but it is striking that Papias is also interested in ἀλήθεια,[10] and Papias's chiliasm very probably—as will appear—could have been nurtured in the soil of early Johannine theology.

4 Cf. the promise that he will come: 2 John 12; 3 John 13–14, and the presbyter's initiative on behalf of the emissaries of the church: 3 John 7–12, etc.

5 Günther Bornkamm, "πρέσβυς, κτλ.," *TDNT* 6 (1968) 671; on the contrary, one must maintain that the constitutional structure of the Christian church could still be different in the various church provinces around the year 100; on this, see Leonard Goppelt, *Christentum und Judentum im ersten und zweiten Jahrhundert* (Gütersloh: Bertelsmann, 1954) 164ff.

6 See Strecker, "Anfänge," 34.

7 The text of Papias (Eusebius *Hist. eccl.* 3.39.3–4) was quoted above (Introduction, part 4). The dating is disputed. Generally, Papias's work is placed around 130 CE; so, for example, by Berthold Altaner and Alfred Stuiber, *Patrologie* (Freiburg/Basel/Vienna: Herder, 1980) 90; Wikenhauser and Schmid, *Einleitung*, 30, 307; Ulrich Körtner, *Papias von Hierapolis: Ein Beitrag zur Geschichte des frühen Christentums* (FRLANT 133; Göttingen: Vandenhoeck & Ruprecht, 1983) 225–26. According to Adolf von Harnack (*Die Chronologie der altchristlichen Literatur bis Eusebius* [2 vols.; Leipzig: Hinrichs, 1897] 1.721), Papias wrote ca. 145–160 CE.

8 Eusebius *Hist. eccl.* 3.39.6.

9 As early as Origen (in Eusebius *Hist. eccl.* 6.25.10); Muratorian Canon, lines 68–69 (see Introduction, part 1, above).

10 Cf. above, Introduction, part 1, n. 8.

One can, then, consider the possibility that the presbyter of the Johannine Letters is the same witness with whom Papias came in contact and who became his teacher.[11]

The presbyter's two letters are no abstract deliberations; they take a stand on concrete situations. In this, 2 John strikes a more basic note than 3 John. If 2 John may have been given to the presbyter's emissaries as a letter of introduction, and therefore is more general in character, 3 John, in contrast, intervenes in a particular conflict, namely, between Diotrephes and the presbyter. There are no elements of the circular letter in 2 John.[12] It is a true community letter, as is clear from the address, *ἐκλεκτῇ κυρίᾳ*, which designates the community to whom the letter is written as the "elect lady." In the NT, believers are often regarded as the community of "the elect" (cf. 1 Pet 1:1; Rev 17:14). Thus an individual congregation can also be thought of as "elect" (also in 1 Pet 5:13). The Christian community has been chosen by God's intervention in the world, by the Christ-event in which God's mercy is revealed.[13]

It is not very likely that the expression *ἐκλεκτῇ κυρίᾳ* represents the name of a female person, so that the letter would either have been addressed to the "Lady Electa" (so Clement of Alexandria *Hyp.*, GCS 17.215) or to "the elect Kyria."[14] It is also improbable that the letter is to a nameless woman called "honored lady," since the address to the *κυρία* corresponds to that to the *τέκνα τῆς ἀδελφῆς σου τῆς ἐκλεκτῆς* ("children of your elect sister," v. 13) and therefore suggests a metaphorical sense. Again, because of the positioning of those greeted, over against the *ἀδελφή* who greet them, this cannot be an address to "the whole church." Rather, one should think of a particular Christian community. Even if it is not possible to establish with certainty that the author has a "house-church" in mind (so Brown, *Epistles*, 654), the community addressed is, in any case, within the circle of influence of the presbyter and his school.

11 It is widely acknowledged that the presbyter was an outstanding personality of great importance for the Johannine tradition. Brown, who does not wish to exclude the possibility of identifying the author with John the presbyter in Papias's testimony, thinks that he may have been a pupil of the eyewitnesses, more precisely "a disciple of the Beloved Disciple" (*Epistles*, 679); Schnackenburg considers him "the bearer of apostolic tradition, in which capacity . . . all knew him. . . . who represents the Johannine tradition and upholds it" (*Epistles*, 272–73). Bultmann is also of the opinion that "[*ὁ πρεσβύτερος*] designates the author as one of the *πρεσβύτεροι* . . . whom Papias (in Eusebius, *Hist. eccl.* 3.39.3f) calls the bearers and transmitters of the apostolic tradition" (*Epistles*, 95). Cf. also Vielhauer, *Geschichte*, 481 ("leader for many years of the Johannine circle"). Bousset wished to identify Papias's presbyter John with the author of Revelation and the presbyter of the shorter Johannine letters, said to have been written ten years after Revelation (*Offenbarung Johannis*, 43–44). Hermann Lüdemann differs, believing that 2 and 3 John were developed in dependence on Papias's remarks, under the (unspoken) name of John the presbyter, and regarding 1 John as the initial, and the Fourth Gospel as the completed identification with the apostle John ("Zur Erklärung des Papiasfragments," *JPTh* 5 [1879] 365–84, 537–76, at 568–73). On the idea of presbyters, see also Eusebius *Hist. eccl.* 3.23.3: "all the [presbyters] who in Asia came in contact with John, the Lord's disciple" (= Irenaeus *Adv. haer.* 2.22.5); also Irenaeus's letter to Florinus: "Such notions the presbyters of an earlier generation, those taught by the apostles themselves, did not transmit to you" (Eusebius *Hist. eccl.* 5.20.4; the reference is probably to Polycarp, who was supposed to have had contact with John, the disciple of the Lord). It is different with the generation of presbyters to whom Clement of Alexandria appeals (Eusebius *Hist. eccl.* 6.13.9; 14.4 = the generation of Melito, Irenaeus, etc.). Eusebius also uses the word "presbyter" for the sources of his tradition; in contrast, he counts Irenaeus among the "historians of the church" (*Hist. eccl.* 5.8.1).

12 Contrary to Bultmann, *Epistles*, 108.

13 Cf. v. 3. The adjective *ἐκλεκτός* appears in the Johannine corpus only at 2 John 1 and 13; the plural noun in the NT generally refers to Christians (Rom 8:33; Luke 18:7; Col 3:12; 2 Tim 2:10; Titus 1:1; 1 Pet 1:1), especially in a future eschatological perspective (Matt 22:14; 24:22, 24, 31 par.; also Rev 17:14, where it is synonymous with *κλητοί*; different in Matt 22:14). The adjectival singular usage can apply to individual Christians (Rom 16:13: Rufus) or to the church as a whole (1 Pet 2:9: *γένος*); cf. also *Mart. Pol.* 16.1; 22.1.

14 Thus, for example, Johann Albrecht Bengel, *Gnomon of the New Testament* (5 vols.; Edinburgh: Clark, 1858) 5.155–56.

It is a practice known from antiquity to the present day that cities, nations, or countries are personified and given women's names (cf. Dodd, *Epistles*, 144–45). This could suggest the possibility here, too, of addressing an individual Christian community as "Lady," all the more since the word κυρία had already been applied in secular Greek to designate an ἐκκλησία ("assembly") in Aristophanes *Acharnenses* 19: κυρία ἐκκλησία (see also the absolute ἡ κυρία in Photius I, Saint, Patriarch of Constantinople ca. 820–ca. 891, *Lexeon synagoge* [Cantabrigiae] Sumptibus Colegii Trinitatis Cantabrigiae, excudit A. J. Valpy, venuent apud J. Mawman, 1822. 2 vols. Edited by P. P. Dobree. Microfilm ed. New York: Columbia University Libraries, 1992; BAGD 458). The expression κυρία πατρίς was an honorific designation for a political community in an inscription in the church of St. George at Gerasa (ca. 115–16 CE): "In honor of the emperor, Titus Flavius, the son of Flavius Cerialios, has erected (this image) to Kyrina Flaccos, the Lady his Native City."[15] "Lady" could have been transferred from the pagan, secular realm to the Christian community. In the *Shepherd of Hermas* the church, who is represented as an aged woman (*Herm. Vis.* 1.2.2; 2.4.1–2) could be called κυρία (*Herm. Vis.* 3.1.3), and Tertullian refers to a particular church in Carthage with the name "Domina mater ecclesia" (*Ad mart.* 1.1).

One can only speculate why the author addresses the community as "Lady." Probably his relationship to it is not that of community founder, for that would have made father-child terminology more likely.[16] He writes from outside the community and respects its independence, even if—as the concluding greeting shows—he regards himself as one with the members of his own community in his address to it (v. 13).

The community is κυρία because, through God's election, it shares in the lordship of the *kyrios*, Jesus Christ. Since political communities could also receive the honorable title κυρία, this address is, in addition, intended to express the author's respect for the addressee. Although he has authority in the community, he does not promote his rank in an authoritarian way. This is clear from his request to the "lady" (v. 5) and from the fact that the concluding greeting does not come directly from the author but is expressed in the name of the "elect sister" (v. 13). The constitutional structure of the church is ecclesial. Autonomous communities greet one another, are in contact with one another, and are obligated to one another in the Christian spirit. The τέκνα (vv. 1, 4, 13) are members of the individual congregations that work out their existence as Christians in the reality of Christian community. Thus the constitutional structure is one in which individual congregations enter into communion with one another. In the various congregations individuals like the presbyter emerge as prominent figures. Even such normative teachers know that the basis of their authority is ecclesially conditioned, since everything they seek to achieve must always refer back to the community itself.

The relationship of the presbyter to the community he addresses is expressed in the very first verse, οὓς ἐγὼ ἀγαπῶ ἐν ἀληθείᾳ. The same expression appears in 3 John 1, although not with reference to all the members of the community. There it refers only to the "beloved Gaius" and reflects the presbyter's consciousness of his authority, which is expressed as affection. At the same time, two key concepts appear that are not only decisive for the relationship between the author and the community but are fundamental terms in early Johannine theology: ἀλήθεια and ἀγάπη.

Roland Bergmeier attempts to clarify the relationship of 2 and 3 John to the Fourth Gospel and 1 John on the basis of the concept of ἀλήθεια.[17] He thus distinguishes between a dualistic character given to this concept in the Fourth Gospel and 1 John and the usage in 2 and 3 John, which goes beyond a dualistic view. Similarly to the interpretation of the concept of πίστις in the Pastorals, he finds that "truth" in the two

15 Cf. F. J. Dölger, "Domina Mater Ecclesia und die 'Herrin' im zweiten Johannesbrief," *Antike und Christentum* 5 (1936) 214.

16 Cf. 1 Cor 4:14; Gal 4.19, Werner Foerster, "κυρία," *TDNT* 3 (1965) 1095.

17 Bergmeier, "Zum Verfasserproblem des II. und III. Johannesbriefes," *ZNW* 57 (1966) 93–100.

smaller Johannine writings refers to "teaching," and thus expresses the truth of what is taught. This interpretation seems to conform to the fact that "walking in the truth" (2 John 4; 3 John 4) is equated with "abiding in the teaching of Christ" (2 John 9). From this point of view the community becomes the refuge of truth against the false teachers, and the concept of truth in 2 and 3 John fits within the sphere of early Catholic thought.[18]

The truth that marks the presbyter's ἀγαπᾶν in relationship to the community can be "known," but not in a detached sense, as if one could step aside from it and examine it critically in order to decide whether one wishes to acknowledge it. Instead, Johannine γινώσκειν has in common with Hebrew ידע that knowledge and acknowledgment are one and the same. Knowledge of the truth is not taking in a particular quantity of information; it means instead that one places oneself at the service of the truth. Knowledge is possible only as a surrender of the human being to the truth. This truth is, in the final analysis, not an uncovering of realities previously hidden, nor the making accessible of genuine facts that were formerly unknown. Instead, what the truth does is to uncover God's own reality for us.

Excursus: Γινώσκειν[19]

Although the noun γνῶσις ("knowledge") is absent from the Johannine writings, the verb γινώσκειν appears in 83 places in the Fourth Gospel and the Johannine Letters[20] (57 times in the Gospel, 25 times in 1 John, and once in 2 John). On the one hand, the knowing subject is manifold in the Fourth Gospel: the world or those who live in it (4:53; 17:23), the disciples (6:69; 17:3, 7, 8, and frequently), or Jesus (2:24; 4:1; 19:4, and frequently). On the other hand, with two exceptions (1 John 3:20: "God knows everything"; 1 John 3:1: "The reason the world does not know us is that it did not know [God]") the knowing subject in the

18 The conclusion that, because of their different concepts of truth, 2 and 3 John have a different author from 1 John is shared by Vielhauer (*Geschichte*, 481). However, this is clear enough from the very fact of the different prescripts. In contrast, Rudolf Schnackenburg ("Zum Begriff der 'Wahrheit' in den beiden kleinen Johannesbriefen," *BZ* n.s. 11 [1967] 253–58) has established that the concept of truth in 2 and 3 John is richer and more comprehensive than appears from Bergmeier, *ZNW* 57 (1966) 93–100. This eliminates the concept of "truth" as criterion for authorship. For further discussion, see the excursus on "Early Catholicism" below.

19 Literature: Klaus Berger, "Gnosis/Gnostizismus I," *TRE* 13 (1984) 519–35; Otto Betz, *Offenbarung und Schriftforschung in der Qumransekte* (WUNT 6; Tübingen: Mohr [Siebeck], 1960); G. Johannes Botterweck, *"Gotterkennen" im Sprachgebrauch des Alten Testaments* (BBB 2; Bonn: Hanstein, 1951); idem, "ידע," *TDOT* 5 (1986) 461–81; Bousset, *Kyrios Christos;* Brown, *Epistles*, 277–81; Bultmann, "γινώσκειν," 689–719; Hans Jonas, *Gnosis und spätantiker Geist* (2 vols.; 2d ed.; Göttingen: Vandenhoeck & Ruprecht, 1954); Friedrich Nötscher, *Zur theologischen Terminologie der Qumran-Texte* (BBB 10; Bonn: Hanstein, 1956); Norden, *Agnostos Theos;* John Painter, *John: Witness and Theologian* (London: SPCK, 1975); Ernst Percy, *Untersuchungen über den Ursprung der johanneischen Theologie* (Lund: Gleerup, 1939); Eugen Prucker, Γνῶσις Θεοῦ (Classiciacum 4; Würzburg: Rita, 1937); Walter Schmithals, *Neues Testament und Gnosis* (EdF 208; Darmstadt: Wissenschaftliche Buchgesellschaft, 1984)]; idem, "γινώσκω," *EDNT* 1 (1990) 248–51; Schnackenburg, *Epistles*, 90–95; Bruno Snell, *Die Ausdrücke für den Begriff des Wissens in der vorplatonischen Philosophie* (Philologische Untersuchungen 29; Berlin: Weidmann, 1924); idem, *Der Weg zum Denken und zur Wahrheit* (Hypomnemata 57; Göttingen: Vandenhoeck & Ruprecht, 1978); Georg Strecker, "Judenchristentum und Gnosis," in Karl-Wolfgang Tröger, ed., *Altes Testament, Frühjudentum, Gnosis* (Gütersloh: Mohn, 1980) 261–82; Karl-Wolfgang Tröger, "Die hermetische Gnosis," in idem, *Gnosis und NT*, 97–119; Robert McL. Wilson, "Gnosis/Gnostizismus II," *TRE* 13 (1984) 535–50; Walther Zimmerli, *Erkenntnis Gottes nach dem Buche Ezechiel* (AThANT 27; Zürich: Zwingli, 1954); ET: "Knowledge of God According to the Book of Ezekiel," in idem, *I Am Yahweh* (trans. Douglas W. Stott; ed. Walter Brueggemann; Atlanta: John Knox, 1982) 29–98.

20 Schmithals ("γινώσκω," 248–51) tentatively attributes the absence of the noun in the Johannine writings to the desire to wrest the concept of "gnosis" from the Gnostics. This reasoning is, however, problematic because of the unclarity in the definition of the phenomenon of "gnosis" or "gnosticism" in the history of religions, and because of the lack of any demonstration of the existence of mythological gnosis in the early Christian period. Jonas (*Gnosis*, 143) attempted to describe the phenomenon of "gnosis" in terms of a special interpretation of the human self and of the world: "an enormous

letters is always the community of believers. The object of knowledge is generally described in 2 John as "the truth." The author of 1 John gives a more differentiated account of the object of knowledge, although knowledge of the "last hour" (2:18) is set apart from the other objects. Otherwise "knowledge" in 1 John is directed to Jesus or his *agapē* (3:6; 3:16), the Father or the Father's *agapē* (2:3, 4, 13–14; 4:6, 7, 16; 5:20; cf. 4:13), the Spirit (4:2, 6), the origin or self-understanding of the believers (2:5, 29; 3:19, 24; cf. 4:13), or the understanding of one's own actions (5:2). This last verse refers to the connection, known also to the fourth evangelist, between knowledge and action (cf. John 7:17; 13:35; 16:3). This connection is treated at length in 1 John.[21] Where the commandments are not kept (2:4), where there is sin (3:6b), or where there is no love (4:8), there is no knowledge or acknowledgment of Christ or God. On the contrary, "keeping the commandments" (2:3, 5) and "loving" (3:18–19; 4:7, 12–13, 16; 5:2) show that one has this knowledge, that one abides in God (3:6, 24). It can be seen from Christ's actions that Christ has loved the community by giving his life for it. From this follows the obligation to be ready to surrender one's own life (3:16). The christological confession is also established as a criterion. It shows whether one possesses the Spirit of God, or whether one is not from God (4:2–3).

According to Greek thinking, the objects of knowledge are being (ὄν) and truth (ἀλήθεια): "And we are assured . . . that the fully real is or may be fully known" (Plato *Rep.* 5.477a). "Every one sees that the principle by which we learn is always wholly directed to [knowing] (εἰδέναι) the truth" (Plato *Rep.* 9.581b). Here truth is "the reality underlying all appearances as true reality."[22] The goal is the discovery of criteria and principles that constitute and support reality. To reach that goal, ancient philosophical schools developed different approaches to a theory of knowledge.[23] The literature frequently emphasizes the purely intellectual intention and purpose of such knowledge.[24] But Bultmann also points to the difficulty of equating the Greek idea of γνῶσις with the idea of the βίος θεωρητικός,[25] for no matter how much being and truth

insecurity about one's existence, human anxiety over this world, fear of the world and of oneself." He believed that it was only the objectivizing of this self-concept that led to the development of a gnostic mythology. The self-understanding itself was an "immanent myth" (p. 259), which constituted the "fully developed kernel of all gnostic mythology" (p. 260). Schmithals correctly opposes this existential description of gnosis: "The number and kind of possible mythical objectivations of this concept of existence are, in principle, unlimited. Therefore one cannot achieve a concept of gnosis that is of any use for comparative religion by means of an existential interpretation alone" (*Neues Testament und Gnosis,* 3). On the contrary, he emphasizes that gnosis was an independent religious phenomenon whose essential features were "a well-developed conception of the world and of the self expressed by a characteristic mythology" (ibid.). But even if we were to suppose that a gnostic conception of existence, a gnostic mission, and the fundamentals of a gnostic mythology existed in the apostolic and postapostolic periods (p. 4), the historical location of gnosis remains unclarified; its beginnings and history are still to be regarded as an open question. Consequently, a conclusive definition of the phenomenon of "gnosis" is also open, since a religio-historically correct definition of gnosis requires both a phenomenological and a historical description. Even if one can give a comprehensive description of the phenomenon of "gnosis" with the aid of a variety of criteria (cf. Strecker, "Judenchristentum und Gnosis," in Tröger, ed., *Altes Testament, Frühjudentum, Gnosis,* 266–68) that extend beyond the inadequate definition on the basis of "gnostic self-understanding," one cannot "determine its origin and sources or the precise stages of its development," and in the last analysis one can discern only lines of development "which culminate in the developed systems of the second century" (Robert McL. Wilson, "Gnosis/Gnostizismus II," *TRE* 13 [1984] 536, 43–46).

21 Schmithals ("γινώσκω," 251) takes for granted that 1 John reflects a terminology "clearly shaped by the Church. Christians face the problem of their sins and must confirm their faith." This assurance is achieved through their recognition that they know God when they keep God's commandments.

22 Bultmann, "γινώσκειν," 692.

23 Cf. Prucker, Γνῶσις Θεοῦ, 20–25.

24 Thus Norden (*Agnostos Theos,* 97) thinks that the purpose of knowledge in Hellenism was "intellectual understanding by rational means"; Bultmann ("γινώσκειν," 690) also emphasizes that γινώσκειν, as distinct from αἴσθησις, is "knowledge deriving from the νοῦς or λόγος."

25 Bultmann, "γινώσκειν," 692.

are the objects of knowledge in the Hellenistic Greek environment, it must still be emphasized that γνῶσις and γινώσκειν can also express an involvement, and therefore represent the precondition for ethical behavior.[26] In the Stoa, knowledge of God led to a demand for obedience to God.[27] This corresponds to the circumstance that secular language used γινώσκειν to describe people's ordinary experience of the world around them.[28] Thus knowledge by no means exists solely for the sake of a purely intellectual understanding that can be divorced from one's historical environment or one's own person. Instead, γινώσκειν includes personal involvement with the object of knowledge which, when one integrates and applies what is known, leads to correct action.

In the LXX, γινώσκειν is the usual translation for ידע. In addition to its extensive secular use,[29] ידע is also found especially in connection with a concrete demand by God (e.g., Isa 1:3; Jer 9:23; 22:16). It implies acknowledgment of God's power (Deut 11:2; Isa 41:20; Mic 6:5)[30] and presupposes the idea of God's special relationship to Israel or to individual members of the people of Israel. Knowing God means "a practical, religio-ethical relationship."[31] The behavior corresponding to this relationship is a reaction to the knowledge of God's actions in history, which demand that God be acknowledged.[32] Thus OT ידע includes the idea of a direct sequence of "knowing, acknowledging, acting."[33]

In general, this combination was maintained in the later development of Judaism, although subject to limited corrections. Thus in rabbinic Judaism there is a knowledge (ידיעה) of God in the absolute sense. The basis and content of this knowledge are the traditions of the nation, especially the Torah. This brings to the fore the idea that knowledge gained from study of the

---

26 On this point, see Bruno Snell, *Der Weg zum Denken und zur Wahrheit* (Hypomnemata 57; Göttingen: Vandenhoeck & Ruprecht, 1978) 23–24; on the meaning of the imperative in the development of Greek thought see ibid., 19–20.

27 Cf. Epictetus *Encheiridion* 31.1: "In piety towards the gods, I would have you know, the chief element is this, to have right opinions about them . . . and to have set yourself to obey them."

28 Cf. Homer *Od.* 15.537; 21.35; *Il.* 18.270; Plato *Rep.* 5.466c; Xenophon *Anabasis* 1.7.4; also Plato *Rep.* 1.347d, where ὁ γινώσκων describes one who is "wise about living."

29 In this regard Botterweck emphasizes that the act of knowing is preceded by a visual or auditory perception ("ידע," 461–81). The "heart" has a variety of functions in this; it "supports understanding and decision on the basis of what is perceived" (462); it provides the basis for judgment and responsible action with respect to what is perceived. "In the heart, the various objects of perception become concentrated to form insight into the true nature of the world, on the basis of which people may consciously frame their lives" (463). The human being should give great attention to the object of knowledge, which must be fundamentally knowable (Prov 8:17), and should seek it (Jer 5:1). Knowledge can be the outcome of a systematic search (Ps 139:1, 23) or a testing (Jer 6:27; 12:3). There is emotional knowledge in the sense of "coming to know," "acquaintance," "participation," and "having concern for," and ידע can also describe sexual intercourse between men and women in the sense of "love."

30 Bultmann ("γινώσκειν," 697) explains this by a comparison with the differing objects of knowledge in Greek based on different ideas of what is reality. In Hellenism truth constituted reality, and this corresponds to the OT idea that reality is founded on "a qualified action of God, or of [human beings] in relation to God" (697).

31 Botterweck, "ידע," 469.

32 In describing the events in 1 Kgs 18:36–40, Zimmerli says (*I Am Yahweh*, 66–67) that the process of knowing is not an internal intellectual or soul process, nor the blossoming of a new insight: "It is a process of acknowledgment that becomes concrete in confession and worship and leads directly to practical decisions" (p. 67).

33 Cf. G. Johannes Botterweck, *"Gotterkennen" im Sprachgebrauch des Alten Testaments* (BBB 2; Bonn: Hanstein, 1951) 42–49. Bultmann ("γινώσκειν," 712–13) distinguishes Johannine γινώσκειν from OT ידע and offers the following reasons: (1) It is combined with verbs of seeing, with which the author opposes groups that emphasized a direct vision of God. Bultmann sees these groups as Gnostics (cf. "γινώσκειν," 712 n. 80). (2) Johannine γινώσκειν has to do with a dogmatic conflict in which the emphasis is to be placed on the historical nature of revelation. (3) Obedience is said to be the criterion for γινώσκειν, and as such is not part of the concept of knowledge, as is the case with ידע. (4) "Knowing" is said to be closely connected with "believing" in John, in such a way that "knowing" is a "constitutive element in πιστεύειν" (Bultmann, "γινώσκειν," 713) in the sense of "faith's own understanding." Schnackenburg (*Epistles*, 90–95) thinks along similar lines. According to him the author "ties in with that cultural current to which this slogan lent its name (p. 90), but has "completely purged [it] of all non-Christian elements." Percy (*Untersuchungen*, 344–45) criticizes Bultmann's point of view.

Torah furnishes the basis for obedience and piety.[34] Something similar was the case with the Qumran sect.[35] There also, the object of knowledge is the Law, the Torah. Personal insights and individual knowledge are, of course, supposed to serve the community, but this knowledge must be clarified by the truth of the Law.[36] It must "be religiously directed and employed according to the spirit of the community."[37] The goal is the purification of the "knowledge of the heart," which can approach "the approximation of the concept of conscience."[38] Knowledge of God is possible (cf. 1QH x.20; xi.17), but it is inconceivable that it can exist without having an effect on practical piety. This "knowledge of the heart" and this "recognition" are determinative of religious consciousness.[39] Hellenistic Judaism also connects with the knowledge and acknowledgment of the power and the works of God (Sir 36:22[17]) the idea that, on the one hand, such knowledge must lead to a way of life corresponding to the norms of wisdom (Sir 18:29; Wis 9:9–10), just as, on the other hand, ignorance of the ways of the Lord leads to error and sin (Wis 5:7). The concept of knowledge in Philo is more syncretistic-Hellenistic than OT-Jewish in character. For him, knowledge of God is the summit of religion.[40] This knowledge is attained not so much by study of the Scriptures, as practiced by the rabbis, but through a direct gift of God.[41]

In the field of Hellenistic-syncretistic literature, "knowing" is distinct from the Greek understanding of the term.[42] The object of knowing is no longer being or truth, but the deity, and the goal of all knowledge is likeness to God: "This is the final good for those who have received knowledge: to be made god" (*Corp. Herm.* 1.26).[43] This takes place in the framework of a raw dualism. As "spirit and matter, the invisible and visible worlds are powers at enmity with one another,"[44] only knowing God, or being equal to God, makes it possible to know the world and human beings[45] and to overcome the world for the sake of God. It is obvious that this "knowledge" is nothing detached and theoretical, but always has to do with the acknowledgment of or involvement with what is known, and with personal activity.[46]

As we have seen, a connection between "knowing," "acknowledging," and "acting" is especially marked in the OT ידע, but it is by no means restricted to OT-Jewish tradition, nor is Greek *γινώσκειν* to be thought of apart from its environment. A distinction between an abstract theoretical knowledge devoid of any personal involvement (= *γινώσκειν*) and a historically concrete knowledge presupposing personal acknowledgment and involvement (= ידע) is more than questionable. The personal involvement that gives rise

34 Prucker (Γνῶσις Θεοῦ, 49) sees in this development a tendency to increasing hellenizing and intellectualizing of the OT ידע.

35 On this, see especially Nötscher, *Zur theologischen Terminologie*, 42–46.

36 1QS i.11–12: "All . . . shall bring all their knowledge, powers, and possessions into the community of God that they may purify their knowledge in the truth of God's commandments."

37 Nötscher, *Zur theologischen Terminologie*, 45.

38 Ibid., 46. 1QS x.24–25: "I will cause vanities to cease from my lips, uncleanness and crookedness from the intention of my heart. I will [impart] knowledge with discretion and will prudently hedge it within a firm bound to preserve faith and strong judgment in accordance with the justice of God."

39 1QH iv.32–33: "to make perfect a way for the children of [humanity], that all . . . creatures might know the might of His power, and the abundance of His mercies toward all the [children] of His grace."

40 Philo *Deus imm.* 143: "the goal . . . is the recognition and knowledge of God."

41 Philo *Abr.* 80: "That is why we are told not that the Sage saw God, but that God was seen by him. For it were impossible that anyone should by himself apprehend the truly Existent, did not He reveal and manifest Himself."

42 On this, cf. esp. Bultmann, "*γινώσκειν*," 692–96. He characterizes the thought in syncretistic Hellenism that he summarizes under the concept of "gnosis," in distinction from Greek thought, as follows: (1) Γνῶσις can be used absolutely without a supplementary genitive. It means the knowledge of God, which is attained only by turning away from the world. (2) Γνῶσις is not a methodical activity but a gracious gift (*χάρισμα*). It is often experienced in an ecstatic vision of God. (3) Γνῶσις no longer merely brings one close to the deity, but invests the Gnostic with the divine nature and immortality.

43 On this, cf. Tröger, "Die hermetische Gnosis," in Tröger, *Gnosis und NT*, 119.

44 Bousset, *Kyrios Christos*, 183.

45 Norden, *Agnostos Theos*, 97–98.

46 Cf. *Corp. Herm.* 1.30: "I have arrived, inspired with the divine breath of truth. Therefore, I give praise to god the father from my soul and with all my might." *Corp. Herm.* 1.32: "Grant my request not to fail in the knowledge that befits our essence; give me power; and with this gift I shall enlighten those who are in ignorance, brothers of my race, but your sons" (translation by Brian P. Copenhaver, *Hermetica* [Cambridge/New York: Cambridge University Press, 1992] 7).

to an action appropriate to the object of knowledge is also included in the meaning of the Greek γινώσκειν. The different objects of knowledge are of crucial importance for interpretation. The basis and content of the conjunction of "knowing," "acknowledging," and "acting" in the Johannine Letters are given in the different objects of knowledge.[47] The mutual relationship of knowledge and action that is central to Johannine theology points to the object of knowledge that is presumed in every individual case. This not only demands acknowledgment by individual Christians and by the whole community, but from it also follows the necessity of ethical behavior.

The later Johannine dualism is not yet visible in 2 and 3 John. There is still no ontological opposition between truth and the world that denies the truth (cf. John 14:17), nor is there an ethical separation, such that false teaching is a lie because it does not come from the truth (first in 1 John 2:21). Instead, everything here is directed toward the community of human beings with God,[48] the Father of the Son, from whom come all good things that exist within the realm of truth and love (2 John 3). The same must be determinative for the church. It is the concrete sphere in which eschatological truth and love are realized. Teaching is part of this: its function is to aid truth and love to attain the victory, but this cannot be reversed, that is, truth and love cannot be made the slaves of dogma.[49]

That individual Christians and the community as a whole are defined by the truth, and only secondarily by

47 Cf. also Percy, *Untersuchungen*, 344–46.

48 Even though the concept of κοινωνία is not found in the lesser Johannine letters, nor in the Fourth Gospel, but only in 1 John 1:3, 6–7 (2 John 11 does, however, attest the secular sense of the verb), the thing itself is found in the prepositions ἐν and μετά in our text: the community between sender and addressee is the community of all those who have recognized the truth (v. 1). This truth not only joins human beings with one another (v. 2) but is the gift that, like all the good things of salvation, is comprehended as the gift of God in the Son (v. 3).

49 That truth is represented in v. 2 as "abiding" (according to Codex A as "indwelling") indicates that there is a temporal dimension. This is expressed in what follows as "abiding in the teaching" (v. 9). On this, cf. the excursus on "Early Catholicism" below. Eduard Schweizer may serve as an example of those who posit a relationship in which the Fourth Gospel is characterized by the alternative of "faith or unbelief," the theology of the Johannine Letters, in contrast, by the conflict of true and false belief, with the criterion of true faith being the abiding in the (old) teaching ("Der Kirchenbegriff im Evangelium und den Briefen des Johannes," *StEv* 1 [TU 73; Berlin: Akademie-Verlag, 1957] 363–81; cf. also Roland Bergmeier, *Glaube als Gabe nach Johannes* [BWANT 112; Stuttgart/Berlin: Kohlhammer, 1980] 200–205). This position, however, is unconvincing. It is true that no acute conflict with false teachers is attested in the Fourth Gospel, although it appears to be present in the Johannine Letters, since these speak of deceivers (2 John 7) or "those who would deceive you" (1 John 2:26; 3:7), and of "the spirit of error" (1 John 4:6). However, it is improbable simply on the basis of the dating that the author of the Fourth Gospel is unacquainted with the problem of false teaching. Since that author is concerned with a christological presentation rather than an ecclesiological one, that is, with the revelation of the Logos at that particular time, the later problems of the church could be dealt with only indirectly. The differentiation between faith and unbelief in the Fourth Gospel is also marked by its fundamental christological intention (although the noun πίστις appears in our literature only in 1 John 5:4; on this point, see above). Faith is oriented to the person of the Logos. If there are no direct confrontations with false teachers, there is nevertheless a content to faith: that Jesus is the Christ (John 20:31). It is connected to the confession of Christ, while unbelief denies that very confession (cf. 9:22). Moreover, "abiding in that which was from the beginning" (cf. 2 John 9) is a problem not only of 2 and 3 John but also of 1 John (cf. 1 John 1:1; 2:24) and even of the Fourth Gospel (cf. John 8:31; 15:7, 27), just as the concept of διδαχή is not unknown to the fourth evangelist (also in John 7:16–17; 18:19). I conclude that the fact that the concept of faith is understood in a very basic way in the Fourth Gospel does not indicate that it belongs to a period earlier than that of the Johannine Letters; this phenomenon has its basis in the transfer of the concept to the christological level, which is determinative for the Gospel.

doctrine, that they are entirely filled by truth, and in turn are oriented to truth and live in the sphere of truth—all this is also clear from the resumption of ἐν ἡμῖν by μεθ' ἡμῶν with a future orientation (ἔσται εἰς τὸν αἰῶνα). Truth is thus an absolute, comprehensive reality, not only in space but in time. It defines and leads the community on its way into the future forever. In the future will occur that which has already been acknowledged and confessed by the community: that the truth, as God's reality, is with and in it, and that it is lifted up in it as the community of all those who have come to know the truth.

■ **3** What the community experiences today through its being-in-the-truth, and what accompanies it on its journey into the future, is a concrete, saving reality. The author formulates this in imitation of the formulas of blessing in the early Christian letters. Paul had already spoken of the χάρις ("grace") he wishes for his readers, thereby adapting the greeting formula of Hellenistic Greek letters. He also mentions εἰρήνη ("peace"), which recalls the Hebrew *shalom,* so that in the Pauline formula of blessing there are echoes of both Hellenistic and Jewish elements, and through it eschatological saving realities are promised to the readers.[50] The author of 2 John presents a formula richer in its content, adding ἔλεος (= God's "mercy"); such broader and more inclusive expressions are also found in 1 Tim 1:2 and 2 Tim 1:2, a further sign that the presbyter is writing in the postapostolic generation.[51]

These are the concrete experiences of salvation that the community will have, just as ἀλήθεια will remain an abiding reality for it. But the author does not pray for a blessing. Instead, he makes a statement about the future, one in which he includes himself.[52] These saving gifts will be present μεθ' ἡμῶν ("with us"). This is true not only for the future—they are already present, just as the community is already living in the realm of truth and the knowledge and acknowledgment of God. One may not make a separation here between more theological and more anthropological aspects. Obviously, the saving gift applies primarily to the community between God and the human being, but the concept of "peace" in particular suggests that the reality of salvation is not something mystical. Communion with God does not mean a dissolution of human reality. Instead, it is worked out in the relationship between human beings; it has ethical consequences.

It is not only the absolute division between dogmatics and ethics, between divine and human reality that is eliminated; the spheres of theological and christological thinking are interleaved. The giver is God, "the Father," and he is Jesus Christ, "the Father's Son."[53] Although the persons are distinguished, the thing that is here expressed is identical. God's reality encounters us in no other way than in the Son, and the Son is nothing in himself, but is always the Son of the Father.

That community with God, as being in the truth, has an ethical consequence is illustrated by the concept of ἀλήθεια. The τέκνα, the members of the community, "walk in the truth" (2 John 4; 3 John 3–4); their way of life is defined by truth. The concept of truth thus covers the sphere of concrete human life as well; it cannot be restricted to a theological or dogmatic aspect. The same is true to an even greater degree of the associated concept of ἀγάπη. This does not establish any particular theological accent in the two shorter Johannine letters, although the author probably could have paraphrased the idea of God's reality with the word ἀγάπη also, as occurs in 1 John 4:8, 16. What is decisive is that ἀγάπη / ἀγαπᾶν characterizes the manner of Christians' existence. The presbyter "loves" his fellow Christians in the truth (2 John 1; 3 John 1; cf. 3 John 2, 5, 11) and knows that the eschatological saving gifts will abide "in truth and love" (2 John 3). Such *agapē* is directed to the sisters and brothers; it is realized in life together and can be attested and praised before the community (3 John 6). This love is the fulfillment of the "commandment . . . from the beginning" (2 John 6).

50 "Grace" and "peace": Rom 1:7; 1 Cor 1:3; 2 Cor 1:2; Gal 1:3; Phil 1:2, and elsewhere; also in the post-Pauline letters: 2 Thess 1:2; Titus 1:4; 1 Pet 1:2; 2 Pet 1:2, and elsewhere.

51 The word ἔλεος is also found with εἰρήνη in the superscription of Polycarp's *Letter to the Philippians;* cf. the further examples in BAGD 250.

52 The case is different with the *v.l.* μεθ' ὑμῶν in v. 3; it is poorly attested and apparently an imitation of the prayer for blessing.

53 Codices ℵ² P, 𝔐, and some Latin, Syriac, and Coptic manuscripts add κυρίου (in a few witnesses replacing τοῦ υἱοῦ τοῦ πατρός). This is a secondary clarification.

Admonition to Mutual Love

**4 I was overjoyed to find some of your
children walking in the truth, just as we
have been commanded by the Father.
5/ But now, dear lady, I ask you, not as
though I were writing you a new
commandment, but one we have had
from the beginning, let us love one
another. 6/ And this is love, that we walk
according to [God's] commandments;
this is the commandment just as you
have heard it from the beginning—you
must walk in it.**

As is customary in other early Christian letters, including the Paulines, the prescript is followed by an expression of joy or thanksgiving for the readers. At this point the letters of Paul usually have thanks for the community's condition of salvation.[1] In v. 4 (as also in the same words in 3 John 3: ἐχάρην λίαν) the body of the letter is introduced with the word "joy."[2] The presbyter now arrives at the real purpose of his remarks, namely, the admonition to practice *agapē*. This is introduced by the statement that already "(some) of your children" (= some of the community) are walking in the truth. This is not an indirect criticism, and probably not a *captatio benevolentiae* either. It is a statement based on the community's existing state of well-being, and intended to prepare for the exhortation regarding future behavior.[3]

Although the article is missing from ἀληθείᾳ, it can be inferred. "Walking in the truth" describes a realization of existence in *the* truth; ἐν ἀληθείᾳ is thus not identical with ἀληθῶς ("really," "authentically").[4] It corresponds, rather, to v. 6. Walking in truth is, concretely, walking according to God's commandments. The community's ethical way of life is fulfilled in obedience to the Father's ἐντολή. Since v. 4b represents a transition to what follows, ἐντολή is not to be understood in a generic sense[5] but as the *agapē* commandment, which is now the subject. The love commandment has a divine origin; it is an eschatological commandment, for it comes "from the Father."[6] There is no indication of an OT background (such as Lev 19:18), nor is there a reference to the double love commandment in the Synoptics (Mark 12:28–34 par.). The issue here is neither the Synoptic double commandment nor its second part, the OT and Jewish commandment of love of neighbor. The *agapē* commandment is, instead, the commandment of mutual love (2 John 5); it appears in this way also in John 13:34–35, in the commandment of the Revealer to his disciples. The concept of "love of the brothers and sisters" appears neither in the Fourth Gospel nor in 2 and 3 John, but it is in 1 John. This suggests a distinction within the history of the Johannine tradition: the two shorter Johannine letters (as well as the Fourth Gospel) here offer a less developed version than that found in 1 John.

Excursus: The Commandment of Mutual Love

2 John 4–6 is dominated, grammatically speaking, by

1 Cf. εὐχαριστῶ τῷ θεῷ in Rom 1:8; 1 Cor 1:4; Phil 1:3 (as introduction to the proemium); Col 1:3 (plural); 1 Thess 1:2 (plural); 2 Thess 1:3 (plural).

2 Cf. the "epistolary formula" λίαν ἐχάρην in a papyrus from the Fayûm in Deissmann, *Light from the Ancient East*, 184, 185 n. 6.

3 The presbyter avoids saying that *all* the members of the community he is addressing are walking in the truth (cf., by contrast, πάντες in v. 1). This may be a hint regarding the community's situation. If it is correct to suppose that 3 John 9 is a reference to this letter, it may be that the conflicts in the community of Diotrephes are intimated here.

4 Schnackenburg differs (*Epistles*, 279: "almost . . . synonymous with ἀληθῶς"); Bultmann, *Epistles*, 96; Heise, *Bleiben*, 167. But see v. 3 (ἐν ἀληθείᾳ), where the article is also to be inferred.

5 Thus Schnackenburg, *Epistles*, 282 ("commandments coming from outside").

6 The idea that the "commandment" was "received from the Father" can be derived from traditions of the Johannine school; cf. John 10:18.

the first person plural; the presbyter submits himself (cf. also the first person singular in v. 5) to the commandment alongside the community (cf. 2 John 1–3). However, the second person also occurs (v. 5: singular; v. 6b: plural), whereby the author sets himself in external relationship to the community. This is combined with a typically Johannine series of key words.[7] As to the content, the love commandment is not a new one, but that which was given "from the beginning." That beginning is established by the διδαχὴ Χριστοῦ.[8] This represents a direct attack on the πλάνοι (v. 7), who do not abide in the teaching of Christ, but go beyond it (προάγων).[9] The antiquity of the commandment and the tradition is thus emphasized in contrast to the progressive movement of the opponents.[10] The commandment "from the beginning" leads to a division between the community and false teaching (vv. 10–11). The interpretation of the commandment's content is shaped in terms of a broad parallelism: "Having received the commandment from the Father" means "walking in the truth" (v. 4), that is, walking "according to [God's] commandments," namely, in love,[11] and "abiding in the teaching of Christ" (v. 9), which means "loving one another" (v. 5b).

2 John 4–6	1 John 2:7–11	John 13:34–35
4/ . . . walking in the truth, just as we have been commanded by the Father; 5/ but now . . . I ask you, not as though I were writing you a new commandment, but one we have had from the beginning, let us love one another. 6/ And this is love, that we walk according to [God's] commandments; this is the commandment just as you have heard it from the beginning—you must walk in it.	7/ Beloved, I am writing you no new commandment, but an old commandment that you have had from the beginning; the old commandment is the word that you have heard. 8/ Yet I am writing you a new commandment that is true in him and in you, because the darkness is passing away and the true light is already shining. 9/ Whoever says, "I am in the light," while hating a brother or sister, is still in the darkness.	34/ I give you a new commandment, that you love one another. Just as I have loved you, you also should love one another.

7 The Johannine style is visible in 2 John 4–6 in the accumulation of concepts such as ἐντολή (vv. 4, 5), ἀγαπῶμεν (v. 5) and ἀγάπη (v. 6a), τὰς ἐντολάς (v. 6a), ἡ ἐντολή (v. 6b). Cf. also Schnackenburg, *Epistles*, 282 ("Verses 5f. are typically Johannine, both in style and thought"). However, one does not yet find here the artful interweaving of parallelisms typical of the later Johannine literature (e.g., John 14–17; 1 John 2:7–14).

8 Cf. 2 John 9. Regarding the question whether this refers to the beginning of the community's Christian life or, in a historical sense, to the "teaching of Christ," see at 2 John 9 and 1 John 2:7.

9 At this point the problem of the relationship of the πλάνοι (2 John 7) to the love commandment arises. Do they offend against Christian *agapē* by damaging the sisters' and brothers' self-understanding through their libertine way of life? Or does their offense against the love commandment consist in the very fact of division, whereby the unity of the congregation is broken? Cf. also 1 John 2:7 and 2 John 9.

10 Reflection on tradition had evidently become an important problem for the church at the time that 2 John was written. It is addressed in a different way by the author of the (later) 1 John when that author—differently from the presbyter—presents himself as an eye- and ear-witness (against Heise, *Bleiben*, 169, the "message . . . always in need of renewed proclamation" of 1 John cannot be employed as a criterion for detecting an earlier initiative in contrast to the time in 2 John, when holding the line is required).

11 In v. 6b ἐν αὐτῇ does not refer to ἐντολή but to ἀγάπη (v. 6a); thus also Schnackenburg, *Epistles*, 283; Brown, *Epistles*, 684; Wendt, *Johannesbriefe*, 18. Windisch and Preisker (*Die Katholischen Briefe*, 138) also refer ἐν αὐτῇ to ἀγάπη, but preserve the grammatically closer reference to ἐντολή by equating "commandment" with the demand to practice love. For the question of the relationship between the singular ("the commandment") and plural ("commandments") in v. 6, see above at 1 John 3:22–23.

10/ Whoever loves a brother or sister lives in the light,	35/By this everyone will know that you are my disciples, if you have love for one another.
. . .	
11/ But whoever hates another believer is in the darkness.	

The passage in 1 John 2:7–11 is dominated by the second person plural throughout. The author of 1 John addresses the readers and expresses himself in a deliberate Johannine dialectic. The formal analysis of vv. 9–11 distinguishes three-part sentences arranged antithetically and thus differentiated both from a *parallelismus membrorum* and also from the antitheses of the OT stylistic tradition.[12] But vv. 7–8 are also artistically constructed of antitheses, as is particularly clear from the dialectic between old and new commandments.

When the author of 1 John begins with an antithesis ("I am writing you no new commandment, but an old commandment"), he is apparently thinking of a concrete dialogue partner. But it is improbable that he is facing the same opponents as the presbyter in 2 and 3 John. Instead, he stands within the living tradition of the Johannine school. The presbyter's rejection of a new commandment and insistence on the commandment from the Father that had been maintained in the community from the beginning was part of that tradition. Now, in a characteristic development of Johannine dialectic, it is emphasized that the commandment that existed from the beginning is the *old* commandment. Moreover, the author emphasizes that the commandment is not only old and existing from the beginning but is also a *new* commandment. In this way the traditional opposition of "old" and "new" is reshaped and, in typically Johannine fashion, the validity of both is asserted.

Unlike the presbyter in the two shorter Johannine letters, but also unlike the Fourth Gospel, the author of 1 John says that this commandment is one of *love for the brothers and sisters* (v. 10). This love for the sisters and brothers is a favorite theme in 1 John.[13] It is true that this is only a terminological precision, since there is no deviation from the content of the *agapē* commandment, that is, the commandment to mutual love, as expressed in 2 John and in the Fourth Gospel. Yet the fact of the dialectical classifying of the love commandment seems to indicate a more advanced, reflective level of tradition within the Johannine school than in 2 and 3 John.

Many scholars regard John 13:34–35 as a secondary interpolation.[14] However, the love-commandment was already anticipated in 13:15,[15] and the style is clearly Johannine.[16] Moreover, the possibility that sayings fragments can be extracted from their context is not a decisive argument in light of the additive style of Johannine composition.

The Fourth Gospel is also acquainted with the idea of something being "from the beginning" (John 15:27) and the "witness" of the disciples that is associated with

12 Thus Bultmann, *Epistles*, 17–18 n. 10 (tracing vv. 9–11 to the "source").

13 It is also in 1 John 3:10–18, 23; 4:7, 11–12, 20–21; cf. 5:16. Schnackenburg (*Epistles*, 107) also describes the commandment of love for the sisters and brothers as "[one of the] favorite theme[s]" of the author of 1 John.

14 Thus Schnackenburg, *John*, 3.53: he believes that the love commandment was introduced redactionally at this point ("although it is very much in the spirit of the evangelist and fits in well"), because Peter's question refers directly to v. 33 and takes no note of vv. 34–35. It is said that there is no other reference to the love commandment in the farewell discourses in the Fourth Gospel. Jürgen Becker says something similar in "Die Abschiedsreden Jesu im Johannesevangelium," *ZNW* 61 (1970) 215–46: the smooth connection between John 13:33 ("ὑπάγειν") and Peter's question in v. 36a is interrupted by vv. 34–35. The injunction to mutual love is out of place in the context of 13:31–38 (p. 220). Michael Lattke differs (*Einheit im Wort* [SANT 41; Munich: Kösel, 1975] 207): vv. 34–35 cannot be shown to be "embedded," and therefore should be retained.

15 According to Bultmann, also (*John*, 475), 13:15 is "an anticipation of the exposition (in 13:34; 15:12) of the command of love as the last testament of the departing Revealer." The verse is said to be the work of the evangelist (p. 475 n. 3).

16 Thus Bultmann, *John*, 525 n. 1, according to whom 13:34–35 are the work of the evangelist. Among the characteristic features he finds are καθώς in a causative sense (382 n. 2; cf. 13:15, 34 and elsewhere), the double ἵνα clause and the motif of ἀγάπη.

it (John 19:35). It would thus have been entirely possible for the fourth evangelist to have Jesus speaking of the old commandment, or the commandment "from the beginning."[17] However, the evangelist places full emphasis on the fact that Jesus taught the *new* commandment. This newness cannot be tested historically or in terms of comparative religions; it is grounded in the eschatological event of revelation. It is motivated by the fact that Jesus is the Logos-Revealer and what he proclaims creates a new situation, the possibility for a new existence, especially since he himself represents that new existence. Such representation consists not only in Jesus' relationship to God (John 14:31: he loves the Father), but also in his love for human beings (John 13:34). His eschatological mission is the expression of his own love for the world and that of his Father (John 3:16–17).

From this point of view it is clear why the fourth evangelist, unlike 2 John 5, can and must speak of a new commandment. This commandment achieves its newness as an essential expression of the Christ-revelation, just what the evangelist wishes to describe in his book. If the revelation of the Logos represents an eschatological event, it is beyond any basis in time and space, and the love commandment can for that very reason be called "new." The christological thrust of this statement is the characteristic sign of the theology of the Fourth Gospel, even in relation to the theology of the Johannine Letters. *Agapē* is already fulfilled in the appearance of the Revealer, but at the same time it represents a demand. It is expected of the disciples that they will actualize *agapē* because it is the "criterion of discipleship."[18] Here there appears to be a trace of the effects of the situation of conflict with heretics in which, as in 2 John, the issue is a division between what is and is not the community. The evangelist does not, however, attack particular heretical groups directly. Rather, he thinks of the universal mission of the Son to the world. Thus "all" will recognize and acknowledge the Christian community as such, whenever mutual love is a reality within it.[19]

No matter how different the tendencies and intended messages in representing the *agapē* commandment as the one "from the beginning" (2 John 7), the "old and new" (1 John 2:7–8), or the "new commandment" (John 13:34), at one point the tradition is the same. This commandment is addressed to the community and must be practiced there.[20] It regulates the relationship to the fellow Christian. It is not addressed to the civic community, but is an essential feature of the ecclesiology of the Johannine circle. It is not only determined by the relationship of human beings to God but implies the demand for ethical action, namely, the work of *agapē*. Here there is an indication that the ecclesiological demand has a christological foundation (John 13:34: "Just as [καθώς] I have loved you . . . "), which settles the problem of indicative and imperative. And we have already seen that the *agapē* commandment, although it has its original location in the ecclesiology of the Johannine circle, contains a positive and universalist tendency, and thus points beyond the boundaries of the ἐκκλησία.[21]

17 It is true that the word παλαιός does not appear in the Fourth Gospel. This is an indication that the dialectic in 1 John ("old" vs. "new") is unknown to the evangelist.

18 Thus Bultmann, *John*, 527: "new" is the essential label of the eschatological community, whereby "reciprocal love within the community" represents "the criterion of the discipleship of Jesus."

19 Cf. Matt 5:13–16: the city on the hill, the light of the world (the external impact of the community is emphasized especially in v. 16). According to Schrenk ("ἐντολή," 555) the passages in 1 John 2:7–8 and 2 John 5 sound like meditations on John 13:34–35. But the weight is on the other side: 2 John 5 contains the most concrete statement and constitutes the tradition-historical basis for the extended reflections in John 13:34–35 and 1 John 2:7–8. That John 13 also shows evidence of being dependent on Synoptic tradition (for this passage: Luke 22:24–27) has been demonstrated by M. Sabbe ("The Footwashing in Jn 13 and Its Relation to the Synoptic Gospels," *EThL* 58 [1982] 279–308) and Karl Theodor Kleinknecht ("Johannes 13, die Synoptiker und die 'Methode' der johanneischen Evangelienüberlieferung," *ZThK* 82 [1985] 361–88).

20 Cf. also Walter Bauer, *Das Johannesevangelium* (HNT 6; 3d ed.; Tübingen: Mohr [Siebeck], 1933) 177: "For the period of separation Jesus gives his own an instruction that, unlike 1 John 2:7; 2 John 5, is called 'new.'" He also equates the love that is demanded with love within the community: "Instead of love for neighbor, [one finds] that what is demanded here is Christian love for the brothers [and sisters]." The adjective καινός refers to this community in love, and thus characterizes the commandment given to the community.

21 Cf. above on 1 John 4:8 (excursus: "Ἀγάπη").

Warning against Deceivers

7 **[For] many deceivers have gone out into the world, those who do not confess that Jesus Christ [will come] in the flesh; any such person is the deceiver and the antichrist! 8/ Be on your guard, so that you do not lose what we have worked for, but may receive a full reward. 9/ Everyone who does not abide in the teaching of Christ, but goes beyond it, does not have God; whoever abides in the teaching has both the Father and the Son. 10/ Do not receive into the house or welcome anyone who comes to you and does not bring this teaching; 11/ for to welcome is to participate in the evil deeds of such a person.**

■ **7** While in vv. 4–6 the author warned that those who are obligated to the truth are to realize the commandment of mutual love, it appears that the subsequent warning against the πλάνοι (vv. 7–11) is awkwardly attached. However, the introductory causal ὅτι makes clear that the author sees a close connection between the *agapē* commandment and the appearance of the false teachers: insofar as the deceivers preach their doctrine in opposition to that of the presbyter, they offend against the demand for ἀγάπη and ἀλήθεια. No matter how important the author finds the struggle against the ideas contained in the false teaching (cf. v. 7), what is decisive for him is that the false teachers are endangering the unity of the community, which is based on love and truth.

In order to meet this danger, the presbyter refers to the tradition he represents. Central to his writing is not a new commandment but the one "we have had from the beginning" (v. 5), "just as you have heard it from the beginning" (v. 6). The ἀρχή to which he refers is not thought of in an absolute sense, as the beginning of the world's creation,[1] but describes the beginning of the church, the founding of the Christian community. The construction with the first or second person plural excludes an identification with Christ's preaching, although the Christ-event represents the foundation of the community's faith. But even in this case it is clear that the idea of tradition implies the notion of a past time to which the presbyter can refer in order to give binding instructions for the present.

That the author by no means sees human existence as simply an isolated mathematical point having no connection with history, but that instead he locates human beings within a process of history that includes both past *and* future, is also clear from the use of the concept of "abiding" (2 John 2) and the future statement that God's saving gift will be (2 John 3: ἔσται) with us, that is, in the community including the presbyter. This community thus has a perspective on the future. The content of its expectation is expressed in its conflict with the deceivers. They have "gone out into the world";[2] they are active as itinerant preachers, similar to what is said in Matt 10:5; Luke 10:1 of the disciples sent out by Jesus; they go about in the world[3] and proclaim a false doctrine, recognizable by the fact that they do not confess Ἰησοῦν Χριστὸν ἐρχόμενον ἐν σαρκί (v. 7).

1 As in John 1:1–2; cf. 8:44 (of the devil); also 1 John 1:1; 2:13 (Christ); 3:8 (the devil).

2 The reading εἰσῆλθον εἰς τὸν κόσμον (= "they have come into the world"), as in 𝔐 K L P and others at 2 John 7, has a different import. It is, however, possible that this was influenced by the following εἰς (cf. also Schnackenburg, *Epistles*, 284). The word ἐξέρχεσθαι appears frequently in the Fourth Gospel: the Revealer has "come from" the Father (cf. John 8:42; 13:3; 16:27, 28, 30). No analogous idea of preexistence is demonstrable in 2 John, and the same must be said with regard to the reference to the "deceivers." There is a close parallel in 1 John 4:1. In this regard, one may ask whether the author of 1 John presupposes that the docetic opponents originally belonged to the Johannine community and

According to many interpreters, the content of this sentence agrees with 1 John 4:2 ("every spirit that confesses that Jesus Christ has come [ἐληλυθότα] in the flesh is from God"). This would mean that the opponents in 1 John deny the earthly incarnation of Christ. They represent a docetic christology,[4] saying that Jesus, as the Christ, did not assume an earthly and material form of existence but only appeared to live on earth (cf. Ignatius *Trall.* 10: Εἰ δέ, ὥσπερ τινὲς ἄθεοι ὄντες, τουτέστιν ἄπιστοι, λέγουσιν, τὸ δοκεῖν πεπονθέναι αὐτόν, αὐτοὶ ὄντες τὸ δοκεῖν, ἐγὼ τί δέδεμαι, τί δὲ καὶ εὔχομαι θηριομαχῆσαι; "But if, as some affirm who are without God,—that is, are unbelievers—say, his suffering was only a semblance [but it is they who are merely a semblance], why am I a prisoner, and why do I even long to fight with the beasts?"). Although 1 John deals with a false teaching in docetic form, the situation in 2 John cannot be equated with that in 1 John. Instead, 2 John 7 differs formally and in its content from 1 John 4:2 by the use of the present participle ἐρχόμενον, in contrast to the perfect participle ἐληλυθότα. It is simply a confession of bafflement to assert that the copyist was unfamiliar with Greek or failed to reproduce the exact expression.[5] The participle contains no statement about the past and cannot be translated with "has come." It has either a present or a future meaning.[6]

On the one hand, in a present interpretation, the deceivers deny that Jesus Christ "comes" in the flesh. This could suggest a denial of the real presence of Christ in the sacrament. The extended interpretation of the Lord's Supper in John 6:53–54, which is at the same time a foundation for the hope of resurrection, gives rise to the question whether the Fourth Gospel was opposing a similar kind of spiritualistic dissolving of the sacra-

---

have gone out from it into the world. In the present passage one cannot determine with absolute certainty what the presbyter considers to be the starting place of the false teachers. It is true that even in this verse there is an emphasis on "unrestrained appearance in public all over the world" (Schnackenburg, *Epistles*, 199, on 1 John 4:1), and yet in NT usage ἐξέρχεσθαι everywhere implies a local idea (cf. Rev 20:7–8: Satan comes out from his prison), so that the question where the deceivers are coming from is entirely legitimate. Since the opponents are identified with the antichrist, they could scarcely be said to come from him (against Bultmann, *Epistles*, 112). It seems better to think of the realm of the antichrist, from which they have come forth. Although our text leaves this question unanswered, in any case the purpose of their emergence is obvious. They have come for the people who live in the world and for whom the presbyter feels responsible: cf. also 1 John 2:19.

3 No dualistic notion of the world is evident here. It is different in John 1:9; 1 John 2:15–17; 4:5 (where the false teachers are "from the world"); 4:9; the neutral idea is also present, as in 1 John 4:1 ("they have gone out into the world"), which apparently presupposes 2 John 7.

4 For the idea and concept of "docetism," see above (excursus on "The False Teachers in 1 John," at 1 John 2:22–23).

5 Cf. Dodd, *Epistles*, 149; Schunack, *Briefe*, 115 (the use of the present participle "at most indicates that the author did not need to listen or speak more carefully because the opposing fronts were already fixed"). Brown correctly emphasizes (*Epistles*, 670) that it is improbable that a copyist would change a grammatically correct perfect to a present. Here he writes particularly in opposition to Bultmann (*Epistles*, 112), who regards the ways in which 2 John 7–9 varies from 1 John 2:18–27; 4:1–6 as proof of the secondary character of 2 John in relation to 1 John, and wishes to see the present participle ἐρχόμενος as a timeless characteristic of Jesus, as in John 3:31; 6:14; 11:27.

6 The future meaning of the participle ἐρχόμενος occurs frequently in sayings of a prophetic nature; cf. Dan 7:13; Rev 1:4, 8; 7:14; Matt 21:9 par.; John 12:13 (quoting Ps 118:25–26); John 6:14 (*the* prophet who is to come into the world). Although Lieu (*Epistles*, 84–85) also is of the opinion that the formulations in 2 John were written on the pattern of 1 John, she emphasizes that the former presumes a quite different situation, and that a future meaning for the present participle ἐρχόμενον in 2 John 7 is possible.

ment,[7] all the more since 1 John 5:6 specifically emphasizes the union of Christ with the sacraments (elements: water and blood), although it is true that here the aorist participle *ἐλθών* appears ("Jesus Christ *has come* in water and blood"). The author of 1 John presupposes that in the environment of the Johannine school there were opposing, spiritualistic teachers who deviated both christologically *and* sacramentally. But in the two shorter Johannine letters there is no indication of a conflict over the interpretation of the sacraments. For that reason a present-tense reading of *ἐρχόμενον* is improbable.[8]

On the other hand, the future-tense interpretation would mean that the deceivers do not confess that Jesus Christ "will come" in the flesh.[9] Such a future interpretation is grammatically permissible, as I have already said. It cannot be objected, with reference to John 17:2–5; Phil 3:20–21; Rom 8:17–18, that in the perspective of the NT authors the future parousia of Christ would occur not in the flesh but "in glory,"[10] because this objection presupposes an "orthodox" eschatological-apocalyptic idea that by no means held the field without opposition in the first and second centuries of Christian theology. Instead, a differentiated set of apocalyptic expectations can be demonstrated even in the NT; for example, the idea transmitted by Paul that a messianic reign would be established before the arrival of the end of the world. (According to 1 Cor 15:23–24 three phases are to be distinguished: the resurrection of Christ; the resurrection of Christians at the parousia of Christ, with the introduction of the messianic reign; and then the

7 Extending the thesis of Peder Borgen (*Bread from Heaven* [NovTSup 10; 2d ed.; Leiden: Brill, 1981]), Schnelle (*Antidocetic Christology*, 194–208, at 208) has demonstrated that the discourse on the bread of heaven and the eucharistic section in John 6:30–58 are to be regarded as the composition of the fourth evangelist, who for antidocetic purposes asserted the unity of incarnation and Eucharist and "in John 6 . . . has taken up some traditions of his school that are independent of one another, but have a related theme and set of motifs, and has shaped them into a compositional unit."

8 This seems to be the opinion now of Balz, "Johanneische Theologie," 54 (the participle "complexively [joins] the history of Jesus Christ and his present meaning"—but he gives no further rationale). François Vouga is of the opinion that the present participle in 2 John 7, like the perfect in 1 John 4:2, "evoke[s] a lasting state" ("The Johannine School: A Gnostic Tradition in Primitive Christianity?" *Bib* 69 [1988] 372–73). Although one might insert a question mark here, since this opinion flies in the face of the difference of tenses, what is especially problematic is the thesis that 2 John 7 represents a combination of quotations from John (1:14 and 6:51–58) and 1 John (4:2), for this contradicts the probable sequence: 2 John first, 1 John later; it also neglects the fact that the combination of *ἐν σαρκί* with the verb is not found in the Fourth Gospel (cf. the difference in *Barn.* 6.7, and frequently).

9 The future interpretation was advocated by Schwartz, *Über den Tod*, 47 n. 3 (cf. idem, *Aporien im vierten Evangelium* [NGWG; Berlin: Weidmann, 1907] 1.368 n. 3). In addition, this confirms the view that 2 and 3 John are genuine letters, in contrast to 1 John and the Fourth Gospel. However, Schwartz's work is too hypothetical when he posits that the presbyter's true name was "cut out," and that this presbyter was the author of John 21 (*Über den Tod*, 49). Lieu (*Epistles*, 85) also says that there was antidocetic polemic in the early church having to do not only with the physical incarnation, death, resurrection, and ascension of Christ, but also his return in the flesh (with reference to Irenaeus *Adv. haer.* 3.16.8 and Tertullian *De Carne Christi* 16.1; 24.4). The counterargument, that the context has no reference to the parousia (ibid.), disregards that the "antichrist" is an apocalyptic figure. The future interpretation of the participle is found also in Westcott, *Epistles*, 218; Charles Gore, *The Epistles of St. John* (London: Murray; New York: Scribner's, 1920) 226–27; in addition, it is in F. W. Bullinger, *Figures of Speech Used in the Bible* (London: Eyre and Spottiswoode, 1898; 9th ed.; Grand Rapids: Baker, 1982) 643; (Pseudo-) Oecumenius: *τοὺς ἀθετοῦντας λέγει τὴν δευτέραν τοῦ κυρίου παρουσίαν*; Π. Ν. *Τρεμπέλας*, *Ὑπομνήματα εἰς τὰς ἐπιστολὰς τῆς καινῆς Διαθήκης* III (Athens, 1982) 532. (For the last two references I am grateful to my colleague, Prof. Otfried Hofius, in Tübingen.) Cf. also the correct translation by Walter Bauer, *Die Katholischen Briefe des Neuen Testaments* (Religionsgeschichtliche Volksbücher; Tübingen: Mohr [Siebeck], 1910) 61 ("the one coming in the flesh"); so also Otto Baumgarten, *Die Johannesbriefe* (SNT 4; 3d ed.; Göttingen: Vandenhoeck & Ruprecht, 1918) 225.

10 Thus Bultmann, *Epistles*, 112; Schnackenburg, *Epistles*, 284; also Balz, "Johannesbriefe," 213.

end, when Christ will hand over his rule to God.) Since the intervening messianic reign was reckoned at a thousand years, it was understood as a millennial messianic dominion, and the teaching about it was called "chiliasm."[11] At one point in the NT this expectation is specifically expressed: in Rev 20:1–3 an angel binds the dragon, Satan, for a thousand years. This idea appears much more frequently in post-NT times. In the second century it was especially vivid in places where Montanist influences can be detected, but it also occurs independently of them. Justin interpreted Isa 7:14 and 8:4 in this sense: Jerusalem will be rebuilt and the church will dwell there with Christ in a reign of peace (*Dial.* 81).[12] In contrast, chiliasm was energetically opposed by Origen, Hippolytus, and others. Papias, however, was also a chiliast.[13] This agrees with the fact that he was instructed by John the presbyter. It was also said of the gnostic Cerinthus that he was a chiliast; for it had been revealed to him by angels that, after the resurrection, the rule of Christ would be established on earth and the bodies of those in Jerusalem would be revived. People would once again give themselves up to lust and pleasure, and a period of a thousand years would be spent in a joyful wedding festival.[14]

That the presbyter at this point is presenting the chiliastic idea of an intervening messianic reign can be seen as probable if one compares this passage with the pseudepigraphical *Epistle of Barnabas*.[15] The author expects that the six thousand years which are the sum total of those allotted to the world are coming to an end, and with the beginning of the seventh millennium will come the dawning of Christ's reign of peace (15.4–5). It is significant that this expected coming of Christ is described as an appearance *ἐν σαρκί* (6.9: he hopes *ἐπὶ τὸν ἐν σαρκὶ μέλλοντα φανεροῦσθαι ὑμῖν ᾿Ιησοῦν* ["in that Jesus who will be manifested to you in the flesh"]; similarly 7.9: they will see him "on that day with the long scarlet robe 'down to the feet' on his body [*περὶ τὴν σάρκα*]").[16] This

11 From Greek *χίλια ἔτη* ("a thousand years"). For the Jewish apocalyptic foundations of this idea, cf. H. Kraft, "Chiliasm," *RGG*^{3} 1 (1957) 1651–52 (according to which the thousand years were arrived at by combining the seven days of creation with Ps 90:4); also Walter Bauer, "Chiliasmus," *RAC* 2 (1954) 1073–78; H. Bietenhard, *Das tausendjährige Reich: Eine biblisch-theologische Studie* (2d ed.; Zurich: Zwingli, 1955); Otto Böcher, "Katechismus," *TRE* 17 (1981) 723–29; idem, "Das tausendjährige Reich," in idem, *Kirche in Zeit und Geschichte* (Neukirchen-Vluyn: Neukirchener Verlag, 1983) 133–43.

12 Cf. also n. 9 above (Irenaeus, Tertullian).

13 Cf. Eusebius *Hist. eccl.* 3.39.12; also Irenaeus *Adv. haer.* 5.30.1; 33.3–4; 36.1–2; 61–62.

14 Eusebius *Hist. eccl.* 3.28.2 (according to Gaius). Dionysios of Alexandria has a similar report of Cerinthus (according to Eusebius *Hist. eccl.* 3.28.4–5: the content of Cerinthus's teaching is said to be that "the kingdom of Christ would be on earth, and being fond of his body and very carnal [*σαρκικός*] he dreamt of a future according to his own desires, . . . given up to the indulgence of the flesh, that is, eating and drinking and marrying, and to those things which seem a euphemism for these things, feasts and sacrifices and the slaughter of victims").

15 The author of the *Epistle of Barnabas* wrote, according to the generally accepted scholarly opinion, ca. 130–135 CE (so Hans Windisch, *Der Barnabasbrief* [HNT Ergänzungsband; Tübingen: Mohr (Siebeck), 1920] 412; Klaus Wengst, *Didache, Barnabasbrief, Zweiter Klemensbrief, Schrift an Diognet: Schriften des Urchristentums* [Munich: Kösel, 1984] 2.115: dating at 130–132 CE; Berthold Altaner and Alfred Stuiber, *Patrologie* [Freiburg/Basel/Vienna: Herder, 1980] 54: "certainly before 140"); it presumes the destruction of the Jerusalem Temple: "Gnosis is already known, but not yet as a danger threatening Christianity; it is also obvious from *Barnabas* that the church has definitively separated from the synagogue" (R. Schütz, "Barnabasbrief," *RGG*^{3} 1 [1957] 880). All this agrees with the situation of Papias as a contemporary.

16 For the interpretation of that letter, cf. Hans Windisch, *Der Barnabasbrief* (HNT Ergänzungsband; Tübingen: Mohr [Siebeck], 1920) 346, 364–65. Of course, the problem at hand cannot be dismissed with the assertion that this passage in 2 John 7 is a "dogmatic formulation" (cf. Windisch and Preisker, *Die Katholischen Briefe*, on 2 John 7: *ἐρχόμενον ἐν σαρκί* would, according to them, be the same as *ἐν σαρκὶ ἐληλυθότα*). Schnackenburg differs (*Epistles*, 281 n. 71), rejecting a relationship between *Barn.* 6.9 and 2 John 7, because he prefers to think simply of a "prophetic foresight" as in *Barn.* 6.7. However, the presentation of the past, present, and future are interwoven (5.3), and the incarnation is an anticipatory figure of Christ's future appearing; for the latter is the foundation of hope in the coming resurrection of the dead, which will bring the rule of believers over the "land" (6.13). The expression *ἐν σαρκί* is therefore not to be referred to the incarnation in the *Epistle of Barnabas*, but rather—as the context indicates—the fulfillment of the prophetic promise

future eschatological expectation, directed toward a messianic reign to be established on earth, is apparently the object of the presbyter's teaching as well. He is concerned with earthly reality, the empirical fact of the substance of apocalyptic hope.

The "deceivers," by contrast, deny the real substance of the apocalyptic expectation. Paradoxically, as a result they themselves become the representatives of an apocalyptic figure, namely, the antichrist, the opponent of Christ. Apocalyptic Judaism was familiar with the idea of a negative counterpart to the coming Messiah. In the NT the expression appears only here and in 1 John. Of course, it originally referred only to *one* antichrist. The plural interpretation in terms of a number of deceivers is secondary. It means that the deceivers, with their false teaching, represent in themselves the distresses of the end time that must precede the appearance of Christ.

Excursus: The Antichrist[17]

The word ἀντίχριστος is attested in the NT only in 2 John 7; 1 John 2:18, 22; 4:3 (singular); and 1 John 2:18 (plural). It is either a creation of the presbyter, or else it comes from the existing tradition as he knew it.[18] The prefix "anti-" can designate either "replacing (substituting for) someone" or hostile opposition.[19] Among the Apostolic Fathers, the word is found only in Polycarp (*Phil.* 7.1) in a passage that rests on 1 John 4:2–3. Here it is used for a person who denies "that Jesus Christ has come in the flesh," and is clearly distinguished from διάβολος and σατανᾶς, that is, from

in the appearance of the Incarnate One anticipates the future appearing of Christ, which is also expected ἐν σαρκί. That the author is not only looking backward to the incarnation, but also forward to the parousia, and sees a concrete connection between the two, is grounded in his parenetic intention. For the future eschatological expectation of a seventh millennium in the *Epistle of Barnabas*, cf. also Johannes Quasten, *Patrology*, vol. 1: *The Beginnings of Patristic Literature* (Utrecht: Speculum, 1966) 89.

17 Literature: Hans Bietenhard, *Das tausendjährige Reich: Eine biblisch-theologische Studie* (2d ed.; Zurich: Zwingli, 1955); Otto Böcher, "Antichrist II," *TRE* 3 (1978) 21–24; idem, "Die teuflische Trinität," in idem, *Die Johannesapokalypse* (EdF 41; Darmstadt: Wissenschaftliche Buchgesellschaft, 1975) 76–83 (= idem, *Kirche in Zeit und Ewigkeit* [Neukirchen-Vluyn: Neukirchener Verlag, 1983] 90–96); Bousset, *Antichrist;* Bousset and Gressmann, *Die Religion des Judentums*, 254–56; Josef Ernst, *Die eschatologischen Gegenspieler in den Schriften des Neuen Testaments* (BU 3; Regensburg: Pustet, 1967); David Flusser, "The Hubris of the Antichrist in a Fragment from Qumran," *Immanuel* 10 (1980) 31–37; Sven S. Hartmann, "Antichrist I," *TRE* 3 (1978) 20–21; Ernst Lohmeyer, "Antichrist," *RAC* 1 (1950) 450–57; Beda Rigaux, *L'Antichrist et l'opposition au royaume messianique dans l'Ancien et le Nouveau Testament* (Gembloux: Duculot; Paris: Gabalda, 1932); Heinrich Schlier, "Vom Antichrist: Zum 13. Kapitel der Offenbarung Johannis," in Ernst Wolf, ed., *Theologische Aufsätze: Karl Barth zum 50. Geburtstag* (Munich: Kaiser, 1936) 110–23 (= Schlier, *Die Zeit der Kirche: Exegetische Aufsätze und Vorträge* [2d ed.; Freiburg: Herder, 1958] 1.16–29); J. Schmid, "Der Antichrist und die kommende Macht (2 Thess 2,1–12)," *ThQ* 129 (1949) 323–43; Willy Staerk, *Soter: Die biblische Erlösererwartung als religionsgeschichtliches Problem*, vol. 1: *Der biblische Christus* (BFCTh 2/31; Gütersloh: Bertelsmann, 1933); Gustav Stählin, "Die Feindschaft gegen Gott und ihre Stelle in seinem Heilsplan für die Welt," in Otto Michel and Ulrich Mann, eds., *Die Leibhaftigkeit des Wortes: Festschrift für Adolf Köberle* (Hamburg: Furche, 1958) 47–62; Richard C. Trench, *Synonyms of the New Testament* (ed. Robert G. Hoetber; Grand Rapids: Baker, 1989) 119–21; Trilling, *Der zweite Brief*, 81–105; Geo Widengren, *Religionsphänomenologie* (Berlin: de Gruyter, 1969) 130–46; Roy Yates, "'The Antichrist,'" *EvQ* 46 (1974) 42–50.

18 If the presbyter, as the authority within the Johannine school, is the originator of the word, then 1 John 2:18 (καθὼς ἠκούσατε) can refer to this tradition, perhaps directly to 2 John 7. If it is a pre-Johannine creation, it probably comes from the primitive Christian tradition of the last decade of the first century CE, since it is unknown to the older Christian apocalyptic literature.

19 In Greek a good many individual names or nouns designating persons are constructed with ἀντι-. Two meanings should be distinguished: (1) "instead of," "being in place of someone": the king's representative during an interregnum is called ἀντιβασιλεύς, and the substitute for the herald is ὁ ἀντικήρυξ; (2) "against" expresses a relationship of enmity: in Heliodorus *Aeth.* 4.7 ἀντίθεος means "godlike" (describing an enemy god). Wicked powers appear when mistakes are made in a ritual of invocation (cf. also Iamblicus *De mysteriis* 3.31; P. Lond. 121, 634–35, and others).

the power from which the antichrist comes (ἐκ τοῦ διαβόλου) and to which he belongs (ἐστι τοῦ σατανᾶ). Thus Polycarp, like the author of 1 John, is acquainted with the figure of the διάβολος, who is distinct from the antichrist and is considered to be the very prototype of the sinner and the opponent of God (1 John 3:8, 10; cf. John 6:70; 8:44; 13:2). The "satan" (cf. Mark 3:23 and elsewhere) appears in the NT under the name "Beliar,"[20] the "evil one" (Matt 6:13, and elsewhere), διάβολος (Matt 4:1–11 par., and elsewhere), "ruler of this world" (John 12:31 and elsewhere), and "dragon"[21] and is *the* adversary of God. But the NT is also acquainted with concrete *human* apocalyptic opponents of God: wonder-working false Christs and prophets (Mark 13:6, 22 par.), the "lawless one" (2 Thess 2:3–12), ὁ ἄλλος (John 5:43), the second beast in the apocalypse (Rev 12:18—13:10; 13:11–18), and ὁ κοσμοπλάνος, the "deceiver of the world," who does signs and wonders like the Son of God (*Did.* 16.4).[22] An identification of Satan with Antichrist occurs in early Christian literature only outside the NT and in the post NT period.[23] The expectation that the adversary of God would appear as a human person made possible the identification of the antichrist with the πλάνοι (2 John 7), and in turn occasioned the plural ἀντίχριστοι in 1 John 2:18. This is undoubtedly a secondary interpretation, because the primary object of the apocalyptic viewpoint known to the presbyter was "the" antichrist.

Primitive Christianity knew as apocalyptic figures one or more[24] false prophets.[25] Except in the Johannine literature the expectation is that they will be accompanied by "signs and wonders," which will cause people to fall away.[26] This notion may be based on an idea in Jewish tradition about the false prophets of the end time as opponents of the true prophets; however, there is no prior clear example on which to base this supposition.[27] It is nonetheless possible that Deut 13:2–6 LXX was already eschatologized in Judaism and that—just as there was an expectation of a prophet

20 This is only in a post-Pauline passage: 2 Cor 6:15. The background is the OT expression Belial ("wickedness," "ruin": Nah 1:11 and frequently elsewhere), which was secondarily personified and equated with Satan, as at *Jub.* 1.20 (Belial as the accuser before God; cf. 1 Chr 21:1; *1 Enoch* 11.7; Rev 12:10); 15.33; *T. Levi* 3.3; CD iv.13, and frequently. See Hans Windisch, *Der zweite Korintherbrief* (KEK 6; 9th ed.; 1924; reprinted Göttingen: Vandenhoeck & Ruprecht, 1970) 215; Ernst, *Gegenspieler*, 288.

21 Rev 12:9–17; 20:2. For the mythological background of the various symbols ("dragon," "serpent," etc.), which are contrasted with messianic symbols (e.g., "bull," "lion"), cf. S. H. Hooke, "The Myth and Ritual Pattern in Jewish and Christian Apocalyptic," in idem, *The Labyrinth* (London: SPCK; New York: Macmillan, 1935) 213–33, esp. 227–29.

22 Cf. Böcher, "Antichrist," 22–23. The dragon, the first beast, and the second beast become a "devilish trinity." The dragon stands against God, the first beast (Rome, which assumes divine honor for itself) against Christ, and the second beast (propagandists for the imperial cult?) against the spirit of early Christian prophecy; see also Schlier, "Vom Antichrist," 21–29, and what follows below (pp. 240–41).

23 *Sib. Or.* 3.63–74 (Christian, end of the first century; cf. Herbert Newell Bate, *The Sibylline Oracles, Books III–V* [London: SPCK; New York: Macmillan, 1918] 22; cf. John J. Collins, "Sibylline Oracles," in *OTP* 1.317–26; on book 3: pp. 354–61, esp. 360); and *Asc. Isa.* 4.1–18. The background is always the figure of Nero as the incarnation of Satan.

24 God's apocalyptic adversary can appear as a single person (2 John 7; 2 Thess 2:3–12) or as a number of people (Mark 13:6, 22 par.; Revelation 13; 1 John 2:18).

25 Cf. Mark 13:22; 2 Thess 2:9–10; 1 John 4:1–3; Rev 13:11–18; 16:13; 19:20; 20:10; indirectly also John 5:43. Trench (*Synonyms*, 121) clarifies the distinction as follows: "The distinction is plain: the *antichristos* denies that there is a Christ; the *pseudochristos* affirms himself to be the Christ. Both make war against Christ, and though under different pretenses, each would set himself on the throne of glory."

26 Cf. *Did.* 16.3–4; *Sib. Or.* 3.63–74; *Asc. Isa.* 4.5, and elsewhere. See the further examples in Ernst, *Gegenspieler*, 42.

27 Nevertheless, Bousset and Gressmann (*Die Religion des Judentums*, 256), Staerk (*Soter*, 71), Lohmeyer ("Antichrist," 453), Brown (*Epistles*, 335), and Trilling (*Der zweite Brief*, 104) believe that this tradition exists. Trilling excludes Christian material; cf. the list in Ernst, *Gegenspieler*, 42. Billerbeck differs (Str-B 3.637–38) as does Schnackenburg (*Epistles*, 137–39). According to Schnackenburg, Judaism had an idea of a reigning political figure opposed to God, but without the features of one who seduces through false signs or as a false prophet. Whether the diversity of apocalyptic notions in the NT (the false signs are traced to opponents [2 Thess 2:9–10], false messiahs and false prophets [Mark 13:22], or the second beast [Rev 13:13–14]) suggests that the

at the end-time derived from Deut 18:15, 18[28] —an idea of apocalyptic false prophets had developed as well. This was elaborated in the Christian Pseudo-Clementine novel, under gnostic influence, to a system of syzygies or pairs in which false and true prophets are juxtaposed as hostile opponents throughout the course of human history.[29]

Apart from the Johannine literature, the other NT texts relevant for understanding the image of the antichrist contain elements drawn mainly from the Jewish apocalyptic expectation of an eschatological *world ruler* as the adversary of God or the Messiah. Thus the expression βδέλυγμα τῆς ἐρημώσεως ("abomination of desolation," Mark 13:14) rests primarily on Dan 8:13; 9:27; 12:11. While the latter refers to Antiochus Epiphanes IV (174–164 BCE), who in his arrogant defiance of God (2 Macc 9:12; Dan 8:11; cf. 8:25) erected an altar to Zeus (1 Macc 1:54), Mark uses the perfect participle ἑστηκότα ("standing") to interpret βδέλυγμα apparently in reference to the antichrist.[30] The persecution of the faithful/saints unto death (Mark 13:9–13) is depicted in Dan 7:25; 8:10, 24 as the work of the "king of the north" (11:40: Antiochus Epiphanes IV), and the "suffering such as has not been from the beginning" is mentioned both in Mark 13:19 and in Dan 12:1. In its description of the

antichrist tradition was strengthened and developed independently on the basis of particular sayings of the Lord in the service of a concrete expectation of the parousia may be set aside at this point (cf. Schnackenburg, *Epistles,* 138–39).

28 Cf. Joachim Jeremias, "Μωϋσῆς," *TDNT* 4 (1967) 858–59. For the NT background: Mark 8:28 par.; Acts 3:21–23; 7:37; John 1:21, 25; 5:46; 6:14; 7:40 (cf. also Jürgen Becker, *Johannes der Täufer und Jesus von Nazareth* [Biblische Studien 63; Neukirchen-Vluyn: Neukirchener Verlag, 1972] 41–42, 50–51); in addition: *Ps.-Clem. Rec.* 1.54.5; 57.1, 5; 3.53.3; 7.33, as well as Origen *C. Cels.* 1.57. Judaism frequently applied Deut 18:15–22 to contemporary events: cf. 1 Macc 14:41 (cf. 4:46); 4QTestim 5–8; as well as the notes in Josephus *Ant.* 20.97 and 20.169 on two messianic revolutionary movements whose leaders called themselves prophets.

29 Cf. Georg Strecker, *Das Judenchristentum in den Pseudoklementinen* (TU 70; 2d ed.; Berlin: Akademie-Verlag, 1981) 145–46, 154–55. For the interpretation of Deut 13:2–6, see *Ps.-Clem. Hom.* 16.13.2–3 par. *Rec.* 2.45.7–8, though the parallel must be regarded as secondary. The "antichrist" is found as a female partner in the syzygy, who "must come towards the end" in *Ps.-Clem. Hom.* 2.17.5 (hapax legomenon going back to the original document); the parallel in *Rec.* 3.61.3 is shown by its shorter formulation to be secondary.

30 Thus Joachim Gnilka, *Das Evangelium nach Markus* (EKKNT 2; Zurich: Benziger; Neukirchen-Vluyn: Neukirchener Verlag, 1979) 2.195 n. 11; Schnackenburg, *Epistles,* 137–38; Nikolaus Walter, "Tempelzerstörung und synoptische Apokalypse," *ZNW* 57 (1966) 43; Walter Grundmann, *Das Evangelium nach Markus* (ThHKNT 2; 8th ed.; Berlin: Evangelische Verlag, 1980) 358. Differently Rudolf Pesch, *Naherwartungen: Tradition und Redaktion in Markus 13* (Düsseldorf: Patmos, 1968) 140 (cf. n. 472, with literature); idem, *Das Markusevangelium* (HThKNT 2, 2; 2d ed.; Freiburg im Breisgau, Basel, Vienna: Herder, 1980) 289; and Dieter Lührmann, "Markus 14,55–64: Christologie und Zerstörung des Tempels im Markusevangelium," *NTS* 27 (1981) 467, 473 n. 70. The argument that this concerns only events in the Jewish war, and that there is no apocalyptic flavor (whereby the participle ἑστηκότα is referred to Titus, not to the antichrist) is unpersuasive, since the antichrist is thought of precisely as a military conqueror, and the second evangelist deliberately refers to future events in Mark 13:14–27. More important is the assertion that Mark includes the pseudochrists and pseudoprophets alongside the tradition in vv. 14–20 without indicating any connection (Egon Brandenburger, *Markus 13 und die Apokalyptik* [FRLANT 134; Göttingen: Vandenhoeck & Ruprecht, 1984] 84–85). But that we find here no messiah as an opponent of the antichrist (ibid., p. 85) is not a genuine counterargument, since in Judaism the figure of the antichrist by no means always requires a messianic adversary (see the following note). Brandenburger supposes that in Mark 13:14–23 there is an actualization of the apocalyptic ideas in Daniel, which Mark applied to describe the events of the Jewish war, events that for him were already in the past (ibid., p. 84). This would be possible only if the hermeneutic horizon in Mark 13:14–23 is a historical one. The extension of time from the appearance of the antichrist (vv. 14–23) to the real end (vv. 24–27) need not contradict a Markan intent to speak apocalyptically; the same is true of Dan 12:11–12. In any case the two motifs appertaining to the antichrist tradition have been worked into Mark 13:6, 22 and 13:14–27, however one may understand Mark's interpretation of them.

"lawless one" as one who "opposes and exalts himself above every so-called god," 2 Thess 2:4 is an almost literal recapitulation of Dan 11:36. The arrogance of the eschatological adversary, directed against God in person, appears also in 4QpsDan ar^a, where it is said that the opponent will be worshiped by all as the "Son of God" and "Son of the Most High." In that day "people shall trample upon people, city upon city" (cf. Mark 13:8).[31] Rev 13:1–11 depicts the Roman Empire in the guise of a beast rising from the sea as antichrist,[32] using elements borrowed from Daniel 7, where they were applied to the Greek empire, especially that of the Seleucids.[33]

Probably on the basis of Daniel, other Jewish apocalypses recognize the figure of an antimessiah as an eschatological ruler.[34] In the Syriac *Apocalypse of Baruch* (written ca. 100–130 BCE)[35] this royal eschatological figure is opposed to the messiah and is characterized as follows: "(1) The last ruler who is left alive at that time will be bound, whereas the entire host will be destroyed. And they will carry him on Mount Zion, and my Anointed One will convict him of all his wicked deeds and will assemble and set before him all the works of his hosts. (2) And after these things he will kill him and protect the rest of my people who will be found in the place that I have chosen."[36]

The eschatological ruler who brings disaster on the people of God is also described in Jewish apocalyptic without any confrontation with the messiah, for example, in the *Assumption of Moses:*[37]

And there shall come upon them (a second) retribution and wrath,
such as has not befallen them
from the beginning until that time,
when he will stir up against them the king of the kings of the earth,
a man who rules with great power,
who will crucify those who confess their circumcision.
And those who deny it he will torture
and put in chains and imprison.[38]

After a description of the resistance of the pious (whose father is the Levite, Taxo), the text continues without any transition:[39]

31 The fragment 4QpsDan ar^a was first published by Joseph A. Fitzmyer, who interprets the "son of God" mentioned there as the expected messiah ("The Contribution of Qumran Aramaic to the Study of the New Testament," *NTS* 20 [1974] 382–407, at 391–94; reprinted in idem, *A Wandering Aramean: Collected Aramaic Essays* [SBL Monograph Series 25; Missoula: Scholars Press, 1979] 85–113, at 90–93). By contrast, Flusser ("Hubris of the Antichrist," 31–37) makes it seem probable that the reference is to an "antichrist figure" who, however (as in *As. Mos.* 8–10) is opposed not by a messiah but by God in person, or by the people of God. For the motif of the arrogant defiance of the ruler at enmity with God cf. Isa 14:12–13; Ezek 28:2. Cf. also 4QTestim 23–24, where, after a series of messianic figures prophesied in sayings drawn from the OT, there is the announcement of "an accursed one, one from Belial" who will be "a net to catch his people and a horror to all his neighbors," and who will manifest himself openly in two "instruments of violence."

32 See the detailed remarks in Schlier, "Vom Antichrist," 21–23; and Bousset, *Offenbarung Johannis,* 358–65.

33 Cf. Rev 13:1 with Dan 7:3; Rev 13:2 with Dan 7:4–6; Rev 13:5 with Dan 7:8–11; Rev 13:7 with Dan 7:21.

34 The tradition of the assault of the nations lacks an antichrist figure. It is therefore at most to be adduced, in a mediated fashion, where individual motifs produce fleeting connections with the antichrist tradition. Thus in Ezekiel 38—39 an eschatological general (Gog) leads the enemy armies against Jerusalem; in *Ps. Sol.* 17.23–27 as in 2 Thess 2:8 the Messiah (= the Christ of the parousia) destroys *the* enemies or *the* enemy "with the breath of his mouth." One should not, however, combine the two traditions into one (against Brown, *Epistles,* 334–35), for while the tradition of the assault of the nations eschatologizes the experience of the attacks of foreign nations against Zion and depicts that assault as being wrecked (after an initial success) by its collision with God or the Messiah (e.g., Zech 14:2), the antichrist tradition reflects the really existing, cruel domination of one or more wielders of power like Antiochus Epiphanes, Pompey, Herod the Great, Caligula, or Nero as the final and ultimate rise of that which is anti-God. Hence Hugo Gressmann's description of Assyria (in Micah and Isaiah) and Gog (in Ezekiel) as "antichrists" is problematic (*Der Messias* [Göttingen: Vandenhoeck & Ruprecht, 1929] 125, 240, 252).

35 Cf. Albertus Frederik Johannes Klijn, "Die syrische Baruch-Apokalpse," in *Apokalypsen* (JSHRZ 5/2; Gütersloh: Mohn, 1976) 114.

36 *2 Bar.* 40.1, 2; translation by Klijn in *OTP* 1.633.

37 The *Assumption of Moses* was apparently written "very shortly after 6 CE" (Egon Brandenburger, "Himmelfahrt Moses," in *Apokalypsen,* 60).

38 *As. Mos.* 8.1–2, translation by R. H. Charles, revised by J. P. M. Sweet, in Sparks, *Apocryphal OT,* 611–12; the text is also known as the *Testament of Moses;* see John Priest, "Testament of Moses," *OTP* 1.919–34.

39 4QpsDan ar^a is equally lacking in transitions; see n. 31 above.

And then shall his kingdom appear throughout all his creation,

And then shall the devil meet his end,

And sorrow shall depart with him.

Then shall be consecrated the angel who has been appointed chief,

Who will immediately avenge them of their enemies.[40]

Although the Satan is mentioned in this section, that does not mean that the description in chap. 8 refers to a "devil's regiment," or that the Satan was identified with the "king of the kings of the earth."[41] A closer parallel occurs in Dan 8:24: Antiochus Epiphanes IV acts "not of his own power," and hence from the power of Satan,[42] who, together with the figure of the dragon, is already known in the OT as the "evil one from the beginning."[43] Hence Wilhelm Bousset's judgment that "the saga of the antichrist now appears to me to be simply a humanizing of that old dragon myth"[44] is not adequate to the complexity of the situation. There are a number of roots to the history of this tradition. The identity of dragon and antichrist can be demonstrated only at a fairly late period, and the (historical) figure of the antichrist is much more clearly delineated than that of the mythological dragon or Satan.[45]

The specific actualization in this instance is in Revelation 12—13: The first beast, as the antichrist, receives power from the dragon (13:2), who is the devil himself. In this, the two traditions about the antichrist as "godless, tyrannical ruler or as false, deceitful prophet"[46] have been systematized. The first beast from the sea is a countertype of Christ and, in a strict sense, the antichrist, while the second beast from the land, as a false prophet, is the propagandist for the first beast and appears as the adversary of the prophetic

40 *As. Mos.* 10.1–2.

41 This was the opinion of Bousset and Gressmann, *Die Religion des Judentums,* 254–55; Bousset, *Antichrist,* 88–89; Staerk, *Soter,* 71–72; Lohmeyer, "Antichrist," 451–52. Against this position is Schnackenburg (*Epistles,* 138–39), who correctly emphasizes that Satan, the old dragon, is also clearly distinguished from the antichrist in Revelation. *As. Mos.* 10.8 ("the eagle") suggests that chap. 8 refers to the Roman Empire, whose destruction (10.8–10) precedes the fall of Satan (10.1).

42 Cf. also 4QTestim 21–30, where the two antimessiahs are traced to Belial (see n. 31 above); also Rev 13:2; 2 Thess 2:9; Polycarp *Phil.* 7.1.

43 An identification of the "dragon" with the antichrist is most likely in *Ps. Sol.* 2.29[25]ff. It is true that this text speaks figuratively of Pompey (v. 30[26]), so that there can scarcely be a mixture of the mythological figure of Satan with the historical figure (cf. Svend Holm-Nielsen, *Die Psalmen Salomos* [JSHRZ 4/2; Gütersloh: Mohn, 1977] 66). The idea of a dragon or monster that was bound at the beginning of creation and will be set free again at the end of the world before being finally destroyed appears in many cultures. (Cf. Sven S. Hartmann, "Antichrist I," TRE 3 [1972] 20–21; Lohmeyer, "Antichrist," 451.) Besides the tradition of the killing of Rahab (Isa 51:9; Ps 74:13; 89:11), this notion is apparently behind Job 3:8; 7:12; and especially Isa 27:1, and influences later apocalyptic as well (e.g., *T. Ash.* 7.3; *Ps. Sol.* 2.24[22]ff.), especially the Revelation of John, where the dragon is expressly identified with Satan, the devil (Rev 20:2). On the idea of the dragon in Revelation, cf. Bousset, *Offenbarung Johannis:* under the influence of Iranian eschatology the victory over the dragon, originally located at the beginning of creation, has been shifted to the end of history (337, 351, 379, 436). The figure of Satan (also Beliar, διάβολος, πνεῦμα ἀέριον) as God's adversary was already known in the OT (prologue to the book of Job) and appears increasingly in the intertestamental literature in place of the dragon as the eschatological opponent of God or the Messiah (*Jub.* 10.8; 23.29; *As. Mos.* 10.1; *T. Dan* 4.7; 5.1; *T. Ash.* 1.8; *T. Levi* 18.12; *T. Jud.* 25.3; *1 Enoch* 68.4; *2 Enoch* 29.4).

44 Bousset, *Antichrist,* 53.

45 Cf. also Bousset and Gressmann, *Die Religion des Judentums,* 254–55, on *As. Mos.* 8: "Here a figure composed of Antiochus IV and Herod has been woven together, and is now depicted without particular reference to any given period of time as the tyrant of the end-time who will rule the whole world." Antichrist figures in Jewish texts include: *As. Mos.* 10.8; 4QpsDan A^a; Isa. 11:4; *4 Ezra* 5.6 ("and one shall reign whom those who inhabit the earth do not expect"); 12.11–12; 14.17 (the eagle = the imperial power of Rome), and elsewhere; Bousset, *Antichrist,* 63. Christian texts include: *Barn.* 4.4– 5; *Did.* 16.3–4; *Asc. Isa.* 4.2–4; *Apocalypse of Elijah* 32.9–33.10; *Sib. Or.* 2.167–68; 3.63–65; 5.33–34, 214–27; 8.140–50; also the texts of the "Saga of Nero" in *Sib. Or.* 4.119–24, 137–39; 5.137–54, 361–85 (with no application to the "antichrist" according to Bousset and Gressmann, *Die Religion des Judentums,* 255; Ernst, *Gegenspieler,* 265).

46 Bousset and Gressmann, *Die Religion des Judentums,* 254.

Spirit of Christ, thus also representing an antichrist figure.[47]

The two antichrist traditions appear, unsystematized but united by the common theme of the apocalyptic event, in Mark 13, if βδέλυγμα τῆς ἐρημώσεως ("abomination of desolation" v. 14) refers to the antichrist (see above), and the ψευδόχριστοι and ψευδοπροφῆται ("false christs and false prophets," v. 22; cf. v. 6) are to be regarded as concretizations of the expectation of false prophets in a variety of guises. In this way they are comparable to the secondary plural form ἀντίχριστοι in 1 John 2:18.

The earliest text in which the two antichrist traditions can be shown to have been fused to produce a single figure is 2 Thess 2:3–12. The characterization of the adversary of the coming Christ as ἄνθρωπος τῆς ἀνομίας ("the lawless one") and υἱὸς ἀπωλείας ("one destined for destruction," 2:3) takes up the tradition from Daniel about the arrogant and violent ruler and develops it in what follows, asserting that the ἀντικείμενος will set himself in place of God (cf. v. 4 with Dan 11:36). His description as one who comes in the power of Satan, who deceives human beings not only with "signs, lying wonders" but also every kind of ἀπάτη ἀδικίας (v. 10), draws on the tradition of the false prophets in Deut 13:2–6.[48] It is characteristic of him that his appearance is identical with the spread of infidelity and causes ἀποστασία (v. 3), made possible by an ἐνέργεια πλάνης ("powerful delusion," v. 11). Such πλάνη, which is equated with the denial of Christ and the acceptance of the antichrist, represents the eschatological apostasy that is typical of apocalyptic expectations.[49] It is the crucial threat to the Christian community.

That in Revelation, Mark and its parallels, and 2 Thessalonians the two expectations of the antichrist have been used with different emphases can be explained from the circumstance that at one point it is political danger (as in Revelation), at another time religious temptation that appears as the most acute danger to the community, even though the two may be closely connected. What is specific to the Johannine Letters is that in them the political dimension is not considered, and the action of the ἀντίχριστος appears as leading the community astray through false teaching, specifically a false christology.

■ **8** The community, confronted by false teaching, is in an apocalyptic situation. This is the basis for the "eschatological admonition"[50] βλέπετε ἑαυτούς ("be on your guard!"). The appearance of the deceivers means that the very existence of the community is at risk. It is called to decide whether it will lose everything it has and is—the state of its faith, its existence in truth and love[51] —or whether it will arrive at that toward which it is striving, the "full reward"—another apocalyptic term that completes the image.[52] Undoubtedly the coming of Christ in the flesh also implies the rewarding of those who belong to him. Those who have acknowledged him in word and deed will receive a heavenly reward that is

47 Cf. Böcher, "Antichrist," 23.

48 Cf. Trilling, *Der zweite Brief*, 83, 104. In addition to the Christian interpretation, the antichrist tradition in *Did.* 16.4 also rests on the combination of motifs from Daniel and Deuteronomy: "and then shall appear the deceiver of the world (κοσμοπλάνος) as a Son of God, and shall do signs and wonders and the earth shall be given over into his hands and he shall commit iniquities which have never been since the world began."

49 Cf. Trilling, *Der zweite Brief*, 81–82. Dan 11:32; 1 Macc 2:15; *As. Mos.* 8.2–5; Mark 13:6; 2 Thess 2:3; 1 John 2:19; Rev 13:14, and elsewhere.

50 Schnackenburg, *Epistles*, 285 (with reference to Rev 3.11, cf. also Mark 13:5, 9 par.).

51 Εἰργασάμεθα must not be understood in the sense of an accomplishment (on the contrary, cf. also John 6:27, 29). Both the first and second person plural are equally well attested (2d person plural in ℵ A Ψ 0232^vid, 33, 81, 323 (614), 630, 1241, 1505, 1739, 2495; al; latt; sy; bo. 1st person plural in B(*) P, 𝔐, sy^hmg; sa); the first person plural is to be preferred as the *lectio difficilior* because of the stylistic unevenness (cf. ἀπολάβητε). Hartwig Thyen differs ("Johannesbrief," *TRE* 17 [1987] 196). He thinks this is an "ecclesial we," to be distinguished from the use of the "authorial we" in 1 John 1:1–5 (see above). So also Brown, *Epistles*, 671 ("we Johannine Christians").

52 The word μισθός appears only here in the Johannine Letters. Cf. Rev 3:11 ("that no one may seize your crown"); 11:18 ("for rewarding your servants"); there is a present interpretation in John 4:36 ("the reaper is already receiving wages"); future in Matt 6:1; 10:41–42. On this subject, see the articles by Herbert Preisker, "The Concept of Reward in Later Judaism" and "The Concept of Reward in the New Testament," *TDNT* 4 (1967) 712–28, which are rich in material but too one-sided in their theology.

identical with eternal life, life in community with Christ.

■ 9 The apocalyptic horizon within which the presbyter's theology is located is also characterized by a specific, realistic anticipation of the parousia. On the one hand, it is understandable that in its later development the Johannine school, beginning from this starting point, drew further realistic conclusions, with respect, for example, to its understanding of the earthly Jesus (colossal miracles) as signs of the Revealer's *doxa,* or to the interpretation of the sacraments (Lord's Supper: John 6; Baptism and Lord's Supper: 1 John 5:5–9). On the other hand, however, it is equally understandable that theological resistance was ignited at an early stage and that innovators opposed the presbyter's traditional theology. These were people who did not share that theology and did not abide in the "teaching of Christ," that is, people who were not able to regard the presbyter's message as an appropriate interpretation of the Christ-event.[53] The old theology represented by the presbyter is opposed by "deceivers," who consider themselves "progressive."[54] They seek new things, deviating from the old. Theirs is an attitude that will later be stigmatized in the church as heresy.

In the presbyter's view, the Christ-*didachē* that he represents possesses a superior theological binding force. As those who do not abide in the teaching of Christ have no community with God, the reverse is also true. Community with the Father and the Son exists only where that teaching is preserved. The antithetical sequence is striking: a negative statement is followed by an affirmative parallel (an antithetical *parallelismus membrorum*). This means that the beginnings of Johannine antithesis, the specific form of Johannine thought as later developed in the Fourth Gospel and in 1 John, are already attested in the writing of the presbyter. This style, together with certain Johannine "key concepts" such as community with God, truth, and *agapē,* was to become an essential characteristic of the Johannine school.

The expression θεὸν ἔχειν is not a specifically Christian term, but is connected primarily with Greek models[55] and is also found in Hellenistic Jewish tradition.[56] This manner of speaking is more marked by Hellenistic than by Jewish traits and was only Christianized at a later stage, when "having God" or "having the Father" (2 John 9; 1 John 2:23) was complemented by "having the Son" (2 John 9; 1 John 5:12; cf. Heb 4:14–15; 8:1: "we have a high priest"). This kind of Christianization is also evident in 2 John. No real distinction is drawn between community with God and community with Christ; both these ideas are more strictly paralleled than in 1 John.[57]

On the basis of the fact that the πλάνοι regard themselves as innovators (cf. also 2 John 5: rejection of a "new" commandment), some have concluded that what is

53 The question whether τοῦ Χριστοῦ is an objective or subjective genitive should be answered in favor of the former; just as the "confession" has Jesus Christ as its object, so also the teaching represented by the presbyter. The concept of διδαχή refers to the concrete situation of the presbyter's community. His teaching about Christ is contrasted with "false" teaching. It is characteristic of the more theoretical attitude of 1 John that the concept of διδαχή does not appear there (cf., besides 2 John 9–10, only John 7:16–17; 18:19); on the contrary, it is asserted in 1 John 2:27 that the community has no need of being taught by anyone: instead, the χρῖσμα teaches them everything!

54 2 John 9: πᾶς ὁ προάγων (this should be the reading; codices P Ψ 𝔐 sy smooth it to παραβαίνων) is resumed in what follows by τις (v. 10); it is not a question of a particular "leading personality in the community" (thus Hans Hinrich Wendt, *Die Johannesbriefe und das johanneische Christentum* [Halle: Waisenhaus, 1925] 21), but of *the* false teaching in general. The singular is partly explained by the connection with the singular ἀντίχριστος, whose conceptual content stems from the apocalyptic tradition (see above at v. 7).

55 See, for example, the itinerant philosopher Epictetus, who lived around the turn of the century and was therefore a contemporary of the presbyter: *Moral Discourses* 2.8.17: ἐκεῖ τὸν θεὸν οὐκ ἔχεις (namely, in the things of nature); also 1.9.7; 4.1.145: Epictetus's students are those who "have the great Lord (= God)."

56 Cf. Hermann Hanse, "ἔχω," *TDNT* 2 (1964) 823: reference to the LXX Add Est 4:17; also 2 Macc 8:36; 11:10; 3 Macc 7:16; also *T. 12 Patr.* (e.g., *T. Dan* 5; *T Iss.* 7); Josephus *Ant.* 8.227; cf. 10.250 (ἔχων τὸν θεῖον).

57 Cf. the series of stages in 1 John 2:23, ascending from Son to Father. 2 John 9 (but cf. also the variant reading in this verse) is closer to the original than 1 John 2:23; similarly 1 John 5:12 ("whoever has the Son has life"); cf. John 3:15–16, 36; 5:24, 26; 6:40, 54); also differentiated is 1 John 1:3: fellowship with the Father and with his Son Jesus Christ. In any case,

at issue here is a gnostic doctrine.[58] However, the idea of "the new" is broadly attested in the religious writings of antiquity, and Jesus himself, according to Mark 2:21 par. Matt 9:17, used the image of new wine and new wine-skins to express the idea of the new thing that had begun with his preaching. So also Paul interpreted the Christ-event as the foundation of the καινὴ κτίσις ("new creation," 2 Cor 5:17).[59] The claims of the "deceivers" are thus located within a general religious conceptual field. One cannot determine from the context that these are Gnostics. The opponents are not accused of teaching dualistic or other specifically gnostic doctrines.

■ **10** At the beginning of the second century there was no clear separation between gnosis and the great church, between orthodoxy and heresy, that would allow us to infer the presence of this heresiological confrontation in 2 and 3 John. Besides, the organization of Christian communities was still flexible in the presbyter's time. The "deceivers" are described not as community officials but as itinerant preachers; they are thus in accord with the church structure that was also important for the presbyter and his community (3 John 2–8: the "brothers and sisters" [*NRSV*: "friends"] as emissaries of the presbyter). The presbyter's unusually harsh order to the community not to receive the false teachers into their houses, and not even to greet them, shows that they represent an acute threat to the existence of the Johannine communities. A similar withdrawal of community fellowship is described in the missionary discourse in Matt 10:14 par., but there it is the unbelieving Jews who refuse to accept the message of the disciples: as a sign of the coming judgment, Jesus' disciples shake off the dust that their shoes have transported out of such a city. In the present passage the people referred to are fellow Christians who, in the opinion of the presbyter, are going astray. If they are to be denied the usual greeting, this indicates internal tensions within the church, more radical than the division between Christians and Jews. One may ask whether this passage presupposes the idea of "excommunication."[60] One cannot, however, discern any overarching constitutional structure for all communities that would make it possible for disciplinary actions, once decided upon, to be applied in every individual community. The presbyter is probably acquainted with a disciplinary institution of exclusion in the communities with which he is associated (3 John 10: Diotrephes is applying it against insubordinate members of the community), but, as the example shows, this can be practiced only in individual communities, and there is no evidence of its extension to the church as a whole. The communities thus have a significant degree of autonomy. It is just this that explains the presbyter's efforts to obtain entry for his ideas into Diotrephes' community.[61]

there is no suggestion in this passage that 2 John is dependent on 1 John (against Bultmann, *Epistles*, 113); it seems rather to suggest a dependence of 1 John on 2 John (cf. at 1 John 2:14: ἔγραψα); also Hermann Hanse, "ἔχω," *TDNT* 2 (1964) 823 (the two verses are "almost identical and are certainly related"); however, he does not take account of the Johannine school tradition.

58 A close parallel to this text is provided, for example, by the document *The Concept of Our Great Power* among the Nag Hammadi texts (NHC 6,4). According to this, "wickedness" arose "when the times were completed" "to nullify . . . the words of the true wisdom [Sophia]," who represents "the old" (44,10–29); cf. Hans-Martin Schenke, "Gnosis: Zum Forschungsstand unter besonderer Berücksichtigung der religionsgeschichtlichen Problematik," *VF* 32 (1987) 2–21.

59 For the concept and idea of "newness" in the OT, cf. esp. Isa 65:17 (new heavens and new earth) and Jer 31:31 (new covenant). Examples from Greek literature are found in BAGD 394–95; also Johannes Behm, "καινός, κτλ.," *TDNT* 3 (1965) 447–50; Jörg Baumgarten, "καινός," *EDNT* 2 (1991) 229–32. The expression ἀπ' ἀρχῆς (2 John 5) is Hellenistic Greek; cf. Herodotus 2.104; Pindar *Pyth.* 8.25; however, the thing itself is also found in the OT: see W. Beuken and U. Dahmen, "ראש," *ThWAT* 7.271–84.

60 For details, see Ingrid Goldhahn-Müller, *Die Grenze der Gemeinde: Studien zum Problem der Zweiten Busse im Neuen Testament unter Berücksichtigung der Entwicklung im zweiten Jahrhundert bis Tertullian* (GThA 39; Göttingen: Vandenhoeck & Ruprecht, 1989) 73–74.

61 The presbyter cannot have recourse to an independent official structure; instead, here as well as in the case of the visit announced in 3 John 14, he must rely on his personal persuasive and argumentative skills. This is correctly observed by Lieu, *Epistles*, 114–15; also Dodd, *Epistles*, 165; Schnackenburg, *Epistles*, 287–88, 295–96.

■ 11 The order to refuse welcome, and with it every kind of human contact, is explained by the statement that the one who welcomes the deceivers is thereby identified with τοῖς ἔργοις . . . τοῖς πονηροῖς ("the evil deeds") of those people. The context does not indicate that the πλάνοι are guilty both of false teaching and of immoral lifestyle. The "evil deeds" of the false teachers consist in the fact that their teaching does not match the presbyter's confession of Christ. However, this originally theoretical controversy also has an eminently practical face to it: false teaching is an offense against the *agapē* that should characterize the community, and this is true because with the false teaching quarrels and the accompanying phenomena (even suspicion and hatred) have been introduced into the community. In this way, the opposing teachers sin against the love commandment that is meant to bring the community together in unity of faith and action. This, then, is the ethical aspect of false teaching. It is itself an "evil deed" because it threatens to split the unity of the congregation and to destroy the love that marks the community of Christians.[62] One can obviously also argue, in reverse, that the *agapē* of the Christian community must be strong enough to support different teachings: for not only can doctrine be a guide to *agapē*, but *agapē* can also contribute to the definition of doctrine. In view of the fact that the continuing existence of his work is apparently at stake, such a relativizing of his teaching could scarcely be expected of the presbyter at this crucial moment. In his opinion, the "teaching of Christ" that he represents has an unconditional claim to be heard.

Excursus: Early Catholicism[63]

Before one can address the question of "early Catholic" tendencies in the Johannine Letters one must first clarify the concept of "early Catholicism." This is a difficult task,[64] not least because the term was

62 The presbyter's accusation against Diotrephes, that his ἔργα consist, among other things, in spreading λόγοις πονηροῖς (3 John 10), is also to be understood in this sense. There is a different use of the expression τὰ ἔργα . . . πονηρά in the Fourth Gospel, where it is related to the dualism of light and darkness (John 3:19; 7:7); and in 1 John, where the "works" of Cain are described as "evil" (1 John 3:12).

63 Literature: Carl Andresen, *Die Kirchen der alten Christenheit* (Theologische Wissenshaft 6; Stuttgart: Kohlhammer, 1971) 17–115; idem, *Geschichte des Christentums* (6 vols.; 2d ed.; Stuttgart/Berlin/Cologne/Mainz: Kohlhammer, 1986) 1.5–21; C. Clifton Black II, "The Johannine Epistles and the Question of Early Catholicism," *NovT* 28 (1986) 131–58; Bultmann, *Theology*, 2.95–142 (§§ 51–55)]; Hans Conzelmann, *An Outline of the Theology of the New Testament* (trans. John Bowden; New York: Harper, 1969) 321–32; idem, *History of Primitive Christianity* (trans. John E. Steely; Nashville: Abingdon, 1973) 13–20; Ferdinand Hahn, "Das Problem des Frühkatholizismus," *EvTh* 38 (1978) 340–57; idem, "Frühkatholizismus als ökumenisches Problem," *Catholica* 37 (1983) 17–35; Adolf von Harnack, "The Present State of Research in Early Church History," in idem, *Ausgewählte Reden und Aufsätze* (2 vols.; Giessen: Töpelmann, 1906; reprinted in one volume; Berlin: de Gruyter, 1951) 2.217–35; idem, *Entstehung und Entwicklung der Kirchenverfassung und des Kirchenrechts in den ersten zwei Jahrhunderten* (1910; reprinted Darmstadt: Wissenschaftliche Buchgesellschaft, 1980) 173–87; idem, *Aus der Werkstatt des Vollendeten* (ed. Axel von Harnack; Giessen: Töpelmann, 1930) 109–213; idem, *History of Dogma* (trans. Neil Buchanan, from 3d ed.; New York: Russell & Russell, 1958 (repr. Dover, 1961) 2.1–93; Ernst Käsemann, "Ministry and Community in the New Testament," in idem, *Essays on New Testament Themes* (SBT 1/41; trans. W. J. Montague; London: SCM; Naperville: Allenson, 1964) 63–94; idem, "The Canon of the New Testament and the Unity of the Church," in ibid., 95–107; idem, "Paul and Early Catholicism" (trans. Wilfred F. Bunge), in idem, *New Testament Questions of Today* (trans. W. J. Montague and Wilfred F. Bunge; Philadelphia: Fortress, 1969) 236–51; Hans Küng, "Der Frühkatholizismus im Neuen Testament als kontroverstheologisches Problem," in Ernst Käsemann, ed., *Das Neue Testament als Kanon* (Göttingen: Vandenhoeck & Ruprecht, 1970) 175–204; Ulrich Luz, "Erwägungen zur Entstehung des 'Frühkatholizismus,'" *ZNW* 65 (1974) 88–111; Willi Marxsen, *Der Frühkatholizismus im Neuen Testament* (BST 21; Neukirchen: Kreis Moers, 1958); Karl H. Neufeld, "'Frühkatholizismus'—Idee und Wirklichkeit," *ZKTh* 94 (1972) 1–28; idem, "'Frühkatholizismus'—Woher?" *ZKTh* 96 (1974) 353–84; idem, "'Frühkatholizismus'—systematisch," *Gregorianum* 62 (1981) 431–66; Alexander Sand, "Überlegungen zur gegenwärtigen Diskussion über den 'Frühkatholizismus,'" *Catholica* 33 (1979) 49–62; Karl Hermann Schelkle, "Spätapostolische Briefe als frühkatholisches Zeugnis," in Josef Blinzler, Otto Kuss, and Franz Mussner, eds., *Neutestamentliche*

introduced and applied with highly critical intent, and even today frequently fulfills this critical function.[65] The concept and idea of "early Catholicism" attempt to describe developments in the Christian communities at the time of transition from the apostolic to the post-apostolic period and, beyond that, to depict the principles underlying the church as it thus emerged.[66] Indisputably, there are discernible developments in early Christianity toward an "early Catholic theology," and also principles that marked the "early Catholic church" as such. While at the beginning of Christian theology one finds the kerygma of the cross and resurrection of Jesus Christ, and in the early period of the church a related pneumatic awareness attesting to the presence of the Spirit of God in the community of those who believe in Christ, coupled with an overwhelming and intensive expectation of the immediate parousia, at the end of this development one recognizes the emergence of an established great church characterized by office, canon, and credo.[67]

In any case, the theological evaluation of this development can be done only with the greatest circumspection. One can scarcely expect to summarize it exhaustively by applying the "theory of decline," which describes the falling away of Catholicism from a normative early Christianity.[68] One must rather say that this development leading to the Catholic church represented a factual necessity. Even Adolf von Harnack thought that the achievement of early Catholicism consisted in the overcoming of gnosis,[69] and Rudolf Sohm asserted that the development of canon law was intended to eliminate what he sees as the

---

Aufsätze: Festschrift für Prof. Josef Schmid zum 70. Geburtstag (Regensburg: Pustet, 1963) 225–32; idem, *Die Petrusbriefe. Der Judasbrief* (HThKNT 13/2; 2d ed.; Freiburg: Herder, 1964) 241–45; Heinrich Schlier, *Die Zeit der Kirche: Exegetische Aufsätze und Vorträge* I (2d ed.; Freiburg: Herder, 1958); Hermann-Josef Schmitz, *Frühkatholizismus bei Adolf von Harnack, Rudolph Sohm und Ernst Käsemann* (Düsseldorf: Patmos, 1977); Siegfried Schulz, *Die Mitte der Schrift* (Stuttgart/Berlin: Kreuz, 1976); Heinz Schürmann, "Auf der Suche nach dem 'Evangelisch-Katholischen,'" in Paul-Gerhard Müller and Werner Stenger, eds., *Kontinuität und Einheit: Für Franz Mussner* (Freiburg/Basel/Vienna: Herder, 1981) 340–75; Rudolf Sohm, *Kirchenrecht* (2 vols.; Systematisches Handbuch der deutschen Rechtswissenschaft 8, 1892; reprinted Berlin: Duncker & Humbolt, 1970); Ernst Troeltsch, "Die Soziallehren der christlichen Kirchen und Gruppen," *Gesammelte Schriften* (4 vols.; 1912–25; reprinted Tübingen: Mohr [Siebeck], 1977). See further bibliography in the articles by Sand (49 n. 1), and Schürmann (340 n. 1).

64 Karl H. Neufeld observes correctly that "all the newer specialized reference works reveal a gap where the corresponding term should be" ("'Frühkatholizismus,'" *ZKTh* 94 [1972] 1; here the reader will also find an extensive discussion of the origin and development of the concept of "early Catholicism"). For a more recent reference, however, cf. Paul-Gerhard Müller, *Lexikon Exegetischer Fachbegriffe* (Stuttgart: Katholisches Bibelwerk, 1985) 106ff.

65 On this, cf. Schürmann, "Auf der Suche," 340–41. According to him the concept is intended to summarize the principle underlying features unique to the early church that were regarded as erroneous by the Reformation churches. In the process, the "theory of a 'rupture,' a 'falling away,' or 'apostasy' [was] . . . imputed more or less reflexively from the beginning."

66 Luz ("Erwägungen," 89–90) distinguishes these two aspects with the terms "emerging early Catholicism" and "early Catholicism."

67 On this, see von Harnack, *History of Dogma* 2.19. He observes that it is necessary to focus on three norms for the church: "the apostolic doctrine, the apostolic canon of Scripture, and the guarantee of apostolic authority, afforded by the organization of the Church, that is, the episcopate, and traced back to apostolic institution."

68 Schmitz, *Frühkatholizismus*, 206: "At least since F. Christian Baur decline in the sense of a historical-theological scheme has ceased to exist as a category: even in Baur's work Catholicism, as a historical phenomenon, has its own indisputable legitimacy, not superseded until the Reformation." Cf. the extensive treatment of this theme in Karl H. Neufeld, "'Frühkatholizismus,'" *ZThK* 96 (1974) 353–84.

69 Thus von Harnack: "That we know anything at all of original Christianity is entirely due to the fixing of the tradition, as found at the basis of Catholicism." If this stabilization, occasioned by Gnosticism, had not taken place, "we would in all probability know next to nothing of original Christianity today. How much we would have known may be seen from the *Shepherd of Hermas* (*History of Dogma* 2.9 n. 1).

problem experienced by primitive Christianity in identifying the visible and invisible church.[70] According to Ernst Käsemann, it was only because of the new organization forced on them by their struggle against enthusiastic movements that the Christian communities "were able to repel the assault and survive as churches of Christ."[71] The Christian communities became the early Catholic church by involving themselves with the world.[72] This was required when it became clear that they must confront history for an indeterminate length of time. The only alternative that could have been seriously considered by the developing great church would have been the ahistorical enthusiasm of the gnostic movement, and they were required by their own history to set up defenses and secure themselves against that.

Problematic tendencies in the direction of early Catholicism can be observed when and if the exercise of office suppresses the Spirit or makes the latter, in principle, an attribute of the former, when history is no longer regarded as open to the coming of the eschaton and the church makes itself an absolute institution and an end in itself, including a situation in which it regards itself in a sacramental sense as *Christus prolongatus.* A balanced judgment is required to decide if and when we are confronted by an absolute understanding of the church as institutionalized salvation, the consequence of which is that the church as a sociological entity is closed to the demands of the kerygma. The normal course of the movement of church history is a dialectic between office and Spirit, between the church as an earthly *societas* and its eschatological destiny; for both are necessary as long as the church lives in the world. Marked by this dialectic, Christian faith articulated itself anew in early Catholicism in a way corresponding to the given historical situation.

It follows from what has been said that no exact historical delimitation of "early Catholicism" can be made.[73] This is reflected in the present state of research. Definitions whose content rests on divergent criteria for differentiation lead to different sets of historical limits. Adolf von Harnack's "hellenization thesis" held that Catholicism and its dogmatic theology resulted from a marriage of Christianity and antiquity. He claimed the second and third centuries as the time period for this development.[74] For R. Sohm the break between "primitive Christianity" and "church" occurred in the conflict over the episcopal office, a dispute which is said to be documented as early as *1 Clement.*[75] When Käsemann interprets "early Catholicism" as the transition from primitive Christianity to the ancient church accomplished in conjunction with "the disappearance of the imminent expectation [of the

70 For Sohm (*Kirchenrecht,* 1.458), the question of canon law responds to "a historically existing, apparently unavoidable need arising indirectly from moral issues"; such a canon law secures "the order and teaching of the church"; it was "the power that clothed a series of self-deceptions with the force of historical necessity and, consequently, the force of victory." This need is explained as follows: "In the struggles to maintain and preserve a community life governed by custom (the administration of the Eucharist and of church property), and to uphold the original Christian truth (in conflict with Gnosticism, Montanism, and heresy), legal order was set up within the *ekklēsia* as a strong bulwark against the enemy powers" (ibid., 456).

71 Käsemann, "Paul and Early Catholicism," 247.

72 Troeltsch ("Die Soziallehren der christlichen Kirchen und Gruppen," in idem, *Gesammelte Schriften* [4 vols.; 1912–25; reprinted Tübingen: Mohr (Siebeck), 1977] 1.83ff.) interpreted this process in the sense of a narrowing of the idea of Christianity, which originally aimed at individualism and universalism. However, he saw such a narrowing as demanded by sociological necessities.

73 Schmitz (*Frühkatholizismus,* 11–13) traces the lack of clarity on this point not least to a terminological difference: "early Catholicism" means, on the one hand, the conclusion of a development toward fully formed Catholicism, which however is dubbed "old Catholicism"; on the other hand, "early Catholicism" can be used as a historical concept describing the period from the end of the first century through the second.

74 Adolf von Harnack ("The Present State of Research in Early Church History," in idem, *Ausgewählte Reden und Aufsätze* (2 vols.; Giessen: Töpelmann, 1906; reprinted in one volume; Berlin: de Gruyter, 1951) 2.229–30): "The ensuing Catholicism which became fully formed in the third century, is therefore not to be understood either on the basis of Paulinism or of Jewish Christianity, or apprehended as a compromise between the two; but the Catholic Church is rather that form of Christianity in which every element of the ancient world which Christianity could in any way take up into itself without utterly losing itself in the world was successively assimilated." Something similar is true of doctrine: "As Catholicism, from every point of view, is the result of the blending of Christianity with the ideas of antiquity, so the Catholic dogmatic . . . is Christianity conceived and formulated from the standpoint of the Greek philosophy of religion" (von Harnack, *History of Dogma* 2.13–14); cf. also Harnack's introductory lecture to the Akademie der Wissenschaften, 1890

parousia]," the question of early Catholicism is retrojected into the NT.[76]

While no explicit definition can offer an easy answer to the question about early Catholic elements in the Johannine Letters, various characteristic signs of early Catholicism, or of the beginnings of the Catholic church, can be identified.[77] First, one detects an interest in the effort to give foundation to authority and to make it secure. This appears in exemplary fashion in the pseudepigraphical writings; early Catholic theologians regard themselves in those works as vehicles of the "apostolic" tradition and attempt to make the authority of the apostle effective in their own time. The development and concretizing of this tendency led to the building up of a system of church offices and a presbyterial constitution, at the end of which stand the monarchical episcopate and a hierarchical community order. By means of the notion that the apostles existed "primarily as guarantors and mediators of the tradition, the Church's 'deposit-in-trust' . . . they come to be regarded in the same light as were the congregational officials, upon whom, next after the apostles, the responsibility for preserving the tradition rests. Hence, the notion can now arise that the apostles must have successors."[78] When the installation of πρεσβύτεροι and ἐπίσκοποι was traced to the apostles, office appeared all the more to be that which is "*constitutive of the Church.* The whole Church rests upon the office-bearers, whose office is held to go

(in *Aus der Werkstatt des Vollendeten,* 209–13, esp. 211).

75 According to Sohm (*Kirchenrecht,* 1.158–60), the purpose of *1 Clement* was "to put an end to the primitive Christian order of things in the church." From then on, the selection and ordination to the office of bishop had a legal significance, so that this letter at the end of the first century announces the beginnings of canon law. But since canon law could only have been brought forward as the divine law for the church, "the birth of canon law is equivalent to the birth of Catholicism" (ibid., 161). "The beginning of canon law is the most important event in the whole development of the church. It is obvious that other circumstances may have contributed to the birth and advancement of Catholicism. But the birth of (divine) canon law is the crucial shift that determined and made possible everything else" (ibid.).

76 Käsemann, "Paul and Early Catholicism," 237. Käsemann underscores the flexibility of the question by his statement that early Catholicism and the NT are not coextensive but overlapping. "The designation, 'sub-apostolic age,' formerly used for the last phase of the period covered by the New Testament, is inadequate, since all New Testament writings except Paul must be placed in this category. It is also imprecise, in that it provides for no distinction from what follows and no criterion for its actual content" (ibid., 237 n. 1). Marxsen differs: according to him early Catholicism is a phenomenon outside the canon, that is, the result of a particular way of dealing with canonical statements. From the results of his analysis of 2 Pet 1:19–21; Jas 2:14–26; and Matt 16:13–20, he draws the conclusion: "If a statement in an 'early Catholic' writing is binding on the basis of a 'so it is written,' that statement *becomes,* by such usage, early Catholic. But if I can interpret the same statement historically, as an aid against degeneration, going astray, and so on, then the formulation may give an impression of early Catholicism, but in fact not be such"(Willi Marxsen, *Der "Frühkatholizismus" im Neuen Testament* [Biblische Studien 21; Neukirchen: Kreis Moers, 1958] 70).

77 On this, cf. Black, "Johannine Epistles," 132. Luz ("Erwägungen," 90–91) draws another distinction when he lists as "typical characteristics of early Catholicism": (1) "deliberate reference back to the 'apostolic' era," (2) "a distinction between orthodoxy and heresy as between true and false doctrine," (3) "emphasis on ethics, which become independent," and (4) "the securing of true doctrine by the visible, official church." Schürmann ("Auf der Suche," 347–48) differs, replacing the concept "early Catholic" with "pre-Catholic," and describing this period as the epoch in which the Christ-revelation was disappearing. Within this epoch, an apostolic and a postapostolic period are distinguished; they conclude with the end of the composition of the canonical Scriptures. A further distinction is made between that which is "'pre-Catholic, always remaining normative for all churches," and nonnormative "catholicisms" and "protestantisms." Here it is clear that the final, critical instance for interpretation of Scripture (in good "Protestant" style!) is the Christ-event.

78 Bultmann, *Theology,* 2.106.

back in uninterrupted succession to the apostles (= the Twelve)."[79]

Second, an attempt was made to clarify and fix the understanding of Christian faith. In the controversies among various Christian groups and their theological ideas, a distinction developed between a true doctrine, which claimed to possess the truth, and a false doctrine, represented by apostates and heretics. The necessity for this arose not only from the differences that could be found within the communities, but also because of the influences exercised from outside individual congregations. Doctrine was authoritatively interpreted by the church's officeholders, as the appointed links in the chain of apostolic tradition.[80]

Third, one observes an interest in church unity and the consolidation of the Christian communities. In this, an effort toward a visible realization of unity existed together with the spiritual foundation adduced for it. It was expressed within the congregations when the church community, in its administration of the sacraments, increasingly took on the features of an institution, and when an ecclesial penitential institution was developed on the basis of initiatives going farther back in time.[81] In addition, it is visible in the progressive expansion of the primitive Christian confession of faith into a generally acknowledged basis for church doctrine, and the collection of the NT writings into a canon, the shaping of which was in a transitional phase in the early Catholic period, something that is documented in exemplary fashion for the second half of the second century by the Muratorian Canon.[82]

Fourth, one should observe that the primitive Christian apocalyptic eschatology was sharply modified, as is evident from the disappearance of the expectation of the parousia. More clearly than is evident in primitive Christianity, the early Catholic communities are living in an interim period. The "not yet" of eschatological anticipation retreats in favor of the emphasis on the "already" of the presence of salvation, and the way is clear for those whose intention would be to expound Christian self-understanding in overarching historical accounts.[83]

On the whole, one may say that these characteristic features are typical of the transitional period between primitive Christianity and the Catholic church. As such, they are typical of early Catholicism and can be applied as critical norms in the interpretation of the NT writings. But since a final theological evaluation of early Catholicism has not been made, it seems questionable whether one may describe writings in which such features are found as "early Catholic writings" and, by the use of this concept, avoid the critique that is still required.[84]

One should also consider that the features of early Catholicism that have been listed occur in the beginnings of the NT corpus of writings as well. The problem arises even in Paul's work, which came into existence because of a slackening in the unbroken anticipation of the parousia (1 Thess 4:13–18; 1 Cor 15:1–34; 2 Cor 5:1–5; Phil 1:23). Paul also appeals to his official authority as an apostle of Jesus Christ (Gal 1:11–12; 1 Cor 15:8–10; 2 Cor 4:1), quotes traditional creeds, and applies tradition in his preaching as the bond that unites the communities (1 Cor 11:23–26; 15:1–7; Rom 1:3–4). From this point of view it is not surprising that there are elements also in 2 and 3 John that can be understood as indicating an early Catholic tendency in both letters. Thus Siegfried Schulz points out that, for one thing, the use of ἀλήθεια and διδαχή indicate a dogmatizing and ethicizing of the Johannine dualism.[85] The presbyter is said to oppose heresy by means of a doctrine containing concrete ethical demands. In addition, 3 John 10 is said to indicate that

79 Bultmann, *Theology*, 2.107.

80 Bauer impressively demonstrated that, in all this, theological motives were intertwined with the drive for political power (*Orthodoxy and Heresy*).

81 Cf. Goldhahn-Müller, *Die Grenze der Gemeinde*.

82 See above, Introduction, pp. xxix–xxx.

83 Cf., on the one hand, Luke's historical work, and on the other hand, Irenaeus's construction of history in terms of the economy of salvation; on this, see Hans Conzelmann, *The Theology of St. Luke* (trans. Geoffrey Buswell; 1961; reprinted Philadelphia: Fortress, 1982). See also Alfred Bengsch, *Heilsgeschichte und Heilswissen* (Erfurter Theologische Studien 3; Leipzig: St. Benno, 1957) 51–163; Norbert Brox, *Offenbarung, Gnosis und gnostischer Mythos bei Irenäus von Lyon* (Salzburg: Pustet, 1966) 180–89.

84 The suggestion of Black, that one could describe an NT writing as early Catholic if it can be shown to possess a majority of the criteria for early Catholicism, is worth consideration and appears to be methodologically exact, but it ignores the problems in the concept of "early Catholicism" itself, and it leaves out of account the question of the overall theological tendency of a given NT writing.

85 Siegfried Schulz, *Die Mitte der Schrift* (Stuttgart/Berlin: Kreuz, 1976) 248–49. For the question of early Catholic features in the Johannine Letters, see esp. Black, "Johannine Epistles," 131–58.

the communities behind the Johannine Letters live under an episcopal constitution that includes canon law and a praxis of excommunication. But an analogy to the exclusion of community members that is reported of Diotrephes can be demonstrated for Paul also (1 Cor 5:1–5; 2 Cor 2:6; 7:11). It is also problematic to describe the relationship between the presbyter and Diotrephes as one of opposition between Spirit and office. In that case, it would not be 3 John but evidently the community of Diotrephes that would have to be characterized as "early Catholic," for apparently the presbyter and Diotrephes belong to different communities. Moreover, there is no evidence at all in 3 John for the supposition that Diotrephes exercised an authority of office that was legalized by the principle of succession. Instead, the relationships are not yet constitutionally fixed. This is especially evident from the fact that itinerant preachers visit the communities as emissaries of the presbyter (3 John 3–8). From an "early Catholic" presbyter one would expect a clearer reference to the apostolicity of his tradition and its claim to universal validity as legally secured by office and succession than is in fact the case. It is therefore inappropriate to see early Catholic tendencies in 2 and 3 John on the basis of a supposed "structure of offices."

Does the relationship between ἀλήθεια and διδαχή, however, permit one to recognize early Catholic thinking here? It cannot be denied that the word ἀλήθεια, which is used with special frequency in 2 and 3 John (2 John 1–4; 3 John 1, 3–4, 8, 12), is connected in its meaning to the concept of διδαχή. While the latter is not described as "right" or "true" teaching and is not opposed to a "false doctrine," διδαχή has a clear function: it marks the division between heresy and church. However, this task of theological teaching was not discovered for the first time in the early Catholic period. Even for Paul, "teaching" has a double meaning: Διδαχή is the apostolic admonition to the community, and the community is such only in obedient listening to the word as taught (1 Cor 14:6, 26; cf. Rom 6:17). This kind of theologically considered instruction is a *conditio sine qua non* for the existence and endurance of the church. It is part of the earliest beginnings of Christianity. In addition, διδαχή has the task of distinguishing between the true community of Christ and the deceivers, between true proclamation of the gospel and false teaching. This distinction is also found as early as the letters of Paul (Rom 16:17; cf. Gal 1:12). As regards the concept and function of "teaching," the standpoint of the Johannine letters is not far removed from what one encounters in the Pauline writings.

Finally, it cannot be shown in the Johannine Letters that an exclusive claim to truth is made on behalf of the teaching, and that orthodox doctrine has become the sole criterion for theology. Instead, the concept of διδαχή describes the "teaching of Christ" (2 John 9). It is subject to no one's control and is not exhausted within the sphere of the church, since it is christologically and not ecclesiologically oriented. This teaching is concerned with truth; for those who abide in the teaching of Christ (2 John 9) know the truth, and the truth remains in them (2 John 2–3), just as also the encounter between the author and his fellow Christians is an encounter of love in truth (2 John 1). This ἀλήθεια is like a space that surrounds and encompasses Christian existence, and remains identical with it as long as it remains secure within this sphere. Hence, it can be said, in an almost mystical formulation, not only that we are "in the truth," but also that the truth abides "in us" (2 John 2; cf. Gal 2:20).

Conclusion of the Letter

12 **Although I have much to write to you, I would rather not use paper and ink; instead I hope to come to you and talk with you face to face, so that our joy may be complete. 13/ The children of your elect sister send you their greetings.**

■ **12-13** In early Christian literature the conclusion of a letter usually contains two elements: first greetings, and then a blessing. There is no wish-formula here, although one was added by some secondary manuscript witnesses.[1] Instead, a brief greeting concludes the letter (v. 13). The image of the community as a *κυρία ἐκλεκτή* (v. 1) is recapitulated, but now with reference to the presbyter's community as senders of the letter. That community is the "elect sister" of the addressees; its members, as her children,[2] send greetings.

This is preceded in v. 12 by the presbyter's announcement of his coming. This is also in accordance with letter style, but is not merely a customary literary flourish: it is to be understood as the expression of the author's real intention to make the journey.[3] The presbyter hopes to achieve more through personal encounter and oral communication than can be obtained by a letter. The announced visit is undoubtedly intended to give force to the warning against false teachers. This at the same time means that the relationship between the community being addressed, on the one hand, and the presbyter and his community, on the other hand, is to be strengthened. The *ἵνα* clause expresses this intention more concretely: "so that our joy may be complete." This formula was not invented by the presbyter. It is also found in the rabbinic writings,[4] and it makes clear that the author's Christianity is rooted not only in the Hellenistic sphere but in Judaism as well. The formulation at this point is presupposed by 1 John 1:4; it is also used in the Fourth Gospel, both as a description of Jesus' person (3:29; 15:11) and for the state of discipleship (15:11; 16:24; 17:13). "Complete joy" in Jewish tradition is the joy of the messianic age.[5] In a Christian sense, the expression describes the eschatological assurance of salvation, which is said to be "fulfilled," "perfected," "complete"[6]—not that an imperfect earthly joy must be consciously perceived as its opposite. The community lives in this joy as long as it lives in truth and love and abides in the teaching of Christ. Therefore, it has nothing fundamentally new to expect from the presbyter's coming, but it appears to be his intention to strengthen the community in this, its eschatological existence.

1 Thus in a number of minuscules, and in the Ethiopian, Armenian, and Latin (Vulgate) translations. The Syrian Harclensis adds the petition for grace in asterisks to show that it is an addition; it is also attested by Pseudo-Oecumenius (10th century) and Theophylact (11th century). Only an *ἀμήν* was added in 𝔐 and in some Vulgate manuscripts and the Syrian Philoxeniana.

2 The *τέκνα* are the members of the community; so also in 2 John 1, 4; 3 John 4; otherwise nowhere in the Johannine writings; cf. instead *τὰ τέκνα (τοῦ) θεοῦ*: 1 John 3:1–2, 10; 5:2; John 1:12; 11:52; and *τεκνία*: 1 John 2:1, 12, 28; 3:7, 18; 4:4; 5:21; John 13:33.

3 It thus corresponds to Rom 15:32; 1 Cor 16:5–9; 2 Cor 13:10.

4 Cf. the examples in Str-B 2.566. It is true that the reading *ὑμῶν* is attested by codices Alexandrinus and Vaticanus, as well as some minuscules and Latin manuscripts, but there can be no doubt that it represents a smoothing of the more difficult *ἡμῶν*.

5 Cf. Str-B 2.429–30.

6 The active of the verb *πληροῦν* as "complete," "fulfill," "make whole" with accusative object is found in Matt 5:17 (*τὸν νόμον*); the combination with *χαρά* is, apart from the Johannine passages listed above, found in the NT only in Phil 2:2. The passive in the sense of "full," "fulfilled," "completed," is also in 2 Cor 10:6 (of *ὑπακοή*); with *τέλειοι* in Col 4:12 *v.l.*

3 John

The situation of 3 John, especially the relationship between the presbyter and Diotrephes within the context of the Johannine school tradition, can be clarified by a comparison with 2 John. What is significant is, first of all, the difference in the addressees. While 2 John is a community letter in which the author addresses particular problems in the situation of the community, especially that of false teachers, 3 John, in contrast, is a personal writing directed to an otherwise unknown Gaius and containing, in particular, a recommendation for Demetrius (3 John 12).

In spite of the difference in the addressees, the kinship between the two letters is remarkably close. Both retain the same Johannine language and style. The terms ἀλήθεια, τέκνα, and ἀγάπη occur in both letters, and the word ἐξέρχεσθαι is used for the false teachers or the itinerant community members (2 John 7; 3 John 7). The same phrases appear: ἐχάρην λίαν (2 John 4; 3 John 3); ἐν ἀληθείᾳ περιπατεῖν (2 John 4, 3 John 3–4); there are word-for-word correspondences in the prescripts (2 John 1; 3 John 1) and in the conclusions (2 John 12; 3 John 13–14). Not least, there is the same sender (ὁ πρεσβύτερος). The situation in which the two letters are written is also similar. Here, as in 2 John, the presbyter announces his coming. In both letters it is said of the addressees that they "walk in the truth" (2 John 4; 3 John 3–4), and an independent charismatic lifestyle or the activity of itinerant preachers is presupposed: both for the false teachers (2 John 7) and with regard to the "brothers and sisters" [*NRSV:* "friends"] who are sent out (3 John 5–10). From all this one may draw the same conclusion as is recorded in the works of Eusebius and Jerome:[1] the two smaller Johannine letters were written by the same author. The great similarity in the form of the letters is explained by the fact that the two are quite close in time. The chronological sequence is: 2 John, 3 John, as is apparent from 3 John 9 (ἔγραψά τι). The community letter the presbyter mentions is evidently 2 John.

It cannot be objected against this conclusion that the letter presupposed by 3 John 9 was a letter of recommendation for the sisters and brothers and that 2 John is not that kind of letter.[2] Rather, what is clear from 3 John 9 is only that the author has already written to the community once before. The immediate context does not refer to the brothers and sisters who are recommended to the community of Diotrephes, but to the fact that "we," that is, the presbyter and the group he represents, have been rejected by Diotrephes (3 John 10a). This can be applied, without

1 Cf. Eusebius *Hist. eccl.* 3.39.4–5; Jerome *De viris illustribus* 9.18. On this, see also Wikenhauser and Schmid, *Einleitung*, 630 (Eusebius distinguishes between the author of 1 John, who is the apostle and evangelist John, and the author of 2 and 3 John, who is John the presbyter). A common authorship for the three Johannine Letters is posited by Schnackenburg, *Epistles*, 268–69; Brown, *Epistles*, 16; and as early as Theodor Zahn, "Apostel und Apostelschüler in der Provinz Asien," in idem, *Forschungen zur Geschichte des neutestamentlichen Kanons* (Erlangen/Leipzig: Deichert, 1900) 6/1.182 (positing identity also with the author of the Fourth Gospel); also Wilhelm Michaelis, *Einleitung in das Neue Testament* (2d ed.; Berne: Haller, 1954) 300. Critical on this point are Haenchen, "Neuere Literatur," 283–86; Alfred Loisy, *Le quatrième Évangile* (2d ed.; Paris: Nourry, 1921) 8–9; Karl P. Donfried, "Ecclesiastical Authority in 2–3 John," in Marinus de Jonge, ed., *L'Évangile de Jean* (BEThL 44; Gembloux: Duculot, 1977) 325–33.

2 So, among others, Bultmann, *Epistles*, 100; Schnackenburg, *Epistles*, 296; Schunack, *Briefe*, 120; Wengst, *Brief*, 248 (with reference to Acts 18:27); Adolf von Harnack, *Über den dritten Johannesbrief* (TU 15/3b; Leipzig: Hinrichs, 1897) 11; Haenchen, "Neuere Literatur," 307; Wendt, *Johannesbriefe*, 26: according to him, Diotrephes is to be equated with the "'leader' already referred to by the letter-writer in II.9." An identification of the letter mentioned in 3 John 9 with 2 John is also inferred by B. Vernon Bartlet, "The Historical Setting of the Second and Third Epistles of St. John," *JTS* 6 (1905) 204–16; although Marshall (*Epistles*, 88) objects that in that case Diotrephes must have sympathized with the false teachers, and that this is not evident from 3 John, the brief note in 3 John 9–11 does not allow one to infer the contrary, either.

difficulty, to a previous denial of the presbyter's claim to authority, like that advanced in 2 John. The rejection of the sisters and brothers who have been sent out is only secondarily related to this, to the extent that the emissaries, along with the letter, represent a further demonstration of the presbyter's intention to exercise authority.

Beginning of the Letter

1 **The elder to the beloved Gaius, whom I love in (the) truth. 2/ Beloved, I pray [first of all] that all may go well with you and that you may be in good health, just as it is well with your soul.**

■ **1** The letter begins with a prescript. As was customary in both secular and Christian letter forms, first the sender (*ὁ πρεσβύτερος*) is named, then the addressee. The letter is directed to an otherwise unknown Gaius.[1] That he is called "beloved" indicates that he is a fellow Christian with whom the author is on good terms.[2] In what follows, Gaius's behavior is praised (vv. 3–4), in particular his hospitality to traveling sisters and brothers (vv. 5–6), and he is requested to give further support (v. 6b). It is possible that Gaius had been converted by the presbyter,[3] or was baptized by him, since he is counted among *τὰ ἐμὰ τέκνα*.[4]

1 Gaius (older form: Caius) is a common Roman first name, often attested in Greek as well (e.g., Diodorus Siculus *Bibliotheca historica* 11.60.1; 13.104.1; 19.73.1; cf. BAGD 149). It is thus not surprising that in the NT period Christians bearing this name often appear: 1 Cor 1:14 (a member of the Corinthian community baptized by Paul; Paul was living at his house when he wrote Romans 16: see Rom 16:23); according to Acts 19:29 a Macedonian Christian named Gaius accompanied Paul to Ephesus; Acts 20:4 speaks of a companion of Paul, "Gaius from Derbe," who travels with the apostle through Macedonia; cf. also the name of the man who copied the *Martyrdom of Polycarp* (22.2). Attempts to identify one of those named with the addressee of 3 John are too hypothetical (against John Chapman, "The Historical Setting of the Second and Third Epistles of St. John," *JTS* 5 [1904] 366). The later tradition reports that Gaius was appointed bishop at Pergamon by the apostle John (*Ap. Const.* 7.46.9); according to Origen, Gaius was the first bishop of Thessalonica (*Comm. in Rom.* 16:23 [10.41]).

2 The adjective *ἀγαπητός* is rare in the Johannine writings; in this letter it is used as an absolute form of address (vv. 2, 5, 11); similarly, the plural appears in 1 John as address to the readers (2:7; 3:2, 21; 4:1, 7, 11; cf. Jude 3; 1 Pet 2:11; 4:12; 2 Pet 3:1, 8, 14, 17, and frequently). As a designation for a fellow Christian, it is also found in Phlm 16 (*ἀδελφὸν ἀγαπητόν, . . . καὶ ἐν σαρκὶ καὶ ἐν κυρίῳ*, "a beloved brother, . . . both in the flesh and in the Lord"); similarly in Col 4:7; Eph 6:21, and frequently elsewhere; in the prescript of letters also in Phlm 1 and 2 Tim 1:2 (singular); Rom 1:7 (plural); beyond this, in general application to the Christian community (cf. 1 Thess 2:8; 1 Cor 10:14; 15:58; 2 Cor 7:1; 12:19; Phil 2:12; 4:1; Heb 6:9). In the Johannine writings, this word stem has a close relationship both to the idea of the revelation of God's *agapē* toward the community and the world (John 3:16; 1 John 3:16) and to the commandment of mutual love (see above at 2 John 4–6), and is based on these. The connection is enunciated in 1 John 4:11, and is established in 3 John 1 by the author's addition of the phrase *ὃν ἐγὼ ἀγαπῶ ἐν ἀληθείᾳ*. Bultmann differs (*Epistles*, 95–96), denying any theological implication of *ἀλήθεια* (in combination with *ἀγαπῶ*) in this passage and ascribing to the latter the meaning "in reality, authentically." In that case *ἀγαπητός* would simply be "a common characterization and form of address among Christians"; Lieu writes similarly (*Epistles*, 102). But it is difficult to suppose that the presbyter's choice to express himself by juxtaposing the key Johannine concepts of "truth" and "love" was accidental (cf. above at 2 John 1).

3 Thus Bultmann, *Epistles*, 95. One can refer to Paul's usage for the thesis that Gaius was converted to the Christian faith by the presbyter: 1 Cor 4:14 (*τέκνα μου ἀγαπητά*); Gal 4:19; Phlm 10; Smalley, *1, 2, 3 John*, 348. It is difficult to object (with Brown, *Epistles*, 707) that it appears from v. 3 "that the Presbyter has never met Gaius," and that in Johannine thought it is God, not a human preacher, who brings forth Christians "as His children" (John 1:13; 3:3, 5). This is an overinterpretation of v. 3, and the idea of being born of God is unknown to the shorter Johannine letters.

4 3 John 4. The personal pronoun *ἐμός* is found in the Johannine Letters only here, but frequently in the Fourth Gospel (e.g., John 5:30: *ἡ κρίσις ἡ ἐμὴ δικαία ἐστίν*), although this way of speaking cannot be explained as something peculiar to the Koine of Asia

The relationship between Gaius and the community of Diotrephes can be reconstructed to some degree. The addressee is apparently not a member of that community, at least not of its clerical component; otherwise the presbyter would not have needed to tell him of a previous letter and its rejection by Diotrephes (vv. 9–10). But there is some relationship between Gaius and that community, for the presbyter wishes, by means of this letter, to assure himself of Gaius's support in order to gain a foothold in the community of Diotrephes in spite of the difficulties that have arisen (vv. 8–10). Presumably Demetrius (v. 12) is the middleman between the presbyter and the community; he is to receive Gaius's particular support. The expected visit of the presbyter, which will bring him to Gaius (vv. 13–14), is also intended, in the wake of the first, unsuccessful attempt, to be part of another try at securing influence over the community of Diotrephes.[5]

■ **2** This verse replaces the blessing[6] that follows the prescript in other early Christian letters; but differently from the Pauline Letters, for example (see Phil 1:2), the linguistic usage[7] corresponds to that in secular Greek letters.[8] This accords with the Hellenistic Greek character of 2 John and is a further argument for the identity of the presbyter as the author of both letters. The word *ψυχή* can also be explained on the basis of Greek usage: differently from the other Johannine writings, where the expression has an OT and Jewish flavor and should be translated "life,"[9] here, although an anthropological body-soul dualism is not expressed in so many words, it is

---

Minor: it "does not have the same usage in other literature from Asia Minor from that period (Revelation, *Acts of Paul*)" (Eckhard Plümacher, "*ἐμός*," *EDNT* 1 [1990] 444). The use of *ἐμός* is, rather, a characteristic of the Revealer's speech in the Fourth Gospel (cf. also John 3:29; 4:34; 5:47, and frequently). The prior placement of the personal pronoun does not necessarily imply a distinction from other "children," but expresses a close relationship (cf. Schnackenburg, *Epistles*, 293; BDR § 285 n. 1); the form *τέκνα* (in contrast to the address with *τεκνία* in 1 John 2:1, 12, 28, and frequently elsewhere) is further evidence of the independence of the lesser Johannine letters (cf. 2 John 1, 4, 13).

5 It is possible, on the basis of the almost identical formulations in 2 John 12 and 3 John 13, that 3 John was written soon after 2 John. This was apparently done as soon as the failure of 2 John to achieve its intended effect was reported to the presbyter by the brothers and sisters who also attested to Gaius's favorable attitude (3 John 3).

6 The verb *εὔχομαι* can be translated "pray" (as in the majority of cases in the NT: 2 Cor 13:7–9; Rom 9:3; Acts 26:29) or "wish," "desire"—the latter meaning is often constructed with accusative plus infinitive: Acts 27:29 ("they wished for day to come" [*RSV* and *NRSV:* "prayed"]); so also in Greek private letters; cf. the almost word-for-word equivalent in P. Oxy. 2.292, 11–12 (*πρὸ δὲ πάντων ὑγιαίνειν σε εὔχομαι*). In light of these parallel texts, one should not think here of a prayer for the sick (as in Jas 5:15), and it is questionable whether the idea of a petitionary prayer is implied, for in that case one would expect a dative construction ("to God"); moreover, the verb *προσεύχομαι* is usual in such cases (cf. esp. in the proemium of NT letters: Phil 1:9; Col 1:3, 9; 2 Thess 1:11). *Περὶ πάντων* can be translated in two ways: (1) "in all parts" (so Plato *Gorgias* 467D); (2) more common is the expression "first of all," or "primarily" (Homer *Il.* 1.287; 21.566; cf. BDR § 229 n. 4).

7 The verb *εὐοδοῦσθαι* is attested in classical Greek (since Sophocles, Herodotus, and also in the papyri and the LXX); the passive has an indeterminate sense (thus not: "being led on a good path") and describes "making good progress," "being well." In the NT it is also in Rom 1:10 and 1 Cor 16:2 in the sense of "succeed." The verb *ὑγιαίνειν* is also good Greek ("be healthy"); it is frequently found in the greetings section of letters: *BGU* 27, 38, 423, 846; *Ep. Arist.* 41; for bodily health also Luke 5:31; Matt 8:13 *v.l.* The Fourth Gospel uses the adjective *ὑγιής* (John 5:6, 9, 14–15; 7:23). In this passage one should not think of the metaphorical sense that appears in the Pastorals, i.e., the "right," sound teaching (1 Tim 1:10; 2 Tim 4:3; Titus 1:9; 2:1); this corresponds to Titus 1:13; 2:2 (*ὑγιαίνειν* [*ἐν*] *τῇ πίστει*).

8 Cf. Funk, "Form and Structure," esp. 425; the wish that the recipient may be well, usual in secular Greek letters (thus also P. Oxy. 14.1680) is not attested elsewhere in the NT or in the Apostolic Fathers.

9 1 John 3:16; John 10:11; 13:37–38; 15:13, and frequently; cf. Eduard Schweizer, "*ψυχή* D: The New Testament," *TDNT* 9 (1974) 642; for the OT and Jewish background, see Edmund Jacob, "*ψυχή*: Anthropology of the Old Testament," *TDNT* 9 (1974) 617–31; Eduard Lohse, "נפש/*ψυχή* in Palestinian Judaism," *TDNT* 9 (1974) 635–37.

nevertheless clear that ψυχή is the "seat and center of life that transcends the earthly"[10] and stands over against the earthly sphere in the relationship of the internal to the external. The wish that it may go well with Gaius in the external sense of bodily health as well is combined with the assertion that it is already well with his soul, because he lives in truth and love.[11]

10 BAGD 893 (with references to Plato *Phaedo* 28, 80AB; Pausanius *Description of Greece* 4.32.4: ἀθάνατός ἐστιν ἀνθρώπου ψυχή: "the soul of man is immortal"); for the NT one can consider this meaning when the subject is the saving of the "soul" by the word of Jesus (John 12:25), by conversion (Jas 5:20), or by faith (1 Pet 1:9; Heb 10:39); cf. also Mark 8:35 par. This is said in disagreement with Schnackenburg, *Epistles*, 292, who wishes to refer this and other passages to the "salvation of the whole person"; but his qualifying phrase "in the totality of his or her being" shows that ψυχή is contrasted with corporeality, and therefore does not refer to the whole human being. Eduard Schweizer is more correct ("ψυχή D: The New Testament," *TDNT* 9 [1974] 651) in calling it "the true life before God." This corresponds to the Hellenistic Greek idea "of the soul as an immaterial or at least invisible essential core of [the human being] that can be thought of as distinct from the body. It gives worth and duration to the human self beyond the limits of physical existence" (Albert Dihle, "ψυχή," *TDNT* 9 [1974] 632).

11 The context suggests that ψυχή is not to be understood simply as "noble spirit" (Brown, *Epistles*, 704), but has the theological content sketched above. The presbyter loves Gaius "in truth" (v. 1), and the sisters and brothers attest that Gaius "walk[s] in the truth" (v. 3); this is heavily underscored by the assertion that "it is well with your soul." There is a parallel in Philo *Rer. div. her.* 285, where a "calm, unclouded life, a life of true bliss and happiness" (γαληνὸν καὶ εὔδιον κτησάμενος βίον, εὐδαίμον' ὡς ἀληθῶς καὶ μακάριον) is described. This is to be found when "there is welfare (εὐοδῇ) outside us (τὰ ἐκτός), welfare in the body (τὰ σώματος), welfare in the soul (τὰ ψυχῆς), the first bringing ease of circumstance and good repute, the second health (πρὸς ὑγίειαν) and strength, the third delight in virtues." The close relationship of this verse to 2 John is especially obvious in the contrasting of σῶμα and ψυχή and in the style of the expressions. The conjunction καθώς in the Johannine Letters usually introduces a comparison that at the same time has an explanatory function: 2 John 4, 6; 1 John 2:6, 18, 27; 3:3, 7, 23; 4:17, and frequently. It is different in 3 John 3, where καθώς means the same as ὡς after verbs of saying and introduces indirect discourse; cf. Acts 15:14; BAGD 391. For the usage especially in the Fourth Gospel, see Brown, *Epistles*, 262–63.

Praise of Gaius

3 **I was overjoyed when some of the brothers
and sisters arrived and testified to your
faithfulness to the truth [or: your being in
the truth; *RSV:* the truth of your life],
namely how you walk in (the) truth. 4/ I
have no greater joy than this, to hear that
my children are walking in the truth. 5/
Beloved, you do faithfully whatever you
do for the brothers and sisters, even
though they are [or: those who are]
strangers to you; 6/ they have testified to
your love before the church. You will do
well to send them on in a manner worthy
of God; 7/ for they began their journey for
the sake of Christ [Greek: for the Name],
accepting no support from nonbelievers.
8/ Therefore we ought to support [or:
welcome] such people, so that we may
become coworkers with the truth.**

■ **3–8** The presbyter has learned from otherwise unnamed "brothers and sisters" that Gaius had welcomed them. The "truth" (ἀλήθεια) in which Gaius is so exemplary is thus a matter not only of right doctrine but equally of right action.[1] This action is the realization of *agapē*, affection and care for fellow Christians.[2] It is, of course, not merely "simple human sympathy"; rather, such activity is carried out within the realm of truth. Ethical concern for the neighbor cannot be severed from its theoretical basis, which is community with God and knowledge of God "in the truth" (cf. v. 11: ἐκ θεοῦ; 2 John 1–3).

That the "truth" practiced is made concrete in "love" is attested by the Christian strangers[3] who had an oppor-

---

1 Regarding the construction μαρτυρούντων σου τῇ ἀληθείᾳ: the verb μαρτυρεῖν is used with the dative of the thing to which testimony is given (cf. John 5:33: "testify to the truth"). BAGD 492: "testify to the truth of you(r way of life)"; but this yields a tautology with the end of v. 3 ("how you walk in the truth") and the end of v. 4, where the "imperative" is implicit, whereas here the thought expressed is intended more in an ontological, indicative sense. Hermann Menge ethicizes: "because of your truthfulness" (in idem, *Die Heilige Schrift des Alten und Neuen Testaments* [Stuttgart: Württembergische Bibelanstalt, 1949] 384).

2 The expression πιστὸν ποιεῖς is an indicative paraphrase of Gaius's behavior (against Bultmann, *Epistles*, 98, who reads v. 5 as an admonition); πιστός appears three times in the Johannine corpus: of the "faithful and just" God who is ready to forgive (1 John 1:9); of the doubting, therefore not "believing," Thomas (John 20:27); and 3 John 5. Here the adverbial accusative refers to the actions of the Christian Gaius, and does not retain the meaning of "believing"; one should rather think of a translation like "faithful." This corresponds to the formula καλῶς ποιήσεις (v. 6b; cf. Phil 4:14; Jas 2:8, 19; Acts 10:33; P. Oxy. 1.119, 11). This frequently appears in Greek letters as the introduction to a request; hence the praise in v. 5, which goes back as far as v. 3 (cf. 2 John 4), may represent the immediate background to the request in v. 6b; see Funk, "Form and Structure," 427. Compare Ignatius's praise of the Smyrnaeans (10.1): "It was good of you [or: you did well] (καλῶς ἐποιήσατε) to welcome (ὑποδεξάμενοι) Philo and Rheus Agathopus as deacons of the Christ God. They accompanied me in God's cause."

3 Καὶ τοῦτο ("and even")—the reading εἰς τοὺς (P 𝔐) is an accommodation to the following ξένους—takes up the relative pronoun and expresses an intensification: Gaius has shown himself hospitable even to sisters and brothers who are strangers to him. The clause confirms that the emissaries sent by the presbyter appeared as itinerant teachers or preachers who visited unfamiliar communities in order to spread the presbyter's message; they are contrasted with the traveling "deceivers" who contradict the διδαχή of Christ (2 John 7, 9).

tunity to praise Gaius's Christian way of life "before the church" (v. 6). Ἐκκλησία appears in the Johannine writings only here and in vv. 9–10. It always means the local congregation or its assembly, not the church as a whole; this corresponds to 2 John 1 (κυρίᾳ) and 2 John 13 (ἀδελφῆς), where the presbyter refers to a local community. The author is probably thinking not of the community of Diotrephes, even though it will be the subject in vv. 9–10, but of that of the presbyter, for v. 3 has already spoken of the return of the travelers and their witness, which occasioned the presbyter's joy.

Gaius's *agapē,* as practiced toward the Christian strangers and attested before the presbyter's community, consists in προπέμπειν, that is, assisting, outfitting, and sending forth the brothers and sisters on their journey.[4] The presbyter expresses a hope that Gaius will also continue to act this way in the future.[5] Such behavior is "worthy of God."[6] The following causal clause (v. 7a: γάρ) explains why Gaius's action is fitting and worthy of God. It consists in the support of emissaries who have gone out "for the Name." In the thinking of the ancients, ὄνομα and the person it represents, as well as that person's cause, are inseparable. With the "name"—undoubtedly this means the name of Jesus Christ—the thing it represents is also present.[7] The cause of Jesus Christ, which the sisters and brothers serve, forbids the itinerant preachers to depend on the "Gentiles" for their sustenance.[8] The Christian community, because it was founded on "the truth," is different from all other religions; it is—to use the words of the author of the *Kerygma Petrou*—a "third race" alongside the Jews and Gentiles.[9] It preserves its independence in part by the fact that its missionaries are cared for by their fellow Christians.[10] The situation has advanced beyond that of

4 This is the only appearance of this word in the Johannine corpus; it is also found in the same sense in Titus 3:13 (combined with σπουδαίως); 1 Cor 16:11 (with accusative); in the passive: Acts 15:3; 2 Cor 1:16; Rom 15:24; the more general sense of "escort" is found in Acts 20:38 and 21:5. The combination of an aorist participle with a future indicative is striking, since the aorist properly describes what must have preceded the future action; however, on the basis of papyrus findings it can be shown that an aorist form can indicate a simultaneous action (cf. Brooke, *Epistles,* 185); possibly the aorist also emphasizes the confident expectation of the writer, as if Gaius's assistance is already as good as given (Brown, *Epistles,* 711). The reading ποιήσας προπέμψεις (Codex C) exchanges the endings without simplifying the grammatical construction.

5 The expression καλῶς ποιεῖν in the sense of "do right," "act rightly" is also in 1 Cor 7:37–38; Acts 10:33; Phil 4:14; Jas 2:8; 2 Pet 1:19; Ignatius *Smyrn.* 10.1; *Ps.-Clem. Ep.* 3.3; cf. *Ps.-Clem. Hom.* 1.16.2; 8.10.1; 11.25.2; 31.1; 33.4; 15.2.4; this serves to recapitulate the preceding πιστὸν ποιεῖς (v. 5a).

6 The adverb ἀξίως with genitive of the person also occurs in 1 Thess 2:12 (τοῦ θεοῦ); Col. 1:10 (τοῦ κυρίου).

7 It is also found in combination with ὑπέρ in Acts 5:41; 9:16; 15:26; 21:13; cf. in the same line 1 John 2:12; 3:23; 5:13.

8 Ἐθνικός appears in the NT only here (the variant ἐθνῶν is apparently a secondary smoothing) and at Matt 5:47; 6:7; 18:17. There the "Gentiles," with the tax collectors, are identical with unconverted people, that is, non-Christians. The author of the *Didache* has another situation in mind in warning against "false prophets" who misuse their position for their own advantage, in order to enrich themselves at the expense of the Christian community (cf. *Did.* 11.3—12.5). In our text the traveling brothers and sisters do not appear as itinerant philosophers or begging priests who accept pay from anyone for their services (cf. Schnackenburg, *Epistles,* 295–96), but as missionaries who rely on the Christian communities and thus achieve freedom for their preaching, not being forced to rely on unbelievers.

9 *Kerygma Petrou* 2 (ἡμεῖς δὲ οἱ καινῶς αὐτὸν τρίτῳ γένει σεβόμενοι Χριστιανοί: "But we are Christians, who as a third race worship him in a new way"); cf. *Diogn.* 1 (καινὸν τοῦτο γένος: "this new race"); Adolf von Harnack, *The Expansion of Christianity in the First Three Centuries* (2 vols.; trans. and ed. James Moffat; Freeport: Books for Libraries Press, 1972) 2.300–352.

10 3 John 8. The verb ὑπολαμβάνειν (*v.l.* ἀπολαμβάνειν: "receive"; cf. 2 John 8) is frequently used in a metaphorical sense in the NT: "suppose," "infer" (Luke 7:43; Acts 2:15); also for "reply" (Luke 10:30); however, the realistic meaning also occurs, as in the present passage and in Acts 1:9 (a cloud "received him"). It is possible that a play on words is intended, with λαμβάνοντες (3 John 7); cf. similarly Acts 1:8–9. In this regard cf. Matt 10:10 ("laborers deserve their food") par. Luke 10:7 ("their wages"); also 1 Tim 5:18; *Did.* 13.1. The ascetic lifestyle of the apostle

the early days of Christianity. One may suppose that Christian communities are widely distributed throughout the country and can represent bases of support for the itinerant preachers. The Christian missionaries see themselves as distinct from the itinerant gentile philosophers.[11] They do not teach for their own benefit, but for the sake of the truth.[12] Therefore, they also lay claim to brotherly and sisterly love, all the more[13] because all Christians are obligated to work together on behalf of the truth.[14]

Paul, who did not wish to be a burden to anyone and supported himself by the work of his own hands (1 Cor 4:12; 9:18; 2 Cor 11:7), did not obviate, even in Paul's own thinking, the fundamental principle of primitive Christianity that, according to the Lord's own teaching, "those who proclaim the gospel should get their living by the gospel" (1 Cor 9:14).

11 This self-understanding is expressed in the demonstrative pronoun *οἱ τοιοῦτοι* ("such people," "people of that kind"). It refers to the preceding sentence and designates the sisters and brothers who refuse to accept support from Gentiles and allow themselves to be aided only by Christian communities (v. 7).

12 Cf. *Did.* 11.6 (*ἐὰν δὲ ἀργύριον αἰτῇ ψευδοπροφήτης ἐστί*: "if he asks for money, he is a false prophet") and 11.10 (*πᾶς προφήτης διδάσκων τὴν ἀλήθειαν*: "every [true] prophet teaches the truth").

13 The particle *οὖν* joins v. 8 to v. 7 and indicates the drawing of a conclusion. From the exemplary missionary activity of the sisters and brothers (v. 7) follows the Christian obligation (v. 8): *οὖν* occurs 194 times in the Fourth Gospel, but in the Johannine Letters only at 3 John 8, and in the secondary readings in 1 John 2:24 and 4:19; on this, see Smalley, *1, 2, 3 John*, 352; BDR § 451, 1. Dodd questioned, on the basis of this very different attestation, whether the Fourth Gospel and the Johannine Letters could have had the same author ("The First Epistle of John and the Fourth Gospel," *BJRL* 21 [1937] 129–56). One can scarcely object that the Gospel is a narrative text and that this particle occurs most frequently in the "gospel" genre (so Brown, *Epistles*, 23), for *οὖν* is also common in the Pauline Letters (esp. Romans), while it is rare in the Gospel of Mark.

14 Verse 8b: *ἵνα συνεργοὶ γινώμεθα τῇ ἀληθείᾳ*. The verb *γίνεσθαι* ("become") often has the meaning of *εἶναι* ("be"), and can be so understood here: "so that we may be coworkers with [or: for] the truth," that is "show ourselves to be" such (thus Bultmann, *Epistles*, 99; Schnackenburg, *Epistles*, 296). That means: we should bring to fruition what we in fact are, incorporated into the sphere of truth which is God's reality. However, *γίνεσθαι* can also have an independent meaning, as in 2 John 12 ("arrive," "come" to you; this corresponds to 1 John 2:18: "many antichrists have come"); also in the Fourth Gospel: becoming disciples (John 9:27; 15:8); becoming children of God (1:12); becoming blind (9:39); becoming healthy (5:6, 9), becoming children of the light (12:36). The word may be used to express a clear opposition, e.g., in John 16:20: "your pain will turn into joy." If one begins with the idea of "becoming," the emphasis lies on the unfinished state of Christian existence, and the indicative of being incorporated into the sphere of the truth is not understood as perfected. There is a further emphasis on the necessary activity of Christians: cooperation with the truth is a goal (*ἵνα*!) set as an obligation for every individual Christian, just as v. 8a expressed an obligation with *ὀφείλειν* (cf. also 1 John 2:6). For the expression *συνεργοὶ τῇ ἀληθείᾳ* cf. *Ps.-Clem. Hom.* 17.19.7 (*τῇ ἀληθείᾳ συνεργῆται*). The word *ἀλήθεια* describes the revealed reality of God in which the human being can share, or in which he or she can exist (cf. *σου* in v. 3). When the presbyter tells the addressee, Gaius, that he "loves [him] in (the) truth," their mutual relationship is determined by God's reality (v. 1). Verse 12 shows that the concept can be personified. This can also be inferred in v. 8, and translated: "so that we may become coworkers with the truth" (the dative corresponds to the preceding *συν[εργοί]*). For locating the presbyter historically it is not without importance that Papias, in his report on the presbyter tradition in Asia Minor, also uses the concept of truth in a personified sense (parallel to *κυρίου*): see Eusebius *Hist. eccl.* 3.39.3: *ἀπ' αὐτῆς παραγινομένας [ἐντολὰς] τῆς ἀληθείας*: "[the commandments] coming to us from truth [her]self." "Truth" is not identical with Christian preaching, even though the context might suggest that interpretation. Instead, the language allows one to infer a personal character. One need not decide whether the author is thinking of God, Christ, or the Spirit (thus Brown, *Epistles*, 715; de la Potterie, *La vérité*, "spirit of truth"), since in any case it is a question of commitment on behalf of God's reality, which is understood as "truth."

Warning against Diotrephes

9 **I have written something to the church; but Diotrephes, who likes to put himself first, does not acknowledge our authority. 10/ So if [or: when] I come, I will call attention to what he is doing in spreading false charges against us. And not content with those charges, he refuses to welcome the brothers and sisters [*NRSV:* friends], and even prevents those who want to do so and expels them from the church.**

■ **9** The assertion that Christians are obligated to work together introduces a transition to the description of the conflict that has broken out between the presbyter and his emissaries on the one side, and the community in which Diotrephes[1] works on the other.

Excursus: Diotrephes and the Presbyter

The conflict between Diotrephes and the presbyter is not merely an episode occurring at the margins of the church's history. It is representative of a fundamental controversy in the earliest period of the church, corresponding to the struggle between Spirit and office, church order and the independent charismatic life. Walter Bauer's groundbreaking work[2] rescued 3 John from the shadowy status to which research had long relegated it and sought particularly within its context to establish the thesis that, contrary to later church opinion, "orthodoxy" did not represent the theology of the earliest times. Instead, "heresy" existed from the beginnings of church history in many communities and provincial churches. Hence what the patristic authors asserted in their polemic writings was incorrect: namely, that heresy was nothing but the product of "corruption" of the original, orthodox teaching, or a "deviation from the genuine." On the contrary, what later appeared as correct, as the teaching of the orthodox great church, had first been forced to win out in a struggle against other theological views and other communities who, in turn, understood their own doctrine as orthodox. As is evident from the extensive tradition, surviving only in fragments but recoverable from the reports of the church fathers, the "heretics" were far more numerous than the "orthodox." The community in the imperial capital, Rome, was an essential factor influencing the outcome of these conflicts. From the beginning, Rome was the center and major source of strength for the "orthodox" movement within Christianity. What ultimately triumphed as orthodoxy was Roman Christianity.

Walter Bauer attempted to demonstrate, on the basis of witnesses from various provincial churches (Syria, Egypt, Asia Minor, and Rome), that in many provinces of the church heresy was originally the primary, and orthodox Christianity the secondary, phenomenon. The demonstration was essentially based on documents outside the NT; an exception, however, was 2 and 3 John. Here Bauer believed he could demonstrate his thesis in the relationship between Diotrephes, who did not receive the presbyter's emissaries (3 John 10), and the presbyter, who opposed false teaching (2 John 7). Thus Diotrephes is a heretical leader who knows he has the majority of community members behind him,[3] while the presbyter is the representative of orthodoxy who attempts to influence the community from outside and intends to assist the victory of orthodoxy. For Bauer, this makes 3 John "especially valuable and instructive for us in that it represents the attempt of an ecclesiastical leader to gain influence in other communities in order to give

1 "Diotrephes" occurs only here in the NT. The name ("child of Zeus") indicates Greek roots; it is frequently attested in ancient literature. Cf. the examples in BAGD 199.

2 Bauer, *Orthodoxy and Heresy.*

3 Similarly, Wendt (*Johannesbriefe*, 27) assigns Diotrephes "to the trend of gnostic innovators" whom the author condemned in 2 John 7 as "the deceiver and the antichrist."

assistance to like-minded persons within those communities, and if possible, to gain the upper hand."[4] Therefore, the situation in this letter reveals a still-unfinished stage in the course of church history. Orthodoxy is on the attack but has not yet conquered; the issue of the struggle is still entirely open.

In his inaugural lecture at Göttingen in 1951, Ernst Käsemann adopted this position of his predecessor but with essential modifications.[5] According to him Diotrephes is not a heretical leader but a "monarchical bishop who sees himself opposing a false teacher and acts accordingly." He exercises "the power of church discipline against the presbyter and his adherents, including those in his own community." By contrast, the presbyter is an isolated figure who cannot appeal to status as a disciple of the Lord "or sacrosanct tradition, but has only the Spirit on his side." He is not only the author of the Johannine Letters but also of the Fourth Gospel, "a Christian Gnostic who has the unimaginable boldness to write a Gospel about the Christ of his own experience projected into the world of gnosis." Both the presbyter's teaching and his Gospel, in which one sees "Christ bestriding the world in the brilliance of his miracles and his heavenly majesty," are diagnosed as heretical, and the acceptance of the Fourth Gospel into the NT canon is to be regarded as contrary to the church position that was responsible for the establishment of a canon.

The idea that a dogmatic controversy underlies the dissension between the presbyter and Diotrephes has certainly been contested. With some frequency the opinion is offered that the disagreement rests merely on a practical, disciplinary conflict.[6] However, on the basis of the common authorship of the two smaller Johannine letters, the sequence 2 John → 3 John, and the statement in 2 John 7 that, as a result, must be seen as a fundamental principle for both letters, a dogmatic background seems probable (even if no exclusive significance can be attached to it).[7] And Käsemann's question remains: Was the presbyter a heretic or a witness?[8]

On the basis of what has been said about 2 John, the question whether the presbyter was more inclined to the heretics or the orthodox must be answered in favor of the former. The chiliastic features of his christology make him an outsider from the perspective of the

4 Bauer, *Orthodoxy and Heresy*, 93.

5 Käsemann, "Ketzer und Zeuge"; citations from 173–74 and 177–78.

6 Cf. von Harnack, *Johannesbrief*, 21, who suspects a controversy over church law: "it is the struggle of the old patriarchal and provincial missionary organization against the consolidating individual communities who, for the purpose of their consolidation and strict delimitation over against outsiders brought forth the monarchical episcopacy in their midst." Cf. also Schnackenburg, *Epistles*, 272 ("practical discipline"); Haenchen, "Neuere Literatur," 308. Brown takes a mediating stance (*Epistles*, 738): Diotrephes shared the presbyter's "anti-secessionist policy," as expressed in 2 John 10–11, but pursued it farther. According to Smalley (*1, 2, 3 John*, 356), the organizational conflict escalated into a dogmatic struggle. Lieu (*Epistles*, 154–55) denies the dogmatic aspect of the conflict, with reference to 2 John 10 where the presbyter would otherwise have discussed his differences with Diotrephes. But 2 John 10–11 refers to itinerant false teachers, while Diotrephes must be thought of as a resident community functionary. In addition, when writing 2 John the presbyter may not yet have anticipated a hostile reaction by Diotrephes; it is possible that it arose only as a result of 2 John. Abraham J. Malherbe ("The Inhospitality of Diotrephes," in Jacob Jervell and Wayne A. Meeks, eds., *God's Christ and His People: Studies in Honour of Nils Alstrup Dahl* [Oslo, Bergen, and Tromsø: Universitetsforlaget, 1977] 222–32) denies both a doctrinal and a church-legal background for the conflict. It is not a question of church authority but of hospitality (228: "The subject with which 3 John deals is hospitality"), which Diotrephes refuses to extend (ἐκβάλλει), in his own house, to Christians who disagree with him. He misuses hospitality for his own advantage (229). The thorough obscuring of the theological implications of 3 John did not succeed in preserving the author from the charge of writing a "Socioreligiological Sociopolitology of Early Christianity" rooted in "German" usage (Bruce J. Malina, "The Received View and What It Cannot Do: III John and Hospitality," *Semeia* 35 [1986] 171–89, at 181). Jens Wilhelm Taeger ("Der konservative Rebell," *ZNW* 78 [1987] 267–87) supposes an "internal Johannine conflict" (275). A conservative believer (Diotrephes), who recognizes the leading of the Spirit and the authority of Jesus Christ in himself and his community alone, resists an ecclesial innovator (the presbyter), who wishes to make himself the head of the Johannine communities in order to organize and preserve them. On this subject, see also Brooke, *Epistles*, lxxxx, 288.

7 Cf. Bauer, *Orthodoxy and Heresy*, 93; also Ehrhardt, *Framework*, 151–99, at 185–86, who points out that the controversy between Diotrephes and the presbyter is closely related to the disturbances connected with the appearance of itinerant Montanist philosophers in already established communities ("a doctrinal conflict undoubtedly had existed"); the citations of anti-Montanist polemic writings in Eusebius (Melito of Sardis at *Hist. eccl.* 4.26.2; Apollonius at 5.18.14; Apollinaris at 5.19.1–

orthodox development of doctrine. The nonorthodoxy in his teaching may have been one of the prime factors in his conflict with Diotrephes, who accordingly stands closer to the orthodox side. Up to this point, one must agree with Käsemann against Bauer. Of course, it would not be right to project the relationships within the later, legally organized official church into the time of 2 and 3 John. As Günther Bornkamm has shown,[9] while Diotrephes is depicted as φιλοπρωτεύων ("puts himself first," 3 John 9), and while he undoubtedly occupied an influential position in his community, one cannot deduce from 3 John that he was a monarchical bishop. Moreover, the thesis that the presbyter appears as a "Gnostic" in his struggle with Diotrephes cannot really be derived from these letters. It is more likely that his opponents represented gnosticizing or spiritualizating tendencies contrary to the presbyter's apocalyptic teaching about Christ. From this point they would have developed a docetic christology like that which 1 John first presupposes as existing within the Johannine school, and then opposes in 1 John 2:18–27 and 4:1–3. This shaped the Johannine tradition in a gnosticizing, but not least in an antidocetic, direction. It was found at this stage by the fourth evangelist and reworked in his writing under the conditions imposed by the gospel genre. If this development within the history of the Johannine school tradition has its seed in the conflict between Diotrephes and the presbyter, it was only in the later stages of tradition that it acquired a definite form.

The presbyter has written "something" (τί) to Diotrephes' community.[10] The little word τί refers to a previous letter. As I have already said, this was 2 John,[11] which in fact is addressed to an ἐκκλησία (2 John 1: κυρία). The attempt made by the presbyter in that letter to establish a closer relationship with the community was foiled by Diotrephes. Although he is not described as a monarchical bishop, he does, as the author says, wish to be foremost in the community,[12] and in any case he exercises so much influence that he can successfully defend himself against the presbyter's authority.

The plural ἡμᾶς (as an ecclesial "we") refers to the presbyter's following. Thus the author of 3 John unites himself, as in what has gone before, with the rest of the community (v. 8: ἡμεῖς). But it is significant that "we" alternates with "I" (vv. 2–4, 10). One may conclude from this that the presbyter's "I" also determines the community's "we"; consequently the calumnies[13] that

2) are enlightening.

8 Cf. Käsemann, "Ketzer und Zeuge," 187.

9 Günther Bornkamm, "πρέσβυς," *TDNT* 6 (1968) 651–80, at 671, against Käsemann, "Ketzer und Zeuge," 173–74.

10 That the letter was directed not to Diotrephes in particular but to the (whole) community does not permit any conclusions about the structure of the community; nor is it possible from this information to shed any light on the question whether, at the time that letter was written, the presbyter was acquainted with the community official Diotrephes. Cf. Brown, *Epistles*, 715. On the relationship of Gaius to this community, see above (at v. 1).

11 See the Introduction to 3 John above. The copyists smoothed the text: the reading ἔγραψας ("you have written") presumes that the unsuccessful letter could not have been written by this author, who can be thought of as John the apostle. The same can be presumed of the reading ἔγραψα ἄν ("I would have written"); for the contrary-to-fact construction supposes that the letter was not written.

12 The literal translation of φιλοπρωτεύειν; the verb occurs only here in the NT and is not attested in Hellenistic Greek literature. The adjective φιλόπρωτος appears, with the same meaning ("eager to be first"), in Plutarch *On Tranquility of Mind* 471D; *Solon* 29.5; Artemidorus *Oneirocritica* 2.32, and elsewhere; the noun φιλοπρωτεία is in Porphyry *Vita Plotini*, and elsewhere; see the references in BAGD 860–61; φιλοπρωτία is in Julianus *Caesares* 319D. The verb may be the presbyter's own construction. That he thereby "disparagingly avoids or replaces the real title of Diotrephes, i.e., ἐπίσκοπος" (Bultmann, *Epistles*, 100), remains a suspicion without a demonstrable basis. In any case, the word (as the cited texts from Plutarch and Solon also show) has a negative, disqualifying tone: Diotrephes is characterized as ambitious; cf. also Windisch and Preisker, *Die Katholischen Briefe*, 142; Wengst, *Brief*, 248; Lieu, *Epistles*, 111.

13 Φλυαρεῖν ("to bring unjust accusations") appears only here in the NT. The verb is attested with some frequency in Greek literature; with βλασφημεῖν, for example, in Xenophon *Hell.* 6.3.12; also in Philo *Som.* 2.291; *Leg. Gaj.* 363. There are numerous derivatives, e.g., φλυαρία (as accusative with φλυαρεῖν) at Plato *Apologia* 19C; φλύαρος ("gossipy"), also 1 Tim 5:13; cf. BAGD 862; LSJ 1945–46; Ceslas Spicq, *Notes de lexicographie néo-testamentaire* (OBO 22/2; Fribourg: Editions universitaires; Göttingen: Vandenhoeck & Ruprecht, 1978) 2.949.

Diotrephes utters in spreading "false charges" against "us" have been primarily directed against the presbyter. ■ **10** It thus appears that Diotrephes has rejected the presbyter's claim. This is expressed not only in slanders but also by his refusal to welcome the itinerant "friends" and by his turning against the members of his community who make common cause with them. Diotrephes thus stands on the side of the presbyter's opponents.[14] One may suspect that he sympathizes with the πλάνοι whom the presbyter attacks, those who deny that "Jesus Christ will come in the flesh" (2 John 7), and that he is allied with the developing orthodox church tradition,[15] although nothing further can be discerned regarding his theological views. In any case he has a strong position in his community, so that he can set in motion and carry out the "excommunication" of disobedient members.[16] In light of the presumed situation, when the presbyter announces his impending arrival (v. 14), it is—as I have already said regarding the nearly identical verse 2 John 12—not a literary flourish but a serious intention. The presbyter's purpose is to strengthen his own position in the community against Diotrephes, and to bring the members of the community over to his side.

14 The word ἐπιδέχεσθαι (as early as Herodotus 8.75) has various meanings: "to receive as a guest" (v. 10) and "acknowledge" (v. 9). Both can be expressed in the same English word, i.e., "receive," or "welcome"; in each case the issue is that Diotrephes permits no access (in the literal and in the metaphorical sense). The verb is a hapax legomenon in the NT; it corresponds to ἀποδέχεσθαι (Luke 8:40; 9:11; Acts 18:27; 24:3, and frequently); cf. Ehrhardt, *Framework*, 169 n. 4; BAGD 292.

15 Cf. also Bultmann, *Epistles*, 100–101, and above (excursus: "Diotrephes and the Presbyter").

16 In the NT the verb ἐκβάλλειν occurs primarily in connection with the expulsion of demons; cf. Mark 3:15, 22–23 par.; 7:26, 29–30; 9:18, 28, 38 par.; Matt 7:22; 8:31; 9:33; 12:27, and frequently. In the Fourth Gospel it often has a neutral meaning: John 2:15 (the money changers); 9:34 (the man who had been healed); 10:4 (the sheep); it is also said of the Revealer that he will "never drive away" his own (6:37), or of the "ruler of this world" that he "will be driven out" (12:31: ἐκβληθήσεται ἔξω; cf. 1 John 4:18: "perfect love casts out fear": ἔξω βάλλει). In the Johannine Letters the verb appears only at 3 John 10. It describes the act of expulsion from the community and is analogous to the disciplinary measures of the synagogue in Judaism and early Christianity: cf. Luke 6:22; Matt 18:17; 1 Cor 5:2; Josephus *Bell.* 2.143; P. Oxy. 1.104, 17. One may question whether John 9:34–35 should be counted among these, in harmony with the "Johannine love of multiple meaning" (BAGD 237); cf. ἀποσυνάγωγος in John 9:22; 12:42; 16:2. In "expelling" the members of the community, Diotrephes anticipates the later church process of excommunication, but it is impossible to determine from this passage whether and how his measures were hierarchically based or justified in law by a fundamental community legal structure (cf. Matt 18:15–20; 1 Cor 5:1–5; Heb 6:1–10; 1 John 5:16–17; 2 John 10–11; Ingrid Goldhahn-Müller, *Die Grenze der Gemeinde: Studien zum Problem der Zweiten Busse im Neuen Testament unter Berücksichtigung der Entwicklung im zweiten Jahrhundert bis Tertullian* (GThA 39; Göttingen: Vandenhoeck & Ruprecht, 1989) 74–75. The problem can scarcely be solved by supposing that ἐκβάλλει is a "conative present" and describes an action that has been attempted but not accomplished (BDF § 319). This would explain why Gaius apparently is not one of those expelled, since the presbyter's communication would otherwise be superfluous (cf. Schnackenburg, *Epistles*, 298). But it is not apparent from 3 John that Gaius is subject to Diotrephes; against this interpretation is also that the preceding present-tense verbs ἐπιδέχεται and κωλύει describe a real event.

Recommendation for Demetrius

11 **Beloved, do not imitate what is evil but imitate what is good. Whoever does good is from God; whoever does evil has not seen God. 12/ Everyone has testified (favorably) about Demetrius, and so has the truth itself. We also testify for him, and you know that our testimony is true.**

■ **11–12** Apparently the presbyter has a well-founded hope that he will be able to achieve his purpose in the community. This hope is attached to the person of Demetrius.[1] If he is some kind of contact between the presbyter and Gaius, he may (as one of the traveling "brothers") be the bearer of this letter (3 John). He is apparently supposed to clear the field ahead of time and discuss with Gaius the possible measures that the presbyter is considering (v. 10a). Demetrius is recommended in the highest terms: he is favorably attested by everyone, even by truth herself (ἀλήθεια, "truth," is here clearly used in a personified sense); that means that he is completely defined by the truth. The presbyter also affirms this, and those who know him know that his word is ἀληθής; his testimony is not only "correct,"[2] but corresponds to the "truth" and can stand in face of God's truth.

The presbyter is using typical Johannine terminology here. This is true not only of the concepts of witness and truth but also of the preceding admonition, which enunciates Gaius's duty to do what is good.[3] If he remains in the realm of truth and walks in the truth (v. 3), this implies the demand that he reject every evil deed (cf. 1 John 2:15–17; 3:16–18). Christian existence is understood as "being from God." Doing good is necessarily a part of this, just as, according to another of the author's sayings, truth and love are united (2 John 1–3). Of those who have recognized the truth (2 John 1) it can be said that they have "seen God";[4] they will also practice love and do good. By contrast, those who do evil show that they have not seen God and have not recognized the truth (v. 11).

As was the case in 2 John 9, this passage reveals elements of a dualism that will appear more clearly in the later Johannine writings. This kind of dualistic thinking is combined with an ontological style of expression, as the idea of ἐκ θεοῦ εἶναι indicates; however, they are not conceived in a rigidly substantive fashion, but are

1 The Greek name "Demetrius" is frequently attested in the NT environment (cf. BAGD 178); in the NT it occurs in Acts 19:24, 38 as the name of a silversmith in Ephesus, the ringleader of a group fomenting a riot against Paul. The Demetrius named here can scarcely be identified with Paul's companion Demas (Phlm 24; Col 4:14; 2 Tim 4:10) (against Chapman, "Historical Setting," 364–66). It would be difficult to demonstrate that he was the "leader of the opposition party" together with Gaius (thus Windisch and Preisker, *Die Katholischen Briefe*, 142). In post-NT literature he appears as the bishop of Philadelphia, installed by John the apostle (*Ap. Const.* 7.46.9).

2 The word is interpreted in this sense by Wendt, "Johannesbriefe," 29; also Schnackenburg, *Epistles*, 300, who, because of the presbyter's authority, prefers the translation "trustworthy." The world of ideas in the Fourth Gospel is close in spirit to these verses. One may recall especially John 19:35 and 21:24 ("his testimony is true"). However, this agreement does not furnish a basis for the thesis that the presbyter is identical with the (ecclesiastical) redactor of the Fourth Gospel (cf. Dodd, *Epistles*, 168), for the fourth evangelist is also acquainted with this language. The "testimony" of the Revealer is "true" (8:14; cf. 3:11), just as his Father's testimony to him is "true" (5:32); something similar can be said of the testimony of John the Baptizer (10:41); by contrast, the Pharisees' accusation against Jesus is that his testimony about himself is "not true" (8:13; cf. 5:31; more distantly: 8:17; Titus 1:13). The Johannine school thus reveals the use of the terminology of witness and truth in all the layers of its tradition (cf. also 1 John 2:8, 27).

3 Verse 11; cf. John 5:29. Funk is correct as regards the form when he separates v. 11, as "parenesis," from v. 12 ("Form and Structure," 424–30), because the former expresses a universally valid ethical statement. In the existing composition, however, the verse is related to what follows it: the admonition to Gaius to do what is good (v. 11) is made concrete by Demetrius's example (v. 12).

4 Cf. above at 1 John 1:1–3 (esp. pp. 12–15).

intimately combined with historical and ethical content. The author is concerned not to describe a cosmic or mystical existence but to issue a warning to do good and avoid evil. It is true both that those who live in the sphere of truth, and therefore come from God, do what is good, and also that those who do evil demonstrate by that very fact that they do not belong to the truth. Since these ideas are expressed in the form of parenesis it is clear that what is at issue is not believers' habitual way of existing; instead, each individual Christian has freedom to choose whether he or she will behave responsibly, according to the truth as revealed.

This kind of ontologically founded dualism of decision is intensified by the apocalyptic trajectory of Johannine theology, something that is expressed in 2 John as an anticipation of reward (v. 8) and a realistic hope in the coming of Christ (v. 7). "Being from God" thus means being oriented to the coming of God, in the future sense as well. But alongside this, and no less weighty, is the enlightening of the present time: the truth given by God manifests itself "already" in the life of believers, in the *agapē* they practice. The existence of a Christian is determined both by the "already" and the "not yet"; it is experienced and accomplished dialectically in time.

Conclusion of the Letter

13 **I have much to write to you, but I [prefer not to write] with pen and ink; 14/ instead I hope to see you soon, and we will talk together face to face. 15/ Peace to you. The friends send you their greetings. Greet the friends there, each by name.**

■ **13–14** The conclusion of the letter corresponds word for word, in part, with 2 John 12–13, with the difference that it is not the community but Gaius who is addressed, in the second person singular. The language, here as in 2 John, is rich in imagery.[1] The beginning deviates from 2 John 12 by the use of the imperfect εἶχον (in place of ἔχων); it describes the "duty" or "necessity" that the sender feels.[2] The indicative οὐ θέλω ("I prefer not to") expresses, more decisively than the reticent aorist οὐκ ἐβουλήθην ("I would rather not") in 2 John 12, the author's determination that the mutual relationship should not be relegated merely to paper. What is new here is the OT and Jewish εἰρήνη, which can be translated both "peace" and "salvation."[3] The anticipation that the sender will soon see and speak with the recipient of the letter, as well as the greeting of peace, express the close relationship between the presbyter and Gaius. The fact that formulaic traditional material is used here[4] does not mean that the author's expressed intention to visit Gaius is only rhetorical. Instead, what is stated here is an earnest desire for a personal encounter, intended to lend emphasis to the presbyter's purpose.

■ **15** The designation of the Christians as φίλοι ("friends"), which occurs very seldom in the NT,[5] is striking; it is

1 These are not exaggerated expressions such as are frequently found at the end of written works (e.g., John 20:30; on this, see Bultmann, *John*, 697 n. 2; Str-B 2.587, on John 21:25: "reed" and "ink" as the materials with which the rabbis wrote). The author really did use "paper and ink," or "ink and reed." See the combination κάλαμον καὶ χάρτην καὶ μέλαν in Synesius *Ep.* 157 (p. 294B), or κάλαμος and μέλαν in P. Oxy. 2.326; cf. Plato *Phaedrus* 276C; Themistius *In Constant.* 31C. Τὸ μέλαν is "ink" (in the NT, besides 2 John 12 and 3 John 13, only 2 Cor 3:3); the Greek linguistic character of this concluding verse is evident, among other things, from the fact that the word is used as a borrowed term in the rabbinic literature. Χάρτης is "paper," prepared from the papyrus plant; cf. Job 8:11; Isa 35:7. In the NT it occurs only here and at 2 John 12. It is possible that the "books" mentioned in 2 Tim 4:13 included not only parchments (μεμβράνας = parchment codices) but also papyrus books (Deissmann, *Light from the Ancient East*, 30; see further citations in BAGD 879). Κάλαμος originally designated the reed itself (Job 40:21; Matt 11:7; 12:20; Luke 7:24) that was used as a stick or rod (Mark 15:19, 36 par.), as a measuring rod (Rev 11:1; 21:15–16), and as a writing tool ("reed pen," or simply "pen," or "stylus" in English). This last usage is found also in Ps 44:2 LXX; 3 Macc 4:20).

2 Cf. BDR § 358; this is also the motivation for use of the aorist infinitive γράψαι (more strongly attested than γράφειν, the "Majority Text" reading); 2 John 12 has γράφειν. Cf. Schnackenburg, *Epistles*, 310 n. 148.

3 It occurs frequently in NT blessings; also in the epistolary introduction at 2 John 3 (see above); cf. Rom 1:7; 1 Cor 1:3, and frequently (with χάρις); the concluding greeting in 1 Pet 5:14 ("peace to all of you who are in Christ") is especially close to this one.

4 For στόμα πρὸς στόμα λαλεῖν cf. Num 12:8 (YHWH says of Moses: "With him I speak face to face—clearly, not in riddles"); also Jer 39:4; and the magical text in *PGM* 1.40. Since στόμα is used in close connection with καρδία (cf. Matt 12:34 par., "out of the abundance of the heart the mouth speaks"), the same expression can describe both oral dialogue and personal encounter; cf. the English "heart-to-heart talk" (Brown, *Epistles*, 725); similarly in 1 Cor 13:12: "face to face" (Deut 34:10).

5 The reading ἀδελφοί (A, minuscules) is a secondary smoothing. Closest to the present passage are statements in which Jesus names his "friends": Luke 12:4 and John 15:14–15; cf. Acts 27:3 (friends of Paul). The verb φιλεῖν is not attested in the Johannine Letters, but it is in the Fourth Gospel: of the

more strongly Hellenistic Greek in its character than the other names given to the members of the community,[6] and emphasizes the community-consciousness of fellow Christians. Not only is their existence defined by truth and love, but this fundamental character also supports their actions, that is, their mutual love (2 John 6), such as the presbyter hopes for from Gaius and presupposes on his part (3 John 1–2). The request that he welcome the friends remains quite general. It is in harmony with the given situation in the church's politics, for it is apparently not yet definite who is to be counted among the friends of the presbyter in Gaius's neighborhood and in Diotrephes' community. That they are to be greeted *κατ' ὄνομα* ("by name"),[7] without a list of names being included at this point, accords with this situation and characterizes the presbyter's desire for a Christian community founded on *agapē*, which bridges all distance, removes uncertainty, and eliminates conflict.

love of God for the Son (5:20) or for the disciples (16:27); of the love of Jesus for his own (11:3, 36; 20:2), and of the disciples for the Revealer (16:27; cf. 21:15–17). In its content, it corresponds to ἀγαπᾶν (cf. 21:15–16, alternating with φιλεῖν): of the love of God for the Son (3:35; 10:17, and frequently) and for Jesus' disciples (14:21; 17:23, and frequently), and the love of Jesus for his own (11:5; 13:1, 23, and frequently). This interchangeability is not (yet) evident in the shorter Johannine letters, where the members of the community (2 John 1) or Gaius (3 John 1) are the objects of the presbyter's ἀγαπᾶν and the adjective ἀγαπητός is applied only to Gaius (3 John 2, 5, 11; see above at v. 2). In repeating the commandment of mutual love the author also employs the usual ἀγαπᾶν (2 John 5; cf. John 13:34; 1 John 2:10; 3:11, 23; 4:7, and frequently). The unusual description of the members of the community as φίλοι at the conclusion of 3 John is possibly explained by the ancient letter formula, on which Titus 3:15 may also rest (ἄσπασαι τοὺς φιλοῦντας ἡμᾶς ἐν πίστει), something that otherwise has only been observed in post-NT letters as οἱ φιλοῦντες ἡμᾶς and similar expressions (cf. Gustav Stählin, "φιλέω, κτλ.," *TDNT* 9 [1974] 137 n. 214). The expression φίλοι is parallel in form and content to the designation of the community members as τέκνα (2 John 1, 13) and corresponds to the indeterminate situation in which the presbyter finds himself with respect to the community, since he failed to achieve the goal he aimed at in 2 John. Both terms make evident, on different levels, that there is an intimate relationship between the presbyter and the community, but this in itself does not suggest that the presbyter wished to teach "an *ecclesiola in ecclesia* as the form of community supportive of it" in his writings (cf. in this regard, rather, the Johannine concept of *agapē*, in the excursus on *agapē* above: against Käsemann, "Ketzer und Zeuge," 179). That the presbyter distinguishes a circle of "friends" in either the sending or receiving community who were especially close to him (thus von Harnack, *Johannesbrief*, 13) cannot be read out of this text.

6 E.g., ἐκλεκτοί ("elect"): Mark 13:20, 22, 27; Matt 24:22, 24, 31; Luke 18:7; Rom 8:33; Col 3:12; 2 Tim 2:10; 1 Pet 2:9; *1 Clem.* 6.1; κλητοί ("called"): Matt 22:14; Rom 1:1, 6–7; 8:28; 1 Cor 1:1, 24; Jude 1; Rev 17:14; ἅγιοι ("saints"): 2 Cor 1:1; Phil 1:1; Col 1:2; Acts 9:13, and frequently; πιστοί ("believers"): Acts 16:1; 2 Cor 6:15; 1 Tim 4:3, 10, 12; Titus 1:6; *1 Clem.* 48.5; 62.3, and frequently; ἀγαπητοί ("beloved"): Rom 1:7; 11:28; 12:19; 1 Cor 10:14; 15:58; 1 John 2:7; 3:2, 21; 4:1, 7, 11; Jude 3, 17, 20, and frequently (see also above at 1 John 3:2 and frequently elsewhere).

7 Κατ' ὄνομα means "individually by name," as in the papyri (esp. in greetings); John 10:3; Ignatius *Smyrn.* 13.2b; *1 Clem.* 43.2b. It is not presumed that the presbyter knows by name all the friends who are to be greeted. Ignatius *Smyrn.* 13.2b also has a general direction that does not suggest full knowledge of everyone's name; this is evident from the addition of πάντας ("everyone, each by name"). Haenchen ("Neuere Literatur," 303) points to the formulaic quality of the expression, which "can easily [sound] more personal to us than it is." The presbyter addresses his greeting to the Christians who are members of Gaius's circle, who are known to him, and to whom he is requested to speak.

Bibliography
Indices

In this bibliography, commentaries are listed first, by century or era (chronologically, up to the 19th century; thereafter, alphabetically). Primary sources, handbooks, encyclopedia articles, monographs, and periodical articles are placed alphabetically under the names of the authors or editors. In the notes, the literature is cited in abbreviated form using the author's name and a key word or words from the title.

1. Commentaries

a. The Ancient Church

Clement of Alexandria (Titus Flavius Clemens, ca. 150–215)
Adumbrationes in Epistolas Canonicas (GCS 17; 2d ed.; ed. Otto Stählin, Ludwig Früchtel, and Ursula Treu; Berlin: Akademie-Verlag, 1970) 3.209–15.

Ps.-Didymus of Alexandria
Brevis Enarratio in Epistolas Canonicas. PG 39.1775–1812. (Cf. Friedrich Zoepfl, *Didymi Alexandrini in Ep. canonicas brevis enarratio* (NTAbh 4/1; Münster: Aschendorff, 1914] 37–88.)

John Chrysostom († 407)
Fragmenta in Epistolas Catholicas. PG 64.1059–62.

Augustine (Aurelius Augustinus, bishop of Hippo, 354–430)
In Epistolam Joannis ad Parthos Tractatus 10. PL 35.1977–2062; ET: *Love One Another, My Friends: St. Augustine's Homilies on the First Letter of John: An Abridged English Version* (trans. John Leinenweber; San Francisco: Harper & Row, 1989).

Cyril of Alexandria (ca. 370–444)
Fragmenta ad Epistolam I Divi Joanni. PG 74.1022–23.

Cassiodorus, Flavius Magnus Aurelius (ca. 487–580)
Complexiones in Epistolas Apostolorum. PL 70.1369–76.

Cramer, John Anthony
Catenae graecorum patrum in Novum Testamentum, vol. 8: *In Epistolas Catholicas et Apocalypsin* (Oxford: Oxford University Press, 1844; reprinted Hildesheim: Olms, 1967) 105–52. (Cf. Karl Staab, "Die griechischen Katenenkommentare zu den katholischen Briefen," *Bib* 5 [1924] 296–353; Robert Devreesse, *DBSup* 1.1224–28.)

b. The Middle Ages

Bede (Beda Venerabilis, 673–735)
In I.–III. Epistolas S. Joannis. PL 93.85–124.

Ps.-Oecumenius (bishop of Tricca in Thessaly, 10th century)
Joannis Apostoli I.–III. Epistola Catholica. PG 119.617–704.

Ps.-Theophylact (Theophylactus, archbishop of Okhrid in Bulgaria, fl. 1078)
Expositio in Epistulam I.–III. S. Joannis. PG 126.9–84.

Dionysius Bar Salibi († 1171)
In Apocalypsim, Actus et Epistulas Catholicas (ed. Jaroslav Sedlacek; CSCO 60, Scriptores Syri 20; 1910; 2d ed.; Louvain: Secrétariat du Corpus SCO, 1954) 120–28.

Euthymius Zigabenus (12th century)
Commentarius in XIV Epistolas S. Pauli et VII Catholicas (2 vols.; ed. Nikephoros Kalogeras; Athens: Typis Fratrum Perri, 1887) 2.590–646.

Ps.-Hilarius of Arles
Tractatus in septem Epistolas Catholicas (ed. Ambrogio Amelli; Spicilegium Casinese 3/1; Monte Cassino: Tipografia de Montecassino, 1897) 205–60.

Martin of Leon († 1203)
Expositio in I. Epistulam B. Joannis. PL 209.253–98.

Glossa Ordinaria. PL 114.693–704.

Stephen Langton († 1228)
Unpublished (cf. Georges Lacombe and Beryl Smalley, "Studies on the Commentaries of Stephen Langton," *Archives d'histoire doctrinale et littéraire du moyen âge* 5 [1930] 1–266).

Barhebraeus, Gregorius (Grighor Abu a-Faraj, called Bar-Hebraeus, 1226–1286)
Martini Klamroth, "In Actus apostolorum et Epistulas Catholicas adnotationes Syriace" (diss., Göttingen, 1878).

De Gorran, Nicolaus (Nicolao Corrano, 1232–ca. 1295)
In Acta Apostolorum et Singulas Apostolorum Iacobi, Petri, Johannis et Judae canonicas Epistolas et Apocalypsim Comentarii (Antwerp, 1620) 135–62 (1 John), 163–66 (2 John), 167–69 (3 John).

Meister Eckhart († 1327)
Wilhelm Schöpff, ed., *Ausgewählte Predigten und verwandte Schriftstücke* (Die Predigt der Kirche; ed. Gustav Leonhardt; 31 vols.; Leipzig: Richter, 1889) 8.34–40 (1 John 3:1).

Nikolaus of Lyra († 1349)
Postillae perpetuae in Vetus et Novum Testamentum (Rome: Conradus Swehnheym and Arnoldus Pannartz, 1471–72; Antwerp, 1634).

Jan Hus (ca. 1369–1415)
Opera omnia (3 vols.; ed. Wenzel Flajshans; Prague: J. Bursik, 1903–1907) chap. 35 (1 John 3:7–8 and 3:10), chap. 72 (1 John 4:16).

Dionysius the Carthusian (Denis le Chartreux, 1402–1471)
Opera omnia, vol. 14: *Epistolae Iohannis* (Montreuil-Tournay: Typis Cartusiae S. M. de Pratis, 1901) 3–64.

Savonarola, Hieronymus (1452–1498)
W. von Langsdorff, ed. "Predigt über 1 Joh 1,1," in *Ausgewählte Predigten* (Die Predigt der Kirche;

ed. Gustav Leonhardt; 31 vols.; Leipzig: Richter, 1890) 11.1–7. Also in E. Carin, P. G. Ricce, and Roberto Ridolfi, eds., *Edizione Nationale delle opere di G. Sav.* (Rome: Belardetti, 1955–).

c. Reformation

Zwingli, Huldrich (1484–1531)
Opera 6/2 (ed. M. Schuler and J. Schultheiss; Zurich: Schulthessium, 1829–42; Paris, 1898) 320–40.

Cajetan, Tommaso de Vio (Cardinal Tommaso de Vio, called Gaetano, 1469–1534)
Notae in epistolam II. Petr, I.–III. Joannis, Jud. (Rome, 1532).

Luther, Martin (1483–1546)
In primam epistolam Johannis. WA 20.592–801.
In primam epistolam Johannis scholia. WA 48.313–23.
Epistel-Auslegung, vol. 5 (ed. Hartmut Günther and Ernst Volk; Göttingen: Vandenhoeck & Ruprecht, 1983) 255–378.

Calvin, John (1509–1564)
Opera, vol. 55: *Commentarius in Johannis Apostoli Epistulam (1 Joh). Joannis Calvini opera* (CR 83; ed. William Baum, Eduard Cunitz, and Eduard Reuss; Braunschweig: Schwetschke, 1896) 293–376.

Brenz, Johannes (the Elder, 1499–1570)
P. Prossel, ed., *Ausgewählte Predigten* (Die Predigt der Kirche; ed. Gustav Leonhardi; 31 vols.; Leipzig: Richter, 1893) 24.70–73 (1 John 4:16–21; 5:4–10).
Frühschriften (vol. 2; ed. M. Brecht, et al.; Tübingen: Mohr [Siebeck], 1974) 124ff. (1 John 4:1ff.).

Bullinger, Heinrich (1504–1575)
In epistolam Ioannis apostoli et evangelistae canonicam, breuis, et catholicae expositio (Tiguris, 1532).

Salmeron, Alfonso (1515–1585)
Disputationes in epistulas Canonicas. Opera omnia (16 vols.; Cologne: Apud Antonium Hierat et Ion. Gymni, 1613).

Zanchius, Hieronymus (Girolamo Zanchi, 1516–1590)
Opera 8 (Geneva: Crispin, 1617–1619).

Benedict Arias Montanus (Benito Arias Montano, 1527–1598)
Elucidationes in omnia Sanctorum Apostolorum scripta: Eiusdem in S. Johannis Apocalypsim significationes (Antwerp: ex officina Christophori Plantini, 1588).

d. The 17th–18th Centuries

Socinus, Faustus (Fausto Sozzini, 1539–1604)
Commentaria in Epistolam Iohannis Apostoli Primam. Racoviae: Sternacianis, 1614.

Estius, Wilhelm (1542–1613)
In omnes B. Pauli Epistolas, item in Catholicas Comentarii (3 vols.; ed. Joannes Holzhammer; Mainz: Kirchhem, 1858–59) 3.674–804.

Justiniani, Benedict (Benedetto Guistinano, 1550–1622)
In omnes Epistolas Catholicas explanatio (Lyons: Cardon & Cauellat, 1621).

Lorinus, Johannes (Jean de Lorin, 1559–1634)
In catholicas tres B. Joannis & duas B. Petri epistolas commentarii (Lyons: Cardon, 1609) 1–168.

Lapide, Cornelius à (Cornelius van den Steen, 1567–1637)
In Acta Apostolorum, epistolas canonicas et Apokalypsim (3 vols. in one; Antwerp: Martinum Nutium, 1627–29) 2.411–529 (1 John), 2.520–27 (2 John), 2.528–34 (3 John).

Gomarus, Franciscus (1563–1641)
Opera Theologica Omnia (Amsterdam: ex officina Joannis Janssonii, 1664) 719–39 (1 John), 739–42 (2–3 John).

Crell, Johann (Johannis Crelli, 1590–1663)
Opera (4 vols.; Bibliotheca Fratrum Polonorum; Amsterdam, 1656), vol. 3.

Schmidt, Sebastian (1617–1696)
Commentarius in primam Joannis Epistolam (Frankfurt am Main and Leipzig: Lipper, 1687).

Spener, Philipp Jakob (1635–1705)
Des hocherleuchten Apostels und Evangelisten . . . Johannis erste Epistel (Halle: Weysenhauses, 1699).

Simon, Richard (1638–1712)
Opera (Rotterdam: Renier Leers, 1665) 2.173–428 (1 John).

Lange, Joachim (1670–1744)
Exegesis Epistolarum Joannis (Halle: Literis et Impensis Orphanotrophei, 1713).

Wettstein, Johann Jakob (1693–1754)
Novum Testamentum Graecum editionis receptae, vol. 2: *Continens Epistolas Pauli, Acta Apostolorum, Epistolas Canonicas et Apocalypsim* (Amsterdam: Dommeriana, 1752; reprinted Graz: Akademische Druck- und Verlagsanstalt, 1962) 713–31.

Bengel, Johann Albrecht (1687–1752)
Gnomon Novi Testamenti (3d ed., 1773; reprinted Berlin: Schlawitz, 1860) 648–64 (1–3 John); ET: *Gnomon of the New Testament,* vol. 5 (trans. Andrew R. Fausset, et al.; ed. Andrew R. Fausset; Edinburgh: Clark, 1858).

Semler, Johann Salomo (1725–1752)
Paraphrasis in I. Epistolam Joannis, acc. de Jo. Sal. Semlero eiusque ingenio narratio Jo. Aug. Nösseli. (Riga: Hartknochium, 1792).

Lange, Samuel Gottleib (1767–1823)
Die Schriften Johannis, vol. 3: *Die drey Briefe Johannis nebst drey Abhandlungen über Johannis Charakter, Schriebart und Theologie* (Weimar: Industrie-comptoire, 1797).

e. The 19th Century

Alford, Henry (1810–1871)
How to Study the New Testament, vol. 3: *The Epistles (second section) and the Revelation* (5th ed.; London: Strahan, 1872).

Bisping, August (1811–1884)
"Erklärung der sieben katholischen Briefe," in idem, *Exegetisches Handbuch zum Neuen Testament*, vol. 8 (Münster: Aschendorff, 1871).

Braune, Karl (1810–1879)
Die drei Briefe des Apostels Johannes (THBW 15; 3d ed.; Bielefeld: Velhagen & Klasing, 1885; ET: *The Epistles General of John* [trans. J. Isidor Mombert; New York: Scribner, 1867]).

De Wette, Wilhelm Martin Leberecht (1780–1849)
"Kurze Erklärung des Evangeliums und der Briefe Johannis," in idem, *Kurzgefasstes exegetisches Handbuch zum Neuen Testament*, vol. 1/3 (ed. Bruno Brückner; 5th ed.; Leipzig: Hirzel, 1863).

Düsterdiek, Friedrich Hermann Christian (1822–1906)
Die drei johanneischen Briefe (Göttingen: Dieterich, 1852–54).

Ebrard, Johannes Heinrich August (1818–1888)
Die Briefe Johannis (Olshansens biblischer Kommentar 6/4; Königsberg: Unzer, 1859).

Erdmann, L. F. D.
Primae Johannis epistolae argumentum, nexus et consilium (Commentatio exegetica; Berlin, 1855).

Ewald, Heinrich (1803–1875)
Die johanneischen Schriften, vol. 1: *Des Apostels Johannes Evangelium und drei Sendschreiben* (Göttingen: Dieterichs, 1861).

Haupt, Erich (1841–1909)
Der erste Brief des Johannes: Ein Beitrag zur biblischen Theologie (Kolberg: Jancke, 1869); ET: *The First Epistle of St. John* [trans. W. B. Pope; Edinburgh: Clark, 1893]).

Hilgenfeld, Adolf (1823–1907)
Das Evangelium und die Briefe Johannis (Halle: Schwetschke, 1849).

Hofmann, Johann Christian Konrad von (1810–1877)
Die heilige Schrift Neuen Testamentes, vol. 9: *Zusammenfassende Untersuchung der einzelnen neutestamentlichen Schriften* (ed. Wilhelm Volck; Nördlingen: Beck, 1881) 9.365–72 (1–3 John).

Holtzmann, Heinrich Julius (1832–1910)
Evangelium, Briefe und Offenbarung des Johannes (HKNT 4; 2d ed.; Freiburg im Breisgau and Leipzig: Mohr, 1893).

Holtzmann, Heinrich Julius (1832–1910) and Walter Bauer (1877–1960)
Johannesbriefe (HKNT 4/2; 3d ed.; Tübingen: Mohr [Siebeck], 1908).

Huther, Johann Eduard (1807–1880)
Kritisch-exegetisches Handbuch über die drei Briefe des Apostels Johannes (KEK 14; 4th ed.; Göttingen: Vandenhoeck & Ruprecht, 1880; ET: *Critical and Exegetical Handbook to the General Epistles of James, Peter, John, and Jude* [trans. Paton J. Gloag, D. B. Croom, and Clarke H. Irwin; ed. Timothy Dwight; New York: Funk & Wagnalls, 1887] 782–823).

Jachmann, C. R.
Kommentar über die Catholischen Briefe (Leipzig: Barth, 1838).

Karl, Wilhelm Adam
Johanneische Studien I: Der erste Johannesbrief (Freiburg im Breisgau, Leipzig, and Tübingen: Mohr, 1898).

Lias, John James (1834–1923)
The First Epistle of St. John with Exposition and Homiletical Treatment (Chicago/London: Nisbet, 1887).

Lücke, Friedrich (1791–1855)
Commentar über die Briefe des Evangelisten Johannes (3d ed.; ed. E. Bertheau; Bonn: Weber, 1856).

Luthardt, Christoph Ernst (1823–1902)
"Die Briefe Johannis," in Hermann L. Strack and Otto Zöckler, eds., *Kurzgefasster Kommentar zu den Heiligen Schriften Alten und Neuen Testamentes, sowie zu den Apokryphen* (14 vols. in 9; 2d ed.; Munich: Beck, 1895), pp. 211–80.

Mayer, G. K.
Commentar über die Briefe des Apostels Johannes (Vienna: Braumüller, 1851).

Neander, Johann August Wilhelm (1789–1850)
Der erste Brief Johannis (Berlin: Wiegandt & Grieben, 1851).

Paulus, Heinrich Eberhard Gottlob (1761–1851)
Die drey Lehrbriefe des Johannes (Heidelberg: Winter, 1829).

Plummer, Alfred (1841–1926)
The Epistles of St. John (CBSC; Cambridge: Cambridge University Press, 1889).

Poggel, Heinrich (1858–1928)
Der zweite und dritte Brief des Apostels Johannes (Paderborn: Ferdinand Schoningh, 1896).

Rickli, J.
Johannes erster Brief (Lucerne: Meyer, 1828).

Rothe, Richard (1799–1867)
Der erste Brief Johannis (ed. K. Mühlhäusser; Wittenberg: Hermann Roelling, 1878).

Sadler, Michael F. (1819–1895)
The General Epistles of Sts. James, Peter, John and Jude (New York: James Pott & Co., 1890; London: Bell, 1889, 1891).

Sander, Immanuel Fredrich Emil (1797–1859)
Commentar zu den Briefen Johannis (Elberfeld: W. Hassel, 1851).

Storr, Gottlob Christian (1746–1805)
Über den Zweck der evangelischen Geschichte und der Briefe Johannis (Tübingen: Jakob Friedrich Heerbrandt, 1786).

Weiss, Bernhard (1827–1918)
Die drei Briefe des Apostel Johannes (KEK 14; 6th ed.; Göttingen: Vandenhoeck & Ruprecht, 1899).

Westcott, Brooke Foss (bishop of Durham, 1825–1901)
The Epistles of St. John (2d ed.; London: Macmillan, 1886; new ed. with introduction by Frederick F.

Bruce; Abingdon: Marcham Manor; Grand Rapids: Eerdmans, 1966).
Wolf, Carl August
Ein exegetischer und praktischer Kommentar zu den drei Briefen St. Johannis (Leipzig: Koessling, 1881).

f. The 20th Century

Alexander, Neil
The Epistles of John (TBC; London: SCM, 1962).
Alexander, William
The Epistles of St. John (New York: Armstrong; London: Hodder & Stoughton, 1905).
Ambroggi, Pietro de
Le Epistole Cattoliche (La Sacra Bibbia; 2d ed.; S. Garofalo/Turin/Rome: Marietti, 1949).
Asmussen, Hans
Wahrheit und Liebe: Eine Einführung in die Johannesbriefe (UCB 22; 3d ed.; Hamburg: Furche, 1957).
Auvray, Paul
Saint Jean nous parle (Thèmes Bibliques 10; Paris: Apostolat des éditions, 1972).
Balz, Horst R.
"Die Johannesbriefe," in Horst Balz und Wolfgang Schrage, *Die "Katholischen" Briefe: Die Briefe des Jakobus, Petrus, Johannes und Judas* (NTD 10; 2d ed.; Göttingen: Vandenhoeck & Ruprecht, 1980) 156–222.
Baumgarten, Otto
Die Johannesbriefe (SNT 4; 3d ed.; Göttingen: Vandenhoeck & Ruprecht, 1918) 185–228.
Belser, Johannes Evangelist
Die Briefe des heiligen Johannes (Freiburg im Breisgau: Herder, 1906).
Bonnard, Pierre
Les épîtres johanniques (CNT 2/13c.; Geneva: Labor et Fides, 1983).
Bonsirven, Joseph
Épîtres de Saint Jean (VS 9; 1936; 2d ed.; Paris: Beauchesne, 1954).
Braun, François-Marie
"Les Épîtres de Saint Jean," in François-Marie Braun and Donatien Mollat, *L'Évangile et les épîtres de Saint Jean* (*SBJ;* 1953; 3d ed.; Paris: Cerf, 1973) 231–77.
Brooke, Alan England (1863–1939)
A Critical and Exegetical Commentary on the Johannine Epistles (ICC 43; New York: Scribner, 1912; reprinted Edinburgh: Clark, 1957).
Brown, Raymond E.
The Epistles of John (AB 30; Garden City: Doubleday, 1982).
Bruce, Frederick Fyvie
The Epistles of John (Old Tappan: F. H. Revell, 1970).
Büchsel, Friedrich
Die Johannesbriefe (ThHKNT 17; Leipzig: Deichert, 1933).
Bultmann, Rudolf
Die drei Johannesbriefe (KEK 14; 2d ed.; Göttingen: Vandenhoeck & Ruprecht, 1969; ET from the 2d ed. by R. Philip O'Hara with Lane C. McGaughy and Robert W. Funk, *The Johannine Epistles* [ed. Robert W. Funk; Hermeneia; Philadelphia: Fortress, 1973]).
Calmes, Th.
Épîtres Catholiques, Apocalypse (1905; Paris: Librairie Bloud, 1907).
Camerlynck, Achille
Commentarius in Epistolas Catholicas (Bruges: Car. Beyaerte, 1909).
Carpenter, Joseph Estlin
The Johannine Writings (London: Constable; New York/Boston: Houghton Mifflin, 1927).
Chaine, Joseph
Les épîtres catholiques (EtB; 2d ed.; Paris: Gabalda, 1939).
Charue, André-Marie
Les Épîtres de S. Jean (*SB* [PC]; Paris: Letouzey, 1946–61) 12.373–582.
Dodd, Charles Harold
The Johannine Epistles (MNTC; 2d ed.; London: Hodder & Stoughton, 1947).
Findlay, George G.
Fellowship in the Life Eternal: An Exposition of the Epistles of St. John (London: Hodder & Stoughton, 1909; reprinted Grand Rapids: Eerdmans, 1955).
Gärtner, Bertil
"Johannesbreven," in Bo Reicke and Bertil E. Gärtner, eds., *De Katolska Breven Fokening* (Folkning av Nyatestament 10/2; Stockholm: Verbum, 1970).
Gaugler, Ernst
Die Johannesbriefe (Auslegung neutestamentlicher Schriften 1, aus dem Nachlass; ed. M. Geiger und K. Stalde; Zurich: EVZ, 1964).
Gore, Charles
The Epistles of St. John (London: Murray; New York: Scribner's, 1920).
Grayston, Kenneth
The Johannine Epistles (NCB; Grand Rapids: Eerdmans, 1984).
Haas, C., Marinus de Jonge, and J. L. Swellengrebel
A Translator's Handbook on the Letters of John (HeTr 13; London: United Bible Societies, 1972).
Häring, Theodor
Die Johannesbriefe (Stuttgart: Calwer, 1927).
Hauck, Friedrich
Die Kirchenbriefe: Die Briefe des Jakobus, Petrus, Judas und Johannes (NTD 10; 8th ed.; Göttingen: Vandenhoeck & Ruprecht, 1957) 113–62.
Horn, Fritz
Der erste Brief des Johannes (Munich: Kaiser, 1931).
Hoskyns, Edwyn C.
"The Johannine Epistles," in *A New Commentary on Holy Scripture including the Apocrypha,* Part 3: *The*

New Testament (ed. Charles Gore, et al.; 4th ed.; London: SPCK, 1937) 658–73.

Houlden, James Leslie
A Commentary on the Johannine Epistles (Black's New Testament Commentaries; London: Black; HNTC; New York: Harper & Row, 1973; 2d ed.; London: Black, 1994).

Jonge, Marinus de
De brieven van Johannes (2d ed.; Nijkerk: Callenbach, 1973).

Klauck, Hans-Josef
Der erste Johannesbrief (EKKNT 23/1; Zurich: Benzinger; Neukirchen-Vluyn: Neukirchener Verlag, 1991).

Kohler, Marc
Le coeur et les mains: Commentaire de la première épîtres de Jean (Neuchâtel: Delachaux & Niestle, 1962).

Lauck, Willibald
Das Evangelium und die Briefe des heiligen Johannes (Die heilige Schrift für das Leben erklärt; Freiburg: Herder, 1941).

Law, Robert
The Tests of Life: A Study of the First Epistle of St. John (Kerr Lectures 1909; 3d ed.; Edinburgh: Clark, 1914).

Lieu, Judith M.
The Second and Third Epistles of John: History and Background (Studies of the New Testament and Its World; ed. John Riches; Edinburgh: Clark, 1986).

Loisy, Alfred F.
Le Quatrième évangile; les épîtres dites de Jean (2d ed.; Paris: Nourry, 1921).

Love, Julian P.
The First, Second and Third Letters of John (Richmond: John Knox, 1960).

Mann, Dietrich
Mit dem Neuen Testament im Gespräch, vol. 2: *Die Briefe und die Offenbarung des Johannes* (Arbeitsbücherei für den Hauskreis 2; Konstanz: Christliche Verlagsanstalt, 1986).

Marshall, I. Howard
The Epistles of John (NICNT; Grand Rapids: Eerdmans, 1978).

Michi, J.
Die Katholischen Briefe (RNT 8; 2d ed.; Regensburg, 1986).

Moody, Dale
The Letters of John (Waco: Word, 1970).

Perkins, Pheme
The Johannine Epistles (New Testament Message 21; Wilmington: Michael Glazier, 1979).

Perkins, Pheme
"The Johannine Epistles," in Raymond Brown, et al., eds., *New Jerome Biblical Commentary* (Englewood Cliffs: Prentice-Hall, 1990) 986–95.

Plummer, Alfred (1841–1926)
"The Epistle of St. John," in Arthur J. Mason, Alfred Plummer, and W. M. Sinclair, eds., *The Epistles of St. Peter, St. John and St. Jude* (Ellicott's Bible Commentary 11; 2d ed.; London/New York: Hodder & Stoughton, 1903).

Rennes, Jean
La Première Épître de Jean (Geneva: Labor et Fides, 1968).

Reuss, Joseph, and Eduard Schick
Briefe des Apostels Paulus. Die Briefe an Timotheus und Titus. Der Brief an Philemon. Der Brief an die Hebräer. Die katholischen Briefe. Die Apokalypse (EB; reprinted; Würzburg: Echter, 1968).

Ross, Alexander
The Epistles of James and John (NICNT; London: Marshall, Morgan & Scott; Grand Rapids: Eerdmans, 1954).

Ruckstuhl, Eugen
Jakobusbrief: 1.–3. Johannesbrief (EB 17–19; Würzburg: Echter, 1985).

Schlatter, Adolf
Die Briefe und die Offenbarung des Johannes (Erläuterungen zum NT 10; 1938; Stuttgart: Calwer, 1976).

Schnackenburg, Rudolf
Die Johannesbriefe (HThKNT 13/3; 7th ed.; Freiburg: Herder, 1984; ET: *The Johannine Epistles: Introduction and Commentary* [trans. Reginald and Ilse Fuller; New York: Crossroad, 1992]).

Schneider, Johannes
Die Briefe des Jakobus, Petrus, Judas und Johannes: Die Katholischen Briefe (NTD 10; 9th ed.; Göttingen: Vandenhoeck & Ruprecht, 1961).

Schunack, Gerd
Die Briefe des Johannes (ZBK NT 17; Zurich: Theologischer Verlag, 1982).

Shepherd, Massey H., Jr.
"The Letters of John," in *The Interpreter's One-Volume Commentary on the Bible* (ed. Charles M. Laymon; Nashville: Abingdon, 1971) 935–41.

Smalley, Stephen S.
1, 2, 3 John (WBC 51; Waco: Word, 1984).

Stott, John R. W.
The Epistles of John (TNTC 19; Grand Rapids: Eerdmans, 1964).

Thüsing, Wilhelm
Die Johannesbriefe (Geistliche Schriftlesung 22; Düsseldorf: Patmos, 1970).

Vawter, Bruce
"The Johannine Epistles," in Raymond Brown, et al., eds., *The Jerome Biblical Commentary* (Englewood Cliffs: Prentice-Hall, 1968) 404–13.

Vouga, François
Die Johannesbriefe (HNT 15/3; Tübingen: Mohr [Siebeck], 1990). (See also Georg Strecker's review in *Bib* 73 [1992] 280–86.)

Vrede, Wilhelm
"Die briefe des heiligen Johannes," in *Die Katholischen Briefe* (trans. and ed. Max Meinertz and Wilhelm Vrede; HSNT 9; 4th ed.; Bonn:

Hanstein, 1932) 143–92.
Wengst, Klaus
Der erste, zweite und dritte Brief des Johannes (ÖTK 16; Gütersloh: Mohn, 1978).
Wilder, Amos N.
"Introduction and Exegesis of the First, Second, and Third Epistles of John," in *IB* 12 (New York/Nashville, 1957) 207–313.
Williams, Ronald R.
The Letters of John and James: Commentary on the Three Letters of John and the Letter of James (CNEB; Cambridge: Cambridge University Press, 1965).
Windisch, Hans (1881–1935)
Die Katholischen Briefe (HNT 15; 1911; 3d ed.; ed. Herbert Preisker; Tübingen: Mohr [Siebeck], 1951).

2. Studies

Aland, Kurt, and Barbara Aland
Der Text des Neuen Testaments: Einführung in die wissenschaftlichen Ausgaben sowie in Theorie und Praxis der modernen Textkritik (Stuttgart: Deutsche Bibelgesellschaft, 1982; ET: *The Text of the New Testament: An Introduction to the Critical Editions and to the Theory and Practice of Modern Textual Criticism* [trans. Erroll F. Rhodes; Grand Rapids: Eerdmans, 1987; 2d ed., 1989]).
Alfaro, G.
"Cognitio Dei et Christi in I. Jo," *VD* 39/2 (1961) 82–91.
Altaner, Berthold, and Alfred Stuiber
Patrologie: Leben, Schriften und Lehre der Kirchenväter (9th ed.; Freiburg/Basel/Vienna: Herder, 1981; ET: *Patrology* [trans. Hilda C. Graef from the 5th ed.; New York: Herder, 1960]).
Ambroggi, Pietro de
"La teologia delle epistole di S. Giovanni," *La Scuola Cattolica* 76 (1946) 35–42.
Amphoux, Christian-Bernard
"Note sur le classement des manuscrits grecs de 1 Jean," *RHPhR* 61 (1981) 125–35.
Baird, Joseph Arthur, and David Noel Freedman, general editors; Andrew Queen Morton and S. Michaelson, concordance editors
The Johannine Epistles: A Critical Concordance (Computer Bible 3; Edinburgh: University of Edinburgh, 1971).
Balz, Horst R.
"Johanneische Theologie und Ethik im Licht der 'letzten Stunde,'" in Wolfgang Schrage, ed., *Studien zum Text und zur Ethik des Neuen Testaments: Festschrift zum 80. Geburtstag von Heinrich Greeven* (BZNW 47; Berlin: de Gruyter, 1986) 35–56.
Barrett, Charles Kingsley
The Gospel according to St. John (London: SPCK; New York: Macmillan, 1955; 2d ed.; Philadelphia: Westminster, 1958).
Barrett, Charles Kingsley, ed.
New Testament Background: Selected Documents (London: SPCK, 1956; New York: Macmillan, 1957; rev. ed.; San Francisco: Harper & Row, 1989).
Bauer, Walter
"Johannesevangelium und Johannesbriefe," *ThR* 1 (1929) 135–60.
Bauer, Walter
Das Johannesevangelium (HNT 6; 3d ed.; Tübingen: Mohr [Siebeck], 1933).
Bauer, Walter
Griechisch-deutsches Wörterbuch zu den Schriften des Neuen Testaments und der übrigen urchristlichen Literatur (5th ed.; Berlin/New York: Töpelmann, 1958; ET: *A Greek-English Lexicon of the New Testament and Other Early Christian Literature* [trans. William F. Arndt and F. Wilbur Gingrich; adapted from the 4th ed.; Chicago: University of Chicago Press, 1958; 2d ed. rev. by F. Wilbur Gingrich and Frederick W. Danker from Bauer's 5th ed.; Chicago: University of Chicago Press, 1979]).
Bauer, Walter
Rechtgläubigkeit und Ketzerei im ältesten Christentum (ed. Georg Strecker; BHTh 10; 2d ed.; Tübingen: Mohr [Siebeck], 1964; ET: *Orthodoxy and Heresy in Earliest Christianity* [trans. by a team from the Philadelphia Seminar on Christian Origins; ed. Robert A. Kraft and Gerhard Krodel; Philadelphia: Fortress, 1971]).
Bauer, Walter
Die Briefe des Ignatius von Antiochia und der Polykarpbrief (HNT 18; 2d ed.; ed. Henning Paulsen; Tübingen: Mohr [Siebeck], 1985).
Baur, Ferdinand Christian
"Die johanneischen Briefe: Ein Beitrag zur Geschichte des Kanons," *ThJb* 7 (1848) 293–337.
Baur, Ferdinand Christian
"Das Verhältnis des ersten johanneischen Briefes zum johanneischen Evangelium," *ThJb* 16 (1857) 315–31.
Berger, Klaus, and Carsten Colpe
Religionsgeschichtliches Textbuch zum Neuen Testament (NTD Texte zum Neuen Testament 1; Göttingen: Vandenhoeck & Ruprecht, 1987).
Bergmeier, Roland
"Zum Verfasserproblem des II. und III. Johannesbriefes," *ZNW* 57 (1966) 93–100.
Bergmeier, Roland
Glaube als Gabe nach Johannes (BWANT 112; Stuttgart: Kohlhammer, 1980).
Beutler, Johannes
"Das Hauptgebot im Johannesevangelium," in Karl Kertelge, ed., *Das Gesetz im Neuen Testament* (QD 108; Freiburg: Herder, 1986) 222–36.
Beutler, Johannes
"Die Johannesbriefe in der neuesten Literatur (1978–1985)," *ANRW* 2.25.5 (1988) 3773–90.
Beyer, Klaus
Semitische Syntax im Neuen Testament 1/1 (1962; 2d ed.; Göttingen: Vandenhoeck & Ruprecht, 1968).

Black, Carl Clifton, II
"The Johannine Epistles and the Question of Early Catholicism," *NovT* 28 (1986) 131–58.

Blank, Josef
Krisis: Untersuchungen zur johanneischen Christologie und Eschatologie (Freiburg: Lambertus, 1964).

Blank, Josef
Das Evangelium nach Johannes (Geistliche Schriftlesung 4/1a; Düsseldorf: Patmos, 1981; ET: *The Gospel according to St. John* [trans. Matthew J. O'Connell; vols. 2–3 of John J. Huckle and Paul Visokay, eds., *The Gospel according to St. John;* The New Testament for Spiritual Reading, John L. McKenzie, gen. ed., vols. 7–9; New York: Crossroad, 1981]).

Blass, Friedrich, and Albert Debrunner
Grammatik des neutestamentlichen Griechisch, rev. Friedrich Rehkopf (16th ed; Göttingen: Vandenhoeck & Ruprecht, 1984; ET: *A Greek Grammar of the New Testament and Other Early Christian Literature* [trans. and rev. Robert W. Funk; from the 9th–10th German ed., incorporating supplementary notes of A. Debrunner; Chicago: University of Chicago Press, 1961]).

Bogart, John
Orthodox and Heretical Perfectionism in the Johannine Community as Evident in the First Epistle of John (SBLDS 33; Missoula: Scholars Press, 1977).

Boismard, Marie-Émile
"La connaissance de Dieu dans l'Alliance Nouvelle d'après la première lettre de S. Jean," *RB* 56 (1949) 365–91.

Boismard, Marie-Émile
"The First Epistle of John and the Writings of Qumran," in James H. Charlesworth, ed., *John and Qumran* (London: Geoffrey Chapman, 1972) 156–65.

Bonnard, Pierre
"La première épître de Jean est-elle johannique?" in Marinus de Jonge, ed., *L'Évangile de Jean* (BEThL 44; Gembloux: Duculot, 1977) 301–5.

Bonsack, Bernhard
"Der Presbyteros des dritten Briefs und der geliebte Jünger des Evangeliums nach Johannes," *ZNW* 79 (1988) 45–62.

Botterweck, G. Johannes, and Helmer Ringgren, eds.
Theologisches Wörterbuch zum Alten Testament (Stuttgart: W. Kohlhammer, 1970– ; ET: *Theological Dictionary of the Old Testament* [trans. John T. Willis, et al.; Grand Rapids: Eerdmans, 1977–]).

Bousset, Wilhelm
Der Antichrist in der Überlieferung des Judentums, des Neuen Testaments und der Alten Kirche (Göttingen: Vandenhoeck & Ruprecht, 1895; ET: *The Antichrist Legend: A Chapter in Christian and Jewish Folklore* [trans. with prologue on the Babylonian dragon myth by A. H. Keene; Satanism series; London: Hutchinson, 1896]).

Bousset, Wilhelm
Kyrios Christos: Geschichte des Christusglaubens von den Anfängen des Christentums bis Irenaeus (FRLANT 21; 6th ed.; Göttingen: Vandenhoeck & Ruprecht, 1967; ET: *Kyrios Christos: A History of the Belief in Christ from the Beginnings of Christianity to Irenaeus* [trans. John E. Steely; Nashville: Abingdon, 1970]).

Bousset, Wilhelm
Die Offenbarung Johannis (KEK 16; 1906; 6th ed.; Göttingen: Vandenhoeck & Ruprecht, 1966).

Braun, François-Marie
"La Réduction du Pluriel au Singulier dans l'Évangile et la Première Lettre du Jean," *NTS* 24 (1977) 40–67.

Braun, François-Marie
"Le péché en monde selon Saint Jean," *RThom* 65 (1965) 181–201.

Braun, Herbert
"Literar-Analyse und theologische Schichtung im ersten Johannesbrief," *ZThK* 48 (1951) 262–92 (reprinted in idem, *Gesammelte Studien zum Neuen Testament und seiner Umwelt* [3d ed.; Tübingen, Mohr (Siebeck), 1971] 210–42).

Braun, Herbert
Qumran und das Neue Testament (2 vols.; Tübingen: Mohr [Siebeck], 1966).

Brown, Raymond E.
The Gospel according to John (2 vols.; AB 29, 29A; Garden City: Doubleday, 1966, 1970).

Brown, Raymond E.
"The Qumran Scrolls and the Johannine Gospel and Epistles," *CBQ* 17 (1955) 403–19, 559–74 (reprinted in Krister Stendahl, ed., *The Scrolls and the New Testament* [New York: Harper, 1957] 183–207; and in Brown, *New Testament Essays* [Milwaukee: Bruce, 1965] 138–73).

Brown, Raymond E.
"The Relationship of the Fourth Gospel Shared by the Author of I John and by His Opponents," in Ernest Best and Robert McLean Wilson, eds., *Text and Interpretation: Studies in the New Testament Presented to Matthew Black* (Cambridge/New York: Cambridge University Press, 1979) 57–68.

Bruce, Frederick Fyvie
"St. John at Ephesus," *BJRL* 60/2 (1978) 339–61.

Büchsel, Friedrich
Der Begriff der Wahrheit in dem Evangelium und den Briefen des Johannes (BFCTh 15/3; Gütersloh: Bertelsmann, 1911).

Büchsel, Friedrich
"Zu den Johannesbriefen," *ZNW* 28 (1929) 235–41.

Bultmann, Rudolf
"Analyse des ersten Johannesbriefes," in Rudolf Bultmann and Hermann Freiherr von Soden, eds., *Festgabe für A. Jülicher zum 70. Geburtstag* (Tübingen: Mohr, 1927) 138–58; reprinted in Erich Dinkler, ed., *Exegetica: Aufsätze zur*

Erforschung des Neuen Testaments (Tübingen: Mohr [Siebeck], 1967) 105–23.

Bultmann, Rudolf
"Die kirchliche Redaktion des ersten Johannesbriefes," in Werner Schmauch, ed., *In Memoriam E. Lohmeyer* (Stuttgart: Evangelisches Verlagswerk, 1951) 189–201; reprinted in Erich Dinkler, ed., *Exegetica: Aufsätze zur Erforschung des Neuen Testaments* (Tübingen: Mohr [Siebeck], 1967) 381–93.

Bultmann, Rudolf
Das Evangelium des Johannes (KEK 2; 19th ed.; Göttingen: Vandenhoeck & Ruprecht, 1986 [Ergänzungsheft, 1968]; ET: *The Gospel of John: A Commentary* [trans. G. R. Beasley-Murray, et al.; from the 1964 edition with the supplement of 1966; London: Blackwell; Philadelphia: Westminster, 1971]).

Bultmann, Rudolf
Theologie des Neuen Testaments (ed. Otto Merk; 9th ed.; Tübingen: Mohr [Siebeck], 1984; ET: *Theology of the New Testament* [trans. Kendrick Grobel; 2 vols.; New York: Scribner's, 1951, 1955]).

Bultmann, Rudolf
"Johannesbriefe," *RGG*[3] 3.836–39.

Cassem, N. H.
"A Grammatical and Contextual Inventory of the Use of *κόσμος* in the Johannine Corpus with Some Implications for a Johannine Cosmic Theology," *NTS* 19 (1972–73) 81–91.

Cernuda, Antonio Vicent
"Engañan la oscuridad y el mondo; la luz era y manifiesta lo verdadero," *EstBib* 27 (1968) 153–75, 215–32.

Chapman, John
"The Historical Setting of the Second and Third Epistles of St. John," *JTS* 5 (1904) 357–68, 517–34.

Chmiel, Jerzy
Lumière et charité d'après la Première Épître de Saint Jean (Rome: Institut Pontifical des recherches ecclésiastiques, 1971).

Clavier, Henri
"Notes sur un mot-clef du johannisme et de la sotériologie biblique: Ἱλασμος," *NovT* 10 (1968) 287–304.

Clemen, Carl C.
"Beiträge zum geschichtlichen Verständnis der Johannesbriefe," *ZNW* 6 (1905) 271–81.

Coetzee, J. C.
"Life (Eternal Life) in John's Writings and the Qumran Scrolls," *Neot* 6 (1972) 46–66.

Coetzee, J. C.
"The Holy Spirit in I John," *Neot* 13 (1979) 43–67.

Conzelmann, Hans
Die Mitte der Zeit (BHTh 17; 6th ed.; Tübingen: Mohr [Siebeck], 1977; ET: *The Theology of St. Luke* [trans. Geoffrey Buswell; New York: Harper, 1961; Philadelphia: Fortress, 1982]).

Conzelmann, Hans
"'Was von Anfang war,'" in Walther Eltester, ed., *Neutestamentliche Studien für Rudolf Bultmann* (BZNW 21; Berlin: Töpelmann, 1957) 194–201; reprinted in Conzelmann, *Theologie als Schriftauslegung: Aufsätze zum Neuen Testament* [BEvTh 65; Munich: Kaiser, 1974] 207–14).

Conzelmann, Hans
"Was glaubte die frühe Christenheit?" in idem, *Theologie als Schriftauslegung: Aufsätze zum Neuen Testament* (BEvTh 65; Munich: Kaiser, 1974) 106–19.

Conzelmann, Hans
History of Primitive Christianity (trans. J. E. Steely; Nashville/New York: Abingdon, 1973).

Court, John M.
"Blessed Assurance?" *JTS* 33 (1982) 508–17.

Culpepper, R. Alan
The Johannine School (SBLDS 26; Missoula: Scholars Press, 1975).

Culpepper, R. Alan
1 John, 2 John, 3 John (Knox Preaching Guides; Atlanta: John Knox, 1985).

Deissmann, Gustav Adolf
Licht vom Osten: Das Neue Testament und die neuentdeckten Texte der hellenistisch-römischen Welt (4th ed.; Tübingen: Mohr, 1923; ET: *Light from the Ancient East* [trans. Lionel R. M. Strachan; New York: George H. Doran, 1927]).

Dibelius, Martin
"Johannesbriefe," *RGG*[2] 3.346–49.

Dibelius, Martin
Geschichte der urchristlichen Literatur (ThBü 58; 1926; ed. Ferdinand Hahn; Munich: Kaiser, 1975; ET: *A Fresh Approach to the New Testament and Early Christian Literature* [New York: Scribner's, 1936; London: Nicholas and Watson, 1937]).

Duplacy, Jean
"'Le Texte Occidentale' des Épîtres Catholiques," *NTS* 16 (1969–70) 397–99.

Ehrhardt, Arnold
The Framework of the New Testament Stories (Cambridge: Harvard University Press, 1964).

Eichholz, Georg
"Glaube und Liebe im 1 Johannesbrief," *EvTh* 4 (1937) 411–37.

Eichholz, Georg
"Der 1 Johannesbrief als Trostbrief und die Einheit der Schrift," *EvTh* 5 (1938) 73–83.

Eichholz, Georg
"Erwählung und Eschatologie im 1 Johannesbrief," *EvTh* 5 (1938) 1–28.

Feuillet, André
"The Structure of First John: Comparison with the 4th Gospel," *BTB* 3 (1973) 194–216.

Filson, Floyd Vivian
"First John: Purpose and Message," *Int* 23 (1969) 259–76.

Francis, Fred O.
"The Form and Function of the Opening and Closing Paragraphs of James and I John," *ZNW* 61 (1970) 110–26.

Freed, Edwin D.
"Variation in the Language and Thought of John," *ZNW* 55 (1964) 167–97.

Funk, Robert W.
"The Form and Structure of I and II John," *JBL* 86 (1967) 424–30.

Gaugler, Ernst
Die Bedeutung der Kirche in den johanneischen Schriften (Bern: Stämpfli, 1925).

Giurisato, Giorgio
"Struttura della prima lettera di Giovanni," *RivB* 21/4 (1973) 361–81.

Goldhahn-Müller, Ingrid
Die Grenze der Gemeinde: Studien zum Problem der Zweiten Busse im Neuen Testament unter Berücksichtigung der Entwicklung im zweiten Jahrhundert bis Tertullian (GThA 39; Göttingen: Vandenhoeck & Ruprecht, 1989).

Haenchen, Ernst
"Neuere Literatur zu den Johannesbriefen," in idem, *Gesammelte Aufsätze*, vol. 2: *Die Bibel und Wir* (Tübingen: Mohr [Siebeck], 1968) 235–311 (= *ThR* 26 [1960] 1–43, 267–91).

Hahn, Ferdinand
"Sehen und Glauben im Johannesevangelium," in Hans Baltensweiler and Bo Reicke, eds., *Neues Testament und Geschichte: Historisches Geschehen und Deutung im Neuen Testament: Oscar Cullmann zum 70. Geburtstag* (Zurich: Theologischer Verlag; Tübingen: Mohr [Siebeck], 1972) 125–41.

Hanse, Hermann
"Gott haben" in der Antike und im frühen Christentum (RVV 27; Berlin: Töpelmann, 1939).

von Harnack, Adolf
Über den dritten Johannesbrief (TU 15/3b; Leipzig: Hinrichs, 1897) 3–27.

von Harnack, Adolf
"Zur Textkritik und Christologie der Schriften des Johannes: Zugleich ein Beitrag zur Würdigung der ältesten lateinischen Überlieferung nach der Vulgata," SPAW.PH 5/2 (Berlin: Reimer, 1915) 534–73 (reprinted in *Studien zur Geschichte des NT und der Alten Kirche*, vol. 1: *Zur neutestamentlichen Textkritik* [AKG 19; Berlin: de Gruyter, 1931] 105–52).

von Harnack, Adolf
Lehrbuch der Dogmengeschichte, vol. 1 (5th ed.; Tübingen: Mohr [Siebeck], 1931; ET: *History of Dogma*, vol. 1 [trans. Neil Buchanan, from 3d ed.; New York: Russell & Russell, 1958; reprinted New York: Dover, 1961]).

Heise, Jürgen
Bleiben: Menein in den johanneischen Schriften (HUT 8; Tübingen: Mohr [Siebeck], 1967).

Hennecke, Edgar, and Wilhelm Schneemelcher
Neutestamentliche Apokryphen (Tübingen: Mohr [Siebeck]; vol. 1, 4th ed. 1968; vol. 2, 4th ed. 1971; rev. ed., 1990; ET: *New Testament Apocrypha* [trans. A. J. B. Higgins, et al.; ed. Robert McL. Wilson; 2 vols.; Philadelphia: Westminster, 1963–66; rev. ed.; Cambridge: Clarke; Louisville: Westminster/John Knox, 1991–93]).

Hirsch, Emanuel
Studien zum vierten Evangelium (BHTh 11; Tübingen: Mohr [Siebeck], 1936).

Hoffmann, Thomas A
"1 John and the Qumran Scrolls," *BTB* 8 (1978) 117–25.

Holtzmann, Heinrich Julius
"Das Problem des ersten johanneischen Briefes in seinem Verhältnis zum Evangelium I," *JPTh* 7 (1881) 690–712; II, *JPTh* 8 (1882) 128–43, 316–42, 460–85.

Johnson, S. E.
"Parallels between the Letters of Ignatius and the Johannine Epistles," in Edgar W. Conrad and Edward G. Newing, eds., *Perspectives on Language and Text: Essays and Poems in Honor of Francis I. Andersen's Sixtieth Birthday;* Winona Lake: Eisenbrauns, 1987) 327–38.

Jonas, Hans
The Gnostic Religion: The Message of the Alien God and the Beginnings of Christianity (2d ed.; Boston: Beacon, 1963).

Jonge, Marinus de
Jesus: Stranger from Heaven and Son of God: Jesus Christ and the Christians in Johannine Perspective (SBL Sources for Biblical Study 11; Missoula: Scholars Press, 1977).

Jonge, Marinus de
"The Use of the Word Χριστός in the Johannine Epistles," in *Studies in John Presented to Dr. J. N. Sevenster on the Occasion of His Seventieth Birthday* (NovTSup 24; Leiden: Brill, 1970) 66–74.

Jonge, Marinus de, ed.
L'Évangile de Jean: Sources, rédaction, théologie (BEThL 44; Gembloux: Duculot, 1977).

Jülicher, Adolf, and Erich Fascher
Einleitung in das Neue Testament (7th ed.; Tübingen: Mohr [Siebeck], 1931).

Käsemann, Ernst
Jesu letzter Wille nach Johannes 17 (4th ed.; Tübingen: Mohr [Siebeck], 1980; ET: *The Testament of Jesus* [trans. Gerhard Krodel; Philadelphia: Fortress; London: SCM, 1968]).

Käsemann, Ernst
"Ketzer und Zeuge," *ZThK* 48 (1951) 292–311 (reprinted in *Exegetische Versuche und Besinnungen* [2 vols.; 6th ed.; Göttingen: Vandenhoeck & Ruprecht, 1970] 1.168–87).

Katz, Peter
"The Johannine Epistles in the Muratorian Canon," *JTS* n.s. 8 (1957) 273–74.

Kilpatrick, George D.
"Two Johannine Idioms in the Johannine Epistles," *JTS* n.s. 12 (1961) 272–73.

Kittel, Gerhard, and Gerhard Friedrich, eds.
Theological Dictionary of the New Testament (10 vols.; trans. G. W. Bromiley; Grand Rapids: Eerdmans, 1964–1976).

Klauck, Hans-Josef
"Die Hausgemeinde als Lebensform im Urchristentum," *MThZ* 32 (1981) 1–15.

Klauck, Hans-Josef
"Gemeinde ohne Amt?" *BZ* 29 (1985) 193–230.

Klein, Günther
"'Das wahre Licht scheint schon.' Beobachtungen zur Zeit- und Geschichtserfahrung einer urchristlichen Schule," *ZThK* 68 (1971) 261–326.

Klöpper, Albert
"1. Joh. 5,6–12," *ZWTh* 43 (1900) 378–400.

Klöpper, Albert
"Zur Lehre von der Sünde im 1. Johannesbrief, Erläuterung von 5,16 fin," *ZWTh* 43 (1900) 585–602.

Klos, Herbert
Die Sakramente im Johannesevangelium (SBS 46; Stuttgart: Katholisches Bibelwerk, 1970).

Koester, Helmut
Einführung in das Neue Testament (Berlin: de Gruyter, 1980; ET: *Introduction to the New Testament*, vol. 1: *History, Culture, and Religion of the Hellenistic Age;* vol. 2: *History and Literature of Early Christianity* [Philadelphia/Berlin/New York: de Gruyter, 1982]).

Kügler, Joachim
"Die Belehrung der Unbelehrbaren (zu 1 Joh)," *BZ* 32 (1988) 249–54.

Kühner, Raphael, and Bernhard Gerth
Ausführliche Grammatik der griechischen Sprache (2 vols.; 4th ed.; Leverkusen: Gottschalk, 1955).

Kümmel, Werner Georg
Einleitung in das Neue Testament (1964; 21st ed.; Heidelberg: Quelle & Meyer, 1983; ET: *Introduction to the New Testament* [trans. Howard Clark Kee; 3d ed.; Nashville: Abingdon, 1975]).

Langbrandtner, Wolfgang
Weltferner Gott oder Gott der Liebe (BBET 6; Frankfurt: Lang, 1977).

Lattke, Michael
Einheit im Wort (SANT 41; Munich: Kösel, 1975).

Leconte, R.
"Jean, Épîtres de Saint," *DBSup* 4 (1949) 797–815.

Leipoldt, Johannes
Geschichte des neutestamentlichen Kanons, vol. 1: *Die Entstehung;* vol. 2: *Mittelalter und Neuzeit* (Leipzig: Hinrichs, 1907–1908).

Léon-Dufour, Xavier
"Bulletin de littérature johannique," *RechSR* 68 (1980) 271–316.

Lidzbarski, Mark
[Sidhra de Yahya] *Das Johannesbuch der Mandäer.* 2 vols. in 1. (Giessen: Alfred Töpelmann, 1915).

Lindskrog, Christian
Fortolkning til første Johannesbrev (Copenhagen: Gyldendal, 1941).

Lohmeyer, Ernst
"Über Aufbau und Gliederung des ersten Johannesbriefes," *ZNW* 27 (1928) 225–63.

Lohse, Eduard, ed.
Die Texte aus Qumran: Hebräisch und deutsch (4th ed.; Munich: Kösel, 1986).

Malatesta, Edward
Interiority and Covenant: An Exegetical Study of εἶναι ἐν and μένειν ἐν in the First Letter of Saint John (AnBib 69; Rome: Biblical Institute Press, 1978).

Mealand, David L.
"The Language of Mystical Union in the Johannine Writings," *DRev* 95 (1977) 19–34.

Moody, D.
"The Theology of the Johannine Letters," *SWJT* 13 (1970) 7–22.

Moule, Charles Francis Digby
"The Meaning of 'Life' in the Gospel of St. John: A Study in the Story of Lazarus, John 11:1–44," *Theology* 78 (London, 1975) 114–25.

Moulton, James Hope, et al.
A Grammar of New Testament Greek (3 vols.; 3d ed.; Edinburgh: Clark, 1908–63).

Müller, Ulrich B.
Die Geschichte der Christologie in der johanneischen Gemeinde (SBS 77; Stuttgart: Katholisches Bibelwerk, 1975).

Mussner, Franz
ΖΩΗ. *Die Anschauung vom "Leben" im vierten Evangelium* (MThS 1/5; Munich: Zink, 1952).

Nauck, Wolfgang
Die Tradition und der Charakter des ersten Johannesbriefes (WUNT 3; Tübingen: Mohr [Siebeck], 1957).

Norden, Eduard
Agnostos Theos: Untersuchungen zur Formgeschichte religiöser Rede (Leipzig/Berlin: Teubner, 1913; reprinted Darmstadt: Wissenschaftliche Buchgesellschaft, 1974).

O'Neill, J. C.
The Puzzle of 1 John: A New Examination of Origins (London: SPCK, 1966).

Painter, John
John, Witness and Theologian (London: SPCK, 1975).

Painter, John
"The 'Opponents' in 1 John," *NTS* 32 (1986) 48–71.

Pecorara, George
"De verbo 'manere' apud Ioannem," *DT* 40 (1937) 159–71.

Perkins, Pheme
"Johannine Traditions in *Ap. Jas.* (NHC I,2)," *JBL* 101 (1982) 403–14.

Perkins, Pheme
"Koinonia in 1 John 1:3–7: The Social Context of Division in the Johannine Letters," *CBQ* 45 (1983) 631–41.
Piper, Otto A.
"1 John and the Didache of the Primitive Church," *JBL* 66 (1947) 437–51.
de la Potterie, Ignace
La vérité dans Saint Jean (2 vols.; AnBib 73–74; Rome: Biblical Institute Press, 1977).
Radermacher, Ludwig
Neutestamentliche Grammatik: Das Griechisch des Neuen Testaments im Zusammenhang mit der Volkssprache (HNT 1; 2d ed.; Tübingen: Mohr [Siebeck], 1925).
Reim, Günter
"Zur Lokalisierung der johanneischen Gemeinde," *BZ* 32 (1988) 72–86.
Reitzenstein, Richard (1861–1931)
Die hellenistischen Mysterienreligionen nach ihren Grundgedanken und Wirkungen (3d ed.; Leipzig/ Berlin: Teubner, 1927; ET: *Hellenistic Mystery-Religions: Their Basic Ideas and Significance* (trans. John E. Steely; Pittsburgh: Pickwick, 1978).
Rese, Martin
"Das Gebot der Bruderliebe in den Johannesbriefen," *TZ* 41 (1985) 44–58.
Richards, William L.
The Classification of the Greek Manuscripts of the Johannine Epistles (SBLDS 35; Missoula: Scholars Press, 1977).
Robinson, John A. T.
"The Destination and Purpose of the Johannine Epistles," *NTS* 7 (1960) 56–65.
Rudolph, Kurt
Die Gnosis: Wesen und Geschichte einer spätantiken Religion (2d ed.; Göttingen: Vandenhoeck & Ruprecht, 1980; ET: *Gnosis, The Nature and History of Gnosticism* [trans. and ed. R. McL. Wilson; 3d ed.; San Francisco: Harper & Row, 1990).
Schenke, Hans-Martin
"Determination und Ethik im ersten Johannesbrief," *ZThK* 60 (1963) 203–15.
Schlier, Heinrich
Das Ende der Zeit (Freiburg: Herder, 1971).
Schlier, Heinrich
"Die Bruderliebe nach dem Evangelium und den Briefen des Johannes," in Albert Descamps and André de Halleux, ed., *Mélanges bibliques en hommage au R. P. Beda Rigaux* (Gembloux: Duculot, 1970) 235–45.
Schmithals, Walter
Johannesevangelium und Johannesbriefe: Forschungsgeschichte und Analyse (BZNW 64; Berlin/New York: Herder, 1992).
Schnackenburg, Rudolf
"Wahrheit in Glaubenssätzen nach dem ersten Johannesbrief," in Karl Rahner, ed., *Zum Problem Unfehlbarkeit* (QD 54; Freiburg: Herder, 1971) 134–47.
Schnackenburg, Rudolf
"Die johanneische Gemeinde und ihre Geisterfahrung," in Rudolf Schnackenburg, Josef Ernst, and Joachim Wanke, eds., *Die Kirche des Anfangs: Für Heinz Schürmann* (Freiburg/Basel/Vienna: Herder, 1977) 277–306.
Schnackenburg, Rudolf
Das Johannesevangelium (3 vols.; HThKNT 4/1–3; Freiburg: Herder, 1965–84; ET: *The Gospel according to St. John* [trans. Kevin Smyth, et al.; 3 vols.; New York: Crossroad, 1982]).
Schnackenburg, Rudolf
Das Johannesevangelium: Ergänzende Auslegungen und Exkurse (HThKNT 4/4; Freiburg: Herder, 1984).
Schnelle, Udo
Antidoketische Christologie im Johannesevangelium (FRLANT 144; Göttingen: Vandenhoeck & Ruprecht, 1987; ET: *Antidocetic Christology in the Gospel of John* [trans. Linda M. Maloney; Minneapolis: Fortress, 1992]).
Schottroff, Luise
Der Glaubende und die feindliche Welt (WMANT 37; Neukirchen-Vluyn: Neukirchener Verlag, 1970).
Schwartz, Eduard (1858–1940)
Über den Tod der Söhne Zebedai: Ein Beitrag zur Geschichte des Johannesevangeliums (AGWG.PH 7/5; Berlin: Weidmann, 1904; reprinted Göttingen: Kraus, 1970).
Schwartz, Eduard
"Johannes und Kerinthos," *ZNW* 15 (1914) 210–19.
Schweizer, Eduard
"Die hellenistische Komponente im neutestamentlichen Sarx-Begriff," *ZNW* 48 (1957) 237–53.
Schweizer, Eduard
"Der Kirchenbegriff im Evangelium und den Briefen des Johannes," *StEv* 1 (TU 73, 1957) 363–81.
Schwyzer, Eduard
Griechische Grammatik: Auf der Grundlage von Karl Brugmanns griechischer Grammatik, vol. 2 (completed and ed. Albert Debrunner; 2d ed.; Munich: Beck, 1959).
Seeberg, Reinhold
"Die Sünden und die Sündenvergebung nach dem 1. Brief des Johannes," in Robert Jelke, ed., *Das Erbe Martin Luthers und die gegenwärtige theologische Forschung* (Festschrift for L. Ihmels. Leipzig: Dörffling & Franke, 1928) 19–31.
Segalla, Giuseppe
"L'esperienza cristiana in Giovanni," *StPat* 18 (2d ed. 1971) 299–342.
Segovia, Fernando F.
"The Love and Hatred of Jesus and Johannine Sectarianism," *CBQ* 43 (1981) 258–72.
Segovia, Fernando F.
Love Relationships in the Johannine Tradition:

Agapē/Agapan in I John and the Fourth Gospel (SBLDS 58: Chico: Scholars Press, 1982).

Smalley, Stephen S.
"What about 1 John?" *StB* 1978 (JSNTSup 3; 3 vols.; ed. E. A. Livingstone; Sheffield: JSOT, 1980]) 3.337–43.

Smit Sibinga, Joost
"A Study in I John," in *Studies in John Presented to Dr. J. N. Sevenster on the Occasion of His Seventieth Birthday* (NovTSup 24; Leiden: Brill, 1970) 194–208.

Smith, Dwight Moody
"Johannine Christianity: Some Reflections on Its Character and Delineation," *NovT* 21 (1975) 222–48.

Soltau, Wilhelm
"Die Verwandtschaft zwischen Evangelium Johannis und dem I. Johannesbrief," *ThStK* 89 (1916) 229–33.

Spicq, Ceslas
Agapē dans le Nouveau Testament (3 vols.; Paris: Gabalda, 1958–59).

Strecker, Georg
Der Weg der Gerechtigkeit (FRLANT 82; 3d ed.; Göttingen: Vandenhoeck & Ruprecht, 1971).

Strecker, Georg
Eschaton und Historie: Aufsätze (Göttingen: Vandenhoeck & Ruprecht, 1979).

Strecker, Georg
"Judenchristentum und Gnosis," in Karl-Wolfgang Tröger, ed., *Altes Testament, Frühjudentum, Gnosis* (Gütersloh: Mohn, 1980) 261–82.

Strecker, Georg
Die Bergpredigt: Ein exegetischer Kommentar (2d ed.; Göttingen: Vandenhoeck & Ruprecht, 1985; ET: *The Sermon on the Mount: An Exegetical Commentary* [trans. O. C. Dean, Jr.; Nashville: Abingdon, 1988]).

Strecker, Georg
"Die Anfänge der johanneischen Schule," *NTS* 32 (1986) 31–47.

Strecker, Georg
"Gottes- und Menschenliebe in Neuen Testament," in G. F. Hawthorne and Otto Betz, eds., *Tradition and Interpretation in the New Testament: Essays in Honor of E. Earle Ellis* (Grand Rapids: Eerdmans; Tübingen: Mohr [Siebeck], 1987) 53–67.

Strecker, Georg
"Neues Testament," in Georg Strecker and Johann Maier, *Neues Testament—Antikes Judentum* (GKT 2; Urban-Taschenbücher 422; Stuttgart: Kohlhammer, 1989) 9–136.

Strecker, Georg
"Chiliasm and Docetism in the Johannine School," *Australian Biblical Review* 38 (1990) 45–61.

Strecker, Georg
Literaturgeschichte des Neuen Testaments (Uni-Taschenbücher 1682; Göttingen: Vandenhoeck & Ruprecht, 1992).

Theobald, Michael
Die Fleischwerdung des Logos (NTAbh n.f. 20; Münster: Aschendorff, 1988).

Thüsing, Wilhelm
Die Erhöhung und Verherrlichung Jesu im Johannesevangelium (NTAbh n.f. 21, heft 1/2; 2d ed.; Münster: Aschendorff, 1970).

Thyen, Hartwig
"'. . . denn wir lieben die Brüder' (1 Joh 3,14)," in Johannes Friedrich, Wolfgang Pöhlmann, and Peter Stuhlmacher, eds., *Rechtfertigung: Festschrift für Ernst Käsemann zum 70. Geburtstag* (Tübingen: Mohr [Siebeck], 1976) 527–42.

Thyen, Hartwig
"Johannesbriefe," *TRE* 17 (1987) 186–200.

Thyen, Hartwig
"Entwicklungen innerhalb der johanneischen Theologie und Kirche im Spiegel von Joh 21 und der Lieblingsjüngertexte des Evangeliums," in Marinus de Jonge, ed., *L'Évangile de Jean* (BEThL 44; Gembloux: Duculot, 1977) 259–99.

Trench, Richard C. (1807–1886)
Synonyms of the New Testament (1880; reprinted London: Clarke, 1961; Grand Rapids: Baker, 1989).

Troeltsch, Ernst
The Social Teaching of the Christian Churches (2 vols.; London: Allen & Unwin, 1931; reprinted Chicago: University of Chicago Press, 1981).

Tröger, Karl-Wolfgang
"Die hermetische Gnosis," in idem, ed., *Gnosis und Neues Testament* (Gütersloh: Mohn, 1973) 97–119.

Tuñí, O.
"Motivacions ètiques de la 1 Jn: La 1 Jn i el Jesús històric," *Revista Catalana de Teologia* 4 (1979) 285–308.

Vellanickal, Matthew
The Divine Sonship of Christians in the Johannine Writings (AnBib 72; Rome: Biblical Institute Press, 1977).

Vielhauer, Philipp
Geschichte der urchristlichen Literatur (Berlin/New York: de Gruyter, 1975).

von Campenhausen, Hans
Kirchliches Amt und geistliche Vollmacht in den ersten drei Jahrhunderten (BHTh 14; 1953; Tübingen: Mohr [Siebeck], 1963; ET: *Ecclesiastical Authority and Spiritual Power in the Church of the First Three Centuries* [London: Black, 1969]).

von Dobschütz, Ernst
"Johanneische Studien I," *ZNW* 8 (1907) 1–8.

Vouga, François
"The Johannine School: A Gnostic Tradition in Primitive Christianity?" *Bib* 69 (1988) 371–85.

Vouga, François
Le cadre historique et l'intention théologique de Jean (2d ed.; Paris: Beauchesne, 1981).

Ward, Ronald Arthur
"The Theological Pattern of the Johannine

Epistles," *SWJT* 13 (1970) 23–39.
Watson, Duane Frederick
"A Rhetorical Analysis of 2 John according to the Greco-Roman Convention," *NTS* 35 (1989) 104–30.
Watson, Duane Frederick
"A Rhetorical Analysis of 3 John: A Study in Epistolary Rhetoric," *CBQ* 51 (1989) 479–501.
Weir, J. Emmette
"The Identity of the Logos in the First Epistle of John," *ExpT* 86 (1974–75) 118–20.
Weiss, Konrad
"Orthodoxie und Heterodoxie im 1. Johannesbrief," *ZNW* 58 (1967) 247–55.
Wendt, Hans Hinrich
"Der 'Anfang' am Beginne des I Johannesbriefes," *ZNW* 21 (1922) 38–42.
Wendt, Hans Hinrich
Die Johannesbriefe und das johanneische Christentum (Halle: Buchhandlung des Waisenhauses, 1925).
Wengst, Klaus
Häresie und Orthodoxie im Spiegel des ersten Johannesbriefes (Gütersloh: Mohn, 1976).
Wengst, Klaus
"Probleme der Johannesbriefe," *ANRW* 2.25.5 (1988) 3753–72.
Wengst, Klaus
Bedrängte Gemeinde und verherrlichter Christus (Biblisch-theologische Studien 5; 1981; 4th ed.; Neukirchen-Vluyn: Neukirchener Verlag, 1992).
Wengst, Klaus, ed.
Didache, Barnabasbrief, Zweiter Klemensbrief, Schrift an Diognet: Schriften des Urchristentums, vol. 2 (Munich: Kösel, 1984).
Wikenhauser, Alfred, and Josef Schmid
Einleitung in das Neue Testament (6th ed.; Freiburg: Herder, 1973).
Wischmeyer, Otto
"Vorkommen und Bedeutung von Agape in der ausserchristlichen Antike," *ZNW* 69 (1978) 212–38.
Witherington, Ben, III
"The Waters of Birth: John 3.5 and 1 John 5.6–8," *NTS* 35 (1989) 155–60.
Wohlenberg, Gustav
"Glossen zum ersten Johannesbrief," *NKZ* 21 (1901) 581–83, 746–48; 13 (1902) 233–40, 632–45.
Woll, D. Bruce
Johannine Christianity in Conflict: Authority, Rank, and Succession in the First Farewell Discourses (SBLDS 60; Chico: Scholars Press, 1981).
Zahn, Theodor
Geschichte des neutestamentlichen Kanons (2 vols.; Erlangen: Deichert, 1888–92).
Zahn, Theodor
Grundriss der Geschichte des neutestamentlichen Kanons: Eine Ergänzung zu der Einleitung in das Neue Testament (2d ed.; Leipzig: Deichert, 1904).
Zerwick, Maximilian
Biblical Greek; Illustrated by Examples (4th ed.; trans. Joseph Smith; Rome: Biblical Institute Press, 1963).

Indices

1. Passages

a / Old Testament and Apocrypha

b / Old Testament Pseudepigrapha and Other Jewish Literature

d / Early Christian Literature and the Ancient Church

e / Greek and Latin Authors

2. Greek Words

3. Subjects

In the design of the visual aspects of *Hermeneia*, consideration has been given to relating the form to the content by symbolic means.

The letters of the logotype *Hermeneia* are a fusion of forms alluding simultaneously to Hebrew (dotted vowel markings) and Greek (geometric round shapes) letter forms. In their modern treatment they remind us of the electronic age as well, the vantage point from which this investigation of the past begins.

The Lion of Judah used as visual identification for the series is based on the Seal of Shema. The version for *Hermeneia* is again a fusion of Hebrew calligraphic forms, especially the legs of the lion, and Greek elements characterized by the geometric. In the sequence of arcs, which can be understood as scroll-like images, the first is the lion's mouth. It is reasserted and accelerated in the whorl and returns in the aggressively arched tail: tradition is passed from one age to the next, rediscovered and re-formed.

"Who is worthy to open the scroll and break its
seals. . . ."
Then one of the elders said to me
"weep not; lo, the Lion of the tribe of David,
the Root of David, has conquered,
so that he can open the scroll and
its seven seals."
Rev. 5:2, 5

To celebrate the signal achievement in biblical scholarship which *Hermeneia* represents, the entire series will by its color constitute a signal on the theologian's bookshelf: the Old Testament will be bound in yellow and the New Testament in red, traceable to a commonly used color coding for synagogue and church in medieval painting; in pure color terms, varying degrees of intensity of the warm segment of the color spectrum. The colors interpenetrate when the binding color for the Old Testament is used to imprint volumes from the New and vice versa.

Wherever possible, a photograph of the oldest extant manuscript, or a historically significant document pertaining to the biblical sources, will be displayed on the end papers of each volume to give a feel for the tangible reality and beauty of the source material.

The title-page motifs are expressive derivations from the *Hermeneia* logotype, repeated seven times to form a matrix and debossed on the cover of each volume. These sifted-out elements will be seen to be in their exact positions within the parent matrix. These motifs and their expressional character are noted on the following page.

Half-titles to introduce the volume in question are further derivations from the main title and may include other expressive or pictorial elements.

Horizontal markings at gradated levels on the spine will assist in grouping the volumes according to these conventional categories.

The type has been set with unjustified right margins so as to preserve the internal consistency of word spacing. This is a major factor in both legibility and aesthetic quality; the resultant uneven line endings are only slight impairments to legibility by comparison. In this respect the type resembles the handwritten manuscripts where the quality of the calligraphic writing is dependent on establishing and holding to integral spacing patterns.

All of the type faces in common use today have been designed between A.D. 1500 and the present. For the biblical text a face was chosen which does not arbitrarily date the text, but rather one which is uncompromisingly modern and unembellished so that its feel is of the universal. The type style is Univers 65 by Adrian Frutiger.

The expository texts and footnotes are set in Baskerville, chosen for its compatibility with the many brief Greek and Hebrew insertions. The double-column format and the shorter line length facilitate speed reading and the wide margins to the left of footnotes provide for the scholar's own notations.

Kenneth Hiebert

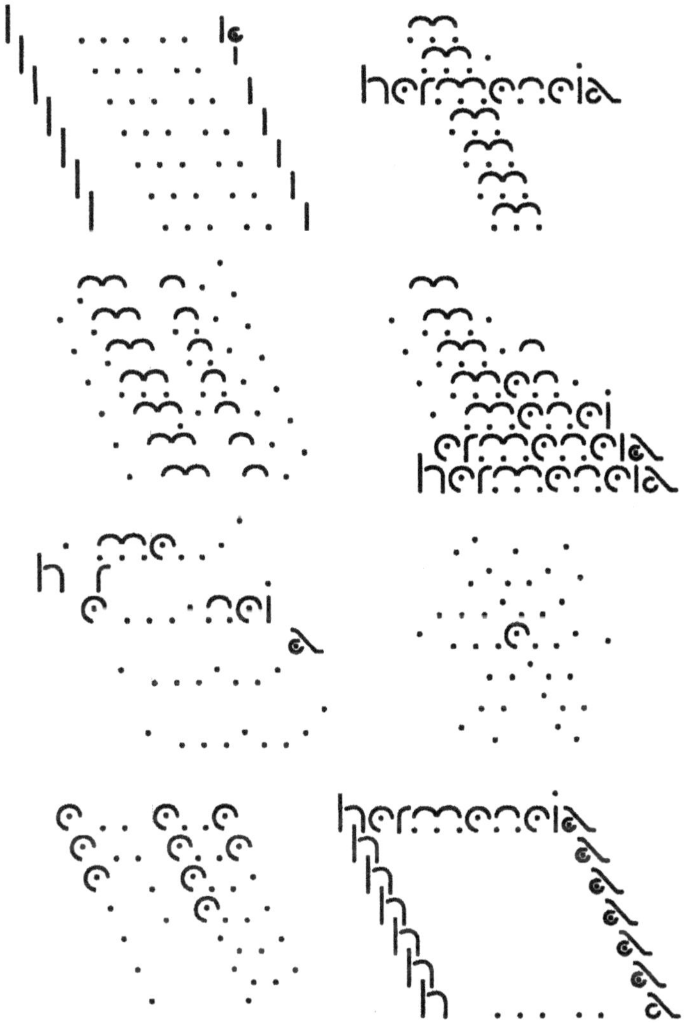

Category of biblical writing, key symbolic characteristic, and volumes so identified.

1
Law
(boundaries described)
- Genesis
- Exodus
- Leviticus
- Numbers
- Deuteronomy

2
History
(trek through time and space)
- Joshua
- Judges
- Ruth
- 1 Samuel
- 2 Samuel
- 1 Kings
- 2 Kings
- 1 Chronicles
- 2 Chronicles
- Ezra
- Nehemiah
- Esther

3
Poetry
(lyric emotional expression)
- Job
- Psalms
- Proverbs
- Ecclesiastes
- Song of Songs

4
Prophets
(inspired seers)
- Isaiah
- Jeremiah
- Lamentations
- Ezekiel
- Daniel
- Hosea
- Joel
- Amos
- Obadiah
- Jonah
- Micah
- Nahum
- Habakkuk
- Zephaniah
- Haggai
- Zechariah
- Malachi

5
New Testament Narrative
(focus on One)
- Matthew
- Mark
- Luke
- John
- Acts

6
Epistles
(directed instruction)
- Romans
- 1 Corinthians
- 2 Corinthians
- Galatians
- Ephesians
- Philippians
- Colossians
- 1 Thessalonians
- 2 Thessalonians
- 1 Timothy
- 2 Timothy
- Titus
- Philemon
- Hebrews
- James
- 1 Peter
- 2 Peter
- 1 John
- 2 John
- 3 John
- Jude

7
Apocalypse
(vision of the future)
- Revelation

8
Extracanonical Writings
(peripheral records)